LIST OF SYMBOLS

SYMBOL	MEANING
$\overleftrightarrow{AB}$	Line
$\overline{AB}$	Line segment
$\overrightarrow{AB}$	Ray
$\overline{AB}$	Half-line
$\parallel$	Parallel
$\perp$	Perpendicular
$\angle ABC$	Angle ABC
AB	Measure of line segment
$m\angle ABC$	Measure of an angle
π	Pi
$60°$	60 degrees
$14°16'17''$	14 degrees, 16 minutes, 17 seconds
$\triangle ABC$	Triangle ABC
$\cong$	Is congruent to
$\sim$	Is similar to
$|a|$	Absolute value of a
$P(E)$	Probability of event E
$\bar{x}$	Mean

ELEMENTARY MATHEMATICS FOR TEACHERS

Second Edition

ELEMENTARY MATHEMATICS FOR TEACHERS

DONALD F. DEVINE
JUDITH OLSON
MELFRIED OLSON

WILEY
John Wiley & Sons

New York   Chichester   Brisbane   Toronto   Singapore

Cover design: Karin Gerdes Kincheloe
Text design: David L. Levy

Library of Congress Cataloging in Publication Data:

Devine, Donald F.
    Elementary mathematics for teachers / Donald F. Devine, Judith Olson, Melfried Olson.
        p.   cm.
    Includes bibliographical references.
    ISBN 0-471-85947-8
    1. Mathematics.   2. Mathematics—Study and teaching (Elementary)
    I. Olson, Melfried.   II. Olson, Judith.   III. Title.
    QA107.D474   1990
    372.7—dc20   89-24816
                                                                                    CIP

Printed in the United States of America

10 9 8 7 6 5 4 3 2 1

PREFACE

This textbook was written for teachers and prospective teachers of elementary school mathematics. The choice of content is based on an analysis of current elementary school mathematics programs, recent developments in mathematics education research, recommendations of the NCTM Standards, and methods and materials available for use in activity-based learning programs. We have been strongly influenced by our experiences in working with children and interactions with teachers through workshops and professional meetings. The recently published NCTM's Curriculum and Evaluations Standards for school mathematics provide a philosophical, pedagogical, and content basis for the directions we have chosen in the writing of this text.

The style of presentation used in this book enables the student to become an active learner. The writing style is informal and asks the student to react to questions and to attempt to relate concepts and relationships before formal statements or definitions are given. We firmly believe that the learning of mathematics is an internal process for each student and is dependent on experience with real-world situations. We have included problem-solving activities throughout the book because we believe that such problems motivate the development of concepts and help learners to become more confident of their abilities as they solve problems. The writing style is meant to be conversational in nature and provides informal discussion of concepts. This is in complete agreement with the NCTM Standards' emphasis on good communication, reasoning, and problem-solving skills in mathematics.

CONTENT FEATURES

Use of Set Concepts.

Set concepts are used to develop our understanding of other concepts, not as an end in themselves. We have incorporated many informal and intuitive approaches similar to those actually used with children. Many real-world encounters with collections of things are used to develop mathematical concepts.

Use of Informal Arguments to Build Mathematical Structure.

We have made every effort to engage the student in mathematical reasoning of an informal and intuitive nature to develop concepts, thereby providing some sort of reasonable justification for the resulting statements. The structure of the development is kept in view by statements of definitions and properties but certainly not developed in any sort of rigorous fashion. Logic is introduced in the second chapter and is referred to frequently throughout the remaining chapters.

Problem-Solving Activities.

Problem solving is the focus throughout the text. We have incorporated some problem-solving activities to motivate the development of concepts and others as places to apply those concepts. We encourage the learner to be active in reasoning with mathematical ideas and to approach new situations with a minimum of prompting in order to develop confidence in problem-solving ability and to increase mathematical power. We have included two chapters *entirely* focused on problem solving. One is designed to deal with problem-solving strategies and uses problems intended to be easily solved. The thirteenth chapter is also devoted to problem solving but with problems that are more dependent on concepts developed in the text. Some teachers might wish to draw from one or both chapters as an introductory unit or some might incorporate the problems as they proceed through the book.

Meaningful and Challenging Problem Sets.

We have made a sincere effort to produce problem sets that are useful to the instructor and meaningful to the students. In the problem sets we have included basic reinforcement exercises and problems designed to ask thought-provoking questions and to extend ideas. Other problems are designed to continue the development of problem-solving strategies. We have included a special category of problems referred to as Pedagogical Problems and Activities for those who wish to look at some activities closely related to activities appropriate for children; many require hands-on involvement by the student.

Use of Calculators and Computers.

We have recommended the use of a calculator throughout the text. Some problems have been specifically designated as places where the calculator would be most useful. It could also be used in a variety of other places at the discretion of the instructor. We have included one chapter relating to the use of LOGO to teach mathematical concepts. A sufficient number of problems have been included to enable the computer to be easily used throughout the book if desired.

SPECIAL FEATURES

We want to emphasize the following special features of this text.

1. Problem solving is stressed throughout the text. Virtually every problem set throughout the text contains problem-solving activities. Each chapter begins with a problem that can be effectively solved on completion of that chapter.
2. We have attempted to bring in the calculator in a very natural way as a useful tool. We have identified some problems specifically for use of a calculator, but hope that it would be used in many other places as well.
3. We have included specific computer experiences with LOGO. Although we have not identified problems to solve throughout the text that utilize

the computer, we have included many that could be so designated. We would hope that teachers would use the material on computers where appropriate and incorporate its use into a variety of problems.

4. We have attempted to encourage the students to be active learners rather than passive. We have attempted to ask questions and lead developments in such a way that they will be asked to use mathematical reasoning throughout the development.

5. We have not become engaged in formal proofs but have chosen to use less formal reasoning processes. Logic concepts were introduced in Chapter Two, then integrated in the text as needed.

6. The chapters on probability and statistics reflects the increasing emphasis of these topics in the curriculum of the elementary school. We have included work with these topics as separate chapters incorporating some of the recently developed approaches such as the Quantitative Literacy Series.

7. Problem sets are a real strength of the book. There are a sufficient number of problems included to enable a teacher to use some in class discussions and to assign others.

8. We have included special problems designated as Pedagogical Problems and Activities in the problem sets. Some of these pose pedagogical situations, others have the students actually make and use materials applicable for use with young children, whereas still others are problems of the types found in elementary texts. These problems provide great flexibility for instructors because they can be omitted without loss of continuity of concepts, can be used only as time permits, or can be used extensively.

9. Many examples have been included in the development of the materials. Students are given the opportunity to attempt a solution and then relate their work to suggested solutions in the text.

10. A great many figures are included to provide a pictoral representation of concepts under discussion and are keyed into the reading materials.

11. We have attempted to produce materials that are readable by students. The format of the book is designed to be open and appealing to the reader.

12. The book is designed in such a way that it can be used in a variety of course settings. There is sufficient content for a two-semester sequence or for a three-quarter course sequence. However, the nature of the chapters would enable one to effectively teach several different one-semester courses if so desired. We believe that the organization of the content of this book and the flexibility of the problem sets provide instructors with a way of adapting the book to their needs.

13. We have attempted to call attention to the NCTM Standards throughout the book. Each chapter addresses specific recommendations from the

standards in some way, often being reflected in the manner of the presentation of the materials being developed.

14. The writing style, the wide choice of topics covered, the examples and illustrations, and the problems incorporated in this text make it appropriate for use with preservice or inservice teachers and will make an excellent book for use in their teaching career.

ACKNOWLEDGMENTS

We want to thank all the students who have used many of these materials in earlier editions to this book. They have provided valuable assistance in helping us refine the material in this text. We also want to thank the following reviewers who took the time to provide feedback to the many questions asked in the review process.

Harald M. Ness	University of Wisconsin Center
Josie Hamer	Western Connecticut State University
Ed Enochs	University of Kentucky
Boyd Henry	College of Idaho
Jerry Young	Boise State University
Mack L. Whitaker	Radford University
Leland Knauf	Youngstown State University
Carol Achs	Mesa Community College
Joe Wise	Southwest Missouri State University
Louis J. Chatterley	Brigham Young University
Mary Alter	University of Maryland—College Park
Carol Dean	Pasadena City College
Judith Jacobs	California State Polytechnic University
Jane Schielack	Texas A & M University

We are appreciative of the care they took in examining the materials as well as for the thoughtful suggestions. We want to thank the staff at John Wiley, especially Gilda Stahl and Elizabeth Austin, for the pleasantness and cooperation they exhibited as we worked together to produce this text. Finally, a special thanks to Nancy Ancelet for continual assistance above and beyond the call of duty.

Donald F. Devine
Judith K. Olson
Melfried Olson

CONTENTS

CHAPTER 7
GEOMETRIC SHAPES   349

CHAPTER 8
LINEAR AND ANGULAR MEASUREMENT   397

CHAPTER 9
AREA AND VOLUME   485

1 PROBLEM SOLVING: THE PLACE TO BEGIN

We are currently experiencing demands for changes in the teaching of mathematics. Our presentation of the mathematical concepts and topics currently advocated for inclusion in the elementary school curriculum may at times appear different from your own personal experience with them. The methods of presentation were chosen to encourage you to explore, investigate, and reason mathematically. It is essential that we develop an ability to communicate effectively with regard to mathematical ideas, and we will attempt to connect your learning of mathematics to a wide variety of your educational experiences. We want you to develop your mathematical knowledge and power to use a variety of mathematical methods to solve nonroutine problems. We hope you will enjoy exploring interesting problems and ideas using important mathematical ideas.

As you study from this text, keep the following diagram in mind:

Posing of the problem → Development of concepts → Reinforcement for understanding of concepts → Applications of concepts

Concepts are introduced in a variety of ways, often making use of techniques and activities that can be effectively used with children. In many instances we will extend topics, use symbolism, or employ reasoning processes that are not appropriate for use with elementary school children, but that will enhance your understanding of the concepts to be taught to children. We will commonly encounter a problem situation that prompts us to develop new concepts with which to attack the problem more effectively.

As has been expressed so forcefully by the NCTM in their *Agenda for Action in 1980* and again in their new publication, *The NCTM Standards*, problem solving must be the focus of school mathematics. This first chapter is designed to provide some focus on problem-solving strategies that will be of help to you in the following chapters in this book as well as in situations in other courses of study and in everyday life.

As illustrated in Figure 1.1, a total program requires three areas of development. As was mentioned in the Preface of this book, a great deal of attention will be focused throughout the book on the development of mathematical ideas. You should always attempt to relate new ideas to the ones that you already have developed. Remember, learning mathematics is an *active* pursuit, not a passive one. The learner must be willing to become actively engaged in using manipulatives, in trying things, in making hypotheses, and in testing them.

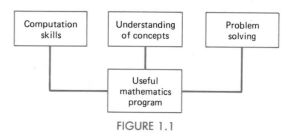

FIGURE 1.1

The same argument can be made regarding problem solving. The tendency on the part of many students is to have some degree of apprehension about anything that seems to fit under the general heading of problem solving. This first chapter of work is intended to help get you started with problem solving. There are some useful techniques that can be used to get started once we encounter a "mathematical problem." Indeed, these same general strategies will also be useful in nonmathematical situations, whether they be related to science, social studies, or other areas encountered in everyday life.

Problem solving has always been a primary goal of the teaching of mathematics at all levels. Therefore, we, as mathematics teachers, must constantly strive to improve our own problem solving skills as well as to devise ways of helping others develop their problem solving abilities.

Volumes have been written on the topic of problem solving, but certainly one of the best known sources is George Polya's book *How To Solve It*. In this book, Polya suggests the following four phase plan for solving problems.

1. *Understanding* the problem
2. *Devising a plan* to solve the problem
3. *Carrying out the plan* to solve the problem
4. *Looking back* at the completed solution to review and discuss it, then consider extensions to the problem

Let us comment briefly on each of the phases and offer some suggestions for following the plan.

Understanding the Problem

Read the problem carefully, making certain you understand the meanings of all the words. Be especially alert for any technical terms used in the statement of the problem. Often it is helpful to sketch a figure, diagram, or chart to visualize and organize the conditions of the problem. Determine the known and unknown facts, including the "units" used to express these facts, and if one of the previously mentioned pictorial devices is used, record these facts in the appropriate places. You may also find it helpful to restate the problem in your own words.

Devising a Plan

This is the "key" part of the four phase plan. There are numerous strategies and techniques that can be used to solve problems. We will discuss some of these strategies at various places throughout this text; however, at this time let us consider a list of questions that you can use to help devise a problem-solving plan. Keep in mind that many of these questions will take on more meaning later in actual problem solving situations.

1. Could you use objects to illustrate the problem or act out the problem?
2. Is there a figure, diagram, chart, or some other *visual aid* that will help organize the data in this problem?
3. Is there a *relationship* suggested by the visual aid that can be used as a guideline for solving the problem?
4. Is there a basic *formula* that applies in this situation?
5. Is this a problem you have previously solved but that now appears in a new setting, perhaps even stated in different vocabulary?
6. Is this a "counting" problem for which you need to *organize the counting process?*
7. Can you make up an *analogous but simpler* problem and learn something from solving it that might apply to this problem?
8. If it is a general-type question, have you tried some *specific cases?*

9. Is there a *related problem* you can solve that can be used to solve this problem?
10. Have you used the "trial and learn from your errors" process?
11. Could you work backward from the answer to get an insight into a procedure that might be useful in solving the problem?

No list of problem-solving strategies will ever be complete. Every problem solver has his or her own special techniques; individual ingenuity is to be encouraged. The intent for such a list is only to give you some ideas from which to start as you become involved with a given problem.

Carrying Out the Plan

If phase two has been successfully completed in detail, then carrying out the plan should be a simple matter of organizing and doing the necessary computations. Confidence in the plan creates a better working atmosphere for carrying it out. Mental calculation is often helpful in making preliminary decisions about whether the approach being used is apt to produce reasonable results. It is also at this phase that the calculator or computer may become a valuable tool. As our prime interest is in the selection of an efficient way to handle the problem, the type of data and the complexity of computation will influence decisions about how to proceed.

Looking Back

This is an important but often overlooked part of problem solving. Again, let us consider a list of questions that suggest some things to think about in this phase.

1. Is your answer to the problem a *reasonable* answer?
2. Is there a way of *checking* your answer?
3. Looking back over your solution, do you now see another plan that could be used to solve the problem?
4. Do you see a way of generalizing your procedure for this problem that could be used to solve other problems of this type?
5. Do you now see that this problem is closely related to another problem you have previously solved?
6. Have you "tucked away for future reference" the technique used to solve this problem?

Looking back over the solution of a newly solved problem can lay important groundwork for the solving of problems in the future. Thus, looking back also has the component "looking ahead."

The remainder of this chapter is devoted to illustrations of the various strategies just listed. All the problems included here can be solved using only the concepts found in the K–8 mathematics program. We encourage you to attempt each example before reading the suggested solution. We also advocate the use of group work as you do these problems. In general, it has been found that groups of two or four people work well. Do not be afraid to be inventive—try to use your own ideas, then test to see if the results are reasonable.

Strategy 1.1

Use real objects or act out the problem.
This approach is asking for a physical model or for action on the part of yourself and perhaps of others.

EXAMPLE 1

Pete has toy train engines and cabooses. He has a red engine and a blue engine and three cabooses, one yellow, one green, and one orange. How many different ways can Pete make a train with one engine and one caboose? (Grade 1)

Solution Take colored blocks of the appropriate color and arrange them into the six possible trains.

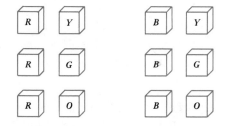

EXAMPLE 2

Is the number 7 even or is it odd? (Grade 1)

Solution Get seven children to stand up. Then line them up in pairs. Because one child will not have a partner, the number seven must be an odd number.

Strategy 1.2

Use a figure, diagram, chart, or other visual aid to organize the data.
The sketch of a figure often helps to get ideas about how to approach a problem.

EXAMPLE 1

Given five points in a plane arranged so that no more than two are in any one straight line, how many segments can be drawn? (Grade 5)

Solution From point **A** draw segments to the other points, **B**, **C**, **D**, and **E** (Fig. *a*). Now from **B**, draw segments to the remaining points **E**, **D**, and **C** (Fig. *b*). Then, from **C** draw $\overline{CE}$ and $\overline{CD}$. (Fig. *c*).

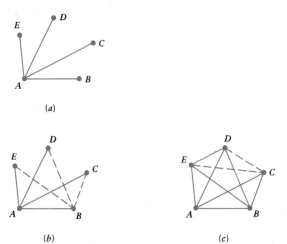

Now, from **D** only one segment $\overline{DE}$ remains to be drawn. Thus, we have $4 + 3 + 2 + 1 = 10$ segments.

EXAMPLE 2

Carl's mother said that he may order one sandwich and one drink for lunch. How many different lunches might he order from this menu? (Grade 5)

Sandwiches	Drinks
Hamburger	Juice
Hot Dog	Milk
Peanut Butter and Jelly	

Solution

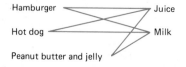

There are six paths, so six different lunches are possible.

> REMARK Notice that this problem is really similar to Example 1 for Strategy 1.1, but the solution employed is somewhat more abstract.

A chart is often helpful in organizing data and determining all possible solutions.

EXAMPLE 3

What number between 130 and 140 has digits whose sum is 13? (Grade 4)

Solution List all possible cases; then select those that satisfy the conditions.

Possible numbers	Sum of digits
131	5
132	6
133	7
134	8
135	9
136	10
137	11
138	12
139	→ 13

The solution is evidently the number 139

EXAMPLE 4

When 25 is added to a number greater than 70 but less than 76, the answer is odd. What number is it? (Grade 3)

Solution 1 Make a list of all possibilities.

Numbers Possible	Sum
71	96
72	97 ←
73	98
74	99 ←
75	100

In this case we have two possible solutions, 72 or 74 because 72 + 25 = 97 and 74 + 25 = 99.

Solution 2 If the sum of two numbers is to be odd, then we know that exactly one of the two addends must be odd. (The sum of two even numbers is even, as is the sum of two odd numbers; i.e., 5 + 7 = 12, etc.) Because 25 is odd, the other addend must be even. This leaves us with 72 and 74, both viable choices.

EXAMPLE 5

A tractor is pulling two trailers on an interstate highway. The tractor is half as long as the first trailer. The second trailer is as long as the tractor and first trailer combined. The total length of the tractor and two trailers is 24 m. What is the length of each trailer? (Grade 6)

Solution

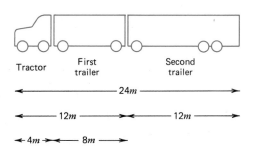

The tractor must be 4 m in length, the first trailer 8 m, and the second trailer 12 m.

EXAMPLE 6

How many different ways can you make change for a quarter? (Grade 4)

Solution

NUMBER OF COINS

Dimes	Nickles	Pennies
2	1	0
2	0	5
1	3	0
1	2	5
1	1	10
1	0	15
0	5	0

NUMBER OF COINS (*continued*)

Dimes	Nickles	Pennies
0	4	5
0	3	10
0	2	15
0	1	20
0	0	25

There are 12 ways to make change for a quarter.

EXAMPLE 7

A group of children and their dogs walked by on their way to the park to play. If there were 46 legs visible, how many dogs could there have been if we are assured that no child had more than one dog and there is at least one dog? (Grade 5)

Solution

No. of Dogs	Dog Legs	No. of Children	Children's Legs	Total No. of Legs
1	4	21	42	46
2	8	19	38	46
3	12	17	34	46
4	16	15	30	46
5	20	13	26	46
6	24	11	22	46
7	28	9	18	46
8	32	7	14	46

Any of the listed combinations of children and dogs would satisfy the problem. (Note that a given number of dogs was selected. Then the number of children was determined so the total number of legs would be 46.) Why was the row with 8 dogs and 7 children crossed out?

EXAMPLE 8

Pete lives in a town with square city blocks. He left his home and rode his bike two blocks east, then four blocks north to the YMCA. He then rode one block west and one block north to get a coke, after which he rode three blocks south and one block west to visit his friend Carl. How many blocks must Pete ride to get home from Carl's house if he takes the shortest route?

Solution A diagram clearly helps in a problem like this. The two boys live just two blocks apart.

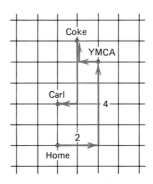

Strategy 1.3

Use a visual aid to obtain a relationship to help in solving the problem.
    Sometimes a pattern exists that becomes apparent as we work with a visual aid.

EXAMPLE 1

Suppose we have a sequence of dots as follows.

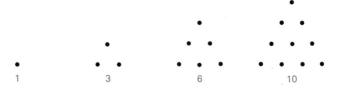

What will be the number of dots in the seventh figure? (Grade 6)

Solution Each new triangle is obtained by adding a new set of dots along one side. It becomes intuitively clear that one additional dot is added each time.

Ordinal Number of the Triangle	*Number of Dots*
1	1
2	3) 2
3	6) 3
4	10) 4

Ordinal Number of the Triangle	Number of Dots
5	15) 5
6	21) 6
7	28) 7

The seventh figure should therefore have 28 dots.

EXAMPLE 2

The 18 pupils in a classroom are seated in a circle. If they are evenly spaced and numbered in order, which pupil is directly opposite pupil number 1? Pupil number 7? Pupil number 13? (Grade 6)

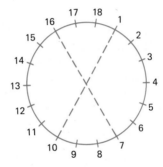

Solution Apparently pupil 10 is directly across from pupil 1, because if we count nine spaces either way from 1 we reach position 10. Across from 7 we find 16, once again obtained by finding 7 + 9. Across from 13 we expect to find one differing from 13 by 9. Thus, pupil 4 is across from pupil 1.

Strategy 1.4

Apply a basic formula.
    Sometimes the problem uses a well-known formula for the key to the solution.

EXAMPLE 1

Ken starts jogging at 5 miles per hour. One half hour later Lisa starts on her bicycle, on the same route, traveling 7 miles per hour. How long will it take for Lisa to overtake Ken? (Grade 6)

Solution 1 The basic formula that relates distance, rate, and time is $d = rt$. Because Ken had a half hour head start, the distance traveled before

Lisa started was $d = 5 \times \frac{1}{2} = \frac{5}{2} = 2\frac{1}{2}$ miles. A diagram helps to illustrate the distance being compared. In slightly more than one hour Lisa will overtake Ken.

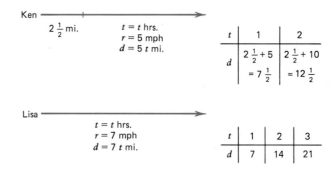

Solution 2   We will again consider the hours t after Lisa departs that she will overtake Ken. The distance traveled by Ken in t hours is $5t$. But in the half hour head start he traveled $2\frac{1}{2}$ miles. So $d = 2\frac{1}{2} + 5t$ is an expression for the distance Ken traveled while Lisa traveled $d = 7t$. Because Lisa traveled the same distance as Ken,

$$7t = 2\frac{1}{2} + 5t$$

$$2t = 2\frac{1}{2}$$

$$t = 1\frac{1}{4} \text{ hours}$$

Note that in $1\frac{1}{4}$ hours, Ken travels $d = 5 \times 1\frac{1}{4}, = 5 \times \frac{5}{4} = \frac{25}{4} = 6\frac{1}{4}$ miles and Lisa travels $d = 7 \times 1\frac{1}{4} = 7 \times \frac{5}{4} = \frac{35}{4} = 8\frac{3}{4}$ miles $= 6\frac{1}{4} + 2\frac{1}{2}$.

EXAMPLE 2

Joe is paid two times his normal rate for each hour worked over 40 hours in a week. Last week he worked 48 hours and earned $252. What is his hourly wage rate? (Grade 6)

Solution   Wages earned (w) is found by using the formula $w = r \cdot t$, where r is the hourly rate and t is the number of hours worked. If r is the hourly rate, then $40r$ is the number of dollars earned in 40 hours and $8(2r) = 16r$ is the number of dollars earned in the 8 hours of overtime. Thus, $w = 40r + 16r = 56r$, so $252 = 56r$. Thus, $r = \frac{252}{56} = 4.5$. That is, $4.50 per hour is the base rate and $9.00 per hour for overtime.

> REMARK Notice that Example 1 and Example 2 both involved "rates." However, one involved distance and time and the other wages earned. Many different kinds of problems relate to this basic idea. We will return to it in other problems from time to time.

The formula that provides the key to a solution for some problems may simply be a relationship that provides necessary information. For example, children are introduced to the idea of multi-digit numerals in the primary grades and are able to use these ideas in problem solving. The following problem was proposed by a fourth grade child.

EXAMPLE 3

I am thinking of a two-digit number. This number is even. The tens digit is twice as large as the ones digit. If you add them together the sum will be 12. What is my number?

Solution 1 A two-digit number, like 23 for example, is made by placing digits (the 2 and the 3) in place-value slots (the tens and the units). The desired number has two digits with the tens digit twice as large as the units digit. Let us use a table to list all the two-digit numbers having the tens digit twice the ones digit.

Tens Digit	Ones Digit
~~2~~	~~1~~
4	2
~~6~~	~~3~~
8	4 ←

Do you agree that only these four are potential solutions? Now it becomes apparent that only the 8 and 4 give the sum 12, so the two-digit number is 84.

Solution 2 We could represent the units digit by some variable, say a. Then the tens digit must be $2a$. The sum of the digits is 12, so $2a + a = 12$. Thus $3a = 12$, so $a = 4$ and $2a = 8$. The number must be 84.

> REMARK It should be clear that Solution 1 is more basic and will be the approach used by most fourth-grade students. As we approach problems we may well start at that level, then consider a variety of other solutions possible. Remember, any reasonable approach is acceptable.

Strategy 1.5

Note a problem previously solved but now in a new setting.

We often see things that at first appear to be quite different, then on closer study discover they are really the same. Consider the following example.

EXAMPLE 1

Six boys appeared in the gym to practice basketball. They decided to practice using a one-on-one format. That is, two boys would compete with each other, then two others would take the floor to compete. If each boy is to compete with each other boy, how many matches will there be? (Grade 5)

Solution This is really the same problem as the one identified as Example 1 for Strategy 1.2. The first boy could be paired with each of the other five and so on. Thus, we expect $5 + 4 + 3 + 2 + 1 = 15$ such pairings.

The next example was proposed by a fourth-grade student.

EXAMPLE 2

I am a three-digit number. All of my digits are even. My first and last digits are the same. When the digits are added they equal 8 and when multiplied they equal 16. What number am I?

Solution 1 This is a digit problem, so it should remind us of Example 3 for Strategy 1.4. A table should be of help, as we consider the three-digit number $c\ b\ a$. The table will reflect the fact that all digits must be even and the units and hundreds the same. Now let us locate instances where the sum of the digits is 8. Two such possibilities exist. Because the product must be 16, only the digits 2, 4, and 2 will work. (Why must you discard 4, 0, 4?) The number must be 242.

Hundreds Digit	Tens Digit	Ones Digit
2	0	2
2	2	2
2	4	2←

Hundreds Digit	Tens Digit	Ones Digit
2	6	2
~~4~~	~~0~~	~~4~~
4	2	4
4	4	4
4	6	4
4	8	4
6	0	6
6	2	6
6	4	6
6	6	6
6	8	6
8	0	8
8	2	8
8	4	8
8	6	8
8	8	8

Solution 2 With some experience students will refine the table-building procedure. For example, they might search for even digits with a sum of eight all in one step. Such a table would contain only two entries and only the digits 2, 4 and 2 will produce the required product.

Hundreds Digit	Tens Digit	Ones Digit
2	4	2 ←
4	0	4

Strategy 1.6

Organize the counting process.

Sometimes it becomes important that we actually tabulate all possible options in order to effectively count the resulting number.

EXAMPLE 1

Suppose five girls are at a Girl Scout meeting to work on a project. When they are finished, three girls are expected to serve as a clean-up committee.

How many such committees could be made?

> *Solution* Let us tabulate the committees possible. To simplify the process, let us identify the girls as A, B, C, D, and E. Note that the committee ABC is the same as ACB, so we must be careful not to duplicate the listings. Consider the following tabulations.

ABC	ACD	ADE	$3 + 2 + 1 = 6$
ABD	ACE		
ABE			
BCD	BDE		$2 + 1 = 3$
BCE			
CDE			$1 = 1$
			Total 10

Do you agree that this list contains all possible committees?

EXAMPLE 2

Four adjacent spaces are available for rent in a shopping center, numbered 1, 2, 3, and 4. A restaurant, a sporting goods store, a pet shop, and a jewelry store would like to rent them. However, zoning laws will not allow the pet store and the restaurant to be located adjacent to each other. How many different ways can these four businesses occupy the four spaces available in the shopping center?

> *Solution* Let us use just the first letter of the name as we make our listing. That is R for restaurant, S for sporting goods, P for pet shop, and J for jewelry store. The following chart should list all possible arrangements.

R in Space One	S in Space One	P in Space One	J in Space One
RSPJ	~~SRPJ~~	~~PRSJ~~	JRSP
RSJP	SRJP	~~PRJS~~	~~JRPS~~
~~RPSJ~~	~~SPRJ~~	PSRJ	~~JSRP~~
~~RPJS~~	SPJR	PSJR	~~JSPR~~
RJSP	~~SJRP~~	PJRS	~~JPRS~~
RJPS	~~SJPR~~	PJSR	JPSR

Now cross out any arrangement having R and P together. There are 12 possible arrangements for the stores.

Strategy 1.7

Use an analogous but simpler problem to suggest a solution.

Sometimes a problem is stated that would be very difficult to analyze from a tabulation or a table because of a large number of cases to consider. The following example might effectively illustrate this.

EXAMPLE 1

Twenty-five people appeared at a political rally. Because politicians always like to shake hands, the first order of business is for every person to shake hands with everyone else present. How many handshakes will there be?

Solution To act this out or to make a tabulation to illustrate the hand-shakes would be time consuming. So let us look at a simpler case, perhaps with five people present. Call them *A*, *B*, *C*, *D*, and *E* for convenience and make a tabulation of the possible handshakes.

AB				
AC	BC			or 4 + 3 + 2 + 1 = 10 handshakes
AD	BD	CD		
AE	BE	CE	DE	

In fact, you may have recognized this as being essentially the same as Example 1 for Strategy 1.2, where we drew the line segments between points, and Example 1 for Strategy 1.5. The basic idea is that one person, say *A*, can shake hands with everyone else present. Thus *A* can shake hands with 24 people, then *B* with 23, and so on. We expect to have 24 + 23 + · · · + 3 + 2 + 1 handshakes. A bit of calculator time will produce the answer 300 handshakes.

EXAMPLE 2

The average yearly rainfall in one locality was 15.6 in. based on records over the past 25 years. This year they registered 20.2 in. of rain. What is the average rainfall for the 26-year period?

Solution Perhaps it is not immediately clear how to handle this data. So try a simpler problem. Suppose that the average for a 2-year period was 15 in. per year and this year 20 in. were recorded. To find the average rainfall we must find the total of the rain over the 3-year period, then divide by the number of years to find the *average* rainfall. This would be 2 × 15 + 20 = 50 in. of rain in 3 years or $\frac{50}{3}$ = 16.7 in. per year. So, in our problem, we find 25 × 15.6 + 20.2 = 410.2 in. over the 26-year period. That is an average of 410.2 ÷ 26 = 15.8 in. per year over the 26-year period.

EXAMPLE 3

How many terms are between 1 and 125 in the sequence 1, 2, 3, 4 . . . 125?

Solution Suppose we look at a shorter sequence, like 1, 2, 3, 4, 5. There are a total of five terms, thus 3 *between* 1 and 5. Therefore, between 1 and 125 we expect 125 − 2 = 123 numbers.

Strategy 1.8

Look at specific cases when encountering general-type questions.
   Generalizations are usually difficult for children to state. We often gain insight into general statements by considering individual examples.

EXAMPLE 1 .

We are given an ordinary circular pizza. We are instructed to cut the pizza using cuts that go completely across the pizza in a straight line. What is the greatest number of pieces that can be obtained from six cuts?

Solution Consider the two *one*-cut results. Both produced the same number of pieces of pizza. With *two* cuts we would have several choices of how to arrange the cuts.

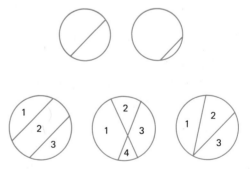

We apparently get more pieces if we use intersecting cuts, providing they intersect inside the pizza rather than on an edge. Now let us try it for *three* cuts.

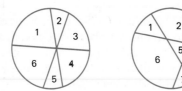

We learned above that lines should intersect inside the pizza rather than be parallel or intersect on the edge. We now also know that to get the maximum number of regions, the cuts should not all pass through a single point. Do you see a pattern in the table? Would you guess that for four cuts we would get 11 pieces? Let us check that out.

No. of Cuts		No. of Regions
1		2
2		4
3		7
4		

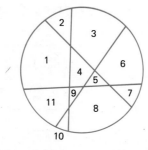

The figure confirms that all 11 regions are formed. So let us answer the original question using an extension of the table.

No. of Cuts		No. of Regions
1		2
2		4
3		7
4		11
5		16
6		22

> REMARK In this last example, you may have seen another pattern in the table. In the number of regions column there was an increase of 2, then 3, then 4, and so on. This is a perfectly good approach that will yield the same results. If you noticed that pattern, it is just as good as the one suggested in the given solution.

EXAMPLE 2

Suppose blocks are stacked as illustrated. How many blocks will be in the nth layer? (Grade 7)

Solution The first layer has one block in it, the second three blocks, and the third six blocks. What do you expect for the fourth layer? Apparently whatever number we had in the third layer plus four blocks placed out in front, giving a total of 10.

Layer Number	Number of Blocks
1	1
2	3 = 1 + 2
3	6 = (1 + 2) + 3
4	10 = (1 + 2 + 3) + 4

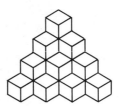

The fifth layer then should have the number found in the fourth layer (1 + 2 + 3 + 4) plus the five put down "out front," so a total of $1 + 2 + 3 + 4 + 5 = 15$ blocks. By the same reasoning in the tenth layer, we would expect $1 + 2 + 3 \cdots + 10 = 55$ blocks. So in the nth layer we expect $1 + 2 + 3 \cdots + n$ blocks.

Strategy 1.9

Relate the problem to another similar problem.

We can often decide how to handle one problem by considering another problem already done that resembles it. The following problem was written by a fifth grade student.

EXAMPLE 1

I am an even number with four digits. My first and last numbers are the same. My tens digit is half as much as my hundreds digit. When you add my digits together, my sum is 16. When you multiply my digits together the product is 128. What number am I?

Solution   This digit problem is similar to Example 2 in Strategy 1.5. Thus we can proceed with place value considerations $d\ c\ b\ a$. Because this is to be an even number, the units digit must be even. Let us build a table, then select those entries where the sum of the digits is 16.

Thousands Digit	Hundreds Digit	Tens Digit	Unit Digit
2	2	1	2
2	4	2	2
2	6	3	2
2	8	4	2 ←
4	2	1	4
4	4	2	4
4	6	3	4
4	8	4	4
6	2	1	6
6	4	2	6
6	6	3	6
6	8	4	6
8	2	1	8
8	4	2	8
8	6	3	8
8	8	4	8

Only one entry will work as the number must be 2842.

EXAMPLE 2

Although production records for each year are not available, we do know that the average corn yield over the past 10 years on a certain midwest farm was 142 bushels per acre. Last year the yield was 160 bushels per acre. What is the new 10-year average?

> *Solution* This problem is much like the rainfall problem encountered in Example 2 for Strategy 1.7. Because we do not know the production for the first year, we will simply drop off the average yield for 1 year. In 10 years, 1420 bushels were produced, so in 9 years we would expect 1420 − 142 or 1278 bushels. Adding the new yield gives a 10-year yield of 1438 bushels, or an average of $\frac{1438}{10}$ = 143.8 bushels per acre.

Strategy 1.10

Use a trial and error process where appropriate.

We simply try some value and observe the results. We then modify our guess based on the information accumulated.

EXAMPLE 1

A square has an area of 115 square inches. What is the length of one side? (to the nearest tenth of an inch) (Grade 5)

> *Solution* The area of a square can be found by using the formula $A = s^2$, where s is the length of a side. Let us guess that $s = 5$. Then $A = 5^2 = 25$, which is much too small. Suppose we let $s = 10$. Then $A = 10^2 = 100$, which is still too small, although much closer. We should pick a larger value for s, say 12. Then $A = 12^2 = 144$. At this point we know the desired value for s is between 10 and 12. Again, a table helps as we contrive to select values of s. The value $s = 11$ is a reasonable choice for our next trial. The value of s must be between 10 and 11 and would appear to be close to 11. If $s = 10.9$, then $A = 118.8$. If $s = 10.8$, $A = 116.64$, which is closer to the area desired. If $s = 10.7$, then $A = 114.49$. Because 10.8 gives an answer that is 1.64 larger than desired and 10.7 produces an answer which is 0.51 smaller than desired, we should select 10.7 as the closest answer. (To the nearest tenth)

r	A
5	25
10	100

r	A
10.7	114.49
10.8	116.64
10.9	118.8
11	121
12	144

EXAMPLE 2

Jessica scored three times as many points as Colleen in a basketball game. Colleen scored eight points less than Jessica in that game. How many points did Jessica score?

Solution Make a guess. Jessica (14) Colleen (6)

$$\text{Check. } 14 - 6 = 8$$
$$14 \neq 3 \cdot 6$$

Second guess. Jessica (16) Colleen (8)
$$\text{Check. } 16 - 8 = 8$$
$$16 \neq 3 \cdot 8$$

Third guess.   Jessica (20) Colleen (12)
$$\text{Check. } 20 - 12 = 8$$
$$20 \neq 3 \cdot 12$$

The product is not getting closer to checking. Let us try a smaller value.

Fourth guess. Jessica (12) Colleen (4)
$$\text{Check. } 12 - 4 = 8$$
$$12 = 3 \cdot 4$$

Jessica scored 12 points and Colleen scored 4.

Strategy 1.11

Work backwards to find the answer.
     We sometimes need to "unravel" the problem by reversing the steps. The following problem was suggested by a fourth-grade child.

EXAMPLE 1

I am a three-digit number. If you multiply me by 52 and add 8, I will equal 7080. What number am I?

Solution One approach would be to just reverse the steps.

$$7080 - 8 = 7072$$

$$\frac{7072}{52} = 136$$

To check this answer, simply multiply 136 times 52, then add 8. (136 × 52) + 8 = 7072 + 8 = 7080.

EXAMPLE 2

Keri's father, Bill, was a baker. Out of his usual morning batch of chocolate chip cookies, Bill burned the first two dozen cookies. He gave half of what was left to Keri to take to school. He wrapped up half of the remaining cookies and gave them to the gas station crew next door. He gave half of what was left to the policeman on the beat. If Bill had only 7 cookies left, how many cookies were in the batch of chocolate chip cookies?

Solution Again let us work from the final results. If Bill gave half to the policeman and still had 7 remaining, he must have given the policeman 7 cookies. His 7 plus those given to the policeman must be the same number as was given to the gas station crew. This accounts for 28 cookies. Thus Keri must have received 28 cookies. There must have been 56 unburned cookies. These along with the 24 that were burned make a total of 80 cookies.

A diagram helps to visualize this process.

EXAMPLE 3

For what number x is $3x - 6 = 18$?

Solution How big would the number $3x$ have to be in order that when 6 is subtracted, the result is 18? Apparently $3x$ should be 24. Then determine what number that when multiplied by 3 gives 24. Of course the answer is 8. We can check our answer by replacing x by 8 in the equation.

$$3 \cdot 8 - 6 = 8$$
$$24 - 6 = 18$$
$$18 = 18$$

Problems with Problem Solving

When problems are drawn from real-world settings, we often find situations where either too much or too little data are presented. Sometimes the problem solvers will need to search out additional information before they can proceed. The following is an example of a problem written by a fourth-grade student.

EXAMPLE 1

I am thinking of a two-digit number. The sum of the digits is 11. Add 11 to the number and it equals 58. Subtract 8 and your answer is 39. What is the number?

Solution Presumably the second sentence means that the sum of the digits is 11. But does one need this information to answer the question? Would not just the information of either of the next two sentences suffice to provide an answer? (That is, $58 - 11 = 47$ has completed the solution as would $39 + 8$.)

EXAMPLE 2

A railroad track from Los Angeles to Buffalo is 3000 miles long. Each railroad tie has four spikes in it. How many railroad spikes have been used in building this railroad?

Solution We really cannot do much until we know more about how the ties are spaced.

Application of
Polya's Plan for
Problem Solving

From the discussion thus far, it should seem evident that no set of examples of problem solving can be exhaustive. We are constantly confronted by new problems or interesting variations on existing problems. You will find that many elementary school textbooks provide students with sets of problem-solving strategies. These are in general very similar to the 11 strategies posed earlier in this chapter.

To become really comfortable in doing problem solving, one must have experience with solving a variety of problems. In the preceding discussion, the methods of solution were purposely tied to the specific procedure identified. In general, as we meet problems we will likely need to spend a lot of time in the "devising a plan" stage. In some cases we will have a variety of approaches that could be used, but in other cases we may be hard pressed to find even one approach that seems reasonable. Let us consider a plan of attack that you might find useful as you work with the problems encountered in this book and elsewhere. The first example is one that a fourth-grade pupil proposed.

EXAMPLE 1

I have three even numbers and, when added, they equal 14. When multiplied, they equal 64. They come between 20 and 1. What are the numbers?

1. Understanding the problem:
   We are searching for three numbers, all even, whose sum is 14 and whose product if 64. The numbers are all between 1 and 20.

2. Devising a plan:
   Plan a: We could build a table consisting of combinations of even numbers between 1 and 20. Because there are 9 even numbers between 1 and 20, if we used all possible combinations for three numbers we would have a *big* table of values.

   Plan b: We could build a table using just those numbers whose sum is 14. Then select those from this list whose product is 64.

   Plan c: Just guess and check to see if we can zero in on a solution quickly.

   Plan d: Try to use a prime factorization of 64, and use these factors to build the three numbers.

   Plan e: Write equations and solve them.

3. *Solution a* I would rather not because the table would have $9 \times 9 \times 9 = 729$ entries.

Solution b Let the three numbers be named a, b, and c for ease of reference. We will start with a value for one variable, say a, then choose all permissible values for b and c that provide the sum $a + b + c = 14$. We must now select those numbers whose product is 64. Apparently the numbers must be 2, 4, and 8.

a	b	c
2	2	10
2	4	8 ←
2	6	6
2	8	4
2	10	2
4	2	8
4	4	6
4	6	4
4	8	2
6	2	6
6	4	4
6	6	2
8	2	4
8	4	2
10	2	2

Solution c We can save time by trying only even numbers where the sum is 14, then check the product. We will start with a guess, say $a = 4$, $b = 4$, and $c = 6$. The product is 96, which is too large.

Let us select one factor that is smaller, say $a = 2$, $b = 4$, and $c = 6$. Then $a \cdot b \cdot c = 48$. We apparently need to increase a factor. Try $a = 2$, $b = 6$, and $c = 6$. Then we have a product of 72, which is too large. Try $a = 2$, $b = 4$, and $c = 8$ and note that the product is 64.

a	b	c	$a \cdot b \cdot c$
4	4	6	96
2	4	6	48
2	6	6	72
2	4	8	64 ←

Solution d Note that $64 = 8 \times 8 = 2 \times 2 \times 2 \times 2 \times 2 \times 2$. We need to group these to make three numbers. We could select $(2) \times (2) \times (2 \times 2 \times 2 \times 2)$ or $2 \times (2 \times 2) \times (2 \times 2 \times 2)$ or $(2 \times 2) \times (2 \times 2) \times (2 \times 2)$ as the only three possibilities. These three are expressible as $2 \times 2 \times 16$, $2 \times 4 \times 8$ and $4 \times 4 \times 4$. Note that $2 + 2 + 16 = 20$, so that solution will not work. $4 + 4 + 4 = 12$, which can also be discarded, leaving us with $2 + 4 + 8 = 14$, which does work. The numbers are 2, 4, and 8.

Solution e Let a, b, and c represent the numbers. Then the two equations are $a + b + c = 14$ and $a \cdot b \cdot c = 64$. Because algebraic solutions for these are not very straightforward, we will not proceed with a solution.

4. Looking back:
   The use of tables to organize the data is often very helpful. As a result of this organization we may be able to identify a strategy that will allow us to proceed with the solution.

EXAMPLE 2

There are seven students in a physical education class who expressed a desire to play tennis. Each student is to play one match with each of the other persons. How many matches will there be?

1. Understanding the problem:
   The nature of a tennis match is that two people share the act, thus person *A* playing with person *B* is the same as *B* playing with *A*. It is also understood that a person does not play a match with oneself.

2. Devising a plan:
   Plan a: We could get seven people and ask them to act out the problem.
   Plan b: We could locate seven points, preferably not more than 2 in a line, and then draw the segments connecting pairs of points.
   Plan c: We could identify the seven people by some convenient symbol, then tabulate all possible pairs.
   Plan d: We could treat the problem more abstractly and recognize that person *A* would be paired with all 6 other people. Then *B* would be matched with all those but person *A*, etc.

3. *Solution a* Suppose we decide to "act it out" and actually have seven people form the possible pairings. Suppose the first initial of the names of the seven people are *A*, *B*, *C*, *D*, *E*, *F*, and *G*. Suppose that *A* plays with *B*, *C*, *D*, *E*, *F*, and *G*. Then *B* plays with *C*, *D*, *E*, *F*, and *G* and *C* plays with *D*, *E*, *F*, and *G*. *D* now must meet *E*, *F*, and *G* whereas *E* plays with *F* and *G*. Finally *F* plays with *G*. There are a total of $6 + 5 + 4 + 3 + 2 + 1 = 21$ matches.

Solution b Rather than have people get up and actually pair up, we could simply make a drawing that illustrates the tennis matches. Note that *A* is connected with *B, C, D, E, F,* and *G,* producing six line segments, as indicated in Figure 1.2*a*. In Figure 1.2*b*, *B* is connected with *C, D, E, F,* and *G* by line segments.

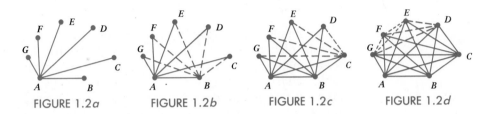

FIGURE 1.2*a*   FIGURE 1.2*b*   FIGURE 1.2*c*   FIGURE 1.2*d*

In Figure 1.2*c*, *C* is connected with *D, E, F,* and *G*. In Figure 1.2*d*, *D* is now connected with *E, F,* and *G*. Moving to vertex *E*, we can draw segments $\overline{EF}$ and $\overline{EG}$ and then from *F* we can draw $\overline{FG}$. The use of the drawing clearly illustrates the possible pairing and even suggests the numerical pattern $6 + 5 + 4 + 3 + 2 + 1$ in the solution.

Solution c We simply recognize this as a basic "counting" problem and systematize our counting process by listing pairs of letters.

AB AC AD AE AF AG	6 pairings
BC BD BE BF BG	5 pairings
CD CE CF CG	4 pairings
DE DF DG	3 pairings
EF EG	2 pairings
FG	1 pairing
Total	21 pairings

Solution d Suppose we start by simply recognizing that to make a tennis match we need a pair of people. We have seven choices for the first player and then any of the six remaining persons could be the second player. Apparently we could have 42 such arrangements. But notice that this could result in *A* as first and *B* second and also as *B* first and *A* second. Because we count both pairings as being the same, we must simply discard the duplicate and thus consider $\frac{7 \times 6}{2} = 21$ distinct tennis matches.

4. Looking back:
We should recognize the fact that in many situations a variety of possible approaches can be found. Students in the elementary school should be encouraged to look for a variety of ways to solve a problem. Eventually

we may find that one mode of attack is superior to others and will tend to use it most freuqently. For example, if 1000 people were at a meeting and we wanted to know how many tennis matches would be involved, we would likely decide not to "act it out" or to draw a diagram. In this case, Solution c or d would be much easier to handle, particularly if we are allowed to use a calculator. We will return to this consideration in later problem sets.

The intent of this chapter has been to present a variety of strategies that may be of help as you attempt to solve problems. You will find them to be useful in problems that will be encountered throughout this book. In general, tables, charts, and diagrams are useful initial steps in problem solving. They allow us to organize data and frequently provide insights regarding further treatment of the information in order to solve the problem. The strategies presented here will allow you to get involved in some potentially helpful approaches.

PROBLEM SET

A. Try each of the following on your own. If you need a hint, consider the examples cited in the chapter.

1. Twelve children went to a movie. The snack bar at the movie only sold popcorn and peanuts. All of the children made a purchase at the snack bar. Some of them bought popcorn; some bought peanuts; some bought both. As they sat down to watch the movie, eight children were carrying only popcorn, three children were carrying both popcorn and peanuts.
   a. How many children were carrying peanuts?
   b. How many children were carrying only popcorn?
   c. How many children were carrying only peanuts?
   (*Hint:* Try acting it out.)

2. I am thinking of a number between 150 and 270. The product of the digits is 81. What is the number? (*Hint:* Check Strategy 1.6. A table should be helpful.)

3. How many three member committees can be formed from Al, Bob, Carol, Dawn, Eve, Faye, George, and Harvey, if Al and Bob refuse to serve on the same committee? (*Hint:* Strategy 1.9 should be of help along with Strategy 1.6.)

4. How many even numbers are between 17 and 243? (*Hint:* Try Strategy 1.7 for help.)

5. a. At what time are the sum of the digits on a digital clock the greatest? (*Hint:* Strategy 1.2 should be of help.)
   b. At what times will the sum of the digits equal 10?

6. A box of blocks was sitting on a table in a classroom. Mindy decided to play with the blocks and took one third of them to her desk. John thought this was a great idea and took one third of the blocks that remained in the box. A moment later Jim took one third of what then remained, leaving 16 blocks in the box.

 a. How many blocks were in the box before any were removed?

 b. How many did each of the children have to play with? (*Hint:* Try to work backward on this one. Check Strategy 1.11.)

7. How many angles are formed by nine rays having a common endpoint? (*Hint:* Consider Strategy 1.5.)

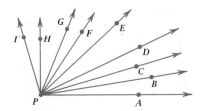

8. How many different choices of three odd numbers will yield seven as the sum? (*Hint:* A tabulation should be of help. Check Strategy 1.6.)

9. a. Ice cream cones are available at the cafeteria in school. Two kinds of cone, sugar and regular, and four flavors of ice cream are provided. How many different ice-cream treats are there to choose from? (*Hint:* Try making a diagram.)

 b. Joe's Pizza Parlor boasts of having three kinds of crust available and eight different toppings. There are four different sizes of pizza to choose from. How many different ways can a customer obtain pizza at Joe's place?

 (*Hint:* Try a diagram like in Strategy 1.3.)

10. I am thinking of a three-digit number. When these three digits are added together, the sum is 14. The product of the number and 5 is 2275, and the quotient of the number and 5 is 91. The number is between 400 and 700. What is my number? (*Hint:* Lots of extra information here. What part do you need to get a solution?)

11. a. Jim leaves point A on his bicycle riding toward point B traveling at a rate of 12 miles per hour. One hour later Pete departs from A riding on the same route traveling 15 miles per hour. After Pete has been riding for 2 hours, how far is he behind Jim? (*Hint:* Make a diagram, or refer to Strategy 1.4.)

 b. Kirk starts jogging at 5 miles per hour. One-half hour later Nancy starts jogging on the same route at 7 miles per hour. How long will it take Nancy to catch Kirk (*Hint:* Check Strategy 1.5.)

12. Find two numbers whose sum is 84 and whose product is 1728.
(*Hint:* Make a chart.)

B. Try your skill on the following problems.

13. When you add the digits of this number you get 11. When you multiply this number by 3 you get a multiple of 8 and the new number is less than 170. When you divide this number by 2, you get a multiple of 4. What is the number?

14. I am thinking of an odd number between 250 and 260. The sum of the digits is 12. What is the number?

15. I am thinking of a three-digit number that is less than 299. It is reversible, and if you divide it by 2, that number is reversible also. What is the number? (By reversible we mean that it is the same when read from left to right as it does when read from right to left.)

16. In the United States it is common to write the date July 4, 1989, as 7/4/89 (or 7-4-89). In many European countries, the date is read 4 July 1989 and written as 4-7-89. During a year, how many dates are in danger of being confused?

17. A table-tennis tournament has 100 contestants. As players lose matches they are dropped out of the tournament. How many matches are needed to complete the tournament?

18. Suppose that on a trip you get 24 miles per gallon average fuel consumption without the use of the air conditioner, but only 20 miles per gallon with air conditioning turned on. With an interstate speed of 65 miles per hour and gasoline costing $0.98 per gallon, what is the cost per hour for air conditioning?

19. Supppose you are building a board fence. To get adequate support, posts most be placed 8 feet apart. How many posts will be needed to enclose a rectangular area that is 40 feet long and 24 feet wide?

20. Find the smallest two-digit counting number whose square contains four even digits.

21. How many 3's must you add to 39 to get 99?

2 | SETS AND WHOLE NUMBERS

Sample Problem

Using 180 dots, make an arrangement that has 150 in the circle and 90 in the square.

2.1.   THE LANGUAGE OF SETS

The NCTM Standards stress the need for using mathematics to communicate. To do this, it is essential that vocabulary be associated with concepts and that symbols that represent these concepts be developed to help us with written communication. As we proceed with the various topics, we will endeavor to allow you to make new mathematical associations with real things as much as possible in order to involve you directly in the development. We will attempt to provide problems and situations where you will have an opportunity to read, write, and discuss ideas using mathematical terms and symbols in a natural way.

The casual observer of the elementary school mathematics program may assume that "number" or perhaps "counting" is the most basic of the mathematical concepts encountered. This is not the case. Ideas about sets are even more basic, and we begin our development with this topic.

The notion of a set, or a collection of things, is not particularly profound. All of us have had many experiences with groups of things. Basketball teams, church congregations, your family, the students in your class, the coats in your closet, the books in the library, and the set of forks in the cafeteria are all commonplace examples. Even the preschool child has notions about sets. A child can often recognize that a toy is missing from the toy box even before he or she can determine how many toys belong to the collection.

As we proceed with this development it is highly desirable for us to be able to have a common understanding of the terms and symbols used. For this reason we will often provide definitions for terms being used—simply to be sure that we all share the same understanding of the meaning intended. This must, of course, be done using words and concepts more basic than the one being defined. It should be apparent that we cannot define every word used; that would take too long, and, more important, it would not be possible to do so without using circular definitions. Thus, we will leave some words undefined, and the term *set* will be the first such word encountered. Although it is undefined, you must surely recognize that we are speaking of a collection of objects or symbols possessing some property or some characteristic that enables us to determine whether a given object belongs to the set.

We call attention to the fact that some situations exist that make it difficult to determine whether an object belongs to a given set. For example, suppose we are interested in the set of "handsome dogs." However, we do not really have a definition for handsomeness in dogs. The person who dearly loves a Mexican hairless might not be inclined to consider a basset hound a handsome dog. Thus, given some specific dog, it would be difficult to decide whether it belongs to our set. In our work in this book, we will simply choose to avoid such sets where we cannot make decisions about membership on a logical basis. We will work only with sets with which when given any object, we can make a decision regarding membership in the set. Such sets are normally referred to as *well-defined sets*.

The types of sets that we encounter will naturally vary greatly. Some sets, such as a set of toy teacups, a set of fish in a pond, a set of seals in the zoo, or a set of crayons in a box, would probably be familiar to most children. In each case, given some object, we could easily determine whether it belonged to the set. But other sets are more complex. For example, the set consisting of the numeral 6, the letter *z*, and the word ice would not display any relationship between the elements beyond the condition that they belong to the set. Some sets have sets as their only elements. For example, the National Football League is a set, each member of which is itself a set of players comprising a team. Some sets have many elements, such as the people living on the earth at a given instant. Indeed, some sets, such as points on a line, have an unlimited number of elements and are said to be *infinite sets*. Other sets are restrictive in members, such as the set of persons who can run a mile in less than 4 minutes. In fact, the set of living mastodons has no members at all. We commonly refer to such a set with no elements as the *empty set*, or the *null set*. In general, those sets that are empty or that have a limited number of elements are called *finite sets*.

It is essential that we develop some terminology and symbolism so that we may communicate about sets. Sometimes we will simply use a diagram or a picture to illustrate a set. This is commonly done in elementary school materials. At other times we will list the elements of a set. For example, if we are interested in the vowels of our alphabet, we might write {*a, e, i, o, u*}. The braces are a universally accepted symbol denoting a set. We would say that we have produced the set of vowels in a *roster* or *tabulation* form. In our everyday conversation we often refer to collections of things and need no special vocabulary to call attention to this fact. Our dinner plates are part of the set of dishes, yet we need not be formal about such a referral as we place the plates on the table. Likewise, as we write about sets we may often be informal yet still communicate accurately. At other times it is more convenient or more precise to use set symbols. Let us agree that in our work we will always use capital letters to refer to sets. Thus, we might write $L =$ {Huron, Ontario, Michigan, Erie, Superior}, which means that the set comprising "the Great Lakes" is being represented by the letter L. We might then state that Huron is a *member* of the set, or is an *element* of the set. We would write Huron $\in L$. The fact that Lake Tahoe is not one of the Great Lakes would be written as Tahoe $\notin L$.

REMARK Some parts of the symbolism involved in mathematics carry over to many aspects of the subject. The use of the slash mark to deny a statement is one of these. Thus, you will encounter it often as you proceed with the work in this book.

Sometimes it is more efficient to use a set in its tabulated form; at other times a verbal description is more useful. For example, suppose we are discussing my fourth-period mathematics class. We might simply refer to it as my Math 201-4 class, or perhaps just as my fourth-hour class. However, if reference is being made to the scores achieved on the last test, then the class roster is much more useful. Suppose a set contains four elements, a star, the letter w, the Greek letter β, and a triangle. It would be convenient simply to write $A = \{*, W, \beta, \triangle\}$.

There are occasions when we wish to do a tabulation but do not wish to write all the elements in the set. To identify the set of counting numbers less than or equal to 100, we might write $\{1, 2, 3, \ldots, 100\}$. We simply begin by writing enough elements to establish a pattern; then the three dots indicate that the set continues in that pattern. The final entry indicates the last element. If we write $\{1, 2, 3, 4, \ldots\}$, the set clearly begins with the counting numbers 1, 2, 3, and 4. The three dots indicate that it continues in a like manner forever.

There are occasions when it is useful to refer to sets using *set-builder notation*. The set of Great Lakes would be written as $\{l \mid l$ is one of the Great Lakes$\}$. This is read as the set of all l's such that l is one of the Great Lakes. The letter l is a place holder to be replaced by names of lakes; any symbol could have been chosen in its place. The vertical slash means "such that." This symbolism has commonly been used in many algebra texts, for example.

EXAMPLE 1

The set of whole numbers would be written as $\{c \mid c$ is a whole number$\}$.

EXAMPLE 2

$\{k \mid k$ is an odd number$\}$ would be read as the set of all numbers k such that k is an odd number.

Several conventions exist for listing elements within a set. One is that because we are merely indicating the elements that are in the set, we do not repeat entries. Thus, if we wish to list the letters found in the word *element*, we would write $\{e,l,m,n,t\}$. The fact that e is contained in the word three times does not matter in the least. Also, it does not matter in what order the elements are written; thus, the set $\{c,a,t\}$ and the set $\{t,a,c\}$ are the same. We make special note of this by stating that any two sets containing the same elements are *equal sets*.

We should call attention to two special sets. As we enter into any particular discussion, it will be convenient to identify the set of objects that may be considered. This set is called the *universal set*, or simply the universe, and is usually denoted by U. In many cases the universe will be specifically indicated, but it is sometimes merely implied. The second special set is the one mentioned earlier as the empty set. Recall that it is a set with no elements. The symbol $\emptyset$ is commonly used for the empty set. It is sometimes helpful simply to represent the empty set by using the braces with no elements inserted. Thus, if P is the set of living tyrannosaurs, we might write $P = \{ \}$ $= \emptyset$. Using set-builder notation, if $B = \{\triangle \mid \triangle + 2 = \triangle + 1$ for any number $\triangle\}$, we could write $B = \emptyset$ because for no number $\triangle$ does $\triangle + 2 = \triangle + 1$.

PROBLEM SET 2.1

1. Let $A = \{1,2,3,4, \ldots 10\}$ and $B = \{1,3,5,7, \ldots \}$. Classify each as true or false.

    a. $4 \in A$ **b.** $12 \in A$ **c.** $15 \notin A$

    d. $6 \in B$ **e.** $11 \notin B$ **f.** $\frac{3}{5} \in A$

2. Write each of the following statements using roster notation:

    a. Distinct letters in the word mathematics

    b. The set of whole numbers greater than three but less than nine

    c. The set whose elements are △, □, ○, 2, and 6

    d. The months having exactly 30 days

    e. The whole numbers x such that $x + 2 = x + 5$

    f. The set whose elements are $a, b, \{a\}, \{b\}$, and $\varnothing$

3. Which of the following sets are well defined?

    a. The set of great musicians

    b. The set of good movies

    c. The set of students enrolled in this class

    d. The set of whole numbers less than 1000

4. Rewrite each of the following using appropriate mathematical symbols.

    a. D is the set whose members are $a, b, c,$ and d

    b. e is not an element of D

    c. b is an element of D

    d. Set E is an empty set

5. Tabulate the following sets:

    a. Whole numbers between 5 and 15

    b. Even whole numbers greater than 0 and less than 14

    c. Whole numbers greater than 500

    d. Whole numbers between 1 and 10 that are divisible by 11

    e. Odd whole numbers

6. Mark each statement either true or false.

    a. $7 \in \{a \mid a$ is a whole number and $a + 2 = 5\}$

    b. $a \in \{a,b\}$

    c. $a \in \{a\}$

    d. $\varnothing \in \{a\}$

    e. $\{1\} \in \{1,2,3\}$

    f. $1 \in \{1,2,3\}$

    g. $\{1\} \in \{\{1\}, \{2\}, \{3\}\}$

    h. $\{a,b\} \in \{a,b,c\}$

    i. $\{a,b\} \in \{\{a\}, \{b\}, \{c\}, \{a,b\}, \{a,c\}, \{b,c\}, \varnothing, \{a,b,c\}\}$

7. What might be an appropriate universal set for each of these sets?

    a. The set of students taking mathematics this term

    b. The set of Ford cars

    c. The set of Orlon sweaters

    d. The set of whole numbers between 10 and 20

8. Suppose six people are in a group and want to shake hands with everyone else.

    a. Find five other persons to help act out the solution.

    b. Show how to use a diagram to obtain a solution.

    c. Use a tabulation to solve the problem.

9. To find the sum $1 + 2 + 3 + \cdots + 12$ is easy enough, but the sum $1 + 2 + 3 + \cdots + 120$ is not so easy, even using a calculator. An alternate approach is the following. Simply write the sequence backward and note that each corresponding pair has the same sum, 10 in this example. There are

$$1 + 2 + 3 + 4 + 5 + 6 + 7 + 8 + 9$$
$$9 + 8 + 7 + 6 + 5 + 4 + 3 + 2 + 1$$

9 such pairs giving a total of $9 \times 10 = 90$. Because we have included the sequence $1 + 2 + 3 + \cdots + 9$ twice, we must now divide by two to obtain the desired sum. Thus $1 + 2 + 3 + \cdots + 9 = \dfrac{9 \times 10}{2} = 45$.

    a. Use this procedure to find $1 + 2 + 3 + \cdots + 15$. Check your answer by adding using your calculator.

    b. Find the sum $1 + 2 + 3 + \cdots + 25$.

    c. Find $1 + 2 + 3 + \cdots + 1200$.

10. If 1000 persons are at a convention and everyone is asked to shake hands with everyone else, how many handshakes would be involved? (*Hint:* Use the technique developed in Problem 9.)

Pedagogical Problems and Activities

11. Young children need to be provided with experiences that allow them to sort objects into sets based on some criteria. For example, one set of blocks, commonly referred to as attribute blocks, is produced in four shapes (circle, diamond, square, and triangle), in four colors (red, green, blue, and yellow), and in two sizes (large and small). Thus, there is one large red circle, one large red square, and so on.

    a. Which pieces would be in the set of blue things?

    b. Which pieces are in the set of yellow triangles?

    c. Suggest two additional ways that a child might be asked to sort these pieces.

    d. If there is one large circle with each color, how many large circles are there? How many small circles? How many pieces in the set?

12. Buttons are often used for sorting. Suggest four different attributes of buttons that could be used to sort them.

13. Sets exist that we cannot see. For example, the attribute might be sounds, in which case we might begin our list with things like: {the school bell, a church bell, a whistle, . . . }.

    a. List five more things in the set of sounds.

    b. Suppose we consider the sense of smell. Children could list smells like a flower (rose?), orange peel, and so on. List other items that might appear in this list.

    c. We could use the sense of touch to determine a set. Tabulate some things in this set.

    d. What other sensory-type sortings might you consider?

14. Suggest a sorting activity based on function, which could be used with the following set of materials: {chair, pencil, soap, crayon, stool, spoon, chalk, table, paper, towel, cup, marble, umbrella, ballpoint pen}.

15. Suppose that in a box we place a pencil, an eraser, and a box of crayons. Tabulate the sets, each having at least one member, that could be made from these materials.

16. A scout troop has six members. We could form two-member cleanup committees or three-member committees. Are there more two-member committees or more three-member committees? Justify your answer.

17. Suggest an appropriate name to describe each set.

    a. {cow, calf, pig, sheep}

    b. {dog, hamster, kitten, turtle}

    c. {grape, peach, apple}

    d. {pencil, crayon, tablet, notebook}

18. Children in the fifth and sixth grades are intrigued with infinite sets. Which of the following are infinite sets?

    a. The set of beans in a jar

    b. The grains of sand in the bottom of an aquarium

    c. The grains of sand on the local beach

    d. The grains of sand on all the beaches on the earth

    e. The number of people living on the earth at a given instant

    f. The number of seconds in 10 years

    g. The whole numbers

    h. The whole numbers bigger than 1,000,000

2.2. RELATIONS ON SETS

Suppose we are given the set $A = \{0, 1, 2, 3, 4, 5, 6, 7, 8, 9\}$ and $B = \{x \mid x$ is a whole number less than 10}. It should be evident that we have simply named the same set in two different ways. Likewise, if $C = \{a, e, i, o, u\}$ and $D = \{k \mid k$ is a vowel}, we have again simply named a set in two ways, and we are referring to the same entity. When two sets are so related we refer to them as *equal sets*. Let us state this relation as the first formal definition in our development.

Definition 2.1 Two sets A and B are *equal* (written $A = B$) if and only if every element of A is an element of B and every element of B is an element of A.

> **REMARK** Notice that in stating the definition we used the words *if and only if*. This tells us two things: (1) if sets A and B are equal, then every element of A is in B and every element of B is in A; and (2) if we have two sets such that every element of the first set is in the second and every element of the second is in the first, then the sets are equal. Every definition will be of this form, or equivalent to it. Thus, the "if and only if" statement is a nice compact way to state two separate "if-then" statements. We call these two "if-then" statements *converses* of each other.

When you wish to apply the definition for equality, it is necessary to use it carefully. For example, suppose $A = \{a, b, c, d\}$ and $B = \{c, d, b, a\}$. Then clearly every element of A is in B and, furthermore, every element of B is in A. Thus, $A = B$. Suppose $C = \{c, a, b\}$. Even though every element of C is in B, it is not true that $C = B$. Indeed, $C \neq B$ because the second criterion, that every element of the second set be in the first, was not met.

Compare $D = \{2, 4, 6, 8, 10, 12\}$ with $E = \{x \mid x$ is an even counting number greater than 1 and less than 12}. We would claim that $D \neq E$ because $12 \in D$ but $12 \notin E$. Notice that we may be certain that two sets are not equal if some element of one set turns out not to be an element of the second set. Thus, with sets D and E we satisfy only one of the two conditions imposed by Definition 2.1. This relationship between sets is of general interest to us. We normally speak of set E as being a *subset* of set D.

Definition 2.2 The set A is a *subset* of set B (written $A \subseteq B$) if and only if every element of A is an element of B.

Referring back to the sets identified earlier, note that $\{c, a, b\} \subseteq \{c, d, b, a\}$ and $\{2, 4, 6, 8, 10\} \subseteq \{2, 4, 6, 8, 10, 12\}$. Let us also agree that $A \subseteq B$ is equivalent to stating that $B \supseteq A$. (We usually read the latter statement as "B is a superset of A" or "B contains A.")

We could now compare sets in four different ways. Either $A = B$ or $A \neq B$, and either $A \subseteq B$ or $A \not\subseteq B$. Be careful, however; knowing that A is not a subset of B does not allow us to conclude that B is a subset of A. For example, let $A = \{a, b, c\}$ and $B = \{b, c, d\}$. Clearly A is not a subset of B (because of the element a), and B is not a subset of A (why?). Suppose $C = \{c, a, b\}$. Then it is perfectly correct to write $A \subseteq C$ even though we might also assert that $A = C$. (Intuitively, the symbol used for subset indicates the possibility for equality.)

Let us observe two examples.

1. $\{a, b, c\} \subseteq \{b, a, c\}$
2. $\{r, s, t\} \subseteq \{r, s, t, u, v\}$

Certainly both statements are true. However, in the first instance the conditions for equality were met, whereas in the second statement equality was not possible. We often wish to distinguish between the two possibilities and will refer to this relation of "subset but not equality" as a *proper subset*.

Definition 2.3 Set A is a *proper subset* of set B (written $A \subset B$) if and only if every element of A is an element of B and B has at least one element not in A.

Thus, we could write $\{r, s, t\} \subset \{r, s, t, u, v\}$ but $\{a, b, c\} \not\subset \{b, a, c\}$. Notice that in Definition 2.3 we imposed two conditions on the sets. The connective "and" makes it essential that both conditions be met. Thus, $\{a, b\} \not\subset \{b, c, d\}$ because $a \notin \{b, c, d\}$, which violates the first condition, and $\{a, b\} \not\subset \{b, a\}$ because there is no element in the second set that is not in the first set, thus violating the second condition. Let us agree that $A \subset B$ and $B \supset A$ are equivalent statements.

It is often helpful to use pictures of sets. If you look at the typical mathematics text prepared for first- or second-grade children, you will find a great many examples of such pictures. In this text we will use a technique similar to this, but a bit more sophisticated. We will associate points in the interior of a rectangle with elements of the universal set, then points in the interior of a circle with elements of a given set. Thus, if $A = \{1, 2, 3, 4\}$ and $U = \{1, 2, 3, \ldots 10\}$ we would be interested in 10 points in a rectangle. Inside set A we would want those points associated with the numbers 1–4. Such an arrangement is illustrated in Figure 2.1. These diagrams are called Venn diagrams.

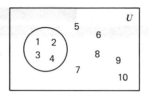

FIGURE 2.1

There will be many other instances when we will not wish to designate the specified points but will still find the Venn diagram of value. Suppose $B = \{vowels\}$ and $U = \{alphabet\}$. This time U consists of 26 points in a rectangle and set B must contain 5 elements. A diagram such as Figure 2.2*a* is sufficient to illustrate this configuration. Suppose $C = \{a, e, i, o, u, w\}$. Then $B \subseteq C$. Figure 2.2*b* illustrates a diagram where set B is a subset of set C. However, we could assert in our example that $B \subset C$ because $w \in C$ and $w \notin B$. This fact is denoted in Figure 2.2*c;* that dot outside of B indicates that at least one point exists in that region, and thus that set C has at least one element that is not in B.

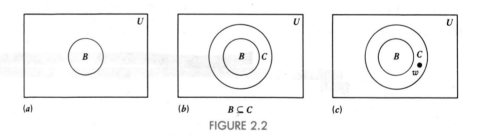

(a)   (b) $B \subseteq C$ (c)

FIGURE 2.2

Consider the diagram in Figure 2.3. Could any element of A be a element of B? It would clearly be impossible. Such sets with no elements in common are referred to as *disjoint sets.*

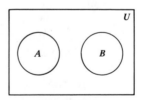

FIGURE 2.3

Definition 2.4   Sets A and B are disjoint if and only if no elements of A are in B.

With the information we now have, we might make some interesting deductions. For example, for any set A, $A \subseteq A$ but $A \not\subset A$. Is it clear why this is true? Do you see that the only way $A \subseteq A$ could be false is if some element in the left-hand set were not in the right, which is clearly impossible? Also, note that $A \not\subset A$ because if $A \subset A$, then there must be some element in the right member that is not in the left.

We might also argue that the empty set is a subset of every set. This can be shown by arguing that $A \not\subseteq B$, only if some element of A fails to be in B. As there are no elements in the empty set, we could not possibly have an element that fails to appear in B. Thus, $\emptyset \subseteq B$. However, note that $\emptyset \not\subset \emptyset$. Why is this true? In fact, $A \not\subset A$ for any set A. This must be true because the definition for a proper subset requires that for A to be a proper subset of B, B must have an element not in A. Clearly this is not possible in this instance.

Suppose we are given three sets A, B, and C and are told that $A = B$ and $B = C$. Could we then conclude that $A = C$? A moment of thought should convince us that we can draw this conclusion. Because $A = B$, both sets must contain precisely the same elements, and because $B = C$, every element of one is in the other. Thus, A and C contain the same elements and $A = C$. Let us state this finding as a property.

PROPERTY 2.1   **For any sets A, B, and C, if $A = B$ and $B = C$, then $A = C$.**

This same pattern will be seen many times in our study of mathematics. It is referred to as the *transitive property of a relation*. It appears once again in Property 2.2, but this time the relation happens to be subset.

PROPERTY 2.2   **For any sets A, B, and C, if $A \subseteq B$ and $B \subseteq C$, then $A \subseteq C$.**

Let us verify this pattern by the use of Venn diagrams. In Figure 2.4a we see the diagram for $A \subseteq B$ and in 2.4b that for $B \subseteq C$. It then follows that $A \subseteq C$ because every element of A is in C.

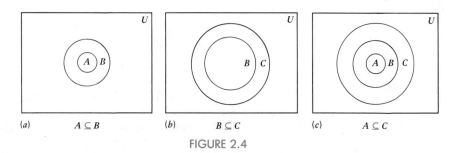

(a) $A \subseteq B$ (b) $B \subseteq C$ (c) $A \subseteq C$

FIGURE 2.4

PROPERTY 2.3   **For any sets *A*, *B*, and *C*, if *A* ⊂ *B* and *B* ⊂ *C*, then *A* ⊂ *C*.**

> **REMARK** Venn diagrams provide a very convenient pictorial represen-
> tation for many set relations. We will use such diagrams to argue many
> of the set properties we find useful. It is worth noting that such arguments
> are not very "mathematically rigorous," and your friends who are math-
> ematics majors might use other techniques to verify the patterns. Even so,
> it does provide an opportunity for you to reason mathematically.

Before we turn to the problems, let us briefly examine one additional concept. Consider the sets $A = \{1, 2, 3\}$ and $B = \{3, 4, 5\}$. Clearly the sets are not
equal. (Why is this true?) Yet we can tell at a glance that the sets are related
in such a way that each element from set *A* can be paired with an element
in *B*, and each element in *B* can be paired with one in *A*. Such a relationship
between the elements of two sets is referred to as a *one-to-one correspondence*. We refer to the sets *A* and *B* as *equivalent sets* and write $A \approx B$.

Definition 2.5   Two sets *A* and *B* are said to be *equivalent sets* $(A \approx B)$ if
and only if there exists a one-to-one correspondence between the elements of
the two sets.

EXAMPLE 1

Let $A = \{1, 2, 3, 4, 5\}$ and $B = \{r, s, t, u, v\}$. We may pair 1 with *r*, 2 with *s*, 3
with *t*, 4 with *u*, and 5 with *v*. Thus a one-to-one correspondence exists, and
we may state that *A* is equivalent to *B* and write $A \approx B$.

EXAMPLE 2

Let $C = \{1, 3, 5\}$ and $D = \{a, c, i, o\}$. Because no one-to-one correspondence
between the elements of the set exists, we will state that $C \not\approx D$.

EXAMPLE 3

Let $E = \{2, 4, 6, 8\}$ and $F = \{8, 4, 2, 6\}$. We could match the elements in the
obvious way: $2 \leftrightarrow 2, 4 \leftrightarrow 4, 6 \leftrightarrow 6, 8 \leftrightarrow 8$. Then $E \approx F$.

> **REMARK** You will note from Example 3 that if two sets are equal then
> they are equivalent. However, as evidenced by Example 1, knowing that
> two sets are equivalent will not permit us to state that they are equal.

PROBLEM SET 2.2

1. Let $A = \{a, b, c, d, e\}$, $B = \{a, b, c\}$, $C = \{d, e\}$, $D = \{c, d, e, f, g\}$, and U = $\{a, b, c, d, e, f, g, h\}$. Classify each of the following as true or false.

a. $B \subseteq A$ b. $A = D$ c. $C \subset D$

d. $B \subseteq U$ e. $\emptyset \subseteq B$ f. $\emptyset \in B$

g. $\{c\} \subset B$ h. $\{c\} \in D$ i. $A \subset U$

2. Draw a Venn diagram to represent the sets. Then describe the relationship between A and B.

a. Let $U = \{\text{human beings}\}$, $A = \{\text{women}\}$, $B = \{\text{mothers}\}$

b. $U = \{\text{human beings}\}$, $A = \{\text{fathers}\}$, $B = \{\text{grandfathers}\}$

c. $U = \{\text{all college students}\}$, $A = \{\text{women in college}\}$, $B = \{\text{elementary education majors}\}$

d. $U = \{\text{human beings}\}$, $A = \{\text{truck drivers}\}$, $B = \{\text{men}\}$

3. Use appropriate symbols from the set $\{\in, \subseteq, \subset, =\}$ or the denial of these symbols to make each statement true.

a. $2 \underline{\quad} \{1, 2, 3\}$ b. $\{2\} \underline{\quad} \{1, 2, 3\}$

c. $\emptyset \underline{\quad} \emptyset$ d. $\{1, 2\} \underline{\quad} \{1, 2, 3\}$

e. $\{1, 2, 3\} \underline{\quad} \{1, 2, 3\}$ f. $\{1, 2, 3\} \underline{\quad} \{1\}$

g. $\emptyset \underline{\quad} \{1, 2, 3\}$ h. $0 \underline{\quad} \{1, 2, 3\}$

i. $\{\{1\}, \{2\}\} \underline{\quad} \{\{1\}, \{2\}, \{3\}\}$ j. $\emptyset \underline{\quad} \{\emptyset, \{1\}, \{2\}, \{3\}\}$

4. Let $A = \{\text{whole numbers less than 12}\}$. Classify each of the following as true or false.

a. $5 \in A$ b. $12 \in A$

c. $\{2\} \in A$ d. $\{2\} \subset A$

e. $\{\} \subseteq A$ f. $\{1\} \in A$

g. $\{1, 2, 3, \ldots 11\} \subseteq A$ h. $50 \in A$

i. $A \subseteq \emptyset$ j. $\emptyset \subset A$

5. Let $U = \{1, 2, 3, 4, \ldots, 20\}$.

a. Select the subset A consisting of all even numbers in U.

b. Select the subset B consisting of all the elements that are multiples of four.

c. What relationship is there between sets A and B?

6. Classify each as true or false.

a. $\{5, 7, 9, 11, \ldots\} \subseteq \{1, 3, 5, \ldots\}$ b. $\emptyset = \{\}$

c. $\emptyset \subseteq \{\}$ d. $\emptyset \in \{\}$

e. $\{1\} \in \{1, 2\}$ f. $1 \in \{1, 2\}$

g. $\{1\} \subseteq \{1, 2\}$ h. $\{1\} \in \{1, 2, \{1\}, \{2\}, \{1, 2\}\}$

   i. $\{a, b\} \subset \{x \,|\, x$ is a letter in the word *bat*$\}$

   j. $\{1, 2\} \subseteq \{1, 2, \{1\}, \{2\}, \{1, 2\}\}$

7. a. We are told that $A \subseteq B$. Is it possible that $A = \emptyset$? Is it possible that $B = \emptyset$?

   b. We are told that $C \subset D$. Is it possible that $D = \emptyset$? Is it possible that $C = \emptyset$?

   c. Suppose $E \subseteq F$. If $F = \emptyset$, what can you conclude about E?

   d. Suppose $G \not\subseteq H$. Could it be the case that $G = \emptyset$? Could it be the case that $H = \emptyset$?

   e. Suppose $I \not\subseteq J$ and $J \neq \emptyset$. Can we conclude that $I \neq \emptyset$?

8. a. Give an example of a set B for which $A \in B$ and also $A \subseteq B$, where $A = \{a, b\}$.

   b. Give an example of two sets A and B such that $a \in A$, $A \in B$, and $a \in B$.

9. If we are given the set $\{a, b, c\}$, we can choose exactly three two-element subsets, $\{a, b\}$, $\{a, c\}$, and $\{b, c\}$. With the four-element set $\{a, b, c, d\}$ we organize the two-element subsets as follows:

$$\{a, b\}$$
$$\{a, c\}\ \{b, c\}$$
$$\{a, d\}\ \{b, d\}\ \{c, d\}$$

Thus, there are six possible two-element subsets. These results are entered into the following table.

Set	Tabulation of Two-Element Subsets	Number of Two-Element Subsets
$\{a, b\}$	$\{a, b\}$	1
$\{a, b, c\}$	$\{a, b\}$	$2 + 1 = 3$
	$\{a, c\}\ \{b, c\}$	
$\{a, b, c, d\}$	$\{a, b\}$	$3 + 2 + 1 = 6$
	$\{a, c\}\ \{b, c\}$	
	$\{a, d\}\ \{b, d\}\ \{c, d\}$	

   a. Extend the table for sets $\{a, b, c, d, e\}$ and $\{a, b, c, d, e, f\}$.

   b. If a set contained the letters $\{a, b, c, d, e, f, g\}$, how many two-element subsets would you expect? (Do not write them; just speculate from your findings above.)

   c. If a set had 20 elements, how many two-element subsets could be formed?

10. This problem is similar to Problem 9 except we are now interested in three-element subsets. Three cases are illustrated in the table.

Set	Tabulation of Three-Element Subsets	Number of Three-Element Subsets
{a, b, c}	{a, b, c}	1
{a, b, c, d}	{a, b, c} {a, c, d}	2 + 1 = 3
	{a, b, d}	
	{b, c d}	1 = 1
		Total = 4
{a, b, c, d, e}	{a, b, c} {a, c, d} {a, d, e}	3 + 2 + 1 = 6
	{a, b, d} {a, c, e}	
	{a, b, e}	
	{b, c, d} {b, d, e}	2 + 1 = 3
	{b, c, e}	
	{c, d, e}	1 = 1
		Total = 10

a. Continue the table for the set {a, b, c, d, e, f}.

b. If the set contains {a, b, c, d, e, f, g}, how many three-element subsets do you expect?

c. If the set contains 10 elements, how many three-element subsets should you have?

11. Let A = {1, 2, 3}, B = {0, 1, 2}, C = {3, 1, 2}, D = {a, b, c}, E = {1, 2}, F = {0, 1, 2, 3}, and G = {whole numbers between 0 and 4}.

a. Which of the sets are equal to set A?

b. Which of the sets are equivalent to set A?

c. If H and I are sets such that H = I, can we conclude that H ≈ I? Explain your answer.

d. If J and K are sets such that J ≈ K, can we conclude that J = K? Explain your answer.

12. a. Suppose A = {1, 2}. Give an example of a set B such that A ⊆ B.

b. Give an example of a set C such that A ⊆ C and C ⊄ A.

c. Give an example of two sets D and E such that D ⊆ E and E ⊆ D. What seems to be true of the sets D and E?

13. a. If A ⊄ B, can we then conclude that B ⊄ A? Justify your answer.

b. If A ⊄ B, can we then conclude that A ≠ B? Justify your answer.

14. In which of the following sets can the elements be placed in a one-to-one correspondence?

a. {1, 2, 3, 4, 5, 6} and {2, 4, 6, 8, 3, 5}

b. {a, b, c, . . . , h} and {1, 2, 3, 4, . . . , 8}

c. {1, 3, 5, 7, . . . , 15} and {0, 1, 2, . . . , 7}

d. {1, 2, 3, 4, . . . , 97} and {101, 102, 103, . . . , 197}

e. {r, i, m, e, s} and {m, i, s, e, r}

f. {x | x + 2 = 5} and the set of distinct letters in "three"

15. Replace each box with the appropriate numeral so the sets will be equivalent.

a. {1, 2, 3, 4, 5, 6, 7, 8} and {4, 5, 6, 7, . . . , □}

b. {1, 2, 3, 4, 5, . . . , 17} and {4, 5, 6, 7, . . . , □}

c. {1, 2, 3, 4, . . . , □} and {0, 1, 2, 3, 4, . . . , 8}

d. {1, 3, 5, 7, . . . , □} and {0, 1, 2, 3, 4, . . . , 11}

e. {0, 1, 2, 3, 4, 5, . . . , 42} and {0, 3, 6, 9, 12, . . . , □}

f. {0, 1, 2, 3, 4, 5, . . . , □} and {0, 3, 6, 9, 12, . . . , 21}

16. Given the sets $A = \{a,b\}$ and $B = \{r,s\}$, the pairing $a \leftrightarrow r$, $b \leftrightarrow s$ is a one-to-one correspondence of the elements of set A with those of set B. But a second one-to-one correspondence may also be made with the pairing $a \leftrightarrow s$, $b \leftrightarrow r$. A convenient way to tabulate these one-to-one correspondences is as follows:

For three element sets $C = \{a,b,c\}$ and $D = \{r,s,t\}$ we could make the following tabulations:

Apparently there are six different one-to-one correspondences possible between the elements of two 3-member sets.

a. Tabulate all possible one-to-one correspondences for each pair of sets.

　(i) {a} and {1}　　　　　　**(ii)** {a,b} and {1,2}

　(iii) {a,b,c,} and {1,2,3}　　**(iv)** {a,b,c,d} and {1,2,3,4}

b. How many one-to-one correspondences do you expect if each of the two sets has five elements? Six elements?

  c. How many one-to-one correspondences do you expect if each set has eight elements?

17. Another viewpoint for determining the number of one-to-one correspondences might result from asking a slightly different question. Given two sets, $A = \{a,b,c\}$ and $B = \{1,2,3\}$, we might start by asking "how many choices do we have from set B to match with the letter a?" Of course the answer is three because any of the numbers 1, 2, or 3 could be selected. Then "how many choices remain for b" would have the answer, two. Thus c has to take the remaining element of set 3, and so, has but one choice. The number of one-to-one correspondences, 6, is thus found by using the product $3 \times 2 \times 1$.

  a. Try this approach as you determine how many possible one-to-one correspondences exist between the elements of the two sets.

     (i) $\{a\}$ and $\{1\}$ **(ii)** $\{a,b,c\}$ and $\{1,2,3\}$ **(iii)** $\{a,b,c,d\}$ and $\{1,2,3,4\}$

  (How does your answer compare with that obtained from the tabulation in Problem 16?)

  b. How many one-to-one correspondences do you expect if each of two sets have 10 elements? 11 elements?

  c. How many if each set has 17 elements? (Leave your answer as an indicated product.)

  d. How many if each set has n elements?

Pedagogical Problems and Activities

18. Young children need to have considerable experience with one-to-one correspondence and with collections of objects before they can be expected to master number concepts. For example, the "as-many-as" relation between sets behaves as follows.

   (i) If A is a set, then A has as many as A (Reflexive property)

   (ii) If A and B are sets, and A has as many as B, then B has as many as A (Symmetric property).

   (iii) If A, B, and C are sets, and A has as many as B and B has as many as C, then A has as many as C (Transitive property).

   Property **i** could be illustrated by taking a box with some balls in it and then causing the balls to roll about. Note that none are removed, thus there are as many now as when we started.

  a. Suggest two sets of objects that could be used to illustrate the symmetric property.

  b. Suggest three specific sets of objects that could be used to illustrate the transitive property.

19. a. Suppose the children are to investigate a more-than relation. Do all three properties discussed in Problem 18 apply to the more-than relation?

   b. Give examples using sets to illustrate your conclusions in part **a.**

20. In each of the following, what property is called to mind as the given child responses are recorded? Is the response correct?

   a. Children are given three sets of "people pieces," one of moms, one of dads, and one of little boys. By one-to-one matching they find that there are as many moms as dads and as many dads as little boys. Therefore, there are as many moms as little boys.

   b. Every girl has a mom. Therefore, there is a one-to-one correspondence between girls and moms.

   c. Johnny prefers to put his candy mints in a dish rather than a cup. That way he gets more.

   d. Three sets of blocks are on the table. A matching test illustrates that there are more red blocks than blue blocks. Another matching shows that there are fewer green blocks than blue blocks. The child concludes that there must be more red blocks than green blocks.

21. **a.** Remember the game of musical chairs? (Each child has a seat, then one chair is removed and the children walk around the chairs until the music stops.) In what way does one-to-one correspondence enter into this game?

   b. "Cake walks" are sometimes used as a money-making project. Each person who is in the game stands on a number. Music is played while people walk around the circle stepping on numbers. When the music stops, one number is drawn from a box to determine the winner. In what way does one-to-one correspondence enter into this activity?

22. One of the local lakes has a canoe rental system in which a tag is placed on a board when a canoe is rented. When the canoe is returned, the tag is removed. In what way does one-to-one correspondence help the person in charge to tell whether the canoes have all been returned at closing time?

23. Suppose a shepherd boy does not know how to count. He must, however, be able to determine whether all of his flock is in the corral each night. Describe how one-to-one correspondence could be of use to him.

2.3   CARDINAL NUMBERS

From the preceding sections it would appear that the concept of a set is even more basic than that of a number. Many of the notions explored in sets will be used in developing number concepts. It might be noted that even the "counting process" makes use of sets and one-to-one correspondence.

Let us comment briefly about one very important point before we proceed with the development of number concepts. Most elementary mathematics textbooks make a distinction between "numbers" and "numerals." Numbers have to do with an idea or a concept. They are a mental construct. Numerals are the symbols used to express the idea. When we write the symbol 5, we are writing a numeral. Clearly the numeral conveys a "manyness" idea that is common to all who read it. Thus, a numeral is a name for a number. It should not be surprising to find that a number may have more than one name. For example, the number "five" could be expressed as $4 + 1$, $7 - 2$, $15 \div 3$, V, and so on. In this chapter we concentrate on sets and on the resulting number concepts. In Chapter 3 we will consider the topic of numeration. Children typically learn to count using the "counting numbers," 1, 2, 3, 4, ... These early encounters with sets and their cardinality lead to the development of concepts involving the system of whole numbers 0, 1, 2, 3, ...

REMARK   Loosely speaking, *cardinal numbers* are numbers that answer the question "how many?" Sometimes we are interested in the relative position of some specific members of a set rather than the cardinality of the set. For example, we might state that a book is fourth from the end, or that Jack sits in the second row. We are using "fourth" and "second" as *ordinal numbers*.

It will be necessary for us to agree on some symbols to be used in order to communicate about sets and their *cardinality*. Certainly a set and the cardinal number for a set are distinct things. That is, if $A = \{a, b, c\}$, then the set is $\{a, b, c\}$ and the cardinal number is three. Let us agree to represent the cardinal number of A as $n(A)$. Then, if $B = \{a, b, c, d\}$, we may write $n(B) = 4$. Likewise, $n(\{r, s\}) = 2$ and $n(\emptyset) = 0$. It should be apparent that if $A \approx B$, then $n(A) = n(B)$. (What does this statement say?) The converse of this statement is also true: if $n(A) = n(B)$ then $A \approx B$.

Let us return now to the problem-solving issue we raised earlier, only now centering our attention on the cardinality of the resulting sets. In each of the last two problem sets you have encountered problems concerning the selection of subsets of a given set. As you noted while you were doing the problems, it helps to just "get organized." The use of a table to organize your data is often a worthwhile approach because it enables you to see patterns more clearly. In the last problem set, we found that two-element subsets were easy to find. Given a six-element set such as $\{a, d, c, d, e, f\}$, we found that the letter "a" could be paired with any of the other five; thus there were five two-element subsets involving the "a." We could then pair "b" with c, d, e, or f

to obtain new subsets and so on. The tabulation might be displayed as follows:

{a, b}				
{a, c}	{b, c}			
{a, d}	{b, d}	{c, d}		
{a, e}	{b, e}	{c, e}	{d, e}	
{a, f}	{b, f}	{c, f}	{d, f}	{e, f}

Clearly there are $5 + 4 + 3 + 2 + 1 = 15$ such sets.

Now suppose that our task is to determine the number of four-element subsets that could be selected from a six-element set. We could, of course, use a direct approach and start listing the possible sets, $\{a, b, c, d\}$, $\{a, b, c, e\}$, $\{a, b, d, e\}$, ... But stop just a moment. Look at the subset $\{a, b, c, d\}$. It should be evident that if we list four of the six elements, then *two* of the elements are *not* listed. Indeed, each four-element subset corresponds to a unique two-element subset. The number of four-element subsets will be the same as the number of two-element subsets. It is therefore easier to determine the number of four-element subsets by looking at corresponding two-element sets. In this case, there should be 15 four-element sets. Could you use a similar reasoning to determine the number of five-element subsets? It should compare rather easily with one-element subsets. Thus there should be six of them.

Let us now examine a problem in which the procedures just described will be of help in analyzing the results.

EXAMPLE

If a set has six elements, how many subsets does it have?

	Number of Subsets Having							Total Number
Set	0 el.	1 el.	2 el.	3 el.	4 el.	5 el.	6 el.	of Subsets
{a, b, c, d, e, f}	1	6	15		15	6	1	

Solution

The values entered into the table were apparent from our previous discussion. Our remaining task is to determine the three-element subsets.

Using the format suggested in the preceeding problem set we could make the following tabulation.

$\{a, b, c\}$
$\{a, b, d\} \{a, c, d\}$
$\{a, b, e\} \{a, c, e\} \{a, d, e\}$
$\{a, b, f\} \{a, c, f\} \{a, d, f\} \{a, e, f\}$ $4 + 3 + 2 + 1 = 10$
$\{b, c, d\}$
$\{b, c, e\} \{b, d, e\}$
$\{b, c, f\} \{b, d, f\} \{b, e, f\}$ $3 + 2 + 1 = 6$
$\{c, d, e\}$
$\{c, d, f\} \{c, e, f\}$ $2 + 1 = 3$
$\{d, e, f\}$ $1 = 1$
Total $= 20$

With this information in mind, the total number of subsets for a six-element set is $1 + 6 + 15 + 20 + 15 + 6 + 1 = 64$. We will return to this idea in the Problem Set and consider the pattern that results from looking at several examples.

PROBLEM SET 2.3

1. Find each of the following:
   a. $n(\{a, b, c\})$ b. $n(\{2, 4, 6, 8, 10\})$
   c. $n(\{a, b, c, \ldots, f\})$ d. $n(\{a, b, c, \ldots, z\})$
   e. $n(\{1, 2, 3, \ldots, 52\})$ f. $n(A)$, where $A = \{6, 7, 8, \ldots, 20\}$
   g. $n(B)$, where B is the set of counting numbers between 1 and 8
   h. $n(\{\text{the Great Lakes}\})$
   i. $n(\{x \mid x$ is one of the United States of America$\})$
   j. $n(\{1, 2, \{1\}, \{2\}\})$

2. If $A \approx B$ and $n(B) = 51$, find $n(A)$.

3. a. Is it true that if $A = B$, then $n(A) = n(B)$? Justify your answer.
   b. Is the converse true (the converse is: if $n(A) = n(B)$, then $A = B$)? Justify your answer.

4. If $A \subset B$, could it be true that $n(A) = n(B)$? Justify your answer.

5. If we know that $n(A) = 3$ and $n(B) = 5$, can we conclude that $A \subset B$? Justify your answer.

6. For each of the following, indicate whether a cardinal or an ordinal number is being used.
   a. The dorm is nineteen stories high.
   b. Sue lives on the fifth floor of her dorm.
   c. September has thirty days.

    d. My birthday is on the sixteenth day of the month.

    e. The teacher said, "Please turn to page fifty."

    f. Our insurance program requires twenty payments, and I just paid the third installment.

    g. Columbus discovered America in 1492.

7. **a.** What is the difference between the empty set and the number zero?

    b. Is there any difference between {0} and $\emptyset$?

    c. Is $\emptyset \subseteq \{\ \}$?

    d. Is $\emptyset \in \{\ \}$?

    e. Is $\emptyset \subset \{\ \}$?

8. Criticize each of the following:

    a. Each child has just one mother, so the number of children is equal to the number of mothers.

    b. Pair each boy who is the oldest son in his family with his father. This is a one-to-one correspondence, so the number of oldest sons is equal to the number of fathers.

9. **a.** The set $A = \{a,b,c\}$ has three elements. It has the following subsets:
$\{\emptyset, \{a\}, \{b\}, \{c\}, \{a,b\}, \{a,c\}, \{b,c\}, \{a,b,c\}\}$

    Enter this data into the chart

Set	Number of Subsets Having				Total Number of Subsets
	0 el	1 el	2 el	3 el	
{a,b,c}					

    b. Complete the table for a four element set.

Set	Number of Subsets Having					Total Number of Subsets
	0 el.	1 el.	2 el.	3 el.	4 el.	
{a, b, c, d}						

    c. Build a similar table for a five-element set.

    d. What would the table consist of if the original set has only 2 elements? 1 element? 0 elements?

10. **a.** Use the data from Problem 9 to complete the following table.

Set	Number of Elements in Original Set	Number of Subsets
{ }	0	
{a}	1	
{a, b}	2	
{a, b, c}	3	8
{a, b, c, d}	4	
{a, b, c, d, e}	5	
{a, b, c, d, e, f}	6	64
{a, b,c, d, e, f, g}	7	

b. Is there a set that has exactly five subsets?

c. If a set had 8 elements, how many subsets would you expect?

d. Suppose a set had 12 elements. Find the number of subsets without first determining the number of subsets for 10-element sets and 11-element sets.

e. In general, if a set has n elements, how many subsets does it have?

Pedagogical Problems and Activities

11. The number 0 commonly causes trouble for young children. For this reason it is common to introduce at least the numbers 1 through 5 before introducing 0.

    a. To represent 5 we need to use a variety of sets, all having appropriate numbers of elements. Make a collection of at least 10 different sets that represent fiveness.

    b. The number 0 must be associated with the empty set. One first-grade teacher developed this idea by having children toss bean bags into a circle drawn on the floor. After each trial, the bags inside the circle were counted and the number recorded. Then the distance from the circle was increased for the next toss. Eventually no bean bags landed in the circle. Thus, an empty set relating to the number 0 was produced. Suggest five other situations that produce the number 0.

12. The number 10 is of great importance in our numeration system. Mathematics texts written for use at the first- and second-grade levels use a variety of pictures to represent tenness. Examples of this might be the following:

Suggest two or three additional pictorial representations for tenness.

13. Use one-to-one correspondence on sets to verify that four objects are fewer than seven objects.

14. **a.** A patio is to be made using square patio blocks. A design is to be made using one block in the first row, two in the second, each row increased by one until the middle row is reached, then decreases again. If we have 50 blocks for use in this project, how many should be placed in the middle row in order to have the fewest number of blocks left over?

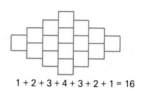

$$1 + 2 + 3 + 4 + 3 + 2 + 1 = 16$$

   b. Discuss your method of solution with other members of your class. Did you find a variety of approaches being used?
   c. Suppose 100 blocks are available. Does this assure us that twice the number of blocks will be used in the middle row? Verify your answer.
   d. How many blocks are there in the center row?

2.4 OPERATIONS ON SETS

In Section 2.2 we concentrated our attention on "comparing" sets. We called such a comparison a *relation*. Recall that in arithmetic we commonly compare two numbers by claiming that they are equal or that one is larger than the other. An entirely different sort of thing is involved when we state that 2 + 6 corresponds with 8, 7 − 3 with 4, and 8 × 3 with 24. Such correspondences are called *binary operations*. The term *binary* applies because two elements are involved in the pairing and the term *operation* because the pair of numbers produce a single number. We wish now to do a similar sort of thing with sets.

Suppose $A = \{1, 2, 3, 4, 5\}$ and $B = \{2, 4, 6, 8\}$. Let us consider that set whose members are found in set A and also in set B. That is, only those elements found in both set A and set B will appear in our new set. This set would be tabulated as $\{2, 4\}$ and is normally referred to as the *intersection* of sets A and B.

Definition 2.6   The intersection of two sets A and B (written $A \cap B$) is the set of all elements that are in both A and B.

An alternate statement that is perhaps more compact is the following. Given sets A and B, $A \cap B = \{x \mid x \in A$ and $x \in B\}$. You may use whichever form you prefer. Notice that the connective "and" is an important part of the definition. For an element to be in the set $A \cap B$ it must be in *both* set A and set B.

EXAMPLE 2

Suppose the set of officers of a club is $O = \{$John, Marsha, Mary, Pete$\}$ and the set of members of the first program committee was $P = \{$Jim, John, Pat, Mary$\}$. Then the committee members who were also officers are $\{$Mary, John$\}$ $= O \cap P$.

EXAMPLE 3

Suppose $D = \{1, 2, 3, 4, 5, 6, 7, 8, 9, 10\}$, $E = \{1, 3, 5, 7\}$, $F = \{4, 5, 6, 7, 8, 9, 10, 11, 12\}$ and $G = \{6, 8, 10, 12\}$, tabulate the sets $D \cap E$, $E \cap F$, $D \cap F$, and $E \cap G$.

Solution:

$$D \cap E = \{1, 3, 5, 7\}$$
$$E \cap F = \{5, 7\}$$
$$D \cap F = \{4, 5, 6, 7, 8, 9, 10\}$$
$$E \cap G = \emptyset$$

We often find Venn diagrams to be useful. In Figure 2.5 we illustrate the diagram for the set $A \cap B$. Note that we have marked set A and set B and that the region containing both sets A and B is marked both vertically and horizontally.

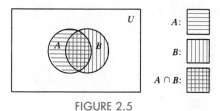

FIGURE 2.5

REMARK When we draw a diagram, we make it as specific as the data will allow. If no specific information is given, care must be taken not to assume its existence.

Sometimes we wish to consider operations on three or more sets. In Figure 2.6 we illustrate the set $(A \cap B) \cap C$. You should note that the three sets are in a general configuration with no special properties claimed. Because intersection is a binary operation, we can operate on only two sets at a time. The parentheses direct us first to obtain the set $A \cap B$ and then operate on the two sets $(A \cap B)$ and C.

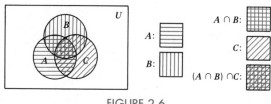

FIGURE 2.6

A second binary-set operation should be identified for our use. Suppose set $E = \{1, 2, 3\}$ and $F = \{3, 5\}$. Let us specify that any element in either set will be placed in our new set. Thus, we obtain the set $\{1, 2, 3, 5\}$. This set is called the *union* of the two sets.

Definition 2.7   The union of sets A and B (written $A \cup B$) is the set of all elements that are in A or in B (or in both).

An equivalent way to say this would be: Given sets A and B, $A \cup B = \{x \mid x \in A \text{ or } x \in B\}$.

REMARK   The word *or* is another technical word coming from logic. We accept an "or" statement as true when either of the two parts is true as well as when both are true. Legal documents recognize this form of "or" and will typically write "and/or" to make the meaning clear.

EXAMPLE 1

Let $A = \{a, b, c, d, e, f\}$ and $B = \{a, e, i\}$. Then $A \cup B = \{a, b, c, d, e, f, i\}$.

EXAMPLE 2

Let $C = \{2, 4, 6\}$ and $D = \{1, 3, 5, 7\}$. Then $C \cup D = \{1, 2, 3, 4, 5, 6, 7\}$.

EXAMPLE 3

Suppose $G = \{1, 2, 3, 4, 5, 6, 7, 8\}$, $H = \{6, 7, 8, 9, 10\}$, $I = \{1, 3, 5\}$, and $J = \{2, 4, 6, 8\}$. Tabulate the sets $G \cup H$, $H \cup I$ and $I \cup J$.

Solution:

$$G \cup H = \{1, 2, 3, 4, 5, 6, 7, 8, 9, 10\}$$
$$H \cup I = \{1, 3, 5, 6, 7, 8, 9, 10\}$$
$$I \cup J = \{1, 2, 3, 4, 5, 6, 8\}$$

We again use Venn diagrams to represent unions. In Figure 2.7*a* we illustrate the set $A \cup B$. Notice that we called it *the* set $A \cup B$. It is a set whose members are all the elements from set A along with the members of B. In Figure 2.7*b* we illustrate the set $(A \cup B) \cup C$.

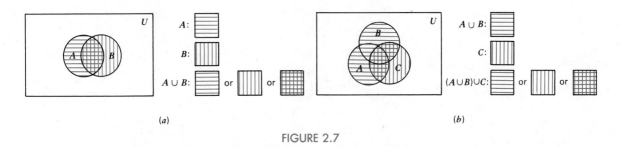

FIGURE 2.7

Let us define one more operation on sets. We sometimes have a particular universal set in mind as well as a set selected from the universe, but then desire to speak of the set of remaining elements. Suppose a ball team has 12 players on the traveling squad. We may assign the numbers 1–12 to players. Let us suppose that we have enough red socks for players in the set $A = \{1, 2, 3, 4, 5, 6\}$, but that the others must use white socks. The players having white socks will be in the set $B = \{7, 8, 9, 10, 11, 12\}$. This set is usually referred to as the *complement* of set A.

Definition 2.8   Given the universal set U and set A, $A \subseteq U$, the complement of A (written A') is the set of all the elements of U that are not in A, ($A' = \{x \mid \in U \text{ and } x \notin A\}$.)

The Venn diagram for the complement of a set is illustrated in Figure 2.8*a*. In Figure 2.8*b* we represent the set $(A \cup B)'$. Notice that the operation "com-

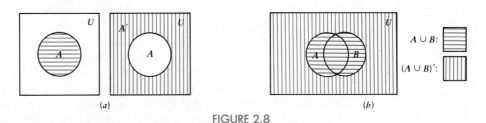

FIGURE 2.8

plement" requires that we work with a *single* set and then take those elements from the universe that are not in the set.

REMARK Complementation is the only unary set operation that we will encounter. We have many examples of unary operations in arithmetic. For example, given a number such as 3, we might associate with it its cube, 27; with the number 4, we may associate the number 64, and so on. Each of these operations associates a single number with another number. Can you think of other unary operations from arithmetic besides cubing?

EXAMPLE 1

Suppose our universal set is the alphabet and A is the set of vowels. Then A' is the set of consonants.

EXAMPLE 2

Let $U = \{0, 1, 2, 3, \dots\}$ and $B = \{x \mid x$ is an even number$\}$. Then B' is the set of whole numbers that are not even, or the odd numbers (i.e., $B' = \{1, 3, 5, \dots\}$).

EXAMPLE 3

Suppose $U = \{1, 2, 3, 4, 5, 6, 7, 8, 9, 10\}$, $D = \{1, 2, 3, 4,\}$, $E = \{1, 3, 5, 7, 9\}$, and $F = \{2, 4, 6, 8, 10\}$. Tabulate D', E', $D' \cap E$, and $E' \cap F'$.

Solution

$$D' = \{5, 6, 7, 8, 9, 10\}$$
$$E' = \{2, 4, 6, 8, 10\}$$
$$F' = \{1, 3, 5, 7, 9\}$$
$$D' \cap E = \{5, 7, 9,\}$$
$$E' \cap F' = \emptyset$$

What would you know about the set $A \cup A'$ for any set A? Would $A \cup A' = U$ for any sets A and U? The answer is apparently yes. We might also conclude that $A \cap A' = \emptyset$ for any set A. What is the complement of the empty set? Since we want all the elements of the universe outside the selected set, if $C = \emptyset$, then $C' = U$. Likewise, $U' = \emptyset$. You should use the definition of complement to convince yourself of this.

Sometimes we need to represent complements where more than two sets are involved. Suppose we wish to represent $A' \cup (B \cap C)$. Let us first identify the set A', then focus on the set $B \cap C$. We then take the union of the two sets illustrated in Figure 2.9. Remember that you must consider the things in parentheses as a single set in performing these operations.

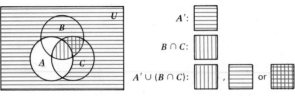

FIGURE 2.9

EXAMPLE 1

Draw the Venn diagram for $A \cup (B' \cap C)$. Note that we first must work with the set enclosed by the parentheses, and then on the union of A with that set (Fig. 2.10).

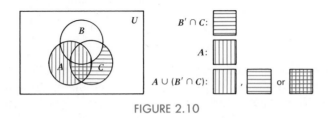

FIGURE 2.10

EXAMPLE 2

Suppose we are given a Venn diagram (Fig. 2.11) and wish to record in set notation the shaded region. We might note that we are interested in the elements that are in A and at the same time in B. Thus, the shaded set must be $A \cap B$.

EXAMPLE 3

Write a set notation formula to describe the shaded region of Figure 2.12. The shaded region does not include any elements of A: thus, it must be in A'. It also contains those elements of A' that are in B. Thus, $A' \cap B$ would be such a representation.

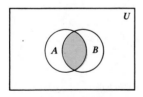

FIGURE 2.11

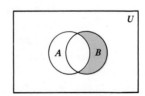

FIGURE 2.12

EXAMPLE 4

Given three sets with the shaded region indicated in Figure 2.13, write the set notation formula. We have no elements of C in the shaded region; thus, we would be interested in the set C'. Also, we note that the shaded region is limited to those points in A or in B, thus in $A \cup B$. Therefore, we have elements in the set $(A \cup B) \cap C'$.

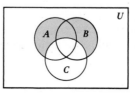

FIGURE 2.13

EXAMPLE 5

We sometimes encounter information about sets that makes it helpful to use diagrams that specifically reflect that situation. Suppose $A = \{$blue vehicles$\}$, $B = \{$sports cars$\}$, and $C = \{$vans$\}$. The diagram presented in Figure 2.14 illustrates these sets. The sets $A \cap B$ and $A \cap C$ are darkened in the figure and are disjoint. This should seem to be reasonable since $A \cap B$ represents blue sports cars and the $A \cap C$ is the set of blue vans and they are indeed disjoint.

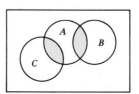

FIGURE 2.14

Venn diagrams are often useful to us as a problem-solving tool in situations where sets overlap. Suppose, for example, that we are told that 30 students are members of the Math Club and 28 students are members of the Science Club. There are 16 students who belong to both clubs. Suppose that the clubs plan a joint picnic. If all the club members attend, how many persons will be present? Because some persons belong to both clubs, we cannot just add 30 and 28 to obtain the answer. Let us refer to the Venn diagram in Figure 2.15a to help sort out this situation. Then, because 16 persons are in region (2) and 30 are in M, 14 must be in region (1). Likewise, because 28 are in S, 12 must be in region (3). Note that regions (1), (2), and (3) are nonoverlapping

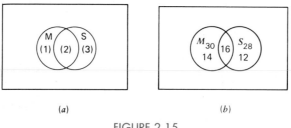

FIGURE 2.15

but account for all the club members. There must therefore be $14 + 16 + 12 = 42$ persons at the picnic.

An alternate form for recording the data is indicated in Figure 2.15b. The symbols M_{30} and S_{28} employ subscripts to indicate that the sets have 30 and 28 elements, respectively. We then write the 16 in the intersection of the two sets. From this information we obtain the other numbers 14 and 12 and write them in the appropriate regions. This results in a diagram that is easier to interpret in many cases.

We can also use Venn diagrams to help analyze problems involving three sets. Consider our summer vacation. On 17 days the temperature was above 95°. It was humid on 13 days and rained on 10 days. On 3 days it was hot (above 95°), humid, and rained. On 4 days it was hot and humid. On 5 days it was hot and rainy. On 8 days it was humid and rained. On how many days was it not hot or humid or rainy? The given data have been recorded in Figure 2.16a. Do the numbers 1, 2, 3, and 5 in their respective regions indeed reflect the use of the given data? In Figure 2.16b we have calculated the numbers that relate to the other regions (i.e., because 17 must be accounted for in the hot circle and we have $1 + 3 + 2 = 6$ already accounted for, there must be 11 in the remaining regions). We can now add the numbers in the nonoverlapping regions to answer the question asked. Thus it was hot or humid or rainy on $11 + 2 + 3 + 1 + 4 + 5 + 0 = 26$ days.

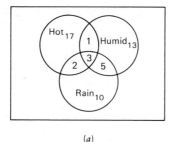

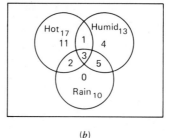

FIGURE 2.16

PROBLEM SET 2.4

1. List the members of the union of each pair of sets.
   a. $A = \{1, 2, 3, 4\}$: $B = \{2, 4, 6, 7\}$
   b. $C = \{0, 2, 4, 6, 8\}$: $D = \{3, 6, 9, 12, 15\}$
   c. $E = \{$Alice, Todd, Beth$\}$: $F = \{$Joe, Jane, Jennifer$\}$
   d. $G = \{\circ, \triangle, \square, *\}$: $H = \{\circ, \triangle, \square, \beta\}$

2. List the members of the intersection of each pair of sets from Problem 1.

3. Let $U = \{0, 1, 2, 3, \ldots, 12\}$. $A = \{1, 2, 3, 4\}$, $B = \{1, 3, 5, 7, 9, 11\}$, $C = \{0, 2, 4, \ldots, 12\}$, and $D = \emptyset$. Tabulate each of the following sets:
   a. $A \cap B$ b. $A \cup B$ c. $B \cap C$ d. $B \cup C$ e. A'
   f. $A' \cap B$ g. $(A \cap B)'$ h. $A' \cup B'$ i. $B \cap D$
   j. $[(A \cup B) \cup C] \cap D$

4. The letters a through p are the members of the universe. Tabulate the elements in the following sets.
   a. $A \cap B$ b. $A \cup B$
   c. $A' \cap B$ d. C'
   e. $(A \cup B \cup C)'$ f. $A \cap B'$

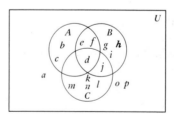

5. Draw a Venn diagram to illustrate each of the following:
   a. $A \cap B$ b. $A \cup B$ c. $A' \cap B$
   d. $(A \cup B)'$ e. $A' \cap B'$ f. $A \cup B'$

6. Draw a Venn diagram to illustrate each of the following:
   a. $(A \cup B) \cup C$ b. $(A \cap B) \cup C$ c. $(A \cap B) \cap C$
   d. $(A \cup B) \cap C$ e. $(A \cup B)' \cap C$ f. $A \cap (B \cup C)$

7. Use set notation to represent each shaded region.

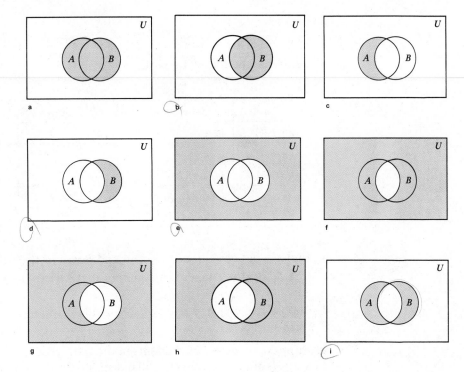

8. Use set notation to represent each shaded region.

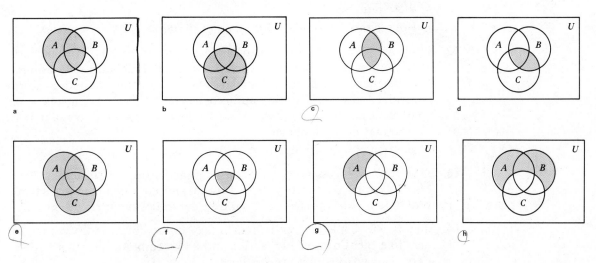

9. Suppose the universe consists of all sixth-grade students at Logan School. Let *M* represent the boys and *F* the girls. Let *R* represent the children with red hair and *B* the ones with brown hair. *C* represents the students with curly hair. Describe the persons in each set.

  a. $C \cap M$ **b.** $F \cap R$ **e.** M'

  d. $(R \cup B)$ **e.** $M \cap F$ **f.** $F \cap (R \cap C)$

10. a. Complete the following table.

Set A	Set B	n(A)	n(B)	n(A ∩ B)	n(A ∪ B)
{a, b, c}	{d, c}	3	2	0	5
{a, b, c, d}	{c, d, c}			2	5
{a, b}	{a, b, c, d}				
{a}	{b, c, d, e, f}				
{a, b, c, d}	∅				

  b. Under what conditions on sets A and B will $n(A) + n(B) = n(A \cup B)$?

  c. If $A \cap B \neq \emptyset$, suggest an equation that relates $n(A)$, $n(B)$, $n(A \cup B)$ and $n(A \cap B)$.

  d. Choose two or three pairs of sets to allow you to test your conjecture from part c.

11. a. Suppose there are 60 students in the sixth grade. In a preference survey, 30 indicated that they like deep-pan pizza, 35 like regular pizza, and 10 like both kinds of pizza. Draw a Venn diagram to illustrate these findings.

  b. How many do not like either kind of pizza?

12. a. We are told that 21 students participated in baseball, 17 wrestled, and 10 were in cross-country. Twelve were in both baseball and wrestling, 6 participated in both baseball and cross-country, and 5 were involved in both wrestling and cross-country. Two students were in all three sports. If all are invited to a sports banquet, how many reservations must be made?

  b. How many participated in exactly one sport?

13. Brian took 14 business trips during the year, always to Toronto or Boston. On four trips he went to both Toronto and Boston and on three trips went only to Toronto. How often did he get to Boston during the year?

14. Suppose 40 people live on the fourth floor of the dorm. Twenty-three of them like Diet Coke, 17 like Sprite, and 8 like both. All the other people prefer Pepsi. How many prefer Pepsi?

15. To raise money for their activities, the local science club sold boxes of assorted cheeses and boxes of fruit. They contacted 50 families in one neighborhood. Twenty bought the cheese box only, and 24 bought fruit boxes only, and 3 families bought both.

a. How many families bought neither?

b. How many families bought cheese boxes?

c. How many bought either cheese or fruit?

16. In an 8th-grade class there were 100 students who received an A in math or science or English. 40 received an A in math, 14 received an A in English and math but not in science, and 16 received only an A in English. Nine received an A in science and math but not in English, 10 received an A in science and English but not in math, and 9 received an A in math only.

    a. How many received an A in English?

    b. How many received an A in all three subjects?

    c. How many received an A only in science?

17. In a certain school, 24 students are enrolled in mathematics, 19 in physics, and 12 in advanced history. Of these, 15 take both mathematics and physics, 8 take both mathematics and history, and 5 take both physics and history. Two students take all three subjects. If the three classes are combined for a field trip, accommodations will have to be made for how many different students?

18. It has been reported that in a sample of 1000 women, 523 used perfume A, 494 used hair spray B, 472 used hand soap C, 177 used both A and B, 235 used both A and C, 228 used both B and C, 65 used all three, and 42 used none of the three. Should you believe the report? (*Hint:* How many elements are in region a? If 177 are in $A \cap B$ and 163 in region a, how many are in region b? How many in region c? Does the sum of the elements in A, in regions a, b, and c, and those outside of $A \cup B \cup C$ total 1000?)

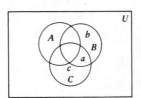

19. A survey of 100 sixth-graders' television-viewing habits showed the following:

    60 see program A

    50 see program B

    50 see program C

    30 see program A and B

    20 see program B and C

30 see program A and C

10 see program A, B, and C

a. How many view A and B but not C?

b. How many view exactly two programs?

c. How many do not view any programs?

20. a. Blood types use a designation based on the presence or absence of three types of antigens, A, B, and Rh. A person is designated as being of type A, B, AB (if both types are present), or O (if he has neither A nor B). He is classified as $+$ if he has the Rh antigen and $-$ if he does not have it. Let us designate the regions as marked in the diagram and let set A represent all persons having antigens A, set B all those having antigen B, and C all those having the Rh antigen. Which regions represent each of the following:

(i) A^+ **(ii)** A^- **(iii)** B^+ **(iv)** AB^+

(v) AB^- **(vi)** O^+ **(vii)** O^-

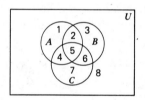

b. Blood types vary for different racial groups. In a Chinese city, a random sample of 100 people yielded 25 with type A blood, 35 with type B, and 10 having type AB. Use the diagram given to find the number having type O blood.

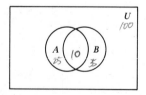

c. In a sample of 100 American whites there were 45 having the type A antigen, 14 had the type B antigen, and 4 had both type A and type B. How many were type O?

d. In a sample of 100 people classified as North American Indians, 8 had the type A antigen, 1 had type B antigen, and 91 had type O blood. How many have blood type AB?

21. Every red car at an auto show was a sports car. Half of all blue cars were sports cars. Half of all sports cars were red. There were 40 blue cars and 30 red cars. How many sports cars were neither red nor blue?

22. In the following diagrams shade the region indicated.

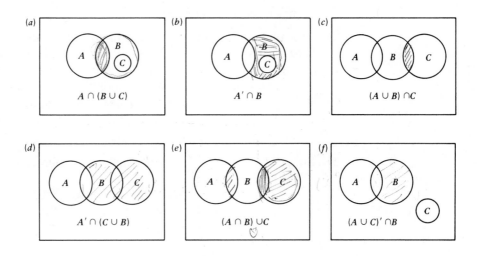

(a) $A \cap (B \cup C)$

(b) $A' \cap B$

(c) $(A \cup B) \cap C$

(d) $A' \cap (C \cup B)$

(e) $(A \cap B) \cup C$

(f) $(A \cup C)' \cap B$

23. Write a description for the region shaded.

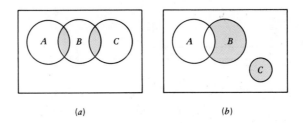

(a)   (b)

Pedagogical Problems and Activities

24. The attribute blocks were mentioned in Problem Set 2.1. (The blocks with four colors, four shapes, and two sizes.) Use the blocks to illustrate each of the following.

  a. {red pieces} ∩ {circles}

  b. {small pieces} ∪ {yellow pieces}

  c. ({triangles} ∪ {squares}) ∩ {small pieces}

  d. {large pieces}

  e. ({red} ∩ {squares}) ∪ {large}

25. From the attribute pieces, select those pieces that satisfy the following:

    a. red and small

    b. not circles

    c. triangles or blue

    d. not (large or red)

    e. not large and (square or circle)

26. The following problems were given to fifth-grade students. Illustrate the type of answer that you would like to obtain from your students.

    Suppose Joe, Frank, Ralph, and Dick are hall monitors and Frank, Ralph, and Dick are lunchroom monitors.

    a. Draw a Venn diagram to illustrate this relationship.

    b. If the hall monitors and lunchroom monitors are combined, show in the diagram the set that results.

27. Suppose there are three clubs having the following membership:

$$A = \{\text{Carol, Ann, Sue, Barb}\}$$
$$B = \{\text{Jane, Carol, Judy, Barb}\}$$
$$C = \{\text{Mary, Sue, Carol, Judy}\}$$

    a. Draw a Venn diagram to illustrate the club membership.

    b. How many girls belong to all three clubs?

    c. How many girls belong to only one club?

2.5   PROPERTIES OF OPERATIONS ON SETS

Certain relationships and patterns permeate much of mathematics; they are very helpful in tying together and organizing many mathematical concepts. Let us consider some properties of sets that will be of particular help to us in the development of operations with whole numbers.

Consider the sets $A \cup B$ and $B \cup A$, where $A = \{1, 2, 3, 4\}$ and $B = \{1, 3, 5\}$. Then $A \cup B = \{1, 2, 3, 4, 5\}$ and $B \cup A = \{1, 3, 5, 2, 4\}$. Clearly $A \cup B = B \cup A$. This is true in general.

It can also be shown that $A \cap B = B \cap A$. These properties are generally referred to as *commutative properties*.

PROPERTY 2.4   **For all sets A and B:**

1. $A \cup B = B \cup A$ (Commutative property of union)

2. $A \cap B = B \cap A$ (Commutative property of intersection)

A second interesting pattern involves the grouping of three sets under the operation of union. Because union is a binary operation, where three sets are involved, we are forced to perform the operation in pairs. Thus, either $(A \cup B) \cup C$ or $A \cup (B \cup C)$ must be chosen. But are the results the same? Venn diagrams are again very useful. In Figure 2.17 we illustrate such a diagram. Notice that we must always first perform the operation enclosed in parentheses, then continue to the next operation. It should be evident that the regions shaded in 2.17a and 2.17b are the same, thus verifying that $A \cup (B \cup C) = (A \cup B) \cup C$. We will show that $A \cap (B \cap C) = (A \cap B) \cap C$ in the next problem set and will summarize this in Property 2.5.

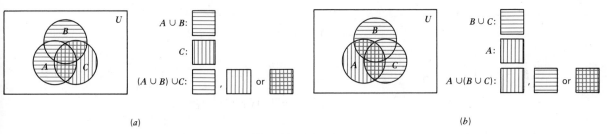

FIGURE 2.17

PROPERTY 2.5   **For all sets, *A*, *B*, and *C*:**

1. $(A \cup B) \cup C = A \cup (B \cup C)$ (Associative property of union)
2. $(A \cap B) \cap C = A \cap (B \cap C)$ (Associative property of intersection)

Each of the patterns, associativity and commutativity, requires the use of a single binary operation. However, some patterns exist that involve two binary operations. Because we have both union and intersection at our disposal, let us check to see whether they may be combined in a single pattern such as $A \cup (B \cap C) = (A \cup B) \cap (A \cup C)$. In Figure 2.18 we develop the sets needed to make a judgment. Notice that in 2.18a we represent $A \cup (B \cap C)$ and in 2.18b we have $(A \cup B) \cap (A \cup C)$. They represent the same region,

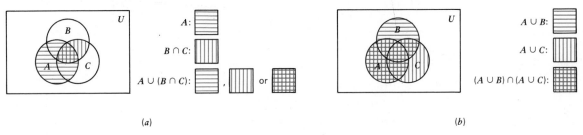

FIGURE 2.18

and we therefore can assert that $A \cup (B \cap C) = (A \cup B) \cap (A \cup C)$ is true. This pattern is referred to as a *distributive pattern*. More specifically, we say that "union distributes over intersection."

Let us carry the investigation one step further. What would happen if we tried $A \cap (B \cup C)$ and $(A \cap B) \cup (A \cap C)$ as our pattern? That is, does a second distributive pattern apply for sets in which intersection distributes over union? We answer the question by making use of Venn diagrams. Note that in Figure 2.19*a* and in 2.19*b* we find the regions are the same. For sets we have two distributive properties that are true. We will summarize these findings in Property 2.6.

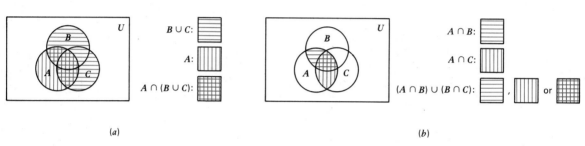

(a)   (b)

FIGURE 2.19

PROPERTY 2.6   For all sets A, B, and C:

1. $A \cup (B \cap C) = (A \cup B) \cap (A \cup C)$ ($\cup$ is distriutive over $\cap$)
2. $A \cap (B \cup C) = (A \cap B) \cup (A \cap C)$ ($\cap$ is distributive over $\cup$)

Other properties could be developed, but because they are not of direct consequence to our development, we will not take the time to do so. We will simply mention one more and let you work with some others in the problem set.

PROPERTY 2.7   For any set A:

1. $A \cup \emptyset = \emptyset \cup A = A$ ($\emptyset$ is the identity of $\cup$)
2. $A \cap U = U \cap A = A$ (U is the identity of $\cap$)

PROBLEM SET 2.5

1. Given $U = \{a, b, c, d, e, f\}$. $A = \{a, b, c\}$, $B = \{a, c, e\}$, and $C = \{c, d, e, f\}$, use tabulations to:
   a. Show that $A \cap B = B \cap A$.
   b. Show that $A \cap (B \cup C) = (A \cap B) \cup (A \cap C)$.

    c. Show that $A \cup (B \cap C) = (A \cup B) \cap (A \cup C)$.

    d. Show that $(A \cap B)' = A' \cup B'$.

2. a. Use Venn diagrams to verify that $A \cap B = B \cap A$.

    b. Use Venn diagrams to verify that $A \cap (B \cap C) = (A \cap B) \cap C$.

3. a. Present some form of argument that $A \cup A' = U$ and $A \cap A' = \emptyset$. (You might wish to use Venn diagrams or perhaps just argue logically from our definitions.)

    b. Verify that $A \cup \emptyset = A$ and $A \cap \emptyset = \emptyset$.

4. Use the definitions and properties, or Venn diagrams, to decide which of the following are true:

    a. $A' \cup B = B \cup A'$

    b. $(A' \cup B) \cup C = A' \cup (B \cup C)$

    c. $(A' \cup B) \cap C = A' \cup (B \cap C)$

    d. $A \cap (B' \cup C) = (A \cap B') \cup (A \cap C)$

    e. $A \cap (B \cup C) = (A \cap B) \cup C$

5. Use the definitions and properties, or Venn diagrams, to write each of the following in a simpler form:

    a. $(A \cup B) \cup B'$ **b.** $(A \cup B) \cup A'$

    c. $(A \cap U) \cup A'$ **d.** $(A \cup U) \cap A'$

    e. $(A \cap B') \cup (A \cap B)$ **f.** $(A \cup \emptyset)' \cup A'$

    g. $(A \cup U)' \cup (A' \cap A)$ **h.** $(A \cup B) \cap (A' \cup B)$

    i. $[A \cup (B' \cap C')] \cap [A \cup (B \cap C)]$

6. Present an argument that for any set A, $(A')' = A$.

7. Let $U = \{1, 2, 3, 4, 5\}$. $A = \{1, 3\}$, and $B = \{2, 3, 4\}$. Tabulate parts a through f. Then use the information to complete the problem.

    a. $A \cup B$ **b.** $(A \cup B)'$ **c.** A' **h.** Does $(A \cup B)' = A' \cap B'$?

    d. B' **e.** $A' \cup B'$ **f.** $A' \cap B'$

    g. Does $(A \cup B)' = A' \cup B'$?

8. a. Is it true that $A \cup B = A \cap B$? (Use a specific set for A and for B to justify your response. A specific substitution used to disprove a statement is referred to as a *counterexample*.)

    b. If we are assured that for a specific pair of sets $A \cup B = A \cap B$, what can you conclude about the sets A and B? Give an example to illustrate your answer.

9. The patterns $(A \cup B)' = A' \cap B'$ and $(A \cap B)' = A' \cup B'$ are referred to as *DeMorgan's laws* in honor of the British mathematician who discovered them in the mid-1800s.

   a. Use a Venn diagram to show that $(A \cup B)' = A' \cap B'$.

   b. Use a Venn diagram to show that $(A \cap B)' = A' \cup B'$.

Pedagogical Problems and Activities

10. Suppose R is the set of red bicycles and T is the set of ten-speed bikes.

   a. Describe the set $R \cap T$. Does a red five-speed belong to this set?

   b. Describe the set $(R \cap T)'$. Does a red five-speed belong to this set?

   c. Describe the set R'.

   d. Describe the set T'.

   e. Describe the set $R' \cup T'$.

   f. "If someone denies that I have a red ten-speed bike, then they are asserting that my bike fails to be red or fails to be a ten-speed." Do you agree with this statement?

11. Use the attribute pieces to illustrate each of the following:

   a. Associative property for $\cup$

   b. Associative property for $\cap$

   c. The distributive pattern for $\{red\} \cap (\{triangles\} \cup \{circles\}) = (\{red\} \cap \{triangles\}) \cup (\{red\} \cap \{circles\})$

2.6   ADDITION OF WHOLE NUMBERS

Earlier in this chapter we discussed the use of cardinal numbers to identify the "manyness" of sets. Some sets of whole numbers do not have a last element, but continue indefinitely and are referred to as *infinite sets*. If a set of whole numbers has a last element we say it is a *finite set*. The following sets have been specially designated:

$\{1, 2, 3, 4, 5, \ldots\}$ the counting numbers (natural numbers)

$\{0, 1, 2, 3, 4 \ldots\}$ the whole numbers.

The first operation on whole numbers that we wish to investigate is addition. What do you think of when someone mentions addition? Perhaps you think of addition facts, such as $4 + 3 = 7$ and $5 + 7 = 12$. But how did you obtain the facts? As elementary teachers you must be able to explain addition from an informal, intuitive viewpoint and also from a somewhat more precise mathematical viewpoint.

Suppose you were to pose the following question to a 5- or 6-year-old child: "If I have four apples and three oranges, how many pieces of fruit do I have?" The child might well take the apples and oranges, place them all in a pile, and then count to see how many pieces of fruit are present. This is probably the most natural approach to the problem, and it is from such experiences that the addition facts arise. No matter what sets are chosen, as long as there are four elements in one set and three in a set disjoint from the first, there will be seven elements in the union. Thus, in general, $4 + 3 = 7$. After some experience with physical objects, the child might well shift his or her attention to work involving pictures of objects or to diagrams of sets. Using this more mature approach, to find $4 + 3$ we might choose a set $A = \{a, b, c, d\}$ and $B = \{e, f, g\}$. Then $A \cup B = \{a, b, c, d, e, f, g\}$ and $n(A \cup B) = 7$.

Let us now attempt to use more precise language to make a statement of what we mean by addition. We are interested in adding two counting numbers, say a and b. To do so, let us select two sets A and B, chosen so that there are a elements in set A, b elements in set B, and the sets A and B are disjoint. Then the sum of a and b is the cardinal number of the set $A \cup B$.

Definition 2.9 Let a and b represent any two whole numbers. Choose disjoint sets A and B such that $n(A) = a$ and $n(B) = b$. Then $a + b = n(A \cup B)$. (We might also write $a + b = n(A) + n(B) = n(A \cup B)$.)

To use the definition to find $5 + 3$, we might choose $A = \{1, 2, 3, 4, 5\}$ and $B = \{6, 7, 8\}$. Then $A \cup B = \{1, 2, 3, 4, 5, 6, 7, 8\}$ and $n(A \cup B) = 8$.

REMARK Note that the definition instructs us to choose any two sets A and B. We are tacitly assuming that sets do exist for which the cardinal numbers are a and b. Second, we are assuming that the answer we obtain is not dependent on which sets are chosen. Any sets will work as long as they are disjoint and their cardinal numbers are correct. Because we commonly work with concrete or semiconcrete materials with young children, the choice of disjoint sets is very natural.

A reasonable question to ask at this point would be, "What properties hold for addition of whole numbers?" The work done with sets would direct our attention in particular directions. For example, does it matter which way we add the two numbers 3 and 5? Note that $3 + 5 = 5 + 3$ since $3 + 5 = 8$ and $5 + 3 = 8$. But is it true in general that if a and b are any whole numbers, then $a + b = b + a$? We should be able to use sets to verify this. By the definition for addition, to add a and b we must choose disjoint sets A and B whose cardinal numbers are a and b, respectively. Then $a + b = n(A \cup B)$. Likewise, $b + a = n(B \cup A)$. But union of sets is commutative, so $A \cup B = B \cup A$. Therefore, $n(A \cup B) = n(B \cup A)$, so in general $a + b = b + a$.

PROPERTY 2.8   The Commutative Property for Addition of Whole Numbers

For all whole numbers a and b, $a + b = b + a$.

Recall from our earlier work that $A \cup \emptyset = A$ for any set A. This fact should suggest to us that $a + 0 = a$ for any whole number a. We refer to 0 as the *identity element* for addition of whole numbers.

PROPERTY 2.9   Identity Element for Addition of Whole Numbers

If a is any whole number, then $a + 0 = 0 + a = a$.

Using the associative property of union of sets, we can also establish that whole numbers are associative under addition. We will allow you to do this in the next problem set.

PROPERTY 2.10   The Associative Property of Addition of Whole Numbers

For all whole numbers a, b, and c, $(a + b) + c = a + (b + c)$.

These properties are frequently helpful in simplifying addition problems. Consider the following examples.

EXAMPLE 1

Find $(23 + 2) + 18$.

$$
\begin{aligned}
(23 + 2) + 18 &= 23 + (2 + 18) \quad \text{Why?} \\
&= 23 + 20 \\
&= 43
\end{aligned}
$$

EXAMPLE 2

Find $(4 + 27) + 26$.

$$
\begin{aligned}
(4 + 27) + 26 &= 26 + (4 + 27) \quad \text{Why?} \\
&= (26 + 4) + 27 \quad \text{Why?} \\
&= 30 + 27 \\
&= 57
\end{aligned}
$$

When doing column addition such as

$$
\begin{array}{r}
4 \\
6 \\
+\ 3 \\
\hline
\end{array}
$$

we often add down, then add up to check. In what way are the properties used in this procedure? As we add down we add $(4 + 6) + 3$, and as we add up we add $(3 + 6) + 4$. Can you verify that $(4 + 6) + 3 = (3 + 6) + 4$? See if you can provide reasons for each step of the following argument.

$$(4 + 6) + 3 = 3 + (4 + 6) \quad \text{Why?}$$

$$3 + (4 + 6) = 3 + (6 + 4) \quad \text{Why?}$$

Thus

$$3 + (6 + 4) = (3 + 6) + 4 \quad \text{Why?}$$

$$(4 + 6) + 3 = (3 + 6) + 4 \quad \text{Why?}$$

We should stop for a moment to consider one more aspect of addition before we turn to some problems. We have tacitly assumed that given two whole numbers we could always find the sum of the two. But is this really true? Apparently the answer is yes, and once again we can turn to sets for our assurance. Given two whole numbers a and b, we can always identify a pair of sets A and B that are disjoint and have the desired cardinality. Then, by definition, $a + b = n(A \cup B)$. Now consider the set $A \cup B$. For *any* sets A and B, $A \cup B$ is a set. Therefore, its cardinal number $n(A \cup B)$ exists. Thus, for any whole numbers a and b we can determine the corresponding whole number $n(A \cup B)$. We say that the set of whole numbers is "closed with respect to addition."

PROPERTY 2.11   The Closure Property for Addition of Whole Numbers

The sum of any two whole numbers is a unique whole number.

The question of closure will come up at other times in our work with the operations. The general idea involved is that if we are given some set S and some binary operation, we must choose an element r from the set, then a second element s (perhaps even the same element again) and perform the given operation. If the resulting answer is always an element of S, no matter how we choose the elements r and s, then we say that the set S is closed with respect to that operation.

Example 1

Let $A = \{0, 1, 2\}$. Is A closed under addition?

Solution Note that $2 + 1 = 3$ and $3 \notin A$. Therefore, A is not closed under addition.

Example 2

Let $B = \{0, 2, 4, 6, 8 \ldots\}$

a. Is B closed with respect to addition?

b. Is B closed with respect to subtraction?

Solution to a If we select two elements, say 4 and 12, the sum is 16, which is even. The sum of 2 evens will always be even. (Let $2 \cdot a$ and $2 \cdot b$ represent any even numbers where a and b are whole numbers. Then $2a + 2b = 2(a + b)$. Because the whole numbers are closed under addition $(a + b)$ is a whole number. Therefore $2(a + b)$ is even.)

Solution to b Note that $(6 - 10) \notin B$. Therefore, B is not closed with respect to subtraction.

EXAMPLE 3

Given $W = \{0, 1, 2, 3, 4, 5 \ldots\}$

a. Is W closed with respect to subtraction?

b. Is W closed with respect to division?

Solution to a To claim that W is closed with respect to subtraction, $(a - b)$ must be an element of W no matter what choice is made for a and b from set W. Note that $(5 - 7) \notin W$. Therefore, W is not closed with respect to subtraction.

Solution to b Consider the fact that $(5 \div 7) \notin W$. The whole numbers are not closed with respect to division.

Sentences such as $x + 2 = 6$, which involve placeholders, are called *open sentences*. One important phase of elementary school mathematics involves finding *truth sets* for various kinds of open sentences. It should be evident that the truth set for $x + 2 = 6$ contains only one element, the number 4. Truth sets are called *solution sets* by some authors. Regardless of the name given the set, before it can be determined we must know the set of permissible values, called the *domain*, from which we can choose solutions. For the remainder of this chapter, unless otherwise specified, we will use the set of whole numbers on our domain. We could tabulate the truth set for $x + 2 = 7$ as $\{5\}$ and $x + 5 = 2$ as $\emptyset$. For much of the work done in elementary school, just a knowledge of number facts and some good, sensible trial-and-error procedures will suffice for finding truth sets.

PROBLEM SET 2.6

1. Use Definition 2.9 to establish each of the following:
   a. $3 + 1 = 4$ b. $5 + 3 = 8$ c. $4 + 3 = 7$ d. $6 + 0 = 6$

2. Which of the following sets are closed with respect to addition?
   a. $S = \{0, 1, 2\}$
   b. $S = \{0, 4, 8, 12, \ldots\}$
   c. $S = \{0\}$
   d. $S = \{0, 1, 4, 9, 16, 25, 36, \ldots\}$
   e. $S = \{1, 3, 5, 7, \ldots\}$
   f. $S = \{7, 8, 9, 10, \ldots\}$
   g. $S = \{0, 3, 6, 9, 12, \ldots\}$

3. State the property being applied in each of the following:
   a. $4 + 6 = 6 + 4$
   b. $(3 + 2) + 4 = 3 + (2 + 4)$
   c. $4 + 0 = 0 + 4$
   d. $4 + 0 = 4$
   e. $(1 + 6) + 4 = 4 + (1 + 6)$
   f. $(1 + 3) + 4 = (3 + 1) + 4$
   g. $[(6 + 4) + 8] + 7 = (6 + 4) + (8 + 7)$
   h. $[(21 + 12) + 15] + 17 = 17 + [(21 + 12) + 15]$

4. a. Can you give an example of two sets A and B such that $n(A \cup B)$ is less than $n(A) + n(B)$?
   b. Give an example of two sets C and D such that $n(C \cup D) = n(C) + n(D)$.
   c. Can you find sets E and F such that $n(E) + n(F)$ is less than $n(E \cup F)$? Justify your answer.

5. Suppose $D = \{1, 3, 5, 7, 9, \ldots\}$. Is D closed with respect to
   a. Addition?
   b. Subtraction?
   c. Mulitplication?
   d. Division?

6. List the elements of the truth set for each of the following using as the domain the set of whole numbers:
   a. $x + 3 = 7$
   b. $x + 4 = 9$
   c. $4 + x = 14$
   d. $92 + x = 101$
   e. $x + 4 = 2$
   f. $6 = 2 + x$
   g. $x + 2 = x + 3$
   h. $x + 4 = 4 + x$
   i. $x = x + 1$

Pedagogical Problems and Activities

7. Unifix materials are often used to illustrate cardinality and basic number facts. These materials make use of soft plastic snap blocks in 10 different colors. To illustrate the addition fact $3 + 4$ the child might take three of the snap blocks Red and another set of four Blue, then just snap them together .
   Red Blue

  a. Describe how the child could use the blocks to show that the commutative property for addition holds for the whole numbers 3 and 5.

  b. Use the Unifix blocks to verify that associativity holds for whole numbers.

  c. Ten is a very important whole number. One of the trays found in the Unifix materials is designed to hold just 10 of the snap blocks. Illustrate the entire set of pairs of whole numbers whose sum is 10.

8. A *number line* is used frequently in elementary school mathematics to aid children in visualizing various mathematical ideas. The association between numbers and points on a line can be introduced in the primary grades. We start with two points on a line with which we associate 0 and 1 as indicated.

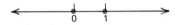

Using the interval between 0 and 1 as a unit segment, we can continue to mark off unit segments to the right of 1 and associate the whole numbers 2, 3, 4, and so on.

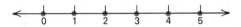

We may then interpret an addition problem such as $2 + 3$ on the number line. Begin at 0 and move to 2, then move 3 more units to the right, ending at 5. Therefore, $2 + 3 = 5$.

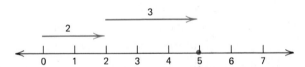

Show a number-line interpretation for each of the following:

  a. $3 + 2 = 5$ **b.** $4 + 1 = 5$

  c. $11 + 3 = 14$ **d.** $5 + 8 = 13$

9. Much of the work with open sentences in elementary schools uses symbols such as □, △, ○, and ◇ as placeholders instead of letters as in Problem 6.

  a. Find the truth set for each of the following:

    (i) □ $+ 2 = 6$

    (ii) ◇ $+ 4 = 4$

    (iii) $(3 + 4) +$ △ $= 3 + (4 +$ △$)$

  b. Would the open sentence □ $+ 2 =$ △ $+ 3$ mean the same as the sentence $x + 2 = x + 3$? Explain your answer.

10. We often check our work in addition by adding down the column of numbers, then adding up. That is, for the sum

$$\begin{array}{r} a \\ b \\ + \; c \\ \hline \end{array}$$

we find $(a + b) + c$ when we add down, then $(c + b) + a$ when we add up. We may use the properties from this section to verify that $(a + b) + c = (c + b) + a$. Provide a justification for each step.

(i) $(a + b) + c = c + (a + b)$

(ii) $\qquad\qquad\quad = c + (b + a)$

2.7 MULTIPLICATION OF WHOLE NUMBERS

Multiplication of whole numbers is often viewed as a natural extension of addition. This is reflected in the approach found in the elementary school mathematics program where 3×2 is considered to be simply a shorter way to write $2 + 2 + 2$. Because multiplication does so closely relate to addition, it is common to find sets used to give a pictorial representation for addition. Thus,

suggests the multiplication fact 4×3 and

is a representation of 3×5. Multiplication, which is viewed from the standpoint of repeated addition, is commonly referred to as the *additive type*.

A second interpretation is found for multiplication, usually beginning at the third grade level. The product 3×5 would be displayed as three rows with five elements in each row, such as

$$\begin{array}{c} \text{X X X X X} \\ \text{X X X X X} \\ \text{X X X X X} \end{array}$$

The answer can be obtained by the child either by using addition facts or by counting. We often refer to this interpretation as the *row by column type* and speak of the row by column representation as an *array*.

Still a third type of multiplication interpretation arises when one encounters two sets of elements and the elements are paired. For example, three kinds of cookies are available, sugar, spice, and oatmeal, and two drinks, milk and juice. How many different kinds of snacks are available if each person gets one cookie and one drink? A tabulation would result in six pairs as illustrated.

(sugar, milk)   (spice, milk)   (oatmeal, milk)

(sugar, juice)   (spice, juice)   (oatmeal, juice)

This interpretation is usually not given strong emphasis until the children are quite secure with the first two. One commonly sees it appearing at the fifth or sixth grade level, although children can model this at an earlier grade level.

We refer to problems of this kind as the *combination type*. One often sees problems of this type related to a diagram that graphically demonstrates the possible combinations.

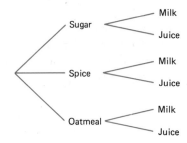

Definition 2.10   Let a and b represent any two whole numbers. Then

$$a \cdot b = \underbrace{b + b + b + \cdots + b}_{a \text{ terms}}$$

REMARK An alternate definition for multiplication could state $a \cdot b$ is the number of elements in the array that contains a rows with b elements in each row.

It should be clear that the two interpretations are closely related. Suppose we had four plates each having three cookies.

Surely the cookies could be rearranged as the array. On the other hand, some real-world problems do not lend themselves to such rearrangement, so it is desirable that children be exposed to both. (For example, in front of the school we have three trees and in the playground there are three more trees. How many trees are there?)

We are once again in the situation where we should try to decide what properties hold for this "new" operation of multiplication. As you will recall, the whole numbers are closed under addition. Because multiplication is merely repeated addition, we can conclude that the set of whole numbers is closed under multiplication. That is, the product of every pair of whole numbers is itself a whole number.

Suppose we use an array to interpret the product 3×5, and write
○○○○○
○○○○○
○○○○○ . Now rotate your paper by a quarter turn. The array now appears
as
○○○
○○○
○○○
○○○
○○○ which is of course 5×3. It is clear that the array was not altered; only the paper was moved. Therefore, in general, the row-column designation changed as a result of the movement of the paper, but not the number of elements, so $a \cdot b = b \cdot a$.

PROPERTY 2.12 The Commutative Property of Multiplication for Whole Numbers

For all whole numbers a and b, $a \cdot b = b \cdot a$.

We identified 0 as the identity element for addition. (Recall that $a + 0 = 0 + a = a$, no matter what whole number a we use.) Do we have a like whole number relative to multiplication? Is there a number that when multiplied by any whole number a gives that number a as the product? Of course, the number 1 satisfies this property.

PROPERTY 2.13 Identity Element of Multiplication for Whole Numbers

If a is any whole number, then $a \cdot 1 = 1 \cdot a = a$.

We can also establish that multiplication of whole numbers is associative. It does not matter in what order we group three whole numbers; the product will be the same. Thus, $(2 \cdot 3) \cdot 4 = 6 \cdot 4 = 24$ and $2 \cdot (3 \cdot 4) = 2 \cdot 12 = 24$.

PROPERTY 2.14 The Associative Property of Multiplication for Whole Numbers

For all whole numbers a, b, and c, $(a \cdot b) \cdot c = a \cdot (b \cdot c)$.

PROPERTY 2.15   The Closure Property for Multiplication of Whole Numbers

The product of any two whole numbers is a unique whole number.

PROPERTY 2.16   Multiplication Property of Zero

What statement can you make about $a \cdot b$ if we know that $b = 0$? Using the repeated addition idea, $3 \cdot 0 = 0 + 0 + 0$.

In general, if a is any whole number, then $a \cdot 0 = 0$ (also $0 \cdot a = 0$).

A direct consequence of Property 2.16 is the following property.

PROPERTY 2.17   For all whole numbers a and b, if $a = 0$ or $b = 0$, then $a \cdot b = 0$.

Property 2.17 asserts that if either of two numbers is zero, then the product is zero. Is the converse also true? That is, if $a \cdot b = 0$, can we be certain that either $a = 0$ or $b = 0$? Apparently that is the case and we will state the following property.

PROPERTY 2.18   For all whole numbers a and b, if $a \cdot b = 0$, then $a = 0$ or $b = 0$.

One additional property should be mentioned at this time. It ties addition and multiplication together. Suppose we have the product of 2 with the sum $3 + 4$ (i.e., $2 \cdot (3 + 4)$). Let us make an array to illustrate $2 \cdot (3 + 4)$ first, such as found in Figure 2.20a. From 2.20b it seems reasonable to rename the array as $(2 \times 3) + (2 \times 4)$. Thus, in this case $2 \cdot (3 + 4) = (2 \times 3) + (2 \times 4)$. This is, of course, the distributive pattern with multiplication distributing over addition. What we have illustrated in this one example is actually true in general, and we will state it as Property 2.19.

$$
\begin{array}{cc}
\circ\,\circ\circ\,\text{x\,x\,x\,x} & \circ\circ\circ\,\}\text{x\,x\,x\,x} \\
\circ\,\circ\circ\,\text{x\,x\,x\,x} & \circ\circ\circ\,\}\text{x\,x\,x\,x} \\
2 \cdot (3 + 4) & (2 \cdot 3) + (2 \cdot 4) \\
(a) & (b)
\end{array}
$$

FIGURE 2.20

PROPERTY 2.19   The Distributive Property

For all whole numbers, a, b, and c, (1) $a \cdot (b + c) = (a \cdot b) + (a \cdot c)$, and (2) $(b + c) \cdot a = (b \cdot a) + (c \cdot a)$.

Some authors refer to part (1) of the distributive property as a "lefthand distributive property" and to (2) as a "right-hand distributive property." We do not need to make this distinction in our work, but we do need both forms.

Even though the distributive property is stated here as a property involving three numbers, it can be extended to four or more numbers.

$$a \cdot (b + c + d) = (a \cdot b) + (a \cdot c) + (a \cdot d)$$

$$a \cdot (b + c + d + e) = (a \cdot b) + (a \cdot c) + (a \cdot d) + (a \cdot e)$$

EXAMPLE 1

$$3 \times 18 = 3 \times (10 + 8) = (3 \times 10) + (3 \times 8)$$
$$= 30 + 24$$
$$= 54$$

EXAMPLE 2

$$4500 + 7200 = 45 \times 100 + 72 \times 100$$
$$= (45 + 72) \times 100$$
$$= 117 \times 100$$
$$= 11,700$$

EXAMPLE 3

$$24 \times 35 = 24 \times (30 + 5)$$
$$= (24 \times 30) + (24 \times 5)$$
$$= (20 + 4) \times 30 + (20 + 4) \times 5$$
$$= (20 \times 30) + (4 \times 30) + (20 \times 5) + (4 \times 5)$$
$$= 600 + 120 + 100 + 20$$
$$= 840$$

PROBLEM SET 2.7

1. Use repeated addition to illustrate each of the following:
   a. 3×5 b. 4×2 c. 3×8 d. 6×3 e. 5×0 f. 4×1

2. Use an array to illustrate each of the following:
   a. 5×3 b. 3×5 c. 4×2 d. 5×1 e. 1×3 f. 5×6

3. Use an array to show each of the following:
   a. $4 \times 3 = 3 \times 4$ b. $6 \times 2 = 2 \times 6$
   c. $4 \times 1 = 1 \times 4$ d. $4 \times 5 = 5 \times 4$

4. In each of the following use repeated addition to verify that multiplication is commutative.
   a. $4 \times 2 = 2 \times 4$ b. $5 \times 3 = 3 \times 5$
   c. $7 \times 2 = 2 \times 7$ d. $6 \times 4 = 4 \times 6$

5. Indicate whether the following sets are closed or not closed with respect to multiplication:

    a. $S = \{1, 2, 3\}$ **b.** $S = \{0, 1, 2, 3, \ldots, 100\}$

    c. $S = \{0, 1, 2, 3, \ldots\}$ **d.** $S = \{0, 1\}$

    e. $S = \{0, 2, 4, 6, 8, \ldots\}$ **f.** $S = \{0, 5, 10, 15, \ldots\}$

    g. $S = \{0, 1, 4, 9, 16, 25, \ldots\}$ **h.** $S = \{1, 4, 7, 10, 13, 16, \ldots\}$

6. Use an array to illustrate each of the following

    a. $4(2 + 5) = (4 \times 2) + (4 \times 5)$ **c.** $6(5 + 2) = (6 \times 5) + (6 \times 2)$

    b. $3(4 + 3) = (3 \times 4) + (3 \times 3)$ **d.** $2(10 + 3) = (2 \times 10) + (2 \times 3)$

7. What property is illustrated in each of the following?

    a. $4 \times 6 = 6 \times 4$ **b.** $7 \times 1 = 7$

    c. $3 \times (4 + 2) = (3 \times 4) + (3 \times 2)$ **d.** $3 \times (4 \times 2) = (3 \times 4) \times 2$

    e. $3 \times (5 + 2) = 3 \times (2 + 5)$ **f.** $4 \times (5 + 2) = (5 + 2) \times 4$

    g. $(4 + 3) \times 5 = (4 \times 5) + (3 \times 5)$

    h. $(4 \times 5) + (4 \times 7) = 4 \times (5 + 7)$

    i. $(75 \times 146) + (75 \times 3) = 75(146 + 3)$

8. Verify each step of the following:

    a. Show that $6 \times (7 \times 5) = (5 \times 6) \times 7$

        i $6 \times (7 \times 5) = (6 \times 7) \times 5$

        ii $= 5 \times (6 \times 7)$

        iii $= (5 \times 6) \times 7$

    b. Show that $(5 \times 4) + (6 \times 5) = (6 + 4) \times 5$

        i $(5 \times 4) + (6 \times 5) = (4 \times 5) + (6 \times 5)$

        ii $= (4 + 6) \times 5$

        iii $= (6 + 4) \times 5$

9. Complete each of the following to demonstrate the distributive property.

    a. $5 \times (\_\_ + \_\_) = (5 \times 3) + (5 \times 4)$

    b. $(7 \times 8) + (9 \times 8) = (\_\_ + \_\_) \times 8$

    c. $8 \times (\_\_ + \_\_) = (\_\_ \times 3) + (\_\_ \times 6)$

    d. $\_\_ \times (5 + 6) = (\_\_ \times 5) + (\_\_ \times 6)$

10. **a.** Make an array to illustrate 3×4.

    b. Make an array to illustrate $2 \times (3 \times 4)$.

    c. Make an array to illustrate $(2 \times 3) \times 4$. [*Hint:* Assume that the commutative property holds and draw an array for $4 \times (2 \times 3)$.]

    d. What property do parts **b** and **c** together illustrate?

11. **a.** When we worked with sets we found that two distributive properties hold. [That is, $A \cup (B \cap C) = (A \cup B) \cap (A \cup C)$ and also $A \cap (B \cup$

$C) = (A \cap B) \cup (A \cap C).$] We have asserted that $a \cdot (b + c) = (a \cdot b) + (a \cdot c)$. Is it also true that $a + (b \cdot c) = (a + b) \cdot (a + c)$? (Use $a = 2$, $b = 3$, and $c = 5$ to test this.)

b. So in general $a + (b \cdot c) \neq (a + b) \cdot (a + c)$. But this does not mean that it *never* works. See if you can find specific values for a, b, and c for which it *will* work. Can you find more than one set of values for a, b, and c for which it will work? (This may be a good time to use the guess-and-check method.)

c. Use algebraic manipulations to try to find a general solution to the problem posed in part **b.**

12. The distributive property allows us to write a quantity as either a sum or as a basic product. The product $2 \times (4 + 5)$ is equal to the sum $(2 \times 4) + (2 \times 5)$. Use the properties that have been developed to write each of the following as a basic product.

a. $(4 \times 3) + (4 \times 5)$ **b.** $(6 \times 8) + (6 \times 2)$

c. $(8 \times 5) + (3 \times 5)$ **d.** $(6 \times 4) + (9 \times 4)$

e. $(8 \times 9) + (9 \times 2)$ **f.** $(4 \times 7) + (3 \times 4)$

g. $(8 \times 6) + (4 \times 8)$ **h.** $(5 \times 2) + (8 \times 5)$

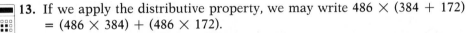 **13.** If we apply the distributive property, we may write $486 \times (384 + 172) = (486 \times 384) + (486 \times 172)$.

a. Use your calculator to find $486 \times (384 + 172)$. (Do the addition first, then the multiplication.)

b. Find $(486 \times 384) + (486 \times 172)$. (Take the products first, then find the sum.)

c. Which was easier to do on your calculator, **a** or **b?**

d. Use your calculator and the observation made in **c** to find $(574 \times 632) + (574 \times 456)$.

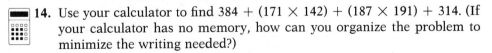 **14.** Use your calculator to find $384 + (171 \times 142) + (187 \times 191) + 314$. (If your calculator has no memory, how can you organize the problem to minimize the writing needed?)

15. Find the truth set for each of the following open sentences using the whole numbers as your domain:

a. $3 \cdot \square = 15$ **b.** $5 \cdot \square = 75$ **c.** $14 = \square \cdot 2$

d. $2 \cdot \triangle + 3 = 7$ **e.** $4 \cdot \triangle + 9 = 37$ **f.** $18 = 6 + 3 \cdot \triangle$

g. $7 \cdot (\square + 6) = 56$ **h.** $(\triangle + 3) \cdot 4 = 24$ **i.** $3 \cdot (\square + 1) = 47$

j. $\triangle \cdot 3 = 3 \cdot \triangle$

16. A box of Boy Scout candy bars is packed with each layer having four rows with three bars in each row. If there are six layers in the box how many candy bars are in the box?

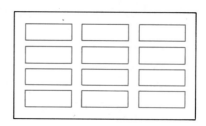

17. Bob has 12 candy bars to sell for his scout troop at 50 cents each. He also has 25 tickets to sell at 20 cents each. If he sells all the candy and tickets, how much money will he give to his troop?

18. a. Two decks of cards are available, one having the letters *a*, *b*, *c*, and *d*, and the other having numbers 1, 2, and 3. You are to draw one card from each deck. How many different hands can you obtain?

     b. In Disneyland the license plates for cars each contain a single letter from the alphabet followed by a single digit. How many different license plates are possible?

19. A farmer raises watermelons to sell at his roadside stand. He has found that his melons produce best if planted with three plants in a cluster. If he has 170 such clusters of plants in his field, how many individual plants must he have in all?

Pedagogical Problems and Activities

20. We stated that three types of multiplication problems are encountered by children: additive type, row by column type, and combination type.

     a. Make up a verbal problem to exemplify each.

     b. Look in elementary school mathematics texts to find an example of each.

21. The repeated-addition approach to multiplication of whole numbers lends itself nicely to work on a number line. For example, $3 \times 2 = 2 + 2 + 2$, which can be pictured on a number line as follows.

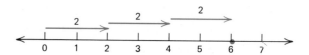

Give a number line interpretation for each of the following:

    a. 3×4 **b.** 2×5 **c.** 5×2 **d.** 3×5 **e.** 5×3

2.8   SUBTRACTION AND DIVISION OF WHOLE NUMBERS

The operation of subtraction can be approached from more than one viewpoint. Many children in first and second grades consider subtraction as it relates to addition. That is, if $5 + 2 = 7$, then we may state that $7 - 5 = 2$ and also $7 - 2 = 5$. The four statements $5 + 2 = 7$, $2 + 5 = 7$, $7 - 5 = 2$, and $7 - 2 = 5$ are often referred to as a *fact family*. Note that the statement $7 - 5 = 2$ is just another way of saying $5 + \underline{} = 7$. For this reason it is common to refer to this concept of subtraction as *the missing addend*. When you consider this type of problem in the real world, it often relates to the question of "how many more are needed?" A typical question might be stated as follows: "Ten children are coming to the birthday party. We have seven candy treats made. How many more do we need?" An answer is suggested when we write $7 + \underline{} = 10$.

A second interpretation of subtraction is that referred to as *take away*. If a child has six toys and two of them are lost, he or she then has four remaining. Children usually find this "take away" idea to be intuitively clear. It is not difficult to picture five birds and show two of them flying away. They may then write the number sentence $5 - 2 = 3$.

Still a third interpretation for subtraction involves a comparison of two sets. The sentence "If John has four marbles and Mary has seven, how many more does Mary have than John?" is an example of this. It is common for children to use two sets of objects and one-to-one correspondence as they answer the question asked. All three of these interpretations arise naturally in the everyday lives of children.

Let us pursue the relationship between addition and subtraction a bit further. Notice that if we add 2 to 6 and then subtract 2 we again get 6. In general, if we add the number b to a and then subtract b, we expect to get a as the result. That is, $(a + b) - b = a$. For this reason, we refer to subtraction as the *inverse operation* of addition.

Note that this is really a restatement of the missing addend idea mentioned previously. Thus $7 + k = 9$ is asking for the number that added to 7 gives 9, and we commonly write it as $9 - 7 = k$. Then, because subtraction is the inverse of addition, $8 - 6$ must be some number x such that $6 + x = 8$. Therefore x must be 2 because $6 + 2 = 8$. Also, $31 - 20$ is that number x that when added to 20 yields 31. Therefore, $31 - 20 = 11$ because $20 + 11 = 31$. Let us use this idea as we define subtraction.

Definition 2.11   For whole numbers a and b, $a - b$ (read "a minus b") is that whole number c (if c exists) such that $b + c = a$ (we could state that $a - b = c$ if and only if $b + c = a$).

It should be clear that this definition does not imply that for every pair of whole numbers we can name a whole number as the difference. For example, $5 - 7$ is to be the number that when added to 7 yields 5. Because no whole number c exists such that $7 + c = 5$, then the subtraction $5 - 7$ cannot be done. Thus, we say that the set of whole numbers is not closed with respect to the operation of subtraction.

We might wonder whether other properties hold for subtraction. Are the whole numbers commutative with respect to subtraction? We noted above that $5 - 7$ did not have an answer in the set of whole numbers, but that $7 - 5 = 2$. Thus, the counting numbers are *not commutative* under subtraction. What about associativity of whole numbers under subtraction? Does $(a - b) - c = a - (b - c)$ for all whole numbers a, b, and c? That is, no matter how we choose three numbers, does $(a - b) - c$ yield the same result as $a - (b - c)$? Suppose $a = 5$, $b = 3$, and $c = 1$. Then $(a - b) - c = (5 - 3) - 1 = 2 - 1 = 1$ and $a - (b - c) = 5 - (3 - 1) = 5 - 2 = 3$. This counterexample allows us to conclude that the whole numbers are *not associative* with respect to subtraction. We might also observe that although $a - 0 = a$, it is not the case that $0 - a = a$. Thus, 0 is not an identity element for subtraction.

Division is much like subtraction in the sense that it can be interpreted in several ways. One important idea is that division may mean repeated subtraction. If I have 25 pop bottles and want to know how many 8 packs I can make to return to the grocery store I could subtract 8 until no more clusters of 8 are available. A second interpretation involves the distribution of items. Suppose I have 18 pieces of bubble gum and five people are coming to the party. How much gum should I give to each? I could simply "deal out" gum to five piles (like dealing cards). This is the distributive idea. Still a third concept comes from the "fact family" idea in a manner very similar to what we considered with subtraction. If $5 \times 3 = 15$, we may also write $3 \times 5 = 15$, $5 \times \underline{\ \ } = 15$ and $\underline{\ \ } \times 3 = 15$. These latter two may be restated as $15 \div 5 = \underline{\ \ }$ and $15 \div 3 = \underline{\ \ }$, respectively. Thus, division can be thought of as a missing factor idea.

The missing factor approach is commonly encountered as the first approach to division. We often refer to division as the *inverse operation of multiplication* when considered from this viewpoint. Using this approach, we can handle a division problem by considering a corresponding multiplication problem; in other words, finding a missing factor. For example, 8 divided by 2 is that number c such that $2c = 8$; therefore, we conclude that 8 divided by 2 is 4. Also, 36 divided by 9 is that number c such that $9c = 36$; therefore, 36 divided by 9 is 4. Let us generalize and state a formal definition for division of whole numbers.

Definition 2.12 For whole numbers a and b ($b \neq 0$), a divided by b (written $a \div b$) is that whole number c (if it exists) such that $bc = a$ (symbolically, $a \div b = c$ if and only if $bc = a$).

Keep in mind that this definition does not imply the existence of a whole number c for every possible choice of a and b. For example, by the definition, $15 \div 7$ is that whole number c such that $7c = 15$, which has no solution in the set of whole numbers. Thus, we say that the set of whole numbers is *not closed* with respect to division. Note that the restriction that a is greater than b would still not assure us of the existence of a whole number solution for $a \div b$ as it did with subtraction.

According to Definition 2.12, $6 \div 0$ is the whole number c such that $c(0) = 6$. We have previously established that $a(0) = 0$ for all whole numbers; therefore, the open sentence $c(0) = 6$ has no solution. We might say that $x \div 0$ for $x \neq 0$ is *meaningless*. Also, according to our definition for division, $0 \div 0$ is that number c such that $c(0) = 0$. The open sentence $c(0) = 0$ is satisfied by all whole numbers c. Consequently we say that $0 \div 0$ is of *indeterminate form*. Frequently in elementary school mathematics the "meaningless" case and the "indeterminate" form are put in one category, and the students are simply told "do not divide by zero." Students should be made aware of the two different situations that are included under such a statement and thus be aware of the fact that division by zero is undefined.

Because $6 \div 2 \neq 2 \div 6$, we can immediately conclude that division is not commutative. Also, because $(18 \div 6) \div 3 = 1$ and $18 \div (6 \div 3) = 9$ we can conclude that division is not associative. We also observe that $a \div 1 = a$ for all whole numbers, but $1 \div a \neq a$ for all whole numbers. Consequently, 1 is not considered to be an identity element for division.

PROBLEM SET 2.8

1. Use Definition 2.11 to find each of the following:
   a. $4 - 1$ b. $12 - 7$ c. $18 - 5$ d. $31 - 25$ e. $17 - 6$ f. $23 - 17$

2. According to Definition 2.11, $5 - x = 3$ may be interpreted to mean "for what number x does $x + 3 = 5$?" The truth set is apparently $\{2\}$. Translate each of the following to an open sentence involving addition and then find the truth set:
   a. $x - 3 = 7$ b. $x - 5 = 9$ c. $4 - x = 1$ d. $43 - x = 32$
   e. $6 - x = 9$ f. $5 - x = 10$ g. $x - 47 = 63$ h. $33 = 17 - x$

3. a. In general, for whole numbers a and b, we state that $a - b \neq b - a$. But that does not necessarily rule out the possibility of some choice of a and b for which $a - b = b - a$. Can you find any replacement for a and b for which $a - b = b - a$? Can you find a second replacement that will work? Can you make a general statement that seems to govern successful choices for a and b?

   b. Try to use a general algebraic expression to verify your conjecture in part **a**.

4. a. If we are told that for certain whole numbers d, e, and f, $(d - e) - f = d - (e - f)$, what can you conclude about f? Give examples to illustrate your answer.

   b. Does the use of algebra verify your conjecture from part **a**?

5. Does $a - a = 0$ for all whole numbers a? Justify your answer.

6. a. Suppose that a whole number k minus 45 = 30. What must k equal?

   b. The difference between some number k and 30 is 15. What number is k?

   c. The difference between some number n and 640 is 763. What number is n?

7. Use Definition 2.12 to find each of the following.

   a. $12 \div 3$ **b.** $14 \div 2$ **c.** $24 \div 6$
   d. $27 \div 9$ **e.** $56 \div 4$ **f.** $17 \div 17$

8. The sentence $32 \div x = 4$ may be translated into the sentence $x \cdot 4 = 32$ by using Definition 2.12. Restate each of the following as a multiplication problem; then find the truth set.

   a. $24 \div x = 4$ **b.** $36 \div x = 9$ **c.** $x \div 4 = 11$
   d. $x \div 5 = 30$ **e.** $21 \div 3 = x$ **f.** $45 \div 15 = x$
   g. $(x + 1) \div 3 = 7$ **h.** $18 \div (x + 2) = 6$

9. a. Does $a \div a = 1$ for *all* whole numbers? Justify your answer.

   b. Can you find some particular numbers a and b such that $a \div b = b \div a$? Can you find a second such pair?

   c. Use an algebraic approach to part **b**. What general statement can you make?

   d. Does $(a \div b) \div c = a \div (b \div c)$ for all nonzero numbers a, b, and c chosen such that $a = b = c$? Can you show a counterexample? (*Hint:* What happens if $a = b = c = 2$?)

   e. Can you find a general solution for part **d** by using an algebraic approach?

10. Sometimes it is helpful to use a table to keep track of the guesses made in attempting to solve a problem. Try this procedure as you solve the following problems.

   a. It costs 15¢ to mail a postcard and 25¢ for a letter. Suppose 15 pieces of mail were sent costing $3.15. How many of each were mailed?

Letters Sent @ 25¢ ea.		Postcards @ 15¢ ea.		Totals	
Number	Cost	Number	Cost	Total Number	Total Cost

b. Suppose a zoo has a "petting pen" with only ducks and goats in it. In all, the animals have 150 legs, and we are assured that there are at least 40 ducks in the pen; what is the largest number of goats that could be in the pen?

11. Find the truth set for each of the following open sentences using the set of whole numbers as your domain:

    a. $3x - 1 = 8$ **b.** $(x + 2) \div 3 = 7$ **c.** $4x - 3 = 9$

    d. $24 \div (x - 2) = 6$ **e.** $48 \div (3x - 2) = 12$ **f.** $(x - 1) \div (x - 5) = 2$

12. a. Use your calculator to find $864 \times (413 - 212)$.

    b. Find $(864 \times 413) - (864 \times 212)$.

    c. Does $864 \times (413 - 212) = (864 \times 413) - (864 \times 212)$?

    d. Does $(672 + 1104) \div 48 = (672 \div 48) + (1104 \div 48)$?

Pedagogical Problems and Activities

13. a. Illustrate with sets the way a second-grade child might find $17 - 8$.

    b. How might you illustrate $45 \div 9$ using sets?

14. A third-grade child states that the difference between 953 and 946 must be greater than the difference between 53 and 46 because 953 is bigger than 53 and 946 is bigger than 46. What might you say?

15. Number lines are frequently used to perform subtraction of whole numbers. The difference $7 - 4$ may be found by answering the question "What must I add to 4 to get 7?" and may be displayed on a number line as illustrated. That is, $7 - 4 = k$ is equivalent to the statement $4 + k = 7$. Use this technique to find the following:

    a. $9 - 4$ **b.** $7 - 5$ **c.** $7 - 3$ **d.** $6 - 6$ **e.** $9 - 1$ **f.** $7 - 2$

16. As you look at primary-level mathematics texts, you will observe several types of subtraction situations. Write a verbal problem that involves:

    a. Take away

    b. Missing addend (how many more are needed)

    c. Comparison

17. a. Some division situations exist in which both a total number of elements and the number in each set are known, and you must determine the number of sets. (There are 48 bottles, 8 in each carton. How many cartons are there?) This is referred to as a *subtractive-type* problem. Write another problem of this type that could be used with fourth-grade children.

b. Another division situation exists in which the total number of elements and the number of sets are known, and you must determine how many are in each set. (There are 30 cookies to be placed in 6 lunch cartons. How many cookies should be placed in each?) This is commonly referred to as a *distributive-type* problem. Suggest another problem of this type that would be suitable for use with fourth-grade children.

18. Another kind of physical setting requiring subtraction arises when we have a set made up of two kinds of things, where we know the number of elements in the set and in one subset. We commonly refer to this as a *partitioning problem.* Consider the following: There are 24 cars in the parking lot, all either Fords or Chevys. If 14 are Fords, how many are Chevys?

2.9   THE ORDERING OF WHOLE NUMBERS

We have introduced the idea of sets and then applied this idea to the development of whole numbers. A number of properties of sets have been discussed and applied to the whole numbers. We have defined the four operations on whole numbers and have considered several of their key properties. We have not yet given any consideration to the process of comparing two whole numbers. Our primary concern in this section is to establish the "less than" and "greater than" relations and to examine a few of their properties.

Children in the primary grades commonly encounter discussion about equality and inequality. Such discussion will very likely make use of sets and one-to-one correspondence. For example, first-grade children may be asked to compare 4 and 7, as illustrated in Example 1.

EXAMPLE 1

Which is greater?

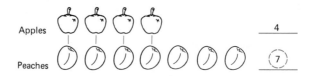

The child can easily use one-to-one correspondence to determine that there are more peaches than apples, and thus the number of peaches is greater than the number of apples.

EXAMPLE 2

Which is less?

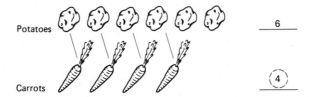

Note that one-to-one correspondence applies to both greater than and less than situations. Children at this age often find it difficult to "reverse" the two inequality situations. Also note that no symbolism was applied to greater than or less than at this stage of development.

Although the one-to-one correspondence idea is useful for the development of concepts of equality and inequality for young children, it is not of great value when working with larger numbers. The fifth-grade child who needs to determine whether 385 is greater than 379 would not find sets to be particularly helpful. A much more useful procedure at this level would be one that considers the two potential differences, $385 - 379$ and $379 - 385$. Only one of these differences will have as a result a nonzero whole number, and this will readily enable us to determine the larger number. That is, because $385 - 379 = 6$, we may conclude that $379 < 385$. Let us state this in a slightly different way. The difference between the two numbers is 6. If 6 is added to the smaller of the two numbers, that sum is equal to the larger number. This is commonly used as a working definition for less than.

Definition 2.13   For any whole numbers a and b, $a < b$ if and only if there exists some nonzero whole number k such that $b = a + k$.

From this definition, we may conclude the following:

$$3 < 4 \text{ because } 3 + \underline{1} = 4$$

$$5 < 12 \text{ because } 5 + \underline{7} = 12$$

$$6 < 20 \text{ because } 6 + \underline{14} = 20$$

$$784 < 846 \text{ because } 784 + \underline{62} = 846$$

Before we continue our discussion of the relation *less than,* let us clarify one important point. If $a < b$, then we can also say that b is *greater than a,* which we denote by $b > a$. Therefore, each time that we examine a property of *less than,* you may assume that there is a corresponding property for *greater than* unless we specify otherwise. Occasionally we will remind you of this fact and perhaps even state the corresponding property of *greater than;* however, try to think constantly in terms of both *less than* and *greater than* properties.

From a pedagogical viewpoint, it is convenient to interpret the relations *less than* and *greater than* on a number line. This helps children to visualize some basic properties. On a number line we agree that $a < b$ means "a is to the left of b," and $a > b$ means "a is to the right of b." For example, in Figure 2.21a $4 < 6$ because 4 is to the left of 6, and $6 > 4$ because 6 is to the right of 4. (We have actually implicitly assumed this earlier when we first introduced the number line.) In Figure 2.21b we have interpreted the inequality in terms of a vertical number line.

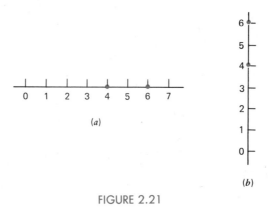

(a)

(b)

FIGURE 2.21

The first property we want to call to your attention is the *trichotomy* property.

PROPERTY 2.20   The Trichotomy Property for Whole Numbers

If a and b are any two whole numbers, then one and only one of the following must be true:

1. $a = b$ **2.** $a > b$ **3.** $a < b$

As a result of the trichotomy property we know that if $a \not< b$ (not less than), then $a = b$ or $a > b$, which we write as $a \geq b$. Similarly, we write $a \leq b$ to mean "$a < b$ or $a = b$." Thus, using the set of whole numbers as our domain, the truth set for $x \leq 3$ is $\{0, 1, 2, 3\}$ and the truth set for $x \geq 4$ is $\{4, 5, 6, \ldots\}$.

We might also observe that the transitive property for inequalities applies to less than situations because the knowledge that $4 < 6$ and $6 < 11$ assures us that $4 < 11$.

PROPERTY 2.21   The Transitive Property for Less Than

For any whole numbers a, b, and c, if $a < b$ and $b < c$, then $a < c$.

Having acquired two new relations, *less than* and *greater than*, we are now able to work with a greater variety of open sentences involving these relations.

Open sentences such as $x + 3 < 5$ can be solved by using substitution procedures much like those used in the intuitive solutions for equalities. That is, if x is replaced by 0, we have $0 + 3 < 5$, which is a true statement; if x is replaced by 1, then $1 + 3 < 5$, which is also true. However, no other whole number, when substituted for x, will result in a true statement. The truth set is $S = \{0, 1\}$.

EXAMPLE 1

Find the solution set for $2x + 3 > 7$.

Solution   If $2x + 3$ must be greater than 7, then $2x$ must be greater than 4. Therefore, x must be greater than 2. Thus $S = \{3, 4, 5, \dots\}$.

EXAMPLE 2

Find the set of whole numbers for which $3x + 2 > 10$.

Solution   If $3x + 2$ is to be greater than 10, then $3x$ must be greater than 8. Note that if $x = 3$, we have $3x = 9$ and $9 + 2 > 10$ is a true statement. Likewise, $x = 4$ will also produce a true statement as will any other whole number greater than 3. Thus, the solution set is $S = \{3, 4, 5, 6, \dots\}$.

See if you agree with the truth sets as indicated for each of the following. Again, the domain is the set of whole numbers.

Open Sentences	Truth Set
$x + 2 > 4$	$\{3, 4, 5, \dots\}$
$x + 1 < 6$	$\{0, 1, 2, 3, 4\}$
$x + 6 > 15$	$\{10, 11, 12, \dots\}$
$2x > 16$	$\{9, 10, 11, \dots\}$
$3x \leqslant 15$	$\{0, 1, 2, 3, 4, 5\}$
$4x \geqslant 16$	$\{4, 5, 6, \dots\}$
$5x + 1 < 21$	$\{0, 1, 2, 3\}$

Now consider the open sentence "$x > 2$ and $x > 5$." Remember that an "and" statement is true only if both parts are true. Replacing x with 1 makes both parts false, so clearly 1 is not in the truth set. If x is replaced by 3, it makes one part true and one part false, therefore, 3 does not belong in the truth set. How about 6? Do you agree that the truth set is $S = \{6, 7, 8, \ldots\}$? Next, consider the open sentence "$x > 2$ and $x < 5$." Does 1 make this sentence true? How about 3? How about 6? Do you agree with the truth set $S = \{3, 4\}$?

Finally, consider the open sentence "$x > 4$ or $x < 2$." Earlier, we commented that an "or" statement is true if either part (or both) are true. Determine whether each of the following is in the truth set: 1, 3, 5, and 6. Do you agree that the truth set consists of those whole numbers that are greater than 4 along with the whole numbers that are less than 2? This truth set can be expressed as the union of two sets $S = \{0, 1\} \cup \{5, 6, 7, \ldots\}$.

Mathematical Structure

Let us pause briefly to take stock of our position in this mathematical development. It should be clear to you that we developed some basic ideas about sets in order to use them to develop the whole numbers and the basic operations for whole numbers. We gave some consideration to the properties that apply to these operations. Many of these properties will be viewed again as we work with integers, rational numbers, and real numbers in later chapters. Perhaps we should attempt to pull together these ideas before we proceed with other work.

We found that the set of whole numbers is closed under addition and multiplication but is *not* closed under subtraction and division. Indeed, this lack of closure for subtraction and division provides at least part of the motivation for extending the number system in later chapters to include integers and rational numbers.

The concept of associativity also permeates a great deal of the development of the real numbers. We have found that the whole numbers are associative under addition and multiplication but not under subtraction and division. Thus, it is clear that $2 \cdot (3 \cdot 4) = (2 \cdot 3) \cdot 4$, but that $5 - (3 - 1) \neq (5 - 3) - 1$. Also, we have found that the whole numbers are commutative under addition and multiplication but not under subtraction and division; that is, $7 + 2 = 2 + 7$, but $6 \div 3 \neq 3 \div 6$.

We also observed that the whole numbers possess the elements referred to as identity elements for both addition and multiplication. The number 0 is the identity for addition, and we observed that $a + 0 = 0 + a = a$ for any choice of whole number a. Similarly, as $a \cdot 1 = 1 \cdot a = a$ for any whole number a, we stated that 1 is the multiplicative identity. In the case of subtraction, we find that $a - 0 = a$ but $= 0 - a \neq a$. For 0 to be the identity for subtraction it would be necessary that $a - 0 = 0 - a = a$. Thus, we have no identity for subtraction. Likewise, we have no identity for division because $a \div 1 = a$ but $1 \div a \neq a$. Thus, neither subtraction nor division has an identity element.

The distributive pattern was found to apply with multiplication distributing over addition. Thus, $2 \times (3 + 4) = (2 \times 3) + (2 \times 4)$, for example. This property ties these two operations together and allows us to relate basic sums with basic products. As with the other properties, we will return to the distributive property many times in further developments.

Properties such as those just reviewed along with some others appearing later are the threads that run throughout mathematics. An understanding of these is very helpful in organizing your thoughts about mathematics.

The basic properties make it possible for us to write expressions involving addition and multiplication in a variety of ways. It is often useful to make use of number sentences involving placeholders. This is, of course, what is commonly done in writing formulas, open sentences, or algebraic expressions. Three notational agreements need to be made before we proceed.

1. Numerals (representing numbers) written in juxtaposition indicate multiplication. For example, $3x$ means $3 \cdot x$, xy means $x \cdot y$, and $5xy$ means $5 \cdot x \cdot y$. This does not imply that writing 56 means that a product is involved. Indeed it does not, but rather $56 = 50 + 6$. Likewise $5\frac{1}{4}$ means $5 + \frac{1}{4}$. Let us agree that if we wish to take the product of 5 and 6 we will write $5 \cdot 6$ or $5(6)$ or perhaps $(5)(6)$. Likewise, $6(\frac{1}{4})$ or $(6)(\frac{1}{4})$ means to perform the indicated multiplication.

2. The concept of exponent is not formally discussed until the next chapter. It suffices here simply to agree that the following statements are true:

$$a^2 \text{ means } a \cdot a$$

$$a^3 \text{ means } a \cdot a \cdot a$$

therefore

$$(a + b)^2 \text{ means } (a + b)(a + b)$$

$$(a + b)^3 \text{ means } (a + b)(a + b)(a + b)$$

3. In general, we perform operations in parentheses first. Unless otherwise indicated, we will perform multiplications and divisions, then additions and subtractions. Thus, when we write $2 \cdot 3 + 4 \cdot 3$ we mean $6 + 12$, but if we write $2 \cdot (3 + 4) \cdot 3$ we mean $2 \cdot 7 \cdot 3$.

> REMARK   When we write $2 + 3 \times 4 + 5$ we intend that the product should be completed first, so $2 + 3 \times 4 + 5 = 2 + 12 + 5 = 19$. When a calculator is used to compute the answer, you may get a different answer. Some calculators simply perform the operations in the order in which they are entered. Thus, it would first add $2 + 3$, then multiply that answer by 4, then add 5, giving the erroneous answer 25. Other calculators are more sophisticated and store the data in memory until all information is entered, then select the procedure that follows the correct order of operations. That is, it first finds the product 3×4, then adds the 2 and the 5, obtaining 19 as the answer.

Let us examine some direct results of the properties; you will note that the distributive property is useful in many of the manipulations.

EXAMPLE 1

$$3x + 2x = (3 + 2)x = 5x$$

$$3b + b = (3 + 1)b = 4b$$

$$5a^2 + 6a^2 = (5 + 6)a^2 = 11a^2$$

$$x + 3x = (1 + 3)x = 4x$$

Many authors refer to expressions such as $x + 2$, $2x + 1$, and $5x + 3y$ as *indicated sums* and expressions such as $3(x + 2)$, $(x + 1)6$, and $(x + 2)(x + 3)$ as *indicated products*. Using this terminology, we see that the distributive property can be used to rewrite an indicated sum as an indicated product or an indicated product as an indicated sum.

EXAMPLE 2

Write each indicated product as an indicated sum:

$$3(x + 4) = 3x + 3(4) = 3x + 12$$

$$a(a + 2) = a \cdot a + a \cdot 2 = a^2 + 2a$$

$$4(a + 2b + 5) = 4(a) + 4(2b) + 4(5) = 4a + 8b + 20$$

Write each indicated sum as an indicated product:

$$3x + 30 = 3(x) + 3(10) = 3(x + 10)$$

$$4a + 6b = 2(2a) + 2(3b) = 2(2a + 3b)$$

In the next example the distributive property is applied twice.

EXAMPLE 3

$$(x + 2)(x + 3) = (x + 2)(x) + (x + 2)(3)$$
$$= x(x) + 2(x) + x(3) + 2(3)$$
$$= x^2 + 2x + 3x + 6$$
$$= x^2 + 5x + 6$$

Do you see that we are allowing $(x + 2)$ to play the role of a in the $a(b + c) = ab + ac$ form of the distributive property? This is permissible since x and 2 are both whole numbers, and because we have closure for addition of whole numbers, $x + 2$ is a whole number. We could also apply the other form of the distributive property if we choose to do so [i.e., $(b + c), a = (b \cdot a) + (c \cdot a)$].

We commented previously about the use of open sentences and the task of finding truth sets for them. You have encountered open sentences involving addition and multiplication in the problem sets. Let us extend this work a bit more by considering some other types of open sentences. Earlier in the chapter we mentioned the logical connectives *and* and *or*. We stated that an "and" statement would be considered true just in those cases where both parts were true. The simple statement "$2 + 3 = 5$" is true, as is the statement "$5 + 2 = 7$." Therefore, "$2 + 3 = 5$ and $5 + 2 = 7$" is also true. However, because "$4 + 3 = 8$" is false, the statement "$2 + 3 = 5$ and $4 + 3 = 8$" is a false statement. Likewise, "$5 + 2 = 6$ and $6 + 4 = 10$" is false, as is "$5 + 2 = 6$ and $4 + 3 = 8$." Now suppose we are interested in finding the truth set for the open sentence "$x + 1 = 3$ and $x + 2 = 4$." If we replace x by the whole number 4, then we have the statement "$4 + 1 = 3$ and $4 + 2 = 4$." Of course, both parts are false, so our "and" statement is false, and 4 is not an element of the truth set. However, because 2 makes both parts true, do you agree that the truth set is $\{2\}$?

Somewhat the same reasoning can be applied in the case of the sentence "$x + 1 = 3$ or $x + 5 = 8$." Recall that an "or" statement is true if *either* part is true. Thus, "$3 + 2 = 5$ or $8 + 1 = 5$" is true, as is "$4 + 1 = 0$ or $3 + 4 = 7$." Thus, replacing x by 2 makes $x + 1 = 3$ true and replacing x by 3 in $x + 5 = 8$ gives a true statement. Apparently the truth set in this case is $\{2, 3\}$.

REMARK Some students find it helpful to recall that an "or" statement is *false* only in case both parts are false. An "and" statement is false if either part (or both parts) is false.

EXAMPLE

Find the truth set for each of the following:

$$x + 2 = 3 \text{ and } x + 5 = 6 \qquad \{1\}$$
$$x + 5 = 7 \text{ and } x + 3 = 9 \qquad \emptyset$$
$$x + 2 = 6 \text{ or } x + 5 = 9 \qquad \{4\}$$
$$x + 2 = 7 \text{ or } x + 5 = 6 \qquad \{1, 5\}$$

In the preceding section, we stated the property "for all whole numbers a and b, if $a \cdot b = 0$, then $a = 0$ or $b = 0$." Note the use of the "or" connective in the statement. Consider the open sentence "$x(x + 3) = 0$." This, according to the property, is equivalent to stating "$x = 0$ or $x + 3 = 0$." If we use only whole numbers as the universe, the solution set is $\{0\}$. We will return to this concept for additional work in a later chapter. Let us turn now to some exercises to allow you to practice with these concepts.

PROBLEM SET 2.9

1. Use sets of objects to verify each of the following:
   a. $2 < 3$ **b.** $4 < 5$ **c.** $6 < 8$
   d. $1 < 5$ **e.** $2 < 9$ **f.** $5 < 7$

2. Use Definition 2.13 to verify each of the following:
   a. $2 < 6$ **b.** $5 < 9$ **c.** $7 < 12$
   d. $17 < 26$ **e.** $84 < 96$ **f.** $463 < 521$

3. Complete the following statement: for any whole numbers a and b, $a > b$ if and only if _____.

4. Use the distributive property and other properties as needed to simplify each of the following expressions;
   a. $7a + 3a$ **b.** $5\triangle + 6\triangle$
   c. $3\square + 2\square + 5\square$ **d.** $8x^2 + 5x^2$
   e. $5a + 3b + 2a + 7b$ **f.** $4x^2 + 3x + 2 + 5x + x^2 + 4$

5. Use the distributive property to change each of the following indicated products to an indicated sum:
   a. $2(x + 2)$ **b.** $a(2a + 3)$
   c. $2x(x + 3y)$ **d.** $3(2a^2 + 3a + 4)$
   e. $2a(a^2 + 4a + 5)$ **f.** $(x + 4)(x + 8)$
   g. $(5x + 2)(2x + 3)$ **h.** $(x + 1)^2$
   i. $(x + 4)^2$

6. Change each of the following indicated sums to an indicated product:

   a. $7x + 14$ b. $5x + 15$

   c. $2ab + 3a$ d. $x^2 + 5x$

   e. $x^2 + 3x + xy$ f. $a(a + 2) + 3(a + 2)$

   g. $2(x + 3) + 5(x + 3)$ h. $x(2x + 3) + y(2x + 3)$

   i. $x^2 + 2x + ax + 2a$

7. Use sets to verify that $0 < 1$.

8. State a transitive property for "greater than" and give an example to illustrate its meaning.

9. Find the truth set for each of the following simple open sentences. Use the set of whole numbers as the domain.

   a. $x + 1 < 11$ b. $x + 11 < 15$ c. $x + 9 > 23$

   d. $4x \leqslant 12$ e. $6x > 24$ f. $3x < 7$

   g. $8x > 57$ h. $2x + 1 \geqslant 5$ i. $3x + 2 > 11$

   j. $5x + 7 < 32$ k. $4x + 7 > 27$ l. $6 < 3x + 3$

   m. $19 \geqslant 2x + 1$ n. $5x + 13 > 163$ o. $7x + 9 < 147$

   p. $6x - 7 < 23$ q. $3x - 4 < 9$ r. $20x - 3 < 11$

10. Find the truth set for each of the following compound open sentences using the set of whole numbers as the domain.

   a. $x > 0$ and $x > 3$ b. $x > 6$ and $x > 4$

   c. $x < 5$ and $x \leqslant 7$ d. $x < 2$ and $x \leqslant 5$

   e. $x > 2$ or $x > 4$ f. $x > 5$ or $x > 3$

   g. $x > 7$ and $x < 5$

11. Find the truth set for each open sentence. Use the whole numbers as the domain.

   a. $x + 5 = 9$ or $x + 3 = 5$ b. $x + 2 = 3$ and $x + 5 = 6$

   c. $2x + 1 = 6$ and $3x + 2 = 8$ d. $4x + 5 = 17$ or $3x + 9 = 21$

   e. $3 + 5x^2 = 18$ and $14 = 2x + 8$ f. $4x + 3 = 14$ or $5x + 1 = 21$

   g. $7x + 9 = 5$ or $9x + 3 = 42$ h. $5 + 2 = 7$ and $2x + 1 = 7$

   i. $5 + 2 = 7$ or $5x + 3 = 4$

12. Suppose a, b, and c are three different nonzero whole numbers and that $a + b = c$. Which of the following are true statements?

   a. $a < b$ b. $b < a$ c. $a < c$

   d. $c < a$ e. $b < c$ f. $c < b$

13. In each case, indicate the grouping symbols needed to produce the indicated answer resulting from operations performed on these numbers $3 + 2 \times 5 + 4$.

   a. 29   b. 45   c. 17   d. 21

14. Replace each of the following statements with a whole number that is equivalent to it.

   a. $4 \cdot (5 + 3) + 2$ b. $3 \cdot 4 + 2$
   c. $3 \cdot 4 + 5 \cdot 6$ d. $5 + (6 \cdot 2) + 7$
   e. $4 \cdot 3 + 8 \cdot 2$ f. $[4 \cdot (3 + 8)] \cdot 11$

Pedagogical Problems and Activities

15. How might you use a number line to explain the trichotomy property to second-grade children?

16. Show how you might employ a number-line argument to convince fifth-grade students that if c, d, and e are whole numbers and $d < e$ and $e < c$, then $d < c$.

17. Show how you might use sets of objects with first-grade children to verify that $5 < 7$. (Be specific in your procedure, using diagrams or drawings if needed.)

18. Use your calculator and Definition 2.13 to verify that $76426 < 76525$.

19. Note that $2(x + 2) = (x + 2) + (x + 2) = 2x + 4$. Contrast this result with that obtained by using the distributive pattern to write $2(x + 2)$ as a basic sum.

20. Suppose a student claims that $2 + 3 \times 4 + 5 \neq 5 + 4 \times 3 + 2$. Is this claim correct? Comment briefly about your answer.

---

*2.10 AN INTRODUCTION TO LOGIC

We constantly use the English language as we do problem solving or as we communicate with others about our thoughts. A brief study of logic will help us to deal with problem solving and in making decisions about the validity of arguments.

A sentence that can be identified as being true or false but not both is referred to as a *statement*. The following are examples of *statements*.

1. $6 + 1 > 2$

2. Some apples are red.

3. Abraham Lincoln was the first president of the United States.

4. All squares are circles.

Expressions like "$4x + 1 = 9$", "He plays basketball," and "Why are you wearing a raincoat?" are not statements because they cannot be assigned truth values.

Compound statements are formed by combining two or more simple statements. The following are examples of compound statements.

1. The sun is shining and the birds are singing.
2. I will play tennis, or I will ride my bicycle.

The connectives "and" ($\wedge$), "or" ($\vee$), and "not" ($\sim$) are commonly encountered. Compound statements may be written in symbolic form or may be stated in words. Suppose we use p and q to represent simple statements.

p: It is cold.
q: The ice rink is open.

We may then write the following compound statements.

$p \wedge q$: It is cold and the ice rink is open.
$p \vee q$: It is cold or the ice rink is open.
  $\sim p$: It is not cold.

EXAMPLE 1

Use p and q as identified above to translate the following into sentences.

a. $p \vee \sim q$
b. $\sim p \wedge q$
c. $\sim(\sim p)$

Solutions

    a. It is cold or the ice rink is not open.
    b. It is not cold and the ice rink is open.
    c. It is not true that it is not cold.

EXAMPLE 2

Use p and q to write each of the following in symbolic form.

a. It is cold and the ice rink is not open.
b. It is not cold or the ice rink is not open.

Solutions

    a. $p \wedge \sim q$
    b. $\sim p \vee \sim q$

Because we are interested in statements, we should define the truth value of compound sentences so they may be included in the set of statements. We will use truth tables to show all possible true-false patterns of statement variables. Truth values of compound statements depend on the truth values of the simple statements that are used. The statement "not p" is said to be the denial of p. Statements p and $\sim p$, which are said to be contradictory statements, are each said to be the negation of the other. If p is true, then $\sim p$ is false, and if $\sim p$ is true, then p is false. The truth table that provides this information is the following.

TABLE 2.1

p	$\sim p$
T	F
F	T

The "and" statement, commonly called a conjunction, should also be expected to meet the test of social usage as we consider the truth-value assignments for the statement variables p and q. Suppose we assign values to p and q as follows:

p: I will take you to the movie.
q: We will go for a pizza.

Then "p and q" is the following statement:

$p \wedge q$: I will take you to the movie, and we will go for a pizza.

Because a promise has been made to do both, we expect $p \wedge q$ to be true just in case both p and q are true.

TABLE 2.2

p	q	$p \wedge q$
T	T	T
T	F	F
F	T	F
F	F	F

The compound statement "p or q" is referred to as a disjunction. We actually have two possible interpretations in everyday language for the "or" statement. The statement "I will go to the movie, or I will go bowling" usually means that one of the two will be done but not both. However, in the sentence "I will order a hamburger or I will get french fries," it is common to interpret the meaning as true if either or both parts are true. This is called the inclusive use of or and is the form most commonly encountered in mathematical usage.

TABLE 2.3

p	q	$p \vee q$
T	T	T
T	F	T
F	T	T
F	F	F

EXAMPLE:

Given the following statements, classify each of the conjunctions and disjunctions as true or false.

$$p: 3 + 4 = 7 \qquad r: 2 \cdot 3 = 6$$

$$q: 4 + 6 = 8 \qquad s: 2 \cdot 5 = 9$$

a. $p \wedge q$ **b.** $q \vee r$ **c.** $p \wedge r$

d. $\sim(p \wedge q)$ **e.** $\sim p \vee r$ **f.** $q \wedge \sim s$

Solutions:

a. p is true and q is false, so $p \wedge q$ is false.

b. q is false and r is true, so $q \vee r$ is true.

c. p is true and r is true, so $p \wedge r$ is true.

d. p is true and q is false, so $p \wedge q$ is false and $\sim(p \wedge q)$ is true.

e. p is true, so $\sim p$ is false and r is true, so $\sim p \vee r$ is true.

f. q is false and s is false, so $\sim s$ is true so $q \wedge \sim s$ is false.

Not only are truth tables useful in summarizing truth values of compound statements, but they also are used to determine whether two statements are *logically equivalent*. Two statements are said to be logically equivalent if and only if they have the same truth value for every substitution of statement variables. Consider the truth table that compares $\sim(p \wedge q)$ with $\sim p \vee \sim q$.

TABLE 2.4

p	q	$\sim p$	$\sim q$	$\sim p \vee \sim q$	$p \wedge q$	$\sim(p \wedge q)$
T	T	F	F	F	T	F
T	F	F	T	T	F	T
F	T	T	F	T	F	T
F	F	T	T	T	F	T

This verifies that $\sim(p \wedge q)$ is logically equivalent to $\sim p \vee \sim q$. We can also show that $\sim(p \vee q)$ is logically equivalent to $\sim p \wedge \sim q$. These two equivalences are referred to as *DeMorgan's laws for statements*.

PROBLEM SET 2.10

1. Decide which of the following are statements and then classify each statement as true or false.
   a. $2 + 6 = 8$
   b. $4 + 1 > 7$
   c. George Washington was born in Texas.
   d. $x + 3 = 5$
   e. How old are you?
   f. $4(x + 2) = 4x + 8$
   g. He is a good driver.
   h. Shut the door.

2. Given the statements p: 5 is an odd number, q: $6 + 4 = 8$, and r: $5 + 1 > 2$, write each of the following symbolically and determine the truth value.
   a. $6 + 4 = 8$ and $5 + 1 > 2$
   b. 5 is an odd number or $6 + 4 = 8$
   c. $5 + 1 > 2$ or 5 is an odd number
   d. $5 + 1 > 2$ or $6 + 4 = 8$
   e. 5 is not an odd number and $6 + 4 = 8$

3. Given that p is true, q is false and r is true, determine the truth value for each of the following.
   a. $p \vee q$ b. $p \wedge r$ c. $(p \vee q) \vee r$
   d. $\sim p \vee r$ e. $p \wedge \sim q$ f. $p \wedge (q \vee r)$
   g. $\sim(p \vee q)$ h. $\sim p \wedge \sim q$

4. Complete the following truth tables.

   a.
p	p	$\sim(\sim p)$
T		
F		

   b.
p	$\sim p$	$p \wedge \sim p$	$p \vee \sim p$
T			
F			

5. Use a truth table to verify that $\sim(p \vee q)$ is logically equivalent to $\sim p \wedge \sim q$.

6. Write each of these statements in symbolic form.
   a. John and Alice are both happy.
   b. Neither John nor Alice is happy.

      c. It is not true that neither John nor Alice is happy.

      d. John is happy or Alice is happy.

   7. a. Verify that $p \wedge (q \wedge r)$ is logically equivalent to $(p \wedge q) \wedge r$.

      b. Verify that $p \vee (q \vee r)$ is logically equivalent to $(p \vee q) \vee r$.

   8. Is it true that $p \wedge (q \vee r)$ is logically equivalent to $(p \wedge q) \vee r$? Use a truth table to verify your answer.

   9. Use truth tables to verify the following:

      a. $p \wedge (q \vee r)$ is logically equivalent to $(p \wedge q) \vee (p \wedge r)$.

      b. $p \vee (q \wedge r)$ is logically equivalent to $(p \vee q) \wedge (p \vee r)$.

*2.11   CONDITIONALS, BICONDITIONS, AND VALID REASONING PATTERNS

Another compound sentence commonly encountered in our reasoning patterns is of the form "if p, then q." Such sentences are called *conditionals* or *implications* and are symbolized as $p \Rightarrow q$. We commonly read such sentences as "p implies q" and refer to the "if" part of the conditional as the *hypothesis* and the "then" part as the *conclusion*. The following are examples of conditionals.

1. If it rains, then I will pick you up after class.

2. If it snows, then I will shovel the walk.

3. If a figure is a square, then it is not a triangle.

4. If a plant is a rose, then it is a flower.

   Because we wish to include such compound sentences in our set of statements, it is essential that we define the truth value for all possible true values for p and q. An implication may be thought of as a promise. Suppose you are told by a friend "If it is raining at 5:00, then I will drive you home from work." Consider the following four possible situations.

TABLE 2.5

p	q	
1. T	T	It is raining: you are driven home.
2. T	F	It is raining: you are not driven home.
3. F	T	It is not raining: you are driven home.
4. F	F	It is not raining: you are not driven home.

The only case in which a promise was broken was in (2) when it did rain but no ride home materialized. If it does not rain, you have no promise, so a ride may or may not be offered. The following truth table summarizes the definition of truth values for implications. Thus, conditionals may also be classified as statements because we can determine the truth value for all substitutions of statement variables.

TABLE 2.6

p	q	$p \Rightarrow q$
T	T	T
T	F	F
F	T	T
F	F	T

Implications may be worded in a variety of ways:

(if p then q): If it has rained then the grass is wet.

(if p, q): If it has rained, the grass is wet.

(q if p): The grass is wet if it has rained.

(p implies q): The fact that it has rained implies that the grass is wet.

(p only if q): It has rained only if the grass is wet.

(p is a sufficient condition for q): Rain having fallen is a sufficient condition for the grass to be wet.

(q is a necessary condition for p): The grass being wet is a necessary condition for it having rained.

It is often helpful to restate these equivalent forms as "if, then" statements when interpreting statements.

Each implication $p \Rightarrow q$ has three related implication statements.

Statement: If p, then q	$p \Rightarrow q$
Converse: If q, then p	$q \Rightarrow p$
Inverse: If not p, then not q	$\sim p \Rightarrow \sim q$
Contrapositive: If not q, then not p	$\sim q \Rightarrow \sim p$

Negatn

EXAMPLE

Write the converse, inverse, and contrapositive for each of the following:

a. If $x + 1 = 3$, then $x = 2$ (true)

b. If you live in Chicago, then you live in Illinois (true)

Solution

a. Converse: If $x = 2$, then $x + 1 = 3$ (true)
Inverse: If $x + 1 \neq 3$, then $x \neq 2$ (true)
Contrapositive: If $x \neq 2$, then $x + 1 \neq 3$ (true)

b. Converse: If you live in Illinois, then you live in Chicago (false)
Inverse: If you do not live in Chicago, then you do not live in Illinois (false)
Contrapositive: If you do not live in Illinois, then you do not live in Chicago (true)

The example illustrates that a conditional and its converse may or may not have the same truth value, but the contrapositive has the same truth value in each instance as did the initial conditional. The following truth table illustrates that a conditional and its contrapositive are logically equivalent as are the converse and inverse.

TABLE 2.7

p	q	$\sim p$	$\sim q$	Conditional $p \Rightarrow q$	Converse $q \Rightarrow p$	Inverse $\sim p \Rightarrow \sim q$	Contrapositive $\sim q \Rightarrow \sim p$
T	T	F	F	T	T	T	T
T	F	F	T	F	T	T	F
F	T	T	F	T	F	F	T
F	F	T	T	T	T	T	T

We frequently wish to consider conditionals where the original statement and the converse have the same truth value. That is, we are interested in the sentence $(p \Rightarrow q) \wedge (q \Rightarrow p)$. The truth table for this expression is as follows.

TABLE 2.8

p	q	$p \Rightarrow q$	$q \Rightarrow p$	$p \Leftrightarrow q$ $(p \Rightarrow q) \wedge (q \Rightarrow p)$
T	T	T	T	T
T	F	F	T	F
F	T	T	F	F
F	F	T	T	T

We usually call the statement $(p \Rightarrow q) \wedge (q \Rightarrow p)$ a *biconditional* and use the symbol $p \Leftrightarrow q$, which is read "p if and only if q," and sometimes written as "*p* iff *q*." Note that a biconditional is true if and only if the truth value for *p* and *q* are the same, both true or both false. It is common to use biconditionals as we define expressions.

In mathematics, as well as in general discussions, we wish to argue from basic premises, assumed to be true, to reach a conclusion. To do this, we should make use of valid reasoning patterns. Although many valid patterns exist, a few of these are used more frequently than others and will be identified at this time.

Consider the pattern of the form "If *p* then *q* is assumed to be true and if *p* is known to be true, then *q* must also be true." This is referred to as the *law of detachment*. Symbolically we may write:

Given: $p \Rightarrow q$	*p* implies *q*
Given: p	and *p*
Conclusion: q	Therefore *q*

We could write this in the form $[(p \Rightarrow q) \wedge p] \Rightarrow q$. Consider the truth table for this statement.

TABLE 2.9

p	q	$p \Rightarrow q$	$(p \Rightarrow q) \wedge p$	$[(p \Rightarrow q) \wedge p] \Rightarrow q$
T	T	T	T	T
T	F	F	F	T
F	T	T	F	T
F	F	T	F	T

The fact that we obtained only Ts in the last column assures us that the law of detachment is a valid reasoning pattern.

EXAMPLE

Determine whether the following argument is valid.

Given: If you are on the basketball team, then you do not smoke.
Given: John is on the basketball team.
Conclusion: John does not smoke.

Solution Suppose:

   p: You are on the basketball team.
   q: You do not smoke.

Then the argument is as follows:

Given: $p \Rightarrow q$
Given: p
Conclusion: q

This is of the form $[(p \Rightarrow q) \wedge p] \Rightarrow q$, so is therefore a valid pattern.

A second form, called the *law of contraposition,* is also frequently encountered. It is of the form

Given: $p \Rightarrow q$
Given: $\sim q$
Conclusion: $\sim p$
This may be written as $[(p \Rightarrow q) \wedge \sim q] \Rightarrow \sim p$.

TABLE 2.10

p	q	$\sim p$	$\sim q$	$p \Rightarrow q$	$(p \Rightarrow q) \wedge \sim q$	$[(p \Rightarrow q) \wedge \sim q] \Rightarrow \sim p$
T	T	F	F	T	F	T
T	F	F	T	F	F	T
F	T	T	F	T	F	T
F	F	T	T	T	T	T

The truth table verifies the validity of the pattern.

EXAMPLE

Determine whether the following argument is valid.

Given: If a triangle has two congruent angles, then it has two congruent sides.
Given: ABC does not have two congruent sides.
Conclusion: ABC does not have two congruent angles.

Solution Let us assign the following:

p: A triangle has two congruent angles.
q: A triangle has two congruent sides.

Then the argument is as follows:

Given: $p \Rightarrow q$

Given: $\sim q$

Conclusion: $\sim p$

This is the form $[(p \Rightarrow q) \wedge \sim q] \Rightarrow \sim p$, which is a valid pattern.

Let us consider one more valid reasoning pattern commonly known as the *chain rule*. It is of the form $[(p \Rightarrow q) \wedge (q \Rightarrow r)] \Rightarrow (p \Rightarrow r)$. A truth table to verify this pattern requires more entries because we have three statement variables p, q, and r.

TABLE 2.11

p	q	r	$p \Rightarrow q$	$q \Rightarrow r$	$(p \Rightarrow q) \wedge (q \Rightarrow r)$	$p \Rightarrow r$	$[(p \Rightarrow q) \wedge (q \Rightarrow r)] \Rightarrow (p \Rightarrow r)$
T	T	T	T	T	T	T	T
T	T	F	T	F	F	F	T
T	F	T	F	T	F	T	T
T	F	F	F	T	F	F	T
F	T	T	T	T	T	T	T
F	T	F	T	F	F	T	T
F	F	T	T	T	T	T	T
F	F	F	T	T	T	T	T

EXAMPLE

Given: If I save my money, then I will take a vacation.

Given: If I take a vacation, then I will get a suntan.

Conclusion: If I save my money then I will get a suntan.

PROBLEM SET 2.11

1. Write each of the following conditionals in "if, then" form.
    a. Whenever it rains, I wear my raincoat.
    b. John will take a ride home if it is raining.
    c. Unless I study, I will fail this course.
    d. We will go on a trip when I get my Christmas bonus.
    e. Every figure that is a square is a rectangle.

2. Use a truth table to verify that $p \Rightarrow q$ is logically equivalent to $\sim p \vee q$.

3. Verify that $\sim(p \Rightarrow q)$ is logically equivalent to $p \wedge \sim q$.

4. If p is true q is false; find the truth value of each of the following:

   a. $p \Rightarrow q$ b. $p \Rightarrow \sim q$

   c. $(p \wedge \sim p) \Rightarrow q$ d. $(\sim p \wedge q) \Leftrightarrow (p \vee \sim q)$

   e. $(p \vee \sim p) \Rightarrow p$

5. Mel makes the statement, "If it does not rain, then I will ride my bike." Does it follow logically that if it does rain, then Mel will not ride his bike?

6. Use a truth table to show that the pattern $[(p \Rightarrow q) \wedge q] \Rightarrow p$ is not a valid reasoning pattern.

7. Is the pattern $[(p \Rightarrow q) \wedge (q \Rightarrow r) \wedge p] \Rightarrow r$ a valid reasoning pattern? Justify your answer.

8. Decide whether each of the following are valid arguments. Justify your answer in each case by using a truth table or by referring to known patterns.

   a. Anyone who is a good speaker will be a good teacher.

      Amy is a good speaker.

      Therefore, Amy will be a good teacher.

   b. If a person makes good grades in mathematics then he or she can balance a checkbook.

      John always gets his checkbook to balance.

      Therefore John makes good grades in mathematics.

   c. If I can not play golf, then we will go shopping.

      I can play golf.

      Therefore, I will not go shopping.

   d. You cry if you are frustrated.

      You are very frustrated.

      Therefore, you are crying.

   e. You will receive your allowance if you take out the garbage.

      You did not receive your allowance.

      Therefore, you did not take out the garbage.

9. a. Is the pattern $[(p \Rightarrow q) \wedge (q \Rightarrow r) \wedge \sim r] \Rightarrow \sim p$ a valid pattern? Justify your answer.

   b. Is the following argument valid? Explain your choice of answer.

      If you use Blondex, then your hair will look nice.

      If your hair looks nice, then you will be well dressed.

      You do not use Blondex.

      Therefore, you are not well dressed.

REVIEW PROBLEM SET

1. Write each of the following using set-builder notation:
   a. The set of third-grade teachers in District 163
   b. {0, 2, 4, 6, 8}
   c. Your siblings

2. Write four elements of each of the following sets:
   a. $\{a \mid a$ is an animal in the zoo$\}$
   b. $\{\triangle \mid \triangle$ is a consonant$\}$
   c. $\{l \mid l$ is one of the Great Lakes)

3. If $A = \{1, 2, 3, 4, 5\}$, $B = \{1, 3, 5\}$, $C = \{3, 4, 5\}$, $D = \emptyset$, $E = \{4, 5, 6, 7\}$, and $U = \{1, 2, 3, 4, \ldots, 10\}$, which of the following are true?
   a. $B \subseteq A$ b. $D \subset E$ c. $C \in U$ d. $E \subseteq U$
   e. $3 \in C$ f. $C \subseteq B$ g. $C \subset A$ h. $A \subseteq U$
   i. $B \approx C$ j. $B = C$

4. Find each of the following:
   a. $n(\{7, 8, 9, 10\})$
   b. $n(\{a, b, c, \ldots, g\})$
   c. $n(A)$, where $A = \{x \mid x$ is a whole number greater than 2 and less than 12$\}$
   d. $n(\{\neq, \{1\}, \{2\}, \{1, 2\}\})$

5. Let $A = \{1, 2, 3, 4\}$, $B = \{1, 3, 5\}$, $C = \{2, 4, 6, 8, 10\}$, $D = \{\alpha \mid \alpha$ is even$\}$, $E = \{k \mid k$ is odd$\}$, and $U = \{1, 2, 3, \ldots, 11\}$. Tabulate the following sets:
   a. $A \cup B$ b. $A \cap B$ c. $B \cap C$ d. $C \cup D$
   e. $C \cup E$ f. $D \cap E$ g. C' h. $(A \cap B) \cap C$
   i. $A' \cup B'$ j. D'

6. Draw a Venn diagram to illustrate each of the following sets:
   a. $A \cap C$ b. $(A \cup B) \cap C$ c. $A' \cup B'$ d. $(A \cap B)'$

7. Use a Venn diagram to verify each of the following:
   a. $(A \cup B) \cap C = (A \cap C) \cup (B \cap C)$
   b. $(A \cup B) \cap C \neq A \cup (B \cap C)$
   c. $(A \cup B')' = A' \cap B$

8. We are preparing to take some students on a picnic. When we polled them, 13 students like Coke best and 15 prefer hot dogs, while 4 like Coke and hot dogs. How many students are there?

9. a. Use the definition of addition (Definition 2.9) to establish that $8 + 6 = 14$.

    b. Use the definition of multiplication (Definition 2.10) to establish that $4 \times 6 = 24$.

10. Which property is being applied in each of the following equalities?

    a. $5 + 3 = 3 + 5$

    b. $(5 + 3) + 2 = 2 + (5 + 3)$

    c. $5 \cdot (2 + 3) = 5 \cdot 2 + 5 \cdot 3$

    d. $(5 + 3) + 2 = 5 + (3 + 2)$

    e. $(5 + 3) + 0 = 5 + 3$

    f. $(5 + 3) + 2 = (3 + 5) + 2$

    g. $(5 + 3) + (2 + 3) = (2 + 3) + (5 + 3)$

11. Find the solution set for each of the following in the set of whole numbers:

    a. $x + 2 = 6$ **b.** $x + 4 = 4$ **c.** $6 + x = x + 6$

    d. $2 \cdot \square = 14$ **e.** $15 = 3 + 4 \cdot \square$ **f.** $x + 2 = 4$ or $x + 4 = 5$

    g. $2x + 3 = 11$ and $4x + 2 = 15$ **h.** $x - 3 = 7$

    i. $x \div 4 = 12$ **j.** $2x + 3 < 9$

12. Use the distributive property to change each of the following from an indicated product to an indicated sum:

    a. $2(a + 3)$ **b.** $x(2x + 4)$ **c.** $3x(2x^2 + 3x)$

    d. $(x + 2)(x + 3)$ **e.** $(x + 2)^2$

13. Change each of the following indicated sums to an indicated product:

    a. $5x + 15$ **b.** $2a + 3ab$ **c.** $x^2 + 4x$

    d. $x(x + 2) + 3(x + 2)$ **e.** $x^2 + 4x + ax + 4a$

14. **a.** Use the definition for subtraction (Defintion 2.11) to find $17 - 9$.

    b. Use the definition for division (Definition 2.12) to find $21 \div 7$.

15. **a.** How many one-to-one correspondences can be made between sets A and B, where $A = \{x, y, z\}$ and $B = \{8, 9, 10\}$?

    b. Show that $D \approx E$, where $D = \{1, 3, 5, 7, 9 \ldots, 19\}$ and $E = \{4, 10, 16, \ldots, 58\}$.

16. **a.** Use sets to verify that $5 < 8$.

    b. Use Definition 2.13 to verify that $265 < 420$.

17. On the last day of school a teacher brought 4 flavors of ice cream and 3 flavors of topping to serve sundaes to his students. How many "different" sundaes, consisting of one scoop of ice cream and one topping, are possible? Can you draw a diagram to justify your answer?

Solution to Sample Problem

Using 180 dots, make an arrangement that has 150 in the circle and 90 in the square.

1. *Understanding the Problem.* When we are finished we expect to satisfy three conditions: Total number of dots is to be 180 with 150 in the circle and 90 in the square.

2. *Divising the Plan.* We could use a guess-and-modify approach to the problem, moving dots from one region to another until they are appropriately positioned. Another possibility would be to use an algebraic statement about the sets:

$$n(A) + n(B) - n(A \cap B) = n(A \cup B)$$

3. *Solution 1.* In Figure *a*, we have positioned 180 dots, 150 are in *A* and 90 are in *B*. Because this uses a total of 240 dots we apparently need to shift some to the overlapping region. In Figure *b*, we have positioned 30 in the overlapping region. Although we again have the correct number in *A* and in *B*, our total, 210, is still too large. Let us move 30 more dots into the overlapping region. In Figure *c*, we see that the three criterion are all met.

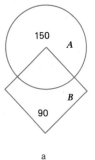
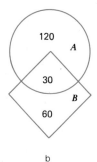
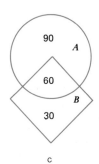

a   b   c

Solution 2. Let us use the equation

$$n(A) + n(B) - n(A \cap B) = n(A \cup B)$$
$$150 + 90 - n(A \cap B) = 180$$
$$240 - n(A \cap B) = 180$$
$$60 = n(A \cap B)$$

Therefore, $n(A \cap B') = 90$ and $n(B \cap A') = 30$.

4. *Looking back.* We can see that the solution is correct because the number can be easily verified. The economy of the equation is also quite noticeable.

3 | NUMERATION SYSTEMS

Sample Problem

A very interesting multiplication algorithm, commonly referred to as the *Russian peasant method*, is often used as an enrichment topic in the middle-grade mathematics program. The product of 42 × 31 is performed as follows:

$$
\begin{array}{rr}
\cancel{42} & \cancel{31} \\
21 & 62 \\
\cancel{10} & \cancel{124} \\
5 & 248 \\
\cancel{2} & \cancel{496} \\
1 & 992
\end{array}
$$

Notice that the numbers in the first column are halved, disregarding remainders if they occur, and the numbers in the second column are doubled. The process is stopped when 1 is reached in the first column. Then each row with an even number in the halving column is marked out. The sum of the remaining numbers in the doubling column is the desired product. Therefore, 42 × 31 = 62 + 248 + 992 = 1302.

Why does this algorithm work? How can we just throw away remainders as we move down the left-hand column and still expect a correct answer? Why should we cross out even numbers in the left column?

121

3.1   INTRODUCTION TO THE HINDU-ARABIC SYSTEM

Once again as we proceed we should look to the NCTM Standards for guidance as we proceed, where a strong plea is made for the development of number sense and numeration. We have developed the materials in this chapter in such a way that you should be able to see something of the history of the development of numeration as well as present-day applications of numeration. We have introduced numeration in bases other than 10 in an attempt to help you to rethink some of the fundamental ideas inherent in a number system. Computation still remains an important ingredient in mathematics. A variety of levels of abstraction are discussed ranging from concrete models through semiconcrete, semiabstract, and finally the abstract format that one typically finds useful.

People have long been interested in numbers. Because any such abiding interest brings about the need for communication, people developed numeration systems. Many different attempts at numeration have been recorded, some very simple in nature and others more complex. The numeration system with which most of us are familiar is the result of centuries of trials and refinements and is the fruit of human inventiveness.

Picture for a moment the young shepherd of ancient times who did well in his chosen profession. He guarded his sheep carefully, turned them out to graze by day, and returned them to their pen at night for protection. As his flock grew larger, it became more difficult to keep an account of them by simple observation. As a bright young man, he may have devised a one-to-one correspondence so that for each sheep that passed through the gate on the way to the pasture in the morning, a pebble was dropped on a pile. At night a pebble was removed for each sheep that returned. This simple scheme enabled him to decide whether to search for strays. Now suppose the young man fell in love with a fair maiden in a neighboring village and wanted to brag about his wealth. How could he communicate with her about the size of the flock? He could hardly be expected to carry the pile of stones. Perhaps he would instead take one flat rock and a stick with a charred end from the fire and make a tally mark for each sheep. The single rock could be easily carried and could communicate readily the number of sheep in the flock.

Of course, the use of tally marks is not very profound. However, this simple start may have been modified and made more effective by the use of *grouping symbols* and other refinements. Although tally marks on the shepherd's rock are admittedly unsophisticated, they are equivalent to many other numerals that could be used to represent the cardinal number of the set. Figure 3.1 illustrates several such numerals.

Let us look more closely at several of these numeration systems in order to understand better our own Hindu-Arabic system. The system we now use must have some characteristics that make it particularly useful, because it

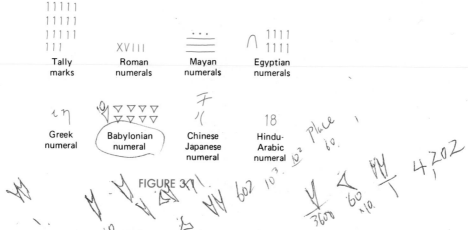

FIGURE 3.1

has replaced other systems throughout most of the world. However, because it is sometimes difficult to study a system with which we are familiar, we will also delve briefly into other systems in order to get a fresh look at ours.

The Hindu-Arabic System

Before we attempt to contrast our Hindu-Arabic system with other systems, let us briefly identify some of the important properties of this system. First, it has a *base of ten*. Numeration of a set is accomplished by placing elements of the set in "piles": each is sufficiently large to be placed in one-to-one correspondence with the fingers on both hands. This choice of base is very likely attributable to this physical confirguation. Although other bases could have just as well been used, the choice of *some* base does have a considerable influence on the ease with which we write numerals and with our ability to perform certain operations.

A second characteristic involves the symbols used in representing numbers. These are the *digit symbols* of our system. The familiar set {0, 1, 2, 3, . . . , 9} is sufficient for our purposes. Of course, questions might be raised about the meaning of these symbols. What does 5 mean? Recall that we used 5 as a cardinal number in the last chapter. Can we still view it this way? The answer is yes. In fact, the digits are associated with sets, and we often refer to these sets as *standard sets*. Figure 3.2 illustrates the standard sets and corresponding numerals used in our base of ten.

Let us now observe the way this base and the digit symbols are used in writing numerals in our Hindu-Arabic system. Consider the numeral 42. This implies that we have four piles of 10 (the base) elements each and two units left over. In general, we write the numerals by inserting the appropriate digit symbols into "positions" or "slots." With our choice of ten as base, the size

Standard Sets	Numeral
{ }	0
{│ }	1
{││}	2
{│││}	3
{││││}	4
{卌}	5
{卌 │}	6
{卌 ││}	7
{卌 │││}	8
{卌 ││││}	9
{卌 卌}-Base	10

FIGURE 3.2

of our groups is as illustrated in Figure 3.3. Thus, a digit inserted in a particular slot indicates the number of piles of that size included in the number.
Then, 342 means that we have three sets each with 100 elements, four sets
each having 10 elements, and two units left over. This use of positions is usually referrred to as *place value.* we often find it useful to write 342 as 300 +
40 + 2. This use of place value is helpful both in recording cardinality and
in performing operations.

	10,000	1000	100	10	1
. . .	Ten-thousands	Thousands	Hundreds	Tens	Units

FIGURE 3.3

Another feature of the Hindu-Arabic numeration system is that we have a
symbol for 0. This is of considerable value to us as we write numerals using
place value. As is true with each of the other digits, 0 is a symbol for a cardinal number and also can serve as a placeholder in our numeration system.
Thus, when we write 402 we are indicating that we have no piles of 10. It is
of interest to note that although the exact date of the invention of 0 as a symbol in our numeration system is not known, there is evidence to support the
theory that it appeared around the eighth century A.D. Thus, it was actually
a latecomer to the set of digit symbols.

It is difficult for most of us to think of operating with a numeration system
different from the Hindu-Arabic system. However, historians tell us that the
system was in limited use for hundreds of years before it gained general
acceptance. They suggest that even as late as the fifteenth and sixteenth cen-

turies the use of the system was rare, as merchants still made use of the Roman system for keeping their accounts.

From this discussion, the four particular properties of the Hindu-Arabic system worthy of special attention are: (1) base of ten, (2) use of place value, (3) a simple digit system, and (4) the availability of a symbol for 0. A useful result of these properties is that we can write numerals in *expanded notation*. That is, $462 = 4 \cdot 100 + 6 \cdot 10 + 2$; $4005 = 4 \cdot 1000 + 0 \cdot 100 + 0 + 10 + 5$, and so forth.

Let us briefly look at some other attempts at numeration in order to contrast them with the Hindu-Arabic system. Recorded history of certain numeration systems dates back to roughly 3500 B.C. The Egyptian system is one of the early systems that should be mentioned. The Rhind Papyrus, a manuscript written in about 1650 B.C., presents a comprehensive description of Egyptian arithmetic. Because Egyptian writing used a system of hieratics, this system of numeration was based on pictures of objects. Some basic symbols in the Egyptian system are presented in Figure 3.4. Notice that one disadvantage of this system is the need for additional symbols to represent larger numbers such as 10 million and 100 million. To use the Hindu-Arabic

Base-ten-symbol	Hieratic symbol	Object represented
1	|	Vertical staff
10	∩	Heel bone
100	9	Scroll
1000	𝑗	Lotus flower
10,000	ſ	Bent reed
100,000	◁	Burbot fish
1,000,000	𝑘	An astonished man

FIGURE 3.4

system to express a number such as 342, we would simply use three digit symbols placed in appropriate positions. However, in the Egyptian system we would use nine symbols. This numeral might appear as illustrated, although there was apparently no real demand for a hierarchy of symbols.

9 9 ∩∩ |
9 ∩∩ |

In fact, symbols were read from right to left instead of from left to right. Notice that the system is clearly more efficient than just using tally marks but is still difficult to manage. To write 9999 would require the use of 36 symbols:

you can verify this yourself. It might be worth making one conversion here. To write 62,862 as an Egyptian numeral first write it in expanded notation, then select appropriate Egyptian symbols. Thus

$$6 \cdot 10{,}000 + 2 \cdot 1000 + 8 \cdot 100 + 6 \cdot 10 + 2 =$$

Additions could be performed using Egyptian symbols. In Figure 3.5 we see the addition procedure for finding the sum of 487 and 2765. In 3.5*a* we show the addition in Hindu-Arabic notation and in 3.5*b* we perform the same operation using Egyptian notation. The result in 3.5*b* might then be regrouped and restated as in 3.5*c*. Would you care to check your bank balance using Egyptian numeration?

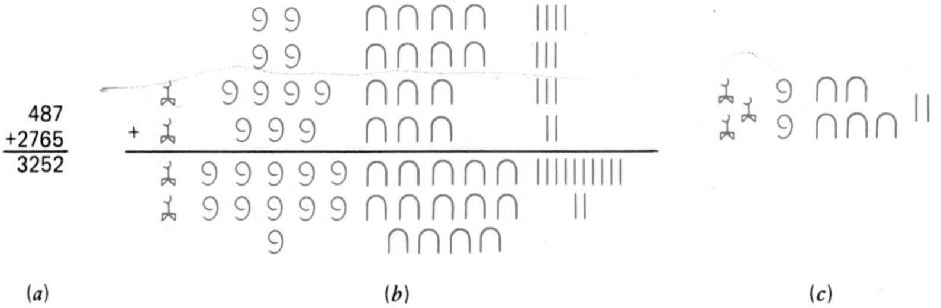

FIGURE 3.5

REMARK Notice that what we really do in adding with this system is to cluster 10 vertical staffs together, trading each bundle for a heel bone. Thus, we have one heel bone and two vertical staffs. Then cluster 10 heel bones and trade for one scroll. In this sense, addition is somewhat similar to what we did in the last chapter.

The Greek influence on numeration systems appears to have extended from roughly 600 B.C. to A.D. 100. The Greeks were mathematicians of the highest caliber, making significant contributions in geometry, logic, and number theory, among other areas of work. Eudoxus is said to have nearly invented the calculus, a most important contribution to mankind that did not follow for nearly 2000 years. The Greek numeration system was extremely cumbersome and unwieldy, a fact that seems highly incongruous. Interestingly, the Greeks used 27 letters to represent numbers, 24 from their own alphabet and 3 from an obsolete alphabet. The symbols identified in Figure

3.6 were written together, as if they were the letters in a word. For example, $\sigma\mu\beta$ means $200 + 40 + 2$ or 242. The "prime" symbol was used to indicate multiplication by 1000. Thus ϵ' is 5000 and $\delta'\rho\lambda\delta$ is the symbol for 4134. Multiplication by 10,000 was achieved by using the additional symbol M. Because the Greek alphabet was used to form both words and numerals, you can imagine one of the problems with such a system! The symbols "$\tau\iota\eta$" as a word mean "why" and as a numeral mean 318. Also, consider that in basic addition, $\epsilon + \theta$ would be represented as $\iota\delta$. Think of the difficulty of addition alone. This is an example of a numeration system that uses a base of ten, but is lacking in other attributes that are needed for it to be effective.

1 α alpha	10 ι iota	100 ρ rho	1000 α'
2 β beta	20 κ kappa	200 σ sigma	2000 β'
3 γ gamma	30 λ lambda	300 τ tau	3000 γ'
4 δ delta	40 μ mu	400 υ upsilon	4000 δ'
5 ϵ epsilon	50 ν nu	500 ϕ phi	5000 ϵ'
6 ρ digamma*	60 ξ xi	600 χ chi	6000 ρ'
7 ζ zeta	70 o omicron	700 ψ psi	7000 ζ'
8 η eta	80 π pi	800 ω omega	8000 η'
9 θ theta	90 $'/$ koppa*	900 $\ni$ sampi*	9000 θ'

FIGURE 3.6   Greek Numerals (Asterisk Indicates Obsolete Symbol)

The Roman system of numeration competed with the Greek system and, by A.D. 100 with the spread of the Roman Empire, it was used throughout Western Europe. This system also used a base of ten. Figure 3.7 indicates the symbols employed. Added economy in writing symbols could be achieved by using both an additivie principle and a subtractive principle. Thus, VI means 6 and IV means 4. In the same way XL means 40 and LX is 60. The basic principle followed is that a symbol for a larger number when preceded by a symbol for a smaller number implies subtraction. To write 3863 as a Roman numeral, first write $3863 = 3000 + 800 + 60 + 3$. Now simply interpret each grouping in the appropriate symbols as MMMDCCCLXIII. In the same way $2,090,849 = 2090 \cdot 1000 + 849 = \overline{\text{MMXC}}\text{DCCCXLIX}$.

I	V	X	L	C	D	M	————
1	5	10	50	100	500	1000	Multiples of 1000

FIGURE 3.7

PROBLEM SET 3.1

1. Express each in expanded notation.
   - **a.** 28
   - **b.** 57
   - **c.** 845
   - **d.** 456
   - **e.** 41,852
   - **f.** 52,134
   - **g.** 452,153
   - **h.** 123,741

2. Express each of the numbers in Problem 1 using Egyptian numeration.

3. Express each of the numbers in Problem 1 using Roman numerals.

4. Express each of the following using Hindu-Arabic numerals:

   - **c.** $\sigma\lambda\delta$
   - **d.** $\epsilon'\phi\pi\theta$
   - **e.** $\overline{\text{MDC}}\text{XCCXVI}$
   - **f.** $\overline{\text{XID}}\text{CCCLXXXVIII}$

5. Suppose you have won $300 from the local lottery and decided to buy some clothes. Your purchases include shoes for $42, jogging sweats for $30, an umbrella costing $14, a coat for $110, and two pairs of jeans costing $18 each.
   - **a.** Write each amount using Egyptian numerals.
   - **b.** Find the total of your bill using only Egyptian numerals.
   - **c.** Use only Egyptian numerals to determine how much money you have remaining from your winnings.

6. Sticker price on a basic model of a car is $6500. Automatic transmission costs an extra $300, the deluxe interior package is $150, power steering is $200, and power brakes are $175. Air conditioning will be an additional $355.
   - **a.** Write these prices using Roman numerals.
   - **b.** Use Roman numerals to determine the cost of the car if you decide not to buy air conditioning.
   - **c.** Use Roman numerals to determine the cost if you decide to take air conditioning.

7. **a.**   **b.**

   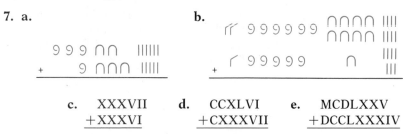

   - **c.**   XXXVII
       +XXXVI
   - **d.**   CCXLVI
       +CXXXVII
   - **e.**   MCDLXXV
       +DCCLXXXIV

8. Use each part of Problem 7 as a subtraction problem and express your answer in the system used.

Pedagogical Problems and Activities

9. The place value feature of our Hindu-Arabic numeration system is useful in making decisions regarding inequality of whole numbers. Consider a = 2463 and b = 2471. Both a and b contain two thousands and four hundreds. However, in the tens place b is larger, thus $b > a$. Use this technique to find the larger whole number in each of the following:

a. $r = 4632$	**b.** $r = 67284$	**c.** $r = 463214$
$s = 4589$	$s = 67290$	$s = 463198$

3.2 EXPONENTIAL NOTATION

When working with numeration systems that use place value, we will find it convenient to make use of exponents. For example, $40,000 = 4 \cdot 10,000 = 4 \times 10 \cdot 10 \cdot 10 \cdot 10$, which can be more conveniently expressed as $4 \cdot 10^4$.

More generally, let us make the following definition.

Definition 3.1   Let a be any whole number and n be a nonzero whole number. Then we define a to the nth power (a^n) as

$$\underbrace{a \cdot a \cdot a \cdot \cdots \cdot a \cdot a}_{\text{to } n \text{ factors}}$$

For example, we would write $5^8 = 5 \cdot 5 \cdot 5 \cdot 5 \cdot 5 \cdot 5 \cdot 5 \cdot 5$ and also $2 \cdot 2 \cdot 2 \cdot 2 \cdot 2 = 2^5$.

Some basic properties are immediately available to us as a result of this definition. For example.

$$2^3 \cdot 2^4 = (2 \cdot 2 \cdot 2) \cdot (2 \cdot 2 \cdot 2 \cdot 2) = 2 \cdot 2 \cdot 2 \cdot 2 \cdot 2 \cdot 2 \cdot 2 = 2^7.$$

In general, if a is any whole number and m and n are nonzero whole numbers, we would write

$$a^m \cdot a^n = \underbrace{(a \cdot a \cdot a \cdot \cdots \cdot a)}_{m \text{ factors}} \cdot \underbrace{(a \cdot a \cdot a \cdot \cdots \cdot a)}_{n \text{ factors}} = \underbrace{a \cdot a \cdot a \cdot \cdots \cdot a}_{m + n \text{ factors}} = a^{m+n}$$

We shall state this as Property 3.1.

PROPERTY 3.1   Given whole numbers a, m, and n with m and n nonzero, $a^m \cdot a^n$ $= a^{m+n}$.

Let us speculate for a moment about a^0. If we wish to define a^0, then it would be convenient to have it agree with an extension of the property just stated. That is, $a^m \cdot a^0 = a^{m+0}$. But because $m + 0 = m$, then $a^m \cdot a^0 = a^m$. Now we know that $a^m \cdot 1 = a^m$; therefore it would be reasonable to state that $a^0 = 1$. Let us define a^0 accordingly.

Definition 3.2   Given a any nonzero whole number, we define $a^0 = 1$.

Two additional properties are worth noting at this time. Consider $5^3 \cdot 4^3 = (5 \cdot 5 \cdot 5) \cdot (4 \cdot 4 \cdot 4)$. Because the whole numbers are commutative and associative under multiplication, we may write $(5 \cdot 5 \cdot 5) \cdot (4 \cdot 4 \cdot 4) = (5 \cdot 4) \cdot (5 \cdot 4) \cdot (5 \cdot 4)$, which may be written as $(5 \cdot 4)^3$. Thus $5^3 \cdot 4^3 = (5 \cdot 4)^3$. In general,

$$a^m \cdot b^m = \underbrace{(a \cdot a \cdot \cdots \cdot a)}_{m \text{ factors}} \cdot \underbrace{(b \cdot b \cdot b \cdot \cdots \cdot b)}_{m \text{ factors}} = \underbrace{(a \cdot b) \cdot (a \cdot b) \cdot \cdots \cdot (a \cdot b)}_{m \text{ factors}}$$
$$= (a \cdot b)^m$$

PROPERTY 3.2   For whole numbers a, b, and n, $a^n \cdot b^n = (a \cdot b)^n$.

In somewhat the same manner we could show that $(2^3)^4 = 2^3 \cdot 2^3 \cdot 2^3 \cdot 2^3 = 2^{3 + 3 + 3 + 3} = 2^{3 \cdot 4} = 2^{12}$.

PROPERTY 3.3   Given whole numbers a, m, and n, $(a^m)^n = a^{m \cdot n}$.

Let us return to the concept of place value. The general scheme for writing any numeral using place value requires that we relate the different positions with powers of the base. Thus, we may write the following and expect it to be applicable for any base b, where b is a whole number greater than or equal to 2. Note that because 10 in general stands for "base," we may use the form illustrated in Figure 3.8c. Because of this we often use a slightly altered form for expanded notation. Thus, $8463 = 8 \cdot 1000 + 4 \cdot 100 + 6 \cdot 10 + 3 \cdot 10^0 = 8 \cdot 10^3 + 4 \cdot 10^2 + 6 \cdot 10^1 + 3 \cdot 10^0$. Also $46,000 = 4 \cdot 10^4 + 6 \cdot 10^3 + 0 \cdot 10^2 + 0 \cdot 10^1 + 0 \cdot 10^0 = 4 \cdot 10^4 + 6 \cdot 10^3$.

Because the associative and distributive properties hold for all whole numbers, they apply also to additions and multiplications involving exponents. Thus, the following statements are true:

1. $5a^2 + 2a^2 = (5 + 2)a^2 = 7a^2$
2. $4a^2 + 2a^2 + 3b + 4b = (4a^2 + 2a^2) + (3b + 4b) = (4 + 2)a^2 + (3 + 4)b$
   $= 6a^2 + 7b$

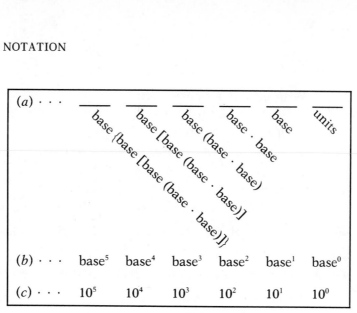

FIGURE 3.8

3. $4 \cdot 10^2 + 3 \cdot 10^2 = (4 + 3) \cdot 10^2 = 7 \cdot 10^2$

4. $3 \cdot 10^2 + 2 \cdot 10^2 + 6 \cdot 10 + 3 \cdot 10 = (3 + 2) \cdot 10^2 + (6 + 3) \cdot 10 = 5 \cdot 10^2 + 9 \cdot 10$

PROBLEM SET 3.2

1. Using exponents, write each in a simple form.
   a. $2 \cdot 2 \cdot 2 \cdot 2$ **b.** $5 \cdot 5 \cdot 5 \cdot 5 \cdot 5 \cdot 5$ **c.** $4 \cdot 8$
   d. $9 \cdot 27$ **e.** $2a \cdot 2a \cdot 2a \cdot 2a$ **f.** $bh \cdot bh \cdot bh$

2. Write each in exponential form using 2, 3, 5, 7, or 11 as a base.
   a. 16   **b.** 27   **c.** 1   **d.** 121
   e. 125   **f.** 49   **g.** 81   **h.** 32

3. Find a value for k for which each statement is true.
   a. $2^3 \cdot 2^4 = 2^k$ **b.** $3^2 \cdot 3^5 = 3^k$ **c.** $3^3 \cdot 3^k = 3^7$
   d. $2^5 \cdot 2^k = 2^7$ **e.** $(5^2 \cdot 5^4) \cdot 5^7 = 5^k$ **f.** $(2^3 \cdot 2^4) \cdot 2^2 = 2^k$
   g. $3^k \cdot 3^k = 1$ **h.** $5^{k+1} = 5^4$ **i.** $2^7 \cdot 3^7 = k^7$
   j. $2^3 \cdot 5^3 = 10^k$ **k.** $2^6 \cdot 3^2 = 2^4 \cdot 6^k$

4. Perform each of the indicated operations.
   a. 3^4 **b.** $2^3 \cdot 3$ **c.** $3^2 \cdot 5^0$ **d.** $(2^3)^4$
   e. $850 \cdot 6542^0$ **f.** $2^4 \cdot 5^4$ **g.** $(2^3 \cdot 3^2)^2$ **h.** $(560 \cdot 435)^0$

5. **a.** Does $a^b = b^a$ if $a = 2$ and $b = 3$?
   b. Can you find any values for a and b for which $a^b = b^a$ will be true?

6. Write each in a simpler form.

a. $5 \cdot 10^3 + 3 \cdot 10^3$ **b.** $3 \cdot 10^4 + 4 \cdot 10^4$

c. $2(3 \cdot 10^2 + 4 \cdot 10^1)$ **d.** $10(10^3 + 2 \cdot 10^2 + 3 \cdot 10)$

e. $5a^3 + 7a^3$ **f.** $4a^4 + 6a^4$

g. $3 \cdot 10^4 + 10^4$ **h.** $10^3 + 4 \cdot 10^3$

i. $4a^2 + a^2$ **j.** $b^5 + 7b^5$

k. $4 \cdot 10^4 + 6 \cdot 10^3 + 2 \cdot 10^2 + 3 \cdot 10^3 + 2 \cdot 10^2 + 7 \cdot 10^1$

7. Use your calculator to verify each of the following equalities.

a. $4^3 \cdot 4^5 = 4^{3+5} = 4^8$ **b.** $5^4 \cdot 6^4 = (5 \cdot 6)^4$ **c.** $(3^2)^5 = 3^{2 \cdot 5} = 3^{10}$

8. Use the calculator to show that $3^4 + 3^5 \neq 3^{4+5}$.

9. Name the place value of the underlined digit in each of the following (refer to Figure 3.3):

a. 4<u>6</u>23   **b.** 5<u>2</u>426

c. 521<u>5</u>8   **d.** 42<u>0</u>50

e. <u>4</u>15236   **f.** 123456<u>1</u>

Pedagogical Problems and Activities

10. Children in the fifth and sixth grades commonly use place value to determine which of the two numbers is larger. For example, 305,751 is greater than 304,973 because if you line up the numbers vertically and compare them digit for digit from left to right, in the thousands place, 5 is greater than 4.

$$
\begin{array}{ccc}
3 & 0 & 5,\,7\;5\;1 \\
3 & 0 & 4,\,9\;7\;3 \\
3 = 3\;\; 0 = 0 & & 5 > 4
\end{array}
$$

Use this procedure to determine which number is greater in each of the following.

a. 430,851; 430,085   **b.** 37,853; 37,835

c. 407,642; 470,642   **d.** 432,059; 432,509

11. Use the procedure discussed in Problem 10 to arrange each of the following sets of numbers in order from least to greatest.

a. 63,890; 63,980; 63,809; 63,089

b. 805,670; 796,670; 804,952; 850,670

c. 3,050,000; 3,050,100; 3,500,900; 3,005,000

d. 46,230; 406,230; 40,623; 46,023

12. A child says "If zero is nothing, then 200, 20, and 2 must all be the same." What do you say?

3.3   POSITIONAL NUMERATION SYSTEMS

Let us now return to the topic of numeration systems that use positional notation. In the Hindu-Arabic system, what do we really mean when we write 26? Apparently we are speaking of two groups with 10 elements in each and then six units. We might picture this as follows. xxxxxxxxxx xxxxxx.
                                                        xxxxxxxxxx xxxxxxxxxx
                                                        xxxxxxxxxx
Likewise, 43 could be represented as xxxxxxxxxx xxx.
                                     xxxxxxxxxx

Suppose that we had a base different from ten. What would positional notation mean if we write 34_{five}? First, it is significant that the base is five. In fact, if we proceed as we did for the base of ten, we should be prepared to consider the standard sets illustrated in Figure 3.9. We must also be prepared to write five numerals to name the sets. Suppose we use the numerals {0, 1,

Standard Sets	Numerals
{ }	0
{ |}	1
{ ||}	2
{|||}	3
{||||}	4
{|||||}-Base	10

FIGURE 3.9

2, 3, 4} in the naming process. This choice is arbitrary; we chose these for the sake of convenience. Note that the symbol for the base set uses the symbol for the set with a single element along with the symbol for the empty set. Thus, when we write 34_{five} we imply that we have three groups with five elements in each, then four units that might be pictured as xxxxx xxxx. Do you
                                                         xxxxx
                                                         xxxxx
see that we have represented three groups, each with "base" elements, and then four additional elements? When we speak of such a number we say "three four base five." (We do *not* say "thirty-four" base five because that names a base-ten number.)

EXAMPLE 1

Let us make an array to illustrate the meaning of 23_{five}. We would need two groups of five and then three units.

            xxxxx
                  xxx
            xxxxx

EXAMPLE 2

Represent 134_{five}. This time we need one cluster of five · five elements, three groups of five, and then four units. Thus we might write

```
XXXXX
XXXXX XXXXX
XXXXX XXXXX XXXX
XXXXX XXXXX
XXXXX
```

EXAMPLE 3

Suppose we are given the array in Figure 3.10a and wish to represent the number of elements using a base of five. We might begin by simply grouping into clusters of five each as illustrated in 3.10b. We have three elements not included in a grouping, and these must be represented as units in our numeral. Next, we should determine whether there are any groups of five × five. We have one group of five × five, two groups of five, and three units as illustrated in 3.10c. Thus, we write 123_{five}.

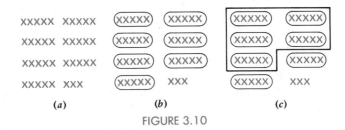

(a)   (b)   (c)

FIGURE 3.10

REMARK We will follow the convention of writing the name of a base as a subscript except in those cases where the base is ten.

EXAMPLE 4

Write 234_{five} as a base-ten numeral. Do this by first making a diagram to associate with the base-five numeral. We need two groups of five × five, three groups of five, and four units. These might be pictured as in Figure 3.11a. In 3.11b we can see the clustering into groups of 10. The number must have 69 as its base-ten numeral.

The significance of the base in a numeration system is that it tells us what size piles to make of our sets. The significance of the positional notation is

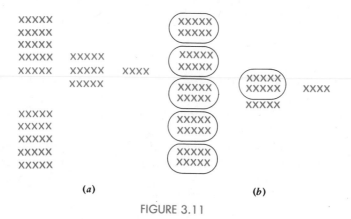

FIGURE 3.11

simply that of looking at progressively larger piles as we move into positions to the left of the units place. Let us look at one more example of this using three as our base. We must again identify the standard sets and numerals for our system. This time we will only need four standard sets and three numerals, as illustrated in Figure 3.12.

Standard Sets	Numeral
{ }	0
{ | }	1
{ | | }	2
{ | | | }-Base	10

FIGURE 3.12

EXAMPLE 1

Given the set, represent its cardinality using a base-three numeral. In Figure 3.13a the elements are clustered into piles of three. Note that there are two units. In 3.13b we have illustrated one set of base $\times$ base. Apparently we have one group of base $\times$ base, two groups of base, and two units, or 122_{three}.

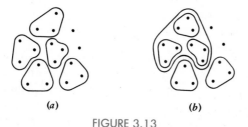

(a)   (b)

FIGURE 3.13

EXAMPLE 2

Write 44_{ten} as a base-three numeral.

Solution Let us first make a diagram showing 44 elements. In Figure 3.14*a* we group into piles of three; note that we have two units remaining. In 3.14*b* we indicate our group of three $\times$ three; note that two groups of three remain unattached. However, we may do one additional grouping of three groups of three $\times$ three, as illustrated in 3.14*c*. Thus, we have one group of three $\times$ three $\times$ three, one group of three $\times$ three, two groups of three, and two units. Therefore, $44_{ten} = 1122_{three}$.

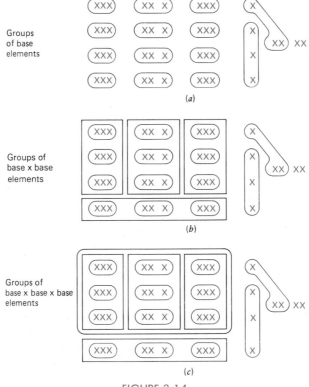

FIGURE 3.14

If you have difficulty seeing the changes we are making, you should try using sets of objects, such as drinking straws, coins, paper clips, or other such things to do these groupings. Children in the primary grades profit tremendously from the use of physical objects as they begin to work with numeration. Several sets of materials are available in the form of kits to serve as models for numeration. We will consider some of these in the next set of exercises.

EXAMPLE 3

Make a diagram to represent 212_{three}. We need two groups of three $\times$ three, one group of three, and two units. Thus we might make the following diagram:

```
              XXX
              XXX
              XXX
                 XXX XX
              XXX
              XXX
              XXX
```

> **REMARK** The frame of reference from which you are working is impor-
> tant in these examples. At times we wish to be positioned in the "tens
> world" and look at a numeral in another base, but at other times we wish
> actually to be working within the "fives world" and view other numerals
> from that perspective. Clearly 32_{five} is different from 32_{ten}.

Let us move from the pictorial representation level to one that uses the same ideas but is less time-consuming. Suppose, for example, that we are given the numeral 43_{five}. Clearly we have four groups of base and three units and might write $43_{five} = (4 \cdot 10 + 3)_{five}$. However, from our base-ten view-point, 10_{five} means 5. Thus, we might write $(4 \cdot 10 + 3)_{five} = (4 \cdot 5 + 3)_{ten}$ because the numeral 4 in the base-five world stands for a set such as $\{||||\}$, which from our base-ten viewpoint is still called 4. Likewise, 10_{five} means $\{|||||\}$, which we call 5 in our base-ten world, so $43_{five} = (4 \cdot 5 + 3)_{ten}$ $= (20 + 3)_{ten} = 23_{ten}$. Perhaps we should look at some other examples similar to this one.

EXAMPLE 1

$$142_{five} = \underline{\hspace{2cm}}_{ten}$$
$$142_{five} = (1 \cdot 10^2 + 4 \cdot 10 + 2)_{five}$$
$$= (1 \cdot 5^2 + 4 \cdot 5 + 2)_{ten}$$
$$= (25 + 20 + 2)_{ten} = 47_{ten}$$

EXAMPLE 2

$$232_{four} = \underline{\hspace{2cm}}_{ten}$$
$$232_{four} = (2 \cdot 10^2 + 3 \cdot 10 + 2)_{four}$$
$$= (2 \cdot 4^2 + 3 \cdot 4 + 2)_{ten}$$
$$= (32 + 12 + 2)_{ten} = 46_{ten}$$

It is sometimes convenient simply to indicate the place value *from our base-ten viewpoint* as follows:

$$\begin{array}{ccc} 2 & 3 & 4 \end{array}_{five} \qquad (2 \cdot 25 + 3 \cdot 5 + 4)_{ten} = (50 + 15 + 4)_{ten} = 69_{ten}$$

EXAMPLE 3

$$\begin{array}{cccc} 1 & 2 & 3 & 1 \end{array}_{four} = \underline{\hspace{2cm}}_{ten}$$
$$64 + 32 + 12 + 1 = 109_{ten}$$

EXAMPLE 4

$$\begin{array}{ccccccc} 1 & 1 & 0 & 1 & 1 & 1 & 0 \end{array}_{two} = \underline{\hspace{2cm}}_{ten}$$
$$64 + 32 + 8 + 4 + 2 = 110_{ten}$$

In each of these examples we changed from a numeral in a base other than ten to a base-ten numeral. Suppose we wish to go the opposite way. If we were asked to write 38_{ten} as a base-five numeral, we could make a set having 38 elements, then group these into piles of five, five × five, and so on. But notice that from our base-ten viewpoint, these are piles of 5, 25, 125, and so on. We could therefore consider one pile of 25 with 13 elements left over. These 13 would make two piles of 5 and have 3 units left over. Therefore, $38_{ten} = 123_{five}$.

EXAMPLE 1

Write 86_{ten} as a base-five numeral. Note that we have three sets of 25, plus two sets of 5, and one still remaining. Thus, $86_{ten} = 321_{five}$. We might write this as follows:

$$86_{ten} = \begin{array}{ccc} 3 & 2 & 1 \end{array}_{five}$$

EXAMPLE 2

$$130_{\text{ten}} = \underline{\hspace{2cm}}_{\text{six}}$$

Let us write

$$130_{\text{ten}} = \overset{3\ 3\ 4}{\underset{216\ 36\ 6}{\diagup\diagup\diagup}}{}_{\text{six}} = 334_{\text{six}}$$

$$\begin{array}{r} 130 \\ -108 \\ \hline 22 \end{array} \qquad \begin{array}{r} 22 \\ -18 \\ \hline 4 \end{array}$$

EXAMPLE 3

$$150_{\text{ten}} = \underline{\hspace{2cm}}_{\text{three}}$$

$$150_{\text{ten}} = \overset{1\ 2\ 1\ 2\ 0}{\underset{243\ 81\ 27\ 9\ 3}{\diagup\diagup\diagup\diagup\diagup}}{}_{\text{three}} = 12120_{\text{three}}$$

$$\begin{array}{r} 150 \\ -\ 81 \\ \hline 69 \end{array} \quad \begin{array}{r} 69 \\ -54 \\ \hline 15 \end{array} \quad \begin{array}{r} 15 \\ -\ 9 \\ \hline 6 \end{array} \quad \begin{array}{r} 6 \\ -6 \\ \hline 0 \end{array}$$

We should consider one more aspect of this work before we introduce the next problem set. This relates to the counting process. Suppose we have the letters in our alphabet and we wish to count them using numerals in the base of five. The cardinal number of the set containing a could be called 1, the sets $\{a, b\}$, $\{a, b, c\}$, and $\{a, b, c, d\}$ could be called 2, 3, and 4, respectively. The set $\{a, b, c, d, e\}$ could be matched with the standard set $\{|\,|\,|\,|\,|\}$ and thus would have the numeral 10 associated with it. Then $\{a, b, c, d, e, f\}$ must contain "base plus one" elements or 11_{five}. Figure 3.15 illustrates the counting process in base five and base three.

The choice of "base" is actually arbitrary, and children may be exposed to a variety of examples in a very natural way. Because the Hindu-Arabic system has a base of ten, it is very important that children recognize the importance of clusters of ten. This is easily demonstrated using a variety of manipulative materials. Although the base of ten is now used for computation worldwide, one should not assume that other bases are not used. Digital computers perform operations in the base of two, and the computer industry makes considerable use of base sixteen. However, when preparing materials to use on a computer, the programmer does not need to rewrite numbers using base two because the "compiler unit" actually makes this change.

$$
\begin{array}{ccccccccccccccc}
a & b & c & d & e & \quad & f & g & h & i & j & \quad & k & l & m & n & o \\
1 & 2 & 3 & 4 & 10 & & 11 & 12 & 13 & 14 & 20 & & 21 & 22 & 23 & 24 & 30
\end{array}
$$

$$
\begin{array}{ccccccccccc}
& p & q & r & s & t & \quad & u & v & w & x & y & \quad & z \\
& 31 & 32 & 33 & 34 & 40 & & 41 & 42 & 43 & 44 & 100 & & 101
\end{array}
$$

Base five
(a)

$$
\begin{array}{ccccccccccccccc}
a & b & c & \quad & d & e & f & \quad & g & h & i & \quad & j & k & l & \quad & m & n & o \\
1 & 2 & 10 & & 11 & 12 & 20 & & 21 & 22 & 100 & & 101 & 102 & 110 & & 111 & 112 & 120
\end{array}
$$

$$
\begin{array}{ccccccccc}
& p & q & r & \quad & s & t & u & \quad & v & w & x & \quad & y & z \\
& 121 & 122 & 200 & & 201 & 202 & 210 & & 211 & 212 & 220 & & 221 & 222
\end{array}
$$

Base three
(b)

FIGURE 3.15

PROBLEM SET 3.3

1. Write the cardinality of the set xxxxx using each of the following as a base. Show the groupings used in each.

   a. Five   **b.** Seven   **c.** Four   **d.** Three   **e.** Eight

2. **a.** Write the base-five numerals from 1_{five} to 31_{five}.
   b. Write the base-eight numerals from 1_{eight} to 31_{eight}.
   c. Write the base-two numerals from 1_{two} to 1111_{two}.

3. Make a diagram to illustrate the meaning of each of the following:
   a. 64_{ten} **b.** 43_{five} **c.** 123_{four} **d.** 48_{ten}
   e. 1011_{two} **f.** 212_{three} **g.** 24_{seven} **h.** 41_{eight}

4. Make a diagram to illustrate the given number, then regroup the sets to determine the new name.

   a. $21_{ten} = \underline{\hspace{1cm}}_{five}$ **b.** $26_{ten} = \underline{\hspace{1cm}}_{eight}$

   c. $23_{ten} = \underline{\hspace{1cm}}_{six}$ **d.** $32_{eight} = \underline{\hspace{1cm}}_{ten}$

   e. $24_{six} = \underline{\hspace{1cm}}_{eight}$ **f.** $32_{four} = \underline{\hspace{1cm}}_{eight}$

   g. $31_{eight} = \underline{\hspace{1cm}}_{three}$ **h.** $28_{ten} = \underline{\hspace{1cm}}_{two}$

   i. $133_{four} = \underline{\hspace{1cm}}_{five}$ **j.** $121_{five} = \underline{\hspace{1cm}}_{six}$

   k. $1011_{three} = \underline{\hspace{1cm}}_{eight}$ **l.** $41_{eight} = \underline{\hspace{1cm}}_{three}$

5. What is the next number after each of the following?
   a. 34_{five} **b.** 104_{five} **c.** 44_{five} **d.** 56_{seven}
   e. 77_{eight} **f.** 1011_{two} **g.** 1222_{three} **h.** 707_{eight}

15   *61*

6. **a.** Which represents the larger number in each of the following?
       (i) 31_{five} or 31_{eight} **(ii)** 100_{five} or 100_{three}
       (iii) 123_{five} or 132_{five} **(iv)** 21_{three} or 14_{five}
   b. If 231_{ten} were restated in base three and also in base five, which numeral would require the use of the greater number of digits?

7. Change each numeral to the desired base without making a drawing.
     a. $85_{ten} =$ _____$_{five}$ **b.** $145_{ten} =$ _____$_{six}$
     c. $160_{ten} =$ _____$_{four}$ **d.** $255_{ten} =$ _____$_{five}$
     e. $413_{five} =$ _____$_{ten}$ **f.** $213_{four} =$ _____$_{ten}$
     g. $1221_{three} =$ _____$_{ten}$ **h.** $110111_{two} =$ _____$_{ten}$
     i. $145_{ten} =$ _____$_{eight}$ **j.** $175_{nine} =$ _____$_{ten}$

8. Find the values for k in each of the following:
     a. $46_{ten} = k6_{eight}$ **b.** $32_{four} = 1k_{ten}$
     c. $11110_{two} = k6_{eight}$ **d.** $25_{six} = 3k_{five}$

9. Suppose we were suddenly transferred to a "rain forest" setting in which it rains much of the time. One hand would likely be employed in holding an umbrella and our toes would be buried in the mud. We might under these circumstances employ a base five numeration system. Suppose we then associate the symbols indicated with the standard sets.

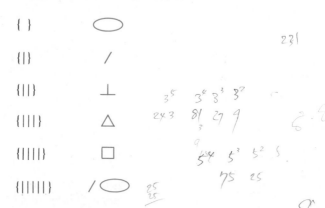

Thus, it is basically a base-five system using positional notation and the symbols as illustrated.

  a. Group the elements in each of the given sets and record the number using "rain forest" numerals.

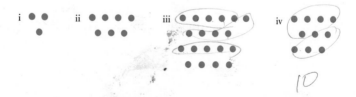

b. Translate the following base-ten numbers into "rain forest" notation:
(i) 7   **(ii)** 32   **(iii)** 125   **(iv)** 425

c. Write each of the following as an equivalent base-ten numeral:

10. Here is a technique often used to change a base-ten numeral to another base. Suppose we wish to change 263_{ten} to a base of four. We would continually divide by 4, recording remainders beside each step, until our quotient was less than 4.

$$4\overline{)263}$$
$$4\overline{)65}\ 3$$
$$4\overline{)16}\ 1\quad \text{Thus } 263_{ten} = 10013_{four}$$
$$4\overline{)4}\ 0$$
$$1\ 0$$

Find 4620_{ten} as a base-six numeral.

$$6\overline{)4620}$$
$$6\overline{)770}\ 0$$
$$6\overline{)128}\ 2\quad \text{Then } 4620_{ten} = 33220_{six}$$
$$6\overline{)21}\ 2$$
$$3\ 3$$

Use this algorithm to make the following conversions.

a. 325_{ten} = _____$_{five}$ **b.** 78_{ten} = _____$_{two}$

c. 450_{ten} = _____$_{eight}$ **d.** 8430_{ten} = _____$_{eight}$

e. 200_{ten} = _____$_{two}$

11. Let us consider a numeration system with the base defined to be a dozen elements. This system of dozen is officially called the duodecimal system. How many standard sets and how many digit symbols will we need for such a system? Because base is defined to consist of a dozen elements, we should expect to find a dozen other standard sets and thus a dozen symbols to use as digits. If we use our base-ten digits, we must still invent two additional symbols. Let us agree to use # and * as digit symbols (see Fig. 3.16). Let us now write 586_{ten} as a duodecimal numeral. Again, the important piles include 1, 12, and 144, and we write 586_{ten} = $4\ 12\ 7$ $_{twelve}$.

Notice that in four piles of 144 we use 576 elements and thus have ten remaining. Because ten is not sufficient to make a pile of 12, they must

Standard Sets	Digit Symbols
{ }	0
{I }	1
{II}	2
{III}	3
{IIII}	4
{卌}	5
{卌 I}	6
{卌 II}	7
{卌 IIII}	8
{卌 IIIII}	9
{卌 卌}	#
{卌 卌 I}	*
{卌 卌 II}-Base	10

FIGURE 3.16

be recorded as units. Thus, $586_{ten} = (4 \cdot 144 + 0 \cdot 12 + 10)_{ten} = (4 \cdot 12^2 + 0 \cdot 12 + 10)_{ten} = (4 \cdot 10^2 + 0 \cdot 10 + \#)_{twelve} = 40\#_{twelve}$. To express the duodecimal $24*_{twelve}$ as a base-ten numeral, we will simply reverse the process just used. That is,

$$24*_{twelve} = (2 \cdot 10^2 + 4 \cdot 10 + *)_{twelve} = (2 \cdot 12^2 + 4 \cdot 12 + 11)_{ten}$$
$$= (2 \cdot 144 + 4 \cdot 12 + 11)_{ten} = (288 + 48 + 11)_{ten} = 347_{ten}$$

a. Write each of the following as base-twelve numerals:

    (i) 36   **(ii)** 144   **(iii)** 556   **(iv)** 1859

b. Write each of the following as base-ten numerals:

    (i) 32_{twelve} **(ii)** 82_{twelve} **(iii)** $\#7_{twelve}$ **(iv)** $\#3*_{twelve}$

12. a. Use the algorithm discussed in Problem 10 to write $350_{ten} = \underline{\hspace{2cm}}_{twelve}$.

b. Use the algorithm to write 250_{ten} as a base-twelve numeral. (Remember, we are renaming the numeral in the base-twelve notation and that $10_{ten} = \#_{twelve}$.)

c. Use the algorithm to write $54,852_{ten}$ as a base-twelve numeral.

13. The Mayan Indians of Central America had an advanced system of numeration in operation before the time that Columbus reached America. Their system, except for one position, used multiples of 20 (perhaps reflecting the fact that the climate was warm and fingers and toes both were available for consideration). Their digit symbols used a dot for one, a horizontal bar for five, and combinations of these for other numbers. Thus represented 6, ⚌ represented 11, and 17 would be written as

‗‗ . They even had a symbol for the cardinal number of the empty set, using ⊂⊃ for that purpose. Positional notation was used with place values going upward. Thus, to represent the number 26, they might write

. That is, we have one group of 20 plus six left over. Their study of astronomy may have prompted the use of numeration to approximate the year as 360 days (plus a special holiday each year of 5 or 6 days!). Their positional notation appears as follows:

☐ 20 · 7200 = 144000
☐ 20 · 360 = 7200
☐ Groups of 18 · 20 = 360
☐ Groups of 20
☐ Units

Using this system to write 450 we would observe that we can make one group of 360 and still have 90 elements left. With these we make four groups of 20 and have 10 units left.

a. Write each of the following as Mayan numerals:
    (i) 49   **(ii)** 558   **(iii)** 8000   **(iv)** 204,850
b. Write each of the following as a base-ten numeral:

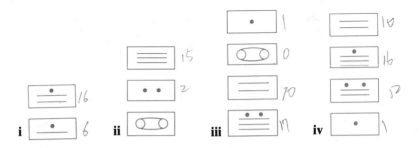

Pedagogical Problems and Activities

14. Multibase blocks are often used as a model for a numeration system. They consist of wooden blocks of various sizes. Small wooden cubes represent units, blocks 10 units long (called longs) represent base, flat blocks 10 units by 10 units—also a unit thick (called flats)—represent hundreds (base × base), and larger cubes—10 units on each edge (called blocks)—represent thousands.

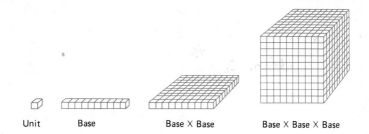

Unit   Base   Base × Base   Base × Base × Base

    a. Sketch or describe the configuration of blocks needed to represent each of the following numbers:

       (i) 24   **(ii)** 142   **(iii)** 431   **(iv)** 2123

    b. What base-ten number is represented by the following?

      (i) Three flats, two longs, and five unit cubes

      (ii) Six blocks, eight flats, seven longs, and three unit cubes

      (iii) Three blocks, four longs, and two unit cubes

    c. What sort of block would be used to represent 10,000? What might you call it?

15. Bundled sticks work well for representing numerals. Single sticks represent units, 10 sticks with a rubber band around them represent 10, 10 bundles tied together represent base · base, and so on.

    a. Describe the way you would use sticks to represent 43.

    b. What would 250 look like in terms of the sticks?

16. **a.** Sam has been saving his money to buy a ball glove. He has only dollar bills, dimes, and pennies in his bank. If he collected 164 aluminum cans and received 1 cent each for them, what is the fewest number of coins and bills that he could put in his bank?

    b. Suppose that Sam saves only pennies, nickels, and quarters. What is the fewest number of coins that he could put in his bank?

17. Base-two numeration can be employed in making a code. The letters of the alphabet are assigned base-ten numerals. The letter D is assigned the numeral 4, E assigned 5, and so on. Each numeral is then expressed in base-two notation and is recorded on a card with a dot meaning 1 and a blank representing 0. To represent the word SIX we would first observe the correspondence S-19, I-9, and X-24. Then, because $19_{ten} = 1 \cdot 16 + 1 \cdot 2 + 1$, we would darken the appropriate dots ($9 = 1 \cdot 8 + 1$ and $24 = 1 \cdot 16 + 1 \cdot 8$).

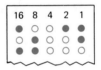

a. Use this code to write the word "FUN."

b. Decode the message given.

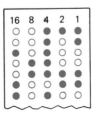

c. Write your name using this code.

18. The following card trick is often presented as if mind reading were involved. Four cards are printed as illustrated. Someone is asked to choose a number from 1 to 15 and then tell you on which of the cards the number appears. The sum of the numbers in the upper-left corner of the designated cards should be the number originally chosen. For example, 13 appears on *D*, *C*, and *A* and 13 = 8 + 4 + 1.

A		*B*		*C*		*D*	
1	9	2	10	4	12	8	12
3	11	3	11	5	13	9	13
5	13	6	14	6	14	10	14
7	15	7	15	7	15	11	15

a. If 10 is the chosen number, which cards are designated?

b. If cards *A* and *C* are selected, what number is involved?

c. Why does this trick work? (The key to this involves the binary representation for numbers.)

d. Expand the procedure to accommodate the numbers 1 through 31. How many cards are needed?

e. If we used a six-card deck, how many numbers could be represented?

19. The structure of the world in which children live demands that they make use of different-sized sets for groupings (different bases).

a. What sized groupings is suggested by each of the following?

(i) School days in a week

(ii) Days in a week

(iii) Months in a year

(iv) Pennies in a nickel

        (v) Hours on a clock face
     (vi) Hours in a day
   (vii) Feet in a yard
 (viii) Inches in a foot

    b. List three more groupings different from those given here.

3.4   THE ADDITION ALGORITHM

In the last chapter we defined the operation of addition on whole numbers. This made it possible for us to determine the sums of whole numbers. In general, we could always add two numbers together by taking the union of properly chosen sets and then counting the number of elements in the union. However, certain other procedures may be used to simplify this process greatly. Any such systematic procedure for performing some mathematical operation is commonly referred to as an algorithm.

Consider the indicated addition $42 + 36$. Using expanded notation, we might write $42 + 36 = (40 + 2) + (30 + 6)$. Because we have both associative and commutative properties for addition, we might then write $(40 + 2) + (30 + 6) = (40 + 30) + (2 + 6)$. Our addition facts assure us that $2 + 6 = 8$ and, furthermore, 4 tens + 3 tens = 7 tens. Thus, $(40 + 30) + (2 + 6) = 70 + 8 = 78$.

In Figure 3.17a we illustrate this same addition problems using a vertical format; in 3.17b we use a partial sums format, and in 3.17c a shortened form. If you look in current elementary school mathematics books, you will find these formats being used or some slight variation of them. It should be pointed out that in early work with the addition algorithm, physical models are very helpful. This is easily illustrated as we consider the regrouping process in addition.

tens	ones
4	2
3	6
7	8

$$
\begin{array}{r}
42 \\
+36 \\
\hline
8 = 2 + 6 \\
70 = 40 + 30 \\
\hline
78
\end{array}
$$

$$
\begin{array}{r}
42 \\
+36 \\
\hline
78
\end{array}
$$

        (a)   (b)   (c)

FIGURE 3.17

Suppose we wish to find the sum $23 + 18$. In Figure 3.18a and b, we illustrate the use of counting rods to find the sum. In 3.18c, we show a semiabstract model using bars to represent ten and dots for units. Figures d, e, and

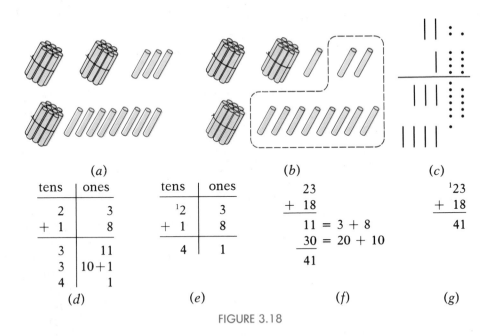

	(a)			(b)			(c)

tens	ones
2	3
+ 1	8
3	11
3	10+1
4	1

tens	ones
^{1}2	3
+ 1	8
4	1

        23
      + 18
        11 = 3 + 8
        30 = 20 + 10
        41

      ^{1}23
    + 18
      41

	(d)			(e)			(f)			(g)

FIGURE 3.18

f are forms of the algorithm that allow us to bridge from the semiabstract format to the standard algorithm illustrated in *g*.

> REMARKS Teachers frequently state that regrouping is one of the most troublesome concepts in the mathematics curriculum. This is why children should begin with concrete materials and progress through a pictoral model before the abstract algorithm is stressed.

The addition algorithm works because we have at our disposal such things as the commutative property, the associative property, and expanded notation. Because this is the case, the algorithm may be logically expanded to handle numbers with three-digit numerals (or more) and to more than two addends. In Figure 3.19 we illustrate the sum 463 + 847 + 252.

Note that any particular addition performed was done using tables you have committed to memory. Indeed, the very fact that you memorized them long ago sometimes allows you to forget that young children do not have them so readily available. They are often allowed to work from tables of facts until they get them firmly committed to memory. To get you to stop and rethink some of the things we have been talking about, we are next going to attempt doing additions in a base other than ten.

Suppose we consider addition in the base of five. Recall that the only digit

Hundreds	Tens	Ones
¹4	¹6	3
8	4	7
2	5	2
15	6	2
	1562	

(a)

$$463$$
$$847$$
$$+\ 252$$

$$12 = 3 + 7 + 2$$
$$150 = 60 + 40 + 50$$
$$\underline{1400 = 400 + 800 + 200}$$
$$1562$$

(b)

$$^1 4^1 63$$
$$847$$
$$\underline{+\ 252}$$
$$1562$$

(c)

FIGURE 3.19

symbols needed will be 0, 1, 2, 3, and 4. What will it mean to write 4_{five} + 2_{five}? Can the definition for addition given in the last chapter still be applied? (If you will recall, at that time we did not specify what base was being used.) Let us identify two sets A and B such that $n(A) = 4$, $n(B) = 2$, and $A \cap B = \varnothing$. Let $A = \{a, b, c, d\}$ and $B = \{e, f\}$. Then $A \cup B = \{a, b, c, d, e, f\}$. We must now find $n(A \cup B)$. We could find this base-five number either by counting or by grouping the elements. It should be apparent that $4_{\text{five}} + 2_{\text{five}} = 11_{\text{five}}$.

REMARK 1 Perhaps an easier, although more sophisticated, procdure would be to write $4_{\text{five}} + 2_{\text{five}} = 4_{\text{five}} + (1 + 1)_{\text{five}} = (4 + 1)_{\text{five}} + 1_{\text{five}} = 10_{\text{five}}$ $+\ 1_{\text{five}} = 11_{\text{five}}$. Children often do this in base-ten work if they forget a particular basic addition fact. For example, $8 + 7 = 8 + (2 + 5) = (8 + 2) + 5 = 10 + 5 = 15$.

REMARK 2 This type of manipulation leads to an understanding called for in the NCTM Standards.

We could proceed to find all the basic base-five facts doing this same thing. In Figure 3.20 we table the values obtained. The values in the table are similar to those found in elementary arithmetic for addition, but involving only the numbers 0, 1, 2, 3, and 4. Notice that commutativity is still exemplified

+	0	1	2	3	4
0	0	1	2	3	4
1	1	2	3	4	10
2	2	3	4	10	11
3	3	4	10	11	12
4	4	10	11	12	13

FIGURE 3.20 Base-five addition facts

by the like entries on both sides of the main diagonal, 0 is still the only number such that $a + 0 = a$ for any number a in the set {0, 1, 2, 3, 4} and so forth.

Let us now consider a sum such as $32_{\text{five}} + 12_{\text{five}}$. Because these numerals also use positional notation, we might write them in expanded form. Thus $32_{\text{five}} + 12_{\text{five}} = (30 + 2)_{\text{five}} + (10 + 2)_{\text{five}}$. The properties of associativity and commutativity were verified in terms of sets and were not dependent on a base of ten. Therefore, they still hold. Thus, $(30 + 2)_{\text{five}} + (10 + 2)_{\text{five}} = (30 + 10)_{\text{five}} + (2 + 2)_{\text{five}} = (40 + 4)_{\text{five}} = 44_{\text{five}}$. The addition process works because we have expanded notation, commutativity, and associativity, and it is *not* dependent on the base used! Figure 3.21 illustrates the different formats applied to a base-five addition.

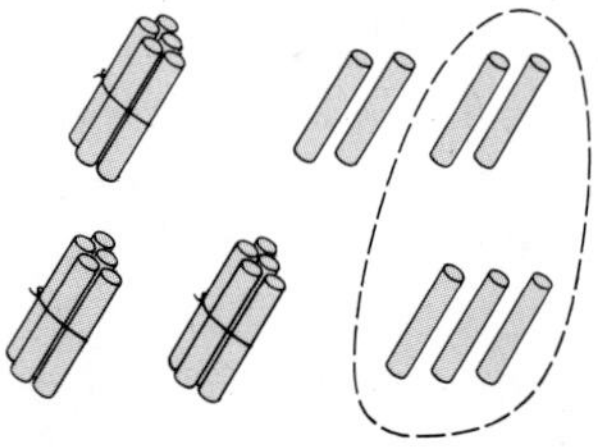

(*a*)

base	units
1	4_{five}
2	3_{five}
3	12
	10 + 2
4	2_{five}

(*b*)

base	units
$^{1}1$	4_{five}
+2	3_{five}
4	2_{five}

(*c*)

$$\begin{array}{r} 14_{\text{five}} \\ +\ 23_{\text{five}} \\ \hline 12 = (4 + 3)_{\text{five}} \\ 30 = (10 + 20)_{\text{five}} \\ \hline 42_{\text{five}} \end{array}$$

(*d*)

$$\begin{array}{r} {}^{1}14_{\text{five}} \\ +\ 23_{\text{five}} \\ \hline 42_{\text{five}} \end{array}$$

(*e*)

FIGURE 3.21

Perhaps we should look at one more example from the base of five. Let us find $(223 + 302 + 133)_{\text{five}}$ using partial sums and then with the shortened algorithm (Fig. 3.22). We would suggest that you not attempt to commit any

$$\begin{array}{r} 223_{\text{five}} \\ 302_{\text{five}} \\ +133_{\text{five}} \\ \hline 13 = (3 + 2 + 3)_{\text{five}} \\ 100 = (30 + 20)_{\text{five}} \\ 1100 = (100 + 300 + 200)_{\text{five}} \\ \hline 1213_{\text{five}} \end{array}$$

Partial sums
(*a*)

$$\begin{array}{rl} {}^{1}2{}^{1}23 & \text{five} \\ 302 & \text{five} \\ +\ 133 & \text{five} \\ \hline 1213 & \text{five} \end{array}$$

Shortened
algorithm
(*b*)

FIGURE 3.22

tables to memory (other than base ten), but rather make a table, then use it as you attempt to do problems in that base.

PROBLEM SET 3.4

1. Use expanded notation similar to that used in Figure 3.19a to find each of the following sums:

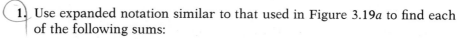

	a.	b.	c.	d.	e.	f.
	23	48	123	156	234	32
	+65	+17	+145	+279	56	46
					+143	51
						+87

2. Use partial sums similar to that used in Figure 3.19b.

	a.	b.	c.	d.	e.	f.
	47	52	143	456	456	51
	+26	+19	+178	+857	35	68
					+157	75
						+49

3. Use the base-five addition table and expanded notation similar to that found in Figure 3.21a to perform the following additions:

   a. 23_{five} b. 12_{five} c. 32_{five} d. 302_{five} e. 124_{five}
      $+14_{five}$ $+33_{five}$ $+43_{five}$ $+234_{five}$ $+233_{five}$

   f. 42_{five}
      13_{five}
      24_{five}
      $+31_{five}$

4. Use the base-five addition table and partial sums to add the following:

   a. 13_{five} b. 32_{five} c. 32_{five} d. 304_{five} e. 134_{five}
      $+24_{five}$ $+23_{five}$ $+24_{five}$ $+143_{five}$ $+142_{five}$

   f. 41_{five}
      13_{five}
      43_{five}
      $+22_{five}$

5. Use the base-five addition table and the shortened format (like Fig. 3.21c) to find each of the following:

   a. 12_{five} b. 14_{five} c. 43_{five} d. 324_{five} e. 432_{five}
      $+22_{five}$ $+23_{five}$ $+33_{five}$ $+142_{five}$ $+144_{five}$

   f. 32_{five}
      141_{five}
      $+231_{five}$

6. a. Use some sets of objects to represent 3_{six} and 5_{six}.
 b. Use the sets from part **a** to find $3_{six} + 5_{six}$.
 c. Use sets to find $4_{six} + 5_{six}$.
 d. Make a base-six addition table.

7. Use your table from Problem 6 to find the following:

a. 42_{six} **b.** 54_{six} **c.** 34_{six} **d.** 301_{six} **e.** 331_{six}
 $+13_{six}$ $+32_{six}$ $+45_{six}$ $+145_{six}$ $+143_{six}$

f. 142_{six} **g.** 1423_{six}
 321_{six} 1204_{six}
 142_{six} $+1332_{six}$
 $+334_{six}$

8. Make an addition table for the base of two, then find the following sums:

a. 101_{two} **b.** 10_{two} **c.** 1101_{two} **d.** 11_{two}
 $+\ 11_{two}$ $+111_{two}$ 101_{two} 101_{two}
                                   $+1001_{two}$ 11_{two}
                                                     $+1010_{two}$

e. 11011_{two} **f.** 110101_{two}
 10010_{two} 1110010_{two}
 $+101101_{two}$ $+1010111_{two}$

9. a. Use sets of objects to represent 7_{twelve} and 8_{twelve}.
 b. Use the sets from part **a** to find $7_{twelve} + 8_{twelve}$.
 c. Use sets to represent 6_{twelve} and 5_{twelve}.
 d. Use the sets from part **c** to find $6_{twelve} + 5_{twelve}$.
 e. Use sets to find $*_{twelve} + \#_{twelve}$.
 f. Make an addition table for the base of twelve.

10. Use your table from Problem 9 to find the following sums:

a. 46_{twelve} **b.** 48_{twelve} **c.** $4\#_{twelve}$ **d.** $4\#_{twelve}$
 $+53_{twelve}$ $+53_{twelve}$ $+93_{twelve}$ $+^*7_{twelve}$

e. $4\#^*{}_{twelve}$ **f.** 59_{twelve} **g.** $14\#3_{twelve}$
 $+34\#_{twelve}$ 43_{twelve} $4^{**}7_{twelve}$
                          $*\#_{twelve}$ $+1509_{twelve}$
                          $+47_{twelve}$

Pedagogical Problems and Activities

11. Base-ten blocks are often used to help introduce addition to children. To add 46 + 38, lay out four longs and six unit cubes in one place and three longs and eight unit cubes below it. Pull the unit cubes together and trade ten of them for one long, leaving four cubes. You then have eight longs and four cubes, or 84. Describe how you might manipulate the blocks to find the following sums:

a. 46   **b.** 75   **c.** 148   **d.** 753
      $+39$ $+87$ $+396$ $+874$

12. Use bundled sticks to illustrate each of the following:

a. 32_{five} **b.** 41_{five} **c.** 34_{five} **d.** 31_{five}
      $+12_{\text{five}}$ $+32_{\text{five}}$ $+32_{\text{five}}$ $+44_{\text{five}}$

13. Regrouping is also easily shown using the bundled-sticks idea. If we add 17 + 15 we would have a tens bundle and 7 sticks in one grouping and 1 tens bundle and 5 sticks in another. When we put the 7 sticks and 5 sticks together, we can then rebundle them to make 1 bundle and have 2 sticks remaining. Thus, we have 3 bundles and 2 sticks, or 32. Describe (or illustrate) how to use this technique in performing each of the following additions:

a. 23   **b.** 48   **c.** 36   **d.** 152   **e.** 107
      $+52$ $+27$ $+48$ $+\ 79$ $+\ 39$

14. Addition could be done moving from left to right instead of starting in the units place and moving to the left. To add 36 + 23, we might first add 3 tens and 2 tens. Then 6 units and 3 units are added and we obtain the answer 5 tens and 9 units, or 59. Even with regrouping we may do this. To add 76 + 48 we may observe that 7 tens plus 4 tens makes 11 tens. Then 6 + 8 = 14. Let us write this as follows:

        76   76
    $+\ 48$ $+\ 48$
    ―――――   ―――――
        11   1̸1̸4
                          2
        (i)   **(ii)**

Consider the problem 2967 + 5897.

    2967   2967   2967   2967
   $+5897$ $+5897$ $+5897$ $+5897$
   ――――――   ――――――   ――――――   ――――――
       7   7̸7̸   7̸7̸5   7̸7̸5̸4
                     8   88   884
     (i)   **(ii)**   **(iii)**   **(iv)**

This algorithm is often referred to as the *scratch method*. Use this technique to find the following sums:

a. 463   **b.** 597   **c.** 467   **d.** 7842
      $+532$ $+875$ $+548$ $+6389$

15. The scratch method is often used by persons who wish a quick estimate to an addition problem.

    a. Estimate the following sums to the nearest hundred. When completed, use a calculator to check how close you came.

       (i) $362 + 816$

      (ii) $7821 + 4350$

    (iii) $2813 + 9135$

    (iv) $1621 + 211$

    b. Using your ability to estimate, insert $<$, $=$, or $>$ between the two additions to make a true statement. Check with the calculator.

       (i) $(453 + 396)$ _____ $(520 + 410)$

      (ii) $(484 + 276)$ _____ $(516 + 223)$

    (iii) $(719 + 293)$ _____ $(614 + 397)$

    (iv) $(658 + 276)$ _____ $(233 + 714)$

3.5   THE SUBTRACTION ALGORITHM

Subtraction is defined in terms of addition, as indicated in the last chapter. As you will recall, we stated if a and b are whole numbers, the whole number c is the solution to $a - b$ if and only if $b + c = a$. Thus, subtraction was at that time related to addition. However, most of you have commonly used subtraction facts when you perform a subtraction. That is, the answer to the problem $17 - 8$ is obtained by recall of a fact memorized at some time. It should be evident that the answer might also be obtained from the addition fact $8 + 9 = 17$. As you work with the subtraction algorithm, try to use both techniques.

> REMARK   Subtraction facts have several interpretations, as was mentioned earlier. The "take-away" idea appears to be easiest for young children to understand. For this reason, the subtraction algorithm typically developed at the second-grade level relies on the take-away interpretation.

Just a knowledge of subtraction facts or of addition facts will not make it easy to find the solution to sentences such as $52 - 17 = n$. No basic addition or subtraction fact alone will answer the question.

Suppose that we want to find $38 - 15$. We could write the problem as $(30 + 8) - (10 + 5) = (30 - 10) + (8 - 5)$. Thus, $38 - 15 = 20 + 3 = 23$. We could illustrate this rather easily by using counting sticks, as was done in Figure 3.23.

Just as in addition, subtraction problems that require regrouping are

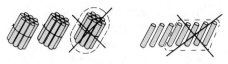

FIGURE 3.23

sometimes more troublesome, but if we continue to emphasize place value, we may increase the understanding. Suppose we want to find 34 − 18. Because it is impossible to subtract 8 from 4, we need to regroup one of the tens in 34, leaving 2 tens and 10 + 4 = 14 units. This is illustrated in Figure 3.24. Note that we can once again choose from one of the three levels of abstraction as illustrated in Fig. 3.24. However, eventually most textbooks written for elementary school mathematics will strive to get the children to use form 3.24c as their final algorithm.

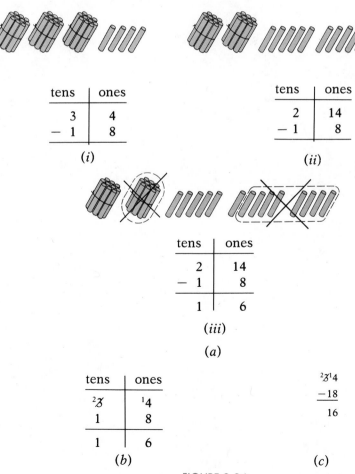

tens	ones
3	4
− 1	8

(i)

tens	ones
2	14
− 1	8

(ii)

tens	ones
2	14
− 1	8
1	6

(iii)

(a)

tens	ones
$^2\cancel{3}$	$^1 4$
1	8
1	6

(b)

$$^2\cancel{3}^1 4$$
$$-18$$
$$16$$

(c)

FIGURE 3.24

Let us turn our attention to subtraction in the base of five. Since the subtraction algorithm is based on expanded notation, will it also apply using a base other than ten? What would we mean by $4_{\text{five}} - 1_{\text{five}}$? We are searching for the number that when added to 1_{five} gives 4_{five}, and thus we want the answer to be 3_{five}. If you look at the table for addition in base five, you can

+	0	1	2	3	4
0	0	1	2	3	4
1	1	2	3	4	10
2	2	3	4	10	11
3	3	4	10	11	12
4	4	10	11	12	13

obtain the answer quickly by locating 1 in the left margin, then reading to the right to 4, and then up to obtain 3. You can also use the table to find that $12_{\text{five}} - 4_{\text{five}} = 3_{\text{five}}$. If you wish to find $43_{\text{five}} - 12_{\text{five}}$ write $(43 - 12)_{\text{five}} = (40$

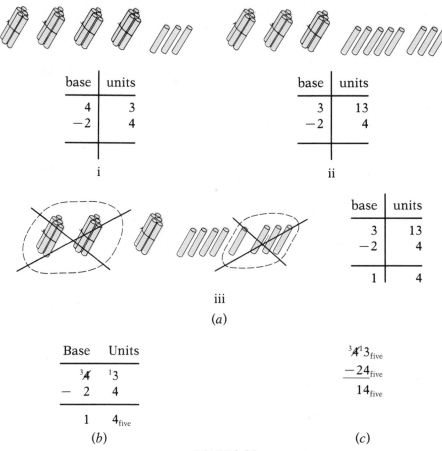

FIGURE 3.25

$+ 3) - (10 + 2)_{\text{five}} = (40 - 10) + (3 - 2)_{\text{five}} = (30 + 1)_{\text{five}} = 31_{\text{five}}$. This is precisely the same format used in the base-ten operation. In Figure 3.25, we illustrate the regrouping process. The only difference in our performance of the subtraction is that since we do not already know base-five subtraction facts, we rely on the additive subtraction process and actually make use of the addition table.

Let us look at one more example before we move to another topic. Suppose we wish to find $4301_{\text{five}} - 344_{\text{five}}$. The regrouping now forces us to move to the base $\times$ base position, leaving 2 in that place and making "10" elements in the "base" column as illustrated in Fig. 3.26a(ii).We then regroup one group of base, leaving 4 groups of base and 11 units. [Fig. 3.26 a(iii)] To complete the subtraction we now once again simply utilize a base five addition table using the missing addend idea.

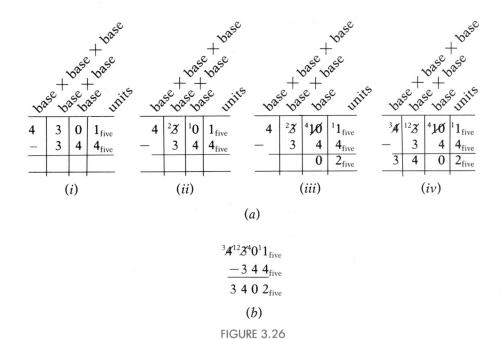

(a)

$$^3\cancel{4}^{12}\cancel{3}^4\cancel{0}^11_{\text{five}}$$
$$-3\ 4\ 4_{\text{five}}$$
$$\overline{3\ 4\ 0\ 2_{\text{five}}}$$

(b)

FIGURE 3.26

PROBLEM SET 3.5

1. Find each difference using a format like that in Figure 3.24b.

   a. $\begin{array}{r} 43 \\ -16 \\ \hline \end{array}$ b. $\begin{array}{r} 75 \\ -38 \\ \hline \end{array}$ c. $\begin{array}{r} 83 \\ -38 \\ \hline \end{array}$ d. $\begin{array}{r} 87 \\ -39 \\ \hline \end{array}$ e. $\begin{array}{r} 302 \\ -127 \\ \hline \end{array}$ f. $\begin{array}{r} 305 \\ -178 \\ \hline \end{array}$

2. Use the base-five addition table to find the following differences. Use a format like that used in Figure 3.25b.

a. 44_{five} **b.** 33_{five} **c.** 42_{five} **d.** 31_{five}
-12_{five} -12_{five} -24_{five} -13_{five}

e. 302_{five} **f.** 2030_{five}
$-\ \ 23_{\text{five}}$ $-\ \ 144_{\text{five}}$

3. Use the base-five addition table and the format found in Figure 3.25c to find the following differences:

a. 33_{five} **b.** 42_{five} **c.** 213_{five}
-14_{five} -14_{five} $-\ \ 31_{\text{five}}$

d. 301_{five} **e.** 131_{five} **f.** 3020_{five}
$-\ \ 23_{\text{five}}$ $-\ \ 42_{\text{five}}$ $-\ \ 143_{\text{five}}$

4. Use your base-six addition table (Problem 6 of Problem Set 3.4) to find each of the following:

a. 54_{six} **b.** 43_{six} **c.** 123_{six}
-15_{six} -25_{six} $-\ \ 44_{\text{six}}$

d. 301_{six} **e.** 412_{six} **f.** 4002_{six}
-125_{six} -135_{six} $-\ \ 453_{\text{six}}$

5. Find the following differences:

a. 101_{two} **b.** 1011_{two} **c.** 11001_{two} **d.** 110101_{two}
$-\ \ 11_{\text{two}}$ $-\ \ 101_{\text{two}}$ $-\ \ 1101_{\text{two}}$ $-\ \ 11010_{\text{two}}$

6. Using the table for the base-twelve addition developed in Problem 9 of Problem Set 3.4, find the following differences:

a.   69   **b.**   93   **c.** 173   **d.**   3#5
-14 $-2*$ $*8$ $-1**$

Pedagogical Problems and Activities

7. Another subtraction algorithm, often referred to as *equal additions*, is performed as follows. To find $54 - 18$ we immediately run into trouble because we cannot find $4 - 8$. Let us write the problem as follows:

$$
\begin{array}{r}
1 \\
54 \\
{}^{2}\cancel{1}8 \\
\hline
36
\end{array}
$$

We may then subtract 8 from 14, getting 6, and 2 from 5, getting 3.
a. Why does this work?

b. Try using it in each of the following:

(i)	(ii)	(iii)	(iv)
40	154	106	458
−26	− 68	− 87	−109

c. Try using this technique to find $413_{\text{five}} - 104_{\text{five}}$. Check your answer.

8. In addition, we used an algorithm called the *scratch method,* where we started on the left and worked right. Let us try a scratch subtraction. To find $56 - 28$, we might begin with 5 tens − 2 tens and obtain 3 tens. But $6 - 8$ is troublesome, so let us increase the 6 to 16 and decrease the 3 tens by one in the difference. The answer is 28. Does it check?

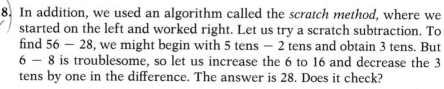

$$\begin{array}{r} 1 \\ 56 \\ -28 \\ \hline \not{3}8 \\ 2 \end{array}$$

a. Use this technique to find the following differences:

(i)	(ii)	(iii)	(iv)	(v)
46	54	85	163	462
−34	−18	−27	− 88	−185

b. Is this subtraction process more like regrouping or more like equal additions?

9. As in addition, the use of the scratch method is also useful in estimating solutions to subtraction problems. Estimate the solution to the following subtractions. Use a calculator to check your accuracy.

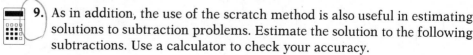

a. $4827 - 357$

b. $4998 - 4259$

c. $7886 - 6517$

d. $2759 - 1243$

e. $3951 - 2480$

f. $6590 - 4820$

10. Children develop intuitive strategies for working with subtraction. Occasionally these strategies are reinforced by occurrences in life. It is common for a street vendor to issue the following statement while making change for a person who paid for a $8.73 purchase with a $10 bill: "Eight seventy-three and two is eight seventy-five; eight seventy-five and twenty-five is nine; nine and one is ten." Translated this is: $8.73 + $0.02 = $8.75; $8.75 + $0.25 = $9.00; $9.00 + $1.00 = $10.00. We call this the *making change algorithm.* It is interesting because the buyer can know he or she has received the correct change, yet often does not know how much change was received. In algorithm

form, making change looks like this:

$$
\begin{array}{r}
10.00 \\
-8.73 \\
\hline
0.02 \quad (8.75) \\
0.25 \quad (9.00) \\
\underline{1.00} \; (10.00) \\
1.27
\end{array}
$$

Use the making change algorithm to compute the following subtractions.

a. $342 - 255$ b. $876 - 293$

c. $8000 - 2345$ d. $3661 - 1873$

11. Another subtraction algorithm is sometimes used for enrichment in the elementary school program. To find $45 - 28$ we must somehow arrange to accommodate subtraction in the units place. To do this we take one of the four tens in 45 and break it into ten parts, eight of which we allow to dribble through our fingers, leaving 2 in our hand. We add these 2 to the 5 and write 7. Then subtract 2 tens from 3 tens and write 1 in the tens place. Thus, $45 - 28 = 17$.

To find $81 - 36$, take 1 ten from 81, leaving 7 tens. Break that ten into 10 parts, then let 6 dribble through your fingers. Add the four that remain to 1 and write 5 into the units place. Then $7 - 3 = 4$, so the tens digit is 4. That is, $81 - 36 = 45$. This algorithm, referred to as the *dribble method*, is of considerable interest to children.

a. Use this technique to find the following:

(i)	(ii)	(iii)	iv)	(v)
43	54	125	346	584
-28	-17	$- 76$	-178	-188

b. Why does this algorithm work?

c. In what sense is this algorithm simpler than the others?

d. Does the dribble method hold for base-six subtraction? Illustrate your answer using $(423 - 145)_{six}$.

12. Another subtraction algorithm has been proposed for use with children who have difficulty with intermixing regrouping and use of subtraction facts. To find $543 - 258$ one normally regroups one ten to get 13 units, then subtracts 8, then regroups one of the hundreds to get 13 tens, then subtracts 5 tens. Use of this new algorithm would find all regrouping being done first, then application of subtraction facts.

$$
\begin{array}{ccc}
5 & 4 & 3 \\
4 & 13 & 13 \\
-2 & 5 & 8
\end{array}
\rightarrow
\begin{array}{ccc}
5 & 4 & 3 \\
4 & 13 & 13 \\
-2 & 5 & 8 \\
\hline
2 & 8 & 5
\end{array}
$$

Use this algorithm to find the following differences:

a. 143
− 97

b. 432
−145

c. 243
− 85

d. 1725
− 956

13. Many student use a form of *compensation* to do subtraction problems mentally. To find 46 − 18 they reason that the answer will be the same as that found in 48 − 20 but the latter is much easier to handle mentally.
a. Does this process really work? (*Hint:* Think of it in terms of bundles of sticks or perhaps on a number line.)
b. Try this technique on the following problems.
   (i) 43 − 17
   (ii) 64 − 15
   (iii) 76 − 18
   (iv) 86 − 19
c. Would this work in the base of five? Use the numbers 32_{five} − 14_{five}.

14. Show or describe how you might use base-ten blocks to find each of the following:

a. 46
−25

b. 245
−132

c. 54
−38

d. 146
− 89

e. 305
−178

15. Use bundled sticks to find the following:

a. 31_{five}
$+12_{five}$

b. 34_{five}
$+32_{five}$

c. 34_{five}
$−12_{five}$

d. 42_{five}
$−13_{five}$

e. 132_{five}
$+ 14_{five}$

f. 122_{five}
$− 34_{five}$

16. Renaming in general is difficult for children. Use some manipulatives to illustrate the renaming in each of the following:

a. 203_{five}
$− 14_{five}$

b. 111_{three}
$− 22_{three}$

c. 123_{six}
$− 54_{six}$

d. 204_{six}
$− 25_{six}$

3.6 THE MULTIPLICATION ALGORITHM

In Chapter 2 we discussed the operation of multiplication on whole numbers. Whether we prefer to think of multiplication in terms of repeated addition or in terms of arrays is immaterial in the development of the algorithm. (Although it is an important consideration as we do problem solving.) Either way we can obtain the basic multiplication facts we have all committed to memory. We also developed the distributive property, which will be very useful to us as we consider the development of the multiplication algorithm.

Suppose that we want to find the product of 4 and 12. Let us make an array to illustrate the meaning of the product. We need to use four rows with 12 objects in each, as illustrated in Figure 3.27a. In 3.27b the product is written using an expanded format, then the distributive property is applied. In 3.27c the format showing the partial products is used, and in 3.27d the shortened format is used. It should be apparent that expanded notation and the distributive pattern are the real key ideas.

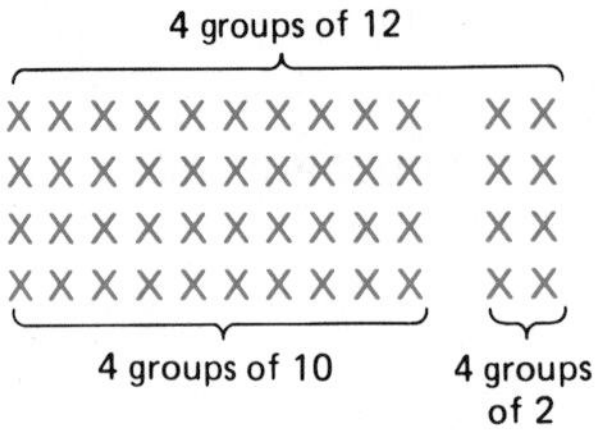

4 groups of 12

```
X X X X X X X X X X   X X
X X X X X X X X X X   X X
X X X X X X X X X X   X X
X X X X X X X X X X   X X
```

4 groups of 10   4 groups of 2

(a)

$$4 \cdot 12 = 4(10 + 2)$$
$$= 4 \cdot 10 + 4 \cdot 2$$
$$= 40 + 8$$
$$= 48$$

(b)

$$
\begin{array}{r}
12 \\
\times\ 4 \\
\hline
8 = 4 \cdot 2 \\
40 = 4 \cdot 10 \\
\hline
48
\end{array}
$$

(c)

$$
\begin{array}{r}
12 \\
\times\ 4 \\
\hline
48
\end{array}
$$

(d)

FIGURE 3.27

Let us consider another example, this time involving some regrouping. Because most of the third- and fourth-grade mathematics texts make use of base-ten blocks as a model, we have used them in this example. To find 3 × 14, let us first represent the array using the base-ten blocks as illustrated in Figure 3.28a. In Figure 3.28b we have illustrated a semi-abstract representation of the problem. Once again note that four levels of abstraction are available for use with children: (1) concrete (use base-ten blocks), (2) semiconcrete (pictures of base-ten blocks), (3) semiabstract (use lines and dots to represent blocks as in b), and (4) abstract (any form using only symbols such as c, d, or e).

> REMARK The different forms of the algorithm are commonly useful in two ways. We will normally begin early work with the algorithm using the array and work toward the shortened form. However, later if we need to do remediation for some students we will again need to go back to some of the more basic forms to build understanding.

The algorithm extends readily to the product of a two-digit number times a two-digit numeral. Let us illustrate this in Figure 3.29 as we consider the product 23 × 24. Note that each of the levels of abstraction is again available for our use.

We should next consider whether this algorithm will hold in another base. For example, should we be able to find $4_{\text{five}} \times 23_{\text{five}}$ using the same techniques that we just applied to base-ten work? First, we should concern ourselves with multiplication facts. What would we mean by $3_{\text{five}} \times 2_{\text{five}}$? If we consider

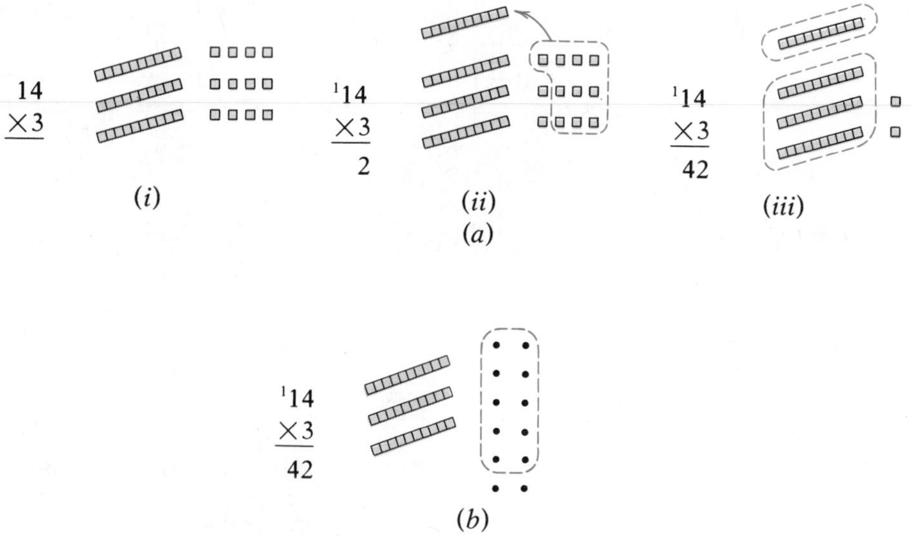

$$
\begin{array}{r} 14 \\ \times 3 \\ \hline \end{array}
\qquad
\begin{array}{r} {}^1 14 \\ \times 3 \\ \hline 2 \end{array}
\qquad
\begin{array}{r} {}^1 14 \\ \times 3 \\ \hline 42 \end{array}
$$

(i)   (ii)   (iii)

(a)

$$
\begin{array}{r} {}^1 14 \\ \times 3 \\ \hline 42 \end{array}
$$

(b)

$$
\begin{array}{l}
3 \times 14 \\
3 \times (10 + 4) \\
(3 \times 10) + (3 \times 4) \\
30 + 12 \\
42
\end{array}
$$

(c)

$$
\begin{array}{r}
14 \\
\times\ 3 \\
\hline
12 \\
30 \\
\hline
42
\end{array}
$$
3 × 4 ones (3 × 4)
3 × 1 ten (3 × 10)

(d)

$$
\begin{array}{r} {}^1 14 \\ \times 3 \\ \hline 42 \end{array}
$$

(e)

FIGURE 3.28

it to be repeated addition, we might write $3_{\text{five}} \times 2_{\text{five}} = (2 + 2 + 2)_{\text{five}} = (4 + 2)_{\text{five}} = 11_{\text{five}}$. Would we have obtained the same results if we had used an array? We would need 2 elements in each row and 3 rows, such as xx. Are there 11_{five} elements in this array?

             xx
             xx

You should check several other base-five facts before you attempt to build a multiplication chart. In Figure 3.30 we enter the basic multiplication facts for the base of five. Notice that as we would expect, $0 \cdot a = 0$ for any a. For this reason multiplication charts sometimes omit the 0 multiplier row and column. Note also that as we go across any given row (or down a column), we find a constant difference from one entry to the next. For example, the row with 2 in the left margin has a constant addition of 2 as we proceed to the right. $2 \cdot 1 = 2, 2 \cdot 2 = 4, 2 \cdot 3 = 11$, which is the same as $4 + 2$, and so on. We often build a multiplication chart by using the addition chart in that base and using the constant addition idea.

We should also consider whether the distributive property holds even if the base is not ten. That is, does $2 \cdot (3 + 4)_{\text{five}} = (2 \cdot 3 + 2 \cdot 4)_{\text{five}}$? We could,

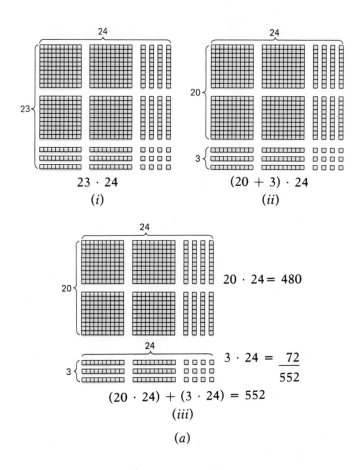

FIGURE 3.29

of course, check this particular pattern using base-five tables, or we could revert to sets again. Does the pattern used in the last chapter still apply?

·	0	1	2	3	4
0	0	0	0	0	0
1	0	1	2	3	4
2	0	2	4	11	13
3	0	3	11	14	22
4	0	4	13	22	31

FIGURE 3.30

Apparently it does not depend on a particular base being used. We should therefore feel confident that the algorithms used to do multiplication in the base of ten will also apply in other bases. Let us return then to the question asked earlier. Can we find $4_{five} \cdot 23_{five}$? We may write $4_{five} \cdot 23_{five} = 4(20 + 3)_{five} = (4 \cdot 20 + 4 \cdot 3)_{five}$. Using our tables we may then write $(4 \cdot 20 + 4 \cdot 3)_{five} = (130 + 22)_{five} = 202_{five}$. The other forms of the algorithm used in our base-ten discussion will still apply and are illustrated in Figure 3.31.

(a)

$$(4 \cdot 23)_{five} = 4(20 + 3)_{five}$$
$$= (4 \cdot 20)_{five} + (4 \cdot 3)_{five}$$
$$= (130 + 22)_{five}$$
$$= 202_{five}$$

(b)

$$
\begin{array}{r}
23_{five} \\
\times\ 4_{five} \\
\hline
22 = 4 \cdot 3_{five} \\
130 = 4 \cdot 20_{five} \\
\hline
202_{five}
\end{array}
$$

(c)

$$
\begin{array}{r}
{}^{2}23_{five} \\
\times\ \ 4_{five} \\
\hline
202_{five}
\end{array}
$$

(d)

FIGURE 3.31

The product of two numbers having two-digit numerals may be accomplished in a manner just like that used for base-ten multiplication. In Figure 3.32 we illustrate the product $12_{five} \times 34_{five}$.

REMARK Just as in the case with addition, we would suggest that you not attempt to memorize any multiplication facts other than those in the base of ten. Instead, quickly build the tables and use them as you do your work.

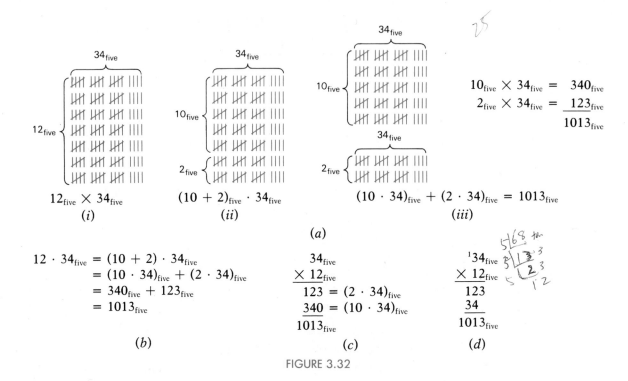

FIGURE 3.32

PROBLEM SET 3.6

1. Use base-ten blocks to make an array that illustrates each of the following products:

    a. 3×23 **b.** 4×17 **c.** 5×13 **d.** 6×23

2. Use the horizontal format (like that in Fig. 3.28c) to find the following products:

    a. 4×19 **b.** 5×23 **c.** 9×16 **d.** 9×17

3. Use the partial product format (like that in Fig. 3.28d) to find the following products:

    a. 3×27 **b.** 4×16 **c.** 9×28 **d.** 8×75

4. **a.** Make an array using base-ten blocks to illustrate the product 21×35.

    b. Show how to use partial products to find 21×35 (Like in Fig. 3.29c.)

5. Find the following products by using the shortened form of the algorithm.

a.	42	**b.**	63	**c.**	176	**d.**	843
	$\times\ 5$		$\times 12$		$\times\ 32$		$\times\ 79$

6. Make an array to illustrate each of the following products:
   a. $(3 \times 24)_{\text{five}}$ **b.** $(3 \times 21)_{\text{five}}$ **c.** $(12 \times 14)_{\text{five}}$ **d.** $(13 \times 23)_{\text{five}}$

7. Find each of the products in Problem 6 using the shortened form of the algorithm.

8. **a.** Show the meaning of $(4 \cdot 3)_{\text{six}}$.
   b. Use an array to verify that $[2 \cdot (4 + 3)]_{\text{six}} = (2 \cdot 4 + 2 \cdot 3)_{\text{six}}$.
   c. Make a multiplication chart for base six. (Use your base-six addition chart to help with this.)
   d. Use the chart to find $(5 \cdot 4)_{\text{six}}$.

9. **a.** Make an array to illustrate $(4 \cdot 23)_{\text{six}}$.
   b. Use the horizontal format to find $(5 \cdot 42)_{\text{six}}$.
   c. Use partial products to find $(3 \cdot 143)_{\text{six}}$.
   d. Use the shortened form of the algorithm to find $(4 \cdot 132)_{\text{six}}$.

10. **a.** The base-two multiplication table is very brief. Make the table for base-two multiplication.
   b. Use it to find the following products.
   (i) 101_{two} **(ii)** 11011_{two} **(iii)** 110010_{two} **(iv)** 111011_{two}
   $\underline{\times\ 11}_{\text{two}}$ $\underline{\times\ 110}_{\text{two}}$ $\underline{\times\ 101}_{\text{two}}$ $\underline{\times\ 1011}_{\text{two}}$

11. The multiplication algorithm can be expanded to take a new look at partial products. For example:

$$
\begin{aligned}
34 \cdot 26 &= (30 + 4) \cdot 26 \\
&= (30 \cdot 26) + (4 \cdot 26) \\
&= 30(20 + 6) + 4(20 + 6) \\
&= (30 \cdot 20) + (30 \cdot 6) + (4 \cdot 20) + (4 \cdot 6)
\end{aligned}
$$

These partial products can be illustrated using an area model that is similar to that illustrated in Figures 3.28a and 3.29a. A model to illustrate 34×26 would appear as follows:

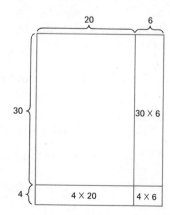

Make an area model to represent each of the following products, then write the four resulting terms implied by the drawing.

a. 24 × 14   **b.** 16 × 23   **c.** 18 × 27   **d.** 15 × 28

12. The four partial products found in Problem 11 are sometimes written as follows:

$$
\begin{array}{r}
26 \\
\times\,34 \\
\hline
24 = 4 \cdot 6 \\
80 = 4 \cdot 20 \\
180 = 30 \cdot 6 \\
600 = 30 \cdot 20 \\
\hline
884
\end{array}
$$

Find each of the following using all of the possible partial products:

a.	**b.**	**c.**	**d.**
32	45	145	654
×17	×83	× 23	× 57

13. A multiplication algorithm, commonly referred to as *lattice multiplication*, is often found in mathematics books written for students in grades 4–6. To multiply 46 × 37 we might set up a chart, or lattice, as follows:

    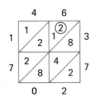

We begin with a blank lattice and find the products of the digits in each intersecting row and column. The 28 in the lower row–column intersection is the product 4 × 7. Other blank spaces are filled in the same manner. Then the numbers are added down the diagonals, using any carry in the next diagonal. Thus, 8 + 4 + 8 = 20, so the 2 is added into the next diagonal, giving the sum of 7 as recorded. The answer, resulting from the sums down the diagonals, is 1702.

a. Use this method to find each of the following:

    (i) 36 · 24   **(ii)** 75 · 63   **(iii)** 176 · 28

b. Explain why this works. (*Hint:* Try writing 36 · 24 using partial products and compare that result with the lattice format.)

14. An algorithm for multiplication, used by the Egyptians before the time of Christ, may be illustrated as follows. Suppose we wish to find 26 × 42. We will form two columns, one headed by 1 and the other by 42. We

will double both numbers until such time as the double in the left column exceeds 26. Then select those entries from the left-hand column whose sum is 26. The sum of the corresponding numbers from the right-hand column is the product.

$$
\begin{array}{rccc}
 & 1 & 42 & \\
\rightarrow & 2 & 84 & 84 \\
 & 4 & 168 & 336 \\
\rightarrow & 8 & 336 & +\ 672 \\
\rightarrow & 16 & 672 & 1092 \\
\end{array}
$$

   a. Use this process to find each of the following:

      (i) 32 · 25   **(ii)** 56 · 12   **(iii)** 48 · 50

   b. Why does this procedure work?

15. Make a multiplication table for base twelve. Find the following products:

    a. 42_{twelve} **b.** 51_{twelve} **c.** $\#3_{\text{twelve}}$ **d.** $13\#_{\text{twelve}}$

      $\times 17_{\text{twelve}}$ $\times 97_{\text{twelve}}$ $\times 19_{\text{twelve}}$ $\times\ \ 5_{\text{twelve}}$

    e. $30*_{\text{twelve}}$

      $\times\ *\#_{\text{twelve}}$

16. Estimate the following products. Use a calculator to check your estimate.

    a. 42 × 95   **b.** 66 × 22

    c. 844 × 161   **d.** 2854 × 71

17. Estimate a range into which the following products will occur. Check using a calculator.

    a. _____ < 61 × 436 < _____

    b. _____ < 52 × 38 < _____

    c. _____ < 62 × 95 < _____

    d. _____ < 452 × 362 < _____

    e. _____ < 737 × 828 < _____

18. Fill in the blank so that the resulting product falls in the specified range.

Product	Range
a. 38 × _____	between 70 and 90
b. 62 × _____	between 900 and 1000
c. 53 × _____	between 250 and 280
d. 76 × _____	between 650 and 710

Pedagogical Problems and Activities

19. Analysis of errors is a most important task for teachers. Suppose a child writes the following:

$$
\begin{array}{r}
34 \\
\times\ 21 \\
\hline
34 \\
68 \\
\hline
102
\end{array}
\qquad
\begin{array}{r}
26 \\
\times\ 32 \\
\hline
52 \\
78 \\
\hline
130
\end{array}
\qquad
\begin{array}{r}
56 \\
\times\ 14 \\
\hline
224 \\
56 \\
\hline
280
\end{array}
$$

   a. What systematic error is being made?

   b. How can you demonstrate to the child that his or her work is incorrect

   c. What would you do to remediate this error? (What form of the algorithm would be useful?)

   d. What basic concept is missing in the childs' use of this algorithm?

20. Suppose a child writes the following:

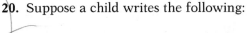

$$
\begin{array}{r}
314 \\
\times\ \ \ 6 \\
\hline
1884
\end{array}
\qquad
\begin{array}{r}
320 \\
\times\ 15 \\
\hline
320
\end{array}
\qquad
\begin{array}{r}
517 \\
\times\ \ 34 \\
\hline
1558
\end{array}
\qquad
\begin{array}{r}
433 \\
\times 226 \\
\hline
878
\end{array}
\qquad
\begin{array}{r}
547 \\
\times\ 463 \\
\hline
2261
\end{array}
$$

   a. What systematic error is being made?

   b. How might you remediate this error?

21. The product of a two-digit number times a one-digit number is often illustrated using an area model. To find the product $6 \cdot 23$, consider the model on the right. The area represented by $6 \cdot 23$ is the same as the sum of the area $6 \cdot 20 + 6 \cdot 3$. Use an area model to find each of the following products.

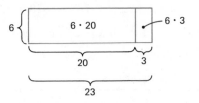

   a. $4 \cdot 35$ **b.** $8 \cdot 23$ **c.** $5 \cdot 42$ **d.** $7 \cdot 84$

22. We could also use an area model to represent the partial products as we do products involving two-digit numbers. For example, to find $26 \cdot 32$, consider the figure on the right. It should be evident that $26 \cdot 32$ represents the same area as the sum of the two rectangles having areas $6 \cdot 32$ and $20 \cdot 32$. Use area models to find each of the following products.

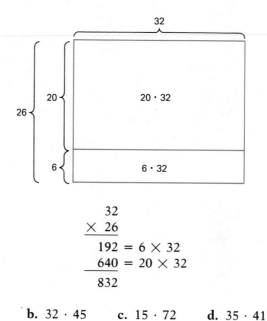

$$
\begin{array}{r}
32 \\
\times\ 26 \\
\hline
192 = 6 \times 32 \\
640 = 20 \times 32 \\
\hline
832
\end{array}
$$

a. $21 \cdot 18$ **b.** $32 \cdot 45$ **c.** $15 \cdot 72$ **d.** $35 \cdot 41$

3.7   THE DIVISION ALGORITHM

Early school exposure to division is often related to multiplication. This was, in fact, the way we defined division in the last chapter. Another application can also be made relating to subtraction. The question $14 \div 4$ can be interpreted to mean "How many sets of four elements each are there in a set of fourteen elements?" We can easily find the answer just by considering the following repeated subtraction:

$$
\begin{array}{r}
14 \\
-\ 4 \\
\hline
10 \\
-\ 4 \\
\hline
6 \\
-\ 4 \\
\hline
2
\end{array}
$$

There are obviously three groups of four and two elements are left over. In teaching the division algorithm, children are usually given considerable experience with repeated subtraction problems.

In some textbook series this subtractive process is carried directly into a division algorithm. We will do this in the next problem set. However, because many recent elementary school mathematics texts are now using a distributive format for division, it is this algorithm that we wish to develop here.

Suppose a child has 5 dimes and 2 pennies he or she wishes to distribute evenly among four friends. There are clearly enough dimes to be distributed, one for each friend. Now the remaining dime is exchanged for pennies, as illustrated in Figure 3.33b, a total of 12 pennies. Now 3 pennies can be given to each friend. Each of the four friends received a dime and 3 pennies, or 13 cents.

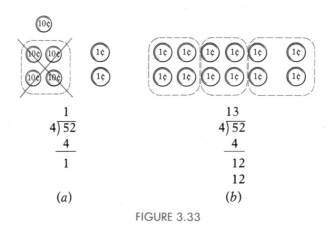

FIGURE 3.33

Base-ten blocks may be used nicely to illustrate this algorithm also. Consider a tougher problem, like 563 ÷ 5. Note that there are enough hundreds blocks (Fig. 3.34a) to distribute evenly to five piles. Now consider the 6 tens in part (b). Note that if we distribute one ten to each of five piles, we still have a ten left. In part (c), we indicate that the remaining 10 provides us with 10 units that, along with the 3 already indicated, gives a total of 13 units. We distribute 2 units to each of 5 piles and have 3 units undistributed. Thus, each of 5 piles have received 112 and 3 remain undistributed.

Even with larger numbers, the procedure is clear. Consider Figure 3.35. There are not enough thousands to distribute to 42 piles, but in 89 hundreds we have enough to distribute 2 to each of 42 piles. The 5 hundreds that remain are broken into tens, giving a total of 54 tens. This number is sufficient to distribute 1 ten to each of 42 piles, as recorded in Figure 3.35b. Now consider the fact that we have 128 units. This is a sufficiently large number to allow us to distribute 3 to each of the 4 piles and 2 remain undistributed.

```
   1    1 hundred distributed
5) 563    to each
   5    Hundreds distributed
   0    Hundreds remaining
```

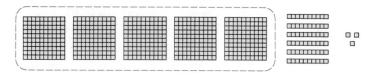

Place 1 of the hundreds blocks in each of the five piles.

(a)

```
   11   1 ten distributed to each
5) 563
   5
   06   Tens
   5    Tens distributed
   1    Tens remaining
```

Place 1 tens block in each of the five piles.

(b)

```
   112  2 units distributed to each
5) 563
   5
   06
   5
   13 Units remaining
   10 Units distributed
   3 Units remaining
```

Place 2 units in each of the five piles.

(c)

FIGURE 3.34

```
    2    Hundreds distributed
42) 8948    to each
   84
    5    Hundreds remaining
```

(a)

```
    21   Tens distributed
42) 8948    to each
   84
   54   Tens to distribute
   42
   12   Tens remaining
```

(b)

```
    213  Units distributed
42) 8948    to each
   84
   54
   42
  128 Units to distribute
  126
    2 Units remaining
```

(c)

FIGURE 3.35

Suppose we are working in the base of five. What do we mean by $13_{\text{five}} \div 4_{\text{five}}$? The interpretation should be the same as was encountered in base ten. One such interpretation is that we have a set of elements that must be placed in piles, 4_{five} in each pile. Using the set $\overline{\left(x\ x\ x\right) x\ x}$ it is clear that there are

2_{five} such piles. What about $22_{\text{five}} \div 4_{\text{five}}$? Again, we might simply use a set and distribute the elements as before. However, if you look at the base-five multiplication table, it is evident that $4_{\text{five}} \cdot 3_{\text{five}} = 22_{\text{five}}$, so the quotient is 3_{five} (i.e., the missing factor).

Now consider the algorithm in a base-five situation. (You will need both your base-five addition and multiplication tables for this work.) Consider $32_{\text{five}} \div 2_{\text{five}}$. We do have enough groups of base to distribute into each of the two piles, as illustrated in Figure 3.36a. The remaining group of base elements is broken into units, make 12_{five} units. If three of these are distributed to the two piles, 11_{five} will be used leaving 1 unit undivided as illustrated in Figure 3.36b.

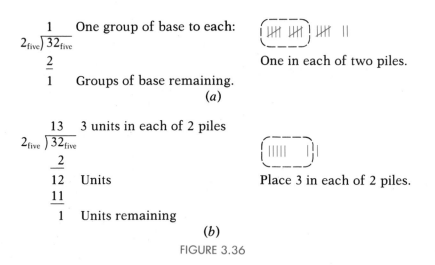

$$
\begin{array}{r}
1 \\
2_{\text{five}}\overline{)\,32_{\text{five}}} \\
2 \\
\hline
1
\end{array}
$$

One group of base to each:

One in each of two piles.

Groups of base remaining.

(a)

$$
\begin{array}{r}
13 \\
2_{\text{five}}\overline{)\,32_{\text{five}}} \\
2 \\
\hline
12 \\
11 \\
\hline
1
\end{array}
$$

3 units in each of 2 piles

Units

Units remaining

Place 3 in each of 2 piles.

(b)

FIGURE 3.36

In Figure 3.37 we illustrate one additional division problem in the base of five.

One further comment should be made regarding the relation between division and multiplication. In our work in the last chapter, we defined division as relating to multiplication. That is $a \div b = c$ if and only if $b \cdot c = a$. What we were seeking was the missing factor. Now we are observing that a remainder sometimes occurs. Consider $563 \div 6$. The quotient is 93, and there is a remainder of 5. That is, 93 was distributed to each of 6 piles and 5 remained undistributed. We note that $(93 \div 6) + 5 = 558 + 5 = 563$. This then is an excellent way to check a division problem to assure ourselves that we did not make an error.

$$
\begin{array}{r}
1_{\text{five}} \\
24_{\text{five}}\overline{)4322_{\text{five}}} \\
\underline{24} \\
14_{\text{five}}
\end{array}
\qquad
\begin{array}{r}
13_{\text{five}} \\
24_{\text{five}}\overline{)4322_{\text{five}}} \\
\underline{24} \\
142 \\
\underline{132} \\
10
\end{array}
\qquad
\begin{array}{r}
131_{\text{five}} \\
24_{\text{five}}\overline{)4322_{\text{five}}} \\
\underline{24} \\
142 \\
\underline{132} \\
102 \\
\underline{24} \\
23
\end{array}
$$

(a) $\qquad\qquad$ (b) $\qquad\qquad$ (c)

FIGURE 3.37

Let us make one additional comment before we close this chapter. All four of the basic algorithms are based on the use of positional notation, commutativity, associativity, the distributive pattern, and so on. Because they do *not* depend on the particular base being used, they carry over nicely to any positional notation system regardless of the base. But we must be cautious about declaring that *everything* that holds for our base-ten system will hold in the other bases. As an example, consider the number 8736216_{ten}. We know immediately that it is an even number simply because the last digit is even. Then let us consider 14_{five}. Its last digit is even. Does that assure us that 14_{five} is even? Recall that for a number to be even it must be the product of 2 and k for some whole number k. What base-five number when multiplied by 2 yields 14_{five}? Let us divide 14_{five} by 2_{five}.

$$
\begin{array}{r}
4_{\text{five}} \\
2_{\text{five}}\overline{)14_{\text{five}}} \\
\underline{13} \\
1
\end{array}
$$

The quotient is 4 with a remainder of 1. Therefore, 14_{five} is *not* even. The test for evenness by checking the last digit does not hold in the base of five. We should continue to think carefully before we draw conclusions. We will return to this problem in the next problem set for further consideration.

PROBLEM SET 3.7

1. Show how to use base-ten blocks and the distributive formula to determine each quotient.

   a. $53 \div 4$ $\qquad$ b. $84 \div 5$ $\qquad$ c. $43 \div 3$

   d. $76 \div 5$ $\qquad$ e. $543 \div 4$ $\qquad$ f. $632 \div 7$

2. Consider $4652 \div 30$.

   a. Are there enough thousands in 4652 to distribute? Are there enough hundreds?

   b. Complete the problem describing the process at each step.

3. Use the distributive format to calculate each of the following quotients:

   a. $42\overline{)584}$ b. $23\overline{)462}$ c. $28\overline{)4932}$

   e. $342\overline{)63254}$ f. $203\overline{)48036}$ d. $103\overline{)9803}$

4. Suppose we are working in a base of five. Illustrate how you would use sets and the distributive procedure to find the following quotients:

   a. $(23 \div 2)_{\text{five}}$ b. $(42 \div 3)_{\text{five}}$ c. $(43 \div 4)_{\text{five}}$

   d. $(34 \div 4)_{\text{five}}$ e. $(102 \div 3)_{\text{five}}$ f. $(114 \div 2)_{\text{five}}$

5. Find the following quotients: (*Hint:* Refer to your base-six addition and multiplication tables.)

   a. $(45 \div 4)_{\text{six}}$ b. $(243 \div 21)_{\text{six}}$ c. $(4325 \div 52)_{\text{six}}$

   d. $(25243 \div 52)_{\text{six}}$ e. $(5324 \div 32)_{\text{six}}$

6. Find the following quotients:

   a. $(101 \div 11)_{\text{two}}$ b. $(1101 \div 101)_{\text{two}}$ c. $(10110 \div 110)_{\text{two}}$

   d. $(111011 \div 1011)_{\text{two}}$ e. $(100100 \div 1001)_{\text{two}}$ f. $(11011010 \div 1011)_{\text{two}}$

7. Perform the following base-twelve divisions:

   a. $(264 \div 12)_{\text{twelve}}$ b. $(4875 \div 87)_{\text{twelve}}$ c. $(4\#3* \div 72)_{\text{twelve}}$

   d. $(4\#30* \div \#3)_{\text{twelve}}$ e. $(11\#23* \div 1\#1)_{\text{twelve}}$

   f. $(\#1* \, 103 \div \#1*)_{\text{twelve}}$

8. a. If $325 = (q \cdot 6) + r$ where q and r are whole numbers and $r < 6$, what is the value for q and for r?

   b. Could there be more than one answer for part a?

9. a. Suppose a and b are whole numbers. If $a \div 7$ gives a remainder of 4 and $b \div 7$ gives a remainder of 5, what remainder do you get when you divide $a + b$ by 7?

   b. Let $a, b, c,$ and d all be whole numbers. Suppose $a \div 6$ gives a remainder of 3, $b \div 6$ has a remainder of 5, $c \div 6$ has a remainder of 2, and $d \div 6$ gives a remainder of 1. What remainder should you expect if $a + b + c + d$ is divided by 6?

   c. Suppose we are working in a base of seven and are told that $a \div 5$ has a remainder of 2 and $b \div 5$ has a remainder of 4. What do you expect to be the remainder when $a + b$ is divided by 5?

10. a. We found that 14_{five} is an *odd* number because $(14 \div 2)_{\text{five}}$ left a remainder of 1_{five}. Complete the following table.

	Quotient	Remainder
$(14 \div 2)_{five}$	4_{five}	1_{five}
$(13 \div 2)_{five}$		
$(12 \div 2)_{five}$		
$(11 \div 2)_{five}$		
$(24 \div 2)_{five}$		
$(23 \div 2)_{five}$		
$(22 \div 2)_{five}$		
$(21 \div 2)_{five}$		

    b. Suggest a rule for testing two digit base-five numbers for evenness. (Test your rule for 34_{five}, 31_{five}, 44_{five}, and 41_{five}.)

11. a. Is 14_{six} even?

    b. Make a table similar to that used in Problem 10 to test some other base-six numbers.

    c. Make a conjecture regarding a test for evenness for base-six numbers.

12. a. Make a conjecture regarding a base-seven rule for evenness.

    b. Do you see a pattern for testing evenness for numbers in other bases? What seems to be happening?

    c. Use counting sticks to verify your conjecture in part b.

13. a. The answer to $84632 \div 584$ is given as 144 with a remainder of 546. Use your calculator to determine whether this answer is correct.

    b. The quotient of $8568 \div 164$ is given as 52 and the remainder of 42. Use your calculator to determine whether the answer is correct.

    c. The answer to the quotient $63842 \div 1562$ is given as 40.871959 on one calculator. Is the whole number part, 40, correct? What remainder would you obtain?

    d. If $143 \cdot b + 22 = 7887$, find b.

    e. What is the remainder if 8432 is divided by 143?

14. Estimate the following quotients and indicate by a $(+)$ or $(-)$ whether you expect the quotient to be larger $(+)$ or smaller $(-)$ than your estimate. Use a calculator to check your answer.

    a. $3231 \div 6$ **b.** $581 \div 4$ **c.** $600 \div 8$ **d.** $58102 \div 42$

15. In an earlier section, we found that we could convert from a base of ten to a base of five by repeated division by five. For example, to write 68_{ten} as a base-five numeral we would perform the following division:

    $5 \underline{|68}$ Change from base ten to base 5

    $5 \underline{|13}$ 3   1. THINK in the base of ten

        2 3   2. DIVIDE by 5.

To change from a base-five representative to base three we should be able to use the same algorithm. For example, to change 32_{five} to its base-three counterpart we will use division.

$3\underline{|32}_{five}$ Change from base five to base 3
$3\underline{|10}$ 2   1. THINK in the base five
$\quad\;\;1$ 2   2. DIVIDE by 3.

That is, $32_{five} = 122_{three}$. (Note that $32_{five} = (3 \times 5 + 2)_{ten} = 17_{ten}$ and $122_{three} = (1 \times 10 \times 10 + 2 \times 10 + 2)_{three} = (1 \times 3 \times 3 + 2 \times 3 + 2)_{ten} = (9 + 6 + 2)_{ten}$. Use this algorithm to convert each of the following.

a. $140_{five} = $ ⸻$_{three}$ b. $54_{six} = $ ⸻$_{three}$

c. $47_{eight} = $ ⸻$_{four}$ d. $54_{six} = $ ⸻$_{three}$

e. $45_{six} = $ ⸻$_{eight}$. (Think in six, but divide by what? How do you name the set having xxxx xxxx as elements from the six point of view?)

f. $2145_{six} = $ ⸻$_{twelve}$

Pedagogical Problems and Activities

16. a. Show how to use counting sticks to find $26 \div 4$ where you use a subtractive format. (How many clusters of four?)

b. Show how to use counting sticks to find $26 \div 4$ where you use the distributive format. (Deal the sticks into four piles.)

17. The subtractive (or scaffolding) format is sometimes used for division. To find $32 \div 5$ we could subtract 5 out at a time to reach the conclusion that there are 6 such sets of 5 in 32 and a remainder of 2. This procedure could be shortened by removing more than one group of 5, such as in ii and in iii. Use this procedure to find the following quotients.

(i) $5\overline{)32}$	(ii) $5\overline{)32}$	(iii) $5\overline{)32}$
$\underline{5}\;\|\;1$	$\underline{10}\;\|\;2$	$\underline{20}\;\|\;4$
27	22	12
$\underline{5}\;\|\;1$	$\underline{10}\;\|\;2$	$\underline{10}\;\|\;2$
22	12	$\;\;2\;\|\;6$
$\underline{5}\;\|\;1$	$\underline{10}\;\|\;\underline{2}$	
17	$\;\;2\;\|\;6$	
$\underline{5}\;\|\;1$		
12		
$\underline{5}\;\|\;1$		
7		
$\underline{5}\;\|\;\underline{1}$		
$2\;\|\;6$		

a. $36 \div 7$ b. $126 \div 25$ c. $254 \div 22$ d. $4932 \div 28$

18. Use base-ten blocks to illustrate the distributive process for 1256 ÷ 8.

19. Egyptian division resembles their multiplication algorithm in that it is dependent on the doubling process. To find 351 ÷ 9 proceed as follows:

$$
\begin{array}{c}
9 \overline{)\,352} \\
\end{array}
\qquad
\begin{array}{ll}
1 \times 9 = 9 \\
2 \times 9 = 18 \\
4 \times 9 = 36 \\
8 \times 9 = 72 \\
16 \times 9 = 144 \\
32 \times 9 = 288 \\
64 \times 9 = 576
\end{array}
$$

9)352		$1 \times 9 = 9$
288	32	$2 \times 9 = 18$
64		$4 \times 9 = 36$
36	4	$8 \times 9 = 72$
28		$16 \times 9 = 144$
18	2	$32 \times 9 = 288$
10		$64 \times 9 = 576$
9	1	
1	39	

Thus, 351 ÷ 9 = 39 with a remainder of 1.
Use this procedure to find the following quotients.
  a. 146 ÷ 6   b. 872 ÷ 8   c. 596 ÷ 7   d. 843 ÷ 5

20. a. Some calculators allow you to choose from two buttons to perform division. When the ÷ button is pushed to find the quotient 45 ÷ 7, the readout is 6.4285714. However, when the button marked INT ÷ is pushed the same quotient produces the answer Q6 R3. Use the INT ÷ button to perform the following divisions.
    (i) 63 ÷ 6   (ii) 89 ÷ 19   (iii) 642 ÷ 31   (iv) 753 ÷ 17
  b. Suppose you find 987 ÷ 47 by using the INT ÷ button. The answer given is Q20 R7. But because 47 × 21 = 987 you apparently entered an incorrect number into the calculator. Suppose you distinctly recall that 987 was entered correctly. What number must have been used in place of 47?

REVIEW PROBLEM SET

1. a. Write 3162 using expanded notation.
   b. Express 3162 using Egyptian numeration.
   c. Express 3162 using Roman numerals.

2. Write each of the following as a base-ten numeral:
   a. $\overline{\text{XIV}}$CCLXVII
   b. ⊂ ⌐ 99 ∩∩∩ ||||
      ⊂ ⌐ 99 ∩∩∩ ||
      99 ∩

3. Write each in exponential form using 2, 3, 5, 7, or 11 as a base.
   a. 72   b. 147   c. 275   d. 300

4. For what number k is each of the following true?

    a. $2^2 \cdot 2^k = 2^6$ **b.** $(5^3 \cdot 5^4) \cdot 5^2 = 5^k$ **e.** $(3^2)^4 = 3^k$

    c. $3^{k+2} = 3^5$ **d.** $2^5 \cdot 7^2 = 2^k \cdot 14^2$

5. Express the cardinality of the set {xxxxx xxxxx xxxxx} using each of the following as a base:

    a. Five   **b.** Three   **c.** Seven

6. Make a diagram to illustrate the meaning of the following:

    a. 24_{ten} **b.** 24_{five} **c.** 212_{three} **d.** 1101_{two}

7. Change each as indicated.

    a. $46_{\text{ten}} = \underline{\hspace{1cm}}_{\text{eight}}$ **b.** $150_{\text{ten}} = \underline{\hspace{1cm}}_{\text{five}}$

    c. $432_{\text{five}} = \underline{\hspace{1cm}}_{\text{ten}}$ **d.** $10101_{\text{two}} = \underline{\hspace{1cm}}_{\text{ten}}$

    e. $175_{\text{ten}} = \underline{\hspace{1cm}}_{\text{six}}$

8. **a.** Find $463 + 284 + 798$ using partial sums.

    b. Find $63 \cdot 26$ using the distributive property twice.

    c. Find $572 \cdot 38$ using the lattice method.

    d. Find $584 \div 23$ using the distributive format.

9. **a.** Make an addition table for the base of four.

    b. Find $313_{\text{four}} + 2133_{\text{four}}$.

    c. Find $231_{\text{four}} - 120_{\text{four}}$.

    d. Find $302_{\text{four}} - 33_{\text{four}}$.

10. **a.** Make a multiplication table for the base of four.

    b. Use the distributive property to find $32_{\text{four}} \times 3_{\text{four}}$.

    c. Find $213_{\text{four}} \times 32_{\text{four}}$.

    d. Find $33_{\text{four}} \div 2_{\text{four}}$.

    e. Find $3023_{\text{four}} \div 23_{\text{four}}$.

11. **a.** Is 23_{four} even or is it odd?

    b. Is 132_{four} even?

    c. Is 132_{five} even?

Solution to Sample Problem

The product of 42×31 was performed

$$
\begin{array}{cc}
\cancel{42} & \cancel{31} \\
21 & 62 \\
\cancel{10} & \cancel{124} \\
5 & 248 \\
\cancel{2} & \cancel{496} \\
1 & 992
\end{array}
$$

Why does this algorithm work? How can we just throw away remainders as we move down the left-hand column and still expect a correct answer? Why should we cross out even numbers in the left column?

1. *Understanding the Problem.* The mechanics of the algorithm are straightforward enough. We use a doubling and halving procedure, stopping when we get a 1 in the halving column. We cross out rows of numbers if an even number appears in the left-hand column. The question to be answered is why this works.

2. *Devising a Plan.* We need to investigate further what is really happening in the algorithm. Perhaps it would help to indicate the doubling that takes place in the right-hand column as it is the sum from that column that produces the answer.

3. *Solution.*

$$
\begin{array}{rll}
59 & 43 = & 1 \cdot 43 \\
29 & 86 = & 2 \cdot 43 \\
\cancel{14} & \cancel{172} = & \cancel{4 \cdot 43} \\
7 & 344 = & 8 \cdot 43 \\
3 & 688 = & 16 \cdot 43 \\
1 & \underline{1376} = & 32 \cdot 43 \\
& 2537 &
\end{array}
$$

Notice that $43 + 86 + 344 + 688 + 1376$ can be restated as:

$$(1 \cdot 43) + (2 \cdot 43) + (8 \cdot 43) + (16 \cdot 43) + (32 \cdot 43)$$
$$= (1 + 2 + 8 + 16 + 32) \cdot 43 = 59 \cdot 43$$

Does the sequence of numbers 32, 16, 8, 4, 2, 1 strike you as being familiar? Of course, they relate to base-two numeration.

$$59_{\text{ten}} = \underset{32}{1}\ \underset{16}{1}\ \underset{8}{1}\ \underset{4}{0}\ \underset{2}{1}\ \underset{1}{1}_{\text{two}}$$

So apparently this algorithm has as its foundation the base of two. Crossing evens in the left-hand column somehow eliminate the places where we have zero digits in the base-two representation of 59.

Let us look at the base-ten–base-two conversion using the "Division" algorithm.

$$
\begin{array}{r}
2\ \underline{|59} \\
29\ 1
\end{array}
$$

The first step involved the odd number 59, producing a remainder of 1. So, 59 being odd guaranteed the remainder, thus assuring us that in the base-two representation we should have a digit 1 in the units place. The same is true of the second step.

$$
\begin{array}{r}
2\ \underline{|59} \\
2\ \underline{|29}\ 1 \\
2\ \underline{|14}\ 1 \\
7\ 0
\end{array}
$$

Note, however, that in the third step, 14 is even, so it produces a zero remainder, thus providing a 0 digit in that corresponding slot in the base-two representation. Thus, we do not really "throw away" remainders at all. They are really the digit 1 that appears in the corresponding base-two representation of the number.

$$
\begin{array}{r}
2\ \underline{|59} \\
2\ \underline{|29}\ 1 \\
2\ \underline{|14}\ 1 \\
2\ \underline{|\ 7}\ 0 \qquad 59_{ten} = 111011_{two} \\
2\ \underline{|\ 3}\ 1 \\
1\ 1
\end{array}
$$

4. *Looking Back.* This is an interesting algorithm in the sense that one can use the algorithm to obtain answers that are correct and never be aware of the role that base-two plays in the process. This is what we usually refer to as a *rote* algorithm. All you do is follow the step-by-step procedure and out pops the answer. People did indeed use this algorithm at one time to do their multiplication. How many of them do you think understood the reasons why it worked?

4 NUMBER THEORY AND INTEGERS

Sample Problem

A group of children are to be seated in a cafeteria. If two children are seated at each table, one child remains unseated. When three are seated at each table, two students are left unseated. When four are seated at each table, three are left, and when five are seated at each table, four remain unseated. What is the fewest number of children that could have been involved for this to happen?

4.1 INTRODUCTION TO DIVISIBILITY CONCEPTS

Patterns, relations, and functions are identified as important ingredients of the school mathematics programs in the NCTM Standards. While you have seen a variety of examples of this work in the preceding chapters, it is worth noting that the content of this chapter is a rich source of such concepts.

We have introduced the basic ideas involving sets and used these concepts to generate the set of whole numbers and to verify some properties of the operations on whole numbers. We have looked at the concept of numeration. It should be clear that when we speak of numbers we are speaking of an

183

abstraction, a mental construct regarding the "manyness" of a set. When we speak of a numeral we are interested in the name for a number.

The first part of this chapter will be devoted to some interesting and useful relationships that exist among whole numbers. We will then turn our attention to the need for other numbers—the integers. We are often interested in knowing whether one number is a multiple of another. We say that 18 is a multiple of 3 because if we take the product of 3 and the whole number 6, we get 18. We might also state that 3 divides 18 (6 also obviously divides 18 as 6 times the whole number 3 is 18). Likewise, 5 divides 15 as 5 times the whole number 3 yields 15. In general, then, one whole number a "divides another whole number b if and only if we can find a whole number that when multiplied times a yields b.

Definition 4.1   Given that a and b are whole numbers, with $a \neq 0$, a divides b (written $a \mid b$) if and only if there exists a whole number k such that $a \cdot k = b$.

REMARK 1 Stating that "a divides b" is equivalent to stating that "b is a multiple of a," that "a is a divisor of b," that "a is a factor of b," or that "b is divisible by a."

REMARK 2 Note the restriction that the number a not be 0. This is necessary since if $b \neq 0$, it is impossible to find a number k such that $0 \cdot k = b$.

REMARK 3 $a \mid b$ is a *statement*, asserting that a divides b. It must not be confused with the *numbers* $a \div b$ and $b \div a$.

Using the symbolism for "divides" we can make the following true statements:

$6 \mid 48$ because if $k = 8$ we have $6 \cdot 8 = 48$

$3 \mid 12$ because if $k = 4$ we have $3 \cdot 4 = 12$

$2 \nmid 9$ because there is no whole number k such that $2 \cdot k = 9$

4 is a factor of 24 because $4 \cdot 6 = 24$

56 is a multiple of 7 because $7 \cdot 8 = 56$

0 is a multiple of 2 because $2 \cdot 0 = 0$

7 divides 0 because $7 \cdot 0 = 0$

$9 \mid 108$ because $9 \cdot 12 = 108$

45 is not a multiple of 12 because there is no whole number k for which
$\qquad 12 \cdot k = 45$

We not only can test specific numbers for the "divides" property, but we also can make some more general claims. For example, $a \mid a$ for any nonzero whole number. We know this is the case because no matter what counting number we choose for a, we can simply use $k = 1$. It should also be fairly evident that 1 divides every whole number. For example, $1|5$ because if $k = 5$, then $1 \cdot 5 = 5$. Also, $1|723$ because if we choose $k = 723$, then $1 \cdot 723 = 723$. Another interesting observation can be made regarding the divisors of 0. Clearly $2|0$ because $2 \cdot 0 = 0$ and $5|0$ because $5 \cdot 0 = 0$. In general, for any nonzero number a, $a|0$ because $k = 0$ will always produce a true statement.

Suppose that we know that $a|b$, and furthermore that $b|c$. Can we conclude that $a|c$? For example, we note that $4|8$ and $8|48$. Can we conclude that $4|48$? Apparently the answer is yes, at least for this case. In general, it seems reasonable that if b is a multiple of a and c is a multiple of b, then c is a multiple of a.

PROPERTY 4.1   **For whole numbers a, b, and c with $a \neq 0$ and $b \neq 0$, if $a|b$ and $b|c$, then $a|c$.**

Do you recognize this pattern? This is the transitive pattern that you saw at work in the earlier chapters. We can readily establish the truth of Property 4.1.

Proof Because $a|b$, we know that for some whole number k, $a \cdot k = b$. Likewise, because $b|c$, we can find a whole number m such that $b \cdot m = c$. By substitution for b in this second equation, $(a \cdot k) \cdot m = c$ so $a \cdot (k \cdot m) = c$. Because $k \cdot m$ is a whole number, $a|c$.

Suppose we are told that a divides some number b and also c. Could we conclude that a divides the sum of b and c? For example, $3|12$ and $3|15$ and $3|(12 + 15)$. (That is, $3|27$). Let us again attempt to establish a general proof for this conjecture.

PROPERTY 4.2   **For whole numbers a, b, and c, $a \neq 0$, if $a|b$ and $a|c$, then $a|(b + c)$.**

Proof $a|b$ implies that $a \cdot k = b$ for some whole number k.
$a|c$ implies that $a \cdot m = c$ for some whole number m.
$$a \cdot k + a \cdot m = b + c$$
Therefore, $$a(k + m) = b + c$$
so $a|(b + c)$ because $k + m$ is a whole number.

Two other properties are closely related to Property 4.2. For example, suppose a divides b and a divides $b + c$, does a necessarily divide c? For example, $3|9$ and $3|(9 + 12)$ and 3 also divides 12. Let us consider a proof for the property.

PROPERTY 4.3 **For whole numbers *a*, *b*, and *c* with *a* ≠ 0, if *a*|*b* and *a*|(*b* + *c*), then *a*|*c*.**

> *Proof* *a*|*b* implies that *a* · *k* = *b* for some whole number *k*.
>   *a*|(*b* + *c*) implies *a* · *m* = *b* + *c* for some whole number *m*.
>   *am* = *ak* + *c* by substitution
> Therefore,   *am* − *ak* = *c*
>   *a* · (*m* − *k*) = *c*
> Because *b* + *c* ⩾ *b*, and *b* + *c* = *a* · m and b = *a* · k we may make
> a replacement for variables and write *am* ⩾ *ak*.
> Therefore *m* ⩾ *k*, so *m* − *k* is a whole number and a|c.

PROPERTY 4.4 **For whole numbers *a*, *b*, and *c* with *a* ≠ 0, if *a*|*b* and *a*∤*c*, then *a*∤(*b* + *c*)**

This property is actually the partial contrapositive of Property 4.3, so it is also true. For example, suppose 3|12 and 3∤13, then note that 3∤(12 + 13).

One additional property is useful to our developments in this next section. It simply assures us that if *a* divides some number *b*, then *a* divides the product of *b* times any whole number *c*. For example, 3|15 and 3|(15 · 2).

PROPERTY 4.5 **For whole numbers *a*, *b*, and *c* with *a* ≠ 0, if *a*|*b*, then *a*|(*b* · *c*).**

This should be evident because the assertions that *a* divides *b* assumes that *a* is a factor of *b*. Thus *a* is clearly a factor of *b* · *k*. For example, 2|6, so 2|(6 · 5) is also true.

It should be pointed out that Properties 4.1 through 4.3 also hold if they are extended. For example, if *a*|*b* and *a*|*c* and *a*|*d*, we may safely conclude that *a*|(*b* + *c* + *d*). Also, if *a*|*b* and *b*|*c* and *c*|*d*, then *a*|*d* is a true statement. Such extensions will be of considerable use to us in the next section.

PROBLEM SET 4.1

1. Classify each of the following as true or false:
    a. 6 is a divisor of 24.
    b. 40 is a multiple of 8.
    c. 12 divides 6.
    d. 6 is a factor of 24.
    e. 8 is a divisor of 12.
    f. 16 is a multiple of 2.

2. Mark each of the following as true or false:
    a. 5|5   b. 7|77   c. 2|0   d. 5|(5 · 23)
    e. 7|91   f. 8|(4 · 6)   g. 5|(11 + 4)

what property belong?

3. Provide four specific examples for each of the Properties 4.1–4.5.

4. If a, b, and c are whole numbers with $a \neq 0$ and $b \neq 0$, can you conclude that if $a|c$ and $b|c$, then $ab|c$? Give examples to substantiate your answer.

5. Classify each of the following as true or false. If it is false, give a counter-example. Let a, b, c, d, and e be whole numbers with $a \neq 0$ and $b \neq 0$.
   a. If $a|c$ and $b|c$, then $(a + b)|c$.
   b. If $a \nmid b$ and $a \nmid c$, then $a \nmid (b + c)$.
   c. If $b > c$, $a|b$ and $a|c$, then $a|(b - c)$.
   d. If $a|b$ and $a|c$ and $a|d$ and $a|e$, then $a|(b + c + d + e)$.
   e. If $a|b$ and $a|c$ and $a|d$ and $a \nmid e$, then $a \nmid (b + c + d + e)$.
   f. If $a|(b \cdot c)$, then $a|b$ or $a|c$.

6. Classify each of the following as true or false. (Think carefully before you answer.) If false, show a counterexample.
   a. If a number is divisible by 2 and by 3, then it is divisible by 6.
   b. If a number is divisible by 3, then it is divisible by 9.
   c. If a number is divisible by 9, then it is divisible by 3.
   d. If a number is divisible by 2 and by 4, then it is divisible by 8.
   e. If a number is divisible by 3 and by 5, then it is divisible by 15.
   f. If a number is divisible by 6 and by 8, then it is divisible by 48.

7. a. Use your calculator to verify that $17|7684$, $17|1326$, and $17|(7684 + 1326)$.
   b. Use your calculator to show that $19|1007$, $19|1600$, and $19|(1007 + 1600)$.
   c. Use $a = 42$, $b = 252$, and $c = 14112$ to illustrate the claim that if $a|b$ and $b|c$, then $a|c$.

8. Suppose a, b, and c are whole numbers with $a \neq 0$.
   a. If $a|b$ and $a|c$, does $a|(b \cdot c)$?
   b. If $a \nmid b$ and $a|c$, does $a|(b \cdot c)$?
   c. If $a \nmid b$ and $a \nmid c$ can we conclude that $a \nmid (b \cdot c)$?
   d. If $a|b$ and $a|(b \cdot c)$, can we conclude that $a|c$?
   e. If $a \nmid b$ and $a|(b \cdot c)$, can we conclude that $a|c$?

4.2 SOME DIVISIBILITY RULES

The divisibility concepts we investigated in the last section will be of considerable use to us in the development of this section. We are going to find it very useful to be able to make decisions about whether a certain given number is divisible by other numbers. In several cases simple tests can be made to answer this question without actually having to divide. In order to accomplish this we will need to make use of expanded notation.

In discussing divisibility rules, it is convenient to use some general representation for certain sets of numbers. For example, every two-digit number can be represented by the form $10b + a$, where $a \in \{0, 1, 2, 3, 4, 5, 6, 7, 8, 9\}$ and $b \in \{1, 2, 3, 4, 5, 6, 7, 8, 9\}$. Thus, we may write 57 as $10 \cdot 5 + 7$ and 73 $= 10 \cdot 7 + 3$. Three-digit numbers can be represented as $100c + 10b + a$, four-digit numbers can be represented as $1000d + 100c + 10b + a$, and so on. In general, the letters $a, b, c, \ldots$ simply represent digits.

REMARK   Some people are very careful about the way they use the words *number* and *numeral*. We realize that such phrases as "three-digit number" are technically incorrect. We should say "the number represented by a three-digit numeral." However, such "abuses" of language do not misrepresent the ideas being communicated and, in fact, many times provide economy of communication.

For our first divisibility rule, let us consider one with which you may already be familiar—the rule for divisibility by two. Would you be prepared to state that 468,438 is divisible by two because the last digit is even? Let us show that this is indeed correct. Suppose we have a three-digit number represented by $100c + 10b + a$. Note that $2 \mid 100$, so no matter what digit c represents, $2 \mid 100c$ (Property 4.5 guarantees this). Also, $2 \mid 10$, so $2 \mid 10b$. Now, if $2 \mid a$, then $2 \mid (100c + 10b + a)$. Therefore, 2 divides the three-digit number (Property 4.2 asserts this). However, if $2 \nmid a$, then $2 \nmid (100c + 10b + a)$ and 2 does not divide the number (refer to Property 4.4). Then clearly the units digit is the key; if it is divisible by 2 (is even), then the number is divisible by 2. Since $2 \mid 1000$, $2 \mid 10,000$, and so on, do you see how this rule extends to any number of digits?

Divisibility Rule for 2 A number is divisible by 2 if and only if the units digit of its base-ten numeral is divisible by 2.

The test for divisibility by 5 is much like that for 2 in the sense that only the units digit is of real concern to us. Because $5 \mid 10$, $5 \mid 100$, and so on, given a three-digit number, we can again write $100c + 10b + a$ and note that $5 \mid 100c$ and $5 \mid 10b$. Therefore, if $5 \mid a$, then $5 \mid (100c + 10b + a)$, but if $5 \nmid a$, then $5 \nmid (100c + 10b + a)$.

Divisibility Rule for 5 A number is divisible by 5 if and only if the units digit of its base-ten numeral is 0 or 5.

5|845 because the units digit is 5

5|4870 because the units digit is 0

5∤4682 because the units digit is not 0 or 5

Let us next consider a rule for divisibility by 3. Consider the three-digit number $100c + 10b + a$ once again. The expanded form is of interest; note that $100c + 10b + a = (99 + 1)c + (9 + 1)b + a$. Let us apply the distributive rule twice and write $(99c + c) + (9b + b) + a$. Then we may rearrange the terms to write $(99c + 9b) + (c + b + a)$. Note that because $3|99$ and $3|9$, then $3|(99c + 9b)$. Therefore, if $3|(c + b + a)$, then $3|[(99c + 9b) + (c + b + a)]$. That is, if 3 divides the sum of the digits, then it divides the number itself. Furthermore, if $3∤(c + b + a)$, then $3∤(100c + 10b + a)$. This rule for a three-digit number can be extended readily to any number of digits since $1000 = (999 + 1)$ and $3|999$, $10,000 = (9999 + 1)$ and $3|9999$, and so on. Let us state the general situation regarding divisibility by 3:

Divisibility Rule for 3 A number is divisible by 3 if and only if the sum of the digits of its base-ten numeral is divisible by 3.

$3|54$ because $3|(5 + 4)$

$3|672$ because $3|(6 + 7 + 2)$

$3∤4811$ because $3∤(4 + 8 + 1 + 1)$

We can develop a divisibility rule for 11 in much the same way that we did for 3. Let us note that a pattern exists that will be of considerable help to us.

$$
\begin{aligned}
10 &= 11 - 1 &\text{and } 11|11\\
100 &= 99 + 1 &\text{and } 11|99\\
1000 &= 1001 - 1 &\text{and } 11|1001\\
10,000 &= 9999 + 1 &\text{and } 11|9999\\
100,000 &= 100,001 - 1 &\text{and } 11|100,001
\end{aligned}
$$

Therefore, given a five-digit number we may write

$$
\begin{aligned}
&10,000e + 1000d + 100c + 10b + a\\
&= (9999 + 1)e + (1001 - 1)d + (99 + 1)c + (11 - 1)b + a\\
&= (9999e + 1001d + 99c + 11b) + (e - d + c - b + a)\\
&= (9999e + 1001d + 99c + 11b) + (e + c + a) - (d + b)
\end{aligned}
$$

Because $11|9999e$, $11|1001d$, $11|99c$, and $11|11b$, then $11|(9999e + 1001d + 99c + 11b)$. Therefore, if $11|[(e + c + a) - (d + b)]$, then 11 divides the five-digit number. However, if $11∤[(e + c + a) - (d + b)]$, then 11 does not divide the number.

Divisibility Rule for 11 A number is divisible by 11 if and only if the difference between the sum of the digits in the odd-numbered places of its base-ten numeral (counting from right to left) and the sum of the digits in the even-numbered places is divisible by 11.

$11\,|\,4290$ because $(9 + 4) - (0 + 2) = 11$ and $11\,|\,11$

$11\,|\,34562$ because $(6 + 4) - (2 + 5 + 3) = 0$ and $11\,|\,0$

$11\,|\,7383926$ because $(6 + 9 + 8 + 7) - (2 + 3 + 3) = 22$ and $11\,|\,22$

$11\,|\,548361$ because $(6 + 8 + 5) - (1 + 3 + 4) = 11$ and $11\,|\,11$

$11\nmid 6432$ because $(3 + 6) - (2 + 4) = 3$ and $11\nmid 3$

REMARK Notice that the rule for 11 does not specify whether to take the sum of the even-placed digits minus the sum of the odd-placed digits or the other way around. In fact, to be assured that we will obtain a difference that is a whole number, we simply state that you should find the sums, then subtract the smaller from the larger. After our work with integers we will be prepared to show why this is true.

We could develop several additional divisibility rules by using arguments similar to these just completed. A rule for 4 would be prompted by the observation that although $4\nmid 10$, 4 does divide 100, 1000, etc. Therefore, $1000d + 100c + 10b + a$ could be broken into two parts where $4\,|\,(1000d + 100c)$ and then question whether 4 divides $(10b + a)$. If $4\,|\,(10b + a)$, then $4\,|\,[(1000d + 100c) + (10b + a)]$, but if $4\nmid(10b + a)$, then $4\nmid[(1000d + 100c) + (10b + a)]$. But note that $(10b + a)$ represents the two-digit number obtained by selecting the two-digit number consisting of the tens digit and the units digit.

Divisibility Rule for 4 A number is divisible by 4 if and only if the number represented by its last two digits is divisible by 4.

REMARK Let us make one additional comment before we begin the next problem set. Your calculator is a very useful tool and may be used in a variety of places to help to develop patterns and ideas. A good example of this arises in the next problem set as we look at divisibility rules for 6 and for 7. We do not claim these to be "useful" rules in the sense that people commonly use them. One is much more likely to simply do a divisibility test for 2 and for 3 to decide about divisibility for 6. However, a nice pattern is available as one considers the development; for this reason, some sixth-grade students would enjoy working with it. Note that the calculator does help to find the patterns. For example, we will wish to write 10,000 as the sum of $a + b$, where $6\,|\,a$ and b is a whole number less than 6. To do this simply divide 10,000 by 6. Thus, $10,000 \div 6 = 1666.66\ldots$, which indicates that we have 1666 whole groups of 6. Then $1666 \cdot 6 = 9996$ accounts for all but 4 of the 10,000. Therefore, $10,000 = 9996 + 4$ is the desired grouping.

PROBLEM SET 4.2

1. Which of the following counting numbers are divisible by 2?

   a. 84   **b.** 76   **c.** 2843   **d.** 7654   **e.** 36,850

   f. 76,545   **g.** 4,628,470   **h.** 420,579   **i.** 8,425,611

2. Which of the numbers in Problem 1 are divisible by 3?

3. Which of the numbers in Problem 1 are divisible by 5?

4. Which of the numbers in Problem 1 are divisible by 11?

5. **a.** Is it true that $11 | 99,999$?

   b. In establishing the divisibility rule for 11, we stated a pattern showing $1000 = 1001 - 1$, $10,000 = 9999 + 1$, and so on. If we continue this pattern, how would we rewrite 1,000,000?

6. When we developed the divisibility rule for 3, we wrote $100c + 10b + a = (99c + 9b) + (c + b + a)$.

   a. Why does $9 | (99c + 9b)$?

   b. If $9 | (c + b + a)$, then $9 | (100c + 10b + a)$. Why is this true?

   c. State a divisibility rule for 9.

7. Which of the following numbers are divisible by 9?

   a. 486   **b.** 528   **c.** 5824

   d. 7997   **e.** 95481   **f.** 4,689,621

8. Determine whether each of the following is true:

   a. If $2 | a$ and $3 | a$, then $6 | a$.

   b. If $2 | b$ and $5 | b$, then $10 | b$.

   c. If $2 | c$ and $6 | c$, then $12 | c$.

   d. If $2 | d$ and $3 | d$ and $5 | d$, then $30 | d$.

   e. If $4 | e$ and $6 | e$, then $24 | e$.

   f. If $2 | f$ and $11f$, then $22 | f$.

9. Determine if each of the following is true without dividing the given numbers (you may wish to refer to Problem 8):

   a. $6 | 3348$ **b.** $15 | 26,475$ **c.** $45 | 783,425$

   d. $33 | 321,465,237$ **e.** $55 | 4,674,945$ **f.** $30 | 468,230$

10. Fill each blank with the largest digit that makes the statement true.

    a. $3 | 46\_\_$ **b.** $5 | 3\_\_0$ **c.** $9 | 2\_\_936$

    d. $3 | 4\_\_23$ **e.** $11 | 5\_\_32$ **f.** $11 | 13\_\_56$

11. Decide whether each is true or false, then justify your answer.

    a. If a number is divisible by 6, then it is divisible by 2.

    b. If a number is divisible by 2, then it is divisible by 6.

  c. If a number is divisible by 2 and by 3, then it is divisible by 6.

  d. If a number is not divisible by 6, then it is not divisible by 2.

  e. If a number is not divisible by 3, then it is not divisible by 6.

12. To devise a divisibility rule for 6, we might proceed as we did when we developed the rule for 3. That is, write each multiple of 10 as a sum, where one of the addends is divisible by 6 and the other is a number less than 6.

  a. Complete the following:

$$10 = 6 + 4$$
$$100 = 96 + 4$$
$$1000 = \underline{\quad\quad}$$
$$10000 = \underline{\quad\quad}$$

  b. Complete the following:

$$10b = (6 + 4)b = 6b + 4b \quad \text{and } 6 \,|\, 6b$$
$$100c = (96 + 4)c = 96c + 4c \quad \text{and } 6 \,|\, 96c$$
$$1000d = (\underline{\quad})d \quad\quad\quad\quad \text{and } 6 \,|\, \underline{\quad}$$
$$10000e = \underline{\quad\quad} \quad\quad\quad\quad \text{and } 6 \,|\, \underline{\quad}$$

  c. Does $6 \,|\, (6b + 96c + \underline{996d} + \underline{9996e})$? Why?

  d. State a divisibility rule for 6.

13. **a.** Note that $8 \,|\, 1000$, therefore $8 \,|\, 1000d$. Does $8 \,|\, 10{,}000$?

  b. Does $8 \,|\, 10{,}000e$? Why?

  c. Is it true that $8 \,|\, (10{,}000e + 1000d)$? Why?

  d. Under what conditions does $8 \,|\, [(10{,}000e + 1000d) + (100c + (10b + a)]$?

  e. What is the significance of the term $(100c + 10b + a)$?

  f. State a divisibility rule for 8.

14. **a.** Does $16 \,|\, 1000$? Does $16 \,|\, 10{,}000$? Does $16 \,|\, 100{,}000$?

  b. Suggest a divisibility rule for 16.

15. Consider the three-digit number $100c + 10b + a$. Let $100 = 98 + 2$ and $10 = 7 + 3$. Then $100c + 10b + a = (98 + 2)c + (7 + 3)b + a = 98c + 2c + 7b + 3b + a = (98c + 7b) + (2c + 3b + a)$.

  a. Can we conclude that $7 \,|\, (98c + 7b)$? Why?

  b. If $7 \,|\, (2c + 3b + a)$, then $7 \,|\, [(98c + 7b) + (2c + 3b + a)]$. Why?

  c. If $7 \nmid (2c + 3b + a)$, then $7 \nmid [(98c + 7b) + (2c + 3b + a)]$. Why?

  d. Suggest a divisibility rule for 7 that will hold for any three-digit number.

e. Test your rule for the following numbers.

(i) 896   **(ii)** 574   **(iii)** 496

 16. a. To make a general divisibility rule for 7, we would need to continue breaking the numbers 10, 100, 1000, and so on apart until a pattern emerged. Use your calculator to continue the following sequences. Find numbers a and b such that $10^n = a + b$, $7|a$, and $b < 7$.

$$10 = 7 + 3$$
$$100 = 98 + 2$$
$$1,000 = 994 + 6$$
$$10,000 = 9996 + 4$$
$$100,000 = \underline{\qquad}$$
$$1,000,000 = \underline{\qquad}$$
$$10,000,000 = \underline{\qquad}$$

b. Suggest a divisibility rule for 7.

c. Use your rule to decide which of the following numbers are divisible by 7.

(i) 7423   **(ii)** 1015   **(iii)** 1953   **(iv)** 12,540   **(v)** 84,632

(vi) 463,845

17. What is the smallest nonzero number that is divisible by all the numbers 1 through 12?

18. Susie has 152 stamps. If she wishes to use six per page, will she have enough stamps to fill each page used in her book? (Can you decide this by using divisibility rules?)

19. John is the grand champion at playing marbles. He now has 2142 marbles in his collection. Can you answer the following questions *without* actually dividing?

(a) Could he divide his marbles evenly among six friends?

(b) Could he divide them evenly among 18 friends?

(c) Could he divide them evenly among 14 friends?

Pedagogical Problems and Activities

20. Describe how you might get a child to discover the divisibility rule for 3 by using a sequence of examples.

21. Suppose we have a three-digit number such that all three digits are even and different. The sum of the digits is 12, and the product is less than 40. The sum of the hundreds digit and the ones digit is less than the tens digit. What is the number?

22. Suppose your favorite football team scored 20 points in its last game. How many different ways could such a score be obtained?

Touchdown (TD): 6 points

Point after touchdown (PAT): 1 point

Field goal (FG): 3 points

Safety (5): 2 points

23. We need to provide problems that can provide problem-solving experience for children at all grade levels. This might be useful at the third- or fourth-grade level.

A dart board has three circles that allow the player to score.

a. Show that a score of 34 can be obtained.

b. What is the *fewest* number of darts that could be thrown to obtain a score of 34?

4.3   PRIME AND COMPOSITE NUMBERS

We now turn our attention to another aspect of counting numbers. The Greeks were quite interested in numbers and their relationships. The Greek invention called the *sieve of Erathosthenes* is used in mathematics to sort out a special subset of the counting numbers. Suppose that we start writing the counting numbers as follows:

$$\begin{array}{cccccc}
1 & 2 & 3 & 4 & 5 & 6 \\
7 & 8 & 9 & 10 & 11 & 12 \\
13 & 14 & 15 & 16 & 17 & 18 \\
19 & 20 & 21 \ldots
\end{array}$$

This scheme simply allows us to write the numbers, six per line, and continue to any number desired. In Table 4.1 we list the numbers through 100 and suggest that you do the following. Discard the number 1 (we will discuss the

TABLE 4.1

1	②	③	4	⑤	6
⑦	8	9	10	⑪	12
⑬	14	15	16	⑰	18
⑲	20	21	22	㉓	24
25	26	27	28	㉙	30
㉛	32	33	34	35	36
㊲	38	39	40	㊶	42
㊸	44	45	46	㊼	48
49	50	51	52	㊾	54
55	56	57	58	㊾	60
㊽	62	63	64	65	66
㊼	68	69	70	㉛	72
㊼	74	75	76	77	78
㉛	80	81	82	㊳	84
85	86	87	88	㊆	90
91	92	93	94	95	96
㉗	98	99	100		

reason for this omission later). Then each number after 2 that is a multiple of 2 is crossed out with a vertical slash |. Note that those numbers crossed out are neatly arranged in columns. Now move past the number 3 and cross out each multiple of 3 with a vertical squiggle. Do you notice again the pattern down the columns? Do the same with 5, again marking out multiples of 5 with a diagonal slash /. Next starting at 7, cross out every seventh number with a diagonal slash \. Do you again recognize a pattern? The next number not yet crossed out is 11. Keep it, but cross out each multiple of 11. The next number would be 13. However, notice that for both 11 and 13, we do not actually find anything new to cross out in the table. This will also be true of 17, 19, and the other numbers not yet crossed out. We are left with the following set:

{2, 3, 5, 7, 11, 13, 17, 19, 23, 29, 31, 37, 41, 43, 47, 53, 59, 61, 67, 71, 73, 79, 83, 89, 97}.

These numbers are said to be the *prime numbers* less than 100.

Definition 4.2   A counting number p, greater than 1, is called a *prime number* if and only if it has no divisors (factors) other than itself and 1. Counting numbers greater than 1 that are not prime numbers are called *composite numbers*.

As a result of this definition, the whole numbers can be partitioned into three mutually disjoint sets consisting of {0, 1}, the set of prime numbers, and the set of composite numbers. In the counting numbers through 100 we found 25 prime numbers. It should be expected that we can find many primes greater than 100. For example, 101 is prime, as is 103. We will soon return to the question of how many primes exist. First let us consider some applications of primes.

The prime factorization of a composite number is frequently of interest in elementary mathematics. Suppose we are asked to write the composite number 15 as a product of prime numbers. We may easily observe that $3 \cdot 5 = 15$ and both 3 and 5 are prime numbers. Also, $33 = 3 \cdot 11$ and $35 = 5 \cdot 7$. However, $12 = 4 \cdot 3$, but 4 is not prime. In this case we might write $12 = 2 \cdot 2 \cdot 3$. Various procedures can be used to find the prime factors of a given composite number. Probably the simplest (at least when working with relatively small numbers) involves factoring into any two easily recognized factors and then continuing to factor each until only primes are obtained. Consider these examples:

$$8 = 2 \cdot 4 = 2 \cdot 2 \cdot 2$$
$$56 = 7 \cdot 8 = 7 \cdot 2 \cdot 2 \cdot 2$$
$$150 = 10 \cdot 15 = 2 \cdot 5 \cdot 3 \cdot 5$$

The divisibility rules are useful in this procedure. For example, suppose we are interested in writing 171 as a product of prime factors. Because the sum of the digits is 9, we know that both 9 and 3 divide 171. Then we may write $171 = 9 \cdot 19 = 3 \cdot 3 \cdot 19$. It should be clear that it does not really matter how we factor the first time. For example, $171 = 3 \cdot 57 = 3 \cdot 3 \cdot 19$, and the same set of prime factors is obtained once again.

We often find a slightly different format for prime factorization employed in elementary-school materials. They use what is commonly referred to as a *factor tree*. Below are three possible "trees" to use in factoring 72 into the product of primes. Note that in each case we finished with the same set of prime factors, three 2's and two 3's (except for the order in which the factors were written). This result of obtaining the same prime factorization is not unique to 72, but is true for any composite number. It is commonly referred to as the *fundamental theorem of arithmetic*.

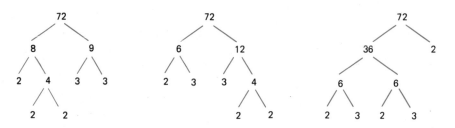

PROPERTY 4.6   **A counting number that is greater than 1 either is prime or is composite and has a unique prime factorization. (Any two prime factorizations of the number are the same except for the order in which the factors occur.)**

> REMARK The reason that we do not wish to call 1 a prime number
> should now be clear. If 1 were classified as a prime number, then Property
> 4.6 would not be true. For example, 10 would not have a unique factoriza-
> tion because 10 = 2 · 5 and also 10 = 2 · 5 · 1, one having two prime
> factors and the other three.

The fundamental theorem of arithmetic does not help us to determine
whether a given counting number is prime. It does, however, assure us that
if it is composite it will have a unique prime factorization. For example, is
161 prime or is it composite? The question could be restated as follows: Does
161 have divisors other than 1 and 161? Surely we will not have to test *every*
number less than 161 to answer the question! In fact, the fundamental theorem of arithmetic again comes to our rescue. If 161 is composite, then it
must have divisors that are primes. Therefore, we only need to test primes.
Our divisibility tests also serve our needs well. We know that $2\nmid161$ because
the units digit is odd, $3\nmid161$ because the sum of the digits is 8 and $3\nmid8$, and
$5\nmid161$ because the units digit is not 0 or 5. Let us divide to test 7. Do you agree
that $7\,|\,161$? Thus, we know that 161 is composite.

Suppose we want to determine whether 323 is prime. We know now that
we only need to test prime numbers, but do we need to test all primes less
than 323? Indeed we do not. Since 2 is the smallest prime, we could actually
not need to try any primes greater than $\frac{1}{2}$ of 323. But we can do even better
than that. Consider the sequences in Table 4.2.

TABLE 4.2

a	b
1 · 36 = 36	1 · 28 = 28
2 · 18 = 36	2 · 14 = 28
3 · 12 = 36	→ 4 · 7 = 28
4 · 9 = 36	7 · 4 = 28
→ 6 · 6 = 36	14 · 2 = 28
9 · 4 = 36	28 · 1 = 28
12 · 3 = 36	
18 · 2 = 36	
36 · 1 = 36	

Notice that after a certain point in each sequence, the first-named factor
simply repeats previously named second factors. Once this "turn around"
point has been reached, no new pairs of factors appear. Applying this bit of
reasoning to our number 323, we should be able to start testing primes and
continue until we find that prime p such that $p^2 \geqslant 323$. If we have found no
factor to that point, the number must be prime. Because $19^2 = 361$, we must
simply test the primes 2, 3, 5, 7, 11, 13, and 17. It is interesting to find that
none of these divides 323 until we get to 17. Thus, $323 = 17 \cdot 19$.

EXAMPLE

Is 473 prime? Because $23^2 = 529$, we must test the primes 2, 3, 5, 7, 11, 13, 17, and 19. We can easily eliminate 2, 3, and 5. Notice, however, that 11 is a divisor. Thus, $473 = 11 \cdot 43$ and so is composite.

As was mentioned earlier, the ancient Greeks were quite interested in number theory. An interesting problem they considered had to do with formulas that would build primes. Some of these are of considerable interest, particularly with a calculator to help do some of the work. Suppose that we use the product of primes to build new numbers as follows:

$$a = 2 \cdot 3 + 1 = 7$$
$$b = 2 \cdot 3 \cdot 5 + 1 = 31$$
$$c = 2 \cdot 3 \cdot 5 \cdot 7 + 1 = 211$$
$$d = 2 \cdot 3 \cdot 5 \cdot 7 \cdot 11 + 1 = 2311$$

Note that each of these numbers is prime. (You should verify this fact.) Now consider $e = 2 \cdot 3 \cdot 5 \cdot 7 \cdot 11 \cdot 13 + 1 = 30031$. This number is composite and may be written as $59 \cdot 509$. It is of interest to note that $2 \nmid e$, $3 \nmid e$, ..., $13 \nmid e$ because each would leave a remainder of 1. That is, the prime divisor 59 is larger than any of the primes used to build the number.

> REMARK The reasoning used in the examples just completed will be returned to shortly as we prove Property 4.6. This is a good example of how arguments made for specific numbers may be extended into a general argument.

Let us consider now the question of the number of primes. To find the primes in the second-hundred counting numbers we could simply continue the sieve idea. In fact, we can imagine it extending indefinitely and can perhaps visualize the crossing out of multiples of the primes as we proceed. Can you imagine actually trying to do this to find the primes between 8600 and 8700? It could be done, but it does not sound like very interesting work. Intuitively, it would seem that the primes would get more scarce as we moved into larger and larger numbers. Although this is indeed true, the Greeks long ago reasoned that we would never find a last prime number. In fact, Euclid proved the set of primes to be infinite over 2000 years ago. We include a proof essentially like that presented by Euclid; observe the simplicity and elegance of his reasoning.

PROPERTY 4.7   **The set of prime numbers is infinite.**

Euclid's Argument

Euclid reasoned that the set of primes either is finite in number or is infinite. He assumed that the set was finite, then showed that this led to a contradiction. Thus, the assumption that the set was finite must be false; therefore, it is true that the set is infinite. More formally, his proof was as follows. Assume that the set is finite and therefore must have a largest prime; call it p_l. Then the set of all primes can be tabulated as $P = \{2, 3, 5, 7, 11, 13, 17, 19, \ldots, p_l\}$. Consider the number formed by taking the product of all the primes 2 through p_l. This number, $2 \cdot 3 \cdot 5 \cdot 7 \cdot \cdots \cdot p_l$, is obviously composite because 2 divides it, as does 3, and so on. However, what about the number $k = 2 \cdot 3 \cdot 5 \cdot 7 \cdot \cdots \cdot p_l + 1$? According to the fundamental theorem of arithmetic, k is either prime or composite. Note that $k \notin P$, so if it is prime it is not included in the set of all primes, which contradicts our hypothesis that p_l is the last prime. If, on the other hand, k is composite, it can be factored into primes. But notice that $2 \nmid k$, $3 \nmid k$, and $5 \nmid k$. In fact, none of the numbers in P will divide k. Thus it must be divisible by some prime greater than p_l, again contradicting our assumption that all the primes were already in P. Thus, the set of primes is not finite. Therefore, the set of primes is infinite.

> REMARK The proof just given is an example of the powerful thinking applied by the ancient Greeks to a variety of subject areas. Does it not seem strange that while these people could reason so clearly, they still had such an unwieldy numeration system?

Even though the set of primes is infinite, we are still faced with the practical problem of deciding whether a given number is prime.

Euclid's argument settles the question about the number of primes. It is an infinite set. There will be no "last prime." However, it tells us nothing about the distribution of primes. Computers have been used to screen for primes. Table 4.3 shows a partial listing of primes.

Some very large primes have been discovered in recent years, most of them of the form $2^p - 1$, where p is a prime. (These are referred to as *Mersenne primes* in honor of the French mathematician Marion Mersenne, 1588–1648.) In 1963, $2^{11213} - 1$ was discovered to be prime at the University of Illinois. This number has 3376 digits! In 1971, Dr. Bryant Tuckerman of IBM found that $2^{19937} - 1$ was a prime, and in 1978 two high-school students, Laura Nickel and Curt Noll of Hayward, California, discovered that $2^{21701} - 1$ is prime. Recently the number $2^{216091} - 1$ was shown to be prime. This number contains 65,050 digits and was discovered by computer scientists while testing a newly installed computer. These are indeed large numbers. Surely Euclid would have been excited if he were with us today!

TABLE 4.3 DISTRIBUTION OF PRIMES

Interval	Number of Primes in the Interval
1 to 100	25
100 to 200	21
200 to 300	16
300 to 400	16
400 to 500	17
500 to 600	14
600 to 700	16
700 to 800	14
800 to 900	15
900 to 1000	14
.	
.	
.	
10^{12} to $(10^{12} + 100)$	4
$(10^{12} + 400)$ to $(10^{12} + 500)$	2
$(10^{12} + 800)$ to $(10^{12} + 900)$	1
$(10^{12} + 900)$ to $(10^{12} + 1000)$	6

PROBLEM SET 4.3

1. Use the sieve method to find all prime numbers between 100 and 150.

2. Make a factor tree for each of the following:
   a. 72   b. 360   c. 120   d. 108   e. 2000   f. 600

3. Use the divisibility rules to help factor each of the following into the product of prime numbers:
   a. 75   b. 84   c. 96   d. 114   e. 119   f. 184
   g. 513   h. 223   i. 512   j. 293   k. 2187   l. 1067

4. Which of the following are prime numbers
   a. 411   b. 737   c. 501   d. 1111   e. 1457   f. 299

5. a. Find four consecutive composite numbers.
   b. Find five consecutive composite numbers.
   c. Find seven consecutive composite numbers.
   d. Find ten consecutive composite numbers.

6. Show that $(7 \cdot 6 \cdot 5 \cdot 4 \cdot 3 \cdot 2) + 1$ has a prime factor larger than 7.

7. a. Use your calculator to determine whether 1517 is prime.
   b. Is 2173 prime?

8. What is the intersection of the set of even counting numbers with the set of prime numbers?

9. Can a number be a product of four different primes and also the product of five different primes? Why?

10. The claim is made that "If the product of two counting numbers is even, then at least one of the two numbers is even." Do you believe this to be true? Justify your answer.

11. **a.** Can we have two consecutive numbers that are prime?
  b. Can we have three consecutive numbers that are prime?

12. How many counting numbers are there with exactly three prime factors? How do you know?

13. **a.** Find all the divisors of 2^6. (*Hint:* Take the factors one at a time, 2 at a time, 3 at a time, and so on. Thus, 1 is a divisor because it divides every counting number, 2 is a divisor, $2 \cdot 2 = 4$ is a divisor, $2 \cdot 2 \cdot 2 = 8$ is a divisor, ... $2 \cdot 2 \cdot 2 \cdot 2 \cdot 2 \cdot 2 = 64$ is a divisor)
  b. Find all the divisors of 3^5.
  c. Write all the divisors of $2^3 \cdot 3^2$.
  d. How many divisors will $2^6 \cdot 3^5$ have?
  e. How many divisors will $p^7 \cdot q^8$ have?

14. Pairs of primes that differ by 2 are called *twin primes.*
  a. List all the twin primes less than 100.
  b. Is it true that for each pair of twin primes listed in part *a*, except for 3 and 5, the composite number between the twin primes is a multiple of 6?
  c. Do you expect the composite number between two primes, except in the case of 3 and 5, always to be a multiple of 6? Can you argue that if p and $p + 2$ are the twin primes, then $p + 1$ (the composite between them) must be a multiple of 2? Why must it be a multiple of 3? (You might try reasoning like that used by the Greeks. If it were not a multiple of 3, what contradiction would be reached?)

15. **a.** A counting number a is called a *perfect square* if and only if there is a counting number b such that $b^2 = a$. (Thus 25 is a perfect square because $5^2 = 25$, and 30 is not a perfect square because no counting number has a square of 30.) Suppose we have a counting number greater than 1 that is a perfect square. What seems to be true of the prime factorization for 36? For 121? For 144?
  b. Could you argue that, in general, each prime factor occurs an even number of times?

Pedagogical Problems and Activities

16. Suppose a sixth-grade student says "If I multiply 2 times itself enough times, I will get a number that is divisible by 3." What do you say?

17. Suppose a child in your fifth-grade class states "If a number is divisible by 8 and also by 6, then it must be divisible by 48." What do you say?

18. Suppose a sixth-grade child says "I know every number that has exactly 3 divisors." What do you say?

4.4 MORE ABOUT NUMBER THEORY

In the last section, we proved that the set of prime numbers is infinite. It has been called to your attention from the sieve of Eratosthenes that 2 and 3 are the only *consecutive* numbers that are prime. However, we have many examples of twin primes such as 5 and 7, and 11 and 13. (Problem 14 in Problem Set 4.3 talked about these.) How many twin primes are there? Is it an infinite set? This question has to date not been answered. Some very large pairs have been found, such as 1,000,000,009,649 and 1,000,000,009,651, but no one has been able to prove that the set of twin primes is infinite.

Let us turn our attention to composite numbers. We know that the set of primes is infinite, and that the primes greater than 3 are never consecutive numbers. Do you suppose it is possible to find four consecutive composite numbers? (You did this in an earlier problem set). You could find the answer simply by looking at the sieve of Erathosthenes. But do you suppose you could find 10 consecutive composites? First, let us recall that if $a = 2 \cdot 3 \cdot 4 \cdot 5$, we may assert that $2|a$, $3|a$, $4|a$, and $5|a$. Therefore, if $n = 11 \cdot 10 \cdot 9 \cdot 8 \cdot 7 \cdot 6 \cdot 5 \cdot 4 \cdot 3 \cdot 2 \cdot 1$, we may state that $11|n$, $10|n$, $9|n$, and so on, down to $2|n$ (1 also divides n, but we will not find that very useful for our purposes). We usually refer to $11 \cdot 10 \cdots \cdots 3 \cdot 2 \cdot 1$ as 11! and call it "eleven factorial." Thus, $5! = 5 \cdot 4 \cdot 3 \cdot 2 \cdot 1$ and $3! = 3 \cdot 2 \cdot 1$. We may then reason that because $2|11!$ and $2|2$, then $2|(11! + 2)$. Likewise, $3|(11! + 3)$, $4|(11! + 4)$, $5|(11! + 5)$, $6|(11! + 6)$, $7|(11! + 7)$, $8|(11! + 8)$, $9|(11! + 9)$, $11|(11! + 10)$, and $11|(11! + 11)$. Therefore, all the numbers $11! + 2$ through $11! + 11$ are composite numbers. Furthermore, they are consecutive numbers, because in each case we are adding just one more to its predecessor. Thus, $(11! + 2)$, $(11! + 3)$, ... , $(11! + 11)$ are 10 consecutive composite numbers. Note that we did not claim that these were the smallest such numbers possible, but the scheme is beautiful. Can we find 800 consecutive composites? Of course we can. Simply use $(801! + 2)$, $(801! + 3)$, ... , $(801! + 801)$ and we have such a set. Could we find 8,000,000 consecutive composites? Of course, but such huge numbers stagger the imagination even though we know they exist!

Because the primes are irregularly positioned in the counting numbers, it is often somewhat difficult to determine whether a specific number is prime. Therefore, the ancient Greeks tried very hard to find a formula that, if numbers were fed into it, would produce a prime number. We will look at one potential formula here and let you try some others in the problem set. Consider the number $k = n^2 - n + 41$, where n is a whole number. If $n = 0$, then $k = 41$, which is prime; if $n = 1$, $k = 41$ again; if $n = 2$, $k = 4 - 2 + 41 = 43$, which is also prime. Several other results are shown in Table 4.4. Notice that in each case the formula did indeed produce a prime number. At first it appears that we have a successful prime-builder for any counting number substituted for n. But what happens when $n = 41$? Then $k = 41^2 - 41 + 41 = 41^2$. But $41^2 = 1681$ and is not prime because 41 divides it. Thus, our formula does not always yield a prime.

TABLE 4.4

n	1	2	3	4	5	6	7	8	9	10
$n^2 - n + 41$	41	43	47	53	61	71	83	97	113	131

Many other interesting relationships hold among numbers; some have been verified and others are still open questions. Goldbach, an eighteenth-century Russian mathematician, conjectured that "every even counting number greater than 2 can be written as the sum of two primes (not necessarily different)." For example, $4 = 2 + 2$, $6 = 3 + 3$, $8 = 5 + 3$, $10 = 7 + 3$ (or $10 = 5 + 5$ if you prefer), and $12 = 7 + 5$. This conjecture has been verified for rather large numbers, but the statement that it is true for all even numbers greater than 2 is still only a conjecture.

Some people find number patterns to be of great interest. The ancient Greeks apparently found them to be so, because a great deal of work was done by them in this area. We have included some problems of this type in the next set of exercises.

Another area of interest to some persons is that of mental calculations. Many calculations can be done easily if we simply apply certain of the basic properties. For example, the product $(24 \cdot 25) \cdot 4$ could be easily accomplished as follows:

$$(24 \cdot 25) \cdot 4 = 24 \cdot (25 \cdot 4)$$
$$= 24 \cdot 100$$
$$= 2400$$

The application of the associative property is of considerable help in this case, as it is in the next example.

$$(21 \cdot 5) \cdot 20 = 21 \cdot (5 \cdot 20)$$
$$= 21 \cdot 100$$
$$= 2100$$

Note that $4 \cdot 53$ can be written as $4 \cdot (50 + 3)$ and then as $4 \cdot 50 + 4 \cdot 3$. Thus, we may write the following:

$$
\begin{aligned}
4 \cdot 53 &= 4 \cdot (50 + 3) \\
&= 4 \cdot 50 + 4 \cdot 3 \\
&= 200 + 12 \\
&= 212
\end{aligned}
$$

We sometimes wish to square a number, such as 31^2. Let us note that $31 = 30 + 1$, therefore $31^2 = (30 + 1)^2$. But

$$
\begin{aligned}
(30 + 1)^2 &= (30 + 1) \cdot (30 + 1) \\
&= (30 + 1) \cdot 30 + (30 + 1) \cdot 1 \\
&= 30 \cdot 30 + 1 \cdot 30 + 30 \cdot 1 + 1 \cdot 1 \\
&= 900 + 30 + 30 + 1 \\
&= 961
\end{aligned}
$$

The pattern involved here is certainly worth noting. Let us look at another example. Suppose that we wish to perform a similar operation on $(a + b)^2$, where a and b are any whole numbers.

$$
\begin{aligned}
(a + b)^2 &= (a + b) \cdot (a + b) \\
&= (a + b) \cdot a + (a + b) \cdot b \\
&= a \cdot a + b \cdot a + a \cdot b + b \cdot b \\
&= a^2 + ab + ab + b^2 \\
&= a^2 + 2ab + b^2
\end{aligned}
$$

Notice that if we want the square of a sum of two numbers, we can find the result by taking the square of the first number plus twice the product of the two numbers, plus the square of the second number.

EXAMPLE

Use the procedure above to find the square of 43.

$$
\begin{aligned}
43^2 &= (40 + 3)^2 \\
&= 40^2 + 2 \cdot (40 \cdot 3) + 3^2 \\
&= 1600 + 240 + 9 \\
&= 1849
\end{aligned}
$$

Another pattern that is useful involves squaring numbers in which the units digit is a five. Any such number may be written in the form $10t + 5$ for some counting number t. For example, $25 = 10 \cdot 2 + 5$, $245 = 10 \cdot 24 + 5$, and $4865 = 10 \cdot 486 + 5$. Then if we square a number with a units digit of 5 we may write $(10t + 5)^2$ and use the patterns discussed in the preceding paragraph. Thus, we may write the following:

$$(10t + 5)^2 = (10t)^2 + 2(10t)(5) + (5)^2$$
$$= 100t^2 + 100t + 25$$
$$= 100t(t + 1) + 25$$

According to this pattern, to square 65 we would write $65^2 = 100(6)(7) + 25 = 4225$. Try using this pattern to square 35. Now try to verbalize the pattern so that you can tell it to someone else.

PROBLEM SET 4.4

1. a. Use the technique described in this section to write 6 consecutive composite numbers. Give your answer as counting numbers without involving factorials.

   b. Indicate 12 consecutive composite numbers (you may leave your answers in factorial form).

2. a. Continue the table until you can demonstrate that $2^n - 1$ is not a formula for producing prime numbers (n is a counting number greater than 1).

n	2	3	4	5
$2^n - 1$	3	7		

   b. Suppose we try $2^n - 1$, where n is itself a prime number. Show why this formula does not always produce a prime number.

n	2	3	5	7	11
$2^n - 1$	3	7	31		

3. Write each of the following as a sum of two primes:
   a. 14   **b.** 16   **c.** 18   **d.** 20   **e.** 22   **f.** 24   **g.** 26

4. Goldbach also conjectured that every odd number greater than or equal to 9 can be expressed as the sum of three odd primes. For example, $9 = 3 + 3 + 3$, $11 = 5 + 3 + 3$, $13 = 7 + 3 + 3$, and $15 = 7 + 5 + 3$. Write each of the following as the sum of three odd primes:
   a. 17   **b.** 19   **c.** 21   **d.** 31   **e.** 55   **f.** 43   **g.** 77

5. Let us define the "proper divisors" of a number to be the divisors not including the number itself. (The proper divisors of 6 are 1, 2, and 3.)

Find the proper divisors of each of the following:

a. 10   b. 15   c. 18   d. 28   e. 56   f. 496

6. If the sum of the proper divisors of a number is equal to the number, the number is called a *perfect* number; if this sum is less than the number, it is called a *deficient* number; if it is greater than the number, the number is an *abundant* number. Classify each of the following as perfect, deficient, or abundant:

a. 6   b. 12   c. 20   d. 26   e. 28   f. 30   g. 72   h. 496

7. a. Write 10 consecutive composite numbers.

  b. Use your calculator to find these counting numbers.

  c. Verify that 11! + 3 is indeed composite by actually dividing that counting number by 3.

8. Use the pattern $(x + y)^2 = x^2 + 2xy + y^2$ to perform the following computations:

a. $(21)^2$ b. $(22)^2$ c. $(24)^2$ d. $(71)^2$ e. $(92)^2$

9. Use the pattern $(10t + 5)^2 = 100t(t + 1) + 25$ to perform the following computations:

a. $(15)^2$ b. $(25)^2$ c. $(35)^2$ d. $(85)^2$ e. $(95)^2$ f. $(135)^2$

10. We have emphasized the importance of discovering patterns in the study of mathematics. The following problems will allow you to practice this.

  a. Complete the following and look for a pattern. Then test to see if it continues for the next problem in the extension of the sequence of problems.

$$(1)(1) = \underline{\hspace{1cm}}$$
$$(11)(11) = \underline{\hspace{1cm}}$$
$$(111)(111) = \underline{\hspace{1cm}}$$
$$(1111)(1111) = \underline{\hspace{1cm}}$$

  b. Complete the following:

(11)(21) = ____	(11)(13) = ____	(11)(17) = ____
(11)(23) = ____	(11)(34) = ____	(11)(42) = ____
(11)(53) = ____	(11)(54) = ____	(11)(35) = ____

  Do you see a pattern for multiplying by 11? Note that in these problems the sum of the digits of the number being multiplied by 11 is less than 10. Now do the following multiplications and see if you can make an adjustment in the pattern:

(11)(47) = ____	(11)(58) = ____	(11)(69) = ____
(11)(75) = ____	(11)(89) = ____	(11)(95) = ____

c. Does the pattern hold for numbers represented by three- or four-digit numerals? Try the following and perhaps some of your own:

$$(11)(195) = \underline{\hspace{1cm}} \qquad (11)(4568) = \underline{\hspace{1cm}}$$

11. a. The Greeks apparently enjoyed working with "polygonal numbers." For example, the arrays of dots indicated gave rise to the "triangular numbers" 1, 3, 6, and 10. What will be the next three triangular numbers?

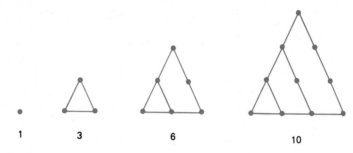

b. What are the first six square numbers?

c. What are the first six pentagonal numbers?

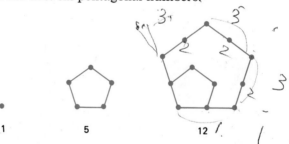

Pedagogical Problems and Activities

12. Suppose that a bright sixth-grade child states that $n! + 1$ produces a prime number for any counting number. What should you say?

13. Observe the following:

$$1 + 3 + 5 + 7 + 9$$

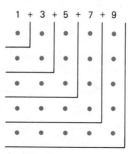

a. Relate the sum of the first three odd numbers $1 + 3 + 5$ to the array suggested here. (*Hint:* You may wish to refer to Problem **11b** for more information.

b. What would be the sum of the first five odd counting numbers?

c. What would be the sum of the first six odd numbers? The first 25? What would be the sum of the first n odd numbers?

d. In part **a** we conjectured that the sum of the first 25 odd counting numbers should be 25^2. Use your calculator to verify that this conjecture is correct.

e. Show that it is also true for the first 30 odd counting numbers.

14. Suppose we have 100 cubes and want to make a pyramid with 1 block on the top, 4 in the next layer, 9 in the next, and so on. What should be the dimensions on the bottom layer in order to use the greatest number of blocks? How many blocks would not be used? (*Hint:* This might be a good time to use blocks and make a model to help organize your thinking.)

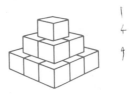

15. Another configuration somewhat like the Greek polygonal numbers are called *dot numbers*. A triangle dot number uses a sequence of dotted figures. Each succeeding triangle simply has one more dot on each side.

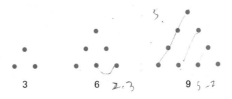

a. What triangle dot number will come next?

b. What triangle dot number has 9 dots on a side?

c. What triangle dot number has 17 dots on a side?

16. Pentagon dot numbers follow the same rules as triangle dot numbers. We have illustrated the first three such numbers.

a. What will be the next pentagon dot number?

b. What will be the sixth pentagon dot number? (7 points on a side?)

c. For the pentagon dot number 45, how many dots are on a side?

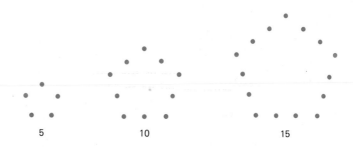

4.5   THE GREATEST COMMON DIVISOR AND LEAST COMMON MULTIPLE

Consider the number 18. We can readily determine that the set of divisors of 18 must be $\{1, 2, 3, 6, 9, 18\}$. Let us call this set D_{18}. Then $D_{24} = \{1, 2, 3, 4, 6, 8, 12, 24\}$. The intersection of these sets is $D_{18} \cap D_{24} = \{1, 2, 3, 6\}$. Therefore 1, 2, 3, and 6 are referred to as common divisors of 18 and 24. Then, by observation, the greatest common divisor of 18 and 24 is 6.

GCD

Definition 4.3   The greatest common divisor of two counting numbers a and b [written as gcd (a, b)] is the largest counting number d such that $d \mid a$ and $d \mid b$.

EXAMPLE 1

Find gcd $(24, 56)$.

$$D_{24} = \{1, 2, 3, 4, 6, 8, 12, 24\}$$
$$D_{56} = \{1, 2, 4, 7, 8, 14, 28, 56\}$$
$$D_{24} \cap D_{56} = \{1, 2, 4, 8\}$$

Then gcd $(24, 56) = 8$.

The concept of greatest common divisor can be extended to more than two numbers.

EXAMPLE 2

Find gcd $(16, 28, 36)$.

$$D_{16} = \{1, 2, 4, 8, 16\}$$
$$D_{28} = \{1, 2, 4, 7, 14, 28\}$$
$$D_{36} = \{1, 2, 3, 4, 6, 9, 12, 18, 36\}$$
$$D_{16} \cap D_{28} \cap D_{36} = \{1, 2, 4\}$$

Therefore, gcd $(16, 28, 36) = 4$.

This procedure is straightforward. For sets like D_{16}, D_{28}, and even D_{36} we have little difficulty in the required tabulation. However, it would be more difficult to find D_{210}. Let us consider a more routine way to find the set of all divisors of 210. We begin by writing 210 as the product of prime factors. Thus, $210 = 2 \cdot 3 \cdot 5 \cdot 7$. The set D_{210} must certainly contain the number 1 because 1 divides every number. Also, we may observe that 2, 3, 5, and 7 are each divisors of 210. Next, let us select the prime factors two at a time and state that $2 \cdot 3 = 6$, $2 \cdot 5 = 10$, $2 \cdot 7 = 14$, $3 \cdot 5 = 15$, $3 \cdot 7 = 21$, and $5 \cdot 7 = 35$ are all divisors of 210. We may then select the factors three at a time and claim that $2 \cdot 3 \cdot 5 = 30$, $2 \cdot 3 \cdot 7 = 42$, $2 \cdot 5 \cdot 7 = 70$, and $3 \cdot 5 \cdot 7 = 105$ are all divisors. Then taking four at a time, we observe that 210 is a divisor. Thus, $D_{210} = \{1, 2, 3, 5, 6, 7, 10, 14, 15, 21, 30, 35, 42, 70, 105, 210\}$.

You may find it helpful, particularly for numbers having many prime factors, to organize your data in a table. We have summarized the discussion just completed in Table 4.5.

why only

TABLE 4.5

| | Prime Factors of 210 Selected: | | |
One at a Time	Two at a Time	Three at a Time	Four at a Time
2	$2 \cdot 3 = 6$	$2 \cdot 3 \cdot 5 = 30$	$2 \cdot 3 \cdot 5 \cdot 7 = 210$
3	$2 \cdot 5 = 10$	$2 \cdot 3 \cdot 7 = 42$	
5	$2 \cdot 7 = 14$	$2 \cdot 5 \cdot 7 = 70$	
7	$3 \cdot 5 = 15$	$3 \cdot 5 \cdot 7 = 105$	
	$3 \cdot 7 = 21$		
	$5 \cdot 7 = 35$		

Let us use the same procedure to write the divisors of 924. The prime factors of 924 are 2, 3, 7, and 11, and we may write $924 = 2 \cdot 2 \cdot 3 \cdot 7 \cdot 11$. Table 4.6 illustrates the selection of prime factors to determine the set of

TABLE 4.6

| | Prime Factors of 924 Selected: | | | |
One at a Time	Two at a Time	Three at a Time	Four at a Time	Five at a Time
2	$2 \cdot 2 = 4$	$2 \cdot 2 \cdot 3 = 12$	$2 \cdot 2 \cdot 3 \cdot 7 = 84$	$2 \cdot 2 \cdot 3 \cdot 7 \cdot 11 = 924$
3	$2 \cdot 3 = 6$	$2 \cdot 2 \cdot 7 = 28$	$2 \cdot 2 \cdot 3 \cdot 11 = 132$	
7	$2 \cdot 7 = 14$	$2 \cdot 2 \cdot 11 = 44$	$2 \cdot 2 \cdot 7 \cdot 11 = 308$	
11	$2 \cdot 11 = 22$	$2 \cdot 3 \cdot 7 = 42$	$2 \cdot 3 \cdot 7 \cdot 11 = 462$	
	$3 \cdot 7 = 21$	$2 \cdot 3 \cdot 11 = 66$		
	$3 \cdot 11 = 33$	$2 \cdot 7 \cdot 11 = 154$		
	$7 \cdot 11 = 77$	$3 \cdot 7 \cdot 11 = 231$		

divisors of 924. Thus, the set of divisors of 924 contains the number 1 along with those in the table making a set of 24 elements and we may write

$$D_{924} = \{1, 2, 3, 4, 6, 7, 11, 12, 14, 21, 22, 28, 33, 42, 44, 66, 77, 84, 132, 154,$$
$$231, 308, 462, 924\}.$$

Then by observation,

$$\gcd(210, 924) = 42.$$

At this point one would hope that there is an easier way to find common divisors than listing the sets of divisors and selecting the largest common factor. This is fortunately the case.

An alternate approach for finding greatest common divisors also uses prime factorization. Suppose that we want to find the greatest common factor in 42 and 70. In factored form we may write $42 = 2 \cdot 3 \cdot 7$ and $70 = 2 \cdot 5 \cdot 7$. Notice that 2 is a factor of both, as is 7. Therefore, $2 \cdot 7$ is the greatest common divisor, so $\gcd(42, 70) = 2 \cdot 7 = 14$.

EXAMPLE 1

Find $\gcd(66, 110)$.

$$66 = 2 \cdot 3 \cdot 11$$
$$110 = 2 \cdot 5 \cdot 11$$

Thus $\gcd(66, 110) = 2 \cdot 11 = 22$.

EXAMPLE 2

Find $\gcd(48, 72, 108)$.

$$48 = 2 \cdot 2 \cdot 2 \cdot 2 \cdot 3$$
$$72 = 2 \cdot 2 \cdot 2 \cdot 3 \cdot 3$$
$$108 = 2 \cdot 2 \cdot 3 \cdot 3 \cdot 3$$

Thus, $\gcd(48, 72, 108) = 2 \cdot 2 \cdot 3 = 12$.

Consider the numbers 14 and 15. Both are composite numbers, but note that $\gcd(14, 15) = 1$. Such numbers are referred to as being relatively prime.

Definition 4.4   If the greatest common divisor of two counting numbers *a* and *b* is 1, we say the numbers *a* and *b* are *relatively prime.*

42 and 55 are relatively prime because $\gcd(42, 55) = 1$.
16 and 24 are not relatively prime because $\gcd(16, 24) \neq 1$.

Let us turn our attention to the multiples of a number. When we speak of the multiples of 3 we mean those numbers obtained by taking the product of some whole number and 3. Thus, 6 is a multiple of 3, 33 is a multiple of 3. Zero is also a multiple of 3. (How can this be true?) We may therefore write $M_3 = \{0, 3, 6, 9, 12, 15, \ldots\}$. Notice that for any whole number a, $0 \in M_a$, and $a \in M_a$. We might also note that M_a is always an infinite set, if $a > 0$.

Consider the two numbers 4 and 6; $M_4 = \{0, 4, 8, 12, 16, \ldots\}$ $M_6 = \{0, 6, 12, 18, 24, \ldots\}$, and $M_4 \cap M_6 = \{0, 12, 24, \ldots\}$. We are often interested in obtaining the smallest nonzero multiple that is an element of both sets. That number, 12, is referred to as the *least common multiple* of 4 and 6.

LCM

Definition 4.5 The least common multiple m of two counting numbers a and b (written as $m = $ lcm (a, b) is the smallest counting number such that $a|m$ and $b|m$.

EXAMPLE 1

Find lcm (8, 12).

$$M_8 = \{0, 8, 16, 24, 32, 40, 48, \ldots\}$$
$$M_{12} = \{0, 12, 24, 36, 48, 60, \ldots\}$$
$$M_8 \cap M_{12} = \{0, 24, 48, \ldots\}$$

Then lcm (8, 12) = 24.

EXAMPLE 2

Find lcm (6, 8, 12).

$$M_6 = \{0, 6, 12, 18, 24, 30, 36, \ldots\}$$
$$M_8 = \{0, 8, 16, 24, 32, 40, 48, \ldots\}$$
$$M_{12} = \{0, 12, 24, 36, \ldots\}$$

Then $M_6 \cap M_8 \cap M_{12} = \{0, 24, 48, \ldots\}$ and lcm (6, 8, 12) = 24.

We might wonder whether two numbers will always have a least common multiple that is less than the product of the numbers. (Do you see that the product is most assuredly a common multiple?) The answer to this question may be easier to arrive at if we first look at another approach to this matter. Consider the numbers 6 and 8. Now $6 = 2 \cdot 3$ and $8 = 2 \cdot 2 \cdot 2$, and we are searching for the least common multiple of 6 and 8. We wish to obtain that counting number m such that m is a multiple of 6. Thus, 2 and 3 must be factors of m. Also, because m is to be a multiple of 8, 2 must be used as a factor three times. Thus, if $m = 2 \cdot 3 \cdot 2 \cdot 2 = 24$, we have a number that is a multiple of both 6 and 8.

EXAMPLE 1

Find lcm (60, 210).

$$60 = 2 \cdot 2 \cdot 3 \cdot 5$$
$$210 = 2 \cdot 3 \cdot 5 \cdot 7$$

Thus lcm (60, 210) = 2 · 2 · 3 · 5 · 7 = 420.

EXAMPLE 2

Find lcm (15, 20, 50).

$$15 = 3 \cdot 5$$
$$20 = 2 \cdot 2 \cdot 5$$
$$50 = 2 \cdot 5 \cdot 5$$

Thus lcm (15, 20, 50) = 3 · 5 · 2 · 2 · 5 = 300. (Do you see that 3 · 5 is a multiple of 15, that (3 · 5) · 2 · 2 is a multiple of 20, and that (3 · 5 · 2 · 2) · 5 is a multiple of 50?)

EXAMPLE 3

Find lcm (15, 14).

$$15 = 3 \cdot 5$$
$$14 = 2 \cdot 7$$

Thus lcm (15, 14) = 3 · 5 · 2 · 7 = 210.

> REMARK   In Example 3 the numbers 15 and 14 were relatively prime. In this case the least common multiple is simply the product of the two numbers. However, if the numbers are not relatively prime, a common multiple can be found that is smaller than the product.

Suppose we are asked to find lcm (a, b), where a is a multiple of b. This type of question that uses a more general set of information is sometimes more difficult to answer than the kind that provides specific data. One good way to approach a problem of this nature is to begin by selecting specific numbers that meet the specifications of the problem. So let us consider specific values for a and b such that a is a multiple of b. Suppose $b = 3$. Then a might be any member of the set of multiples of 3. That is, $a \in \{0, 3, 6, 9, 12, \ldots\}$. What is lcm (6, 3)? (Do you agree that it is 6?) Does lcm (9, 3) = 9?

Now let us select a different value for b, say 5. Again a is to be a multiple of b, so $a \in \{0, 5, 10, 15, \ldots\}$. What is lcm $(15, 5)$? What is lcm $(25, 5)$? In each case it is found to be a. Now we have some feel for the problem and are fairly certain that if a is a multiple of b, then lcm $(a, b) = a$.

REMARK We could argue this directly if we choose to do so. Because a is a multiple of b, we may write $a = bk$ for some whole number k. Then lcm $(a, b) =$ lcm (bk, b). Because bk is the smallest multiple of both bk and b, it must be true that lcm $(bk, b) = bk = a$.

Let us consider one more problem before we close this section. Suppose we are asked to find the smallest counting number that is divisible by 2, 3, 4, 5, 6, and 8. How should one begin a problem such as this? Perhaps one way to start is to consider a simpler problem like it. For example, what is the smallest counting number that is divisible by 2, 3, and 4? Do you agree that 12 is the number that we are seeking? But now we recognize that if some number k is divisible by 2, then k is a multiple of 2. In other words, we were looking for that number that is the smallest multiple of 2, 3, and 4. So we can now proceed with our original question and find lcm $(2, 3, 4, 5, 6, 8)$. We note that $2 \cdot 3$ is a multiple of both 2 and 3. Then $2 \cdot 3 \cdot 2$ is a multiple of 2, 3, and 4 and that $2 \cdot 3 \cdot 2 \cdot 5$ is a multiple of 2, 3, 4, 5, and 6. If we include one more 2 as a factor, we should have the desired number. That is, $2 \cdot 3 \cdot 2 \cdot 5 \cdot 2 = 120$ is the smallest counting number that is divisible by 2, 3, 4, 5, 6, and 8.

PROBLEM SET 4.5

1. Use prime factorization, then select factors one at a time, two at a time, and so on to write the set of divisors for each of the following numbers:
   a. 72   b. 84   c. 92   d. 188   e. 48   f. 56

2. For each of the following, find the greatest common divisor by using the set-intersection approach.
   a. 48 and 72   b. 36 and 56
   c. 84 and 92   d. 72 and 188
   e. 18, 28, and 36   f. 48, 72, and 144

3. For each of the following, find the greatest common divisor by examining the prime factorization of each number involved.
   a. 36 and 48   b. 56 and 72
   c. 54 and 86   d. 36 and 108
   e. 18, 27, and 36   f. 48, 72, and 144

4. Use a Venn diagram and prime factorization to find the greatest common divisor of each of the following:

   a. 36 and 86   **b.** 84 and 72

   c. 16, 48, and 72   **d.** 45, 75 and 110

5. Find the greatest common divisor of a, b, and c. (You may leave your answer expressed as a product of primes.)

$$a = 31^2 \cdot 7^3 \cdot 3 \qquad c = 7^6 \cdot 31^3 \cdot 3^4$$
$$b = 31 \cdot 3^7 \cdot 7^2$$

6. **a.** What is the remainder when $[(2 \cdot 3 \cdot 5 \cdot 7 \cdot 19) + 6]$ is divided by 7?

   b. What is the remainder when $[(2 \cdot 3 \cdot 5 \cdot 7 \cdot 19) + 6]$ is divided by 5?

   c. What is the remainder when $[(2 \cdot 3 \cdot 5 \cdot 7 \cdot 19) + 6]$ is divided by 19?

7. If $a = 2^3 \cdot 3^{17} \cdot 5^{93}$:

   a. List 3 multiples of a.

   b. List 8 divisors of a.

   c. Is $b = 2^2 \cdot 3^{29} \cdot 5^{98}$ a multiple of a?

   d. Is $c = 2^2 \cdot 3^{15} \cdot 5^{71}$ a divisor of a?

8. **a.** If $2^3 \cdot 3^2$ is the least common multiple of $2 \cdot 3^2$ and x, find possible values of x.

   b. If $3^5 \cdot 5^3$ is the least common multiple of $3^2 \cdot 5^2$ and x, find possible values of x.

9. For each of the following, find the least common multiple by using the set-intersection approach.

   a. 8 and 16   **b.** 9 and 12

   c. 12 and 18   **d.** 15 and 21

   e. 6, 8, and 12   **f.** 10, 15, and 25

10. For each of the following, find the least common multiple by examining the prime factorization of each number:

   a. 21 and 56   **b.** 14 and 16

   c. 16 and 42   **d.** 48 and 108

   e. 12, 18, and 26   **f.** 14, 18, 27, and 35

11. Use a Venn diagram and prime factorization to find the least common multiple of each of the following:

   a. 12 and 16   **b.** 15 and 21

   c. 12, 18, and 21   **d.** 14, 18, and 27

12. a. What is the greatest common divisor of a and b if a and b are both prime numbers and $a \neq b$? Explain your answer.

b. What is the greatest common divisor of a and b if a and b are counting numbers and b is a multiple of a? Explain your answer.

13. What is the smallest counting number that is divisible by every number from 1 to 10 inclusive?

14. a. What is the least common multiple of a and b if they are both prime numbers and $a \neq b$? Explain your answer.

b. What is the least common multiple of a and b if they are relatively prime? Explain your answer.

c. If 1 is the greatest common divisor of two numbers, what can you say about their least common multiple?

15. List the counting numbers that are less than the given x and that are relatively prime to x.

a. $x = 11$ **b.** $x = 12$ **c.** $x = 24$ **d.** $x = 23$

16. a. Show that "if a and b are *any* counting numbers and $a|c$ and $b|c$, then $ab|c$" is false. (Try to find counting numbers a and b that both divide a third number c, yet $a \cdot b \nmid c$.)

b. Consider the following statement: "If a and b are counting numbers that are relatively prime, and $a|c$ and $b|c$ then $ab|c$." Give four specific examples that could be used to test this statement. Can you find a counterexample?

c. Which statements are true?

   (i) If $2|k$ and $5|k$, then $10|k$.
   (ii) If $2|k$ and $6|k$, then $12|k$.
   (iii) If $3|m$ and $4|m$, then $12|m$.
   (iv) If $6|n$ and $4|n$ then $24|n$.
   (v) If $14|p$ and $15|p$, then $1210|p$.

17. a. Complete the following table:

a	b	gcd (a, b)	lcm (a, b)	$a \cdot b$
2	3			
3	6			
6	12			
6	15			
12	18			

b. What relationship seems to exist between gcd $(a, b) \cdot$ lcm (a, b) and the number $a \cdot b$?

18. Consider the following data:

n	Prime Factorization of n	Divisors of n	Number of Divisors of n
6	$2 \cdot 3$	1, 2, 3, 6	4
12	$2 \cdot 2 \cdot 3 = 2^2 \cdot 3$	1, 2, 3, 4, 6, 12	6
14	$2 \cdot 7$	1, 2, 7, 14	4
24	$2 \cdot 2 \cdot 2 \cdot 3 = 2^3 \cdot 3$	1, 2, 3, 4, 6, 8, 12, 24	8
60	$2 \cdot 2 \cdot 3 \cdot 5 = 2^2 \cdot 3 \cdot 5$	1, 2, 3, 4, 5, 6, 10, 12, 15, 20, 30, 60	12
70	$2 \cdot 5 \cdot 7$	1, 2, 5, 7, 10, 14, 35, 70	8
80			
84			
100			
210			

    a. Complete the table.

    b. Find a formula that relates the number of divisors for a given number with the exponents found in the prime factorization (i.e., $24 = 2^3 \cdot 3$, so the exponents are 3 and 1).

19. We can think about divisibility and factorization in other bases too. For example: $12_{six} | 24_{six}$ because $12_{six} \cdot 2_{six} = 24_{six}$; 32_{five} is prime; and the prime factorization of 33_{five} is $2_{five} \cdot 3^2_{five}$.

    a. Does $13_{six} | 43_{six}$?

    b. Is 13_{six} a prime number?

    c. Does $12_{five} | 42_{five}$?

    d. What is the prime factorization of 413_{five}?

    e. Give values of x such that $x | 215_{six}$.

Pedagogical Problems and Activities

20. Today Joe mowed the lawn and trimmed the hedge. If the lawn needs to be mowed every 6 days and the hedge trimmed every 8 days, when will Joe again have to do both jobs on the same day?

21. At Shari's birthday party, each child got the same number of cookies. They also each received the same number of candies. If 30 cookies and 40 candies were used, what is the greatest number of persons who could have attended the birthday party? Could fewer persons have attended and still satisfy the given conditions?

22. a. A set of toys can be separated into 6 equal piles. It can also be separated into 14 equal piles. What is the smallest number of toys in this set?

    b. Could any *other* set of toys be separated evenly into 6 and 14 piles?

23. a. If 3 is the greatest common divisor of 12 and another number, what could the other number be?

   b. If 36 is the least common multiple of 18 and another number, what could the other number be?

24. a. Two runners are running on a circular track. One completes a lap every 4 minutes, the other every 6 minutes. If they start at the same place at the same time, in how many minutes will they again be together at the starting point?

   b. Suppose one runs a lap every 4 minutes and the other every 5 minutes. In how many minutes will they again be together at the starting point?

   c. In general, if one runner completes a lap every m minutes and the other runner every n minutes, in how many minutes will they again be together at the starting point?

4.6   INTRODUCTION TO THE INTEGERS AND ADDITION OF INTEGERS

A great deal of mathematics can be done using only the whole numbers. However, there still is a need for numbers that are not whole numbers. Children often become aware of the existence of negative numbers even before they begin their formal schooling. This is particularly true in those regions where cold weather occurs. A temperature of 5 below zero or ⁻5 is a commonplace occurrence. Other very natural uses of negative numbers occur, such as time before and after the birth of Christ, elevations below and above sea level, and assets and liabilities of a bank or a business. Games of various types often involve such numbers, particularly if a player is allowed to "go in the hole" or, as in football, is capable of losing or gaining yardage. The advent of space launches has given us still one more commonplace usage: the familiar countdown, " . . . 0 minus 3, 0 minus 2, 0 minus 1, zero, plus 1, plus 2. . . ."

Early exposure to integers is always at a very intuitive level with no attempt to formalize the concept. "Above or below zero," "B.C. or A.D.," "above or below sea level" are all quite expressive, particularly if accompanied by pictures or other discussion. It is very common today to find "number lines" in elementary school classrooms.

The number line is of considerable help to us as we proceed with this development. The whole numbers may be associated with the points chosen

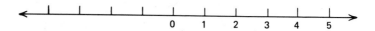

on the number lines as indicated. Let us agree that for each of the nonzero whole numbers we will associate its "image" across the 0 point. Thus, the image of 2 is the point indicated. Let us agree to call this point "negative two" and write ⁻2.

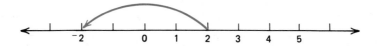

> REMARK Some elementary school texts call this number "the opposite of 2," others refer to it as "the additive inverse of 2."

Care must be exercised so that the meaning of "plus and minus" be separated from that of "positive and negative." "Positive" and "negative" are adjectives telling us whether a number is greater than or less than zero. "Plus" and "minus" are verbs telling us to add or to subtract. Please note that the raised hyphen does *not* imply the operation of subtraction. Thus ⁻2 is read "negative 2", not "minus 2". When we write (⁻5) − (⁻8) = ⁺3 we mean "negative five minus negative 8 equals positive 3.

Each of the nonzero whole numbers can be matched in a similar manner with an image point across the 0 point. (We may state that 0 matches to itself.) The set of whole numbers along with these new numbers, ⁻1, ⁻2, ⁻3, and so on, is referred to as the set of *integers*. Thus, if *I* stands for the set of integers, *I* = { . . . , ⁻3, ⁻2, ⁻1, 0, 1, 2, 3, . . .}. In general, the subset {1, 2, 3, . . .} is referred to as the set of *positive integers*, the subset {0, 1, 2, 3, . . .} as the set of *nonnegative integers*, and the subset { . . . , ⁻3, ⁻2, ⁻1} as the set of *negative integers*. It should be apparent from this that the number 0 is neither positive nor negative.

The idea of "opposite of" or "inverse of" can now be expanded to refer to any integer, not just to the positive integers (nonzero whole numbers). That is, the opposite of ⁻3 is the image of ⁻3 across the 0 point. Thus, the opposite of ⁻3 is 3. We may write this as ⁻(⁻3) = 3. This general matching of integers to their opposites is illustrated here.

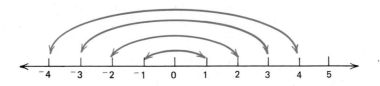

What is ⁻(⁻7)? Do you agree that it is the number 7? Check it out on a numberline if you question it. What is the opposite of ⁻5? Is ⁻(⁻5) = 5?

A word of caution is in order. If we are asked to show where the integer $^-6$ is located on the number line, we simply must identify that point six units to the left of the 0 point. We know that it is a negative integer and that it must be graphed as a point to the left of 0. Likewise, we recognize that the number $^-(^-3)$ is really the same as 3 and may simply mark the point three units to the right of the 0 point. However, what if you are given the integer ^-r? What can be said about its graph? Is it a negative number? The answer is that we cannot tell. We know only that it is the opposite of r. If r is itself positive then ^-r is a negative integer. But if r is a negative integer, then ^-r is a positive integer, as illustrated on the number line. (For example, if $r = ^-7$, then $^-r = ^-(^-7) = 7$.) As a result of this discussion let us agree to the following property.

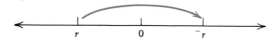

PROPERTY 4.8   **For any integer r, $^-(^-r) = r$.**

Using the number line should make such statements increasingly clear. When you write r you should visualize some point on the line. Then the symbol ^-r calls to mind the image across 0, and $^-(^-r)$ sends you back across 0 to the starting point. Thus, the same point is named both r and $^-(^-r)$.

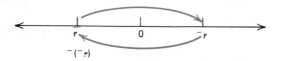

REMARK Note that 0 is its own opposite. That is, $^-0 = 0$. Therefore $^-(^-0) = ^-0 = 0$ so Property 4.7 holds for all integers.

In Chapter 2 we did some problems involving addition of whole numbers using a number line. As you will recall, we agreed to add $3 + 2$ by starting at 0 with our first arrow; then to the terminal point of the first we place the initial point of the second arrow. Thus, we may graph this sum as follows:

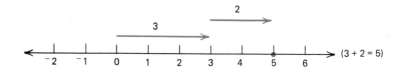

Addition of integers, where both addends are positive or both are negative, is very similar to addition of whole numbers. Suppose we have ⁻4 + ⁻3. We may use the number line as follows:

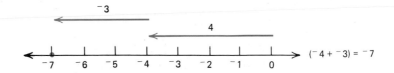

Thus ⁻4 + ⁻3 = ⁻7. Likewise, ⁻5 + ⁻2 = ⁻7.

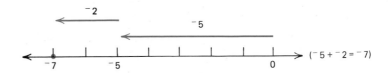

In general, when we add two positive integers, we get a positive integer, and when we add two negative integers we get a negative integer. Do you see how in both cases we use addition facts for whole numbers? Recognizing this fact, we do not need to use the number line to perform additions.

EXAMPLE 1

Find 4 + 7.

Solution This is, of course, just addition of whole numbers and 4 + 7 = 11.

EXAMPLE 2

Find ⁻6 + ⁻14.

Solution We know the answer will be negative. Also 6 + 14 = 20 so ⁻6 + ⁻14 = ⁻20.

Using this same number-line procedure, we may add integers with unlike signs. The integer ⁻4 can be represented by an arrow four units long and extending to the left from 0. Then, to add ⁻4 + 3 we could proceed as follows:

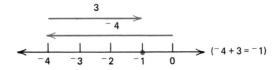

Thus, $^-4 + 3 = ^-1$. Likewise, $^-3 + 5 = 2$, as indicated by the graph.

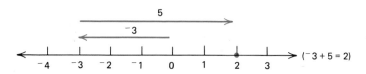

Let us once again emphasize the relationship between an integer and its opposite. What is $^-3 + 3$?

Do you agree that $^-3 + 3 = 0$? What is $5 + ^-5$?

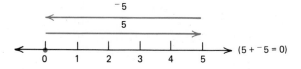

Is it again 0? This is indeed the case. Any integer plus its opposite yields 0. We refer to such a number *b* that when added to another number *a* yields 0 as the additive inverse of *a*. Thus, if *r* is an integer, then ^-r is its additive inverse because $r + ^-r = 0$. But notice also that it is correct to state that *r* is the additive inverse of ^-r. Thus, a number and its opposite are additive inverses of each other. For this reason we often refer to $^-3$ as "the additive inverse of 3." The terminology "negative of," "opposite of," and "additive inverse of" are all quite expressive and should add meaning to your work. Because an integer and its additive inverse are really just mirror images of each other across the 0 point, each integer has exactly one additive inverse.

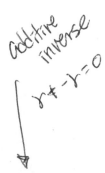

PROPERTY 4.9   **For every integer *r*, there exists a unique integer ^-r, such that $r + ^-r = ^-r + r = 0$.**

This concept of additive inverse is helpful to us in performing additions of integers. Let us find $6 + ^-4$ using a number line. Thus, $6 + ^-4 = 2$.

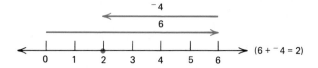

Notice that we might also have written $6 + {}^-4 = (2 + 4) + {}^-4$. If the integers are associative under addition, we may write $(2 + 4) + {}^-4 = 2 + (4 + {}^-4)$. Because $4 + {}^-4 = 0$, we have $6 + {}^-4 = 2 + 0 = 2$. This, of course, agrees with our number-line interpretation. What might we name as the sum of ${}^-7 + 3$? Let us write ${}^-7 + 3 = ({}^-4 + {}^-3) + 3$. (Do you agree that ${}^-4 + {}^-3 = {}^-7$?) Then ${}^-7 + 3 = {}^-4 + ({}^-3 + 3) = {}^-4 + 0 = {}^-4$.

EXAMPLE 1

Find ${}^-6 + 4$.

Solution

$$
\begin{aligned}
{}^-6 + 4 &= ({}^-2 + {}^-4) + 4 & {}^-2 + {}^-4 = {}^-6 \\
&= {}^-2 + ({}^-4 + 4) & \text{Associative property for addition} \\
&= {}^-2 + 0 & \text{Property 4.9} \\
&= {}^-2 & \text{0 is the additive identity}
\end{aligned}
$$

EXAMPLE 2

Find $8 + {}^-15$.

Solution

$$
\begin{aligned}
8 + {}^-15 &= 8 + ({}^-8 + {}^-7) \\
&= (8 + {}^-8) + {}^-7 \\
&= 0 + {}^-7 \\
&= {}^-7
\end{aligned}
$$

Let us summarize what we have done. If we are to find ${}^-16 + {}^-14$, we know the answer will be the negative of $(16 + 14)$. Thus, ${}^-16 + {}^-14 = {}^-30$. To find ${}^-26 + 14$, we may write $({}^-12 + {}^-14) + 14 = {}^-12 + ({}^-14 + 14) = {}^-12 + 0 = {}^-12$. That is, ${}^-26 + 14 = {}^-12$. The sum $25 + {}^-18$ will be positive. In fact, $25 + {}^-18 = (25 - 18) = 7$.

The integers are indeed associative under addition. To illustrate this, consider the three integers ${}^-2$, 3, and ${}^-4$. Does $({}^-2 + 3) + {}^-4 = {}^-2 + (3 + {}^-4)$? Note that $({}^-2 + 3) + {}^-4 = 1 + {}^-4 = {}^-3$ and ${}^-2 + (3 + {}^-4) = {}^-2 + {}^-1 = {}^-3$. We may apply the associative property whenever we find it convenient to do so. We should also note that the integers are commutative under addition. Thus ${}^-5 + 2 = 2 + {}^-5$ as is easily seen on the number lines that follow.

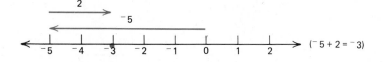

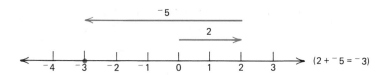

These properties are often used in simplifying addition problems with integers.

EXAMPLE 1

Find $(^-16 + 58) + 16$.

Solution

$$
\begin{aligned}
(^-16 + 58) + 16 &= 16 + (^-16 + 58) \\
&= (16 + {}^-16) + 58 \\
&= 0 + 58 \\
&= 58
\end{aligned}
$$

EXAMPLE 2

Find $(^-26 + 82) + (^-82 + 30)$.

Solution

$$
\begin{aligned}
(^-26 + 82) + (^-82 + 30) &= (^-26 + 30) + (82 + {}^-82) \\
&= 4 + 0 \\
&= 4
\end{aligned}
$$

The question of order has not yet been raised for integers. As you will recall, we asserted in Chapter 2 that the whole numbers possess this property, and we discussed a number-line interpretation at that time. Because the number line has been extended to accommodate the integers, it would seem reasonable to expect that the integers are ordered. As with the whole numbers, let us agree that the integer a that is to the right of a second integer b is the larger, and we will write $a > b$. It should be apparent, therefore, that $5 > {}^-3$, and that $^-4 < 1$. Likewise, we write $^-6 < {}^-4$ and $^-26 < {}^-1$. We may be interested in identifying a set that contains the truth values for an open statement of inequality. Consider the set of elements x such that $x > {}^-4$. We might tabulate the solution set as $\{^-3, {}^-2, {}^-1, 0, 1, 2, \ldots\}$. The graph would appear as follows:

> **REMARK** It should be noted that the statements $a > b$ and $b < a$ are equivalent. To state that $5 > {}^-3$ is equivalent to writing ${}^-3 < 5$. Likewise, ${}^-4 < 1$ says the same thing as $1 > {}^-4$, and $3 < 5$ is equivalent to writing $5 > 3$.

PROBLEM SET 4.6

1. Use a number-line interpretation to find each of the following sums:
   a. $3 + {}^-4$.
   b. $4 + {}^-2$
   c. $4 + 2$
   d. ${}^-5 + {}^-2$
   e. ${}^-3 + {}^-4$
   f. ${}^-5 + 2$
   g. ${}^-7 + {}^-3$.
   h. $5 + {}^-8$
   i. ${}^-4 + 0$
   j. $({}^-2 + {}^-1) + {}^-3$
   k. $({}^-3 + {}^-4) + {}^-2$
   l. $({}^-3 + 5) + {}^-6$
   m. $(5 + {}^-4) + {}^-6$

2. Determine which of the two symbols $<$ or $>$ should be used to make each statement true.
   a. $0 \underline{\quad} {}^-6$
   b. ${}^-4 \underline{\quad} 4$
   c. ${}^-10 \underline{\quad} 1$
   d. ${}^-12 \underline{\quad} {}^-8$
   e. ${}^-8 \underline{\quad} 0$
   f. ${}^-1 \underline{\quad} {}^-3$

3. Use the number line to find the point midway between each of the pairs of points.
   a. 0 and 6
   b. 0 and ${}^-6$
   c. ${}^-1$ and ${}^-9$
   d. ${}^-2$ and 2
   e. 7 and ${}^-7$
   f. ${}^-3$ and 5

4. Find the distance between each of the following pairs of points. (We usually represent distance by a positive value.)
   a. 2 and 7
   b. ${}^-3$ and 3
   c. ${}^-2$ and 7
   d. ${}^-10$ and 10
   e. 0 and 8
   f. ${}^-10$ and ${}^-2$
   g. ${}^-6$ and 1
   h. 0 and ${}^-8$

5. Use a format like that shown to solve each of the following:

$${}^-6 + 4 = ({}^-2 + {}^-4) + 4 = {}^-2 + ({}^-4 + 4) = {}^-2 + 0 = {}^-2$$

   a. ${}^-4 + 6$
   b. $5 + {}^-2$
   c. ${}^-12 + 4$
   d. ${}^-4 + 10$
   e. ${}^-5 + 9$
   f. $7 + {}^-3$

6. Give four examples of everyday situations that may be interpreted as "$6 + {}^-8$."

7. Find each of the following sums without using a number line. (Use the associative and commutative properties where it is helpful to do so.)
   a. ${}^-6 + (6 + {}^-15)$
   b. ${}^-17 + (18 + 14)$
   c. ${}^-16 + {}^-12$
   d. $({}^-3 + 15) + 3$
   e. $(18 + {}^-19) + 3$
   f. $({}^-16 + {}^-12) + (16 + 12)$

g. $21 + (^-21 + ^-43)$ **h.** $^-42 + (^-12 + 42)$

i. $(^-35 + 92) + (35 + ^-90)$

8. a. Suppose we know that x is a negative integer and y is also a negative integer. What kind of integer is $(x + y)$?

b. If x is a negative integer and y is a positive integer, what can be said about the integer $(x + y)$?

9. Find the additive inverse of each of the following:

a. 5 **b.** $^-3$ **c.** $^-7$ **d.** 4

e. $(4 + 3)$ **f.** $(^-4 + ^-2)$ **g.** $(^-3 + 5)$ **h.** $(8 + ^-12)$

i. $4 + (^-6 + 2)$ **j.** $^-(^-3)$ **k.** $^-(^-7)$

10. a. If r is a counting number, what kind of number is ^-r?

b. If s is an integer, what can you say about ^-s?

11. List the elements of the truth set for each of the following open sentences. Use only integers in your work.

a. $x + 4 = 6$ **b.** $x + ^-4 = 0$ **c.** $x + ^-6 = ^-7$

d. $x + ^-6 = ^-4$ **e.** $x + ^-4 = 6$ **f.** $x + 8 = ^-11$

g. $^-4 + x = ^-8$ **h.** $^-17 + x = 18$ **i.** $^-17 + x = 0$

j. $^-12 = y + 14$ **k.** $x + 2 > ^-4$ **l.** $^-1 + x < 4$

12. Graph the solution set for each of the following on a number line. Use only integers in your work.

a. $x + 2 = 3$ **b.** $4 + x = ^-2$ **c.** $5 + 2 = x$

d. $^-6 + x < 10$ **e.** $x + ^-3 > 0$

13. Find the sum by adding in the order in which the integers appear, then check by grouping the positive numbers together and the negative numbers together.

a. $5 + 6 + ^-4 + 3 + ^-7$ **b.** $6 + ^-4 + 8 + ^-9 + 2$

c. $^-7 + 5 + 3 + ^-4 + ^-6$ **d.** $^-8 + ^-7 + 15 + ^-2 + 9$

14. To find the sum of 65, 68, 71, 73, and 69 we might consider the deviation of these numbers from some other number, say 70. That is, consider $^-5 + ^-2 + 1 + 3 + ^-1 = ^-4$. The sum should be $(5 \cdot 70) + ^-4 = 346$. Use this procedure to find the following:

a. $84 + 78 + 82 + 75$

b. $136 + 145 + 142 + 137 + 132$

c. $56 + 63 + 61 + 58 + 52 + 67$

d. $119 + 123 + 121 + 116 + 114 + 128$

15. Many calculators have a button ⊞⊟ called a "change sign" key. If you enter the numeral 6 and push ⊞⊟ the readout on the display will read -6.

Push the indicated sequence of buttons and examine the readout on the calculator.

a. 4 $\boxed{+}$ 3 $\boxed{+/-}$ =   b. 5 $\boxed{+/-}$ $\boxed{+}$ 2 =

c. 5 $\boxed{+/-}$ $\boxed{+}$ 2 $\boxed{+/-}$ =

16. Use the calculator and the $\boxed{+/-}$ key to compute the following:

  a. $(^-5) + (^-2) =$ b. $(2) + (^-3) =$ c. $(^-2) + (^-3) =$

  d. $(^-5) + (2) =$

17. Write an addition statement corresponding to each of the following, then find the answer to the statement:

  a. Corn prices on the board of trade rose 3 cents one day then dropped 8 cents the next day. What was the net change in the value of the corn?

  b. The temperature was 17° but then rose 12°. What was the new temperature?

  c. You have $125 in the bank, then write a check for $30, then deposit $45. What is your new balance?

  d. You have $156 in the bank, then deposit $45. What is your new bank balance?

  e. The temperature is 12°, then drops 20° during the night but rises 8° the next morning. What is the new temperature reading?

  f. The temperature is now less than 41°. It has dropped 10° since this morning. What might the temperature have been this morning?

18. For each of the following identify the truth set, using the set of integers as the domain, then graph the solution set on a number line:

  a. $x > ^-2$ and $x > 1$

  c. $x > ^-3$ and $x < 5$

  e. $x > ^-4$ or $x < 3$

  b. $x \geq ^-2$ or $x > 1$

  d. $x > ^-3$ and $x < ^-6$

  f. $x > ^-2$ and $x > 4$ and $x > ^-1$

19. a. Use your calculator to find each of the following:

    (i) $^-484 + 364$

    (iii) $285 + (^-611) + (^-310)$

    (ii) $2486 + (^-7943)$

    (iv) $^-244 + (^-56) + 284$

  b. What result do you obtain when you find $3 - 8$ on your calculator?

Pedagogical Problems and Activities

20. a. Suggest some activity that would allow fifth grade students to see that addition of integers is commutative.

b. How might you get these same students to see that addition is associative?

21. Suppose the first integer named represents a gain or a loss on one investment and the second named integer is a gain or loss on a second investment. Show how a fifth grade student might use this to interpret each of the following (find the answer in each case):

    a. $4 + 12$ **b.** $^-5 + {^-3}$ **c.** $7 + {^-3}$

    d. $^-6 + 2$ **e.** $(4 + {^-5}) + 6$ **f.** $(3 + 4) + {^-7}$

22. Electrical charges are sometimes used to teach children about integers. When doing so, we say that a positive charge $(+)$ balances a negative charge $(-)$. Imagine a container with 5 positive charges and 2 negative charges. We could also use the integer $(^+3)$ to describe this container. Likewise, a $(^+3)$ container could have 4 positive charges and 1 negative charge.

    a. What integer name can be given the following containers

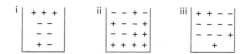

    b. Using charges, draw two different containers, each of which names the desired integer.

       (i) $(^+5)$ **(ii)** $(^+1)$

       (iii) $(^-2)$ **(iv)** $(^-4)$

    c. We can use containers to show addition of integers. For example, $(^+5) + (^-2)$ can be shown as "pouring" the $(^-2)$ container into the $(^+5)$ container.

This results in the following container, which has the name $(^+3)$, and we say $(^+5) + (^-2) = (^+3)$.

Draw a system of containers to show the following additions.

 (i) $(^-4) + (^-5) =$ **(ii)** $(^+7) + (^-5) =$

 (iii) $(^-4) + (^+5) =$ **(iv)** $(^+1) + (^-6) =$

4.7 MULTIPLICATION OF INTEGERS

In this section we consider the operation of multiplication with integers. A product where both numbers are positive integers is precisely like that for whole numbers. Thus, we expect $4 \cdot 3 = 12$. However, what will happen if we take the product of $4 \cdot {}^-3$? We could perhaps proceed as we did with whole numbers when we used repeated addition. Then $4 \cdot {}^-3 = {}^-3 + {}^-3 + {}^-3 + {}^-3 = {}^-12$. Could you suggest the number-line solution to $4 \cdot {}^-3$?

We might also consider a game type of interpretation for these products. Suppose the first number represents the number of plays and the second represents a constant gain or loss per play. Then $4 \cdot 3$ means that at each play we gain 3 points. In four such plays we would expect to gain 12. What would it mean to write $4 \cdot {}^-2$? Apparently we lose two each time we play. Then in 4 plays we would expect to lose a total of 8 points. Thus, $4 \cdot {}^-2 = {}^-8$. How does this result compare with that found by repeated addition? Using this same game situation, let us consider an interpretation for ${}^-3 \cdot 2$. Apparently we are in a situation where we gain 2 each time we play. Then 3 plays ago we had 6 fewer points than we have now. That is, ${}^-3 \cdot 2 = {}^-6$. Using this same procedure, what would be the results of ${}^-4 \cdot 5$?

A second way that the product ${}^-3 \cdot 2$ is sometimes interpreted is to assume that commutativity holds for multiplication of integers (fortunately, this assumption is true). Then, ${}^-3 \cdot 2 = 2 \cdot {}^-3$, and we know how to handle this as repeated addition. Thus, ${}^-3 \cdot 2 = 2 \cdot {}^-3 = {}^-6$.

A third way to approach such multiplication problems would be to use patterns. Consider the following:

$$4 \cdot 3 = 12$$
$$3 \cdot 3 = 9$$
$$2 \cdot 3 = 6$$
$$1 \cdot 3 = 3$$
$$0 \cdot 3 = 0$$

Is it not apparent that a sequence is involved, both in the first factor and also in the right-hand member of each equality? Continuing this we would expect $4, 3, 2, 1, 0, {}^-1, {}^-2, {}^-3, \ldots$ in the left-hand factor and $12, 9, 6, 3, 0, {}^-3, {}^-6, {}^-9, \ldots$ in the right-hand member. Thus, let us continue the pattern as follows:

$$4 \cdot 3 = 12$$
$$3 \cdot 3 = 9$$

$$2 \cdot 3 = 6$$
$$1 \cdot 3 = 3$$
$$0 \cdot 3 = 0$$
$$^-1 \cdot 3 = ^-3$$
$$^-2 \cdot 3 = ^-6$$
$$^-3 \cdot 3 = ^-9$$

This pattern-building procedure is useful in developing the fourth possibility, the product of two negative integers. Consider the following sequence:

$$3 \cdot ^-3 = ^-9$$
$$2 \cdot ^-3 = ^-6$$
$$1 \cdot ^-3 = ^-3$$
$$0 \cdot ^-3 = 0$$

What should the next product be? Apparently $^-1 \cdot ^-3 = 3$ if we are to continue. What is $^-2 \cdot ^-3$?

$$3 \cdot ^-3 = ^-9$$
$$2 \cdot ^-3 = ^-6$$
$$1 \cdot ^-3 = ^-3$$
$$0 \cdot ^-3 = 0$$
$$^-1 \cdot ^-3 = 3$$
$$^-2 \cdot ^-3 = 6$$
$$^-3 \cdot ^-3 = 9$$
$$\cdot$$
$$\cdot$$
$$\cdot$$

Let us contrast this with the game situation mentioned earlier. The product $^-2 \cdot ^-3$ would call to mind the fact that we are to lose three points on each play. The $^-2$ indicates that we are interested in the situation two plays ago. At that time our score was 6 points better than it is now. Thus, $^-2 \cdot ^-3 = 6$.

To summarize our work with multiplication of integers, we might state the following: The product of two positive integers is a positive integer. The product of two negative integers is a positive integer. The product of a positive integer and a negative integer is a negative integer.

$$4 \cdot 6 = 24$$
$$4 \cdot ^-6 = ^-24$$
$$^-4 \cdot 6 = ^-24$$
$$^-4 \cdot ^-6 = 24$$

Now that we know how to add and multiply integers, let us pause for a moment to consider what properties hold in each case. For example, if you are given two integers, do you expect the sum to be an integer? What about the product? In both cases the answer would be yes. Likewise, the integers are commutative and associative with respect to both operations. We mentioned in an earlier section that 0 is a very special number in addition of integers because $r + 0 = r$ for any integer r. The number 1 plays precisely the same role with regard to multiplication because $s \cdot 1 = s$ for any integer s. The numbers 0 and 1 are referred to as *identity elements* with regard to addition and multiplication, respectively. Recall the term *additive inverse*. We stated that 5 is the additive inverse of $^-5$ because $^-5 + 5 = 0$. In fact, every integer has a unique additive inverse. We cannot state the same principle for multiplication because, for example, no integer k can be found such that $3 \cdot k = 1$. This fact will make it desirable for us to expand our number system, which we will do in the next chapter.

Identity elements [handwritten margin note]

We should once again look at the distributive pattern. In the set of integers, multiplication distributes over addition. Thus, $^-2(3 + {}^-4) = (^-2 \cdot 3) + (^-2 \cdot {}^-4) = {}^-6 + 8 = 2$ and also $(3 + {}^-4) \cdot {}^-2 = (3 \cdot {}^-2) + (^-4 \cdot {}^-2) = {}^-6 + 8 = 2$.

Let us summarize these findings as Property 4.10.

PROPERTY 4.10   For all integers r, s, and t:

1. $r + s$ is a unique integer (closure property for addition)
2. $r + s = s + r$ (commutative property for addition)
3. $(r + s) + t = r + (s + t)$ (associative property for addition)
4. $r + 0 = 0 + r = r$ (identity property for addition)
5. For each integer r, there exists a unique integer ^-r such that $r + {}^-r = {}^-r + r = 0$ (additive inverse property).
6. $r \cdot s$ is a unique integer (closure property for multiplication)
7. $r \cdot s = s \cdot r$ (commutative property for multiplication)
8. $(r \cdot s)t = r(s \cdot t)$ (associative property for multiplication)
9. $r \cdot 1 = 1 \cdot r = r$ (identity property for multiplication)
10. $r(s + t) = (rs) + (rt)$ and $(s + t) \cdot r = (sr) + (tr)$ (distributive property of multiplication over addition)

PROBLEM SET 4.7

1. Find the following products:
   a. $4 \cdot 5$ b. $^-4 \cdot 5$ c. $6 \cdot {}^-3$ d. $^-4 \cdot {}^-5$
   e. $^-6 \cdot 5$ f. $^-5 \cdot 0$ g. $^-5 \cdot 3$ h. $^-1 \cdot 7$

2. a. Is the set of negative integers closed with respect to multiplication?
   b. Is the set of negative integers closed with respect to addition?
   c. Find a set of integers closed under multiplication, but not under addition.

3. Perform the computations that follow using the commutative, distributive, and associative properties whenever *helpful*.

   a. $(37 + {}^-4) + 4$ b. $(5 + {}^-37) + {}^-5)$
   c. $(97 + {}^-42) + 3$ d. $^-17 + (40 + {}^-3)$
   e. $(17 \cdot 25) \cdot {}^-4$ f. $(31 \cdot {}^-8) + (31 \cdot {}^-2)$
   g. $^-5 \cdot (2 \cdot {}^-17)$ h. $(25 \cdot {}^-36)(2 \cdot {}^-4)$
   i. $^-42 \cdot (2 + {}^-3)$ j. $(29 \cdot 3614) + (29 \cdot {}^-2614)$

4. a. Use a pattern similar to those used in Section 4.7 to illustrate that $2 \cdot {}^-3 = {}^-6$.
   b. Use a pattern to show that $^-4 \cdot {}^-6 = 24$.

5. a. Does $^-(r + s) = {}^-r + {}^-s$? Use examples to illustrate your answer.
   b. Does $^-(r \cdot s) = {}^-r \cdot {}^-s$? Justify your answer.

6. State the properties that justify each of the following:
   a. $(6 \cdot {}^-4) \cdot {}^-3 = ({}^-4 \cdot 6) \cdot {}^-3$
   b. $^-4(7 + {}^-7) = ({}^-4 \cdot 7) + ({}^-4 \cdot {}^-7)$
   c. $(7 + {}^-8) \cdot 1 = (7 + {}^-8)$
   d. $(6 \cdot {}^-4) \cdot 25 = 6({}^-4 \cdot 25)$
   e. $(5 + {}^-4) \cdot 3 = (5 \cdot 3) + ({}^-4 \cdot 3)$
   f. $(17 + {}^-1) + 0 = (17 + {}^-1)$
   g. $(6 + {}^-5) + {}^-8 = {}^-8 + (6 + {}^-5)$
   h. $(7 + {}^-8) \cdot 1 = ({}^-8 + 7) \cdot 1$
   i. $(6 \cdot {}^-4) + (6 \cdot {}^-2) = 6({}^-4 + {}^-2)$

7. List the elements of the truth set for each of the following, using as your domain the set of integers:

   a. $3x = 15$ b. $3x = {}^-12$ c. $4x = {}^-24$
   d. $^-4 \cdot x = 28$ e. $3x + 2 = {}^-10$ f. $^-2x + {}^-4 = 12$
   g. $^-6x = 38$ h. $3x > {}^-12$ i. $4x < {}^-17$
   j. $^-2x < 6$

8. a. In an Eskimo village in northern Alaska, the temperature has been falling 3° per day for the last 2 weeks. If the temperature is now 42° below 0, what was the temperature 10 days ago? Write a number sentence to describe this.

   b. If the temperature pattern continues, what do you expect 5 days from now? Write a number sentence to describe this situation.

   c. Use a placeholder to state in general the temperature pattern involved.

9. a. If r is an integer such that r is greater than $^-15$ and less than $^-5$, what can you say about $7r$?

   b. What about $r \cdot {}^-4$?

10. Consider $4 + {}^-4 = 0$ as an alternate method to show that $3 \cdot {}^-4 = {}^-12$. Therefore, $3(4 + {}^-4) = 3 \cdot 0 = 0$. Thus, $(3 \cdot 4) + (3 + {}^-4) = 0$ because of the distributive property or $12 + (3 \cdot {}^-4) = 0$. Therefore, $3 \cdot {}^-4$ is the additive inverse of 12, but $12 + {}^-12 = 0$ so ${}^-12$ is the additive inverse of 12. Therefore, $3 \cdot {}^-4 = {}^-12$, because any integer has exactly one additive inverse.

a. Use this technique to argue that $2 \cdot {}^-5 = {}^-10$.

b. Use it to show that ${}^-3 \cdot {}^-4 = 12$

11. Show that ${}^-1 \cdot r = {}^-r$. (*Hint:* Write $1 + {}^-1 = 0$, then $(1 + {}^-1) \cdot r = 0 \cdot r$ and proceed as in Problem 10.)

12. a. Use your calculator to find ${}^-382({}^-186 + 482)$.

b. Find ${}^-36(248 - 184)$.

13. Consider the distributive property $a(b + c) = ab + ac$. Show that this property holds for the following integers.

a. $a = 2, b = 3, c = {}^-2$ **b.** $a = {}^-3, b = {}^-4, c = 1$

c. $a = {}^-5, b = {}^-2, c = {}^-6$ **d.** $a = {}^-3, b = 4, c = {}^-7$

14. Show that the statement $a + (b \cdot c) = (a + b) \cdot (a + c)$ is false if $a = {}^-3, b = 4$, and $c = {}^-2$.

15. The procedures used when multiplying integers can be proved in general. The following sequence of steps can be used to show that ${}^-a \cdot b = {}^-(ab)$. Complete the justifications for each of the steps.

Let a and b be positive integers

$$\begin{array}{ll} {}^-a + a = 0 & \text{Property 4.9} \\ ({}^-a + a) \cdot b = 0 \cdot b & \text{If } r = s, \text{ then } rk = sk \text{ for any } k. \\ ({}^-a + a) \cdot b = 0 & 0 \text{ times anything is 0.} \\ ({}^-a + b) + (a \cdot b) = 0 & \\ \qquad \therefore ({}^-a \cdot b) \text{ is the additive inverse of } (ab) \end{array}$$

But

$$\begin{array}{l} {}^-(ab) + (ab) = 0 \\ \therefore {}^-(a \cdot b) \text{ is the additive inverse of } (ab) \\ \therefore {}^-a \cdot b = {}^-(a \cdot b) \qquad \text{Uniqueness of additive inverse} \end{array}$$

16. Supply a justification for each step of the following proof that $({}^-a \cdot {}^-b) = ab$.

Let a and b be positive integers.

$$\begin{array}{l} {}^-b + b = 0 \\ {}^-a({}^-b + b) = {}^-a \cdot 0 \\ {}^-a({}^-b + b) = 0 \\ ({}^-a \cdot {}^-b) + ({}^-a \cdot b) = 0 \\ ({}^-a \cdot {}^-b) + {}^-(ab) = 0 \qquad \text{Problem 15} \end{array}$$

$\therefore (^-a \cdot ^-b)$ is the additive inverse of $^-(ab)$

$^-(ab) + (ab) = 0$
$\therefore ab$ is the additive inverse of $^-(ab)$
$\therefore (^-a \cdot ^-b) = ab$

Pedagogical Problems and Activities

17. Suppose we are playing a game where points can be gained or lost on each play. When we write $r \cdot s$ let us agree that s represents a constant gain or loss on each play. Then r represents the number of plays. Thus, $3 \cdot 4$ means that 4 points are gained on each play and we make three such plays, thereby increasing our score by 12. Interpret each of the following using the same setting:

    a. $4 \cdot 3$ b. $2 \cdot 6$ c. $4 \cdot ^-2$
    d. $6 \cdot ^-2$ e. $5 \cdot ^-3$ f. $6 \cdot ^-8$

18. Suppose that one of your sixth-grade students comments, "We are so far in debt now that we couldn't possibly get any deeper in debt." What do you say?

19. Use a pattern like the one in the text to show that $^-1 \cdot ^-1 = 1$.

20. Use the calculator and the $\boxed{+/-}$ key to compute the following:

    a. $(5) \cdot (^-2) =$
    b. $(^-5) \cdot (^-2) =$
    c. $(^-12) \cdot (^-15) =$

21. a. We considered the use of a pattern as one way to develop the rule for multiplication of integers. Suppose a child considers the indicated sequence. Can he use it to determine the answer to $(^-1)(^-1)$?

    $$4 \cdot 4 = 16$$
    $$3 \cdot 3 = 9$$
    $$2 \cdot 2 = 4$$
    $$1 \cdot 1 = 1$$
    $$0 \cdot 0 = 0$$
    $$(^-1)(^-1) = ?$$

    b. In what way is this sequence different from those used in our earlier discussion?

4.8   SUBTRACTION AND DIVISION OF INTEGERS

Subtraction is usually closely related to addition. In Chapter 2 we defined subtraction in terms of addition by claiming that if $a > b$ the difference $a - b$ is a whole number c if and only if $b + c = a$. In Chapter 3 we again found this definition to be helpful, particularly when performing subtractions involving bases other than ten. This same approach to subtraction is quite helpful as we work with integers.

Definition 4.6 Given integers r and s, $(r - s)$ is that integer t such that $s + t = r$. ($r - s = t$ if and only if $s + t = r$.)

Using this definition we may make the following statements:

$$
\begin{array}{lll}
7 - 4 = 3 & \text{because} & 4 + 3 = 7 \\
8 - {}^-2 = 10 & \text{because} & {}^-2 + 10 = 8 \\
{}^-6 - 4 = {}^-10 & \text{because} & 4 + {}^-10 = {}^-6 \\
{}^-7 - {}^-1 = {}^-6 & \text{because} & {}^-1 + {}^-6 = {}^-7 \\
0 - 3 = {}^-3 & \text{because} & 3 + {}^-3 = 0
\end{array}
$$

Number-line work can also be done to aid in subtraction. To answer the subtraction question ${}^-6 - 4 = n$, we can return to the definition to ask "What number n must we add to 4 to obtain ${}^-6$?" That is, $4 + n = {}^-6$.

According to the number line, we have one addend, 4, and the answer, ${}^-6$. The missing arrow must be ${}^-10$.

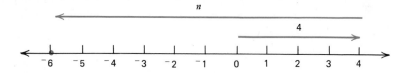

Thus, ${}^-6 - 4 = {}^-10$ because $4 + {}^-10 = {}^-6$.

EXAMPLE 1

Use a number line to find $6 - {}^-3$. Again we are asked to find the number that when added to ${}^-3$ gives 6 (i.e., one addend is ${}^-3$, so ${}^-3 + n = 6$).

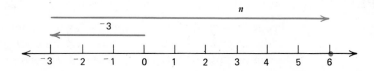

The result must be 9. That is, $6 - {}^-3 = 9$ because ${}^-3 + 9 = 6$.

EXAMPLE 2

Find $^-3 - {}^-5$. The interpretation can again be one of asking what must be added to $^-5$ to obtain $^-3$.

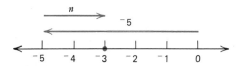

We may conclude that $^-3 - {}^-5 = 2$ because $^-5 + 2 = {}^-3$. We could proceed to perform subtractions in this manner. However, another approach seems easier. Let us make the following observations:

$$
\begin{array}{llll}
4 - 3 = 1 & \text{and} & 4 + {}^-3 = 1 \\
6 - {}^-2 = 8 & \text{and} & 6 + {}^-({}^-2) = 6 + 2 = 8 \\
^-4 - 7 = {}^-11 & \text{and} & ^-4 + {}^-7 = {}^-11 \\
^-9 - 3 = {}^-12 & \text{and} & ^-9 + {}^-3 = {}^-12 \\
^-3 - {}^-8 = 5 & \text{and} & ^-3 + {}^-({}^-8) = {}^-3 + 8 = 6
\end{array}
$$

Note that in each case we have been able to restate the subtraction problem as an equivalent addition problem.

EXAMPLE 1

Find $^-7 - 3$. We can rewrite this as the addition problem $^-7 + {}^-3 = {}^-10$. Thus, $^-7 - 3 = {}^-7 + {}^-3 = {}^-10$. A check shows us that this is indeed correct, since $3 + {}^-10 = {}^-7$.

EXAMPLE 2

Find $^-4 - {}^-6$. Write the addition problem $^-4 + {}^-({}^-6) = {}^-4 + 6 = 2$. We may check by noting that $^-6 + 2 = {}^-4$.

In general, we find that solutions of subtraction problems involving integers can easily be done by replacing the subtraction problem with an equivalent addition statement. Let us formalize this fact as Property 4.11.

PROPERTY 4.11   For all integers r and s, $r - s = r + {}^-s$.

Property 4.11 allows us to approach subtraction more easily by applying the addition process that we already have mentioned. Thus, to find $(6 - 3) - 4$ we may simply rewrite in the equivalent form $(6 + {}^-3) - 4 = 3 - 4 = 3 + {}^-4 = {}^-1$.

> REMARK   Notice that we are finding the answer to a problem calling for
> subtraction by simply adding the additive inverse.

EXAMPLE 1

Use Property 4.11 to find:
a) $(6 - 2) - 5$ b) $6 - (2 - 5)$

$$a)\ (6 - 2) - 5 = (6 + {}^-2) - 5$$
$$= 4 - 5$$
$$= 4 + {}^-5$$
$$= {}^-1$$
$$b)\ 6 - (2 - 5) = 6 - (2 + {}^-5)$$
$$= 6 - {}^-3$$
$$= 6 + {}^-({}^-3)$$
$$= 6 + 3$$
$$= 9$$

EXAMPLE 2

Write $r(s - t)$ as a difference.

$$r(s - t) = r(s + {}^-t)$$
$$= rs + r \cdot {}^-t$$
$$= rs + {}^-(rt)$$
$$= rs - rt$$

Do you see that Example 3 verifies that multiplication distributes over subtraction? What conclusion can be drawn from Examples 1 and 2? Does this
specific example show that the integers are not associative under subtraction? The answer is yes; one such counterexample suffices to make such a
general statement.

Are the integers closed under subtraction? That is, given two integers r and
s, will $r - s$ be an integer no matter how we pick r and s? Intuitively, our
number-line work would seem to make us answer in the affirmative. Property 4.11 provides us with even more forceful evidence. We have asserted
before that the integers are closed under addition, and this property guarantees that each subtraction statement is equivalent to an addition statement.
Therefore, the integers must be closed under subtraction.

The definition for division closely parallels that for division of whole numbers. Division is closely related to multiplication (we previously declared that
$12 \div 6 = 2$ because $6 \cdot 2 = 12$, for example). Let us define division for
integers as follows.

Definition 4.7   For integers r and s, where $s \neq 0$, $r \div s$ is that integer t (if t exists) such that $s \cdot t = r$ ($r \div s = t$ if and only if $s \cdot t = r$).

Using the definition we may make the following statements:

$$14 \div 2 = 7 \quad \text{because} \quad 2 \cdot 7 = 14$$
$$^-14 \div 2 = ^-7 \quad \text{because} \quad 2 \cdot {}^-7 = {}^-14$$
$$14 \div {}^-2 = {}^-7 \quad \text{because} \quad {}^-2 \cdot {}^-7 = 14$$
$$^-14 \div {}^-2 = 7 \quad \text{because} \quad {}^-2 \cdot 7 = {}^-14$$

It should be noted that the integers are not closed under division. For example, $5 \div 2$ does not have an answer in the set of integers. For this reason we must continue with the "if it exists" statement in the definition of division.

PROPERTY 4.12   **For all integers r, s, and t:**

1. $r - s$ is a unique integer (Closure property for subtraction)
2. $(r - s) \div t = (r \div t) - (s \div t)$ (Distributive property)

REMARK We noted in Property 4.12 that with the development of the integers we gained closure under subtraction. However, we still do not have commutative or associative properties under subtraction or division.

1. $r - s \neq s - r$
2. $(r - s) - t \neq r - (s - t)$
3. $r \div s \neq s \div r$
4. $(r \div s) \div t \neq r \div (s \div t)$

PROBLEM SET 4.8

1. Evaluate each of the following using a number line as illustrated in the preceding section:

    a. $5 - 3$ **b.** $4 - 6$ **c.** $^-5 - 2$ **d.** $^-4 - 6$ **e.** $6 - {}^-3$

    f. $8 - {}^-5$ **g.** $^-4 - {}^-3$ **h.** $^-6 - {}^-4$ **i.** $^-3 - {}^-7$ **j.** $^-2 - {}^-4$

2. Use Property 4.11 to solve each of the following:

    a. $6 - 7$ **b.** $^-8 - 5$ **c.** $^-9 - {}^-10$
    d. $14 - {}^-12$ **e.** $^-18 - 6$ **f.** $^-19 - 5$
    g. $6 - (2 - {}^-6)$ **h.** $^-5 + ({}^-6 - 7)$ **i.** $9 - ({}^-5 + 7)$
    j. $^-7(8 - 9)$ **k.** $(7 - 8)({}^-9 - 4)$ **l.** $^-7 - (0 - 2)$

3. **a.** Give two examples different from that given in the text to illustrate that the integers are not associative under subtraction.

    b. Are the integers commutative under subtraction? Justify your answer.

4. Evaluate each of the following:

a. $^-14 \div ^-2$ b. $28 \div ^-7$ c. $^-36 \div 12$

d. $0 \div ^-4$ e. $(^-6 + ^-4) \div ^-2$ f. $(6 \div 2) + (4 \div 2)$

g. $(^-6 \div 3) - (10 \div 2)$ h. $(^-18 + 12) \div 6$ i. $(^-18 \div 6) + (12 \div 6)$

j. $(^-4 \cdot 5) \div 10$ k. $(^-8 \div 2) - (21 \div ^-7)$

5. a. Is division commutative? Justify your answer.

   b. Is division associative? Justify your answer.

6. A deserted shack in Death Valley is 280 feet below sea level. A tree in the Bristlecone Pine Forest stands at a point 11,400 feet above sea level. How much higher is the tree than the shack? Write a mathematical sentence to express this.

7. One Bristlecone pine, named Methuselah, is reported to be 4600 years old. In what year did this tree start to grow?

8. Find the following (you may reduce your work considerably by applying the distributive property for multiplication over subtraction):

a. $(46 \cdot 5812) - (46 \cdot 5812)$ b. $(52 \cdot 78) - (52 \cdot 28)$

c. $(582 \cdot 69) - (582 \cdot ^-31)$ d. $(455 \cdot 62) - (55 \cdot 62)$

e. $(73 \cdot 45) - (13 \cdot 45)$ f. $(482 \cdot 758) - (482 \cdot 158)$

9. List the elements of the truth set for each of the following in the domain of integers:

a. $x - 4 = 7$ b. $x - 4 = ^-10$ c. $6 - x = ^-12$

d. $^-8 = x - 6$ e. $2x - 4 = 12$ f. $x \div 3 = ^-12$

g. $x \div 5 = ^-14$ h. $(x - 2) \div 3 = 12$ i. $(x - 4) \div 5 = 17$

10. Does $a - (b - c) = (a - b) + c$ for all integers a, b, and c?

11. Under what condition does $a \div b = b \div a$?

12. Is the statement $(a - b) \cdot c = (a \cdot c) - (b \cdot c)$ true for each of the following?

a. $a = ^-8, b = 12, c = 2$

b. $a = ^-8, b = ^-12, c = ^-2$

c. $a = 8, b = ^-12, c = ^-2$

d. $a = 21, b = ^-35, c = ^-7$

13. Is the statement $a \cdot (b - c) = (a \cdot b) - (a \cdot c)$ true for each of the following?

a. $a = ^-8, b = 12, c = 2$

b. $a = ^-8, b = ^-12, c = ^-2$

c. $a = 8, b = ^-12, c = ^-2$

d. $a = 21, b = ^-35, c = ^-7$

14. Consider the expressions $(x + y) - (z + w)$ and $(x - z) + (y - w)$. Are the expression equal if:

   a. $x = 9$, $y = 4$, $z = 4$, $w = 2$?
   b. $x = 3$, $y = 6$, $z = {}^-5$, $w = 8$?
   c. $x = {}^-9$, $y = {}^-2$, $z = 6$, $w = {}^-3$
   d. Show that $(x + y) - (z + w) = (x - z) + (y - w)$ for all w, x, y, and z.

15. A product such as $(x - 2)(x + 3)$ may be performed as follows:

   (i) $(x - 2)(x + 3) = (x - 2) \cdot x + (x - 2) \cdot 3$
   $$= x^2 - 2x + 3x - 6$$
   $$= x^2 + x - 6$$
   (ii) $(x - 4)(x - 5) = (x - 4)(x + {}^-5)$
   $$= (x - 4)x + (x - 4) \cdot {}^-5$$
   $$= x^2 - 4x - 5x + 20$$
   $$= x^2 - 9x + 20$$

   Write each of the following indicated products as an equivalent indicated sum or difference:

   a. $(x - 8)(x + 5)$ b. $(x + 6)(x - 4)$
   c. $(x - 2)(x - 3)$ d. $(x - 5)(x - 6)$

Pedagogical Problems and Activities

16. A sixth-grade book poses the following problem: one night the temperature dropped from 2 degrees below 0 to 10 degrees below 0. How much was the drop? If a student writes an equation to express this as ${}^-2 - n = {}^-10$, what do you say?

17. A sixth-grade class has learned to add integers. Explain briefly how you would explain the meaning of $6 - {}^-4$ and ${}^-6 - {}^-4$.

18. Suppose a sixth-grade child tells you that because the integers are not commutative with respect to subtraction, then it is impossible to find any integers r and s such that $r - s = s - r$. What do you say?

19. We can also think of subtraction as finding the difference between two numbers, where we are interested both in how far is it and in what direction do we go to get from the subtrahend to the minuend. That is ${}^-5 - {}^-8$ is asking "how far and in what direction do we go to get from ${}^-8$ to ${}^-5$." The answer is, go to the right 3. (That is ${}^-5 - {}^-8 = 3$.) Use this procedure to find the following:

   a. $4 - {}^-2$ b. ${}^-3 - 5$ c. ${}^-6 - {}^-2$
   d. ${}^-3 - {}^-7$ e. ${}^-5 - 2$ f. ${}^-5 - {}^-4$

20. Use the calculator and the ⊞⊟ key to compute the following;

    a. $(^-4) - (^-3) =$

    b. $3 - (^-4) =$

    c. $(^-12) \div (^-6) =$

    d. $^-59 + (^-5)$

    e. $[18 - (^-3)] \times (^-5) =$

21. Subtraction of integers using electrical charges is best viewed from the "take-away" subtraction. For example, $(^+7) - (^+2)$ is interpreted as "remove two positive charges from the $^+7$ container". We picture this as the following:

The result leaves the container 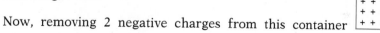, named $(^+5)$, and we say that $(^+7) - (^+2) = (^+5)$. However, when using charges to compute $(^+7) - (^-2)$ we may have a problem. We cannot remove 2 negative charges unless we arrange our container to have 2 negative charges. Hence, we must use a container for $(^+7)$ with at least 2 negative charges, say one like the following

Now, removing 2 negative charges from this container

leaves the container   or $(^+9)$.

Hence, $(^+7) - (^-2) = (^+9)$.

Use a system of charges to compute the following:

    a. $(^-2) - (^-3) =$

    b. $(^+5) - (^-1) =$

    c. $(^-5) - (^+1) =$

    d. $(^-5) - (^-1) =$

4.9 INEQUALITIES AND EQUATIONS

Let us turn now to some properties that are useful in finding solution sets. In Chapter 2 and again in Section 4.6 we discussed basic concepts involving equality and inequality. In Section 4.6 we discussed inequality of integers in terms of number-line representations.

EXAMPLE

7 > 5 and 7 is to the right of 5 on the number line.

As we extended this idea to the integers, we concluded that $^-3 > {}^-5$ because $^-3$ is to the right of $^-5$, which is indeed the case.

Another approach to order might be one that is an extension of the definition used earlier. We stated that $a < b$ if and only if there exists some counting number $k > 0$ such that $a + k = b$. Let us modify this definition slightly and apply it to integers.

Definition 4.8   For any integers r and s, $r < s$ if and only if there exists some positive integer k such that $r + k = s$.

Application of this definition allows us to conclude the following:

$$^-10 < {}^-4 \text{ because if } k = 6, {}^-10 + \underline{6} = {}^-4.$$
$$^-3 < {}^-1 \text{ because if } k = 2, {}^-3 + \underline{2} = {}^-1.$$
$$^-6 < 0 \text{ because if } k = 6, {}^-6 + 6 = 0.$$
$$^-5 < 2 \text{ because if } k = 7, {}^-5 + 7 = 2.$$

Two properties follow immediately from the preceding discussion.

PROPERTY 4.13   **Given integers r, s, and t, if $r < s$ and $s < t$, then $r < t$. (Transitive property for inequality)**

PROPERTY 4.14   **If r and s are integers, exactly one of the following must be true: $r = s$, $r > s$, or $r < s$. (Trichotomy property for integers)**

We have asked you to find solution sets for equalities several times in the first three chapters. In each case we used an intuitive approach where we simply substituted numbers into the given equation to test them. We could of course use the same procedure to obtain solution sets as we work with integers as illustrated in the following example.

EXAMPLE 1

Find the set of integers S such that $2x + 5 = 1$.

We know that $^-4 + 5 = 1$, so $2x$ must equal $^-4$. Thus it must be the case that $x = {}^-2$, so $S = \{^-2\}$.

Although such a procedure is permissible and is intuitively clear, it is often somewhat cumbersome to use. Let us consider an alternate approach, one commonly used in algebra. The following property is useful for this purpose.

PROPERTY 4.15 **For any integers a, b, and c:**

1. If $a = b$, then $a + c = b + c$.
2. If $a = b$, then $ac = bc$.

Let us apply Property 4.15 as we solve the following equations.

EXAMPLE 2

Find the set of integers S such that $2x + 5 = 1$.

Solution

$$2x + 5 = 1$$
$$(2x + 5) + (^-5) = 1 + (^-5) \quad \text{By Property 4.15(1)}$$
$$2x + (5 + ^-5) = 1 + (^-5) \quad \text{Associative property}$$
$$2x + 0 = ^-4 \quad \text{Definition of } + \text{ for integers}$$
$$2x = ^-4 \quad \text{0 is the additive identity}$$
$$x = ^-2$$
$$\text{Thus} \quad S = \{^-2\}$$

You should note that each part of Property 4.15 allows us to state a new equality that is equivalent to the original. That is, each resulting equality will have the same solution set as the original equality. The final equality is one for which the solution set is readily observable (i.e., the solution set for $x = ^-2$ by observation contains just the integer $^-2$, and therefore the solution set for $2x + 5 = 1$ must also contain just the integer $^-2$).

EXAMPLE 3

Find the set of integers S such that $4 - 2x = ^-6$.

Solution

$$4 - 2x = ^-6$$
$$4 - 2x + ^-4 = ^-6 + ^-4$$
$$^-2x + (4 + ^-4) = ^-6 + ^-4$$
$$^-2x + 0 = ^-10$$
$$^-2x = ^-10$$
$$x = 5$$
$$\text{Thus } S = \{5\}$$

Inequalities may be solved in a manner similar to that used above for equalities. Let us state Property 4.16, which will allow us to proceed with this idea.

PROPERTY 4.16   **For any integers a, b, and c:**

1. If $a < b$, then $a + c < b + c$.
2. a. If $a < b$ and $c > 0$, then $ac < bc$.
   b. If $a < b$ and $c < 0$, then $ac > bc$.

Special attention must be called to part 2 of this property. If both sides of an inequality are multiplied by the same positive number the inequality remains in the same order, but if both sides are multiplied by some negative number, the inequality reverses.

a. $1 < 3$ and $4 > 0$,   so $1 \cdot 4 < 3 \cdot 4$
   i.e., $4 < 12$
b. $^-3 < 2$ and $5 > 0$,   so $^-3 \cdot 5 < 2 \cdot 5$
   i.e., $^-15 < 10$
c. $^-5 < ^-2$ and $3 > 0$,   so $^-5 \cdot 3 < ^-2 \cdot 3$
   i.e., $^-15 < ^-6$
d. $2 < 3$ and $^-3 < 0$,   so $2 \cdot ^-3 > 3 \cdot ^-3$
   i.e., $^-6 > ^-9$
e. $^-4 < 2$ and $^-5 < 0$,   so $^-4 \cdot ^-5 > 2 \cdot ^-5$
   i.e., $20 > ^-10$
f. $^-6 < ^-2$ and $^-3 < 0$,   so $^-6 \cdot ^-3 > ^-2 \cdot ^-3$
   i.e., $18 > 6$

EXAMPLE 4

Find the set of integers S such that $2x + 5 < 1$.

Solution

$$2x + 1 < 5$$
$$2x + 1 + {}^-1 < 5 + {}^-1 \qquad \text{Property 4.16(1)}$$
$$2x + 0 < 5 + {}^-1 \qquad \text{Additive inverse}$$
$$2x < 5 + {}^-1 \qquad \text{0 is the additive identity}$$
$$2x < 4 \qquad \text{Definition of addition}$$
$$x < 2 \qquad \text{Definition of multiplication}$$
$$S = \{\cdots, {}^-2, {}^-1, 0\ 1\}$$

EXAMPLE 5

Find the set of integers S such that $2x - 4 < 1$.

Solution

$$2x - 4 < 1$$
$$2x - 4 + 4 < 1 + 4$$
$$2x - 0 < 5$$
$$2x < 5$$
$$x < 3$$
$$S = \{ \cdots, {}^-2, {}^-1, 0, 1, 2\}$$

> REMARK   Let us again emphasize that the statement "a is greater than b" $(a > b)$ is equivalent to the statement "b is less than a" $(b < a)$. Thus, although Property 4.16 is phrased as a less than property, we should recognize that the reverse situation also applies, as will be the case in Example 6.

EXAMPLE 6

Find the set of integers S such that $4 - 3x > {}^-2$.

Solution

$$4 - 3x > {}^-2$$
$$4 - 3x + {}^-4 > {}^-2 + {}^-4$$
$${}^-3x > {}^-6$$
$${}^-1({}^-3x) < {}^-1({}^-6)$$
$$3x < 6$$
$$x < 2$$
$$S = \{ \cdots, {}^-2, {}^-1, 0, 1\}$$

PROBLEM SET 4.9

1. For each pair, decide which is larger.
   a. $7, 9$ b. $^-4, 2$ c. $^-12, ^-14$
   d. $^-8, ^-6$ e. $4 + ^-6, 8 \div ^-2$ f. $^-6 - ^-8, ^-3 \cdot ^-2$

2. State the properties that can be used to justify each of the following:
   a. If $x + 2 = 6$, then $(x + 2) + {}^-2 = 6 + {}^-2$.
   b. If $x + {}^-3 > 8$, then $(x + {}^-3) + 3 > 8 + 3$.
   c. If $x > 4$, then $2 \cdot x > 2 \cdot 4$.
   d. If $x > y$, and $y > z$ then $x > z$.
   e. If $x > {}^-3$, then ${}^-2x < {}^-2 \cdot {}^-3$.

3. Use the properties developed pertaining to equality to aid in determining the truth set for each of the following (the domain is the set of integers):
   a. $x - 3 = 5$ b. $x - 2 = {}^-3$ c. $x + 2 = 5$
   d. $x + 3 = {}^-3$ e. $2x + 3 = 7$ f. $2x - 1 = 5$
   g. $3x - 4 = 11$ h. $3x + 2 = 11$ i. $2 = x + 5$
   j. $5 = 3 + x$ k. $3 = 2x - 5$ l. $4 = 3x - 2$

4. a. In a certain card game, Sally is 20 points in the hole and Brian is 70 points in the hole. Who has the better score?
   b. Later in the game, Sally has 30 points and Brian has 10 points. Who gained the most points?

5. Use the properties developed pertaining to inequality to aid in determining the truth set for each of the following (the domain is the set of integers):
   a. $x - 2 > 4$ b. $x - 4 > {}^-7$ c. $x - {}^-3 < {}^-7$
   d. $2 + x > {}^-6$ e. ${}^-16 > {}^-12 + x$ f. ${}^-14 < {}^-12 + x$
   g. $2x + {}^-1 < {}^-9$ h. $3x - 2 < 19$ i. ${}^-3x - 2 > 19$
   j. $2x - 81 < 133$ k. ${}^-x < 4$ l. ${}^-2x + 3 > {}^-9$

6. Find the truth set in the set of integers for each of the following inequalities:
   a. $3x - 3 > 5$ b. $4x + 1 < 7$ c. $2x + 3 > 6$
   d. $3x + 4 < 5$ e. $2x - 4 > {}^-5$ f. $4x + 1 < 7$

7. Complete the following statements in order to express the "greater than" properties:
   a. If $r > s$ and $s > t$, then _____.
   b. If $r > s$, then $r + t$ _____ $s + t$.
   c. If $r > s$ and $t > 0$, then rt _____ st.
   d. If $r > s$ and $t < 0$, then rt _____ st.

Pedagogical Problems and Activities

8. Present a number-line argument that might convince sixth-grade children that if $r > s$ and $s > t$, then $r > t$.

9. Present an argument based on the number line to verify that if $r > s$, then $r + t > s + t$.

10. a. Show how to use a beam balance to show that $5 < 7$.

   b. Show how to use the balance to illustrate that $5 + 2 < 7 + 2$.

REVIEW PROBLEM SET

1. Which of the following statements are true?

   a. $3 | 3$ **b.** $6 | 0$ **c.** $7 | (7 + 14)$ **d.** $5 | (6 \cdot 7)$

   e. If $6 | a$ and $6 | b$ then $6 | (a + b)$.

   f. If a number is divisible by 5 and by 3, then it is divisible by 15.

2. Use divisibility rules to test whether 32,760 is divisible by each of the following numbers:

   a. 2   **b.** 3   **c.** 5   **d.** 11   **e.** 9   **f.** 6

3. Write each of the following as a product of prime numbers:

   a. 52   **b.** 63   **c.** 486   **d.** 111   **e.** 291   **f.** 47,542

4. Test to see whether 401 is a prime number. What was the largest prime that you needed to try?

5. Find eight consecutive composite numbers.

6. a. Find the greatest common divisor of 56 and 84.

   b. Find the least common multiple of 56 and 84.

   c. The numbers 21 and 110 are relatively prime. What is their greatest common divisor? What is the least common multiple?

7. Perform the indicated operations.

   a. $(^-4) + (^-6)$ **b.** $4 - (^-5)$ **c.** $(^-12)(^-4)$

   d. $^-4(^-3 + 4)$ **e.** $^-12 \div 3$

8. List the elements in the truth set of each of the following open sentences:

   a. $x + 4 = 6$ **b.** $x + ^-4 = ^-2$ **c.** $^-3 + x = 5$ **d.** $2x + 3 = ^-1$

   e. $2x + 1 = 5$ **f.** $3x - 4 = 5$ **g.** $3 + x = ^-2$ **h.** $3x + 9 = 0$

9. a. Are the integers closed under addition? Why is this the case?

   b. Are the integers closed under subtraction? Discuss your answer please.

   c. Are the integers associative under subtraction? Justify your answer.

   d. Why are the integers not closed under division?

10. Which of the following are true?

   a. If $x + 3 = 5$, then $(x + 3) + (^-3) = 5 + (^-3)$.

   b. If $x + 2 < 6$, then $(x + 2) + (^-2) > 6 + (^-2)$.

   c. If $x - 5 > ^-4$, then $(x - 5) + 5 > ^-4 + 5$.

   d. If $x > ^-3$, then $(^-2)x < (^-2)(^-3)$.

11. **a.** Tabulate D_{28} and D_{35}.
    b. Find $D_{28} \cap D_{35}$. What is the greatest common divisor of 28 and 35?
    c. Tabulate the sets M_{28} and M_{35}.
    d. Find $M_{28} \cap M_{35}$.
    e. Find the least common multiple of 28 and 35.

12. Write the additive inverse for each of the following:
    a. 6   **b.** $^-3$ **c.** 0   **d.** $^-(^-3)$
    e. k **f.** ^-m **g.** $(^-4) - (^-2)$ **h.** $^-[(^-3)(^-4)]$

13. Find the truth set for each of the following using the integers as your domain.
    a. $x + 2 > 5$ **b.** $3 - x > 1$ **c.** $4x + 2 \le 7$ **d.** $2x + 1 \le 8$
    e. $3 < x + 5$ **f.** $2 + 3x < 4$ **g.** $2x - 4 > 13$ **h.** $5x - 3 < 1$

14. Consider the expressions $(x \div y) + (x \div z)$ and $x \div (y + z)$.
    a. Are these expressions equal if $x = 12$, $y = 2$, and $z = 4$?
    b. Why can we conclude that $x \div (y + z) \ne (x \div y) + x \div z)$?

15. Consider the expressions $(x + y) \div z$ and $(x \div z) + (y \div z)$.
    a. Are these expressions equal if $x = 12$, $y = 4$, and $z = 2$?
    b. Are they equal if $x = ^-9$, $y = 21$, and $z = 3$?
    c. What if $x = ^-12$, $y = 4$, and $z = ^-2$?

Solution to Sample Problem

A group of children are to be seated in a cafeteria. If two children are seated at each table, one child remains unseated. When three are seated at each table, two students are left unseated. When four are seated at each table, three are left, and when five are seated at each table, four remain unseated. What is the fewest number of children that could have been involved for this to happen?

1. *Understanding the Problem.* The number that we are searching for is clearly *not* a multiple of 2, 3, 4, or 5 because these numbers do not divide it. If n is the number that we are asked to find, then we may write the following where j, k, l, and m are the quotients in each case, so they must be counting numbers.
    a. $n = 2 \cdot j + 1$
    b. $n = 3 \cdot k + 2$
    c. $n = 4 \cdot l + 3$
    d. $n = 5 \cdot m + 4$

2. *Devising a Plan.* We could try a guess-and-check approach where we select numbers that satisfy one of the four conditions listed, then check it in each of the other cases.

   A second possibility would be to see if somehow we could use the ideas from least common multiples or greatest common divisors to attack the problem.

3. *Solution 1.* Let us try a guess-and-check method and use a table to record the numbers as we proceed. Because the greatest divisor to test is to be 5, let us select numbers that satisfy that condition first. Then perhaps recognize that to produce a remainder of 1 when divided by 2 the number must be odd.

n	$rem \dfrac{n}{5} = 4?$	$rem \dfrac{n}{2} = 1?$	$rem \dfrac{n}{3} = 2?$	$rem \dfrac{n}{4} = 3?$
4	yes	no		
9	yes	yes	no	
14	yes	no		
19	yes	yes	no	
24	yes	no		
29	yes	yes	yes	no
34	yes	no		
39	yes	yes	no	
49	yes	yes	no	
54	yes	no		
59	yes	yes	yes	yes

Thus, 59 is the smallest counting number that satisfies the four conditions named.

4. *Solution 2.* The number for which we are searching is not divisible by 2, 3, 4, or 5 because it produces a nonzero remainder in each case when we carry out the division. But notice that in each case the remainder is one less than the divisor. Apparently the number n differs by 1 from the least common multiple of 2, 3, 4, and 5.

$$lcm(2, 3, 4, 5) - 1 = (2 \cdot 3 \cdot 2 \cdot 5) - 1$$
$$= 60 - 1$$
$$= 59$$

5. *Looking Back.* The answer is indeed correct because $\frac{59}{5} = 11\ r4$, $r4$, $\frac{59}{4} = 14\ r3$, $\frac{59}{3} = 19\ r2$, and $\frac{59}{2} = 29\ r1$. The economy obtained from Solution 2 is obvious.

EXTENDED QUESTIONS

a. If you wish to find the next counting number greater than 59 for which the four conditions hold, how could you proceed?

b. Would nonzero multiples of 59 be solutions? (For example, is 2 $\times$ 59 a solution?)

c. Would you expect 590 to be a solution?

5

RATIONAL NUMBERS

Sample Problem

Mathematical ideas were used by the Egyptians long before the time of Christ. They were obviously successful in their work because the pyramids that they built are still standing and are viewed by engineers as marvels of construction, even by today's standards. The Egyptians worked with fractions as well as with whole numbers. They used unit fractions (numerator of 1) for all representations except one. They had one special number, $\frac{2}{3}$, which was also used. They did not repeat a fraction in any representation. Consider the following examples.

$$\frac{3}{4} = \frac{1}{2} + \frac{1}{4}$$
$$\frac{5}{6} = \frac{2}{3} + \frac{1}{6}$$
$$\frac{3}{8} = \frac{1}{4} + \frac{1}{8}$$

How would you write $\frac{11}{12}$? How would you write $\frac{3}{7}$? What about $\frac{39}{42}$?

5.1 INTRODUCTION TO THE RATIONAL NUMBERS

The middle-grade mathematics curriculum should provide an opportunity for continuing development of meaning and representation of number and number relationships. The NCTM Standards recommend that whole num-

251

bers be extended to include fractions and applied to real-world and mathematical problem situations. That is the central theme of this chapter. It
should also be pointed out that concepts developed in the preceding chapter
have rich applications in the development of rational numbers. Prime numbers, least common multiples, and greatest common factors will have important roles to play as we proceed.

The numbers introduced so far allow us to perform many of the day-to-
day arithmetic tasks. However, we are still restricted in some respects. A
child who receives one stick of gum from a package of five sticks is in need
of some expression for the fact that he or she got one of the five pieces. If we
slice an apple into four equal parts, how can we express the amount that we
receive if we get one of the pieces?

We found that the integers fit nicely on a number line. However, how can
we name the point an equal distance from 0 and 1? We might also note that
with only the whole numbers at our disposal, we had closure for addition
and multiplication, but not for subtraction. However, with the extension to
the integers we obtained closure for subtraction. Our next move might well
be prompted by a desire to obtain a set that is closed with respect to division.

You are all aware of the existence of numerals such as $\frac{1}{2}$, $\frac{3}{4}$, and $\frac{4}{5}$. Basic
notions regarding the "fractional number" $\frac{1}{2}$ are commonly formed before
the time a child enters school. Comments from everyday life involving "half
an apple," "a fourth of a candy bar," and so on are fairly common. But as
we have seen in other areas of our work, multiple meanings can be associated with the numeral $\frac{3}{5}$. In Figure 5.1a it is represented by 3 of 5 members
of a set. In 5.1b it represents 3 of 5 equal parts of a region. In 5.1c it is represented by 3 of 5 equal parts between 0 and 1. In 5.1d it is represented as
the quotient of 3 divided by 5, in 5.1e as the number $\frac{3}{5}$, and in 5.1f as three
one-fifths. As children encounter these numbers, they must become familiar
with all of these ideas.

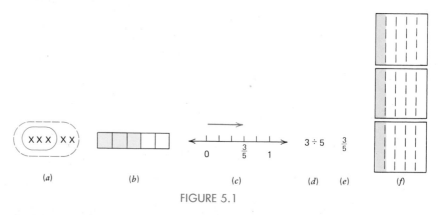

FIGURE 5.1

Let us officially designate the set of numbers that we have been referring
to as the set of *rational numbers.*

Definition 5.1 A rational number is a number that may be represented by an ordered pair of integers a and b, where $b \neq 0$ and is written as $\dfrac{a}{b}$, a/b, or as $a \div b$ $\left(\{\text{rational numbers}\} = Q = \left\{\dfrac{a}{b} \middle| a \text{ and } b \text{ are integers and } b \neq 0\right\}.\right)$

The a is commonly referred to as the *numerator* and the b as the *denominator*. According to the definition, the following is a partial listing of the members of the set of rational numbers: $\frac{1}{2}, \frac{1}{25}, \frac{7}{8}, \frac{5}{18}, \frac{3}{1}, \frac{-6}{5}, \frac{7}{9}, \frac{0}{1}, \frac{2}{2}, \frac{-9}{-3}, \frac{3}{17}, \frac{8}{3}$.

> **REMARK 1** It is sometimes helpful to call special attention to the origin of certain terms. For example, the word "numerator" has come from the same Latin word as "enumerate," and that is precisely its role. It enumerates the number of parts that we have. The denominator comes from the same root word as "nominate" and "denomination." Its role is to name the size of the parts with which we are working.
>
> **REMARK 2** We would like once again to call your attention to the distinction between numbers and numerals. Earlier we stated that numbers are ideas and numerals are the symbols that we use to communicate these ideas. Thus, rational numbers are numbers and fractions are numerals.

To aid in the development of some of the properties of the rational numbers, let us relate the set Q to points on a line. Suppose l is a line with points O and I associated with the integers 0 and 1, respectively, as illustrated in Figure 5.2a. Consider points A and B chosen so the distances between the points O, A, B, and I are all the same (Figure 5.2b). Then we might associate the rational number $\frac{1}{3}$ with the point A and $\frac{2}{3}$ with B. The number $\frac{5}{3}$ would be associated with the point C, which is five of the $\frac{1}{3}$ intervals from point O. In

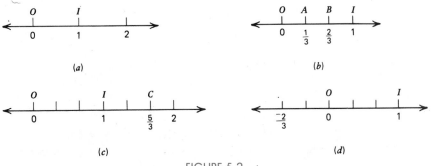

FIGURE 5.2

5.2*d* we see the graph of the number $\frac{-2}{3}$. In general, the denominator of the rational number will indicate the number of divisions to use in our unit length, and the numerator will indicate the number of such segments to use. With this agreement it should be evident that each rational number may be associated with a distinct point on the number line. This is stated as Property 5.1.

PROPERTY 5.1   **Every rational number corresponds to some unique point on a number line.**

Let us make another observation from the number line. In Figure 5.3 segment $\overline{OI}$ again represents a unit interval. Let point P be the point representing the rational number $\frac{1}{2}$. Then point O may be called $\frac{0}{2}$ and I may be named $\frac{2}{2}$. Suppose points A and B are the midpoints of the segments $\overline{OP}$ and $\overline{PI}$, respectively. Then the points O, A, P, B, and I would be associated with the rational numbers $\frac{0}{4}$, $\frac{1}{4}$, $\frac{2}{4}$, $\frac{3}{4}$, and $\frac{4}{4}$, respectively. Likewise, if S and T represent points $\frac{1}{3}$ and $\frac{2}{3}$ of the distance from O to I, respectively, then O, S, T, and I could be named $\frac{0}{3}$, $\frac{1}{3}$, $\frac{2}{3}$, and $\frac{3}{3}$, respectively. If the points U and V are midpoints of $\overline{OS}$ and $\overline{TI}$, then the numbers $\frac{0}{6}$, $\frac{1}{6}$, $\frac{2}{6}$, $\frac{3}{6}$, $\frac{4}{6}$, $\frac{5}{6}$, and $\frac{6}{6}$ are indicated. Note that the point S has been associated with both $\frac{1}{3}$ and $\frac{2}{6}$. Also, P has been named $\frac{1}{2}$, $\frac{2}{4}$, and $\frac{3}{6}$. Indeed, we may assert that $\frac{1}{3}$ and $\frac{2}{6}$ are two names for the same rational number. In fact, any of these points might be named by a variety of fractions. Notice that $\frac{1}{3} = \frac{2}{6}$ and $1 \cdot 6 = 2 \cdot 3$, that $\frac{1}{2} = \frac{2}{4}$ and $1 \cdot 4 = 2 \cdot 2$, that $\frac{2}{4} = \frac{3}{6}$ and $2 \cdot 6 = 3 \cdot 4$. This observation leads us to the following definition.

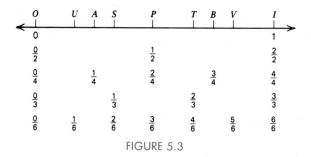

FIGURE 5.3

Definition 5.2   Given rational numbers $\frac{a}{b}$ and $\frac{c}{d}$, $\frac{a}{b} = \frac{c}{d}$ if and only if $a \cdot d = b \cdot c$.

Using this idea, we may note that $\frac{2}{3} = \frac{4}{6}$ because $2 \cdot 6 = 3 \cdot 4$, that $\frac{1}{3} = \frac{5}{15}$ because $1 \cdot 15 = 3 \cdot 5$, and that $\frac{3}{4} \neq \frac{7}{8}$ because $3 \cdot 8 \neq 4 \cdot 7$.

> REMARK We asserted in Property 5.1 that every rational number corresponds to a unique point on a number line. However, that rational number may be named by a great many "equivalent" fractions. Notice that we have *not* asserted that each point on the number line matches a rational number. In fact, we will show later that some points *do not* correspond to rational numbers.

We often find it desirable to change from one name for a rational number to another. You may have noticed that pairs of equivalent fractions such as $\frac{1}{2}$ and $\frac{3}{6}$, and $\frac{2}{3}$ and $\frac{4}{6}$ all have a common characteristic. That is,

$$\frac{1}{2} = \frac{1 \cdot 3}{2 \cdot 3} = \frac{3}{6} \quad \text{and} \quad \frac{2}{3} = \frac{2 \cdot 2}{3 \cdot 2} = \frac{4}{6}$$

Indeed, this technique always produces an "equivalent fraction."

PROPERTY 5.2 **For any rational number $\dfrac{a}{b}$ and any integer c, $c \neq 0$, $\dfrac{a}{b} = \dfrac{a \cdot c}{b \cdot c}$.**

Therefore, we may write

$$\frac{5}{8} = \frac{5 \cdot 2}{8 \cdot 2} = \frac{10}{16} \quad \text{or} \quad \frac{5}{8} = \frac{5 \cdot 3}{8 \cdot 3} = \frac{15}{24}$$

Likewise,

$$\frac{12}{15} = \frac{4 \cdot 3}{5 \cdot 3} = \frac{4}{5} \quad \text{and} \quad \frac{21}{28} = \frac{3 \cdot 7}{4 \cdot 7} = \frac{3}{4}$$

We often refer to this latter process as *reducing fractions*. Note that it is always possible to rename a rational number in a form where the numerator and denominator are relatively prime and the denominator is positive, and we refer to such fractions as being in *reduced form*. We would therefore claim that $\frac{3}{5}$, $\frac{11}{10}$, $\frac{0}{1}$, $\frac{-2}{3}$, and $\frac{6}{35}$ are in reduced form, but that $\frac{6}{10}$, $\frac{22}{20}$, and $\frac{3}{3}$ are not.

Consider the fraction $\frac{24}{30}$. Clearly both numerator and denominator contain a factor 2. Then $\frac{24}{30} = \frac{12 \cdot 2}{15 \cdot 2} = \frac{12}{15}$. But this fraction is still not in reduced form because both 12 and 15 are divisible by 3, so we may write $\frac{12}{15} = \frac{4 \cdot 3}{5 \cdot 3} = \frac{4}{5}$. We could have saved time if we had searched first for the greatest common divisor of 24 and 30 and used it as the common factor in the numerator and denominator. Since $\gcd(24, 30) = 6$, we write $\frac{24}{30} = \frac{4 \cdot 6}{5 \cdot 6} = \frac{4}{5}$.

PROBLEM SET 5.1

1. What rational numbers do the following shaded regions illustrate?

   a.   b.   c.   d.

   e.    f.   g.   h.

2. Locate each of the following on a number line:
   a. $\frac{2}{5}$ b. $\frac{3}{4}$ c. $\frac{5}{8}$ d. $\frac{3}{6}$
   e. $\frac{-2}{3}$ f. $\frac{-5}{6}$ g. $\frac{7}{4}$ h. $\frac{5}{3}$

3. Identify a fraction associated with each figure. Are they equivalent fractions in each case?

   a.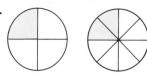

   (i)   (ii)

   b.

   (i)   (ii)

   c.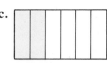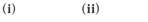

   (i)   (ii)

   d.

   (i)   (ii)

   e.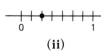

   (i)   (ii)

4. a. Represent $\frac{1}{2}$ as a section of a circular region. Represent $\frac{2}{4}$ as a section of the same circular region. How does the section representing $\frac{1}{2}$ compare with that representing $\frac{2}{4}$?

   b. Represent $\frac{2}{3}$ as a section of a circular region. Represent $\frac{4}{6}$ as a section of the same circular region. How does the section representing $\frac{2}{3}$ compare with that representing $\frac{4}{6}$?

   c. Represent $\frac{1}{5}$ as a section of a rectangular region. Represent $\frac{2}{10}$ as a section of the same rectangular region. How does $\frac{1}{5}$ compare with $\frac{2}{10}$?

d. Represent $\frac{3}{7}$ as a section of a rectangular region. Now represent $\frac{9}{21}$ as a section of the same rectangular region. *Hint:* The easy way to get 21 pieces is to make lines perpendicular to the original lines. For example, if $\frac{2}{3}$ is then $\frac{6}{9}$ is

5. To use sets to represent both $\frac{2}{3}$ and $\frac{4}{6}$ we might consider the following:

a. Use sets to show that $\frac{1}{4} = \frac{2}{8}$.

b. Use sets to show that $\frac{3}{5} = \frac{6}{10}$.

c. Use sets to show that $\frac{2}{3} = \frac{8}{12}$.

d. Use sets to show that $\frac{3}{4} = \frac{9}{12}$.

6. Use a number line to illustrate that:

a. $\frac{1}{2} = \frac{3}{6}$ **b.** $\frac{3}{4} = \frac{6}{8}$ **c.** $\frac{2}{3} = \frac{6}{9}$ **d.** $\frac{3}{5} = \frac{6}{10}$

7. Which of the following are equal?

a. $\frac{4}{1}$ and $\frac{8}{2}$ **b.** $\frac{2}{3}$ and $\frac{4}{6}$ **c.** $\frac{5}{8}$ and $\frac{7}{10}$ **d.** $\frac{-3}{5}$ and $\frac{3}{-5}$

e. $\frac{9}{2}$ and $\frac{0}{1}$ **f.** $\frac{5}{1}$ and $\frac{15}{3}$ **g.** $\frac{9}{4}$ and $\frac{17}{12}$ **h.** $\frac{2a+b}{2c}$ and $\frac{a+b}{c}$

8. Write three fractions that might name each of the following rational numbers:

a. $\frac{3}{5}$ **b.** $\frac{4}{5}$ **c.** $\frac{4}{4}$ **d.** $\frac{2}{3}$ **e.** $\frac{4}{3}$

f. $\frac{0}{4}$ **g.** $\frac{3}{2}$ **h.** $\frac{2}{4}$ **i.** $\frac{3}{4}$ **j.** $\frac{5}{6}$

9. Write each of the following in *reduced form:*

a. $\frac{5}{20}$ **b.** $\frac{18}{24}$ **c.** $\frac{8}{12}$ **d.** $\frac{36}{95}$

e. $\frac{36}{84}$ **f.** $\frac{680}{1240}$ **g.** $\frac{27}{45}$ **h.** $\frac{66}{24}$

i. $\frac{15}{45}$ **j.** $\frac{81}{27}$

10. Find a value for x that will make each of the following statements true:

a. $\dfrac{1}{5} = \dfrac{x}{20}$ **b.** $\dfrac{5}{20} = \dfrac{1}{x}$ **c.** $\dfrac{x}{6} = \dfrac{4}{24}$ **d.** $\dfrac{x}{24} = \dfrac{5}{6}$ **e.** $\dfrac{21}{15} = \dfrac{x}{30}$

f. $\dfrac{x}{3} = \dfrac{x}{2}$ **g.** $\dfrac{x}{9} = \dfrac{1}{x}$ **h.** $\dfrac{6}{9} = \dfrac{3x}{27}$ **i.** $\dfrac{0}{6} = \dfrac{x}{4}$

11. Which of the following fractions are in reduced form?

a. $\frac{6}{8}$ **b.** $\frac{11}{4}$ **c.** $\frac{7}{12}$ **d.** $\frac{8}{12}$ **e.** $\frac{15}{6}$

f. $\frac{13}{26}$ **g.** $\frac{3}{5}$ **h.** $\frac{6}{35}$ **i.** $\frac{8}{17}$ **j.** $\frac{13}{3}$

12. Shade the region associated with the given rational number. If it is impossible to make the association, state why.

a. $\frac{2}{3}$ **b.**

c. $\frac{1}{3}$ **d.**

13.

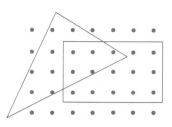

a. What fractional part of the dots is inside the rectangle?

b. What fractional part of the dots is inside the triangle?

c. What fractional part of the dots is inside the rectangle but not in the triangle?

d. What fractional part of the dots inside the triangle is also inside the rectangle?

e. What fractional part of the dots inside the rectangle is inside the triangle?

f. What fractional part of the dots is inside the triangle but outside the rectangle?

14. Write each in reduced form given that a, b, c, d, $(a + b)$, and $(c + d)$ are nonzero integers.

a. $\dfrac{ab}{abc}$ **b.** $\dfrac{ab}{a + b}$ **c.** $\dfrac{ab^2}{a^2bc}$

d. $\dfrac{2c + 6d}{2b}$ **e.** $\dfrac{ad}{bd}$ **f.** $\dfrac{ab(c + d)}{d(c + d)}$

15. a. If $\frac{2}{3} = \frac{4}{6}$ and $\frac{4}{6} = \frac{8}{12}$, does it follow that $\frac{2}{3} = \frac{8}{12}$?

b. If $\frac{5}{8} = \frac{10}{16}$ and $\frac{10}{16} = \frac{30}{48}$, does it follow that $\frac{5}{8} = \frac{30}{48}$?

c. Try to argue in general that if $\dfrac{a}{b} = \dfrac{c}{d}$ and $\dfrac{c}{d} = \dfrac{e}{f}$, then $\dfrac{a}{b} = \dfrac{e}{f}$.

Pedagogical Problems and Activities

16. Suggest six ways that rational numbers arise naturally from the experiences of a third-grade child.

17. In what way does the interpretation of a rational number *differ* when we use a set, a part of a region, and a number line?

18. Suppose a fifth-grade child "reduces" fractions by writing the following: $\frac{16}{64} = \frac{1}{4}$, and $\frac{19}{95} = \frac{1}{5}$. Is the procedure correct? (Could you find a counterexample?)

19. Fraction strips are a concrete set of materials that are easily used to illustrate the fractions $\frac{1}{2}, \frac{1}{3}, \frac{1}{4}, \frac{1}{6}$, and $\frac{1}{12}$. They are simply colored paper strips that may be matched to compare lengths.

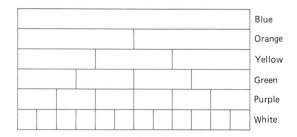

Show how to use the strips to verify the following;

a. $\frac{1}{2} = \frac{3}{6}$ **b.** $\frac{2}{3} = \frac{4}{6}$ **c.** $\frac{3}{4} = \frac{9}{12}$ **d.** $\frac{5}{6} = \frac{10}{12}$

20. Make a set of circular regions to illustrate the same fractions as were represented by the fraction strips in Problem 19. (Pizza boards work well for this.)

21. Make a set of rectangular regions to illustrate the same fractions as were represented by the fraction strips. (Cardborad or poster board works well for this.)

22. a. A common error is for students to assert that $\frac{5}{7}$ is equivalent to $\frac{3}{5}$ because $\frac{3+2}{5+2} = \frac{5}{7}$. How might you convince a student that $\frac{3}{5}$ and $\frac{5}{7}$ are not equivalent.

b. Try to make an argument for part **a.** by using a simpler problem and a model to illustrate that it is in general false to claim that $\frac{a}{b}$ is equivalent to $\frac{a + c}{b + c}$.

c. Under some very special conditions for a, b, and c, it is true that $\frac{a}{b} = \frac{a + c}{b + c}$. Find values for a, b, and c for which it will be true.

23. Another application of rational numbers in the elementary school mathematics program is related to the idea of probability. One example of this application might be the following. Suppose a box contains nine balls, two of which are red. If you randomly select one ball from the box, the chance of selecting a red ball is 2 out of 9. We say the probability of getting a red ball is $\frac{2}{9}$ and may write $P(\text{red ball}) = \frac{2}{9}$.

  a. If you have 3 pennies, 4 dimes, and a quarter in your pocket and one coin falls out, what is the probability that the coin is a dime?

  b. The set A of factors of 24 is as follows: $A = \{1, 2, 3, 4, 6, 8, 12, 24\}$. If a whole number between 0 and 25 is randomly selected, what is the probability that the number selected is a factor of 24?

  c. A cube has the letters A, B, C, D, E, and F on its faces. If the cube is tossed, what is the probability that a vowel will come up?

5.2   ADDITION OF RATIONAL NUMBERS

Let us turn now to some consideration of operations on the set of rational numbers. Because work with rational numbers at lower levels rarely deals with negative rationals, we will restrict our discussions and examples to just those rational numbers formed from ratios of whole numbers with denominators that are nonzero. Our definitions would allow us to include negative rationals if we so desire. As we proceed with this development, we will be careful not to violate any of the structure developed to date as we extend that structure.

We will once again begin by appealing to your intuition. The basic ideas involving rational numbers are often illustrated either by sets, by regions of some geometric figure, or by a number line. Suppose it is $\frac{1}{5}$ of a mile from your dorm to the union and it is $\frac{2}{5}$ of a mile from the union to your classroom building. The distance from your dorm to the classroom building via the student union must be $\frac{3}{5}$ of a mile. Thus, $\frac{1}{5} + \frac{2}{5} = \frac{3}{5}$. See Figure 5.4.

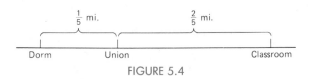

FIGURE 5.4

Consider the case of a child who receives a candy bar divided into six equal segments. He eats three of the segments after lunch and then two more segments later in the afternoon. It can be shown, as in Figure 5.5, that he has then eaten five of the six segments or $\frac{5}{6}$ of the candy. We might write the sentence $\frac{3}{6} + \frac{2}{6} = \frac{5}{6}$.

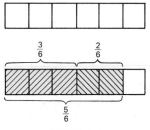

FIGURE 5.5

Let us use sets to illustrate the fact that $\frac{3}{10} + \frac{5}{10} = \frac{8}{10}$. In Figure 5.6a we illustrate $\frac{3}{10}$ and $\frac{5}{10}$. Then the set that is the union of the sets containing three elements and five elements implies the solution. In Figure 5.6b the same addition is illustrated using a number line.

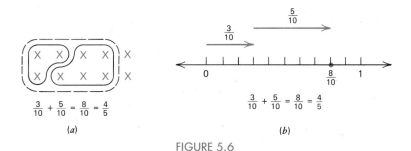

$$\frac{3}{10} + \frac{5}{10} = \frac{8}{10} = \frac{4}{5}$$

(a)

$$\frac{3}{10} + \frac{5}{10} = \frac{8}{10} = \frac{4}{5}$$

(b)

FIGURE 5.6

In the cases considered the denominators were the same, and we observe that the denominator of the sum was the same number. The numerator of the sum was simply the sum of the numerators of the two fractions. This should be apparent because the role of the numerators, 3 and 5, is to count how many parts we have. Because 3 plus 5 of anything is 8 of that same thing, we are simply noting that we have 8 of the named objects, in this case tenths. In essence the denominator only identifies the things referred to by the 8 in the numerator. Let us state this as the definition for addition of rational numbers.

Definition 5.3 For all rational numbers $\dfrac{a}{b}$ and $\dfrac{c}{b}$, $\dfrac{a}{b} + \dfrac{c}{b} = \dfrac{a + c}{b}$.

Note, therefore, as a consequence of this definition, that $\frac{3}{8}$ plus $\frac{4}{8} = \frac{3 + 4}{8} = \frac{7}{8}$, $\frac{5}{12} + \frac{3}{12} = \frac{5 + 3}{12} = \frac{8}{12} = \frac{2}{3}$, and $\frac{5}{7} + \frac{6}{7} = \frac{5 + 6}{7} = \frac{11}{7}$.

Consider the situation that arises if the denominators are not the same. Suppose we wish to add $\frac{1}{3} + \frac{1}{2}$. We can readily identify regions associated with $\frac{1}{3}$

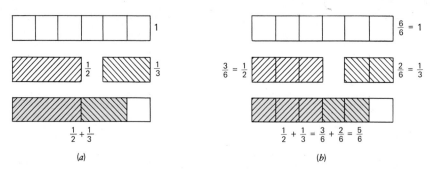

FIGURE 5.7

and $\frac{1}{2}$, as illustrated in Figure 5.7a, but what is the sum? Perhaps we could rename these regions, as suggested in Figure 5.7b.

We might also use sets to obtains the same results. In Figure 5.8a a set that might represent $\frac{1}{2}$ is illustrated, but it will not give a representation for $\frac{1}{3}$. In Figure 5.8b we illustrate another set that could be interpreted as $\frac{1}{2}$, but again we cannot represent $\frac{1}{3}$. However, in Figure 5.8c we have a representation for both $\frac{1}{2}$ and $\frac{1}{3}$. Thus, $\frac{1}{2} + \frac{1}{3} = \frac{5}{6}$.

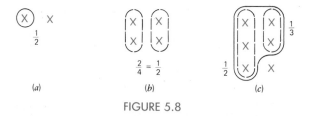

FIGURE 5.8

In each of these examples we are actually finding equivalent fractions whose denominators are the same counting number. To add $\frac{1}{6}$ and $\frac{1}{4}$, we should first search for a common denominator, in this case perhaps 12. Then let us rewrite $\frac{1}{6} = \frac{1 \cdot 2}{6 \cdot 2} = \frac{2}{12}$ and $\frac{1}{4} = \frac{1 \cdot 3}{4 \cdot 3} = \frac{3}{12}$ and write $\frac{1}{6} + \frac{1}{4} = \frac{2}{12} + \frac{3}{12} = \frac{2 + 3}{12} = \frac{5}{12}$.

Suppose that we are asked to find $\frac{1}{15} + \frac{1}{12}$. What might we use as a common denominator? Do you agree that the least common multiple of 15 and 12 would be such a number? Because $15 = 3 \cdot 5$ and $12 = 2 \cdot 2 \cdot 3$, then lcm $(15, 12) = 3 \cdot 5 \cdot 2 \cdot 2 = 60$. Then we may write $\frac{1}{15} = \frac{1 \cdot 4}{15 \cdot 4} = \frac{4}{60}$ and $\frac{1}{12} = \frac{1 \cdot 5}{12 \cdot 5} = \frac{5}{60}$. Thus $\frac{1}{15} + \frac{1}{12} = \frac{4}{60} + \frac{5}{60} = \frac{4 + 5}{60} = \frac{9}{60} = \frac{3}{20}$. Consider the following examples of addition of rational numbers.

EXAMPLE 1

Find the sum
$$\frac{3}{10} + \frac{7}{25}$$

Solution $10 = 2 \cdot 5$ and $25 = 5 \cdot 5$, then lcm $(10, 25) = 2 \cdot 5 \cdot 5 = 50$. Therefore,

$$\frac{3}{10} + \frac{7}{25} = \frac{3 \cdot 5}{10 \cdot 5} + \frac{7 \cdot 2}{25 \cdot 2} = \frac{15}{50} + \frac{14}{50} = \frac{15 + 14}{50} = \frac{29}{50}$$

REMARK We use the number $4\frac{1}{3}$ in Example 2. It should be understood that $4\frac{1}{3}$ means $4 + \frac{1}{3}$ and is commonly referred to as a *mixed number*. Note that $4\frac{1}{3}$ is equivalent to the rational number $\frac{13}{3}$, which is referred to as an *improper fraction*.

EXAMPLE 2

Find $4\frac{1}{3} + 6\frac{1}{4}$.

Solution 1 Because $4\frac{1}{3} = 4 + \frac{1}{3}$ and $6\frac{1}{4} = 6 + \frac{1}{4}$ we might write

$$4\frac{1}{3} + 6\frac{1}{4} = \left(4 + \frac{1}{3}\right) + \left(6 + \frac{1}{4}\right)$$

$$= (4 + 6) + \left(\frac{1}{3} + \frac{1}{4}\right)$$

$$= (4 + 6) + \left(\frac{4}{12} + \frac{3}{12}\right)$$

$$= 10 + \frac{7}{12}$$

$$= 10\frac{7}{12}$$

Solution 2 $4\frac{1}{3} + 6\frac{1}{4} = 4\frac{4}{12} + 6\frac{3}{12} = 10\frac{7}{12}$

Solution 3

$$4\frac{1}{3} = 4\frac{4}{12}$$

$$+ 6\frac{1}{4} = 6\frac{3}{12}$$

$$\overline{\qquad\qquad 10\frac{7}{12}}$$

Solution 4

$$4\frac{1}{3} + 6\frac{1}{4} = \frac{13}{3} + \frac{25}{4} = \frac{13 \cdot 4}{3 \cdot 4} + \frac{25 \cdot 3}{4 \cdot 3}$$

$$= \frac{52}{12} + \frac{75}{12} = \frac{127}{12} = 10\frac{7}{12}$$

The set of rational numbers is closed under addition. Because we defined $\frac{a}{b} + \frac{c}{b}$ as $\frac{a+c}{b}$, certainly the denominator of the sum is a nonzero integer. Because a and c are both integers and the integers are closed under the operation of addition, the numerator is also an integer and thus the sum, $\frac{a+c}{b}$, is a rational number.

Because $\frac{a}{b} + \frac{c}{b} = \frac{a+c}{b}$ and $\frac{c}{b} + \frac{a}{b} = \frac{c+a}{b}$ and $a + c = c + a$, it must be true that $\frac{a+c}{b} = \frac{c+a}{b}$ and $\frac{a}{b} + \frac{c}{b} = \frac{c}{b} + \frac{a}{b}$. You may recognize this as the commutative property for addition of rationals.

Other properties that hold for rational numbers are stated in Property 5.3. One comment should be made about the way Property 5.3 is stated. We defined addition of rational numbers in terms of $\frac{a}{b} + \frac{c}{b}$; that is, where a common denominator is present. We have found it possible to add rational numbers even if they are not specifically stated with a common denominator. We can always rewrite them as equivalent fractions that have a common denominator and then use Definition 5.3. Therefore, when we state that if $\frac{a}{b}$ and $\frac{c}{d}$ are rational numbers, then the sum is a rational number, we are simply asserting that rationals are closed under addition, and we are not restricted to just rational numbers with the same denominator.

PROPERTY 5.3 **The set of rational numbers under addition has the following properties:**

1. Closure: If $\frac{a}{b}$ and $\frac{c}{d}$ are rational numbers, then $\left(\frac{a}{b} + \frac{c}{d}\right)$ is a rational number.

2. Commutative: For all rational numbers $\frac{a}{b}$ and $\frac{c}{d}$, $\frac{a}{b} + \frac{c}{d} = \frac{c}{d} + \frac{a}{b}$.

3. Associative: For all rational numbers $\frac{a}{b}, \frac{c}{d}$, and $\frac{e}{f}$, $\frac{a}{b} + \left(\frac{c}{d} + \frac{e}{f}\right) = \left(\frac{a}{b} + \frac{c}{d}\right) + \frac{e}{f}$.

4. Identity for addition: For any rational number $\frac{a}{b}$, $\frac{a}{b} + \frac{0}{1} = \frac{a+0}{b} = \frac{a}{b}$.

5. Additive inverse property: Each rational number $\dfrac{a}{b}$, $\dfrac{a}{b} + \left(\dfrac{^-a}{b}\right) = \dfrac{a + {}^-a}{b} =$

$\dfrac{0}{b}$.

PROBLEM SET 5.2

1. Use shaded regions of some geometric form to illustrate each of the following:

   a. $\frac{1}{3} + \frac{1}{3}$ **b.** $\frac{3}{5} + \frac{1}{5}$ **c.** $\frac{1}{6} + \frac{4}{6}$ **d.** $\frac{2}{7} + \frac{3}{7}$ **e.** $\frac{1}{8} + \frac{4}{8}$
   f. $\frac{3}{9} + \frac{2}{9}$

2. Use a number line to illustrate each of the following:

   a. $\frac{1}{4} + \frac{2}{4}$ **b.** $\frac{2}{5} + \frac{1}{5}$ **c.** $\frac{3}{8} + \frac{2}{8}$ **d.** $\frac{1}{7} + \frac{2}{7}$ **e.** $\frac{1}{6} + \frac{4}{6}$
   f. $\frac{4}{9} + \frac{1}{9}$

3. We can use the number line to add fractions, even if they do not have common denominators. To find $\frac{1}{3} + \frac{1}{2}$ we can use vectors as indicated.

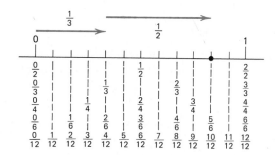

   Use the number line to find the following:

   a. $\frac{1}{3} + \frac{1}{4}$ **b.** $\frac{1}{6} + \frac{1}{4}$ **c.** $\frac{1}{4} + \frac{1}{2}$ **d.** $\frac{5}{12} + \frac{1}{4}$ **e.** $\frac{1}{3} + \frac{1}{6}$

4. **a.** Make a set that will allow you to identify both $\frac{1}{3}$ and $\frac{1}{4}$. Use it to find $\frac{1}{3} + \frac{1}{4}$.

   b. Make a set that will allow you to identify both $\frac{1}{2}$ and $\frac{1}{5}$. Use it to find $\frac{1}{2} + \frac{1}{5}$.

   c. Use a set to find $\frac{1}{3} + \frac{1}{5}$.

5. Add the following, leaving answers in reduced form:

   a. $\frac{2}{5} + \frac{1}{5}$ **b.** $\frac{5}{8} + \frac{1}{8}$ **c.** $\frac{3}{10} + \frac{4}{10}$ **d.** $\frac{5}{11} + \frac{4}{11}$ **e.** $\frac{3}{7} + \frac{4}{7}$
   f. $\frac{5}{9} + \frac{7}{9}$

6. Find the least common denominator for each, then add the fractions.

    a. $\frac{1}{6} + \frac{1}{4}$ **b.** $\frac{5}{6} + \frac{3}{8}$ **c.** $\frac{2}{3} + \frac{7}{8}$ **d.** $\frac{5}{9} + \frac{1}{5}$ **e.** $\frac{2}{5} + \frac{3}{4}$

    f. $\frac{3}{8} + \frac{1}{2} + \frac{1}{4}$ **g.** $\frac{2}{3} + \frac{1}{4} + \frac{5}{6}$

7. Change the following improper fractions to mixed numbers:

    a. $\frac{26}{4}$ **b.** $\frac{15}{7}$ **c.** $\frac{52}{8}$ **d.** $\frac{25}{4}$ **e.** $\frac{140}{6}$ **f.** $\frac{59}{8}$

8. Write each mixed number as an improper fraction.

    a. $2\frac{1}{5}$ **b.** $4\frac{2}{3}$ **c.** $8\frac{1}{5}$ **d.** $1\frac{7}{8}$ **e.** $23\frac{3}{4}$ **f.** $16\frac{3}{5}$

9. Find the following (expressing your answers as mixed numerals with fractions in reduced form):

    a. $4\frac{1}{4} + 3\frac{1}{4}$ **b.** $5\frac{1}{8} + 4\frac{1}{2}$ **c.** $2\frac{1}{3} + 3\frac{1}{4}$ **d.** $2\frac{5}{6} + 1\frac{7}{8}$

    e. $5\frac{1}{5}$ **f.** $2\frac{5}{9}$ **g.** $5\frac{6}{15}$ **h.** $5\frac{5}{24}$

    $\;\;+6\frac{1}{10}$ $\;\;+4\frac{2}{3}$ $\;\;+4\frac{5}{6}$ $\;\;+3\frac{8}{21}$

10. If a, b, c, d, and e are counting numbers, find the following:

    a. $\dfrac{a}{b} + c$ **b.** $\dfrac{a}{b} + \dfrac{c^2}{b}$ **c.** $\dfrac{a^2}{b} + \dfrac{c^2}{d}$

    d. $\dfrac{3}{e} + \dfrac{5}{2e}$ **e.** $\dfrac{4}{ab} + \dfrac{5}{b} + \dfrac{6}{a}$ **f.** $\dfrac{2}{ae} + \dfrac{3}{bc} + \dfrac{4}{ab}$

11. a. To find the sum of $\frac{2}{3}$ and $\frac{4}{5}$ we could write $\frac{2}{3} + \frac{4}{5} = \frac{2 \cdot 5 + 3 \cdot 4}{3 \cdot 5} = \frac{10 + 12}{15} = \frac{22}{15}$. Verify that this answer is correct.

    b. Use this technique to find $\frac{5}{6} + \frac{3}{7}$.

    c. Use this technique to find $\frac{3}{4} + \frac{1}{6}$. Could you have used a denominator smaller than the product of the denominators to do the problem? (This technique is quicker than using the definition if the denominators are relatively prime.)

    d. Use the definition for addition to show in general that $\dfrac{a}{b} + \dfrac{c}{d} = \dfrac{ad + bc}{bd}$.

    e. Use your calculator and this technique to find $\frac{46}{89} + \frac{53}{75}$.

12. Consider the following sequence:

$$\frac{1}{2} + \frac{1}{3} = \frac{5}{6}$$

$$\frac{1}{3} + \frac{1}{4} = \frac{7}{12}$$

$$\frac{1}{4} + \frac{1}{5} = \frac{9}{20}$$

$$\cdot$$
$$\cdot$$
$$\cdot$$

a. Verbalize the pattern. Will it work for $\frac{1}{17} + \frac{1}{18}$?

b. Can you claim that it will work in general? Justify your answer.

13. a. Does $\dfrac{a}{b} + \dfrac{c}{d} = \dfrac{a+c}{b+d}$ for all rational numbers $\dfrac{a}{b}$ and $\dfrac{c}{d}$?

b. In part a. you should have easily produced a pair of rational numbers $\dfrac{a}{b}$ and $\dfrac{c}{d}$ where the sum is not $\dfrac{a+c}{b+d}$. Can you observe any specific substitution for a, b, c, and d for which it *would* be true?

14. a. Use the fractions $\frac{1}{8}$, $\frac{3}{8}$, and $\frac{5}{8}$ to illustrate the associative pattern.

b. Show that the pattern also holds for $\frac{1}{4}$, $\frac{1}{5}$, and $\frac{1}{6}$.

15. Let $S = \{\frac{1}{1}, \frac{1}{2}, \frac{1}{3}, \frac{1}{4}, \frac{1}{5}, \dots\}$. Is S closed under addition? Justify your answer.

Pedagogical Problems and Activities

16. a. To use a number line to find $\frac{1}{3} + \frac{1}{2}$ with fifth-grade students, it would be helpful to have a premarked number line that would allow the students to see thirds, halves, and sixths. Make such a number line, then find $\frac{1}{3} + \frac{1}{2}$.

b. Make a number line to use as you find $\frac{2}{5} + \frac{1}{4}$.

17. Use fraction strips (discussed in Problem 19 of Problem Set 5.1) to find each of the following:

a. $\frac{1}{4} + \frac{2}{3}$ **b.** $\frac{1}{6} + \frac{3}{4}$ **c.** $\frac{1}{6} + \frac{2}{3}$ **d.** $\frac{3}{4} + \frac{1}{2}$

18. a. A child used sets to find $\frac{1}{2} + \frac{1}{3}$ as follows:

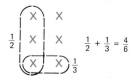

What did the child do incorrectly?

b.

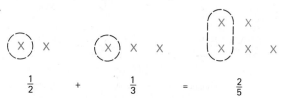

Can this answer be correct?

19. a. Use pizza boards to represent $2\frac{1}{3}$. Verify that this represents $\frac{7}{3}$.

b. Use pizza boards to show that $1\frac{2}{5} = \frac{7}{5}$.

   c. Use pizza boards to show that $3\frac{1}{4} = \frac{13}{4}$.

   d. Use pizza boards to illustrate $\frac{5}{2}$. Show why $\frac{5}{2} = 2\frac{1}{2}$.

   e. Suggest an algorithm that allows you to change a mixed number to an equivalent improper fraction.

20. a. Suppose that we have a spinner made as illustrated. If you spin the pointer, what is the probability that it will point to an odd number?

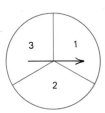

   b. What is the probability that the number will be even?

   c. What is the probability that it will be either even or odd?

21. a. A calculator is sometimes quite effective in reinforcing a concept. Use a calculator that allows you to work with fractions in $\dfrac{a}{b}$ form to find the following.

   (i) $\frac{1}{3} + \frac{1}{4}$ **(ii)** $\frac{1}{3} + \frac{1}{5}$ **(iii)** $\frac{1}{4} + \frac{1}{6}$ **(iv)** $\frac{1}{6} + \frac{1}{9}$

   b. What basic concept is illustrated in part **a**?

22. a. Use a calculator that allows you to work with fractions in $\dfrac{a}{b}$ form to find the following:

   (i) $\frac{1}{3} \times \frac{2}{5}$ **(ii)** $\frac{1}{3} \times \frac{3}{8}$ **(iii)** $\frac{3}{4} \times \frac{2}{5}$ **(iv)** $\frac{5}{6} \times \frac{3}{4}$

   b. Did the calculator use the reduction process (cancellation) as it performed the operations in part **a**?

5.3   MULTIPLICATION OF RATIONAL NUMBERS

Our attention might next be focused on the operation of multiplication. We have previously performed multiplications on whole numbers and on integers. But will we be able to carry these ideas over into the rational numbers? Consider the product of 3 and $\frac{1}{4}$. One approach to multiplication in the set of whole numbers was to consider the operation in terms of repeated addition. Could we then be safe in considering $3 \cdot \frac{1}{4} = \frac{1}{4} + \frac{1}{4} + \frac{1}{4}$? Figure 5.9 illustrates this situation for us. It is apparent that $3 \cdot \frac{1}{4} = \frac{1}{4} + \frac{1}{4} + \frac{1}{4} = \frac{1+1+1}{4} = \frac{3}{4}$.

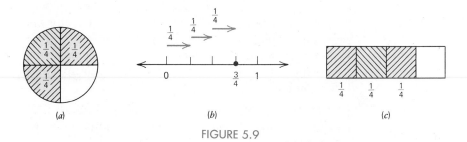

FIGURE 5.9

If we want the product of $\frac{1}{3} \cdot 6$, repeated addition will not help us very much because we agreed that the first-named factor told us how many times to use the second factor. However, if we assume that commutativity will hold, we might then write $\frac{1}{3} \cdot 6 = 6 \cdot \frac{1}{3}$ and apply repeated addition to write $\frac{1}{3} + \frac{1}{3} + \frac{1}{3} + \frac{1}{3} + \frac{1}{3} + \frac{1}{3} = \frac{6}{3} = 2$. We could also have made use of a number line to help with this as illustrated in Figure 5.10a, or even a set as illustrated in Figure 5.10b, by interpreting $\frac{1}{3} \cdot 6$ as "$\frac{1}{3}$ of 6."

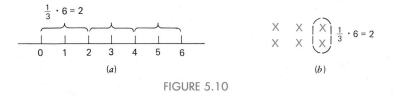

FIGURE 5.10

Suppose that we wish to find the product $\frac{1}{2} \cdot \frac{3}{4}$. A rectangular region is useful in this case. Suppose the entire region in Figure 5.11a represents one unit. The shaded region represents $\frac{3}{4}$ of the rectangle. In 5.11b we can see the region further separated into two congruent parts with $\frac{1}{2}$ of them shaded. The portion shaded twice represents $\frac{1}{2}$ of $\frac{3}{4}$ or $\frac{3}{8}$.

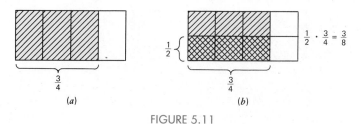

FIGURE 5.11

REMARK 1 Elementary school children usually find this reasonable. If one child has $\frac{3}{4}$ of a candy bar and promises to give a friend half of this, the friend should be satisfied with 3 segments, each of which is $\frac{1}{8}$ of the whole bar. It should be pointed out that multiplication by $\frac{1}{2}$ is the same as division by 2.

REMARK 2 Note how we translated $\frac{1}{2} \cdot \frac{3}{4}$ to $\frac{1}{2}$ of $\frac{3}{4}$. This is similar to what we did with multiplication of whole numbers where we interpreted 3 $\times$ 4 as 3 groups of 4.

Figure 5.12 illustrates the product $\frac{1}{3} \cdot \frac{2}{5}$. In Figure 5.12a we see the unit region divided into five equal parts with two of them shaded. In Figure 5.12b we see the region further divided into three equal parts. The product is represented by the region that is marked twice. Thus $\frac{1}{3}$ of $\frac{2}{5}$ is $\frac{2}{15}$.

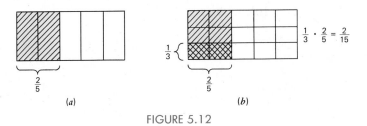

FIGURE 5.12

Perhaps one more example would be helpful. Let us make a diagram to find $\frac{3}{4}$ of $\frac{5}{7}$. In Figure 5.13a we can see the unit rectangular region divided into seven equal parts. Five of these are marked to represent $\frac{5}{7}$ of the original region. In Figure 5.13b we have further separated the rectangular region into four equal parts and shaded three of these parts. The portion shaded twice represents $\frac{3}{4}$ of $\frac{5}{7}$. Thus $\frac{3}{4} \cdot \frac{5}{7}$ produces 15 of the subregions, each representing $\frac{1}{28}$ of the original rectangular region. Thus $\frac{3}{4} \cdot \frac{5}{7} = \frac{15}{28}$.

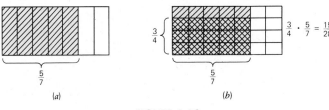

FIGURE 5.13

These examples should make the following definition seem reasonable.

Definition 5.4 For $\dfrac{a}{b}$ and $\dfrac{c}{d}$ any rational numbers $\dfrac{a}{b} \cdot \dfrac{c}{d} = \dfrac{a \cdot c}{b \cdot d}$.

Using the definition for multiplication, we may quickly compute the products of rational numbers. Consider the following examples.

EXAMPLE 1

Find $\dfrac{3}{5} \cdot \dfrac{6}{7}$.

Solution $\dfrac{3}{5} \cdot \dfrac{6}{7} = \dfrac{3 \cdot 6}{5 \cdot 7} = \dfrac{18}{35}$

EXAMPLE 2

Find $\dfrac{3}{8} \cdot \dfrac{2}{5}$.

Solution 1 $\dfrac{3}{8} \cdot \dfrac{2}{5} = \dfrac{3 \cdot 2}{8 \cdot 5} = \dfrac{6}{40} = \dfrac{3 \cdot 2}{20 \cdot 2} = \dfrac{3}{20}$

Solution 2 $\dfrac{3}{8} \cdot \dfrac{2}{5} = \dfrac{3}{4 \cdot 2} \cdot \dfrac{2}{5} = \dfrac{3 \cdot 2}{4 \cdot 5 \cdot 2} = \dfrac{3}{4 \cdot 5} \cdot \dfrac{2}{2} = \dfrac{3}{20}$

(An alternate form for this is $\dfrac{3}{{}_4 8} \cdot \dfrac{2^1}{5} = \dfrac{3}{20}$. This is commonly referred to as *cancellation*.)

> REMARK Cancellation was not discussed in elementary mathematics books for a period of time because students had a tendency to overgeneralize its use. Current texts often refer to it as *simplifying factors*.

EXAMPLE 3

Find $4\frac{1}{3} \cdot 5\frac{3}{8}$.

Solution 1 $4\frac{1}{3} = \frac{13}{3}$ and $5\frac{3}{8} = \frac{43}{8}$.

Thus, $4\frac{1}{3} \cdot 5\frac{3}{8} = \frac{13}{3} \cdot \frac{43}{8} = \frac{559}{24} = 23\frac{7}{24}$.

Solution 2 $4\frac{1}{3} = 4 + \frac{1}{3}$ and $5\frac{3}{8} = 5 + \frac{3}{8}$

Thus using the distributive property $(a + b) \cdot (c + d) = ac + ad + bc + bd$ we write:

$$\begin{aligned}
4\frac{1}{3} \cdot 5\frac{3}{8} &= (4 + \tfrac{1}{3}) \cdot (5 + \tfrac{3}{8}) \\
&= (4 \cdot 5) + (4 \cdot \tfrac{3}{8}) + (\tfrac{1}{3} \cdot 5) + (\tfrac{1}{3} \cdot \tfrac{3}{8}) \\
&= 20 + \tfrac{3}{2} + \tfrac{5}{3} + \tfrac{1}{8} \\
&= 20 + \tfrac{36}{24} + \tfrac{40}{24} + \tfrac{3}{24} \\
&= 20 + \tfrac{79}{24} \\
&= 20 + 3\tfrac{7}{24} \\
&= 23\tfrac{7}{24}
\end{aligned}$$

REMARK Students commonly have added fractions like $4\frac{1}{3} + 5\frac{3}{8}$ by finding $(4 + 5) + (\tfrac{1}{3} + \tfrac{3}{8}) = 9\frac{17}{24}$, which is correct, but then attempt to find the product by using a like procedure. Note that $4\frac{1}{3} \cdot 5\frac{3}{8} \neq (4 \cdot 5) + (\tfrac{1}{3} \cdot \tfrac{3}{8})$. What terms have been omitted?

Some natural questions might once again be raised concerning the properties that hold for multiplication with rational numbers. Does it seem clear that the set of rational numbers is closed under multiplication? That is, does the product of two rational numbers yield a rational number? Apparently the answer is yes, because $\frac{a}{b} \cdot \frac{c}{d} = \frac{a \cdot c}{b \cdot d}$. Because a, b, c, and d are integers, closed under multiplication, we know that $(a \cdot c)$ and $(b \cdot d)$ are integers. Furthermore, because $b \neq 0$ and $d \neq 0$, then $(b \cdot d) \neq 0$. Therefore, $\frac{a \cdot c}{b \cdot d}$ is a rational number. Thus, the set is closed under multiplication. We could verify the other properties that follow, but we will not do so here.

PROPERTY 5.4 If $\frac{a}{b}, \frac{c}{d}$, and $\frac{e}{f}$ are any rational numbers, then the following must be the case:

1. Closure: $\left(\frac{a}{b} \cdot \frac{c}{d}\right)$ is a rational number.

2. Commutative: $\frac{a}{b} \cdot \frac{c}{d} = \frac{c}{d} \cdot \frac{a}{b}$

3. Associative: $\frac{a}{b} \cdot \left(\frac{c}{d} \cdot \frac{e}{f}\right) = \left(\frac{a}{b} \cdot \frac{c}{d}\right) \cdot \frac{e}{f}$

4. Identity for multiplication: $\dfrac{a}{b} \cdot \dfrac{1}{1} = \dfrac{1}{1} \cdot \dfrac{a}{b} = \dfrac{a}{b}$

5. Each nonzero element $\dfrac{a}{b}$ has a multiplicative inverse $\dfrac{b}{a}$. Such that

$$\frac{a}{b} \cdot \frac{b}{a} = \frac{1}{1}.$$

One additional property should be mentioned before we turn to some problems. Observe that $\frac{1}{2} \cdot (\frac{3}{4} + \frac{1}{3}) = \frac{1}{2} \cdot \frac{13}{12} = \frac{13}{24}$, and also $(\frac{1}{2} \cdot \frac{3}{4}) + (\frac{1}{2} \cdot \frac{1}{3}) = \frac{3}{8} + \frac{1}{6}$ $= \frac{9}{24} + \frac{4}{24} = \frac{13}{24}$. Thus, $\frac{1}{2} \cdot (\frac{3}{4} + \frac{1}{3}) = (\frac{1}{2} \cdot \frac{3}{4}) + (\frac{1}{2} \cdot \frac{1}{3})$. Do you recognize this pattern? Of course, it is the distributive pattern. We can state that, in general, multiplication distributes over addition.

PROPERTY 5.5 **For all rational numbers** $\dfrac{a}{b}, \dfrac{c}{d}$, **and** $\dfrac{e}{f}, \dfrac{a}{b} \cdot \left(\dfrac{c}{d} + \dfrac{e}{f} \right) = \left(\dfrac{a}{b} \cdot \dfrac{c}{d} \right) +$ $\left(\dfrac{a}{b} \cdot \dfrac{e}{f} \right).$

PROBLEM SET 5.3

1. Use a rectangular region to illustrate each of the following products.

a. $\frac{1}{2} \cdot \frac{3}{4}$ **b.** $\frac{2}{3} \cdot \frac{1}{5}$ **c.** $\frac{1}{4} \cdot \frac{3}{5}$ **d.** $\frac{3}{4} \cdot \frac{1}{8}$ **e.** $\frac{5}{6} \cdot \frac{2}{3}$ **f.** $\frac{1}{5} \cdot \frac{2}{3}$

2. In each of the following figures a rectangular region has been used to indicate a product of two fractions. Name the fractions and their product.

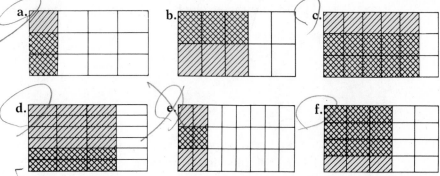

3. Use Definition 5.4 to find the following products (express your answers in reduced form):

a. $\frac{1}{2} \cdot \frac{3}{4}$ **b.** $\frac{5}{6} \cdot \frac{7}{8}$ **c.** $\frac{4}{5} \cdot \frac{10}{12}$ **d.** $5 \cdot \frac{3}{4}$ **e.** $\frac{1}{2} \cdot 3$

f. $3 \cdot \frac{2}{5}$ **g.** $\frac{5}{3} \cdot \frac{6}{8}$ **h.** $\frac{23}{18} \cdot \frac{36}{40}$ **i.** $\frac{2}{3} \cdot \frac{3}{2}$ **j.** $\frac{46}{45} \cdot \frac{45}{46}$

4. Find the following products (express your answers as mixed numerals in reduced form):

a. $2 \cdot 3\frac{1}{3}$ **b.** $4 \cdot 5\frac{1}{4}$ **c.** $\frac{2}{3} \cdot 4\frac{1}{2}$ **d.** $\frac{3}{5} \cdot 5\frac{1}{6}$

e. $4\frac{1}{2} \cdot 5\frac{1}{4}$ **f.** $\frac{4}{3} \cdot 1\frac{7}{8}$ **g.** $3\frac{1}{2} \cdot 4\frac{5}{8}$

5. Find the following products using common factors wherever it is possible to do so.

a. $\frac{2}{5} \cdot \frac{1}{3}$ **b.** $\frac{5}{6} \cdot \frac{6}{7}$ **c.** $\frac{4}{9} \cdot \frac{3}{8}$ **d.** $\frac{9}{2} \cdot \frac{3}{4}$

f. $\frac{7}{9} \cdot \frac{21}{25}$ **g.** $3 \cdot \frac{5}{3}$ **h.** $2\frac{1}{4} \cdot \frac{6}{8}$ **e.** $\frac{9}{2} \cdot \frac{6}{5}$

6. Suppose the distance from your room to the mathematics classroom is $\frac{3}{4}$ of a mile. When you are at a point $\frac{2}{3}$ of the distance from your room to the class, how far are you from your room?

7. A recipe that serve 4 people uses $2\frac{1}{2}$ cups of flour and $\frac{3}{4}$ cup of sugar.

a. If you are cooking for 2, how much of each must you use?

b. How much should you use if you are cooking for 6 persons?

8. What property does each of the following illustrate?

a. $\frac{3}{5} \cdot \frac{5}{7} = \frac{5}{7} \cdot \frac{3}{5}$ **b.** $\frac{1}{3} + (\frac{3}{4} + \frac{1}{2}) = (\frac{1}{3} + \frac{3}{4}) + \frac{1}{2}$

c. $\frac{1}{4} \cdot (\frac{1}{2} + \frac{1}{3}) = (\frac{1}{4} \cdot \frac{1}{2}) + (\frac{1}{4} \cdot \frac{1}{3})$ **d.** $\frac{3}{5} \cdot (\frac{1}{4} \cdot \frac{5}{8}) = \frac{3}{5} \cdot (\frac{5}{8} \cdot \frac{1}{4})$

e. $\frac{3}{4} \cdot (\frac{1}{5} + \frac{3}{8}) = (\frac{1}{5} + \frac{3}{8}) \cdot \frac{3}{4}$

9. Use the distributive property to rewrite each of the following:

a. $12 \cdot (\frac{1}{2} + \frac{1}{3}) =$ **b.** $6 \cdot (\frac{2}{3} + \frac{1}{6}) =$

c. $\frac{5}{3} \cdot (\frac{1}{4} + \frac{1}{2}) =$ **d.** $\frac{3}{5} \cdot (\frac{1}{6} + \frac{5}{12}) =$

e. $\frac{1}{4} \cdot \frac{2}{3} + \frac{1}{4} \cdot \frac{1}{3} =$ **f.** $\frac{2}{5} \cdot \frac{1}{6} + \frac{2}{5} \cdot \frac{1}{4} =$

10. For each part of Problem 9, compute the answer to the problem posed. (In some cases, one set of computations may be easier than the other and would allow you to perform a mental calculation.)

11. To find the product $2 \cdot 3\frac{1}{3}$ we might write the following:

$$
\begin{array}{r}
2 \\
\times 3\frac{1}{3} \\
\hline
6 = 2 \cdot 3 \\
\frac{2}{3} = 2 \cdot \frac{1}{3} \\
\hline
6\frac{2}{3}
\end{array}
$$

a. Use the distributive property to verify this algorithm.

b. Use this algorithm to find each of the following:

(i) 3	**(ii)** 5	**(iii)** 6	**(iv)** 7
$\times 4\frac{1}{2}$	$\times 2\frac{1}{4}$	$\times 3\frac{2}{3}$	$\times 1\frac{3}{5}$

c. Show how to expand the algorithm to find $3\frac{1}{2} \cdot 4\frac{3}{5}$. (You should expect four partial products in this case.)

12. To find $\frac{1}{2} \cdot \frac{2}{3}$ using sets, we might do the following:

Therefore, $\frac{1}{2} \cdot \frac{2}{3} = \frac{1}{3}$.

a. Use sets to find the following:

(i) $\frac{1}{3} \cdot \frac{3}{4}$ (ii) $\frac{1}{4} \cdot \frac{4}{5}$ (iii) $\frac{2}{3} \cdot \frac{3}{5}$ (iv) $\frac{3}{4} \cdot \frac{4}{7}$

b. To find $\frac{1}{2} \cdot \frac{3}{5}$ requires that we use equivalent fractions. Using the set

we cannot represent $\frac{1}{2}$ of $\frac{3}{5}$, so consider the equivalent fraction

$\frac{6}{10}$. 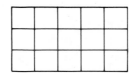 Thus $\frac{1}{2} \cdot \frac{3}{5} = \frac{3}{10}$ Use this idea to find the following:

(i) $\frac{1}{2} \cdot \frac{3}{4}$ (ii) $\frac{1}{2} \cdot \frac{5}{6}$ (iii) $\frac{1}{3} \cdot \frac{2}{5}$ (iv) $\frac{2}{3} \cdot \frac{4}{5}$

13. If a, b, c, and d are nonzero whole numbers, express each of the following as a fraction in reduced form:

a. $\dfrac{a}{b} \cdot \dfrac{a}{d}$ b. $\dfrac{a}{b^2} \cdot \dfrac{b}{c}$ c. $\dfrac{a^2}{b^3} \cdot \dfrac{b^2 d}{ad}$ d. $\dfrac{a^2 + b}{ac^2} \cdot \dfrac{a^2 b}{a^2}$

Pedagogical Problems and Activities

14. A pan of brownies has been cut as illustrated. Explain how you might use this with third-grade children to show the meaning of $\frac{2}{3} \cdot \frac{4}{5}$.

15. a. Show how you might use pizza boards to illustrate that $2 \cdot 1\frac{1}{3} = 2\frac{2}{3}$.
    b. Show how you might use pizza boards to illustrate that $\frac{1}{2} \cdot 2\frac{1}{3} = 1\frac{1}{6}$.

16. a. Suppose that a sixth-grade student states that the product of a rational number and $\frac{3}{4}$ is always less than $\frac{3}{4}$. What could you say?
    b. Suppose the student says that the product of a rational number and $\frac{3}{4}$ is always less than the given rational number. What could you say?

17. Indicate the mathematical sentences that you would expect elementary school children to use in solving the following:

a. Susie had a bottle of cola. She drank $\frac{1}{4}$ of it, then gave her sister $\frac{1}{2}$ of what remained. What part of the bottle of cola did the sister actually receive?

b. Candy is on sale in a store. Five boys find that they can buy a box of Valentine's Day candy holding $1\frac{3}{4}$ pounds at half price. How much candy will each of the five boys receive if they purchase one box and divide it equally?

18. What misconception is involved in each of the following?

a. $\dfrac{1}{\not{4}} + \dfrac{\not{4}}{7} = \dfrac{1}{7}$ b. $\dfrac{1\not{4}}{2\not{4}} = \dfrac{1}{2}$ c. $3\dfrac{2}{\not{3}} = 2$

19. A child reasons as follows:

$3 \cdot \frac{1}{4} = \frac{1}{4} + \frac{1}{4} + \frac{1}{4} =$ $= \frac{3}{12}$

What could you say?

20. A child writes $4\frac{1}{3} \cdot 2\frac{1}{2} = (4 \cdot 2) + (\frac{1}{3} \cdot \frac{1}{2}) = 8\frac{1}{6}$.
What could you say?

21. **a.** The probability of a coin "coming up heads" is $\frac{1}{2}$. If we toss a coin 50 times, we would expect that the number of heads would be $\frac{1}{2} \cdot 50 = 25$. In 1000 tosses, what is the number of heads that would be expected?

b. If a dictionary is opened at random and a page selected, what is the probability that the last digit of the page number will be a multiple of 3? In 20 trials, how many times would you expect the last digit to be a multiple of 3?

22. **a.** Many pencils have six sides. Label each side of a pencil with one of the digits 1, 2, 3, 4, 5, or 6, then roll the pencil on a table and record the top number when it stops. What is the probability that the 2 will come up?

b. How many rolls of the pencil should you expect to make in order to record 2 twelve times?

23. **a.** Is $\frac{7}{15}$ greater or less than half?
b. Which is greater, $\frac{7}{15}$ or $\frac{19}{34}$?
c. Which is closer to $\frac{3}{4}$, $\frac{5}{12}$ or $\frac{11}{12}$?

5.4   SUBTRACTION AND DIVISION OF RATIONAL NUMBERS

Let us turn now to subraction of rational numbers. We would like to have the meaning of subtraction be the same as that applied to whole numbers and integers. For this reason, we make the following definition.

Definition 5.5   If $\dfrac{a}{b}$ and $\dfrac{c}{d}$ are rational numbers, $\dfrac{a}{b} - \dfrac{c}{d}$ is that rational number $\dfrac{e}{f}$ such that $\dfrac{c}{d} + \dfrac{e}{f} = \dfrac{a}{b}.$ $\left(\dfrac{a}{b} - \dfrac{c}{d} = \dfrac{e}{f} \text{ if and only if } \dfrac{c}{d} + \dfrac{e}{f} = \dfrac{a}{b}. \right)$

Using this definition we can feel confident that $\frac{5}{7} - \frac{2}{7} = \frac{3}{7}$, because we know that $\frac{2}{7} + \frac{3}{7} = \frac{5}{7}$.

In practice we usually approach subtraction of rational numbers in a slightly different fashion with children. For example, suppose that a child has $\frac{3}{4}$ of a candy bar and then eats $\frac{1}{4}$ of the bar. He then has $\frac{3}{4} - \frac{1}{4}$ or $\frac{2}{4}$ of the bar remaining, as illustrated in Figure 5.14.

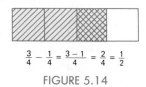

$$\frac{3}{4} - \frac{1}{4} = \frac{3-1}{4} = \frac{2}{4} = \frac{1}{2}$$

FIGURE 5.14

Let us formalize this observation in the following property.

PROPERTY 5.6 If $\dfrac{a}{b}$ and $\dfrac{c}{b}$ are rational numbers, then $\dfrac{a}{b} - \dfrac{c}{b} = \dfrac{a-c}{b}$.

Then if we are asked to find $\frac{4}{5} - \frac{2}{5}$ we could use regions to find the answer, but would very likely use the property instead.

EXAMPLE 1

Find $\dfrac{5}{8} - \dfrac{1}{3}$.

Solution $\dfrac{5}{8} - \dfrac{1}{3} = \dfrac{15}{24} - \dfrac{8}{24} = \dfrac{15-8}{24} = \dfrac{7}{24}$.

EXAMPLE 2

Find $2\frac{1}{3} - 1\frac{1}{4}$.

Solution 1 Because $2\frac{1}{3} = \frac{7}{3}$ and $1\frac{1}{4} = \frac{5}{4}$, we may restate the problem as $\frac{7}{3} - \frac{5}{4}$. Then $\dfrac{7}{3} - \dfrac{5}{4} = \dfrac{28}{12} - \dfrac{15}{12} = \dfrac{28-15}{12} = \dfrac{13}{12} = 1\frac{1}{12}$.

Solution 2

$$\begin{array}{r} 2\frac{1}{3} = 2\frac{4}{12} \\ -1\frac{1}{4} = -1\frac{3}{12} \\ \hline = 1\frac{1}{12} \end{array}$$

EXAMPLE 3

Find $\dfrac{3}{8} - \dfrac{7}{5}$.

Solution $\dfrac{3}{8} - \dfrac{7}{5} = \dfrac{15}{40} - \dfrac{56}{40} = \dfrac{15 - 56}{40} = \dfrac{^{-}41}{40}$.

> **REMARK** The problem illustrated in Example 3 is usually not encountered in the elementary school program. However, you should be aware of the fact that our knowledge of how to subtract rational numbers and our ability to work with subraction of integers allow us to find the difference indicated. The rational numbers are closed with respect to subtraction.

Let us now turn our attention to division. We proceed by extending the development made in prior work and define division in terms of multiplication and state the following:

Definition 5.6   If $\dfrac{a}{b}$ and $\dfrac{c}{d}$ are rational numbers with $\dfrac{c}{d} \neq 0$, $\dfrac{a}{b} \div \dfrac{c}{d}$ is that rational number $\dfrac{e}{f}$ such that $\dfrac{c}{d} \cdot \dfrac{e}{f} = \dfrac{a}{b}$. $\left(\dfrac{a}{b} \div \dfrac{c}{d} = \dfrac{e}{f} \text{ if and only if } \dfrac{c}{d} \cdot \dfrac{e}{f} = \dfrac{a}{b}. \right)$

> **REMARK** Notice that we no longer need the qualifying statement "if $\dfrac{a}{b}$ exists" similar to that used in Definition 4.7 because the nonzero rational numbers are closed under division.

Just as was the case with subtraction of rational numbers, this definition allows us to verify quickly that $\frac{2}{3} \div \frac{5}{6} = \frac{4}{5}$ because $\frac{5}{6} \cdot \frac{4}{5} = \frac{2}{3}$. It is, however, not the working algorithm for division of rational numbers. Such an algorithm follows from Definition 5.6. Because $\dfrac{a}{b} \div \dfrac{c}{d} = \dfrac{e}{f}$ means that $\dfrac{c}{d} \cdot \dfrac{e}{f} = \dfrac{a}{b}$, we may write $b \cdot c \cdot e = d \cdot f \cdot a$. Then $\dfrac{e}{f} = \dfrac{ad}{bc}$ so by substitution $\dfrac{a}{b} \div \dfrac{c}{d} = \dfrac{ad}{bc}$.

A more intuitive observational treatment is commonly found in elementary school mathematics texts. Consider the following examples of division involving fractions. In Figure 5.15 some typical questions are asked. The diagram should make the answer readily available just by counting.

a How many fourths in 2?

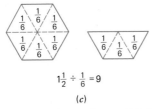

$$2 \div \tfrac{1}{4} = 8$$

(a)

b How many eighths in $\tfrac{3}{4}$?

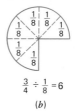

$$\tfrac{3}{4} \div \tfrac{1}{8} = 6$$

(b)

c How many sixths in $1\tfrac{1}{2}$?

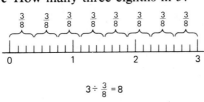

$$1\tfrac{1}{2} \div \tfrac{1}{6} = 9$$

(c)

d How many halves in 3?

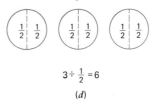

$$3 \div \tfrac{1}{2} = 6$$

(d)

e How many three eighths in 3?

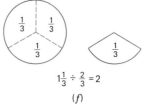

$$3 \div \tfrac{3}{8} = 8$$

(e)

f How many two thirds in $1\tfrac{1}{3}$?

$$1\tfrac{1}{3} \div \tfrac{2}{3} = 2$$

(f)

FIGURE 5.15

Note that we found that $2 \div \tfrac{1}{4} = 8$. (That is, we found 8 $\tfrac{1}{4}$ths in 2.) We also know that $2 \cdot \tfrac{4}{1} = 8$. Likewise, we found $\tfrac{3}{4} \div \tfrac{1}{8} = 6$ and we know that $\tfrac{3}{4} \cdot \tfrac{8}{1} = 6$. In like manner, each of the division statements in Figure 5.15 can be related to a multiplication statement as indicated in Table 5.1.

Another approach is often used to obtain this same observation. Recall that $2 \div 3$ and $\tfrac{2}{3}$ mean the same thing. Then $3 \div \tfrac{4}{5}$ may be written as $\dfrac{3}{\tfrac{4}{5}}$. Since $\tfrac{4}{5}$ $\cdot \tfrac{5}{4} = 1$, we may write the following $\dfrac{3}{\tfrac{4}{5}} = \dfrac{3 \cdot \tfrac{5}{4}}{\tfrac{4}{5} \cdot \tfrac{5}{4}} = \dfrac{3 \cdot \tfrac{5}{4}}{1} = 3 \cdot \tfrac{5}{4}$. In other words, $3 \div \tfrac{4}{5}$ and $3 \cdot \tfrac{5}{4}$ are equivalent statements. We commonly refer to $\tfrac{5}{4}$ as the *reciprocal* of $\tfrac{4}{5}$.

TABLE 5.1

Division	Multiplication
$2 \div \frac{1}{4} = 8$	$2 \cdot \frac{4}{1} = 8$
$\frac{3}{4} \div \frac{1}{8} = 6$	$\frac{3}{4} \cdot \frac{8}{1} = 6$
$\frac{3}{2} \div \frac{1}{6} = 9$	$\frac{3}{2} \cdot \frac{6}{1} = 9$
$3 \div \frac{1}{2} = 6$	$3 \cdot \frac{2}{1} = 6$
$3 \div \frac{3}{8} = 8$	$3 \cdot \frac{8}{3} = 8$
$\frac{4}{3} \div \frac{2}{3} = 2$	$\frac{4}{3} \cdot \frac{3}{2} = 2$

In a very similar manner, we may note that $\dfrac{4}{5} \div \dfrac{7}{8} = \dfrac{\frac{4}{5}}{\frac{7}{8}}$. Then let us mul-

tiply the numerator and denominator by the reciprocal of $\frac{7}{8}$. Then $\dfrac{\frac{4}{5} \cdot \frac{8}{7}}{\frac{7}{8} \cdot \frac{8}{7}} =$

$\dfrac{\frac{4}{5} \cdot \frac{8}{7}}{1} = \frac{4}{5} \cdot \frac{8}{7}$. This reasoning also makes it clear that we may rewrite a division

problem as an equivalent multiplication problem.

PROPERTY 5.7   If $\dfrac{a}{b}$ and $\dfrac{c}{d}$ are rational numbers with $c \neq 0$, then $\dfrac{a}{b} \div \dfrac{c}{d} = \dfrac{a}{b} \cdot \dfrac{d}{c}$.

EXAMPLE 1

Find $\frac{5}{6} \div \frac{2}{7}$.

Solution $\frac{5}{6} \div \frac{2}{7} = \frac{5}{6} \cdot \frac{7}{2} = \frac{35}{12}$.

EXAMPLE 2

Find $1\frac{1}{3} \div \frac{4}{5}$.

Solution $1\frac{1}{3} \div \frac{4}{5} = \frac{4}{3} \cdot \frac{5}{4} = \frac{5}{3} = 1\frac{2}{3}$.

EXAMPLE 3

Find $\dfrac{\frac{5}{2} + \frac{2}{3}}{\frac{1}{4}}$.

Solution 1 Multiply both the numerator and the denominator by 4.

$$\frac{(\frac{5}{2} + \frac{2}{3})4}{\frac{1}{4} \cdot 4} = \frac{\frac{5}{2} \cdot 4 + \frac{2}{3} \cdot 4}{1} = 10 + \frac{8}{3} = 12\frac{2}{3} = \frac{38}{3}$$

Solution 2 Let us perform the addition in the numerator first.

$$\frac{\frac{5}{2}+\frac{2}{3}}{\frac{1}{4}}=\frac{\frac{15}{6}+\frac{4}{6}}{\frac{1}{4}}=\frac{\frac{19}{6}}{\frac{1}{4}}=\frac{\frac{19}{6}\cdot 4}{\frac{1}{4}\cdot 4}=\frac{\frac{19}{6}\cdot 4}{1}=\frac{38}{3}$$

PROBLEM SET 5.4

1. Use a diagram to illustrate the meaning of each of the following:

   a. $\frac{3}{5}-\frac{1}{5}$ **b.** $\frac{5}{6}-\frac{1}{6}$ **c.** $\frac{3}{8}-\frac{1}{8}$ **d.** $\frac{5}{6}-\frac{3}{6}$ **e.** $\frac{3}{4}-\frac{1}{4}$

2. Use Property 5.6 to find the following:

   a. $\frac{5}{7}-\frac{2}{7}$ **b.** $\frac{9}{2}-\frac{5}{2}$ **c.** $\frac{5}{2}-\frac{2}{3}$ **d.** $\frac{7}{2}-\frac{5}{6}$

   e. $\frac{9}{7}-\frac{3}{5}$ **f.** $\frac{11}{7}-\frac{4}{3}$ **g.** $\frac{5}{6}-\frac{1}{8}$ **h.** $\frac{7}{8}-\frac{5}{12}$

3. What division problem is suggested by each of the following?

   a.   **b.**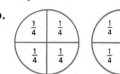

   c.   **d.**   **e.**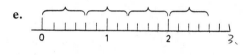

   f.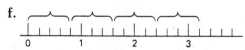

4. Find the following quotients by applying Property 5.7.

   a. $\frac{2}{3}\div\frac{3}{4}$ **b.** $\frac{1}{4}\div\frac{3}{6}$ **c.** $4\div\frac{5}{6}$ **d.** $2\div\frac{2}{3}$

   e. $\frac{5}{8}\div 3$ **f.** $\frac{4}{5}\div 7$ **g.** $\frac{9}{2}\div\frac{3}{4}$ **h.** $\frac{9}{16}\div\frac{5}{2}$

5. Perform the indicated operations.

   a. $(\frac{8}{9}-\frac{2}{9})-\frac{5}{9}$ **b.** $(\frac{8}{5}+\frac{4}{3})-2$ **c.** $\frac{2}{3}\cdot(\frac{1}{2}+\frac{3}{4})$

   d. $(\frac{2}{3}\cdot\frac{1}{2})+(\frac{2}{3}\cdot\frac{3}{4})$ **e.** $4\frac{5}{8}-2\frac{3}{8}$ **f.** $4\frac{3}{5}-1\frac{1}{4}$

   g. $5\frac{1}{6}-2\frac{2}{3}$ **h.** $2\frac{2}{3}\div 4\frac{1}{2}$ **i.** $(\frac{2}{3}+\frac{1}{4})\div\frac{9}{10}$

   j. $(8\div\frac{5}{9})\cdot(\frac{2}{3}\div 4)$ **k.** $\frac{3}{4}+\frac{2}{3}\cdot\frac{3}{8}$ **l.** $\frac{2}{3}+(\frac{1}{4}-\frac{2}{3})$

6. Simplify the following:

   a. $\dfrac{\frac{1}{2}+\frac{3}{5}}{\frac{4}{5}}$ **b.** $\dfrac{\frac{1}{2}+\frac{1}{3}}{\frac{1}{6}+\frac{1}{2}}$ **c.** $\dfrac{\frac{1}{4}}{\frac{1}{2}+\frac{5}{6}}$ **d.** $\dfrac{\frac{2}{3}-\frac{1}{4}}{\frac{5}{6}+\frac{1}{12}}$

7. Let $a, b, c, d,$ and $(a+b)$, be nonzero integers. Perform the indicated operations.

   a. $\dfrac{a}{bc}-\dfrac{d}{bc}$ **b.** $\dfrac{a}{bc}-\dfrac{d}{b}$ **c.** $\dfrac{a}{bc}\div\dfrac{b}{c}$

d. $\dfrac{12}{a+b} - \dfrac{5}{a+b}$ **e.** $\dfrac{5}{ab^2} \div \dfrac{2}{ab}$ **f.** $\dfrac{a^2b}{c} \div \dfrac{bc}{ad}$

8. **a.** Is it correct to write $\dfrac{3}{8} \div \dfrac{3}{4} = \dfrac{3 \div 3}{8 \div 4} = \dfrac{1}{2}$? Justify your answer.

   b. Does $\dfrac{6}{9} \div \dfrac{2}{9} = \dfrac{6 \div 2}{9 \div 9} = 3$? Justify your answer.

   c. Does $\dfrac{5}{11} \div \dfrac{3}{11} = \dfrac{5 \div 3}{11 \div 11} = \dfrac{5}{3}$? Justify your answer.

   d. Show that for any rational numbers $\dfrac{a}{b}$ and $\dfrac{c}{d}$, $\dfrac{a}{b} \div \dfrac{c}{d} = \dfrac{a \div c}{b \div d}$. $\Big($*Hint:*

   Write $\dfrac{a \div c}{b \div d}$ as a complex fraction, then simplify it and show that the

   results are the same as for $\dfrac{a}{b} \div \dfrac{c}{d}$.$\Big)$

   e. This algorithm is particularly useful if a common denominator exists. Use it to find the following quotients.

   (i) $\frac{12}{7} \div \frac{3}{7}$ **(ii)** $\frac{15}{17} \div \frac{5}{17}$ **(iii)** $\frac{13}{17} \div \frac{19}{17}$ **(iv)** $\frac{5}{8} \div \frac{3}{4}$

9. **a.** Does $(\frac{7}{6} - \frac{1}{3}) - \frac{1}{2} = \frac{7}{6} - (\frac{1}{3} - \frac{1}{2})$?

   b. Does an associative property hold for subtraction of rational numbers?

   c. Does $(\frac{7}{6} \div \frac{1}{3}) \div \frac{1}{2} = \frac{7}{6} \div (\frac{1}{3} \div \frac{1}{2})$?

   d. What might you state regarding an associative property for division?

10. **a.** Are the rational numbers commutative under subtraction? Justify your answer.

   b. Are the rational numbers commutative under division? Justify your answer.

11. Find the truth set for each using as your domain the set of rational numbers. (*Hint:* You may obtain the answer in each case by referring back to the definition for the operation involved.)

   a. $x + \frac{1}{2} = \frac{2}{2}$ **b.** $\frac{5}{6} - x = \frac{1}{6}$ **c.** $\frac{5}{6} - x = \frac{1}{2}$
   d. $\frac{3}{4} \div x = \frac{1}{2}$ **e.** $x \div \frac{2}{3} = \frac{1}{5}$ **f.** $3 - x = \frac{5}{2}$

12. **a.** As $\dfrac{a}{b} + \dfrac{c}{d} = \dfrac{ad + bc}{bd}$, argue that the rational numbers are closed

   under addition. (*Hint:* Are you sure that $\dfrac{ad + bc}{bd}$ is a rational

   number?)

   b. Are the rational numbers closed under subtraction? (*Hint:* Property 5.6 helps to answer this.)

   c. Are the rational numbers closed under multiplication?

d. Are the rational numbers closed under division? (*Hint:* Property 5.7 is useful here.)

13. a. Three heirs to an estate are to receive $\frac{1}{5}$, $\frac{1}{4}$, and $\frac{3}{8}$ of the estate, respectively. The remainder is to go to charity. What fraction of the estate is left to charity?

b. If the estate is valued at $600,000, how much money did the charities receive?

14. The will of a deceased collector of antique automobiles specified that his cars were to be left to his three children. Half were to go to his eldest son, $\frac{1}{3}$ to his daughter and $\frac{1}{9}$ to his youngest child. At the time of his death, 17 cars were in the collection. The administrator of his estate borrowed a car to make 18.

$$\frac{1}{2} \text{ of } 18 = 9$$
$$\frac{1}{3} \text{ of } 18 = 6$$
$$\frac{1}{9} \text{ of } 18 = \underline{2}$$
$$\text{Total} \quad 17$$

The borrowed car was then returned. Could this *really* happen? Where is the error?

15. a. One interpretation for division of whole numbers involves repeated subtraction. This same interpretation can be used with rational numbers. For example, $2 \div \frac{1}{3}$ means $2 - \frac{1}{3} = 1\frac{2}{3}$, $1\frac{2}{3} - \frac{1}{3} = 1\frac{1}{3}$, and so on. There must be 6 one-thirds in 2. Use this technique to find each of the following:

(i) $3 \div \frac{1}{2}$ **(ii)** $2 \div \frac{2}{3}$ **(iii)** $\frac{3}{4} \div \frac{1}{4}$ **(iv)** $\frac{9}{2} \div \frac{3}{4}$ **(v)** $2 \div \frac{2}{5}$

b. Consider $3 \div \frac{2}{3}$. Note that $4 \cdot \frac{2}{3} = \frac{8}{3} = 2\frac{2}{3}$, which is less than 3, and $5 \cdot \frac{2}{3} = \frac{10}{3} = 3\frac{1}{3}$ which is greater than 3. We conclude that there are four groups of $\frac{2}{3}$ in 3 with a remainder of $\frac{1}{3}$. This remainder is $\frac{\frac{1}{3}}{\frac{2}{3}}$ of another group of $\frac{2}{3}$, or $\frac{1}{2}$. Thus $3 \div \frac{2}{3} = 3\frac{1}{2}$. Use this reasoning process to find the following quotients.

(i) $\frac{5}{7} \div \frac{2}{7}$ **(ii)** $2 \div \frac{3}{4}$ **(iii)** $\frac{5}{2} \div \frac{2}{3}$ **(iv)** $\frac{15}{4} \div \frac{5}{6}$

16. Notice that

$$\frac{1}{2} - \frac{1}{3} = \frac{1}{6}$$
$$\frac{1}{4} - \frac{1}{5} = \frac{1}{20}$$
$$\frac{1}{5} - \frac{1}{6} = \frac{1}{30}$$

a. Does the pattern apply to $\frac{1}{12} - \frac{1}{13}$?

b. Does it apply to $\frac{1}{31} - \frac{1}{32}$?

c. Do you expect this in general? Justify your answer.

$$\left(Hint: \text{Show that } \frac{1}{a} - \frac{1}{a+1} = \frac{1}{a \cdot (a+1)}. \right)$$

Pedagogical Problems and Activities

17. **a.** Show how you might use a set to illustrate $\frac{5}{7}$.
    b. Use the set from part **a** to illustrate $\frac{5}{7} - \frac{2}{7}$.
    c. Show how to use a set to find $\frac{3}{4} - \frac{1}{6}$.

18. Fraction strips have been used to illustrate equivalent fractions and addition of fractions.
    a. Use fraction strips to find $\frac{5}{6} - \frac{1}{6}$. How can the fraction strips be used to obtain the answer in reduced form?
    b. Use fraction strips to find $\frac{5}{6} - \frac{1}{4}$.

19. Earlier in this section we illustrated that division with fractions relates to the "how many" aspect of division. The division problem $3 \div \frac{1}{2}$ asks the question "how many halves in three?" The answer is of course 6. How would a sixth-grade student use this idea to do the following problems?
    a. $1 \div \frac{1}{3}$ **b.** $2 \div \frac{1}{5}$ **c.** $2 \div \frac{1}{3}$ **d.** $\frac{6}{5} \div \frac{1}{5}$
    e. $5 \div \frac{1}{8}$ **f.** $4 \div \frac{1}{11}$

20. Estimation is important in mathematics. In each of the following, estimate whether the answer is larger than 1 or smaller than 1. (*Hint:* Use the "how many" idea from Problem 19 to answer these.)
    a. $\frac{3}{4} \div \frac{1}{2}$ **b.** $1 \div \frac{7}{8}$ **c.** $\frac{1}{2} \div \frac{3}{4}$ **d.** $\frac{8}{7} \div \frac{7}{8}$
    e. $\frac{2}{3} \div \frac{1}{4}$ **f.** $\frac{3}{5} \div \frac{3}{4}$

21. **a.** Is there a whole 2 in $\frac{1}{3}$?
    b. What part of 2 is in $\frac{1}{3}$?

5.5   ORDER IN THE SET OF RATIONAL NUMBERS

As we work with rational numbers such as $\frac{1}{3}$ and $\frac{3}{4}$, it is intuitively clear that $\frac{3}{4}$ is greater than $\frac{1}{3}$. Young children have had sufficient experience to realize that $\frac{3}{4}$ of an apple is more than $\frac{1}{3}$ of an apple. The fractions $\frac{5}{9}$ and $\frac{6}{9}$ are easy to make order decisions about. Because both speak of ninths, it is obvious that 6 of them are more than just 5 of them. Indeed, one method of making decisions about order of rational numbers is simply to obtain positive common denominators, then compare the numerators. The fraction having the larger numerator is the greater fraction.

EXAMPLE

Which is greater, $\frac{5}{9}$ or $\frac{7}{11}$?

Solution Because lcm (9, 11) = 99, write $\frac{5}{9} = \frac{55}{99}$ and $\frac{7}{11} = \frac{63}{99}$. Then $\frac{7}{11} > \frac{5}{9}$.

Another rather natural way to make decisions about order is exemplified by the following questions. Which is greater, $\frac{5}{6}$ of an apple or $\frac{5}{9}$ of an apple? This time we are to receive the same number of pieces in either case, but the denominators are not equal. However, a sixth of an apple is greater than a ninth of an apple, so $\frac{5}{6}$ is greater than $\frac{5}{9}$.

EXAMPLE

Which is greater, $\frac{7}{11}$ or $\frac{7}{13}$?

Solution Because $11 < 13$, one eleventh is greater than one thirteenth. Therefore, $\frac{7}{11} > \frac{7}{13}$.

We might consider one more approach to the question of inequality for rational numbers. When we considered this same question regarding whole numbers, we stated that $a < b$ if and only if for some whole number $c > 0$, $a + c = b$. The number c could be determined by finding the difference between a and b. Let us do the same for rational numbers.

Definition 5.7 Let $\dfrac{a}{b}$ and $\dfrac{c}{d}$ be rational numbers. Then $\dfrac{a}{b} < \dfrac{c}{d}$ if and only if there exists a rational number $\dfrac{e}{f} > 0$ such that $\dfrac{a}{b} + \dfrac{e}{f} = \dfrac{c}{d}$.

Application of this definition would then yield the following examples.

$\frac{3}{8} < \frac{5}{8}$ because there exists $\frac{2}{8} > 0$ such that $\frac{3}{8} + \frac{2}{8} = \frac{5}{8}$.

$\frac{1}{3} < \frac{3}{4}$ because there exists $\frac{5}{12} > 0$ such that $\frac{1}{3} + \frac{5}{12} = \frac{9}{12} = \frac{3}{4}$.

Although Definition 5.7 is easily understood, it does not tell us how to determine the positive rational number $\dfrac{e}{f}$. The value for $\dfrac{e}{f}$ may be found by considering the two possible differences between $\dfrac{a}{b}$ and $\dfrac{c}{d}$. $\left(\text{That is, } \dfrac{a}{b} - \dfrac{c}{d} \text{ and } \right.$ $\left. \dfrac{c}{d} - \dfrac{a}{b}. \right)$ If the difference is 0, the numbers $\dfrac{a}{b}$ and $\dfrac{c}{d}$ are equal. If the difference is not 0, $\dfrac{e}{f}$ is that positive difference found. Consider $\dfrac{a}{b} = \dfrac{5}{7}$ and $\dfrac{c}{d} = \dfrac{11}{14}$. Note that $\dfrac{c}{d} - \dfrac{a}{b} = \dfrac{11}{14} - \dfrac{5}{7} = \dfrac{1}{14}$. Therefore, $\dfrac{e}{f} = \dfrac{1}{14}$ and $\dfrac{5}{7} + \dfrac{1}{14} = \dfrac{11}{14}$, so $\dfrac{5}{7} < \dfrac{11}{14}$. Thus, finding the difference between the two rational numbers will quickly answer the question of order.

PROPERTY 5.8   For rational number $\frac{a}{b}$ and $\frac{c}{d}$, $\frac{a}{b} > \frac{c}{d}$ if and only if $\frac{a}{b} - \frac{c}{d} > 0.$

EXAMPLE

Which is greater, $\frac{7}{8}$ or $\frac{3}{4}$?

Solution   Because $\frac{3}{4} = \frac{6}{8}$ and $\frac{7}{8} - \frac{6}{8} = \frac{1}{8}$, then $\frac{7}{8} > \frac{3}{4}$.

Any time you are faced with the task of determining the order of two or more rational numbers, you may choose which technique you prefer to use.

Let us observe another interesting property possessed by the rational numbers. Consider the numbers $\frac{2}{3}$ and $\frac{3}{4}$. Note that $\frac{2}{3} < \frac{3}{4}$. We have graphed these numbers on the number line illustrated in Figure 5.16. We can find another rational number $\frac{m}{n}$ that is between $\frac{2}{3}$ and $\frac{3}{4}$. One easy way to do this is to consider common denominators. Because $\frac{2}{3} = \frac{16}{24}$ and $\frac{3}{4} = \frac{18}{24}$, then $\frac{17}{24}$ is one possible selection for $\frac{m}{n}$. But $\frac{2}{3} = \frac{32}{48}$ and $\frac{3}{4} = \frac{36}{48}$, so any of the numbers $\frac{33}{48}$, $\frac{34}{48}$, or $\frac{35}{48}$ could be used as an acceptable value for $\frac{m}{n}$. Indeed, if we are requested to place three rational numbers between $\frac{2}{3}$ and $\frac{3}{4}$, we have a ready-made answer. We could use this same technique to find four rationals between two rationals.

(a)   (b)

FIGURE 5.16

PROPERTY 5.9   **Density Property**

For any two rational numbers, it is always possible to find another rational number between them.

REMARK   Property 5.9 states that between any two rational numbers there always exists another rational number. This is equivalent to stating that between any two rational numbers there are infinitely many rational numbers.

This property assures us that between two rational numbers there always exists another rational number. Therefore, given some rational number it is not possible for us to find the "next larger" one. This is much different from the situation that exists for integers or whole numbers. We are not always able to find another whole number between two given ones. For example, between 3 and 4 there is no other whole number. Furthermore, given any whole number we can always find the next larger one. The whole numbers do not possess the property of density.

PROBLEM SET 5.5

1. Place the symbol $>$, $<$ or $=$ between the given rational numbers in order to make the statement true.

   a. $\frac{3}{5} \bigcirc \frac{4}{5}$ **b.** $\frac{5}{16} \bigcirc \frac{3}{16}$ **c.** $\frac{8}{3} \bigcirc \frac{8}{5}$ **d.** $\frac{14}{11} \bigcirc \frac{14}{9}$

   e. $\frac{3}{8} \bigcirc \frac{19}{24}$ **f.** $\frac{5}{12} \bigcirc \frac{9}{24}$ **g.** $\frac{3}{4} \bigcirc \frac{5}{6}$ **h.** $\frac{27}{28} \bigcirc \frac{13}{14}$

   i. $\frac{35}{72} \bigcirc \frac{35}{71}$ **j.** $\frac{35}{72} \bigcirc \frac{11}{18}$

2. Arrange the following in order of size from smallest to largest:

   a. $\frac{7}{8}, \frac{9}{10}, \frac{17}{18}$ **b.** $\frac{3}{5}, \frac{4}{7}, \frac{8}{11}$ **c.** $\frac{17}{24}, \frac{21}{26}, \frac{35}{40}$ **d.** $\frac{19}{21}, \frac{17}{19}, \frac{37}{42}$

3. Use the common denominator approach to find the following:

   a. Three rational numbers between $\frac{5}{6}$ and $\frac{3}{4}$.

   b. Three rational numbers between $\frac{5}{6}$ and $\frac{7}{8}$.

   c. Four rational numbers between $\frac{1}{2}$ and $\frac{2}{3}$.

4. Use Property 5.8 to determine which is larger:

   a. $\frac{5}{9}$ or $\frac{7}{11}$ **b.** $\frac{7}{8}$ or $\frac{20}{23}$ **c.** $\frac{5}{7}$ or $\frac{7}{9}$ **d.** $\frac{17}{12}$ or $\frac{21}{16}$

5. Given rational numbers $\dfrac{a}{b}$ and $\dfrac{c}{d}$, consider $\dfrac{m}{n} = \dfrac{a+c}{b+d}$.

   a. If $\dfrac{a}{b} = \dfrac{2}{3}$ and $\dfrac{c}{d} = \dfrac{3}{4}$, find $\dfrac{m}{n}$. Locate the numbers $\dfrac{a}{b}, \dfrac{c}{d}$, and $\dfrac{m}{n}$ on a number line.

   b. If $\dfrac{a}{b} = \dfrac{3}{8}$ and $\dfrac{c}{d} = \dfrac{5}{7}$, find $\dfrac{m}{n}$. Locate the numbers $\dfrac{a}{b}, \dfrac{c}{d}$, and $\dfrac{m}{n}$ on a number line.

   c. If $\dfrac{a}{b} = \dfrac{17}{20}$ and $\dfrac{c}{d} = \dfrac{21}{25}$, find $\dfrac{m}{n}$. Locate the numbers $\dfrac{a}{b}, \dfrac{c}{d}$, and $\dfrac{m}{n}$ on a number line.

   d. In general, if $\dfrac{a}{b} < \dfrac{c}{d}$, is $\dfrac{m}{n}$ between $\dfrac{a}{b}$ and $\dfrac{c}{d}$?

6. Fill each blank with $>$, $<$, or $=$ to make a true sentence for each of the following:

   a. $\frac{3}{2} \cdot \frac{2}{3}$ _____ $\frac{3}{2} + \frac{2}{3}$ **b.** $\frac{2}{5} \cdot \frac{5}{2}$ _____ $\frac{4}{5} \cdot \frac{5}{4}$

   c. $8 \div \frac{2}{3}$ _____ $4 \div \frac{1}{3}$ **d.** $2\frac{2}{3} \cdot \frac{1}{4}$ _____ $6 \div \frac{3}{4}$

   e. $5 \div 2\frac{1}{3}$ _____ $1 \div \frac{1}{7}$ **f.** $2\frac{2}{3} \cdot 5\frac{1}{4}$ _____ $4\frac{1}{5} \cdot 3\frac{1}{6}$

7. Suppose $\dfrac{a}{b}$ and $\dfrac{c}{d}$ are rational numbers with $b > 0$ and $d > 0$. Let $\dfrac{r}{s} = \dfrac{1}{2}\left(\dfrac{a}{b} + \dfrac{c}{d}\right)$.

   a. If $\dfrac{a}{b} = \dfrac{2}{3}$ and $\dfrac{c}{d} = \dfrac{5}{6}$, find $\dfrac{r}{s}$. Is $\dfrac{r}{s}$ between $\dfrac{a}{b}$ and $\dfrac{c}{d}$?

   b. If $\dfrac{a}{b} = \dfrac{3}{4}$ and $\dfrac{c}{d} = \dfrac{7}{8}$, find $\dfrac{r}{s}$. Is $\dfrac{r}{s}$ between $\dfrac{a}{b}$ and $\dfrac{c}{d}$?

   c. If $\dfrac{a}{b} = \dfrac{17}{20}$ and $\dfrac{c}{d} = \dfrac{21}{25}$, find $\dfrac{r}{s}$. Is $\dfrac{r}{s}$ between $\dfrac{a}{b}$ and $\dfrac{c}{d}$?

   d. In general, is $\dfrac{r}{s}$ between $\dfrac{a}{b}$ and $\dfrac{c}{d}$?

8. Definition 5.2 stated that $\dfrac{a}{b} = \dfrac{c}{d}$ if and only if $a \cdot d = b \cdot c$. Thus, $\frac{2}{3} = \frac{8}{12}$ because $2 \cdot 12 = 3 \cdot 8$, but $\frac{3}{4} \neq \frac{8}{12}$ because $3 \cdot 12 \neq 4 \cdot 8$.

   a. Show that $\frac{3}{4} > \frac{8}{12}$. Note that $3 \cdot 12 > 4 \cdot 8$.

   b. Complete the statement: $\frac{2}{5}$ _____ $\frac{9}{20}$ and $2 \cdot 20$ _____ $5 \cdot 9$.

   c. Complete the statement: $\frac{5}{9}$ _____ $\frac{25}{44}$ and $5 \cdot 44$ _____ $9 \cdot 25$.

   d. If $\dfrac{a}{b}$ and $\dfrac{c}{d}$ are rational numbers with $b > 0$ and $d > 0$, is it true that

      $\dfrac{a}{b} > \dfrac{c}{d}$ if and only if $ad > bc$? Justify your answer. (*Hint:* Find a com-

      mon denominator for $\dfrac{a}{b}$ and $\dfrac{c}{d}$ and change to equivalent fractions.)

   e. Use your calculator and the technique shown in part **a** to decide whether $\frac{488}{5423}$ is greater than $\frac{323}{3782}$.

Pedagogical Problems and Activities

9. Present an argument that might be used with sixth-grade students to show that the set of points in the line segment AB is dense.

A B

10. Show how you might use a number line to illustrate the property of density to sixth-grade students using the numbers $\frac{1}{6}$ and $\frac{3}{4}$.

11. **a.** How might a third-grade child use a pizza board to show that $\frac{4}{5} > \frac{3}{5}$?
    b. How might fraction strips be used to verify that $\frac{2}{3} < \frac{3}{4}$?
    c. How might a fourth-grade child reason that $\frac{13}{15} > \frac{13}{17}$?

12. **a.** Evaluate $\frac{1}{2}(\frac{1}{4} + \frac{5}{6})$. Show that the resulting number is actually midway between $\frac{1}{4}$ and $\frac{5}{6}$ on a number line.
    b. Is the number $\frac{1}{3}(\frac{1}{4} + \frac{5}{6})$ a third of the distance from $\frac{1}{4}$ to $\frac{5}{6}$ on the number line? Show how a sixth-grade student might handle this question.

13. **a.** Use some type of diagram to illustrate the meaning of $(\frac{2}{4})_{\text{five}}$.
    b. Which is greater, $(\frac{2}{4})_{\text{five}}$ or $(\frac{2}{4})_{\text{ten}}$?

5.6   USING RATIOS TO SOLVE PROBLEMS

We often compare things on the basis of some attribute. One obvious way to do this is to find some numerical value for each item, say length or weight, and then find the difference. Another useful way to make comparisons is to use ratios. If there are 4 blue cars and 6 red cars in a parking lot, we say the ratio of blue cars to red cars is 4 to 6. We could write this as 4:6 or as $\frac{4}{6}$.

REMARK Every fraction $\dfrac{a}{b}$ may be interpreted as the ratio of a to b, but some ratios cannot be written as fractions. The ratio of 5 to 0 would be meaningless as a fraction.

EXAMPLE 1

In the sixth-grade class there are 50 girls and 40 boys. The ratio of boys to girls is 40 to 50, or as a fraction $\frac{40}{50}$. The ratio of girls to boys is 50 to 40 or $\frac{50}{40}$.

EXAMPLE 2

Using Example 1, suppose there are eight cheerleaders selected, all girls. The ratio of girls to boys on the cheerleading squad is 8 to 0, which could be written as 8:0.

EXAMPLE 3

To reconstitute dried milk, one is to use 1 cup dried milk to 3 cups of water. Differing quantities can be made, as indicated in the table.

Cups of dried milk	1	2	3	4
Cups of water	3	6	9	12
Ratio of dried milk to water	$\frac{1}{3}$	$\frac{2}{6}$	$\frac{3}{9}$	$\frac{4}{12}$

Note that any two ratios found in the table for Example 3 are equivalent. The statement of equality of two ratios expressed in fractional form is called a *proportion*.

Definition 5.8   If $\frac{a}{b}$ and $\frac{c}{d}$ are rational numbers, $\frac{a}{b} = \frac{c}{d}$ is a proportion if and only if $ad = bc$.

We often use proportions where one term is missing. It is often convenient to use Definition 5.8 to find the missing term.

EXAMPLE 1

Find the missing term in each of the following.

a. $\dfrac{a}{9} = \dfrac{2}{3}$ **b.** $\dfrac{4}{5} = \dfrac{b}{10}$ **c.** $\dfrac{4}{9} = \dfrac{6}{c}$ **d.** $\dfrac{5}{d} = \dfrac{10}{3}$

Solution

a. $a \cdot 3 = 9 \cdot 2$ **b.** $4 \cdot 10 = 5 \cdot b$ **c.** $4 \cdot c = 9 \cdot 6$
$\qquad a = 6$ $\qquad\quad 8 = b$ $\qquad\quad c = \frac{54}{4} = 13\frac{1}{2}$

d. $10d = 15$
$\qquad d = 1.5$

EXAMPLE 2

On a bicycle the wheels revolve 12 times during the time that the pedals revolve 5 times. In 200 rotations of the wheel, how many rotations will the pedals make?

Solution The ratio of wheel rotation to pedal rotation is 12 to 5. The following proportion expresses the data where n represents the number of pedal rotations needed to cause the wheels to rotate 200 times.

$$\frac{12}{5} = \frac{200}{n}$$
$$12n = 1000$$
$$n = \frac{1000}{12} = 83\frac{1}{3}$$

Suppose a road construction company hires 36 people, 26 men and 10 women. The ratio of women to men is expressed as 10 to 26 or, as a fraction, $\frac{10}{26}$. Let us further suppose that 7 of these people are to act as "flag persons" to control vehicular traffic. One man and 7 women are so employed. The ratio of men to women flag persons is 1:6, or as a fraction $\frac{1}{6}$. Even though ratios are commonly represented by a fraction, there is still a subtle distinction between "ratios" and "fractional parts". A ratio may be used to compare disjoint sets whereas a fractional part may be used to compare a subset with the entire set. Note that $\frac{10}{36}$ represents the fraction of the work force that is female and $\frac{6}{10}$ represents the fraction of women hired who are flag persons. (In each case a subset was compared with the entire set.) The ratio of females who are flag persons to females who have other assignments is $\frac{6}{4}$. (Comparison of two disjoint sets.)

EXAMPLE 1

A set of blocks consists of 3 red blocks and 5 blue blocks:

Find:

a. The ratio of red blocks to blue blocks.
b. The red blocks as a fractional part of the set.
c. The blue blocks as a fractional part of the set.

Solutions

a. The ratio of red blocks to blue blocks is 3:5 or $\frac{3}{5}$.
b. $\frac{3}{8}$ of the blocks are red.
c. $\frac{5}{8}$ of the blocks are blue.

EXAMPLE 2

In a fifth-grade classroom there were 18 girls and 16 boys. $\frac{1}{3}$ of the girls and $\frac{1}{2}$ of the boys had ten speed bikes. What fraction of the class had ten speed bikes?

Solution 1 Suppose we add $\frac{1}{3} + \frac{1}{2} = \frac{5}{6}$. Is this a reasonable answer? Then $\frac{5}{6} \cdot 34 = 28\frac{1}{3}$ students have ten speeds. One should question the results, as $\frac{1}{3}$ of a student is hard to find!

Solution 2 $\frac{1}{3} \cdot 18 + \frac{1}{2} \cdot 16 = 6 + 8 = 14$ is the number of ten speeds. $\frac{14}{34} = \frac{7}{17}$ have ten speed bikes. This seems reasonable since $\frac{7}{17} \cdot 34 = 14$.

EXAMPLE 3

The local YMCA has 300 individual members. The ratio of adults to children is 3 to 2. The ratio of adult men to women is 4 to 1 and for children, the ratio of boys to girls is 1 to 1. Find the number of individual members who are **a.** adults, **b.** adult females, and **c.** males.

Solution

a. $\frac{3}{5}$ of the individual members are adult. $\frac{3}{5} \cdot 300 = 180$ are adults.

b. $\frac{1}{5}$ of the adults were women. $\frac{1}{5} \cdot 180 = 36$ were adult women.

c. There are 180 adult members, $\frac{4}{5}$ of which are men, and 120 child members, $\frac{1}{2}$ of which are male. Thus, $\frac{4}{5} \cdot 180 + \frac{1}{2} \cdot 120 = 144 + 60 = 204$ male members.

In many applications of proportions we find special situations. For example, if one can of Diet Coke cost 45 cents from a vending machine, then 2 cans will cost 90 cents, 3 cans $1.35, etc. We say that the cost "varies directly" as the number of cans purchased. As one increases the number of cans purchased, we expect the price to increase. If n is the number of cans of pop purchased at 45 cents each and the cost is c, then $c = 45n$. We say that c is "directly proportional" to n and that 45 is the constant of proportionality.

Definition 5.9 Given two numbers a and b, a varies directly as b (a is directly proportional to b) if and only if for some constant k, $a = k \cdot b$. We call k the constant of proportionality.

EXAMPLE

The distance traveled in t hours driving 55 mph can be expressed as $d = 55t$. Complete the table:

t	1	2		
d	55		220	330

Solution If $t = 2$, $d = 55 \cdot 2 = 100$ mi
If $d = 220$, $220 = 55t$, so $t = 4$ hrs
If $d = 330$, $330 = 55t$, so $t = 6$ hrs

PROBLEM SET 5.6

1. Solve each proportion.

   a. $\dfrac{3}{5} = \dfrac{n}{25}$ b. $\dfrac{8}{3} = \dfrac{32}{n}$ c. $\dfrac{n}{5} = \dfrac{24}{2}$ d. $\dfrac{n}{2} = \dfrac{15}{5}$

   e. $\dfrac{6}{12} = \dfrac{n}{10}$ f. $\dfrac{2}{5} = \dfrac{30}{n}$ g. $\dfrac{n}{21} = \dfrac{2}{3}$ h. $\dfrac{9}{33} = \dfrac{6}{n}$

   i. $\dfrac{5}{8} = \dfrac{n}{64}$ j. $\dfrac{n}{7} = \dfrac{16}{56}$ k. $\dfrac{5}{n} = \dfrac{30}{48}$ l. $\dfrac{21}{27} = \dfrac{n}{63}$

2. Solve. Use equivalent ratios.

   a. A jet plane flies 2000 miles in 4 hours. How many miles each hour is this?

   b. A new car travels 81 miles on 3 gallons of gasoline. How many miles per gallon is this?

   c. Bill earns $54 in 12 hours. How much does he earn each hour?

   d. Two pounds of bananas cost 56¢. What is the cost of 3 pounds of bananas?

3. a. The cook at a summer camp planned to scramble 7 eggs for every 3 campers. How many eggs would be needed to feed 60 campers?

   b. In one batch of pancakes, 2 tablespoons of oil are used, making 8 pancakes. If campers eat 4 pancakes on the average, how much oil will be needed to feed 60 campers?

4. a. In one of the national forests 24 out of every 100 trees cut are used for firewood. If 42 trees were used for fuel in one winter, how many trees were cut?

   b. A logging truck is used to haul logs out of the forest. If the truck travels 6 miles in 25 minutes, how far can it travel in 2 hours?

5. a. A recipe for chili calls for one 15-ounce can of beans and a 16-ounce can of tomatoes for 1 pound of hamburger (along with water and prepared chili mix). This makes 6 one cup servings. A big batch of chili is to be made to entertain friends after a ball game. If a 128-ounce can of tomatoes is used, how many pounds of hamburger will be needed?

   b. How many 15-ounce cans of beans will be needed?

6. Use proportions to solve the following:

   a. A traffic survey at a given intersection indicated that during a given time interval, the ratio of cars to trucks, was $\frac{15}{4}$. If 88 trucks were counted, how many cars were counted?

   b. The ratio of cars with more than one occupant to just a single occupant was $\frac{11}{4}$. If 240 cars had only one person in each, how many had more than one person?

c. A student can type 28 words per minute. How many minutes will it take to type a 420 word report?

7. There are 36 elementary education majors who are taking an area of concentration in mathematics. One third of these students are men.
 a. What fractional part are women?
 b. What is the ratio of women to men in this area of concentration?
 c. If there are n students in this area of concentration and the ratio of women to men is f to m, write an expression for the number of women.
 d. How many men would there be?

8. A small pulley makes 5 turns for every 3 turns of a larger pulley.

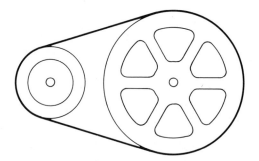

 a. How many turns will the larger pulley make if the smaller pulley makes 30 turns?
 b. How many turns will the smaller pulley make if the larger pulley makes 27 turns?

9. Orange paint can be made by mixing 6 parts of yellow with 2 parts of red.
 a. How much of each would be needed to make 16 grams of orange paint?
 b. How much red paint would need to be added to 8 grams of yellow paint to make orange paint?
 c. If you only have 3 grams of yellow and 3 grams of red, how many grams of orange could you make?

10. a. When a ten speed bike is in first gear, 2 revolutions of the pedals makes 3 revolutions of the wheel. How many pedal revolutions are needed for 156 wheel revolutions?
 b. In tenth gear, 7 revolutions of the pedal make 26 revolutions of the wheel. How many pedal revolutions are needed for 156 wheel revolutions?

c. The bicycle travels 21 meters for every 10 revolutions of the wheel. How many revolutions would the wheel make in a kilometer? (1000 m = 1 km)

d. Suppose it is necessary to climb a slight upward grade in the road. How many pedal revolutions are needed to travel 1 km in tenth gear?

e. If 28.4 km are covered during the first $2\frac{1}{4}$ hour, how long should it take to complete 50 km?

11. a. If 12 gal of gasoline cost $11.76, what should you expect to pay for 15 gal?

b. A car traveled 117 miles in $2\frac{1}{4}$ hours. How long should it take to complete a 260 mile journey?

c. If it takes $2\frac{1}{4}$ hours to travel the first $\frac{1}{3}$ of a trip, how long will it take for the remainder of the trip?

12. A smelter has found that 1935 pounds of raw material produced 1446 pounds of the refined product. How many pounds of refined material can he expect to receive from 1605 pounds of raw material? Set up a proportion to express this relationship. Solve the proportion using your calculator.

13. The following information is known about the students at Highertech University.

1. The ratio of men to women is 3 to 5.
2. The ratio of upperclass to lowerclass students is 7 to 1.
3. The ratio of A grades to grades lower than an A is 1 to 11.
4. The ratio of mathematics majors to nonmathematics majors is 1 to 23.
5. Three-tenths of the students take College Algebra.

If the number of mathematics majors is 250, how many are in each of the following categories?

a. men
b. students
c. lowerclass students
d. A grades
e. College Algebra

14. Suppose a train travels 60 miles traveling at a constant rate of speed. If r is the rate of speed in miles per hour and t is the time in hours, you can write the equation $rt = 60$. A table of values indicate the following data:

r	10	20	30	60
t	6	3	2	1

Notice that when r is doubled, t is halved, when r is tripled it is divided by 3, and so on. For this reason, r and t are said to be inversely proportional. Suppose the rate of speed r of a car varies inversely as the amount of time t it takes to drive a distance of 200 miles.

a. What is the rate of speed if the time is 5 hr?

b. What is the rate of speed if the time is 10 hr?

c. What is the amount of time if the speed is 10 mph?

d. What is the amount of time if the speed is 55 mph?

15. The length (l) of a rectangle with an area of 48 cm² varies inversely as the width (w).

a. What is the length if the width is 4 cm?

b. What is the length if the width is 12 cm?

c. What is the width if the length is 8 cm?

d. What is the width if the length is 24 cm?

Pedagogical Activity

16. a. A child in mixing lemonade for a school party puts in one can of frozen lemonade and two cans of water. When the mixture did not taste quite right he added to this one more can of frozen lemonade and five cans of water. He proceeded to write his actions as follows: $\frac{1}{2} + \frac{1}{5} = \frac{2}{7}$. What do you say?

b. When the spring baseball season in Bozeman, Montana, ended two children were at the top of the batting average category. One child had 14 hits in 29 at bats, a second child had 15 hits in 31 at bats. The person with 15 hits claims that she should win the batting title because of the following addition which she writes: $\frac{14}{29} + \frac{1}{2} = \frac{15}{31}$ Is her answer correct? What do you say to her procedure?

c. Refering back to **b**, which is the better average of the following: 16 hits in 29 at bats or 17 hits in 31 at bats?

17. In 1903 the Wright Brothers produced the first airplane to make a successful flight. It had a wingspan of 12.29 meters and a length of 6.43 meters. If a model of this airplane is to be 0.5 meters long, what should the wingspan be?

18. A Lockheed Vega has a wingspan of 12.50 meters and a length of 8.38 meters. What is the ratio of wingspan to length of this airplane? What is the length of a model that has a wingspan of 3.0 meters?

19. Compute the wingspan and length of a model of a Ford Trimotor if it is $\frac{1}{80}$ the actual size, given that the wingspan is 22.60 meters and the length is 15.19 meters.

REVIEW PROBLEM SET

1. Locate each of the following on a number line:

   a. $\dfrac{3}{5}$ b. $\dfrac{3}{2}$ c. $\dfrac{-4}{3}$ d. $\dfrac{6}{3}$ e. $\dfrac{0}{9}$

2. Show that $\frac{3}{2} = \frac{6}{4}$ by using:

   a. A number line

   b. Definition 5.2

3. a. Write three fractions equivalent to $\frac{5}{8}$.

   b. Write $\frac{135}{315}$ in reduced form.

4. Represent $\frac{5}{8}$ in each of the following ways:

   a. As a section of a circular region

   b. As a rectangular region

   c. As a point on a number line

   d. As a set

5. Perform the indicated operations:

   a. $\frac{3}{5} + \frac{4}{5}$ b. $\frac{3}{5} + \frac{3}{8}$ c. $2\frac{1}{4} + 1\frac{5}{6}$ d. $\frac{3}{5} - \frac{1}{4}$

   e. $2\frac{2}{3} - \frac{7}{8}$ f. $\frac{3}{5} \cdot \frac{2}{7}$ g. $1\frac{1}{3} \cdot \frac{3}{4}$ h. $2\frac{1}{4} \cdot 1\frac{3}{5}$

   i. $\frac{2}{3} \div \frac{3}{5}$ j. $\frac{3}{8} \div 3$ k. $2\frac{1}{2} \div 1\frac{1}{3}$

6. a. Is the set of rational numbers closed under subtraction?

   b. Is the set of rational numbers closed under division?

   c. Are the rational numbers associative under subtraction?

7. Describe how you can be certain that $\frac{5}{6} > \frac{3}{4}$.

8. Insert four rational numbers between $\frac{5}{6}$ and $\frac{7}{8}$.

9. Arrange in order of size from smallest to largest:

   a. $\frac{5}{8}, \frac{7}{10}, \frac{8}{11}$ b. $\frac{3}{5}, \frac{5}{7}, \frac{9}{11}$

10. Find the unknown term in each of the following:

    a. $\dfrac{n}{8} = \dfrac{12}{32}$ b. $\dfrac{n}{14} = \dfrac{4}{7}$ c. $\dfrac{2}{3} = \dfrac{6}{n}$

    d. $\dfrac{9}{n} = \dfrac{3}{8}$ e. $\dfrac{7}{8} = \dfrac{14}{n}$ f. $\dfrac{21}{35} = \dfrac{n}{5}$

    g. $\dfrac{33}{n} = \dfrac{11}{4}$ h. $\dfrac{3}{4} = \dfrac{n}{10}$

11. a. When making lemonade the ratio of lemons to quarts of water is $3:2$. If 12 lemons are available, how many quarts of water should be used?

    b. Six cups of flour are used to make 36 pancakes. How much flour will be needed for 12 pancakes?

c. Four liters of lemon concentrate and 6 liters of lime concentrate are used to make a punch for a party. The ratio of fruit concentrate to water is to be 5 to 8. How many liters of water must be added?

Solution to Sample Problem

The Egyptians worked with many arithmetic operations long before the time of Christ. They were obviously successful in their work because the pyramids that they built are still standing and are viewed by engineers as marvels of construction, even by today's standards. The Egyptians worked with fractions as well as with whole numbers. They used unit fractions (numerator of 1) for all representations except one. They had one special number, $\frac{2}{3}$, which was also used. They did not repeat a fraction in any representation. Consider the following examples.

$$\frac{3}{4} = \frac{1}{2} + \frac{1}{4}$$
$$\frac{5}{6} = \frac{2}{3} + \frac{1}{6}$$
$$\frac{3}{8} = \frac{1}{4} + \frac{1}{8}$$

How would you write $\frac{11}{12}$? How would you write $\frac{3}{7}$? What about $\frac{39}{42}$?

1. *Understanding the Problem.* The fraction in question must be expressed using the sum of fractions having numerators of 1, or using the fraction $\frac{2}{3}$ along with unit fractions. No fraction can be repeated in the sum. That is, we *cannot* write $\frac{3}{4} = \frac{1}{4} + \frac{1}{4} + \frac{1}{4}$.

2. *Deviving a Plan.* Because we are hoping to express a single fraction as a sum of unit fractions, the denominators of the unit fractions must all be divisors of the denominator of the given fraction. But the *sum* of the numerators of the new fraction must equal the numerator of the original fraction. The key ideas therefore seem to be that of divisors and equivalent fractions.

3. *Carry out the Plan.*

$$\frac{3}{4} = \frac{2}{4} + \frac{1}{4} = \frac{1}{2} + \frac{1}{4}$$
$$\frac{5}{6} = \frac{4}{6} + \frac{1}{6} = \frac{2}{3} + \frac{1}{6}$$
$$\frac{3}{8} = \frac{2}{8} + \frac{1}{8} = \frac{1}{4} + \frac{1}{8}$$

These examples may not really shed much light on the process that we need to employ. Let us try $\frac{11}{12}$ in more detail. Note that the divisors of 12 are 1, 2, 3, 4, 6, and 12. Furthermore, $6 + 4 + 1 = 11$. So let us write $\frac{11}{12}$ $= \frac{6}{12} + \frac{4}{12} + \frac{1}{12} = \frac{1}{2} + \frac{1}{3} + \frac{1}{12}$.

In the case of $\frac{3}{7}$ we need to search a bit longer to find acceptable fractions. The divisor of 7 are 1 and 7, which are not much help. But $\frac{3}{7} = \frac{6}{14}$. The divisors of 14 are 1, 2, 7, and 14. However, no selection from them add up to 6. Let us write $\frac{3}{7} = \frac{9}{21}$. Divisors of 21 are 1, 3, 7, and 21 and again we find none that produce 9 when added. Now try $\frac{3}{7} = \frac{12}{28}$. The divisors of 28 are 1, 2, 4, 7, 14, and 28 and $7 + 4 + 1 = 12$. Therefore,

$$\tfrac{3}{7} = \tfrac{12}{28} = \tfrac{7}{28} + \tfrac{4}{28} + \tfrac{1}{28} = \tfrac{1}{4} + \tfrac{1}{7} + \tfrac{1}{28}$$

The same procedure can be used for $\frac{39}{42}$. The divisors of 42 are 1, 2, 3, 6, 7, 21, and 42. Because $21 + 7 + 6 + 3 + 2 = 39$, we may write $\frac{39}{42} = \frac{21}{42} + \frac{7}{42} + \frac{6}{42} + \frac{3}{42} + \frac{2}{42} = \frac{1}{2} + \frac{1}{6} + \frac{1}{7} + \frac{1}{14} + \frac{1}{21}$.

4. *Looking Back.* This is an efficient way to proceed with the writing of unit fractions. This does seem to be a laborious method of expressing fractional quantities, but if you will recall from your work in Chapter 2, the Egyptian numeration system was in general somewhat unwieldy because they did not use positional notation. The existence of the great Pyramids of Egypt serves to be all the more of a marvel!

6 | REAL NUMBERS

Sample Problem

Suppose 100 liters of salt water are set out in the sun. The original solution was 99% water. After a period of time a sufficient amount of water has evaporated, so the brine solution is only 98% water. How much water must have evaporated?

6.1 DECIMAL FRACTIONS

The NCTM Standards emphasize the need for beginning work with fractions and decimals in the K–4 program, extensively using physical materials and diagrams to model these numbers. For grades 5–8, the Standards recommend that fractions, decimals, and percents should be a major component of the mathematics curriculum with learning grounded in experience relating to real life or to the use of concrete materials designed to reflect underlying mathematical ideas. This chapter will provide opportunities to work with decimals and percents in a way compatible with these recommendations.

As we noted in our work with numeration systems, computation is greatly simplified if one makes use of positional notation. The work done at that time can be easily extended to allow us to work with numbers other than the whole numbers. We have commonly referred to such numbers as *decimal fractions* or simply as *decimals*. In the past we have normally encountered such numbers in the elementary school program at the time that we considered representations for money. With the advent of the metric system, more work is appearing with decimal fractions in the elementary school program.

REMARK   Common fractions and decimal fractions are simply different representations of the same thing. Decimal fractions are simply restricted to denominators of 10, 100, ... When we write the common fraction $\frac{7}{10}$ or the decimal fraction 0.7, the numerator is explicitly stated and the denominator is implied by the place-value position of the digits.

Perhaps the most intuitively clear approach to decimal fractions is that which uses diagrams. If we let the square represent 1, and there are 10 strips in the square, then each strip represents one tenth. Consider the diagrams in Figure 6.1. A natural extension of this is to consider the square broken into

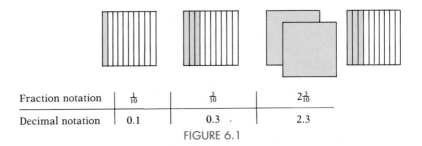

Fraction notation	$\frac{1}{10}$	$\frac{3}{10}$	$2\frac{3}{10}$
Decimal notation	0.1	0.3 ·	2.3

FIGURE 6.1

100 segments, thus making each small square represent one hundredth. This is illustrated in Figure 6.2.

A more mature approach to the decimals may be obtained by considering an extension to the positional notation format used earlier. As should be clear from Figure 6.3*a*, as one moves to the right in the positional notation format, the place values decrease in value, each being one tenth as large. If we continue the pattern, the sequence is as illustrated in Figure 6.3*b*. The decimal point is used as a marker to allow us to identify the place value of any given position. Then to write $\frac{2}{10}$ as a decimal we could note that $\frac{2}{10} = 2 \cdot \frac{1}{10}$ and simply enter the digit 2 in the $\frac{1}{10}$ slot. Thus $\frac{2}{10} = 0.2$. In a like manner, because $\frac{21}{100} = \frac{20 + 1}{100} = \frac{20}{100} + \frac{1}{100} = \frac{2}{10} + \frac{1}{100}$, we might write $\frac{21}{100} = 0.21$. Consider the following examples.

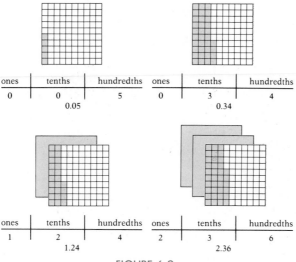

FIGURE 6.2

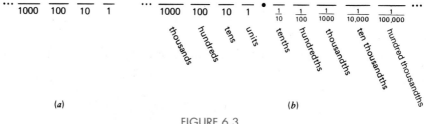

(a)   (b)

FIGURE 6.3

EXAMPLE 1

Write $\dfrac{25}{100}$ as a decimal fraction.

$$\frac{25}{100} = \frac{20+5}{100} = \frac{20}{100} + \frac{5}{100} = \frac{2}{10} + \frac{5}{100} = 0.25$$

EXAMPLE 2

Write $\dfrac{43}{1000}$ as a decimal fraction.

$$\frac{43}{1000} = \frac{40+3}{1000} = \frac{40}{1000} + \frac{3}{1000} = \frac{4}{100} + \frac{3}{1000} = 0.043$$

EXAMPLE 3

Write $\dfrac{2}{1000}$ as a decimal fraction.

$$\frac{2}{1000} = 0.002$$

EXAMPLE 4

Write $\dfrac{483}{100}$ as a decimal fraction.

$$\frac{483}{100} = \frac{400}{100} + \frac{80}{100} + \frac{3}{100} = 4 + \frac{8}{10} + \frac{3}{100} = 4.83$$

EXAMPLE 5

Write $\dfrac{5286}{100}$ as a decimal fraction.

$$\frac{5286}{100} = \frac{5200}{100} + \frac{80}{100} + \frac{6}{100} = 52 + \frac{8}{10} + \frac{6}{100} = 52.86$$

Let us consider 0.42 as a rational number in $\dfrac{a}{b}$ form. Note that

$$0.42 = \frac{4}{10} + \frac{2}{100}$$
$$= \frac{40}{100} + \frac{2}{100} = \frac{40 + 2}{100} = \frac{42}{100}$$

Also

$$0.036 = \frac{3}{100} + \frac{6}{1000} = \frac{36}{1000}$$

and

$$2.3 = 2 + \frac{3}{10} = \frac{20}{10} + \frac{3}{10} = \frac{23}{10}$$

By this same reasoning $0.34 = 0.340$, since $\frac{34}{100} = \frac{340}{1000}$.

The process of translating rational numbers having denominators expressed as powers of 10 into decimal form and of performing the reverse procedure is simple. Note that the positioning of the decimal point is determined by the power of 10. Thus, $\frac{25}{100} = 0.25$ indicates that division by 100 "shifted the decimal point" in 25.0 two places to the left. The real reason for this is explained in terms of the place-value system mentioned previously. This algorithm is useful when making conversions. Consider the following examples.

> REMARK An alternate thought process regarding the placement of the decimal point results from considering the place value systems as being fixed, and digits are shifted to new locations. Thus, the number 25 would appear as 2 5.␣␣ . Dividing by 100 then shifts the digits to the right two places yielding the decimal: ␣0.2 5.

EXAMPLE 1

Write $\dfrac{24}{1000}$ as a decimal fraction.

$\frac{24}{1000} = 0.024$ because the $1000 = 10^3$ suggests that we shift the decimal point three places to the left.

EXAMPLE 2

Write 0.36 as a fraction in $\dfrac{a}{b}$ form.

$0.36 = \frac{36}{100}$ because we shifted the decimal point two places to the right.

Now let us consider an interesting question. Under what conditions will a rational number $\dfrac{a}{b}$ have a terminating decimal representation? It is apparent that $\frac{2865}{1000}$ will have one, as $\frac{2865}{1000} = 2.865$. In fact, wherever the denominator is a power of 10 we should be able to do so. But what if the denominator is not a power of 10? Would you be able to express $\frac{34}{5}$ as a terminating decimal? Of course, the answer is yes, because $\frac{34}{5} = \frac{68}{10} = 6.8$. What about $\frac{2}{3}$? Is it possible to express $\frac{2}{3}$ as an equivalent rational number whose numerator is an integer and whose denominator is an integer that is expressible as $10k$, where k is a whole number? The answer in this case is no, and we will not be able to express $\frac{2}{3}$ as a terminating decimal. (We will return to this discussion in a later section and find that $\frac{2}{3}$ does have a decimal counterpart, it simply does not terminate.) Let us summarize this discussion as Property 6.1.

PROPERTY 6.1   **A rational number $\dfrac{a}{b}$, expressed in reduced form, has a terminating decimal representation if and only if b has only two or five as its prime factors.**

We may apply this property in a variety of ways.

EXAMPLE 1

Write $\dfrac{7}{2}$ as a decimal.

$$\frac{7}{2} = \frac{7 \cdot 5}{2 \cdot 5} = \frac{35}{10} = 3.5$$

EXAMPLE 2

Express $\frac{21}{6}$ in reduced form, then rewrite it as a decimal.

$$\frac{21}{6} = \frac{7 \cdot 3}{2 \cdot 3} = \frac{7}{2} = \frac{35}{10} = 3.5$$

EXAMPLE 3

Write the denominator in factored form, then multiply numerator and denominator by fives in order to build tens in the denominator.

$$\frac{3}{8} = \frac{3}{2^3} = \frac{3 \cdot 5^3}{2^3 \cdot 5^3} = \frac{3 \cdot 5^3}{10^3} = \frac{375}{1000} = 0.375$$

By using diagrams the algorithm for addition can be easily developed. To find $0.2 + 0.34$ we could proceed as illustrated in Figure 6.4a. The alignment of the decimal point is the only new feature of the algorithm and is important. This process of regrouping used in adding decimals is the same as that used for addition of counting numbers. Because 10 of a smaller unit are always equivalent to one of the next larger units, we may proceed with an algorithm just like that used before, but we should be careful about the location of the decimal point.

REMARK The alignment of the decimal point in addition (and later in subtraction) assures that we are aligning the place value positions and are therefore using common denominators.

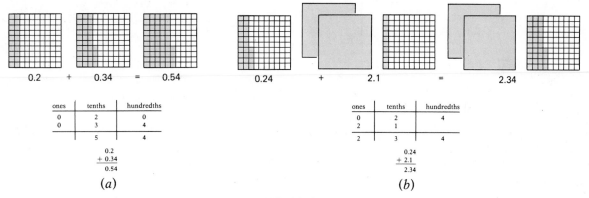

FIGURE 6.4

EXAMPLE 1

Find 3.6 + 12.15.

Solution

$$\begin{array}{r} 3.6 \\ +12.15 \\ \hline 15.75 \end{array}$$

EXAMPLE 2

Find 6.84 + 5.683.

Solution

$$\begin{array}{r} {}^{1}6.{}^{1}84 \\ +\ 5.\ 683 \\ \hline 12.\ 523 \end{array}$$

Subtraction of decimals may also be easily approached using diagrams. Consider the difference 0.46 − 0.12 illustrated in Figure 6.5. As is the case with addition, the key to the subtraction algorithm is that of locating decimal points so that the digits with similar place values are in the respective columns. Consider the following examples.

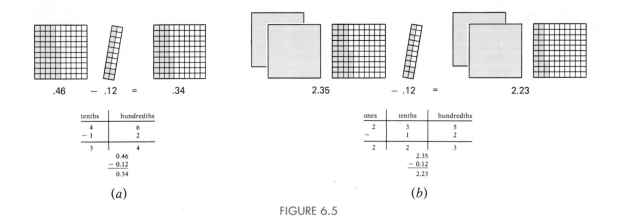

tenths	hundredths
4	6
− 1	2
3	4

0.46
− 0.12
0.34

(a)

ones	tenths	hundredths
2	3	5
−		
2	2	3

2.35
− 0.12
2.23

(b)

FIGURE 6.5

EXAMPLE 1

Find 42.63 − 10.4.

Solution

$$\begin{array}{r} 42.63 \\ -10.4 \\ \hline 32.23 \end{array}$$

EXAMPLE 2

Find 56.83 − 41.16.

Solution

$$\begin{array}{r} 56.\overset{7}{\cancel{8}}{}^{1}3 \\ -41.1\ 6 \\ \hline 15.6\ 7 \end{array}$$

An understanding of the multiplication algorithm is perhaps best obtained by considering the relationship between fractions in decimal form and the equivalent $\frac{a}{b}$ form. For example, consider the product $(0.3) \cdot (0.2)$. Because $0.3 = \frac{3}{10}$ and $0.2 = \frac{2}{10}$, $(0.3) \cdot (0.2) = \frac{3}{10} \cdot \frac{2}{10} = \frac{6}{100} = 0.06$. In the same manner, $(3.4) \cdot (0.53) = \frac{34}{10} \cdot \frac{53}{100} = \frac{1802}{1000} = 1.802$. What we have done is to simply take the product of the numbers 34 and 53, then position the decimal point in the answer three places to the left. In general, if there are m digits to the right of the decimal point in one number and n digits to the right of the decimal point in a second number, simply multiply the two numbers, ignoring the decimal points, then place the decimal point so that there are $m + n$ digits to the right of the decimal point in the answer.

EXAMPLE

Find $(42.1) \cdot (0.34)$.

Solution 1

$$42.1 \cdot 0.34 = \frac{421}{10} \cdot \frac{34}{100} = \frac{421 \cdot 34}{10 \cdot 100} = \frac{14314}{1000} = 14.314$$

Solution 2

$$
\begin{array}{r}
42.1 \\
\times \quad 0.34 \\
\hline
1684 \\
12630 \\
\hline
14.314
\end{array}
$$

The division algorithm for decimals is closely related to the algorithm developed for whole numbers. Suppose that we are interested in the quotients of $55 \div 4$. In Figure 6.6a we illustrate the shortened form for the operation. The answer is 13 r3. But this is equivalent to stating that we have 13 sets of 4 with 3 remaining, or $\frac{3}{4}$ of another group. Thus, $\frac{55}{4} = 13\frac{3}{4}$, but because

$$
\begin{array}{cc}
\begin{array}{r}
13 \\
4\overline{)55} \\
4 \\
\hline
15 \\
12 \\
\hline
3
\end{array}
&
\begin{array}{r}
13.75 \\
4\overline{)55.00} \\
4 \\
\hline
15 \\
12 \\
\hline
30 \\
28 \\
\hline
20 \\
20 \\
\hline
\end{array} \\
(a) & (b)
\end{array}
$$

FIGURE 6.6

$\frac{3}{4} = 0.75$, we may write $\frac{55}{4} = 13.75$. In 6.6*b* we illustrate the extension to the usual algorithm for whole numbers to include the annexation of zeros and continuation of the division process. Notice that the decimal point in the answer is directly above that in the body of the work.

EXAMPLE 1

Find $12.93 \div 25$.

Solution 1

$$
\begin{array}{r}
0.5172 \\
25\overline{)12.9300} \\
12\ 5\ \\
\overline{43} \\
25 \\
\overline{180} \\
175 \\
\overline{50} \\
50 \\
\overline{}
\end{array}
$$

Solution 2

$$
\frac{12.93}{25} = \frac{12.93 \cdot 4}{25 \cdot 4}
$$
$$
= \frac{51.72}{100}
$$
$$
= 0.5172
$$

EXAMPLE 2

Find $46.3 \div 6$.

Solution

$$
\begin{array}{r}
7.71666\ldots \\
6\overline{)46.300000} \\
42 \\
\overline{43} \\
42 \\
\overline{10} \\
6 \\
\overline{40} \\
36 \\
\overline{40}
\end{array}
$$

In this case, because the denominator does not consist only of powers of 2 or 5, we will not have an answer that is a terminating decimal. Notice that the remainder 4 appears in each further step that we take, and thus the 6 will repeat in the quotient. We could round off to whatever decimal accuracy we need.

In many instances we need to find a quotient where the divisor is not a counting number. For example, find $4.2 \div 0.15$. We could rewrite such decimal fractions as a common fraction as follows:

$$4.2 \div 0.15 = \tfrac{42}{10} \div \tfrac{15}{100}$$
$$= \tfrac{42}{10} \cdot \tfrac{100}{15}$$
$$= 28$$

We might also note that $4.2 \div 0.15 = \dfrac{4.2}{0.15} = \dfrac{4.2 \times 100}{0.15 \times 100} = \dfrac{420}{15} = 28$. It is this format that is commonly used in the division algorithm for decimal fraction.

$$0.15\overline{)4.2} \;\rightarrow\; 15\overline{)420.} \;\rightarrow\; 15\overline{)420}$$
$$\underline{30}$$
$$120$$
$$\underline{120}$$

with quotient 28.

EXAMPLE 3

Find $0.8632 \div 1.22$ to the nearest ten thousandth.

Solution We will write the ratio $\frac{0.8632}{1.22}$ in an equivalent form so the denominator is an integer. The quotient is then found to four decimal places of accuracy. Since $\frac{50}{122}$ is less than half, the desired quotient is 0.7075. (if the remainder were half or greater, we would raise the last digit to the next higher number.)

$$\frac{0.8632}{1.22} = \frac{100 \cdot 0.8632}{100 \cdot 1.22} = \frac{86.32}{122}$$

$$122\overline{)86.3200} \quad 0.7075$$
$$\underline{85\ 4}$$
$$920$$
$$\underline{854}$$
$$660$$
$$\underline{610}$$
$$50$$

The work with decimals may be related very naturally with the work done with whole numbers and rational numbers. We have considered the issue of inequality for rational numbers in $\frac{a}{b}$ form. Now let us consider this topic briefly for decimals. Reasoning in terms of diagrams is very convenient for early work of this nature. Clearly 0.3 is less than 0.7 because 0.3 requires only three of the tenth bars whereas 0.7 requires the use of seven bars. But what about numbers like 0.56 and 0.57? Because each contains the same number of tenths, we must look at the hundredths to make a decision. Is it clear that 0.57 > 0.56? Can you use this same procedure to find which is bigger, 0.34682 or 0.34678? Do you agree that because 0.34682 has an 8 in the ten-thousandths place, whereas 0.34678 has only a 7, then 0.34682 > 0.34678? Note that 0.2 > 0.02 because in the tenths place we have the digit 2 in 0.2 but the digit 0 in 0.02.

PROBLEM SET 6.1

1. Identify the decimal represented by each diagram.

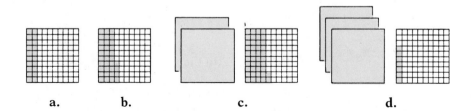

    a.   **b.**   **c.**   **d.**

2. Make a diagram to illustrate each of the following decimals.

    a. 0.6   **b.** 0.07   **c.** 0.23   **d.** 1.26   **e.** 3.14   **f.** 2.03

3. We may write 0.46 as $\frac{4}{10} + \frac{6}{100}$. Write each of the following in a similar expanded notation.

    a. 0.183   **b.** 0.45   **c.** 0.283   **d.** 0.042   **e.** 2.13   **f.** 3.145

4. Place one of the symbols <, >, or = in each of the following to make a true statement:

    a. 35.11 ◯ 35.01   **b.** 0.8 ◯ 0.80   **c.** 19.43 ◯ 19.23

    d. 1.246 ◯ 1.236   **e.** 0.03462 ◯ 0.04462   **f.** 9.3 ◯ 9.30

    g. 4.5 ◯ 4.49   **h.** 0.46 ◯ 0.4599   **i.** 0.08 ◯ 0.18

    j. 1.6 ◯ 1.600   **k.** $3\frac{1}{4}$ ◯ 3.14   **l.** 365.489 ◯ 865.491

5. Express each of the following as a decimal fraction:

   a. $\frac{23}{100}$ b. $\frac{17}{100}$ c. $\frac{5}{10}$ d. $\frac{236}{1000}$ e. $\frac{56}{10}$ f. $\frac{43}{10}$

   g. $\frac{562}{100}$ h. $\frac{584}{100}$ i. $\frac{76}{1000}$ j. $\frac{4}{1000}$ k. $\frac{3542}{100}$ l. $\frac{4321}{1000}$

6. Express each of the following in $\frac{a}{b}$ form.

   a. 0.7   b. 0.23   c. 0.463   d. 2.31   e. 0.62   f. 0.75

   g. 0.034   h. 0.05   i. 1.63   j. 2.14   k. 14.31   l. 0.0032

7. Decide whether each of the following will have a terminating decimal representation. If so, write it as a decimal.

   a. $\frac{6}{20}$ b. $\frac{3}{25}$ c. $\frac{7}{5}$ d. $\frac{15}{4}$ e. $\frac{7}{21}$ f. $\frac{7}{28}$

   g. $\frac{5}{3}$ h. $\frac{3}{5}$ i. $\frac{21}{70}$ j. $\frac{18}{80}$ k. $\frac{28}{42}$ l. $\frac{189}{124}$

8. Perform the indicated operations.

   a. $0.3 + 2.4 + 26.8$ b. $14.63 + 17 + 0.014$

   c. $68.3 - 1.4$ d. $26.72 - 12$

   e. $56.3 - 0.043$ f. $(4.63 + 8.423) - 0.46$

   g. $(0.46 + 2.8) - (0.54 + 0.036)$ h. $582.7 - 6.23$

   i. $(0.4 + 6.0038) - 1.005$

9. Find the following:

   a. $(32.4) \times (1.6)$ b. $(5.26) \times (0.23)$ c. $(0.63) \times (0.02)$

   d. $(0.046) \times (0.032)$ e. $(6.04) \times (0.006)$ f. $118.6 \div 31$

   g. $18.6 \div 29$ h. $18.46 \div 1.3$ i. $0.4862 \div 0.016$

   j. $840 \div 0.021$

10. Arrange the following in order from smallest to largest:

    a. 12.3567, 12.3498, 12.35, 12.3, 12.4

    b. 0.00365, 0.003, 0.0036, 0.003654, 0.00399

    c. 0.4603, 0.4063, 0.4306, 0.4036, 0.4360

    d. 12.402, 14.204, 12.420, 14.024, 12.240

11. We have not yet considered the possible use of negative integers as exponents. A pattern might be used to illustrate that $2^{-3} = \dfrac{1}{2^3}$.

$$2^4 = 16$$
$$2^3 = 8$$
$$2^2 = 4$$
$$2^1 = 2$$

Notice that each successive step reduces the exponent by 1 and takes half of the preceding right-hand member for the new right-hand member.

To continue we would write:

$$2^0 = 1$$

$$2^{-1} = \frac{1}{2} = \frac{1}{2^1}$$

$$2^{-2} = \frac{1}{4} = \frac{1}{2^2}$$

$$2^{-3} = \frac{1}{8} = \frac{1}{2^3}$$

a. Use this approach to show that $6^{-3} = \dfrac{1}{6^3}$.

b. Show that $7^{-4} = \dfrac{1}{7^4}$.

c. Show that $10^{-4} = \dfrac{1}{10,000}$. (*Hint:* Show that $10^{-4} = \dfrac{1}{10^4}$ and that $10^4 = 10,000$.)

d. Complete the sentence: $a^{-n} = \dfrac{1}{a^n}$

12. A number is expressed in *scientific notation* when it is in the form $a \cdot 10^k$, where a is in decimal form and is greater than or equal to 1 and less than 10 and k is an integer. Scientific notation is commonly used when we are working with very large or very small numbers. We may write the number 146,000 as $1.46 \cdot 10^5$ and 0.00000542 as $5.42 \cdot 10^{-6}$. Write each of the following in scientific notation:

    a. 105   **b.** 4800   **c.** 568,000,000   **d.** 0.0016   **e.** 0.000105   **f.** 46.01

13. To add two numbers in scientific notation we might proceed as follows: $4.23 \cdot 10^4 + 2.1 \cdot 10^4 = (4.23 + 2.1) \cdot 10^4 = 6.33 \cdot 10^4$. However, $1.8 \cdot 10^3 + 4.6 \cdot 10^4 = (1.8 + 4.6 \cdot 10) \cdot 10^3 = (1.8 + 46) \cdot 10^3 = 47.8 \cdot 10^3 = 4.78 \cdot 10^4$. Find the following sums and differences:

    a. $1.6 \cdot 10^2 + 2.4 \cdot 10^2$ **b.** $4.8 \cdot 10^5 + 9.6 \cdot 10^5$

    c. $4.8 \cdot 10^5 - 2.9 \cdot 10^5$ **d.** $3.8 \cdot 10^6 - 9.7 \cdot 10^5$

    e. $4.2 \cdot 10^5 + 1.7 \cdot 10^4$ **f.** $6.4 \cdot 10^5 + 3.8 \cdot 10^5$

14. Products and quotients of numbers in scientific notation are also easily performed. For example,

$$(4.6 \cdot 10^3) \times (5.1 \cdot 10^4) = (4.6 \times 5.1) \cdot (10^3 \times 10^4)$$
$$= 23.46 \cdot 10^7 = 2.346 \cdot 10^8$$

Similarly,

$$\frac{200,000}{1000} = \frac{2 \cdot 10^5}{10^3} = 2 \cdot 10^{5-3} = 2 \cdot 10^2$$

Find the following:

a. $(2.3 \cdot 10^4) \times (6.1 \cdot 10^5)$ **b.** $(5.6 \cdot 10^6) \times (3.4 \cdot 10^2)$
c. $(6.2 \cdot 10^5) \times (4.1 \cdot 10^3)$ **d.** $(5.8 \cdot 10^6) \times (7.5 \cdot 10^4)$
e. $(6.5 \cdot 10^6) \times (4.2 \cdot 10^6)$ **f.** $(5.6 \cdot 10^{-5}) \times (6.4 \cdot 10^{-5})$

15 a. Is it true that the sum of two nonnegative decimals is always greater than the smaller of the two?

  b. Is it true that the product of two nonnegative decimals is always greater than the smaller of the two? Give examples to verify your answer.

16. An estate contains 79 acres of land and is assessed at $59,250. The house is assessed at $17,500. A $1500 deduction is available for the Homestead Act on the dwelling. Five acres of the land are allotted to yard and living area. The tax rate is $0.0325 per dollar of assessed valuation. What amount of tax is attributable to the living accomodations? (Use your calculator to solve this problem. Remember, you should organize your work in such a way as to make your work easy.)

17. a. When the product $35,896 \times 98,521$ is found on a scientific calculator the answer is given as 3.5365098 09. To what does 09 refer?

  b. Write an approximation for the product $62,873 \times 48,295$ without using scientific notation. Why is this an approximation?

  c. Use your calculator to find 0.0357×0.041. Now write the answer without scientific notation. Is this answer an approximation?

18. Determine which is larger in each case.
  a. 0.463 or 0.46293   **b.** 2.3643 or 2.3463
  c. 0.2134 or 0.20134   **d.** 42.3621 or 42.362099

Pedagogical Problems and Activities

19. As you may recall from our earlier work, we may add $469 + 784$ by beginning on the left and working to the right.

$$
\begin{array}{r}
469 \\
+ \ 784 \\
\hline
1\cancel{1}\cancel{4}3 \\
{\scriptstyle 2\ 5}
\end{array}
$$

43

  a. Explain how to use the scratch method of addition to find $4.632 + 1.784$.

  b. Can you use the scratch method of subtraction to find

$$
\begin{array}{r}
42.63 \\
-24.79?
\end{array}
$$

Verify your answer.

20. Use base ten blocks to illustrate the following:

   a. 1.43 + 2.34

   b. 0.78 + 2.65

   c. 2.36 − 1.14

   d. 3.74 − 1.36

21. **a.** In using a calculator to divide 2453 by 32 a child obtained 76.65265. He wants to know if there is a way to find the whole number remainder without doing the division "longhand." What do you say?

   b. Use your calculator to find the remainder of each of the following:

   (i) 965 ÷ 23   **(ii)** 1452 ÷ 57

   (iii) 1232 ÷ 15   **(iv)** 8888 ÷ 159

22. When we round off numbers, many elementary books advise us to "increase the last digit if the remainder is half or more." Therefore, rounded to the nearest hundredth, we would write 6.234 as 6.23, 4.738 as 4.74, 6.379 as 6.38, and 2.435 as 2.44. Use this rule to round each of the following to the nearest hundredth.

   a. 0.463   **b.** 0.527   **c.** 6.432   **d.** 52.435

   e. 0.3446   **f.** 0.0352   **g.** 0.055   **h.** 1.414159

23. Suppose the rule were "round up if the next digit to the right is greater than five, leave it unchanged if less than five, but if the digit is exactly five, then round so the last remaining digit is even." Find the value of each rounded to the nearest tenth.

   a. 0.43   **b.** 2.149   **c.** 3.15   **d.** 0.071

   e. 0.335   **f.** 0.7801   **g.** 32.093   **h.** 1.654

24. A child says "0.2301 > 0.235 because 2301 > 235". What could you say?

25. We often wish to use a variety of explanations for mathematical ideas. Let us, for example, use a model to illustrate the product of two decimals rather than to use fractions in $\frac{a}{b}$ form. Then to find 0.5 × 0.3 we can use regions as follows.

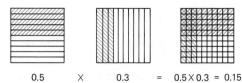

   0.5   ×   0.3   =   0.5 × 0.3 = 0.15

Use this procedure to find the following products.

   a. 0.3 × 0.2   **b.** 0.4 × 0.7   **c.** 0.6 × 0.7   **d.** 0.3 × 0.4

26. **a.** A child asks, "When I read a digital clock and it says 4:32 does the 3 mean 3 tenths?" What do you say?

    b. A child asks, "When I watched the Olympics on television, the announcer used the following numbers—4:32.7 seconds. What does that mean?" What do you say?

6.2   INFINITE REPEATING DECIMALS

We have considered certain types of decimal forms for rational numbers. We stated in Property 6.1 the conditions under which a rational number would have a terminating decimal form. However, what would we expect if we attempted to change a number such as $\frac{5}{7}$ to a decimal form? First, it clearly is not expressible with a denominator which is a multiple of 10; therefore, it will not have a terminating decimal form. Suppose we attempt long division. As indicated in Figure 6.7, the first digit in the quotient will be 7 followed by 1, and so forth. Let us continue the division through some additional steps to see what will happen. Notice that after the 5 in the quotient we have a remainder of 5, which was precisely what we had at the beginning. We

$$
\begin{array}{r}
0.71428571 \\
7\overline{)5.00000000} \\
4\,9 \\
\hline
10 \\
7 \\
\hline
30 \\
28 \\
\hline
20 \\
14 \\
\hline
60 \\
56 \\
\hline
40 \\
35 \\
\hline
50 \\
49 \\
\hline
10 \\
7 \\
\hline
\end{array}
$$

FIGURE 6.7

should then expect to repeat what has been done, proceeding through the cycles over and over. Thus, we state $\frac{5}{7} = 0.714285714285\ldots$. The three dots indicate that it continues in a similar pattern. Another common symbol, which we will use in this book, will be to place a bar over the repeating digits to indicate repetition forever in the given cycle. Thus we write $0.\overline{714285} = \frac{5}{7}$. Please note that this is an infinite repeating decimal that is equal to $\frac{5}{7}$. If we terminate it after any number of decimal places, it will not represent the number $\frac{5}{7}$ exactly.

Let us now represent $\frac{3}{11}$ as a decimal. Again, we are certain that no terminating decimal will be found equal to $\frac{3}{11}$. Let us proceed in the same manner as indicated in Figure 6.8a. Upon the first subtraction, the difference found was certain to be less than 11. Thus, it was necessarily from the set $\{1, 2, 3, \ldots, 10\}$. Let us continue, but remember, if we obtain a remainder that is a duplication of a remainder already received, we know that we are beginning another cycle. In the next place we receive the 3 as a remainder, which is where we started. Thus, our cycles contain two digits and we write $\frac{3}{11} = .\overline{27}$.

$$
\begin{array}{lll}
0.2 & 0.27 & 1.16\cdots \\
11)\overline{3.00000} & 11)\overline{3.0000} & 6)\overline{7.00} \\
2\,2 & 2\,2 & 6 \\
\overline{8} & \overline{80} & \overline{1\,0} \\
 & 77 & 6 \\
 & \overline{3} & \overline{40} \\
 & & 36 \\
 & & \overline{4}
\end{array}
$$

$\qquad\qquad\qquad$ (a) $\qquad\qquad$ (b)

$\qquad\qquad$ FIGURE 6.8

Let us return to our reasoning regarding remainders as we attempt to write $\frac{7}{6}$ in a decimal form. In the first step we get 1 as a remainder (see Fig. 6.8b). The only possible remainders are 1, 2, 3, 4, or 5. Can you be certain that with five or fewer digits in the quotient we will obtain a repetition in the cycle? In fact, we obtain a cycle much sooner than that, because we find $\frac{7}{6} = 1.1\overline{6}$. It is comforting to realize that we would eventually obtain a cycle, and we could even predict the maximum number of decimal places that a cycle could take!

Perhaps one more example would be helpful. The number $\frac{3}{17}$ is a rational number. However, because the denominator is a prime number different from 2 or 5, we are certain that the decimal form will not be a terminating decimal. If we then find the quotient "3 divided by 17," we expect never to receive 0 as a remainder. Thus, any remainder r must be such that $r \in \{1, 2,$

3, ... , 16}. Therefore, in 16 or fewer steps we may be certain to find the infinite decimal form beginning a new cycle. In this case the full 16 digits are needed, and we find $\frac{3}{17} = 0.\overline{1764705882352941}$. Do you agree with this result?

Let us summarize our discussion in the following property, which we will not attempt to prove.

PROPERTY 6.2 If $\dfrac{m}{n}$ is any rational number in reduced form with n having prime divisors other than 2 or 5, then $\dfrac{m}{n}$ has a decimal form that will be an infinite repeating decimal that may be determined by dividing m by n. Furthermore, the number of digits in the cycle may not exceed $n - 1$, where $n > 1$.

The question that should naturally arise at this time would be the following. If every rational number can be expressed as an infinite repeating decimal or as a terminating decimal, does the converse also hold? We have already shown that every terminating decimal may be written as a fraction, but given an infinite repeating decimal, can we always find a rational number that is equal to it? For example, suppose that we start with the decimal $0.\overline{4}$ and wish to find a rational number in $\dfrac{a}{b}$ form that might be associated with it.

Let n represent the rational numbers. Consider the following argument.

$$n = 0.\overline{4}$$
$$n = 0.4444 \ldots$$
$$10n = 10 \times 0.4444 \ldots$$
$$10n = 4.4444 \ldots = 4 + 0.4444 \ldots$$
$$10n - n = (4 + 0.444 \ldots) - 0.4444 \ldots$$
$$9n = 4 + (0.444 \ldots - 0.444 \ldots)$$
$$9n = 4$$
$$n = \tfrac{4}{9}$$

Thus, the rational number $\tfrac{4}{9}$ is the one that we were searching for and we write $\tfrac{4}{9} = 0.\overline{4}$. (You can check this quickly by division!)

REMARK You should recognize the fact that we are tacitly assuming that the property "if $a = b$, then $a \cdot c = b \cdot c$" holds, even for rational numbers. This is true, and we will return briefly to consider it in Section 6.4.

Let us consider the same approach in another situation. Suppose that we are given the decimal $0.\overline{12}$ and wish to identify the common fraction $\frac{a}{b}$ that may be associated with it. In the preceding example each cycle was just one digit long, so by using a multiple of 10 we were able to subtract the decimal portion of the number. Would it seem reasonable in this case, having a decimal that cycles in two digits, to multiply by 100? Consider the following format for the solution.

Let $\qquad n = 0.\overline{12} = 0.12121212\ldots$

Then
$$100n = 100 \times 0.121212\ldots = 12.121212\ldots = 12 + .121212\ldots$$
$$100n - n = (12 + 012.1212\ldots) - 0.121212\ldots$$
$$99n = 12 + (0.121212\ldots - 0.121212\ldots)$$
$$99n = 12$$
$$n = \frac{12}{99} = \frac{4}{33}$$

Thus $\qquad \dfrac{4}{33} = 0.\overline{12}$

EXAMPLE

Find the rational number in $\frac{a}{b}$ form such that $\frac{a}{b} = 3.\overline{16}$.

Solution Let

$$n = 3.\overline{16} = 3.161616\ldots$$
$$100n = 100 \times 3.161616\ldots = 316.1616\ldots$$
$$100n - n = 316.1616\ldots - 3.1616\ldots$$
$$99n = (316 - 3) + (0.1616\ldots - 0.1616\ldots)$$
$$99n = 313$$
$$n = \frac{313}{99}$$

Therefore,

$$\frac{a}{b} = \frac{313}{99} = 3.\overline{16}$$

In each of these situations the decimal point was at the beginning of a cycle. Suppose our infinite repeating decimal is of the form $4.23\overline{5}$. Perhaps our first step should be to get the decimal before a cycle. Thus, we would use a multiplier of 100 in the first step. The format might appear as follows:

Let $\qquad\qquad n = 4.23\overline{5}$

$$100n = 42\overline{3.5} = 423.5555\ldots$$

$$10 \times (100n) = 10 \times 423.5555\ldots$$

Then $\qquad\qquad 1000n = 4235.555\ldots$

Thus $\qquad 1000n - 100n = 4235.555\ldots - 423.555\ldots$

and $\qquad (1000 - 100)n = (4235 - 423) + (0.555\ldots - 0.555\ldots)$

So $\qquad\qquad 900n = 3812$

Then $\qquad\qquad n = \dfrac{3812}{900} = \dfrac{953}{225}$

EXAMPLE

Find a fraction $\dfrac{a}{b}$ that is equal to $0.13\overline{4}$.

Solution

$$\text{Let } n = 0.13\overline{4}.$$

$$100n = 13.\overline{4}$$

$$10 \times (100n) = 10 \times (13.\overline{4})$$

$$1000n = 134.\overline{4}$$

$$1000n - 100n = 134.\overline{4} - 13.\overline{4}$$

$$900n = (134 + 0.\overline{4}) - (13 + 0.\overline{4})$$

$$900n = (134 - 13) + (0.\overline{4} - 0.\overline{4})$$

$$900n = 121$$

$$n = \dfrac{121}{900}$$

> REMARK Note carefully that the key to the procedure used here is the fact that when we get the decimal portions of two numbers to be the same and then subtract, the entire decimal portion is eliminated. Other procedures that appear to be different from this one may be used, but they will very likely be based on this same principle.

Every infinite repeating decimal can be written as a rational number in $\dfrac{a}{b}$ form. Let us summarize this discussion as Property 6.3.

PROPERTY 6.3   **Every rational number can be represented by a decimal fraction that either terminates or repeats in cycles and, conversely, every decimal fraction that terminates or repeats in cycles represents a rational number.**

PROBLEM SET 6.2

1. Express each of the following in decimal form:

    a. $\frac{2}{7}$ **b.** $\frac{13}{16}$ **c.** $\frac{34}{7}$ **d.** $\frac{59}{11}$ **e.** 4

    f. $11\frac{2}{5}$ **g.** $\frac{3}{14}$ **h.** $\frac{1}{17}$ **i.** $\frac{2}{9}$ **j.** $\frac{4}{9}$

2. Express each of the following in $\frac{a}{b}$ reduced form:

    a. $0.\overline{5}$ **b.** $0.\overline{34}$ **c.** $0.\overline{7}$ **d.** $0.\overline{05}$ **e.** $1.\overline{9}$

    f. $0.\overline{109}$ **g.** $0.1\overline{8}$ **h.** $3.2\overline{5}$ **i.** $2.5\overline{24}$ **j.** $0.00\overline{43}$

3. Express in $\frac{a}{b}$ reduced form:

    a. $0.3\overline{5}$ **b.** $2.3\overline{4}$ **c.** $0.10\overline{9}$ **d.** $3.41\overline{5}$ **e.** $0.00\overline{4}$ **f.** $0.13\overline{72}$

4. Write each of the following sets of decimals in order from smallest to largest:

    a. $3.4\overline{5}$, $3.\overline{45}$, $3.\overline{453}$, $3.45\overline{0}$

    b. $0.412\overline{3}$, $0.\overline{4123}$, $0.41\overline{23}$, 0.4123

    c. $1.45\overline{1}$, $1.\overline{451}$, $1.4\overline{51}$, $1.451\overline{0}$

    d. $13.5\overline{62}$, $13.\overline{562}$, $13.56\overline{2}$, $13.\overline{5623}$

5. Find a decimal between each of the following pairs of decimals:

    a. $4.\overline{6}$, $4.\overline{7}$ **b.** $3.6\overline{2}$, $3.6\overline{20}$

    d. $153.2\overline{4}$, $153.\overline{24}$ **c.** $0.13\overline{4}$, $0.1\overline{34}$

6. **a.** Insert five rational numbers between 0.563 and 0.564.

    b. Insert five rational numbers between $0.\overline{563}$ and $0.\overline{564}$.

    c. What property does this exemplify?

7. To find the sum of $0.\overline{13}$ and $0.\overline{4}$ we could use "scratch addition." Consider the sum:

$$0.131313\cdots$$
$$0.44444\cdots$$
$$0.575757\cdots$$

   a. Use this technique to find $0.\overline{45} + 0.\overline{04}$. Does the answer repeat in cycles? How long are the cycles?

   b. Find $a + b$ if $a = 0.\overline{462}$ and $b = 0.\overline{43}$. Does the answer repeat in cycles? How long are the cycles?

   c. Find $0.2\overline{31} + 0.\overline{1423}$. Does the answer repeat in cycles?

d. Find $0.\overline{34} + 0.\overline{1231}$. Does the answer repeat in cycles?

e. Will the sum of two infinite cycling decimals always be a cycling decimal. How can you be sure?

f. If two infinite cycling decimals are added, what will be the length of the cycle of the resulting decimal?

g. Find $0.\overline{143} + 0.\overline{523}$. Why is this *not* a counterexample for your answer to part **f**?

8. Suppose $a = \frac{2}{7}$ and $b = \frac{5}{7}$.

  a. Write a and b each as infinite decimals.

  b. Find $a + b$ using the fractional form.

  c. Find $a + b$ using the decimal form.

  d. Are the two results obtained in parts **b** and **c** equivalent?

9. **a.** Represent $\frac{1}{9}$ as a decimal.

  b. Represent $\frac{1}{99}$ as a decimal.

  c. Represent $\frac{1}{999}$ as a decimal.

  d. What rational number would you next encounter in this pattern? What do you expect of its decimal form? Verify your speculation.

10. We state that the multiplicative inverse of $\frac{3}{5}$ is $\frac{5}{3}$, because $\frac{3}{5} \cdot \frac{5}{3} = 1$.

  a. What is the multiplicative inverse of $\frac{26}{5}$

  b. What is the multiplicative inverse of $0.\overline{65}$?

11. Consider the following pattern:

$$\tfrac{1}{9} = 0.\overline{1} \text{ (one-digit repetition)}$$
$$\tfrac{1}{27} = \tfrac{1}{3} \cdot \tfrac{1}{9} = \tfrac{1}{3} \cdot (0.\overline{1}) = 0.\overline{037} \text{ (three-digit repetition)}$$
$$\tfrac{1}{81} = \tfrac{1}{3} \cdot \tfrac{1}{27} = \tfrac{1}{3} \cdot (0.\overline{037}) = 0.\overline{012345679} \text{ (nine-digit repetition)}$$

What do you expect for $\frac{1}{243}$?

12. Write each of the following in $\dfrac{a}{b}$ form. Use your calculator to change back to decimal form to verify that your answer is correct.

  a. $0.\overline{4}$ **b.** $0.\overline{45}$ **c.** $0.\overline{230}$ **d.** $0.1\overline{426}$ **e.** $1.\overline{23}$ **f.** $0.58\overline{3}$

13. Use your calculator to obtain a decimal approximation for each, in order to determine which is larger.

  a. $\frac{2}{11} \cdot \frac{3}{13}$ **b.** $\frac{5}{7} \cdot \frac{12}{17}$ **c.** $\frac{19}{42} \cdot \frac{23}{51}$ **d.** $\frac{26}{47} \cdot \frac{99}{179}$

Pedagogical Problems and Activities

14. How would you explain to a sixth-grade student that you can find a decimal term approximation for $\frac{12}{7}$ with an error less than 0.0001?

15. Consider the perfect square 36. Write it as a product of prime factors. Notice that each prime factor appears an even number of times ($36 = 2 \cdot 2 \cdot 3 \cdot 3$).

   a. Does this also hold true for 49? For 64? For 144?

   b. Try to present an argument to convince a sixth-grade student that this will hold for any perfect square.

16. Students are sometimes reluctant to accept the statement that $0.\overline{9} = 1$. Consider the following argument. Write $\frac{1}{3}$ and $\frac{2}{3}$ both as decimals. Let $\frac{1}{3} = a$ and $\frac{2}{3} = b$. Then $\frac{1}{3} + \frac{2}{3} = a + b$. What is $\frac{1}{3} + \frac{2}{3}$ in $\frac{a}{b}$ form? What is the sum of the decimals, $a + b$? Does $1 = 0.\overline{9}$?

 17. Calculators use different approaches in how they round off decimals to provide answers. It is important that you know how your calculator works and to understand that "different looking" answers may need to be understood as the same. For example, three different calculators gave the following answers to this question:

$$\tfrac{2}{3} \times 3 = ?$$

   Calculator 1: 1.99999998
   Calculator 2: 1.99999999
   Calculator 3: 2

   a. How do you think calculator 1 is operating?

   b. How do you think calculator 2 is operating?

   c. How do you think calculator 3 is operating?

   d. Using techniques learned earlier in the section, can you show that $1.\overline{9} = 2$?

18. A second procedure for finding the $\frac{a}{b}$ form for a repeating decimal is as follows:

$$\frac{a}{b} = 0.12\overline{1} \qquad 10\,\frac{a}{b} = 1.2\overline{1} = 1.21\overline{1}$$

$$\frac{a}{b} = 0.12\overline{1} = 0.12\overline{1}$$

$$9\,\frac{a}{b} = 1.09$$

$$\frac{a}{b} = \frac{1.09}{9} = \frac{109}{900}$$

   a. Compare this to the method illustrated in this section.

b. Use this procedure to find the rational number for each of the following:

(i) $0.341\overline{3}$ (ii) $0.01\overline{266}$

(iii) $0.56\overline{67}$ (iv) $0.871\overline{2}$

6.3 IRRATIONAL NUMBERS

We have shown that the set of rational numbers is dense. The points on a line are also dense. We stated earlier that every rational number corresponds to some point on a number line. Does each point on the line correspond to a rational number? To answer this, let us proceed along a line of thought as the Greeks are reputed to have done. First, recall that any square has a diagonal that may be recognized as being the hypotenuse of a right triangle. As stated in the Pythagorean theorem, in any right triangle the square of the hypotenuse is equal to the sum of the squares of the legs. Thus, for a square with side of measure s and diagonal of measure d, we could write $d^2 = s^2 + s^2 = 2s^2$. Now let us apply this to a situation related to the number line, as illustrated in Figure 6.9. On the number line, let 0 be at the point O, and 1 be at A. Consider the square $OABC$ having segment $\overline{OA}$ as one side. Note that $\overline{OB}$ is a diagonal. Let us identify as point P that point on the number line whose distance from O is the same as the length of $\overline{OB}$. According to the Pythagorean theorem, if r is the length of $\overline{OB}$, then $m(\overline{OB})^2 = 1^2 + 1^2 = 2$. Therefore, r is a number whose square is 2. This number we normally define as the square root of 2.

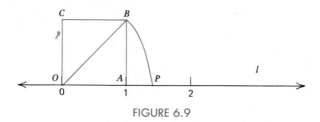

FIGURE 6.9

Definition 6.1 Let k be a whole number. The principal square root of k, denoted $\sqrt{k}$, is that unique positive number that when used as a factor twice yields k.

Thus, in our case, $r = \sqrt{2}$. Now a question arises concerning $\sqrt{2}$. Is it a rational number or is it not rational? Let us offer the following argument.

Clearly, either $\sqrt{2}$ is rational or $\sqrt{2}$ is not rational. If $\sqrt{2}$ were rational then $\sqrt{2} = \dfrac{p}{q}$ for some integers p and q, where $q \neq 0$. Then $(\sqrt{2})^2 = \left(\dfrac{p}{q}\right)^2$ so $2 = \dfrac{p^2}{q^2}$, and $2q^2 = p^2$. Thus, $2 \cdot q \cdot q = p \cdot p$. In the prime factorization of $q \cdot q$, 2 will appear as a factor an even number of times, as will be the case with $p \cdot p$. Therefore in $2 \cdot q \cdot q$ we have an odd number of factors of two, whereas in $p \cdot p$ we have two occurring as a factor an even number of times. This is, of course, not possible. Thus our assumption that the $\sqrt{2}$ is rational is false. We therefore may conclude that $\sqrt{2}$ is not rational.

We defined rational numbers to be numbers expressible in a form $\dfrac{a}{b}$, where a and b are integers with $b \neq 0$. Numbers that are not expressible as ratios of integers are said to be irrational numbers.

Definition 6.2   An irrational number is a number that cannot be represented by an ordered pair of integers a and b.

Let us summarize this discussion by stating the following property.

PROPERTY 6.4   **The number $\sqrt{2}$ is irrational.**

We observed in Chapter 5 that rational numbers always have a decimal form that either terminates or repeats in cycles. We might characterize irrational numbers then as decimal numbers that do not terminate and do not repeat in cycles.

Property 6.4 provides convincing evidence for us that some points on the line are not associated with rational numbers. There are, of course, other such points that are associated with irrational numbers. For example, $2\sqrt{2}$, $3\sqrt{2}$, and $4\sqrt{2}$ are all irrational. So is $\sqrt{2} + 1$, $\sqrt{2} + 2$, $\sqrt{2} + 3$, and so on. We can also show that $\sqrt{3}$, $\sqrt{5}$, $\sqrt{6}$, and $\sqrt{7}$ are irrational. In fact, any counting number that is not a perfect square will have a square root that is irrational. It might also be noted that $\sqrt[3]{2}$, $\sqrt[4]{2}$, $\sqrt[5]{2}$, and so on are also irrational. As you can see, there are a great many irrationals. In fact, it can be shown that there are "more" irrational numbers than there are rational numbers.

Another irrational number that we often encounter is related to a circle. The ratio of the circumference of a circle to its diameter is a constant. No matter what circle we choose, if we measure the distance around the circle and the distance across it, the ratio of the measures will be the same number, approximately equal to $\frac{22}{7}$ or to 3.14 as a decimal. The ratio is actually an irrational number. We commonly refer to it as π (the Greek letter pi).

We stated earlier that any decimal that terminates or repeats in cycles is a rational number. Then any decimal that does *not* terminate or repeat in cycles must be an irrational number. Consider $n = 0.424224222422224....$ The pattern for the number is clear, but it is not repeating in a cycle. We can readily designate irrational numbers using this idea. In many respects this type of irrational number seems more "real" to elementary school children than those mentioned previously.

EXAMPLE

Write an irrational number that is greater than $\frac{1}{2}$ but less than $\frac{2}{3}$.

> *Solution* Because $\frac{1}{2} = 0.5$ and $\frac{2}{3} = 0.\overline{6}$, let us begin by writing a rational number between 0.5 and $0.\overline{6}$ such as 0.54. Then we will begin a series of digits to assure us that it is irrational. For example, $n = 0.5414114111411114...$ is irrational and $\frac{1}{2} < n < \frac{2}{3}$.

The irrationals, as we have mentioned, are more numerous than the rationals. However, they do not possess many of the properties that hold for rationals. For example, the set of irrationals possesses neither an additive identity nor a multiplicative identity because $\sqrt{2} + 0 = \sqrt{2}$ and $\sqrt{2} \cdot 1 = \sqrt{2}$ and 0 and 1 are not irrational numbers. Note also that the irrationals are not closed under addition. If $m = 0.46233323333...$ and $n = 0.53767667666 ...$, then both m and n are irrational. However, $m + n = 0.999...$, which is rational. Thus, the set of irrational numbers is not closed under addition. Likewise, Definition 6.1 would seem to assure us that the set of irrational numbers is not closed under multiplication because $\sqrt{2} \cdot \sqrt{2} = 2$.

> REMARK The irrational numbers may not be as familiar to you as are the other sets of numbers that have been developed. The fact remains, however, that they do occur very "naturally." Indeed, it would be difficult to discuss equations of the form $x^2 = 2$ or $x^3 + 3x^2 - 2x - 6 = 0$ without having irrationals at our disposal. (The solutions for $x^2 = 2$ are $\sqrt{2}$ and $^-\sqrt{2}$, whereas those for the second equation are $\sqrt{2}$, $^-\sqrt{2}$, and $^-3$.)

Let us emphasize the fact that $\sqrt{2}$ is a number. It is exact, not an approximation. However, it does not have a terminating decimal form nor is it associated with a cycling decimal. There are many times when it is convenient to obtain a decimal approximation for an irrational number. In Table 6.1 we have included the approximate square roots of the numbers 1 through 30 correct to the nearest thousandth. Thus, if someone asks for $\sqrt{7}$ rounded to the nearest thousandth, we would respond 2.646. If asked for an approximation to the nearest hundredth, we would write 2.65, and if we were to find $\sqrt{7}$ to the nearest tenth, we would write 2.6. Even if we were asked to find

TABLE 6.1

n	$\sqrt{n}$	n	$\sqrt{n}$
1	1.000	16	4.000
2	1.414	17	4.123
3	1.732	18	4.243
4	2.000	29	4.359
5	2.236	20	4.472
6	2.449	21	4.583
7	2.646	22	4.690
8	2.828	23	4.796
9	3.000	24	4.899
10	3.162	25	5.000
11	3.317	26	5.099
12	3.464	27	5.196
13	3.606	28	5.292
14	3.742	29	5.385
15	3.873	30	5.477

$\sqrt{6.5}$ we could get a close approximation. As 6.5 is half way between 6 and 7, $\sqrt{6.5}$ should be about half way between 2.449 and 2.646, or about 2.547.

Of course the calculator should be used whenever possible. Use your calculator to obtain a rational approximation for $\sqrt{7}$ to whatever number of digits your calculator will display. For example, the following was observed on one model: $\sqrt{7} \doteq 2.645751311$. It should be obvious that the calculator performs the same function as a table because it provides answers to several decimal places of accuracy. The user must simply round the answer off to the desired accuracy.

Even without a calculator to help us, we could employ one of several algorithms that are available to approximate the root. One such procedure works on a bracketing principle. We know that $\sqrt{2} > 1$ because $1^2 = 1$, but $\sqrt{2} < 2$ because $2^2 = 4$. (Recall that $\sqrt{k}$ is a number that when used as a factor twice yields k.) Also, because $1.4^2 = 1.96$ and $1.5^2 = 2.25$, we know that $1.4 < \sqrt{2} < 1.5$. Furthermore, because $1.41^2 = 1.9881$ and $1.42^2 = 2.0164$, we may write $1.41 < \sqrt{2} < 1.42$. Let us use the following format:

$$1 < \sqrt{2} < 2$$
$$1.4 < \sqrt{2} < 1.5$$

$$1.41 < \sqrt{2} < 1.42$$
$$1.414 < \sqrt{2} < 1.415$$
$$1.4142 < \sqrt{2} < 1.4143$$
$$1.41421 < \sqrt{2} < 1.41422$$
$$1.414213 < \sqrt{2} < 1.414214$$

$$\vdots$$

At any given step, the next "bracket" is obtained to a great extent by trial and error. Only by actually squaring the decimals and comparing with $(\sqrt{2})^2 = 2$ can we select the correct pair.

EXAMPLE 1

Find $\sqrt{3}$ correct to the nearest thousandth.

Solution

$$1 < \sqrt{3} < 2 \qquad (1^2 = 1 \text{ and } 2^2 = 4)$$
$$1.7 < \sqrt{3} < 1.8 \qquad (1.7^2 = 2.89 \text{ and } 1.8^2 = 3.24)$$
$$1.73 < \sqrt{3} < 1.74 \qquad (1.73^2 = 2.9929 \text{ and } 1.74^2 = 3.0276)$$
$$1.732 < \sqrt{3} < 1.733 \qquad (1.732^2 = 2.9998 \text{ and } 1.733^2 = 3.0033)$$

We may decide whether 1.732 or 1.733 is the better estimate by choosing the one whose square is nearer to 3. Thus, 1.732 is the better estimate.

EXAMPLE 2

Find $\sqrt[3]{3}$ to the nearest hundredth.

Solution

$$1 < \sqrt[3]{3} < 2 \qquad (1^3 = 1 \text{ and } 2^3 = 8)$$
$$1.4 < \sqrt[3]{3} < 1.5 \qquad (1.4^3 = 2.744 \text{ and } 1.5^3 = 3.375)$$
$$1.44 < \sqrt[3]{3} < 1.45 \qquad (1.44^3 \doteq 2.98598 \text{ and } 1.45^3 \doteq 3.0486)$$

We may select 1.44 as the approximation for $\sqrt[3]{3}$ to the nearest hundredth.

REMARK Even though the bracketing process does not demand the use of a calculator, it is obviously a useful tool and will save you a great deal of time and energy as you work with such problems.

Computers are often used to calculate rational approximations for irrational numbers. The following are approximations for $\sqrt{2}$, $\sqrt{3}$, and π.

$$\sqrt{2} \doteq 1.41421356237309504880168872420969807856967187537690$$
$$\sqrt{3} \doteq 1.73205080756887729352744634150587236694280525381090$$
$$\pi \doteq 3.14159265358979323846264338327950288419716939937510$$

REMARK The rational approximations for these irrational numbers, correct to 50 significant digits are now readily obtained by using a computer. It is easy to forget that only in the last few years have we had such devices available for our use. Even the great mathematical minds of the past could only dream of such conveniences!

PROBLEM SET 6.3

1. Classify each of the following as being rational or irrational:

   a. $\frac{46}{843}$ b. $.46$ c. $0.231231123111\ldots$ d. 4.658342

   e. 5.62 f. $34.1211211121111\ldots$ g. $6.343434\ldots$

   h. $2\sqrt{2}$ i. 6.248 j. $\sqrt{9}$ k. $\sqrt{5}$ l. $\dfrac{\sqrt{5}}{2\sqrt{5}}$ m. $\dfrac{\sqrt{2}}{2}$

   n. $140140014000\ldots$

2. Complete each of the following as indicated:

   a. $2 < \sqrt{6} < 3$ because $2^2 = 4$ and $3^2 = 9$
      $2.4 < \sqrt{6} < 2.5$ because $2.4^2 = 5.76$ and $2.5^2 = 6.25$
      $\underline{} < \sqrt{6} < \underline{}$ because $\underline{}$
      $\underline{} < \sqrt{6} < \underline{}$ because $\underline{}$

   b. $3 < \sqrt{12} < 4$ because $3^2 = 9$ and $4^2 = 16$
      $\underline{} < \sqrt{12} < \underline{}$ because $\underline{}$
      $\underline{} < \sqrt{12} < \underline{}$ because $\underline{}$
      $\underline{} < \sqrt{12} < \underline{}$ because $\underline{}$

   c. $4 < \sqrt{18} < 5$ because $4^2 = 16$ and $5^2 = 25$
      $4.2 < \sqrt{18} < 4.3$ because $4.2^2 = 17.64$ and $4.3^2 = 18.49$
      $\underline{} < \sqrt{18} < \underline{}$
      $\underline{} < \sqrt{18} < \underline{}$

   d. $9 < \sqrt{96} < 10$ because $9^2 = 81$ and $10^2 = 100$
      $\underline{} < \sqrt{96} < \underline{}$
      $\underline{} < \sqrt{96} < \underline{}$
      $\underline{} < \sqrt{96} < \underline{}$

e. $2 < \sqrt[3]{9} < 3$ because $2^3 = 8$ and $3^3 = 27$

$2.0 < \sqrt[3]{9} < 2.1$ because $2.0^3 = 8.0$ and $2.1^3 = 9.261$

$2.08 < \sqrt[3]{9} < 2.09$ because $2.08^3 = 8.998912$ and $2.09^3 = 9.129329$

___ $< \sqrt[3]{9} <$ ___

f. ___ $< \sqrt[3]{17} <$ ___

___ $< \sqrt[3]{17} <$ ___

___ $< \sqrt[3]{17} <$ ___

___ $< \sqrt[3]{17} <$ ___

3. Use the bracketing process to approximate each of the following to the nearest tenth:

a. $\sqrt{5}$ **b.** $\sqrt{13}$ **c.** $\sqrt{84}$ **d.** $\sqrt{840}$ **e.** $\sqrt{750}$ **f.** $\sqrt{1450}$

4. Use your calculator to bracket each of the following between two numbers expressed to hundredths:

a. $\sqrt{4680}$ **b.** $\sqrt{5642}$ **c.** $\sqrt[3]{450}$ **d.** $\sqrt[3]{585}$ **e.** $\sqrt[4]{452}$ **f.** $\sqrt[4]{400}$

5. a. Find $\sqrt{17}$ with an error no more than 0.001.

b. Find a decimal approximation for $5 + \sqrt{5}$ correct to the nearest hundredth.

6. Arrange each in order of decreasing magnitude:

a. 2.33, $2\frac{1}{3}$, 2.333, $\frac{60}{25}$

b. $2\frac{1}{2}$, 2.51 $2.5\overline{1}$, $2.\overline{51}$

c. $3.4623233\ldots$, $\frac{2}{3}\sqrt{15}$, $\frac{08}{20}$, $3.46\overline{23}$

d. $2.\overline{91}$, $\frac{32}{11}$, $2.\overline{9}$, $\frac{455}{154}$

7. a. Place a rational number between $a = 0.456212112111\ldots$ and $b = 0.456303003000\ldots$

b. Place an irrational number between a and b.

8. Let $c = 0.35\overline{8}$ and $d = 0.35\overline{78}$.

a. Place a rational number between c and d.

b. Place an irrational number between c and d.

9. Let $a = 0.434\overline{2}$ and $b = 0.4326202002000\ldots$

a. Insert a rational number between a and b.

b. Insert an irrational number between a and b.

c. What is the additive inverse of a?

d. What is the additive inverse of b?

10. We can prove that $3\sqrt{2}$ is irrational as follows. Either $3\sqrt{2}$ is rational or it is irrational. Let us assume that it is rational. Then $3\sqrt{2} = \dfrac{a}{b}$. Therefore

$\sqrt{2} = \dfrac{a}{3b}$ But $3b$ is an integer, so $\sqrt{2}$ is rational. This is a contradiction of Property 6.4. Therefore $3\sqrt{2}$ is irrational. Use this approach to prove each of the following is an irrational:

a. $2\sqrt{2}$ b. $5\sqrt{2}$ c. $2 + \sqrt{2}$

d. $5 + \sqrt{2}$ e. $4 + 6\sqrt{2}$ f. $\frac{3}{4} + \frac{1}{2}\sqrt{2}$

11. Consider the following proof that $\sqrt{2}$ is irrational. Either $\sqrt{2}$ is rational or $\sqrt{2}$ is not rational. Let us assume $\sqrt{2}$ is rational. That is, $\left(\dfrac{a}{b}\right)^2 = 2$ for some rational number $\dfrac{a}{b}$, where a and b are integers, $b \neq 0$ and a and b are relatively prime. If $\left(\dfrac{a}{b}\right)^2 = \dfrac{a^2}{b^2} = 2$ then $a^2 = 2b^2$. Thus, a^2 is even.

However, if a^2 is even then a is even. (This must be true because the square of an odd number is always odd.) Thus, we might write $a = 2k$ for some integer k. Because $a^2 = (2k)^2 = 4k^2$, we may write $a^2 = 4k^2 = 2b^2$. Therefore, $b^2 = 2k^2$, so b^2 must be even. Thus, b is even. Observe that we would have the situation where a must be even and also b is even. This contradicts our original stipulation that $\sqrt{2}$ is rational and a and b are relatively prime. Therefore, our assumption that $\sqrt{2}$ is rational must be false, and $\sqrt{2}$ is not rational.

a. Use this approach to prove that $\sqrt{3}$ is irrational.

b. Prove that $\sqrt{5}$ is irrational.

12. Another algorithm, often referred to as the "guess-and-average" approach, may be used to find decimal approximations for irrational numbers. To find $\sqrt{15}$ we begin by guessing a number that we think is close to the square root of 15. Suppose we choose $g_1 = 4$. Now let us find the quotient $15 \div 4$. That is $q_1 = \frac{15}{4} = 3.75$. Notice that we are seeking a number whose square is 15. If g_1 is too large, then q_1 is too small. However, the average of g_1 and q_1 is a closer approximation than was either g_1 or q_1. Let this average be our second guess; that is, $g_2 = \dfrac{g_1 + q_1}{2} = \dfrac{4 + 3.75}{2} \doteq 3.88$. Then $q_2 = \dfrac{15}{3.88} \doteq 3.87$. Let us choose our third guess as the average of g_2 and q_2. Then $g_3 = \dfrac{g_2 + q_2}{2} = \dfrac{3.88 + 3.87}{2} = 3.875$.

We may then obtain $q_3 = \dfrac{15}{3.875} \doteq 3.871$. We may infer that $\sqrt{15}$ is 3.87 to the nearest hundredth.

  a. Use the guess-and-average approach to find $\sqrt{86}$ correct to the nearest tenth if $g_1 = 9$.

  b. Find $\sqrt{950}$ correct to the nearest hundredth. Use $g_1 = 30$.

  c. Use the guess and average technique to find:

  (i) $\sqrt{10}$ **(ii)** $\sqrt{35}$ **(iii)** $\sqrt{78}$

  (iv) $\sqrt{830}$ **(v)** $\sqrt{4980}$ **(vi)** $\sqrt{8000}$

Pedagogical Problems and Activities

13. Suppose your sixth-grade students are doubtful of the guess-and-average approach where you make a "wild guess" for g_1: for example, choosing $g_1 = 2$ when you are asked to find $\sqrt{80}$. Show that the algorithm will work, even with such a choice for g_1. (Problem 12 introduces this algorithm.)

14. Select six different circular objects. Measure the circumference and diameter for each, then find the ratio of the circumference to the diameter. Express each ratio as a decimal accurate to the nearest hundredth.

6.4 THE REAL NUMBER SYSTEM

Let us pause briefly to summarize the status of the number system that has been developed. The set of whole numbers was used to develop the integers. The integers were then used to define rational numbers. We have indicated that rational numbers can be written either in an $\frac{a}{b}$ form or in a cycling decimal form (where a terminating decimal is considered to cycle 0's.) We then discussed the irrational numbers and indicated that their decimal counterparts do not terminate and do not cycle. These two sets are disjoint. However, the union of these two sets is of considerable interest to us.

Definition 6.3 The set of real numbers, denoted by R, consists of all rational numbers (Q) in union with all irrational numbers (Ir). (That is, $Q \cup Ir = R$.)

    The real numbers are extremely useful to us. A great amount of mathematics can be done using them. It can be shown that the real numbers can be matched in one-to-one correspondence with points on a line. This fact is of great importance, and we will return to it later.

PROPERTY 6.5   **For each point on the number line there corresponds a real number, and to each real number there corresponds a unique point on the number line.**

Some of the basic properties possessed by the real numbers are summarized in Property 6.6.

PROPERTY 6.6   **Let *R* be the set of real numbers. The following properties are satisifed:**

   1. *R* is closed under addition.
   2. *R* is associative under addition.
   3. *R* has an additive identity (0).
   4. Each element $a \in R$ has an additive inverse in *R*.
   5. *R* is commutative under addition.
   6. *R* is closed under multiplication.
   7. *R* is associative under multiplication.
   8. *R* contains the multiplicative identity (1).
   9. Each nonzero element has a multiplicative inverse in *R*.
  10. *R* is commutative under multiplication.
  11. Multiplication is distributive over addition.
  12. The set *R* is ordered.
  13. The set *R* is dense.

   Furthermore, the properties introduced in previous chapters for solving equations and inequalities can be extended to cover real numbers. Let us restate them at this time for your convenience.

PROPERTY 6.7   **For any real numbers *r*, *s*, and *t*:**

   1. If $r = s$, then $r + t = s + t$.
   2. If $r = s$, then $rt = st$.
   3. If $r < s$, then $r + t < s + t$.
   4. a. If $r < s$ and $t > 0$, then $rt < st$.
      b. If $r < s$ and $t < 0$, then $rt > st$.

   Consider the following examples in which use is made of Property 6.7.

EXAMPLE 1

For what real numbers does $2x + \frac{2}{3} = \frac{5}{6}$?

Solution

$$2x + \frac{2}{3} + \frac{-2}{3} = \frac{5}{6} + \frac{-2}{3}$$

$$2x + 0 = \frac{5}{6} + \frac{-4}{6}$$

$$2x = \frac{1}{6}$$

$$\frac{1}{2} \cdot 2x = \frac{1}{2} \cdot \frac{1}{6}$$

$$x = \frac{1}{12}$$

EXAMPLE 2

For what real number is $2.3x - 1.45 < 5.2$?

Solution

$$2.3x - 1.45 + 1.45 < 5.2 + 1.45$$

$$2.3x + 0 < 6.65$$

$$2.3x < 6.65$$

$$\frac{1}{2.3} \cdot 2.3x < \frac{1}{2.3} \cdot 6.65$$

$$x < 2.89$$

EXAMPLE 3

For what real numbers is $\frac{5}{6} - \frac{2}{3}x > \frac{1}{4}$?

Solution

$$\frac{5}{6} + \frac{-5}{6} - \frac{2}{3}x > \frac{1}{4} + \frac{-5}{6}$$

$$\frac{-2}{3}x > \frac{-7}{12}$$

$$\frac{-3}{2} \cdot \frac{-2}{3}x < \frac{-3}{2} \cdot \frac{-7}{12}$$

$$x < \frac{7}{8}$$

With the completion of the development of the real number system, we have in some sense satisfied our most basic needs for numbers. A great amount of mathematics can be studied using these numbers, and many real-world problems can be solved. We now have closure for addition, subtraction, multiplication, and division involving nonzero divisors. However, certain inadequacies still exist. For example, suppose we wish to find some number x such that $x^2 + 4 = 0$. Clearly $x \neq 2$ because $2^2 = 4$ and $4 + 4 \neq 0$. Likewise $x \neq {}^-2$ because $({}^-2)^2 = 4$. To handle the solution to such an equation, we would need to invent new numbers not yet encountered. These numbers, the complex numbers, are commonly developed in advanced algebra classes where many of you may have become familiar with them. We do not propose that such a development needs to be done at this time or suggest that you will need to use them as you teach in the elementary school or junior high program. It is simply interesting to note that there are a great many further mathematical developments that can be explored given the motivation to do so.

PROBLEM SET 6.4

1. **a.** Is there a greatest counting number less than 10?
    b. Is there a greatest integer less than 10?
    c. Is there a greatest rational number less than 10?
    d. Is there a greatest real number less than 10?
    e. What property is involved here?

2. Use the properties of equality to find the truth sets for the following (the universe is the set of real numbers):
    a. $3x + 1.2 = 4.6$ **b.** $\frac{5}{6}x - \frac{2}{3} = \frac{7}{8}$
    c. $2.6 - 1.6x = 5.2$ **d.** $\frac{5}{6}x - \frac{1}{3} = 2$
    e. $3 - \frac{2}{3}x = \frac{5}{6}$ **f.** $0.8 - 0.4x = 0.3$

3. Use the properties for inequality to find the truth sets for the following (the universe is the set of real numbers):
    a. $3x + 5 > 1.6$ **b.** $2x - \frac{1}{3} < \frac{5}{6}$ **c.** $1.2x - 2.3 < 1.3$
    d. $0.4x - 0.5 > 1.3$ **e.** $\frac{3}{5}x + 4 < 8$ **f.** $\frac{1}{4}x - \frac{1}{2} > \frac{3}{4}$

4. To solve an equation or inequality that contains fractions, it is usually helpful to first multiply both sides by the least common multiple of the fractions in order to simplify the work. To solve $\frac{1}{2}x + \frac{3}{4} = \frac{1}{6}$, first multiply both sides by 12 to obtain $12(\frac{1}{2}x + \frac{3}{4}) = 12(\frac{1}{6})$ so $6x + 9 = 2$. Use this technique to solve the following.
    a. $\frac{2}{3}x + \frac{1}{2} = \frac{1}{3}$ **b.** $\frac{3}{4}x + \frac{1}{3} > \frac{1}{2}$ **c.** $\frac{3}{5}x + \frac{1}{4} = \frac{4}{5}$
    d. $\frac{1}{2}x - \frac{1}{5} < \frac{4}{5}$ **e.** $\frac{2}{3}x - \frac{1}{2} = \frac{3}{5}$ **f.** $\frac{5}{8}x - 3 > \frac{1}{5}$

5. Equations involving decimals may be simplified by multiplying by the

appropriate multiple of 10. For example, the equation $0.3x - 4.23 = 6.3$ could be simplified by multiplying by 100. Thus, $100(0.3x - 4.23) = 100(6.3)$ so $30x - 423 = 630$. Use this technique to help find the solution set in each of the following. Write your answers in decimal form correct to the nearest hundredth.

a. $4x - 0.3 = 0.21$ b. $3.1x - 0.14 = 6.2$
c. $0.42x + 1.3 = 3.14$ d. $0.05x + 0.001 = 4.3$
e. $1.02x - 3.4 = 0.13$ f. $4 - 1.2x = 0.56$

6. If $R = \{$real numbers$\}$, $Q = \{$rational numbers$\}$, $Ir = \{$irrational numbers$\}$, $C = \{$counting numbers$\}$, and $I = \{$integers$\}$, classify each of the following as true or false.

a. $R \cap I = R$ b. $R \cap Q = Q$ c. $I \cap Q = Q$ d. $Q \cup C = C$
e. $Q \cup Ir = R$ f. $Q \subseteq R$ g. $Q \subseteq I$ h. $I \subseteq Q$

7. a. How many counting numbers are between 0 and 5?
   b. How many rational numbers are between 0 and 5?
   c. How many irrational numbers are between 0 and 5?
   d. What property is involved here?

8. Complete the following table.

Number	Counting Number	Integer	Rational Number	Irrational Number	Real Number
$\frac{1}{2}$	No	No	Yes	No	Yes
14.2					
16.23					
$\frac{21}{7}$					
0.343434 · · ·					
0.151551555 · · ·					
$\sqrt{36}$					
0					
$\sqrt{3}$					
$\frac{5}{9}$					

9. Classify each as true or false. If false, give a counterexample.

   a. The sum of a rational number and an irrational number is rational.
   b. The sum of two rational numbers is rational.
   c. The sum of two irrational numbers is irrational.
   d. The product of two irrational numbers is irrational.
   e. The real numbers are closed under addition.

6.5   PERCENT

One application of ratios that is commonly used is percent. The word *percent* means "per hundred." Thus, 30 percent of a quantity means that we take $\frac{30}{100}$ of that amount. Because 30% = $\frac{30}{100}$ and $\frac{30}{100}$ = 0.30 it seems evident that we really have three equivalent forms expressing the same thing. We frequently find one form preferred to the others in everyday usage. The following equivalent forms are illustrated pictorially in Figure 6.10.

$$42\% = \frac{42}{100} = 0.42$$
$$6\% = \frac{6}{100} = 0.06$$
$$120\% = \frac{120}{100} = 1.20$$
$$0.4\% = \frac{0.4}{100} = 0.004$$
$$100\% = \frac{100}{100} = 1$$

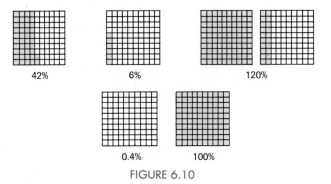

42%   6%   120%

0.4%   100%

FIGURE 6.10

Because work with percent relates so closely with fractions having a denominator of 100, it is natural to illustrate percents with the same models used in the work with decimals. In Figure 6.11, we have illustrated 2% and 20% for example. Is it clear that 20% is ten times as large as 2%? The use of percents gives us a common denominator, which aids in comparisons. However, care must be taken so that we interpret results properly. Although it

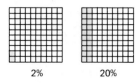

2%   20%

FIGURE 6.11

seems clear that 20% is greater than 2%, as illustrated in Figure 6.11, note that 20% of 10 is less than 2% of 1000. That is, $\frac{20}{100} \cdot 10 = 2$ and $\frac{2}{100} \cdot 1000 = 20$.

The use of percents is widespread. The interest rates on investments or on loans, the sale price of items, sales tax, income tax rates, and so on all make use of percents.

EXAMPLE 1

Write as a fraction in reduced form.

a. 60%   b. 45%   c. 25%   d. 12.5%

Solutions

a. $60\% = \frac{60}{100} = \frac{3}{5}$ b. $45\% = \frac{45}{100} = \frac{9}{20}$

c. $25\% = \frac{25}{100} = \frac{1}{4}$ d. $12.5\% = \frac{12.5}{100} = \frac{125}{1000} = \frac{1}{8}$

EXAMPLE 2

Write as a percent.

a. 0.36   b. 0.03   c. 1.4   d. 0.002

Solutions

a. $0.36 = 36\%$ b. $0.03 = 3\%$

c. $1.4 = 140\%$ d. $0.002 = 0.2\%$

EXAMPLE 3

Write $\frac{7}{8}$ as a percent.

Solution 1

$$\frac{7}{8} = \frac{7}{2^3} = \frac{7 \times 5^3}{2^3 \times 5^3} = \frac{875}{1000} = \frac{87.5}{100} = 87.5\%$$

Solution 2

$$\frac{7}{8} = \frac{n}{100}$$
$$8n = 700$$
$$n = 87.5$$
$$\text{thus, } \frac{7}{8} = \frac{87.5}{100} = 87.5\%$$

Solution 3 Use long division to convert to a decimal.

$$\begin{array}{r} 0.875 \\ 8\overline{)7.00} \\ 64 \\ \hline 60 \\ 56 \\ \hline 40 \\ 40 \\ \hline \end{array}$$

Thus, $\frac{7}{8} = 0.875 = 87.5\%$

Let us now look at some examples of use of percent in real-world problems. It will be helpful to remember that percent means "per hundred" and that proportions are readily applied in our solutions. That is, we are interested in the proportion $\dfrac{\text{part}}{\text{whole}} = \dfrac{\text{part}}{\text{whole}}$, where one of the denominators is 100. More specifically then, we are stating $\dfrac{\text{part}}{\text{whole}} = \dfrac{P}{100}$ where P is the percentage. $\left(\text{or if } A \text{ is the part and } B \text{ the whole, then } \dfrac{A}{B} = \dfrac{p}{100}\right).$

EXAMPLE 1

What is 75% of 48?

Solution 1

$$\frac{75}{100} = \frac{n}{48}$$
$$100n = 3600$$
$$n = 36$$

Therefore 75% of 48 is 36.

Solution 2

$$75\% = \frac{75}{100} = \frac{3}{4}$$
$$\frac{3}{4} = \frac{n}{48}$$
$$4n = 3 \cdot 48$$
$$n = 36$$

EXAMPLE 2

15 is what percent of 75?

Solution 1 The question being asked is equivalent to the question "15 is what fractional part of 75"?

$$\frac{15}{75} = \frac{n}{100}$$
$$75n = 1500$$
$$n = 20$$

Thus, 15 is 20% of 75.

Solution 2 $\frac{15}{75} = \frac{1}{5} = \frac{20}{100} = 20\%$

EXAMPLE 3

25 is 20% of what number?

Solution

$$\frac{20}{100} = \frac{25}{n}$$
$$20n = 2500$$
$$n = 125$$

Thus, 25 is 20% of 125.

EXAMPLE 4

The list price of a car tire was $50, but it was on sale for 30% off. What is the sale price?

Solution 1

$$\frac{30}{100} = \frac{n}{50}$$
$$100n = 1500$$
$$n = 15$$

Thus, the tire is being marked down $15, so it has a sale price of 50 − 15 = $35.

Solution 2 If the tire is being marked down 30%, it must be selling for
70% of the original price.

$$\frac{70}{100} = \frac{n}{50}$$
$$100n = 3500$$
$$n = \$35$$

So the sale price is $35.

EXAMPLE 5

A coat is on sale for $48. This represents a mark down of 20% from the original price. What was the original price of the coat?

Solution Because the coat is marked down 20%, its sale value must be
80% of the original value.

$$\frac{80}{100} = \frac{48}{n}$$
$$80n = 4800$$
$$n = 60$$

The original value of the coat was $60.

EXAMPLE 6

A college football player weighed 240 pounds at the beginning of fall training but weighed only 220 pounds at the end of the training session. What percent loss is this?

Solution The amount of weight lost is 20 pounds. Because it is a weight loss, it must be compared with the original weight.

$$\frac{20}{240} = \frac{n}{100}$$
$$240n = 2000$$
$$n = 8\tfrac{1}{3}$$

Thus, $\dfrac{8\frac{1}{3}}{100} = 8\frac{1}{3}\%$ weight loss.

When working with percent problems it is often helpful to use a calculator. We would encourage you to do so. There are other times when we need to do mental calculations regarding percents. A discount of 25% means $\frac{1}{4}$ off, so it is fairly easy to compute mentally. Often approximations will suffice. An item marked down 44% can be approximated by a 40% discount, which is $\frac{2}{5}$ (or even the less accurate approximation of 50% or $\frac{1}{2}$ may be close enough).

PROBLEM SET 6.5

1. Write each percent as a decimal.

    a. 46%   **b.** 24%   **c.** 18%   **d.** 56%

    e. 3%   **f.** 7%   **g.** 143%   **h.** 135%

    i. 14.2%   **j.** 16.3%   **k.** 0.2%   **l.** 0.6%

2. Write each percent as a fraction in reduced form.

    a. 60%   **b.** 70%   **c.** 48%   **d.** 36%

    e. 55%   **f.** 28%   **g.** 125%   **h.** 150%

    i. 6%   **j.** 4%   **k.** 0.5%   **l.** 0.4%

3. Write each as a percent.

    a. $\frac{1}{4}$ **b.** $\frac{3}{4}$ **c.** $\frac{8}{10}$ **d.** $\frac{7}{10}$

    e. $\frac{5}{100}$ **f.** $\frac{7}{100}$ **g.** $\frac{14}{20}$ **h.** $\frac{16}{20}$

    i. $\frac{21}{1000}$ **j.** $\frac{46}{1000}$ **k.** $\frac{5}{6}$ **l.** $\frac{1}{6}$

4. Complete the chart

Fraction in Simplest Form	Decimal	Percent
$\frac{21}{100}$		
___	0.13	___
___	___	91%
___	___	42%
___	0.03	___
$\frac{3}{10}$	___	___
___	0.7	___
___	___	5%
$\frac{14}{25}$	___	___

5. Use a proportion to solve the following:

    a. Find 60% of 25.

    b. Find 45% of 50.

    c. Find 120% of 85.

    d. Find 150% of 60.

    e. 15 is what percent of 45?

    f. 25 is what percent of 60?

    g. 150 is what percent of 125?

    h. 200 is what percent of 150?

    i. 12 is 25% of what number?

j. 80 is 10% of what number?

k. 125 is 110% of what number?

l. 80 is 120% of what number?

6. Use a proportion to solve each of the following:

   a. There were 30 antique cars at the show in the local mall. Twelve of them were Model T Fords. What percent of the cars were Model Ts?

   b. A small plane makes a landing at the local airport. The runway is a half-mile long but the plane only traveled 25% of it before it stopped. What was the landing distance of the plane? Could it be landed on a football field?

   c. A glass fish bowl is marked $6.98 plus tax. If the sales tax is 8%, what will the fish bowl cost?

   d. In a class of 30 students, 40% play musical instruments. How many students in the class play instruments?

   e. A student has 18 out of 25 problems correct on an assignment. What percent is correct?

   f. Pete made 40% of his shots in the basketball game. If he made 12 baskets, how many times did he shoot?

   g. You must score 90% or better to receive an A on a given test. If there are 40 points on the test, how many must you have right to receive an A?

7. **a.** In a school having an enrollment of 1200 students, 10% of the students are in orchestra or band. The band has 100 members and 20 students are in both band and orchestra. How many students play in the orchestra?

   b. What percent of the band and orchestra members play in both?

8. In 1980 Mount St. Helens erupted, blowing off a portion of the mountain and resulting in an odd-shaped, truncated cone with a height of 8,419 feet. This is about 87% of the original height of the mountain. What was the height before the eruption?

9. **a.** Employees at a local sporting goods store get a 15% discount on all merchandise purchased. A tennis racquet marked for $75 is on sale for 40% off. What would an employee have to pay for the tennis racquet?

   b. Would a discount of 40% followed by a 15% discount be the same as a single discount of 55%? Which would be to the advantage of the employee?

10. Choose the best approximation for each.

    a. 48% of 300   **(i)** 100   **(ii)** 150   **(iii)** 200

    b. 25% of 96   **(i)** 100   **(ii)** 50   **(iii)** 25

    c. 8% of 154   **(i)** 15   **(ii)** 10   **(iii)** 20
    d. 34% of 150 **(i)** 50   **(ii)** 100 **(iii)** 75
    e. 1% of 241   **(i)** 2   **(ii)** 24   **(iii)** 2.4

11. A couch was originally price at $640 but was reduced by 10%. Later the sale price was reduced another 25% for a clearance sale. What single discount would have provided the same clearance sale price?

12. A chair is on sale for 30% off. Sales tax is 6% on all purchases. You have the choice of first adding the tax, then taking the discount or taking the discount, and then adding the tax. Which would be the better deal for you?

Pedagogical Problems and Activities

13. Compare. Use >, <, or = for each following statements.
    a. 18% _____ 81%   **b.** 9% _____ 90%   **c.** 10% _____ 1%
    d. 56% _____ 55%   **e.** $\frac{7}{100}$ _____ 9%   **f.** 71% _____ 0.71
    g. 24% _____ 0.34   **h.** 100% _____ $\frac{100}{100}$

14. Write each as a percent, as a fraction and as a decimal.

a.   **b.**   **c.**   **d.**

15. Estimate what percent of each square is shaded. Compare estimates with a friend.

a.   **b.**   **c.**   **d.**   **e.**

16. A merchant who paid $50 for an item of clothing added a 20% markup to obtain her selling price. When the item did not sell at the price she listed, she reduced the selling price 20%. What is the new selling price?

17. Using graph paper, mark off a square of 100 boxes. Shade in your initials. What percent of the square is shaded?

18. a. Three of the 20 team members missed practice. What percent of the team missed practice?

    b. John answered 37 of the 50 questions correctly. What percent did he answer correctly?

    c. There are 25 cars in the lot. Nine are blue. What percent are not blue?

REVIEW PROBLEM SET

1. Express each in decimal form:

    a. $\frac{5}{4}$ **b.** $\frac{14}{25}$ **c.** $\frac{3}{8}$ **d.** $\frac{21}{120}$ **e.** $\frac{7}{11}$ **f.** $\frac{15}{7}$

2. Write each of the following in $\dfrac{a}{b}$ form:

    a. 0.2   **b.** 0.34   **c.** 0.0015   **d.** $0.\overline{15}$ **e.** $3.12\overline{3}$ **f.** $0.04\overline{3}$

3. Perform the indicated opertions:

    a. $0.23 + 1.4 + 62.5$

    c. $4.26 \cdot 0.013$

    b. $45.2 - 12.14$

    d. $52.63 \div 0.015$

4. Find the solution set for each of the following where the domain is the set of real numbers:

    a. $x + \frac{1}{3} = 2$ **b.** $\frac{1}{2} \cdot x = \frac{5}{2}$ **c.** $\frac{2}{3} + x = \frac{1}{4}$

    d. $\frac{2}{5}x + 1 = 3$ **e.** $3x + \frac{1}{2} = \frac{1}{4}$

5. Arrange in order of size from smallest to largest.

    a. $0.583, 0.5829994, 0.582929\ldots$ **b.** $0.623, 0.6\overline{2}, 0.6\overline{231}$

    c. $\frac{1}{3}, 0.03, 0.335, \frac{1}{4}, \frac{5}{11}$

6. **a.** Find $0.\overline{63} + 4.\overline{756}$.

    b. Find $0.\overline{46} - 0.1\overline{2}$.

    c. Find $2.\overline{46} - 0.\overline{8}$.

    d. Find $3 \cdot 0.\overline{67}$.

    e. Find $0.\overline{3} \cdot 0.\overline{4}$.

7. Write two irrational numbers greater than 0.352 and less than 0.353.

8. Find $0.432322322232222\ldots + 0.456566566656666.\ldots$ Is the sum rational or irrational?

9. Express $\sqrt{15}$ to the nearest tenth:

    a. Using the bracketing procedure

    b. Using the guess-and-average approach

10. **a.** Sue is earning \$18,000 per year and received a 6% raise. What will her salary be for next year?

    b. A dress has been marked down from \$40 to \$32. The discount is what percent of the original price?

11. Write each of the following as a percent.

    a. $\frac{11}{100}$ **b.** $\frac{6}{100}$ **c.** $\frac{67}{100}$ **d.** 0.44   **e.** 0.52   **f.** 0.89

12. Write each as a ratio in lowest terms.

    a. 23%   **b.** 25%   **c.** 70%   **d.** 80%   **e.** 92%   **f.** 35%

13. Write each as a decimal.

    a. 13%   **b.** 37%   **c.** 41%   **d.** 58%   **e.** 79%   **f.** 85%

14. Select the correct answer in each of the following:

    a. 0.4×5.3 **b.** 3.6×1.42 **c.** 0.26×1.4 **d.** 0.082×0.41

       (i) 21.2   **(i)** 5.112   **(i)** 36.4   **(i)** 0.3362

       (ii) 2.12   **(ii)** 51.12   **(ii)** 0.364   **(ii)** 0.03362

15. Fifty percent of the dogsled team were huskies. Express that percent as a ratio in lowest terms.

16. About 80% of the timber cut in Alaska is made into wood pulp. What percent is not used for wood pulp?

17. A digital clock records the time at a given instant to be 3:24. A fourth-grade child says "the 2 has the same meaning as the 2 in the decimal 3.24." What could you say?

18. a. When we divide 25 by 4, we say the quotient is six and the remainder is 1. When the calculator is used to find $462 \div 23$ the calculator display reads 20.086957. What is the quotient and what is the remainder?

    b. Use a calculator with an integer division button to find $468 \div 27$. What is the quotient, and what is the remainder?

19. Write a fraction, a decimal, and a percent for the shaded part of the diagram.

    a.   **b.**   **c.**

Solution to Sample Problem

Suppose 100 liters of salt water are set out in the sun. The original solution was 99% water. After a period of time a sufficient amount of water has evaporated, so the brine solution is only 98% water. How much water must have evaporated?

1. *Understanding the problem.* When we speak of "salt water" we mean the salt has been dissolved in the water—no salt crystals remain in the bottom of the container. When evaporation takes place, only water leaves the solution, leaving all the salt in the remaining "brine."

2. *Devising a plan.* Some visual aid may be helpful to recognize the effects of evaporation. We could then attempt to identify some relationships in the problem that would be of help. For example, the amount of salt did not change as evaporation took place. This might result in an equation or in a proportion that would provide the desired information.

3. *Solution 1.* There must have been 1 liter of salt in the original solution, which will still be in the new solution. Then using the idea of per cent $\frac{2}{100} = \frac{1}{w}$, where w is the amount of water in the new solution. That is, 2% of the new solution is salt, so $\frac{2}{100}$ represents the ratio of salt to solution based on 100 parts. This must be the same as the ratio of salt (1 liter) to the actual number of liters of brine remaining in the new solution. It is clear that 50 liters of brine is in the new solution, so, 50 gal of water must have evaporated.

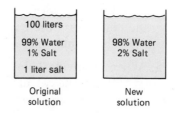

Original solution   New solution

Solution 2 Suppose we trace the water as it changes from the original condition to the new one.

Let x represent the number of liters of water to evaporate. Then $100 - x$ will represent the number of liters of water in the new solution. Therefore:

$$99 - x = 0.98\,(100 - x)$$
$$9900 - 100x = 98\,(100 - x)$$
$$9900 - 100x = 9800 - 98x$$
$$100 = 2x$$
$$50 = x$$

That is, 50 liters of water must be removed.

4. *Looking back.* Does the answer obtained seem reasonable? At first glance it would appear to be a surprisingly large number. To check the result, we could return to the problem. The final brine solution has all the salt remaining, namely, 1 liter. (Because 1% of 100 liters was salt.) The ratio of salt to brine in the final brine solution is $\frac{1}{50}$. This is to be 2% of the solution. Note that $\frac{1}{50} = \frac{2}{100}$ is a true statement, so our answer is correct.

7 | GEOMETRIC SHAPES

Sample Problem

Is there a pyramid that has exactly 55 edges?

7.1 INTRODUCTION AND BASIC IDEAS

There has been a significant amount of research related to how children develop understanding of geometric concepts. Levels of understanding of geometry have been classified by the van Hiele's as: Level 0—Visualization, Level 1—Analysis, Level 2—Informal Deduction, Level 3—Formal Deduction, and Level 4—Rigor. One such description of these levels is found in Table 7.1.

Various studies indicate that most students operate at or below the informal deduction level and need multiple experiences before they can progress to a higher level. We have been cognizant of this research as we prepared the activities for this book. In addition, the material presented here is consistent with the geometry to be included in the mathematics curriculum as envisioned by the NCTM Standards. The Standards suggest geometry experiences be developed so that children can describe, model, draw, and classify

TABLE 7.1

Visualization: Students can learn names of figures and recognize a shape as a whole by physical appearance but not by parts of properties. (Squares and rectangles seem to be different.)

Analysis: Students can identify properties and discern the characteristics of figures. (Rectangles have four right angles.)

Informal Deduction: Students can logically order figures and relationships, but do not operate within a mathematical system. (Deductive arguments can be followed, but proof is not understood.)

Formal Deduction: Students understand the role of postulates, theorems, and proofs and the significance of deduction. (Proofs can be written for meaning and understanding.)

Rigor: Students are able to make abstract deductions and can work in a variety of axiomatic systems. (Students can understand non-Euclidean geometry.)

shapes; develop spatial sense; relate geometric ideas to number and measurement ideas; investigate and predict results of combining, subdividing, and changing shapes; recognize and appreciate geometry as a means of describing the physical world; explore transformations of geometric figures; and understand and apply geometic properties and relationships. It is from these perspectives that we proceed.

At a very early age children encounter geometric shapes such as triangles, rectangles, squares, and circles and are exposed to point, line, line segment, ray, angle, plane, space, and many other geometric concepts and relationships. This exposure is frequently accomplished within the framework of an activity oriented program with emphasis on the use of physical models. At the primary level it may be done without formal use of any sort of measurement concepts; the children are identifying the concepts and discussing various characteristics of them (in their language) in terms of sets of points satisfying certain conditions.

Looking in a dictionary for the meaning of some word may result in what is commonly called *circular reasoning*. For example, do you know the meaning of the word *lacuna?* A dictionary gave the definition as a *hiatus.* Looking up *hiatus* we found it to be a *lacuna.* Thus, our search resulted in ending up where we started; not knowing the meaning of the word *lacuna.*

In any development of geometry, to avoid the problem of circular reasoning, certain basic concepts are used for which no definitions are given. These are frequently called *undefined terms.* It is important not to confuse "undefined" with "meaningless." The undefined terms may refer to meaningful concepts, but because of the circular reasoning pitfall must be accepted without any formal definition. We accept the concepts of *point, plane, line, and space* as undefined terms. Each reader must have an intuitive understanding of these concepts, and this may come from a variety of sources.

Probably the most basic of all geometric concepts is that of a *point.* It is true that a point is simply an idea; it has no dimensions; it cannot be seen or touched. However, the notion of a point has been formulated by observing physical models such as the end of a pencil, the tip of a pin, or the corner of a room. Representing points by dots ∴ and then naming dots with capital letters $\overset{B\cdot}{\underset{A}{}}\,\underset{C}{}$ provides an effective tool for communication purposes.

Flat surfaces such as a sheet of paper, a wall, a desk top, or a floor may be used to help formulate the mathematical concept of a *plane*. Keep in mind *Plane* that a plane, like a point, is simply an idea abstracted from physical models. It is also very important to realize that the physical models of planes mentioned here have bounds or edges; the plane itself does not. It might be helpful to think of an "infinite sheet of paper" or an "infinite wall." Planes are usually represented by drawings of portions of planes such as in Figure 7.1. Naming the planes with letters will then allow us to refer to planes p, q, and r, as in Figure 7.1.

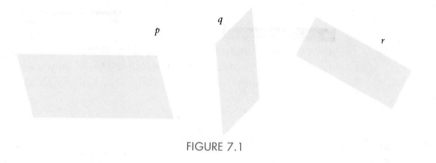

FIGURE 7.1

Space

Space is considered to be the set of all points. Frequently referred to as three-space, this concept is very real to us because the world we live in is three dimensional.

REMARK 1 An easy way to understand what is meant by three-dimensional is to consider an object like this textbook. It has the following *three* attributes, "length," "width," and "height."

REMARK 2 If it is difficult for you to imagine living in any world other than a three-dimensional one, you might enjoy reading the book *Flatland* by Edwin Abbott. In an interesting and humorous fashion he describes what it might be like in a one- or two-dimensional world.

REMARK 3 We also want to mention that the geometry that you will study here is called Euclidean geometry. You may be surprised to know that there are other geometries that can also be studied. A model for one of those geometries is called spherical. One way that this differs from

Euclidean can be seen by considering a "triangle" formed by two different points on an equator of the sphere and the third point of the triangle at the "north pole." This triangle has two right angles, a feat that cannot be obtained in Euclidean geometry. In all that follows, we will deal only with Euclidean notions of geometry.

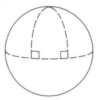

Consider the set of all points in the intersection of two planes, as illustrated in Figure 7.2. (Remember that such drawings indicate only portions of the planes; the planes are unbounded.) The set of points in the intersection of two such planes is called a *line*. Lines are frequently named by choosing two points of the set such as *A* and *B* in Figure 7.2 and then using the symbol $\overline{AB}$ or $\overline{BA}$. "Flatness" is a characteristic of planes and "straightness" is a property of lines. There are really no good physical models of lines in our

line

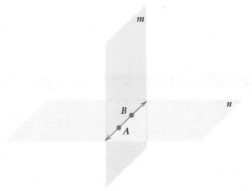

FIGURE 7.2

environment because lines extend without limit in both directions. However, it might be helpful to use models such as the edge of a ruler, a piece of string held tautly, or a pipe cleaner, always keeping in mind the concept of having no endpoints. Pictorial representation of lines should also emphasize this concept of no endpoints by using arrows, as in Figure 7.3.

FIGURE 7.3

Also associated with points on a number line is the notion of betweenness. In Figure 7.4, we would think that 2 is between 1 and 3 and also that there are some points between 1 and 2 even if they are not labeled. These notions are similar to the notions explored with regard to density in previous chapters.

FIGURE 7.4

Having accepted the concepts of point, line, plane, betweenness, and space as undefined terms, it is now possible to formulate a meaningful definition.

Definition 7.1 A *line segment* is the set of all points between two points on a line, including the two points.

Figure 7.5 shows a model of a line segment consisting of points A and B and all points of the line between them. The symbol for the line segment is $\overline{AB}$ (or $\overline{BA}$), and the points A and B are called the endpoints. Thus, it helps children to distinguish between the concepts of a line and a line segment in terms of endpoints: a line has no endpoints, and a line segment has two endpoints. Also, from a child's viewpoint, line segments are more "real" than lines because many physical models of line segments are a part of our real world.

FIGURE 7.5

Because sets of points are involved, it is natural to include set operations (union, intersection, etc.) in the discussions about geometry. For example, in Figure 7.6a suppose that we want to refer to the points indicated with the heavy shading. Using the concept of set union, this set of points could be expressed as $\overline{AB} \cup \overline{CD}$. It also follows from Figure 7.6a that $\overline{AB} \cap \overline{CD} = \phi$. Similarly, in Figure 7.6b, $\overline{BC} = \overline{AC} \cap \overline{BD}$, whereas in Figure 7.6c $\overline{AC} \cup \overline{BD} = \overline{AD}$.

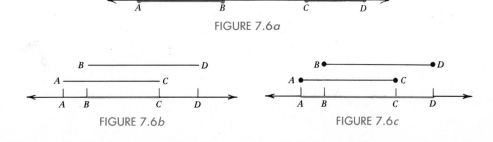

FIGURE 7.6a

FIGURE 7.6b   FIGURE 7.6c

EXAMPLE 1

Determine $\overleftrightarrow{AB} \cap \overline{CD}$

A   B   C   D

Solution $\overline{CD}$.

EXAMPLE 2

Determine $\overline{AC} \cap \overline{AD}$

A   B   C   D

Solution $\overline{AC}$

EXAMPLE 3

Determine $\overline{BA} \cap \overline{BC}$

A   B   C   D

Solution B

EXAMPLE 4

Determine $\overline{AC} \cap \overline{BD}$

A   B   C   D

Solution $\overline{BD}$ $\overline{BC}$

Geometry provides another excellent setting for the development of problem-solving techniques. The fact that most geometric concepts can be "pictured" is a real help for solving geometry problems. Perhaps now would be a good time for you to reread the introductory section of Chapter 1, especially Sections 1.2 and 1.3, where solving problems with the use of pictures is addressed.

EXAMPLE 1

How many line segments are there in Figure 7.7?

Solution To help "systematize" our counting process, let us label the points as shown in Figure 7.8. Now we can consider the points by their

FIGURE 7.7

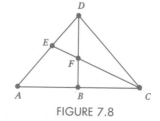

FIGURE 7.8

labels in alphabetical order as *ABCDEF*. Because it takes two points to determine a line segment, we systematically list all two-element subsets of the set {*A, B, C, D, E, F*} and then refer to the figure to see which subsets name line segments in the figure.

{*A, B*}	Yes	{*B, C*}	Yes	{*C, D*}	Yes
{*A, C*}	Yes	{*B, D*}	Yes	{*C, E*}	Yes
{*A, D*}	Yes	{*B, E*}	No	{*C, F*}	Yes
{*A, E*}	Yes	{*B, F*}	Yes		
{*A, F*}	No				
{*D, E*}	Yes	{*E, F*}	Yes		
{*D, F*}	Yes				

Counting the number of "Yes" responses indicates that there are 13 line segments in the figure.

EXAMPLE 2

How many *lines* are determined by three points?

Solution We need to consider two possibilities—namely, (1) the three points are *collinear* (points all on one line are said to be collinear), or (2) the three points are *noncollinear*. As illustrated in Figure 7.9, if the three points *A, B,* and *C* are collinear, then only *one* line is determined. However, if the three points are noncollinear (Fig. 7.10), then *three* distinct lines $\overline{AB}$, $\overline{AC}$, and $\overline{BC}$ are determined.

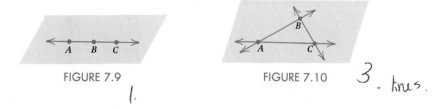

FIGURE 7.9   FIGURE 7.10

EXAMPLE 3

How many *line segments* are determined by three points?

Solution Looking at Figures 7.9 and 7.10, we see that three distinct points *A, B,* and *C* determine three line segments $\overline{AB}$, $\overline{BC}$, and $\overline{AC}$, regardless of the relative positions of the points.

REMARK 1 The statement that "three points determine three line segments" actually means that "three *different* (distinct) points determine three *different* (distinct) line segments." At times we will use the word "distinct" to reemphasize this idea. Regardless of whether or not the word *distinct* or *different* appears, the meaning is to be implied unless indicated otherwise.

REMARK 2 Examples 2 and 3 could be used to help children with their understanding of the concepts of line and line segment as well as for developing problem-solving skills. It is also important to be able to look at a whole figure and discern the important subparts. For example, in Figure 7.10, although there is more to be seen, you should be able to "see" a triangle as well as the three lines.

We have included several "counting-type" problems throughout the problem sets of this chapter. Do not restrict yourself to the use of only the techniques presented in our examples. Use your own counting techniques, *but* be sure to organize your thoughts and be able to explain your procedure to someone else. Many times it is also advisable to do a problem in more than one way for checking purposes.

PROBLEM SET 7.1

1. Give three examples (not the ones given in the text) of physical models that can be used to illustrate each of the following concepts:
   a. Point
   b. Plane
   c. Line segment

2. Given the line with points A, B, C, and D, identify each of the following:

   a. $\overline{AB} \cup \overline{BC}$ b. $\overline{AB} \cap \overline{BC}$
   c. $\overline{BC} \cap \overline{CD}$ d. $\overline{BC} \cup \overline{CD}$
   e. $\overleftrightarrow{BC} \cap \overline{BC}$ f. $\overleftrightarrow{AC} \cap \overline{CD}$ $\overline{CD}$
   g. $\overline{AB} \cup \overrightarrow{BC}$ $\overrightarrow{AB}$ h. $\overleftrightarrow{BC} \cup \overline{AC}$ $\overline{BC}$
   i. $\overline{AB} \cap \overline{CD}$

3. Sketch figures to illustrate that the intersection of a line and a line segment might be:
   a. The empty set
   b. The line segment
   c. A point

4. Name all the line segments in the accompanying figure.

A   B   C   D   E   F

5. Name all the line segments in each of the following figures.

a.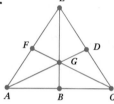

b.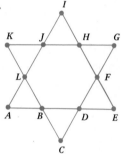

c.

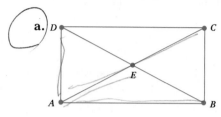

d.

6. Given that no three points lie on the same segment, complete the following table. What is the relationship between the number of points and the number of line segments determined by those points?

Number of Points	Number of Segments
2	1
3	3
4	6
5	9
6	12
7	15
.	
.	
100	
.	
.	
n	

7. a. How many *lines* are determined by four points in a plane located as follows?

(i) $\overset{.}{A}$ $\overset{.}{B}$ $\overset{.}{C}$ $\overset{.}{D}$ **(ii)** A B C D **(iii)**

    b. Could you locate four points in a plane such that the number of lines determined would be something other than one, four, or six?

    c. Would it make any difference if the points were not all in the same plane?

8. Analyze all the possibilities for the number of *lines* determined by five points.

Pedagogical Problems and Activities

9. Describe some activities that could be used with primary-age children to help them understand each of the following:

    a. The concept of "straightness" of a line or line segment

    b. The concept of "flatness" of a plane

    c. The notion that a line has no endpoints

    d. The notion that a line segment has two endpoints

    e. The concept of collinear points

10. Which of the capital letters of the alphabet are frequently made using only line segments?

11. Write numerals for the counting numbers from one to ten, inclusive, using only line segments.

7.2   LINES AND PLANES

In the previous section we focused on the basic concepts of point, line, line segment, plane, and space. It was observed that our environment contains numerous physical models that can be used to help formulate these concepts. For example, something as simple as an ordinary shed, pictured in Figure 7.11, can be used to illustrate such concepts as parallel lines, intersecting lines, skew lines, parallel planes, and intersecting planes. As we discuss these concepts, it might be helpful for you to refer back to Figure 7.11 to identify examples of each concept.

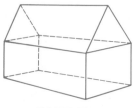

FIGURE 7.11

There are three ways that two lines may be situated in space:

1. They may intersect in a point (Fig. 7.12a). In this case the lines are *copla-nar;* that is, they lie in the same plane.

2. The two lines may lie in the same plane and not intersect. In this case the two lines are called *parallel lines* (Fig. 7.12b). (The symbol ‖ is the conventional one used for parallel. Thus, if two lines $\overleftrightarrow{AB}$ and $\overleftrightarrow{CD}$ are parallel, we write $\overleftrightarrow{AB} \parallel \overleftrightarrow{CD}$). Mathematically we say that two parallel lines determine a plane.   *parallel lines.*

3. The two lines may not intersect because they are in different planes and are then called *skew lines* (Fig. 7.12c).   *skew lines*

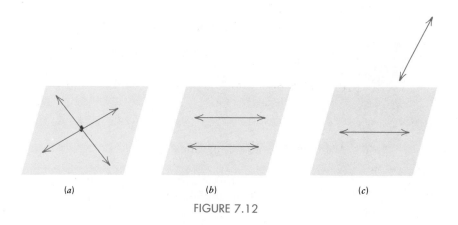

(a)   (b)   (c)

FIGURE 7.12

Although we can identify parallel lines, planes, etc. in the shed, it is easier to communicate ideas about points, lines, and planes if we label our figures. Figure 7.13 is the same figure as Figure 7.11 with the vertices labeled.

In the examples that follow, refer back to Figure 7.13.

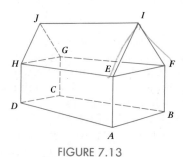

FIGURE 7.13

EXAMPLE 1

Identify two lines that are parallel.

Solution Although several answers are correct, $\overleftrightarrow{AE}$ and $\overleftrightarrow{DH}$, $\overleftrightarrow{IJ}$ and $\overleftrightarrow{EH}$, and $\overleftrightarrow{GF}$ and $\overleftrightarrow{AD}$ are three such pairs.

EXAMPLE 2

Identify two lines that are skew.

Solution $\overleftrightarrow{AB}$ and $\overleftrightarrow{DH}$, $\overleftrightarrow{HJ}$ and $\overleftrightarrow{AE}$, and $\overleftrightarrow{FG}$ and $\overleftrightarrow{DC}$ are three such pairs.

EXAMPLE 3

Identify two lines that intersect in one point.

Solution $\overleftrightarrow{EI}$ and $\overleftrightarrow{FE}$, $\overleftrightarrow{BF}$ and $\overleftrightarrow{IF}$, and $\overleftrightarrow{BC}$ and $\overleftrightarrow{DC}$ are three such pairs.

EXAMPLE 4

Are lines $\overleftrightarrow{AB}$ and $\overleftrightarrow{CG}$ parallel?

Solution No. Although these two lines do not intersect, they do not lie in the same plane and, hence, are not parallel.

REMARK This discussion has been in terms of lines; however, these same ideas can be extended to line segments by thinking in terms of the lines that contain the segments. In other words, *two line segments are parallel* if and only if the lines containing the segments are parallel. Similarly, *two line segments are skew* if and only if the lines containing the segments are skew lines. Thus, using a model such as in Figure 7.13 you might naturally think of line-segment relationships, but then the line segments could be used to think about analogous line relationships.

We may wonder what are the possible relationships of two distinct planes in space. Figure 7.14 gives two different such relationships. What can you observe by examining these drawings?

From Figure 7.14 we may conclude that these are the only two such relationships between two planes, that is, either two planes intersect or they do not intersect. If they intersect, the intersection is a line. In a previous section we tried to help you formulate the concept of a line in terms of intersection of two planes. If the two planes do not intersect, they are called *parallel*

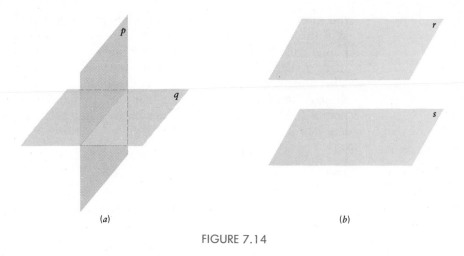

FIGURE 7.14

planes. Note that for two planes we do not have a relationship analogous to skew lines.

Having examined the relationship of two planes, we may wonder what are the possible relationships of a line and a plane in space. Figure 7.15 gives several such relationships. Can you think of any others? What can you observe from these relationships?

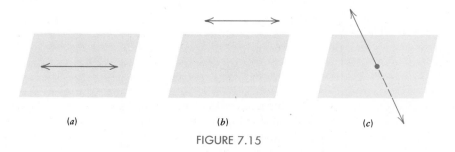

FIGURE 7.15

We see that there are basically three ways that a plane and a line can be situated in space.

1. The plane may contain the line, as illustrated in Figure 7.15*a*.
2. The line and the plane may not intersect, in which case they are said to be *parallel.* This is illustrated in Figure 7.15*b*.
3. The line and the plane may intersect in exactly one point, as pictured in Figure 7.15*c*.

It was previously stated that two parallel lines "determine" a plane. This means that there is one and only one plane that contains the two lines. Furthermore, we concluded that two intersecting lines will determine a plane. Will three points determine exactly one plane? Do you see that the three points must be noncollinear in order that one plane is determined? Because three noncollinear points determine a plane, it is sometimes convenient to label a plane accordingly. For example, in Figure 7.16, the plane containing the bottom of the box could be identified by naming any three of the four points *A*, *B*, *H*, and *G*. In that fashion we could refer to parallel planes *ABH* and *DEF*.

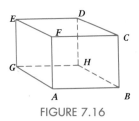

FIGURE 7.16

In the next problem set we provide the opportunity to use physical models and sketches to extend some of the ideas pertaining to lines and planes. Try to think of physical models that are different from the ones we mention. There are many different ways in which some of these ideas can be pictured. Try different sketches and see which ones seem best to convey the idea under consideration.

PROBLEM SET 7.2

1. Give two examples of physical models that can be used to illustrate each of the following:
   a. Two intersecting lines
   b. Two parallel lines
   c. Two skew lines
   d. Two intersecting planes
   e. Two parallel planes
   f. A line intersecting a plane
   g. A line parallel to a plane

2. Think of the lines and planes suggested by the accompanying figure. In order to answer the following, name the lines by two points and the planes by three points:

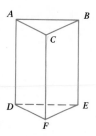

    a. Name a pair of parallel lines.

    b. Name two planes that are parallel.

    c. Name two intersecting lines.

    d. Name two intersecting planes.

    e. Name two skew lines.

    f. Name three planes that intersect in exactly one point, and name the point of intersection.

    g. Name a line and a plane whose intersection is the empty set.

    h. Name a plane and a line whose intersection is the line.

    i. Name a plane and a line whose intersection is exactly one point.

3. Draw a sketch to illustrate each of the following:

    a. Two parallel planes

    b. Two intersecting planes

    c. A line parallel to a plane

    d. A line intersecting a plane in exactly one point

    e. A line contained in a plane

4. If l_1, l_2, and l_3 are three distinct lines in a plane such that $l_1 \| l_2$ and $l_2 \| l_3$, then does it follow that $l_1 \| l_3$? Defend your answer.

5. Suppose that l_1, l_2, and l_3 are three distinct lines in space such that $l_1 \| l_2$ and $l_2 \| l_3$. Answer the following questions:

    a. Are l_1 and l_2 in the same plane? Why?

    b. Are l_2 and l_3 in the same plane? Why?

    c. Must l_1, l_2, and l_3 be in the same plane? Illustrate your answer with a physical model.

    d. Is $l_1 \| l_3$? Sketch a figure to illustrate your answer.

6. If l_1, l_2, and l_3 are three distinct lines in a plane, then these lines may be related to each other in several ways. For example, they may all intersect in exactly one point, as the accompanying figure illustrates. What are the other possibilities? Sketch a figure for each one.

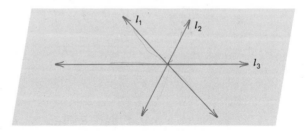

7. If p, q, and r are three distinct planes such that $p\|q$ and $q\|r$, then does it follow that $p\|r$? Illustrate your answer with a sketch. Also illustrate your answer with a physical model.

8. If p, q, and r are three distinct planes, then these planes may be related to each other in several ways. For example, the three planes may all intersect in one line as illustrated in the accompanying figure. What are the other possibilities? Sketch a figure and give a physical model for each possibility.

9. Do a line and a point determine a plane regardless of where the point is located relative to the line? Draw sketches to illustrate your answer.

10. Why is it that chairs having four legs sometimes "rock," whereas three-legged stools never do?

Pedagogical Problems and Activities

11. A child claims $\overline{AB}$ and $\overline{CD}$ below are parallel because they both lie in the same plane and do not intersect. What do you say?

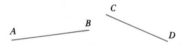

12. Some teachers use various paper-folding activities to help children visualize concepts dealing with points, lines, and planes. For example, try these experiments for yourself.

a. Fold a piece of stiff paper in half. Now let it open up enough so that it will stand on a table with the crease not on the table, but parallel to the table. Do the folded paper and the table top suggest three planes? What is the intersection of all three planes?

b. Now stand the paper on the table so that the crease "intersects" the plane of the table. Are three planes suggested? What is the intersection of all three planes?

c. Now hold the paper so that only the crease is on the table. Are three planes suggested? What is the intersection of the three planes?

13. It is often difficult to visualize how to draw a diagram in a three-dimensional manner. To practice drawing three-dimensional figures, trace each of the following. In tracing, use dashed lines for portions of the figure that cannot be seen and solid lines for portions that can be seen. Because different perspectives are possible, you should try to trace each figure in two different ways, if possible.

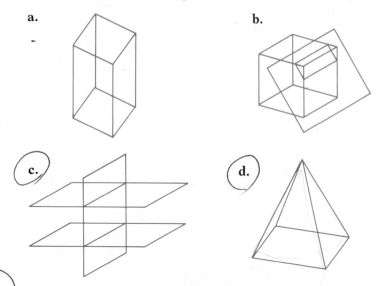

a.   **b.**

c.   **d.**

14. a. The drawing below is made on dot paper. Dot paper is useful to practice sketches from different perspectives. Use the same seven dots to give a different perspective on the cube.

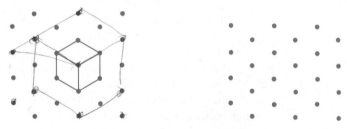

b. Below is the same block drawn from different perspectives.

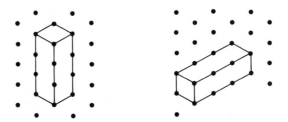

Here is one view of a T. Draw two other views.

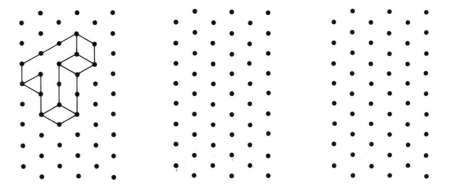

15. a. A child suggests that two planes that do not intersect are parallel. Furthermore, because lines lie in planes, two lines that do not intersect must also be called parallel. What do you say?

b. A child suggest that two planes that do not intersect are parallel. Furthermore, because lines lie in planes, any line in one of two parallel planes will be parallel to any line in the other plane. What do you say?

7.3   SEPARATION, RAYS, AND ANGLES

Consider a line l in a plane m as in Figure 7.17. It seems that any path in plane m joining point A, which is "above" the line, to point B, "below" the line, must intersect the line l.

We express this fact by stating that *a line separates a plane into two half-planes.* In such a case, three disjoint subsets of the plane are formed: the line and two half-planes, as illustrated in Figure 7.18. Note that the line does not belong to either half-plane and is sometimes referred to as the *separation set.* To get from one part of the separated set to the other part of the separated set, one must intersect the separation set. The concept of separation provides another setting to help distinguish between the concept of a line extending indefinitely as opposed to a line segment having two endpoints. Because a

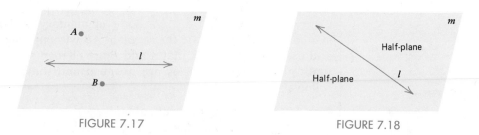

FIGURE 7.17   FIGURE 7.18

line segment "stops," it cannot separate a plane. As illustrated in Figure 7.19, the line segment does not separate the plane, for a path can be found that will join the points A and B and not intersect the segment.

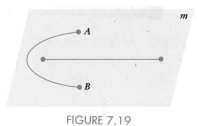

FIGURE 7.19

Figure 7.20 illustrates the concept of a plane separating space into two half spaces, one above the plane and one below the plane. To get from point B above the plane to point A below the plane, one must pass through the plane.

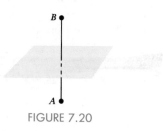

FIGURE 7.20

Consider a line $\overleftrightarrow{AB}$ and a point P between A and B as in Figure 7.21. We say that A and B are on "opposite sides" of P, or, P separates the line into two half-lines. The symbol $\overrightarrow{PB}$ represents the half-line on the B side of P, and $\overset{\circ}{PA}$ represents the half-line on the A side of P.

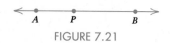

FIGURE 7.21

REMARK 1 Note that $A \notin \overset{\circ}{\overrightarrow{AB}}$. Some elementary textbook series use the symbolism $\overset{\circ\;\;\circ}{AB}$ to indicate the segment AB without the endpoints A and B and use $\overset{\bullet\;\;\bullet}{AB}$ to reinforce that A and B are elements of segment AB. Eventually the darkened circles are dropped and the notation we use, $\overline{AB}$, follows.

REMARK 2 Although we talk about sets that separate, we can also talk about sets that do not separate. For example, although a point may separate a segment, it will never separate a plane. Similarly, a line may separate a plane, but it will never separate space. When we talk about separation, we must keep in mind the set and what we want to consider it to separate.

The concepts of half-line and separation point can now be used to define a ray. A *ray* is the union of a half-line and the point of separation. Thus, a separation point determines two rays of a line. In Figure 7.22 $\overset{\circ}{\overrightarrow{PA}} \cup \{P\}$ is the ray called $\overrightarrow{PA}$, and $\overset{\circ}{\overrightarrow{PB}} \cup \{P\} = \overrightarrow{PB}$.

FIGURE 7.22

Intuitive notions of a ray include thinking of a ray in terms of some point on a line and all the points of the line in "one direction from that point including the point," or "a ray is a set of points in a straight path that goes on without end in one direction."

It is now possible to offer a precise definition of the concept of an angle using the definition of a ray.

Definition 7.2 Given three noncollinear points A, B, and C, the set $\overrightarrow{BC} \cup \overrightarrow{BA}$ is called a *plane angle* (Fig. 7.23a).

ray. (handwritten margin note)

plane angle (handwritten margin note)

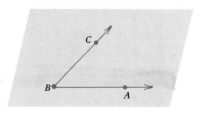

(a)

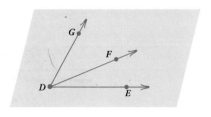

(b)

FIGURE 7.23

> **REMARK** Definition 7.2 has required that the three points be noncollinear, or, in other words, it has excluded the possibility that the two rays form a line. Elementary school textbooks frequently use this same restriction when first discussing angles as sets of points. It avoids confusion when referring to the interior and exterior of an angle. The restriction is omitted later when the measurement concept is introduced, which then allows for a "straight angle."

The common endpoint of the two rays is called the *vertex* of the angle, and the rays are referred to as the *sides* of the angle. If there is no chance for confusion, as in Figure 7.23a we may refer to the angle by its vertex only, thus using the symbol ∠B. Figure 7.23b is an example of a situation where we should *not* use a single letter to name an angle. That is, ∠GDE, ∠GDF, and ∠FDE all have the same vertex, and to name any one as simply ∠D would not indicate which angle is being named.

Referring back to Definition 7.2, you will note that the phrase "plane angle" is used. If only two noncollinear rays are being considered, then there is simply one plane involved—the plane determined by the two rays, as in Figure 7.23a. However, if three or more rays are being considered, then there may be more than one plane involved. In Figure 7.23b we indicated in the drawing that the three rays were *coplanar*, but in Figure 7.24 three different planes are involved.

An angle also serves as a separation set for a plane. As indicated in Figure 7.25, ∠B separates the plane into two subsets called the *interior* (the shaded part) and the *exterior* (the unshaded part). Formally, the concepts of interior and exterior of an angle can be defined as follows.

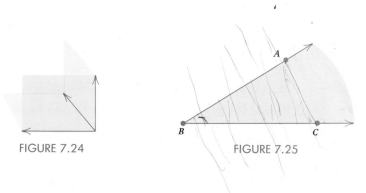

FIGURE 7.24

FIGURE 7.25

Definition 7.3 Given ∠ABC, the *interior* of the angle is the intersection of the half-plane on the A side of $\overleftrightarrow{BC}$ with the half-plane on the C side of $\overleftrightarrow{AB}$. All points in the plane not contained in the interior or in the angle itself are *exterior* points.

interior
exterior

> REMARK You should draw a few different angles and apply Definition 7.3 to determine the interior and exterior of each angle.

EXAMPLE 1

List the angles for which point P lies in the interior.

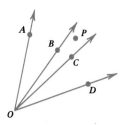

Solution ∠AOC, ∠AOD, ∠BOC, and ∠BOD.

EXAMPLE 2

List 2 angles for which point P lies in the exterior.

Solution ∠AOB and ∠COD.

In Figure 7.26 ∠AOB and ∠COD are such that the rays $\overrightarrow{OB}$ and $\overrightarrow{OC}$ form a line, as do rays $\overrightarrow{OD}$ and $\overrightarrow{OA}$. We say that ∠AOB and ∠COD are *vertical angles*, as are ∠AOC and ∠BOD. In general, two intersecting lines form two pairs of vertical angles.

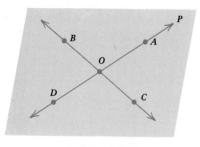

FIGURE 7.26

EXAMPLE

Name five pairs of vertical angles.

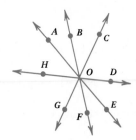

Solution Some pairs are ∠*AOB* and ∠*EOF*, ∠*HOG* and ∠*DOC*, ∠*GOA* and ∠*COE*, and ∠*BOC* and ∠*FOG*.

In Figure 7.27, ∠*AOB* and ∠*BOC* are called *adjacent angles*. Two angles are said to be adjacent if (1) they are coplanar, (2) they have the same vertex, (3) they have a common side, and (4) the intersection of their interiors is empty. In Figure 7.27, ∠*AOB* and ∠*AOC* are not adjacent. Why is this true?

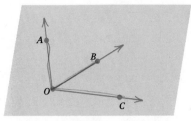

FIGURE 7.27

EXAMPLE 1

Are ∠*AOB* and ∠*AOD* adjacent?

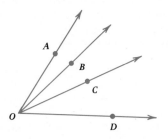

Solution No. Although they have a common vertex, common side, and lie in the same plane, the intersection of their interiors is not empty.

EXAMPLE 2

Are ∠AOB and ∠COD adjacent?

Solution No. Although the two angles lie in the same plane, have a common vertex, and the intersection of their interiors is empty, they do not have a common side.

The concept of a plane angle can be extended to an analogous situation in three-space. Start with a line $\overleftrightarrow{AB}$ and select two half-planes, whose union is not a plane, that have $\overleftrightarrow{AB}$ as a common edge. The set of points that is the union of the two half-planes and the given line is called a *dihedral angle*. In Figure 7.28, $\overleftrightarrow{AB}$ is the common edge, and C and D are points in the two half-planes. The concepts of vertical angles and adjacent angles may be extended to analogous three-space dihedral angle situations. For example, two intersecting planes will form two pairs of vertical dihedral angles.

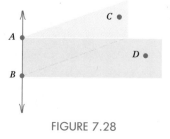

FIGURE 7.28

REMARK The word dihedral means "two faces." Most likely you are now in a room where a side wall and either the floor or the ceiling provide an example of a dihedral angle. Can you identify other examples? Open your book to this page but do not let both covers of the book lie "flat." This is another example of a dihedral angle.

PROBLEM SET 7.3

1. Given the line with points A, B, C, and D on it. Identify each of the following:

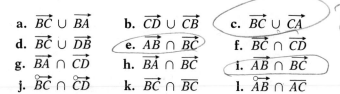

a. $\overrightarrow{BC} \cup \overrightarrow{BA}$ **b.** $\overrightarrow{CD} \cup \overrightarrow{CB}$ **c.** $\overrightarrow{BC} \cup \overrightarrow{CA}$

d. $\overrightarrow{BC} \cup \overrightarrow{DB}$ **e.** $\overleftrightarrow{AB} \cap \overrightarrow{BC}$ **f.** $\overrightarrow{BC} \cap \overrightarrow{CD}$

g. $\overrightarrow{BA} \cap \overrightarrow{CD}$ **h.** $\overrightarrow{BA} \cap \overrightarrow{BC}$ **i.** $\overleftrightarrow{AB} \cap \overrightarrow{BC}$

j. $\overleftrightarrow{BC} \cap \overleftrightarrow{CD}$ **k.** $\overrightarrow{BC} \cap \overline{BC}$ **l.** $\overleftrightarrow{AB} \cap \overline{AC}$

2. Give three examples of physical models that can be used to illustrate each of the following:

   a. Ray

   b. Plane angle

   c. Dihedral angle

3. Use the figure to answer the following:

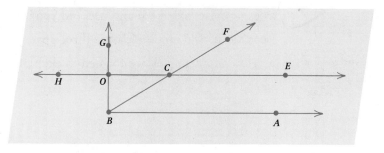

   a. Name two pairs of vertical plane angles.

   b. Name two pairs of adjacent plane angles.

   c. Why are angles *FCE* and *FBA* not adjacent?

   d. Why are angles *GBC* and *GBA* not adjacent?

4. Make sketches to illustrate two plane angles whose intersection is

   a. Empty   **b.** A point

   c. Two points   **d.** A line segment

   e. A ray   **f.** Four points

   g. Three points

5. Name all pairs of adjacent plane angles in the accompanying figure.

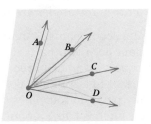

6. Give an example of a physical model to illustrate each of the following:
   a. Vertical dihedral angles
   b. Adjacent dihedral angles
   c. A line and a dihedral angle whose intersection is empty
   d. A line and a dihedral angle whose intersection is two points

7. Make a sketch to illustrate each of the following:
   a. A pair of vertical dihedral angles
   b. A pair of adjacent dihedral angles
   c. A line and a dihedral angle whose intersection is empty
   d. A line and a dihedral angle whose intersection is two points

8. Does a half-line separate a plane? Defend your answer.

9. Does a ray separate a plane? Defend your answer.

10. Does a dihedral angle separate three-space? Explain your answer.

11. a. How many angles are formed in each of the following figures?

   (i)   (ii)

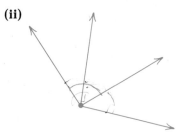

   (iii)   (iv)

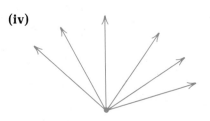

   b. From your work in part **a**, look for a pattern and then use it to find
      how many angles are formed by 10 rays having a common endpoint.

12. In the accompanying figures we demonstrate that (1) one line separates
    a plane into two parts, (2) two intersecting lines separate a plane into
    four parts, and (3) three lines, no two of which are parallel and do not
    intersect in a common point, separate a plane into seven parts. Into how
    many parts do four lines (assume no two lines are parallel and no three
    lines intersect in a common point) separate a plane? How about five

lines? Six lines? *n* lines? Recording your results in a chart such as the following would be helpful.

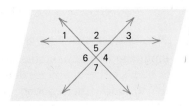

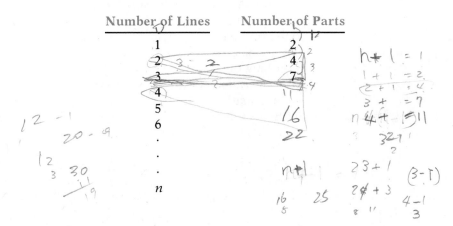

Number of Lines	Number of Parts
1	2
2	4
3	7
4	11
5	16
6	22
.	.
.	.
.	.
n	

Pedagogical Problems and Activities

13. Describe some activities that could be used with children to aid in their understanding of each of the following.

a. A dihedral angle

b. Vertical dihedral angles

c. Adjacent dihedral angles

d. Vertical plane angles

e. Adjacent plane angles

f. A line separating a plane

g. A point separating a line

h. A plane separating three-space

14. Given ∠*AOB* and point *P*, a child claims that point *P* is not in the interior of ∠*AOB*. Can you see why such a claim may be made? What do you say?

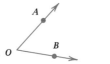

7.4 PLANE CURVES

The language of mathematics contains many technical words for which a reader needs either a precise definition or at least an intuitive understanding in order to follow the sequence of ideas being presented. Consider the question, "How many diagonals can be drawn in a convex dodecagon?" The concepts of diagonal, convex, and dodecagon need to be understood before the problem takes on any meaning. Likewise, some mathematical words have "different" meanings that can only be obtained from the context in which they are placed. For example, consider the word "base." We may use it when describing the "base of a triangle," the "base of a pyramid," or the "base for our numeration system." It is important to know that many understandings of mathematics content rely on context, just as does proper understanding of the English language. In our language, the word "read" has two different pronounciations, whereas the words "read" and "red" may be pronounced the same.

Which of the curves in Figure 7.29 would you describe as being a simple curve? It would not be surprising if you chose Figure 7.29*b* as the simple curve; however, Figure 7.29*a* fits the mathematical definition of a simple

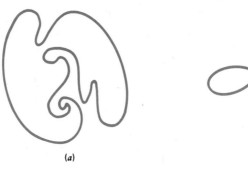

FIGURE 7.29

curve, and Figure 7.29*b* does not. Thus, vocabulary of both the technical nature as well as the mathematical use of common words is a vital part of the study of mathematics.

Let us pursue the concept of a *plane curve.* Suppose you were to take a sheet of paper and draw on it without lifting your pencil and without retracing (except for single points), as illustrated in Figure 7.30. The set of points pictured by the mark on the paper is called a *plane curve.* The fact that there are no breaks in the curve is one important condition, and the restriction that all of the points lie in one plane is a second condition. We could remove the one-plane restriction and discuss space curves, but for now let us keep the restriction and confine our work to plane curves. The condition that the curve does not have any "breaks" is another way of stating that the curve must be connected, that is, the curve may be drawn as a continuous line.

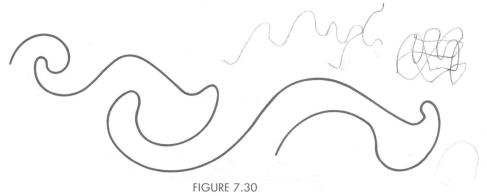

FIGURE 7.30

Figure 7.31 pictures a variety of plane curves. Although in each example the set is continuous, there are some obvious differences between the curves. For example, in (*c*), (*e*), (*f*), (*h*), and (*i*) the curve could be traced by starting and ending at the same point. Such curves are called *closed curves.* Thus, we say that the curves in (*a*), (*b*), (*d*), and (*g*) are not closed. Notice that the closed curves in (*c*) and (*h*) do not intersect themselves, whereas the closed curves in (*e*), (*f*), and (*i*) do intersect themselves. We say that a curve is *simple* if and only if it does not intersect itself. Thus, the curves in (*a*), (*b*), and (*d*) are simple, but not closed, plane curves. The curve illustrated in (*g*) is neither simple nor closed.

The *simple closed plane curve* is of prime importance to our work as well as to a large amount of work with geometry in elementary school programs. Consider the simple closed plane curves illustrated in Figure 7.32. Notice that in each case there is a set of points that we would say is in the interior of the simple closed curve and another set of points in the exterior. In general, every simple closed plane curve *separates* the plane into three mutually disjoint sets: the interior, the exterior, and the curve itself. That is, if two points are chosen, one in the exterior and one in the interior of a simple closed plane

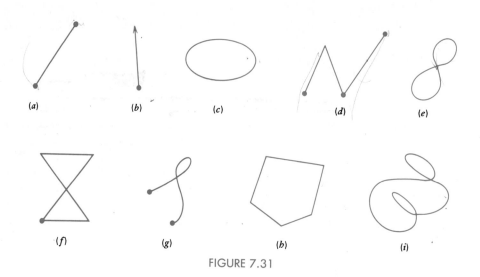

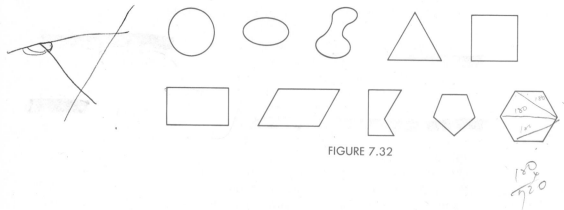

FIGURE 7.31

curve, then any path joining the two points must intersect the separation set (the curve) at least once.

Deciding whether a point is in the interior or the exterior of simple closed curves such as those pictured in Figure 7.32 is fairly easy. However, the issue of interior versus exterior is not always so apparent. Consider point X in Figure 7.33. Do you think point X is in the interior or the exterior? How did you decide? We will investigate more problems of this type in the next set of exercises.

FIGURE 7.32

One very common type of plane curve is composed of line segments. Figure 7.34 illustrates some such curves. We see that 7.34c–7.34f are closed plane curves, and that 7.34d–7.34f are simple closed plane curves. We call any plane curve that is the union of line segments end to end in sequence a *polygonal curve*, and thus a *polygon* is a simple closed polygonal curve.

The number of line segments associated with a given polygon is often of

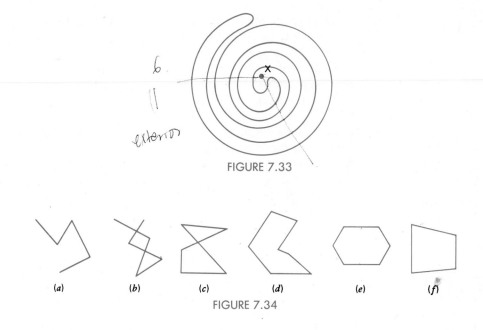

FIGURE 7.33

(a)   (b)   (c)   (d)   (e)   (f)

FIGURE 7.34

considerable interest. Polygons are classified by the number of segments involved. The following names are commonly used:

3 segments	triangle
4 segments	quadrilateral
5 segments	pentagon
6 segments	hexagon
7 segments	heptagon
8 segments	octagon
9 segments	nonagon
10 segments	decagon
12 segments	dodecagon

EXAMPLE

Name the polygons below.

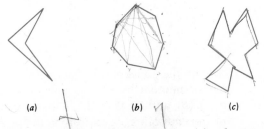

(a)   (b)   (c)

Solution (a) Quadrilateral (b) Heptagon (c) Eleven-gon

When speaking of a polygon, it is common to refer to the line segments as *sides* and the endpoints of the line segments as *vertices*. Thus, a heptagon is a seven-sided polygon and has seven vertices. This allows us to generalize and speak of an *n*-sided polygon. The terminology of *consecutive* (or adjacent) *sides* is used to refer to two sides with a common vertex. Likewise, *consecutive vertices* are any two vertices that are endpoints for a common side.

Sometimes we are concerned with line segments associated with polygons other than the sides. For example, in Figure 7.35 consider the line segment determined by points *A* and *C*. Any line segment connecting nonconsecutive vertices of a polygon is called a *diagonal*. Although only one diagonal has been drawn, the pentagon in Figure 7.35 has five diagonals.

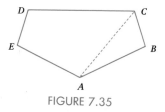

FIGURE 7.35

EXAMPLE

In Figure 7.35

a. Name 2 consecutive vertices.
b. Name 2 nonconsecutive vertices.
c. Name 2 consecutive sides.
d. Is $\overline{AD}$ a diagonal?
e. Is $\overline{EA}$ is diagonal?

Solution

a. *A* and *B*, *A* and *E*, *D* and *C*, *C* and *B*, and *E* and *D*.
b. *A* and *D*, *A* and *C*, *B* and *D*, *B* and *E*, etc.
c. $\overline{AB}$ and $\overline{BC}$, $\overline{AB}$ and $\overline{EA}$, $\overline{EA}$ and $\overline{ED}$, etc.
d. Yes. Refer to **b** above where *A* and *D* are not consecutive vertices.
e. No.

Using the concept of "diagonal," another useful classification of polygons may be made. Observe the polygons represented in Figure 7.36. Notice that in (*a*), (*b*), and (*d*) if we were to draw in all the diagonals, they would, except for the endpoints, lie entirely in the interior of the polygon. However, in both

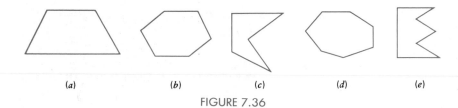

(a) (b) (c) (d) (e)

FIGURE 7.36

(c) and (e) at least one diagonal except for its endpoints would be in the exterior. Any polygon having no diagonals in the exterior is called a *convex polygon*. (A triangle does not have any diagonals and is considered a convex polygons.) Thus (a), (b), and (d) of Figure 7.36 are convex polygons. Polygons that are not convex [(c) and (e) in Fig. 7.36] are called *concave polygons*. Convex polygons usually receive most of the attention in geometry at the elementary and secondary school level.

PROBLEM SET 7.4

1. For each of the following, provide a physical world model:
   a. Plane curve
   b. Convex quadrilateral
   c. Convex octagon
   d. Concave polygon

2. Draw a sketch to represent each of the following:
   a. A simple closed plane curve
   b. A simple plane curve that is not closed
   c. A closed plane curve that is not simple
   d. A convex decagon
   e. A concave octagon
   f. A closed polygonal curve that is not simple

3. (i) (ii) (iii) (iv) (v) (vi)

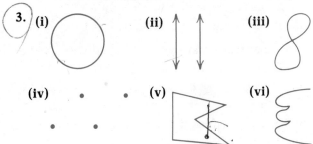

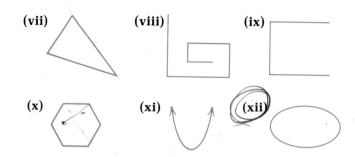

(vii)   **(viii)**   **(ix)**

(x)   **(xi)**   **(xii)**

    a. Which of the figures represent plane curves?

    b. Which represent closed plane curves?

    c. Which represent simple closed plane curves?

    d. Which represent polygonal curves?

    e. Which represent closed polygonal curves?

    f. Which represent polygons?

    g. Which represent convex polygons?

    h. Which represent concave polygons?

4. Which of the elements of the set of capital letters from our alphabet, {A, B, C, . . . , Z}, are simple closed plane curves?

5. **a.** We used half-planes to define interior of an angle. Use the idea of interior of an angle to define interior of a triangle.

    b. Expand this idea to define the interior of any convex polygon.

6. Name one state of the United States whose boundary does not represent a simple closed plane curve.

7. Draw two simple closed plane curves so that their intersection is:

    a. One point   **b.** Two points

    c. Three points   **d.** Four points

8. Draw a line and a simple closed plane curve so that their intersection is three points.

9. Draw two convex polygons whose intersection is

    a. A line segment   **b.** One point   **c.** Two points

    d. Three points   **e.** Four points

10. How many diagonals are associated with each of the following?

    a. Triangle   **b.** Quadrilateral

    c. Pentagon   **d.** Hexagon

    e. Heptagon   **f.** n-gon (n-sided polygon)

    g. Dodecagon (use the formula you found for part **f**)

11. In the polygon below;
    a. Name a diagonal that except for its endpoint lies completely outside the polygon.
    b. Name a diagonal that lies partially inside and partially outside the polygon.

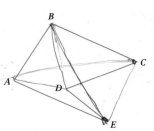

12. Name all the triangles in each of the following figures:

a.

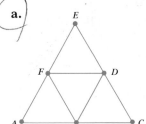

b.

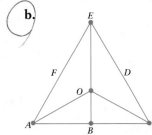

c.

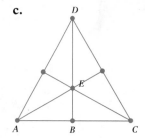

13. For each of the following simple closed plane curves, determine whether point x is in the interior or the exterior of the curve.

a.

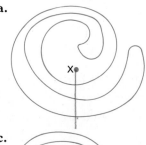

b.

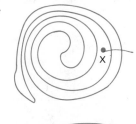

c.

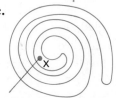

d.

14. a. Explain why the following statement is true: If point X is in the interior of a simple closed plane curve and point Y is in the exterior, then

the line segment determined by X and Y will intersect the curve an *odd* number of times.

b. Use the idea from part **a** to check your results in Problem 13.

15. In each of the accompanying figures, determine whether or not it is possible to draw paths from 1 to I, from 2 to II, and from 3 to III so that the paths do not intersect each other nor do they intersect any of the line segments joining the numerals. Use a diagram to verify your answers.

Pedagogical Problems and Activities

16. Venn-diagram activities are helpful for reinforcing the concepts of polygon, interior, and exterior. Consider the following Venn diagram and answer the questions that follow:

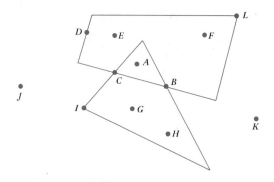

a. Which points labeled are in the interior of the triangle?

b. Which points labeled are in the interior of the qudrilateral?

c. Which points labeled are points of the triangle?

d. Which points labeled are points of the quadrilateral?

e. Which points labeled are in the exterior of the triangle?

f. Which points labeled are in the exterior of the quadrilateral?

g. Which points labeled are points of the quadrilateral and of the triangle?

h. Which points labeled are in the intersection of the interior of the quadrilateral and the interior of the triangle?

i. Which points labeled are in the union of the interior of the quadrilateral and the interior of the triangle?

j. Which points labeled are inside the triangle and outside the quadrilateral?

k. Which points labeled are outside the triangle and inside the quadrilateral?

l. Which points labeled are outside the triangle or outside the quadrilateral?

m. Which points labeled are outside the triangle and outside the quadrilateral?

17. Describe some activities that could be used to help children understand the concepts of polygon, interior of a polygon, and exterior of a polygon.

18. A geoboard is often used in the elementary school to demonstrate several of the situations that have been described thus far in this section. If you have access to a geoboard, try the following problems on it. If you do not have access to a geoboard use the dot paper below.

a. Show two triangles whose intersection is a point.

b. Show two triangles whose intersection is 2 points.

c. Show two triangles whose intersection is 3 points.

d. What is the largest finite number of points of intersection that two triangles may have?

e. Show two triangles whose intersection is a segment.

f. Show two triangles whose intersection is the union of a point and a segment where the point is not on the line segment.

g. Show two triangles whose intersection is the union of two line segments.

h. Show two triangles whose intersection is the union of a line segment and 2 points, where the two points are not on the line segment.

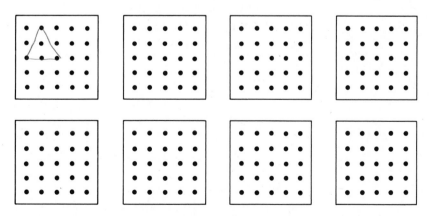

19. In Problem 18 we investigated the intersection of two triangles. In this problem we investigate the intersection of quadrilaterals.

   a. Show two quadrilaterals whose intersection is 3 points
   b. Show two quadrilaterals whose intersection is 10 points. (If you have trouble with this, try considering some concave quadrilaterals.)
   c. What is the largest finite number of points of intersection that two quadrilaterals may have.
   d. Show two quadrilaterals whose intersection is the union of three segments.

20. A child who identifies figure (*a*) as a rectangle does not identify figure (*b*) as a rectangle because it is a square. What do you say?

(*a*)   (*b*)

21. A child asks if the metal spiral binder on her notebook is a simple plane curve. What do you say?

22. Although we usually draw convex figures, on a geoboard it is easy to create concave figures. Here a concave figure with one "inside corner" is shown. If possible, create the following:

   a. A hexagon with 2 inside corners.
   b. An octagon with 3 inside corners.
   c. A pentagon with 2 inside corners.
   d. A heptagon with 3 inside corners.

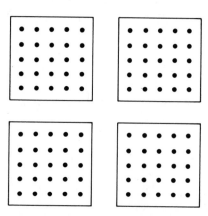

7.5   SETS OF POINTS IN THREE-SPACE

We will restrict our work in this section to a group of three-dimensional figures called *polyhedrons* (or *polyhedra*). In order to describe polyhedrons, we
need one additional concept from our work in the previous section—that of
a polygonal region. The union of a polygon and its interior is called a *polygonal region.*

Figure 7.37 illustrates a variety of models of polyhedrons. We see that each
polyhedron is composed of the union of a finite number of polygonal regions
such that their interiors are disjoint, and each side of a region is a side of
exactly one other region. Each of the polygonal regions is referred to as a
face of the polyhedron. The vertices and sides of the polygonal regions are
called *vertices* and *edges*, respectively, of the polyhedron. A *diagonal* of a
polyhedron is any line segment determined by two vertices that do not lie in
the same face. Thus, in Figure 7.37, (*a*) has no diagonals and (*b*) has four
diagonals. Can you "see" these diagonals even though they are not drawn?
How many diagonals are in each of the other polyhedrons?

Just as polygons are classified by the number of sides, polyhedrons can be
named by the number of faces.

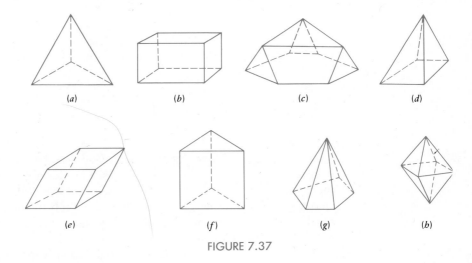

FIGURE 7.37

EXAMPLE 1

Name the polyhedrons in Figure 7.37 according to the number of faces in
each.

Solution

a. Tetrahedron (4 faces)   **b.** Hexahedron (6 faces)

    c. Octahedron (8 faces)   **d.** Pentahedron (5 faces)

    e. Hexahedron   **f.** Pentahedron

    g. Hexahedron   **h.** Octahedron

You should note that the name of the polyhedron tells *only* the number of faces; it does not tell what the shape of the polyhedron may be.

Earlier we saw that polygons encompass a large variety of "shapes." We were able to classify them as being convex or concave. A polyhedron is *convex* if and only if every plane containing a face separates space such that the remainder of the polyhedron is in one half-space. The description may seem a little confusing, but it simply states in mathematical terms the idea that a convex polyhedron may not have any "dents" or "cave-ins." A polyhedron that is not convex is said to be *concave*. Figure 7.38 provides an illustration of a concave polyhedron. The figure is not convex because not all the polyhedron is on the same side of plane *EDH*. As with convex polygons, convex polyhedra receive most of the attention at the elementary and secondary school level.

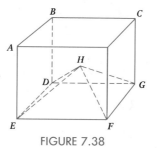

FIGURE 7.38

Many three-dimensional figures you have worked with in the past are actually special kinds of convex polyhedrons. For example, consider the three-dimensional "shapes" in Figure 7.39. Each of these is an example of what is called a *prism*. A prism is a polyhedron in which two congruent polygonal faces lie in parallel planes and the other faces are bounded by parallelograms. These parallel faces are commonly called the bases of the prism. Prisms are classified according to the type of polygons forming the bases. Thus, in Figure 7.39, (*a*) and (*d*) are triangular prisms, (*b*) is a rectangular prism, (*c*) is a pentagonal prism, and (*e*) is a square prism, more commonly called a cube. In Figure 7.40*a* there are three pairs of parallel faces, any of which could be considered bases. Why? However, in Figure 7.40*b*, although there are three pairs of parallel faces, only one pair (the hexagons) may be used as bases. Why?

Figure 7.41 illustrates a variety of polyhedrons called *pyramids*. A pyramid is a polyhedron such that a set of faces intersects in one point and another face intersects all the faces in the set. (This face is commonly called the *base*

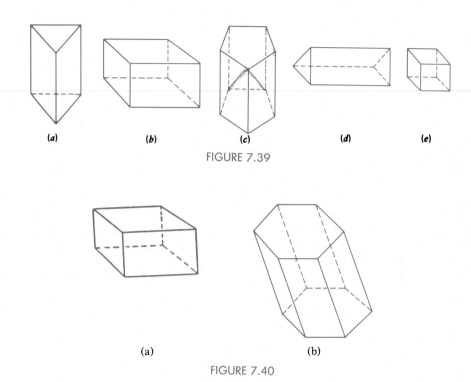

(a)   (b)   (c)   (d)   (e)

FIGURE 7.39

(a)   (b)

FIGURE 7.40

of the pyramid.) It is convenient to classify pyramids according to the base. Thus, in Figure 7.41, (*a*) is a triangular pyramid (also a tetrahedron by our previous classification of polyhedrons), (*b*) is a quadrangular pyramid, (*c*) is a pentagonal pyramid, and (*d*) is a hexagonal pyramid.

It is often difficult for people to sketch three-dimensional figures. If this is the case for you, remember the uses we have made of dot paper, different perspectives, and the use of solid and dotted lines as we drew our figures. There are many different ways of conveying the same idea, so use your imagination and practice with the tools we have provided. In time, your sketches will successfully emerge.

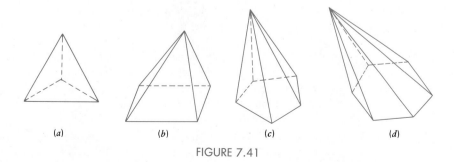

(a)   (b)   (c)   (d)

FIGURE 7.41

PROBLEM SET 7.5

1. **a.** What is the smallest number of faces that a polyhedron may have? Sketch such a polyhedron.
   b. What is the smallest number of faces that a prism may have? Sketch such a prism.
   c. What is the smallest number of faces that a pyramid may have? Sketch such a pyramid.

2. Draw a sketch for each of the following.
   a. A cube
   b. A quadrangular prism that is also not a rectangular prism
   c. A pentagonal prism
   d. An octagonal prism
   e. A tetrahedron
   f. A pentagonal pyramid
   g. An octagonal pyramid

3. Give an example of a physical model for each of the following:
   a. Quadrangular prism
   b. Pentagonal prism
   c. Hexagonal prism
   d. Quadrangular pyramid

4. Give two examples of physical models of polyhedrons different from those in Problem 3 and indicate the number of faces for each.

5. Consider the following geometric solids. For each, count the vertices, faces, and edges. Record your information in the chart and examine the chart for patterns and relationships among the entries.

   a.

Prism	Vertices	Faces	Edges
Triangular			
Square			
Pentagonal			
Hexagonal			
Heptagonal			
Octagonal			
Nineteen-gonal			
n-gonal			

b.

Pyramid	Vertices	Faces	Edges
Triangular			
Square			
Pentagonal			
Hexagonal			
Heptagonal			
Octagonal			
Nineteen-gonal			
n-gonal			

6. A search for patterns is always an integral part of the study of mathematics. Euler, a renowned mathematician of the eighteenth century, was credited with discovering a pattern that exists concerning the number of edges, vertices, and faces of a polyhedron.

   a. Refer to Problem 5 and using v to represent the number of vertices, f the number of faces, and e the number of edges, try to state a relationship using v, f, and e as Euler might have done.

   b. Check your relationship for each convex polyhedron in Figure 7.37.

   c. Check your relationship for each convex polyhedron in Figure 7.39.

7. **a.** A prism with 45 faces has _____ edges?

   b. A pyramid with 76 edges has _____ faces?

   c. A prism with 540 edges has _____ vertices?

   d. Why is there not a prism with exactly 55 edges?

8. Consider the diagonal of the quadrangular prism below. Note that there are four vertices on the base, one diagonal can be drawn from each vertex, giving a total of 4×1 diagonals for the whole prism. For each of the prisms, complete the appropriate cell in the chart.

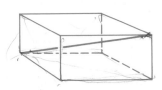
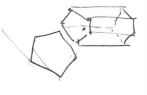

Prism	Vertices per Base	Diagonals per Vertex	Total Number of Diagonals
Quadrangular	4	1	4
Pentagonal	5	2	5×2
Hexagonal			
Heptagonal		$n-2$	$n(n-2)$
Octaganal			
n-gonal			

9. Why would the concept of a diagonal have no meaning for a pyramid?

10. **a.** What does it mean to say that a convex polyhedron separates space?
    b. Does a concave polyhedron separate space?

11. Sketch a concave polyhedron different than the one illustrated in Figure 7.38.

Pedagogical Problems and Activities

12. Elementary school students can be given the opportunity to make physical models of various three-dimensional figures. These models may be made of cardboard, soda straws, commercial toy-building kits, and so on. Make some models of the polyhedra discussed in this section.

13. One objective for the study of three-dimensional geometric concepts is the development of "spatial perception." Various activities may be used to give children an opportunity to develop their abilities to visualize three-dimensional relationships from two-dimensional drawings. For example, the following model can be used to form a box without a lid by folding along the dotted lines.

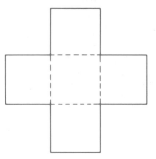

   a. Which of the following patterns will also fold into an open box? Indicate the "folds."

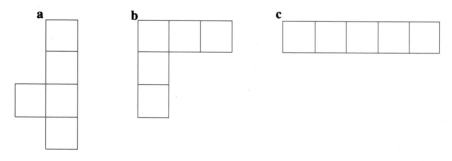

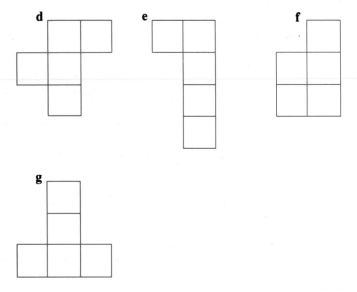

b. Find all other patterns made like those above that will fold into an open box.

c. Using the drawing below as an empty box with *ABCD* as the open face, name the cuts that result in each pattern in **a** and **b** that fold into an open box. For example, cutting segments $\overline{AE}$, $\overline{BF}$, $\overline{CG}$, and $\overline{DH}$ will make the pattern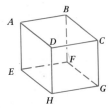

14. Using six squares instead of five as in the previous problem we can draw patterns like those above.

   a. Draw three patterns that will fold into a cube.

   b. Draw three patterns that will not fold into a cube.

15. Five different views of the same "block" are shown:

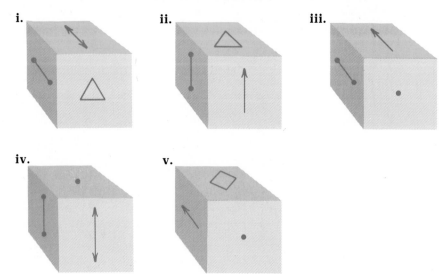

What design is on the face opposite the face with the ray on it? What design is on the face opposite the face with the line segment on it?

16. a. A child asks, "How can a square pyramid also be called a pentahedron?" What do you say.

b. A child concludes that there is no difference between prisms and pyramids because a triangular prism and a square pyramid both are called pentahedrons. What do you say?

17. a. A child says the following sketch is the sketch of a pentagonal pyramid. What do you say?

b. A second child disagrees with the first, and suggests the sketch looks like the one below. What do you say?

c. Where would each child have to be with respect to the pyramid to "see" the pyramid as sketched.

d. A child sketches the pentagonal prism below. What do you say?

e. A child asks if this figure could be a cube. What do you say?

REVIEW PROBLEM SET

1. Sketch each of the following:
   a. Two parallel lines
   b. Two skew lines
   c. Two parallel planes
   d. Two intersecting planes
   e. A dihedral angle
   f. Convex heptagon
   g. Concave octagon
   h. A pentagonal prism
   i. A quadrangular pyramid
   j. A convex polyhedron other than a prism or a pyramid

2. Describe the meaning of each of the following concepts:
   a. Line segment
   b. Ray
   c. Plane angle
   d. Simple closed plane curve
   e. Polygon
   f. Convex polygon
   g. Vertical plane angles
   h. Octagon
   i. Octagonal prism
   j. Octagonal pyramid

3. **a.** If a polyhedron has 12 edges and 8 vertices, how many faces does it have?
   b. A pyramid with 8 faces has how many vertices?
   c. A prism with 14 vertices has how many edges?
   d. A pyramid with 29 vertices has how many edges?
   e. The number of edges on a prism is between 440 and 460. What are the possible values for the number of edges?

4. How many *lines* are determined by four points? How many *line segments* are determined by four points?

5. How many triangles are determined by five points, no three of which are collinear?

6. What does it mean to say that a point separates a line? A line separates a plane? A plane separate space?

7. How many endpoints does a line possess? A line segment? A ray?

8. **a.** Do two parallel lines determine a plane?
   b. Do two intersecting lines determine a plane?
   c. Do two skew lines determine a plane?
   d. Is a plane always determined by three points? Explain your answer.

Solution to Sample Problem

Is there a pyramid that has exactly 55 edges?

1. *Understanding the problem.* What is a pyramid? What is meant by an edge? Is an edge the same thing as a face or a vertex?

2. *Devising a plan.* Because the number given was 55, it does not seem that I could draw this one. This rules out trial and error. Is there any relationship between vertices, faces, and edges that I know? Maybe, I should try a simpler case to see if I can determine any relationship.

3. *Solution.* Let us try the simpler case route. A triangular pyramid has 4 faces, 4 vertices, and 6 edges. A square pyramid has 5 faces, 5 vertices, and 10 edges. A pentagonal pyramid has 6 faces, 6 vertices, and 12 edges. It appears that the number of edges is always a multiple of 2. That being the case, a pyramid with 55 edges is not possible.

4. *Looking back.* The answer is indeed correct, as not only is the number of edges a multiple of 2, the number of edges is always the double of the number of vertices of the base. Furthermore, the number of vertices of the polyhedron and the number of faces is always the same, and the number of faces is always one more than the number associated with the polygonal region used to name the pyramid.

5. *Looking ahead.*
   a. I wonder if there could be a prism with exactly 55 faces?
   b. I wonder if there could be a pyramid with exactly 55 vertices? 55 faces?
   c. Could I make a spatial figure that is not a prism or pyramid that would have 55 edges?

8 | LINEAR AND ANGULAR MEASUREMENT

Sample Problem

How many dollar bills are there in a stack one kilometer tall?

8.1 INTRODUCTION AND STANDARD LINEAR UNITS OF MEASUREMENT

The NCTM Standards are very clear regarding the importance of measurement in the mathematics curriculum. Measurement is used in mathematics to quantify the physical world. As soon as children understand that there are attributes that we measure they should be provided with experiences to make and use measurements and estimates of measurements in everyday situations. In doing so, children will be able to describe, compare, and contrast objects, select appropriate units of measure and appropriate tools to use in measuring to the degree of accuracy desired. The use of measurement activities can assist in changing students' perceptions that mathematics is a static set of rules. Furthermore, an active measurement approach in the elementary classroom reinforces the number concepts component of the curriculum.

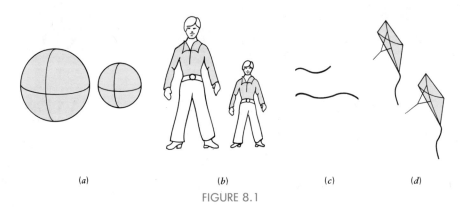

(a)　　　　　　　　(b)　　　　　　　(c)　　　　　(d)

FIGURE 8.1

In Figure 8.1*a* which is the larger ball? Which of the two people is the taller in Figure 8.1*b*? Which of the two pieces of string is the longer in Figure 8.1*c*? Which of the two kites is flying higher in Figure 8.1*d*? Children at a very early age are able to react to questions of this type, even before they have had any formal work with measurement concepts. Experiences in their environment help them to form intuitive meanings for such comparison terms as longer, shorter, larger, smaller, higher, and lower. However, as adults we realize that eventually a more formal approach to measurement is needed to cope with "real-world" problems. In this text, we hope to provide you with a blend of informal and formal measurement ideas.

In Figure 8.2, segment $\overline{AB}$ is longer than $\overline{AC}$ because C is between A and B. Furthermore, $\overline{CB}$ is longer than $\overline{AC}$, even though "betweenness" is not the justification. However, we are likely to hesitate for a moment when working

A　　　　C　　　　　　　　B

FIGURE 8.2

with the lengths of the line segments in Figure 8.3 because it is difficult to decide just by observation which is longer. There are several ways to decide but one method is to compare the two lengths by marking the length of one on the edge of a sheet of paper and then placing the paper beside the other. This would allow us to determine that $\overline{CD}$ is the longer of the two segments.

FIGURE 8.3

Now suppose that in Figure 8.3 we are also interested in how much longer $\overline{CD}$ is than $\overline{AB}$. At this time it becomes convenient to establish some sort of linear unit and then to "measure" each of the line segments by seeing how many times the unit is contained in the segment. In Figure 8.4 an arbitrary linear unit is shown: $\overline{AB}$ is about 4 units long and $\overline{CD}$ is about $4\frac{1}{2}$ units long.

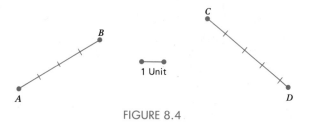

FIGURE 8.4

Therefore, in terms of this choice of a linear unit, $\overline{CD}$ is about $\frac{1}{2}$ unit longer than $\overline{AB}$. If a different linear unit were used for measuring the segments the results would be different from a "number" standpoint. That is, in Figure 8.5, using a different arbitrary linear unit, $\overline{AB}$ is about 2 units and $\overline{CD}$ about $2\frac{1}{4}$ units long.

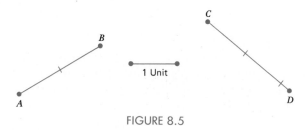

FIGURE 8.5

We hope that from this discussion you see the need for a standardized unit of measure.

REMARK Activities that allow children to measure lengths of various objects in the classroom by choosing their own linear unit (length of a pencil, length of a finger, length of a pice of chalk, etc.) are used by many elementary school teachers. It is felt that such activities using nonstandard units not only help children see the need for standard units but also aid in developing an understanding of the concept of linear measurement.

Two standard sets of measuring units are in use in the United States today: the metric system and the English system. Even though most scientific and business related work is done using the metric system, the English system is used in many aspects of everyday life. The United States continues to be an island in the metric world, but even that is changing owing to world trade. The NCTM Standards suggest that both systems should be taught as measurement systems but that we should not demand that students become proficient in the changing of units from one system to another. Because you are probably less familiar with the metric system, we will provide as much work as possible in this system to assist you in becoming more proficient with metric measurement. The NCTM Standards also suggest that students will not learn a measurement system unless they become actively involved in measurement. The same will be true for you. We suggest that you obtain a metric ruler, or better yet a metric measuring tape, and practice measuring everything in sight until you are comfortable with the metric vocabulary and can efficiently estimate various lengths.

The realization of a need for measurement seems to go back nearly as far as human history. Even though a detailed development of the history of measurement from its very beginning does not seem to be available, there are many accounts of various measurement concepts being used throughout the ages. The Bible indicates the use of such linear measurement concepts as forearm, hand, and finger in early times. It is also reported that such terms as digit, palm, span, cubit, pace, and fathom were used as linear measurement concepts. Apparently, the first standard unit of length used in England was the yard (or girth), according to records dating back to approximately 1000 A.D. The English statute books in the early part of the fourteenth century used the inch, foot, yard, and perch as standard linear units. Table 8.1 lists the part of the English system with which most of us are familiar. Table 8.1 is lacking any "number patterns" that might help in remembering these relationships. Furthermore, we find that calculations using this system frequently become cumbersome. Even a simple problem of changing units can be awkward. For example, suppose that we want to change 10 yards to rods. Because a rod is a longer unit than a yard, this helps us remember to divide by $5\frac{1}{2}$ when changing yards to rods. Thus, 10 yards is the same as $10 \div 5\frac{1}{2}$ or $1\frac{9}{11}$ rods.

TABLE 8.1

12 inches = 1 foot	$5\frac{1}{2}$ yards = 1 rod
3 feet = 1 yard	320 rods = 1 mile
5280 feet = 1 mile	36 inches = 1 yard

The origin of the metric system dates back to the latter part of the eighteenth century when in 1795 the French government authorized the development of a decimal measurement system. The distance from the north pole to the equator was measured along an arc of a great circle, and this unit of length was repeatedly divided by 10 until a convenient unit, the *meter*, was determined. The meter was actually one ten-millionth of the distance mentioned. In 1960, the meter was defined to be the length of 1,650,763.73 wavelengths in a vacuum of the orange-red line of the spectrum of krypton 86. Since 1983, the meter has been defined as the length of the path traveled by light in a vacuum during a time interval of 1/229,792,458th of a second. We point out these changes in definition not that it is important for you to remember the exact definition, but so, as the NCTM Standards suggest, you can see that mathematics is not a static discipline. Furthermore, you may be surprised to know that in the United States all the English units of measure are officially defined in terms of metric units.

Table 8.2 shows some of the basic metric units that apply to linear measure. The metric system has been devised to take advantage of our base-ten numeration system.

TABLE 8.2

10 millimeters	=	1 centimeter
10 centimeters	=	1 decimeter
10 decimeters	=	1 meter
10 meters	=	1 dekameter
10 dekameters	=	1 hectometer
10 hectometers	=	1 kilometer

Referring to Table 8.2, you will note that we underlined some prefixes. Table 8.3 defines them. It would be very helpful for you to memorize the meanings attached to these prefixes. They will be used continuously as we study the metric system in this chapter as well as later. Thus, combining ideas from Table 8.2 and Table 8.3, such statements as "a millimeter is one-thousandth of a meter," "a decimeter is one-tenth of a meter," "a hectometer is one hundred meters," and "a kilometer is one thousand meters" may be made.

TABLE 8.3

milli	0.001 times the basic unit
centi	0.01 times the basic unit
deci	0.1 times the basic unit
deka (deca)	10 times the basic unit
hecto	100 times the basic unit
kilo	1000 times the basic unit

The process of changing units within the metric system is simple once the meaning of the prefixes has been established. For example, suppose that we want to change 17 decimeters to meters. The prefix "deci-" helps us recall that one decimeter is 0.1 of a meter. Thus, 17 decimeters would be $17(0.1) = 1.7$ meters.

Another approach to changing 17 decimeters to meters is based on the fact that if 1 decimeter equals 0.1 of a meter, then 10 decimeters = 1 meter. Because we are changing from a smaller unit (decimeter) to a larger unit (meter), there will be fewer meters than decimeters and therefore we need to divide by 10. So 17 decimeters equals $17 \div 10$, or 1.7 meters. Thinking along these lines, changing meters to decimeters would require multiplying by 10, and thus 5 meters equals 5 times 10 or 50 decimeters.

Table 8.4 is put in at this time for your convenience. We have indicated the common symbols used for the linear metric terms.

TABLE 8.4

millimeter (mm)	dekameter (dam)
centimeter (cm)	hectometer (hm)
decimeter (dm)	kilometer (km)
meter (m)	

One of the unfortunate results of living in a country using two systems of measurement is that at times converting from one system to the other is necessary. You should develop meaningful physical referents for both metric and English units (height of a doorknob is about 1 meter from the floor, etc.) as well as some idea of common relationships between the systems. Table 8.5 provides some of the more common conversion relationships between the English system and the metric system.

TABLE 8.5

($\doteq$ means "is approximately equal to")

1 meter $\doteq$ 39 inches $\doteq$ 3.3 feet $\doteq$ 1.1 yards
1 centimeter $\doteq$ 0.4 inches (1 cm is not quite one-half an inch)
1 kilometer $\doteq$ 0.6 mile (1 km is just over $\frac{1}{2}$ mile)
1 inch $\doteq$ 2.5 centimeters
1 foot $\doteq$ 30 centimeters
1 yard $\doteq$ 91 centimeters $\doteq$ 0.91 meters
1 mile $\doteq$ 1600 meters $\doteq$ 1.6 kilometers

It is not recommended that you memorize the data in Table 8.5, nor even that you try to make use of it for precise calculations. More importantly, you should establish some frames of reference between the two systems so that when a measurement is given in one system you will quickly be able to establish a frame of reference in the other system.

We encourage you to now become proficient in the terminology and use of the metric system with respect to linear measure. We will make extensive use of linear measure when we deal with perimeter and in later chapters when we deal with area and volume.

PROBLEM SET 8.1

1. Convert as indicated within the metric system.
   a. 1 meter = _____ centimeters
   b. 1 meter = _____ millimeters
   c. 1 hectometer = _____ meters
   d. 1 kilometer = _____ meters
   e. 1 centimeter = _____ meter
   f. 1 meter = _____ kilometer

2. Convert as indicated within the metric system.
   a. 17 meters = _____ centimeters
   b. 23 meters = _____ decimeters
   c. 14 dekameters = _____ meters
   d. 6 hectometers = _____ meters
   e. 5 kilometers = _____ meters

3. Convert as indicated within the English system.
   a. 1 yard = _____ inches
   b. 1 rod = _____ feet
   c. 1 mile = _____ yards.
   d. 1 mile = _____ feet
   e. 1 yard = _____ rod

4. Convert as indicated within the English system. Express parts of units in both $\frac{a}{b}$ form and decimal form for rational numbers. For example, 4 feet is the same as $1\frac{1}{3}$ yards, which can also be written $1.\overline{3}$. Use your calculator whenever it is helpful.
   a. 78 inches = _____ feet
   b. 17 feet = _____ yards
   c. 9 rods = _____ yards
   d. 77 inches = _____ yards
   e. $8\frac{1}{4}$ yards = _____ rods
   f. 2000 yards = _____ miles

5. Convert as indicated within the metric system. Express answers in decimal form. For example, 13 decimeters is the same as 1.3 meters.
   a. 19 decimeters = _____ meters
   b. 32 decimeters = _____ meters
   c. 147 centimeters = _____ meters
   d. 73 centimeters = _____ decimeters
   e. 200 meters = _____ kilometer
   f. 8725 meters = _____ kilometers
   g. 71 meters = _____ hectometer
   h. 323 centimeters = _____ meters
   i. 113 decimeters = _____ meters

6. Convert within the metric system.
   a. 5.2 centimeters = _____ millimeters
   b. 0.48 meters = _____ decimeters = _____ centimeters
   c. 0.64 kilometers = _____ meters = _____ centimeters
   d. 367.2 hectometers = _____ kilometers = _____ meters
   e. 456 millimeters = _____ centimeters = _____ decimeters
   f. 2323 meters = _____ dekameters = _____ kilometers
   g. 0.3 meters = _____ dekameters = _____ kilometers
   h. 0.35 centimeters = _____ decimeters = _____ kilometers

7. a. Donna measured the top of the teacher's desk with her pencil and found the desk to be about 7 pencils long. Don measured the same desk with his pencil and found it to be 9 pencils long. Who has the longer pencil?
   b. Rick and Johnny were each measuring the width of a classroom using this textbook. Johnny measured the room using the short side of the book as a unit of measure whereas Rick used the long side. When they completed the task and compared the numerical value found, who has the larger numerical value?
   c. What is the width of a standard sheet of paper in paper-clip units (using regular paper clips)?

8. Which most closely approximates the measure of the following:
   a. Length of a football field
      (i) 40 m   (ii) 90 m   (iii) 200 m
   b. Height of a male university basketball player
      (i) 1 m   (ii) 2 m   (iii) 3 m
   c. Height of an average woman
      (i) 165 cm   (ii) 185 cm   (iii) 205 cm

    d. Driving a car in town
       (i) 30 kph   **(ii)** 50 kph   **(iii)** 70 kph

    e. Driving a car on a two-lane road
       (i) 50 kph   **(ii)** 70 kph   **(iii)** 90 kph

    f. Distance from New York to San Francisco
       (i) 1500 km   **(ii)**3500 km   **(iii)**5500 km

Pedagogical Problems and Activities

9. Children need to be exposed to many different linear measurement situations in their environment. For example, they are always interested in measurements relative to their own bodies. Here is a list of some possible measurements that can be made to aid in formulating linear metric concepts. Fill in the blanks to make a "metric sheet" about yourself.

Height in centimeters _____
Height in meters _____
Sleeve length in centimeters _____
Waist size in centimeters _____
Wrist size in centimeters _____
Hip size in centimeters _____
Length of little finger in millimeters _____
Foot length in centimeters _____

10. We frequently "step off" distances to make approximations. An adult can usually estimate in terms of yard-long strides fairly accurately. Try measuring a stride of one meter and see if you can comfortably step off in terms of meters. If not, perhaps you will need to adjust to half-meters. Now try approximating some distances by "stepping off" in terms of either meters or half-meters. Measure the distances to see how well you are doing.

11. Once children have formulated some mental pictures of how long the basic units are, they may begin to use this information for estimation purposes. Try your estimation skills on the following problems. For each one, first estimate in terms of the indicated unit and then measure to see how well you did. Round off answers to the nearest unit.

Object	Estimation	Actual Measurement
Length of this book (centimeters)	_____	_____
Width of this book (centimeters)	_____	_____
Thickness of this book (millimeters)	_____	_____

Object	Estimation	Actual Measurement
Length of room in which you are now studying (meters)	_____	_____
Width of room in which you are now studying (meters)	_____	_____
Height of room in which you are now studying (meters)	_____	_____
Length of your foot (centimeters)	_____	_____
Length of your normal walking stride (centimeters)	_____	_____
Height of nearest doorway (meters)	_____	_____
Length of pen or pencil that you are now using (millimeters)	_____	_____

12. Decide on an appropriate unit (kilometer, meter, centimeter, or millimeter) that would probably be used to measure the following items.
   a. Thickness of pencil lead
   b. Length of an automobile
   c. Distance from New York to Philadelphia
   d. Width of a street
   e. Diameter of a contact lens
   f. Width of computer screen
   g. Height of a chair
   h. Distance around a running track

13. Order the following from smallest to largest: 88 centimeters, 4.5 meters, 0.34 kilometers, 9.5 decimeters, 559 millimeters.

14. Estimate the length of each segment below in centimeters and in millimeters. Use a ruler to check your estimates.

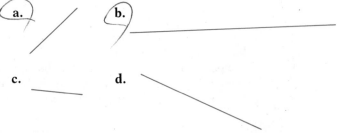

15. Without using a ruler, draw line segments having the following measures. Use a ruler to check your estimates.
   a. 15 centimeters   b. 92.9 millimeters
   c. 65 millimeters   d. 0.12 meters

8.2   MORE ON LINEAR MEASUREMENT AND ESTIMATION

When we speak of the line segment joining two points A and B, we will continue to write $\overline{AB}$, but when we wish to speak of the length of the segment, we will write AB. Thus, the symbol $\overline{AB}$ has reference to the line segment as a set of points, whereas the symbol AB refers to the real number that describes the number of times the unit length must be applied end to end to measure the segment. In Figure 8.6a, the statement may be made that $\overline{AB} = \overline{CD}$, whereas in Figure 8.6b $\overline{AB} \neq \overline{CD}$ but $AB = CD$.

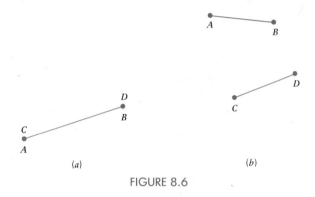

(a)   (b)

FIGURE 8.6

Suppose that a person using a measuring stick with only centimeter markings on it reports that a line segment measured to the nearest centimeter is 8 centimeters long. This simply states that the length of the segment is closer to 8 centimeters than it is to either 7 or 9 centimeters. In other words, the length is somewhere between $7\frac{1}{2}$ centimeters and $8\frac{1}{2}$ centimeters. The shaded region in Figure 8.7 indicates the interval into which the one endpoint of the line segment would fall if the other endpoint is placed at zero. It also indicates that the 8-centimeter measurement can be in error of up to $\frac{1}{2}$ centimeter.

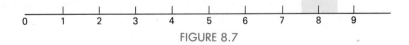

FIGURE 8.7

Now suppose that another person using a measuring stick that has $\frac{1}{2}$ centimeter markings on it reports that the line segment to the nearest $\frac{1}{2}$ centimeter is 8-centimeters long. This states that the length is somewhere between $7\frac{3}{4}$ centimeters and $8\frac{1}{4}$ centimeters. This interval is pictured in Figure 8.8. Again we see the error can be up to $\frac{1}{4}$ centimeter (or $\frac{1}{2}$ of $\frac{1}{2}$ centimeter).

FIGURE 8.8

In these examples, measuring to the nearest $\frac{1}{2}$ centimeter gives a better approximation than measuring to the nearest centimeter. In general, the smaller the unit of measure, the better the approximation will be. This is referred to as *precision*. Precision, refers to the unit of measure being used. It is more precise to measure to the nearest centimeter than to the nearest meter. Similarly, it is more precise to measure to the nearest inch than to the nearest foot, nearest meter than to the nearest kilometer, and the nearest foot than to the nearest yard.

> REMARK It is important to remember that when a measurement is reported it also tells what unit of measure was used and what is the largest possible error. Consider the following examples:

EXAMPLE 1

A measurement of $7\frac{1}{2}$ inches tells us that $\frac{1}{2}$ inch is the unit of measure and the largest possible error is $\frac{1}{2}$ of $\frac{1}{2}$ inch $= \frac{1}{4}$ inch.

EXAMPLE 2

A measurement of 7.5 inches tells us that 0.1 inch is the unit of measure and the largest possible error is $\frac{1}{2}$ of 0.1 inch $= 0.05$ inch.

EXAMPLE 3

A measurement of 3.20 meters tells us that 0.01 meter is the unit of measure and the largest possible error is $\frac{1}{2}$ of 0.01 m $= 0.005$ meter.

The term *accuracy*, or *relative error*, is also used when working with measurement concepts. Accuracy refers to a way of comparing the "seriousness" of errors in different measurements. For example, which is more serious, an error of $\frac{1}{2}$ centimeter in a measurement of 5 centimeters or an error of $\frac{1}{2}$ meter in a measurement of 10 meters? Looking at this from a ratio viewpoint comparing the error to the measurement involved, we have

$$\frac{\frac{1}{2}}{5} = \tfrac{1}{10} = 10 \text{ percent};$$

$$\frac{\frac{1}{2}}{10} = \tfrac{1}{20} = 5 \text{ percent}.$$

Because a 5-percent error is less than a 10 percent error, we say that the measurement of 10 meters to the nearest meter is *more accurate* than the measurement of 5 centimeters to the nearest centimeter.

Finding the measure of a polygonal curve, such as illustrated in Figure 8.9, is simply a matter of being able to add the measures of the line segments involved. Thus, the measure of the polygonal curve from *A* to *F* is given by *AB* + *BC* + *CD* + *DE* + *EF*. This could be accomplished by using a measuring stick on each of the line segments and adding the measures. Another technique is to use a compass to "measure" each segment, placing the segments end to end in a straight line, then measuring the resulting single line segment. Using centimeters, estimate the length of the polygonal curve in Figure 8.9 and then use each of the above measuring procedures to find its length.

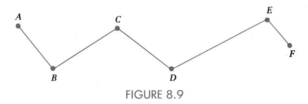

FIGURE 8.9

The length of a nonpolygonal plane curve, such as in Figure 8.10, is more difficult to obtain. One approach is to get a "polygonal approximation." That is, choose a number of points along the curve and consider the measures of the line segments determined by these points. Both the number of points chosen as well as where the points are located will affect the accuracy of the approximation process. Another approach to approximating the length of the curve in Figure 8.10 is to use a string. Lay the string so that it coincides with the curve. Mark the two ends of the curve on the string and then straighten the string and measure it.

Two terms are traditionally used when referring to the "lengths" of simple closed plane curves: *perimeter* and *circumference*. In this book, we will use

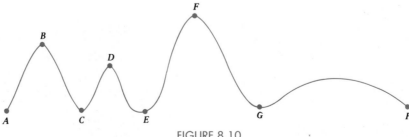

FIGURE 8.10

the term *perimeter* when referring to the "length" of any simple closed plane curve and reserve the term *circumference* for use with the circle only.

The perimeters of the quadrilateral, pentagon, and hexagon in Figure 8.11 are 7.2 cm, 8.2 cm, and 7.0 cm, respectively. Suppose that we desired to have each of the perimeters from Figure 8.11 expressed in terms of meters. The fact that 1 meter = 100 centimeters indicates that to change centimeters to meters we must divide by 100. Thus, the perimeters would be 0.072 meters, 0.082 meters, and 0.070 meters. Likewise, the perimeters given in centimeters could easily be changed to millimeters by multiplying by 10. Thus, we would have 72 mm, 82 mm, and 70 mm.

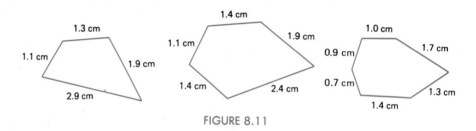

FIGURE 8.11

The concept of linear measurement now allows us to define a familiar geometric figure, the *circle*. A circle is a set of points in a plane that are all at a given distance from some given point in the plane. The given reference point is called the *center* of the circle, and any line segment that connects the center with any point of the circle is called a *radius*. All radii of a circle are equal in length. It should be noted that the center of a circle is not a point of the circle, but merely a reference point.

Any line segment connecting two points of a circle is called a *chord*. If a chord contains the center of the circle then it is a *diameter*. In Figure 8.12, $\overline{OA}$, $\overline{OB}$, and $\overline{OC}$ are radii, $\overline{AB}$ is a diameter, and $\overline{BC}$ is a chord that is not a diameter.

In the preceding development we discussed the idea of approximating the length of a nonpolygonal curve by using a polygonal curve or by superim-

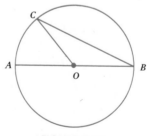

FIGURE 8.12

posing something flexible on the curve and then measuring the item when straightened out. The same techniques would work for approximating the perimeter (circumference) of a circle. Another technique for measuring the circumference of a circle is to roll the circle along a line marking a starting point and the finishing point after one complete revolution. The line segment formed can then be measured.

The procedures described above for measuring the circumference of a circle are used to introduce the concept of π (pi). For several circles we may find the ratio of the measure of the circumference divided by the measure of a diameter. As a result of this type of activity, we conjecture that the ratio of the circumference of any circle to the measure of a diameter of that circle is always the same, or in other words, a constant. That constant was given the name π, and even from these rough approximations, we begin to realize that the value of π must be somewhere near 3. We normally express this relationship as $C = \pi d$ or $C = 2\pi r$, where C is the circumference of a circle, d the length of a diameter, and r the length of a radius.

A few comments regarding the number π are in order. We used π in an earlier chapter as an example of an irrational number. Recall that an irrational number is a number that cannot be expressed in $\dfrac{a}{b}$ form, where a and b are integers, and $b \neq 0$. Equivalently, we decided that in decimal form an irrational number produces a nonrepeating decimal. Thus, we need to realize that when using π for computational purposes we can either express calculations in terms of π or use an appropriate rational approximation for π. As you may know, various approximations are used for π, such as $3\frac{1}{7}$, $\frac{22}{7}$, and 3.14. Students using a calculator button might use 3.1415927 or even a number with more digits. Mathematics textbooks may choose not to use an approximation and write the answer in terms of π. You should be comfortable with all the above uses of π. Consider the following example.

EXAMPLE

Find the circumference of a circle that has a diameter of 5 centimeters.

Solution   Using the formula $C = \pi d$, we obtain $C = 5\pi$ cm. We may simply express the answer as 5π cm or obtain an approximation by using a rational approximation for π. Using $\pi \doteq 3\frac{1}{7}$, we find that $C \doteq 15\frac{5}{7}$ cm. Using $\pi \doteq 3.14$ we find that $C \doteq 15.7$ cm.

The choice of a rational approximation for π in a particular problem technically depends on the concept of precision. Suppose we are attempting to find the circumference of a circle and that we have determined the length of a diameter to be 7.1 cm measured to the nearest tenth of a centimeter. It would seem foolish to use something as precise as 3.1415927 as an approximation for π when our original measurement was merely to the nearest tenth of a centimeter. A more practical approach would be to use 3.14 (precise to the nearest hundredth) and then to round off the final answer to agree with the precision of the given measurement. Thus, we would have $C \doteq (3.14)(7.1)$ or $C \doteq 22.3$ cm.

As we work with measurement concepts, *estimation* plays an important role. Estimations can be used to check for "reasonableness" of answers; and for some purposes an estimated answer may be all that is necessary. Experience plays a large role in the development of estimation skills; however, there are some specific techniques that can be used to help make estimates. We will briefly illustrate four considerations pertaining to estimation involving linear units.

1. Form a mental image of the desired unit and "picture" laying off this unit along the "segment" whose length is to be estimated.

EXAMPLE 1

Estimate the length, in centimeters, of the following segment

•————————————————————————————————————•

We need a "mental image of a centimeter." You may want to use the width of the tip of your little finger as a model. Now you need to mentally picture laying off centimeter lengths along the segment. Try it, and then measure the segment to see how well you did.

2. Use a *convenient unit* as a mental image and then make a conversion if necessary.

EXAMPLE 2

Estimate the perimeter, in centimeters, of the following polygon:

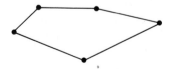

Though the answer is to be expressed in centimeters, if you mentally unwrap this polygon it may resemble a unit with which you are familiar. Estimate the perimeter and then check by measuring.

3. Use an appropriate formula.

EXAMPLE 3

Estimate the circumference, in centimeters, of the following circle:

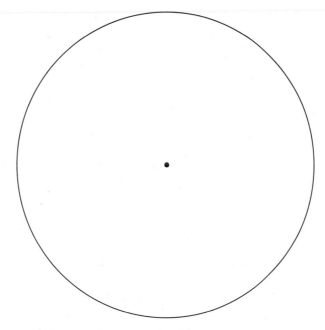

The circumference of a circle is given by the formula $C = 2\pi r$, where r represents the length of a radius. Using 3 as an approximation for π, the formula becomes $C \doteq 6r$. Thus, an estimate of the length of a radius multiplied by 6 yields an estimate for the circumference. Try this approach.

4. Use previous measurement experiences for comparison purposes.

EXAMPLE 4

Estimate the circumference, in centimeters, of the quarter pictured here:

The circumference of the circle in Example 3 is approximately 24 centimeters. By comparison, you should be able to make a fairly good estimate for the circumference of the quarter.

PROBLEM SET 8.2

1. According to the measurement reported, what is the unit of measure being used in each of the following:

   a. 6.3 m   b. 4.2 cm   c. 6.230 km

   d. 5.012 m   e. 6.2 in.   f. $6\frac{2}{3}$ yards

2. For each of the following pairs of measurements, determine which is the more precise:

   a. 5 centimeters or 7 meters

   b. 8 centimeters or 13 millimeters

   c. 14 feet or 6 yards

   d. 13 dekameters or 142 kilometers

   e. 4.1 centimeters or 7.23 centimeters

   f. 5.21 meters or 7.34 meters

3. For each of the following, determine which is the more accurate:

   a. An error of $\frac{1}{2}$ centimeter in a measurement of 6 centimeters or an error of $\frac{1}{2}$ centimeter in a measurement of 8 centimeters

   b. An error of 0.05 meter in a measurement of 5.2 meters or an error of 0.005 meter in a measurement of 7.14 meters

   c. An error of 0.5 millimeter in a measurement of 7 millimeters or an error of 0.5 meter in a measurement of 7 meters

   d. An error of $\frac{1}{4}$ foot in a measurement of $6\frac{1}{2}$ feet or an error of $\frac{1}{6}$ inch in a measurement of $5\frac{2}{3}$ inches

4. Using $C = \pi d$ or $C = 2\pi r$, find the circumference of each of the following circles.

   a. A circle with a diameter of 14 centimeters

   b. A circle with a diameter of 9 millimeters

   c. A circle with a radius of 6 decimeters

   d. A circle with a radius of 16 decimeters

5. a. Find the perimeter for each of the following polygons:

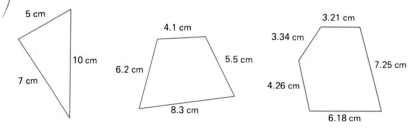

   b. Change each of the perimeters in part a to millimeters.

   c. Change each of the perimeters in part a to meters.

6. Find the perimeter of an octagon if each side is of length 7 millimeters. Express the answer in centimeters.

7. Suppose that I have enough wire to form a circle with a diameter of 1 meter. *How much more* wire would I need to form a circle with a diameter of 3 meters?

8. A metal band is stretched around the earth on a great circle. How many feet of band must be added for the band to be exactly 2 feet above the original position at every spot? Assume the earth has a diameter of 40-million feet.

9. Estimate the length of each of the following. Check your estimate by measuring.

a. •————————————•

_____ cm

b. •————————————————•

_____ mm

c.

_____ cm

d.

_____ mm

10. Estimate each of the following. Check your estimate by measuring.
   a. Circumference of a quarter   _____ cm
   b. Circumference of a penny   _____ cm
   c. Circumference of a dime   _____ mm
   d. Perimeter of a dollar bill   _____ cm

11. The concept of *significant digits* may be explained in terms of unit of measure. For example, consider a measurement of 3.02 centimeters. The unit of measure is 0.01 centimeter, and 3.02 means that we have 302 of these 0.01 centimeter units. Thus, we have three significant digits. Now consider a measurement of 0.024 centimeter. The unit of measure is 0.001 centimeter, and 0.024 means that we have 24 of these 0.001 centimeter units. Here, we have two significant digits. Determine the number of significant digits for each of the following measurements:

a. 14.13 millimeters

b. 0.02 decimeters

c. 4.03 hectometers

d. 0.005 meter

e. 420 kilometers (the unit of measure is 10 kilometers)

f. 420 kilometers (the underlining of the zero indicates that the unit of measure is 1 kilometer)

12. Using a calculator, find an approximation for the circumference of each of the following circles. Use $\pi \doteq 3.14$, and express answers to the nearest tenth of a unit.

a. A circle with a radius of 8.2 centimeters

b. A circle with a radius of 4.7 meters

c. A circle with a diameter of 12.6 centimeters

d. A circle with a diameter of 8.6 meters

13. a. How much larger is the circumference of a circle of radius 2 than the circumference of a circle of radius 1? A circle of radius 3 than a circle of radius 1? A circle of radius 4 than a circle of radius 1?

b. If the equator of the earth was a circle and a person 6 feet tall could walk around the earth at the equator, how much farther would the person's head travel than his feet?

c. If the equator of the earth was a circle and if you could walk around the earth at the equator, how much farther would your head travel than your feet?

Pedagogical Problems and Activities

Problems 14–19 illustrate some measurement and estimation activities that can be used with children in the middle grades.

14. a. Estimate by observation the length of each of the following polygonal curves. Give your estimate to the nearest centimeter.

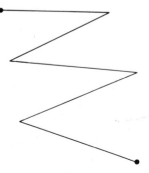

b. Measure the length of each curve in part **a** and compare with your estimate.

15. a. Estimate by observation the length of each of the following curves. Give your estimate to the nearest centimeter.

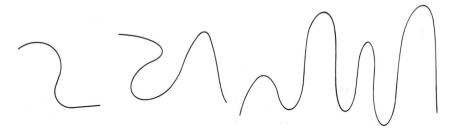

b. For each curve in part **a** select some points on the curve and measure the line segments determined by these points. Use the sum of these measurements as a polygonal approximation of the length of the curve. Compare this result for each curve to your estimation in part **a.**

c. Estimate the length of each curve in part **a** by laying a piece of string along the curve and then measuring the string when straightened out. Compare this to your results from parts **a** and **b.**

16. Use a compass to draw a large circle on a sheet of paper. Estimate by observation the circumference of the circle. Give your estimate to the nearest inch. Then measure a radius of the circle and use the formula $C = 2\pi r$ to get an approximation. Compare this to your original estimation.

17. For each of the following, place a decimal point in the number to make the statement reasonable.

a. The diameter of a pizza is 304 centimeters.

b. The blackboard eraser is 150 decimeters long.

c. The teacher's desk is 800 meters wide.

d. The circumference of an orange is 250 centimeters.

e. The height of a can of pop is 135 centimeters.

f. The length of the classroom is 145 meters.

18. Use a ruler to find the perimeter of the following figures to the nearest mm

a. **b.**

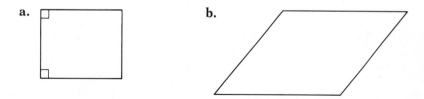

c.   **d.**

19. Using a tape measure a child measures the circumference of a tennis ball. From this measurement she claims to be able to "predict" the height of the can in which the ball was packaged (three tennis balls to a can). What do you say?

20. **a.** How much larger is the circumference of a circle of radius 4 than a circle of radius 2?

    b. How much larger is the perimeter of a square of side 4 than a square of side 2?

    c. How much larger is the perimeter of a square of side $3k$ than a square of side 3?

8.3   ANGULAR MEASURE

In Chapter 7 we restricted our definition of a plane angle so that the two rays that make up the angle could not be in a straight line. This was done to avoid confusion when talking about the interior and exterior of an angle. For measurement purposes we will lift that restriction, as indicated by the following definition.

Definition 8.1   Given two rays $\overrightarrow{AB}$ and $\overrightarrow{AC}$ with a common endpoint A, the set of points $\overrightarrow{AB} \cup \overrightarrow{AC}$ is called a *plane angle*.

Using this as our definition, any of the sets of points in Figure 8.13 fit the concept of being a plane angle. In each case we have labeled the angle $\angle BAC$.

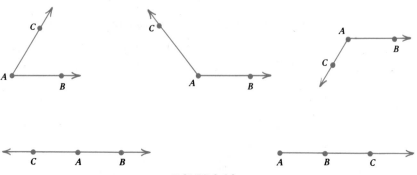

FIGURE 8.13

The idea of "measuring" an angle is analogous to the concept of linear measurement. We need to choose some sort of basic unit that can be used to "measure" angles. In Figure 8.14 we indicate a basic unit angle and then show that this unit can be applied to ∠ABC and its interior five times. In other words, ∠ABC has a measure of five of the unit angles, and this may be written as m∠ABC = 5. A different choice for our basic unit angle would change the number of such angles contained in ∠ABC in Figure 8.14. In other words, we need to agree on some standard units so that an angle of some specific measurement will mean the same to all of us.

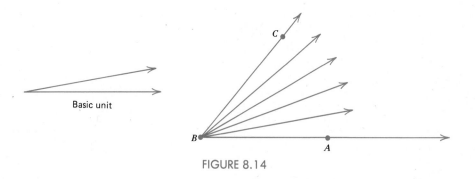

Basic unit

FIGURE 8.14

The common standard units for angle measure are the *degree*, the *grad*, the *mil*, and the *radian*. Because the degree is the unit most frequently used in elementary school mathematics, we will concentrate on it.

REMARK A *mil* is a very small unit that has been used by the United States Army. It is approximately 0.056 of a degree. It also approximates the smallest angle of a right triangle having one side of 1000 units and a second side of 1. This makes for ease in adjusting artillery pieces when in action. The *radian* is used frequently in theoretical mathematics. In fact, those of you who have studied trigonometry may have used radian measure in that connection. One radian is approximately 57.3 degrees. Along with the degree and radian measure, the grad can be found on calculators that have different angle measure capabilities. One-hundred grads = 90 degrees.

Consider a plane angle ∠BAC as in Figure 8.15 such that the rays $\overrightarrow{AB}$ and $\overrightarrow{AC}$ are collinear but $\overrightarrow{AB} \neq \overrightarrow{AC}$. A *degree* is defined to be that basic angle unit so that the measure of ∠BAC in Figure 8.15 is 180. This is written as m∠BAC = 180°; the raised symbol after 180 is the degree symbol. An angle of 180° is called a *straight angle*. Other terminology commonly used pertaining to the "size" of angles is indicated in Figure 8.16.

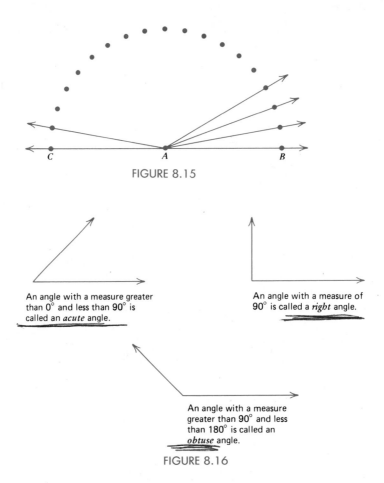

FIGURE 8.15

An angle with a measure greater than 0° and less than 90° is called an *acute* angle.

An angle with a measure of 90° is called a *right* angle.

An angle with a measure greater than 90° and less than 180° is called an *obtuse* angle.

FIGURE 8.16

The measuring device most commonly used for measuring angles is the *protractor*. Figure 8.17 illustrates the protractor as it is being used to indicate that $m\angle AOB \doteq 50°$ and $m\angle AOC \doteq 120°$.

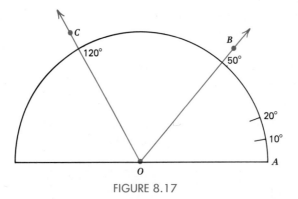

FIGURE 8.17

Our degree system for angle measurement is similar to the hour, minute, and second relationship of our time system. Each degree may be divided into 60 parts, known as *minutes*, and each minute may be further divided into 60 parts called *seconds*. Problems involving degrees, minutes, and seconds frequently require the use of grouping procedures, as indicated by the following example. Suppose that we wish to add (53 degrees and 42 minutes and 37 seconds) to (48 degrees and 51 minutes and 53 seconds). Such a problem may be handled as follows (note the symbolism for minutes and seconds and the use of the facts that 60 seconds = 1 minute and 60 minutes = 1 degree):

$$
\begin{array}{r}
48° \; 51' \; 53'' \\
+ \quad 53° \; 42' \; 37'' \\
\hline
101° \; 93' \; 90'' = 101° \; 94' \; 30'' = 102° \; 34' \; 30''
\end{array}
$$

Numerous angle relationships are involved when working with basic geometric concepts. In this section we will investigate some of these relationships.

If the sum of the measures of two angles is 180°, then they are called *supplementary angles*. If their sum is 90°, they are called *complementary angles*. From the definitions, one must realize that the angles involved when discussing complements and supplements may or may not be adjacent angles, as indicated in Figure 8.18.

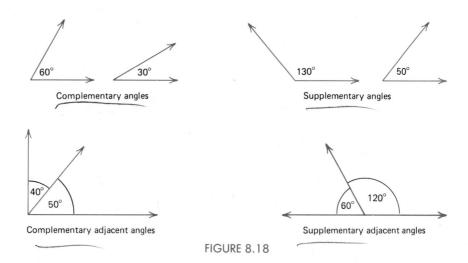

FIGURE 8.18

We can state a relationship pertaining to angles and demonstrate a deductive argument that will verify the property.

PROPERTY 8.1   **Two angles that are complements of the same angle are equal in measure.**

Deductive Argument: First we translate to symbolic form. The property states that "if $\angle A$ and $\angle B$ are both complements of some angle, call it $\angle C$, then $m\angle A = m\angle B$.

Therefore $m\angle A + m\angle C = 90°$ because $\angle A$ and $\angle C$ are complementary
$m\angle B + m\angle C = 90°$ because $\angle B$ and $\angle C$ are complementary
Therefore $m\angle A + m\angle C = m\angle B + m\angle C$ because of transitive property of equality
Therefore $m\angle A = m\angle B$ because of addition property of equality

Three other properties closely related to Property 8.1 are stated next. You may wish to develop an argument to verify each.

PROPERTY 8.2   **Two angles that are supplements of the same angle are equal in measure.**

PROPERTY 8.3   **If two angles are equal in measure, then their complements are equal in measure.**

PROPERTY 8.4   **If two angles are equal in measure, then their supplements are equal in measure.**

Recall from Chapter 7 that two intersecting lines form two pairs of *vertical* angles. In Figure 8.19, $\angle AOB$ and $\angle DOC$ are vertical angles, as are $\angle AOC$ and $\angle BOD$. In Figure 8.20, we illustrate three more vertical angle situations. From these four examples, it appears that a pair of vertical angles must be equal in measure. This conjecture may be easily verified by using some of our previous properties. Referring back to Figure 8.19, we see that $\angle AOC$ and $\angle AOB$ are supplementary angles because $\angle BOC$ is a straight angle, or in other words, equal in measure to $180°$. In a similar fashion, we know that $\angle AOB$ and $\angle BOD$ are supplementary angles. Because $\angle AOC$ and $\angle BOD$ are supplements of the same angle, namely $\angle AOB$, we conclude that $m\angle AOC = m\angle BOD$. We state this as the following property.

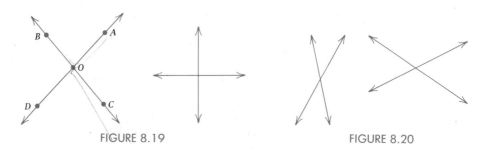

FIGURE 8.19   FIGURE 8.20

PROPERTY 8.5   **If two straight lines intersect, each pair of vertical angles formed are equal in measure.**

In Chapter 7 we established the fact that if two distinct lines are coplanar, then they must be parallel or they intersect. Thus, if two lines $\overleftrightarrow{AB}$ and $\overleftrightarrow{CD}$ are distinct and coplanar, and if both are cut by a third line, one of the possibilities illustrated in Figure 8.21 must exist. Figure 8.21c does not create any interesting relationships beyond vertical angles, so we focus our attention to Figures 8.21a and b.

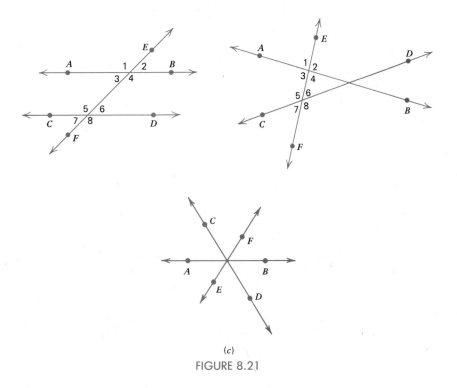

(c)

FIGURE 8.21

Any line that intersects two or more lines is called a *transversal*. In Figures 8.21a and b, $\overleftrightarrow{EF}$ is considered a transversal; in 8.21b each of the lines $\overleftrightarrow{AB}$, $\overleftrightarrow{CD}$ and $\overleftrightarrow{EF}$ is considered a transversal. Special names are commonly given to pairs of angles formed in Figures 8.21a and b. These names are *alternate interior angles*, *alternate exterior angles*, and *corresponding angles*. In general, we call angles located "between" the two given lines interior and those on opposite sides of the transversal alternate. The pairs from Figure 8.21a are given as follows: *Alternate interior* angles in pairs: ∠3 and ∠6, ∠4 and ∠5. *Alternate exterior* angles in pairs: ∠2 and ∠7, ∠1 and ∠8. *Corresponding angles* in pairs: ∠2 and ∠6, ∠4 and ∠8, ∠1 and ∠5, ∠3 and ∠7.

Several relationships pertaining to these pairs of angles exist and are stated in Property 8.6.

PROPERTY 8.6   **If two parallel lines are cut by a transversal, then:**

1. Any pair of corresponding angles are equal in measure.

2. Any pair of alternate interior angles are equal in measure.

3. Any pair of alternate exterior angles are equal in measure.

4. Any pair of interior angles on the same side of the transversal are supplementary.

In Chapter 2 we discussed the concept of a *converse*. Recall that the converse of a statement of the form "if p, then q" is the statement "if q, then p." Also, recall that a true statement may have either a true or a false converse. As it turns out, each of the statements in Property 8.6 has a *true* converse. In fact, we will state these in Property 8.7.

PROPERTY 8.7   **If two lines are cut by a transversal such that**

1. Any pair of corresponding angles are equal in measure, then the lines are parallel.

2. Any pair of alternate interior angles are equal in measure, then the lines are parallel.

3. Any pair of alternate exterior angles are equal in measure, then the lines are parallel.

4. Any pair of interior angles on the same side of the transversal are supplementary, then the lines are parallel.

In Chapter 7, a triangle was defined as a three-sided polygon. Our work with triangles was brief, and none of the special kinds of triangles were named. This we now do. We have arranged the two most common classification schemes in the following chart:

Classification by Angles

Acute triangle   Triangle having three acute angles

Obtuse triangle   Triangle having one obtuse angle

Right triangle   Triangle having one right angle

Classification by Sides

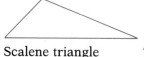

Scalene triangle   Triangle having no two sides of the same measure

Isosceles triangle   Triangle having at least two sides equal in measure

Equilateral triangle   Triangle having all three sides equal in measure

It is possible for triangles to fit both classification schemes—for example, isosceles obtuse triangles. However, the only mixing of classification that is used very often is the concept of an *isosceles right triangle*, which will be discussed later.

Is it possible for a triangle to have two obtuse angles? Is it possible for a triangle to have two right angles? You probably said "no" to both questions, and you are correct. Perhaps you based your answer on attempts to sketch triangles with these conditions, or perhaps you recalled from your past that the sum of the measures of the angles of any triangle is 180°. Either way would exhibit good thinking on your part, and all that we want to do at this time is to show you how this fact may be deduced from some previously established properties.

Consider any triangle $\triangle ABC$ (Figure 8.22). Through point C consider a line l parallel to $\overleftrightarrow{AB}$. Using transversal $\overline{AC}$, we see that $m\angle 1 = m\angle A$, and then using transversal $\overleftrightarrow{BC}$, we now know that $m\angle 2 = m\angle B$ (recall the alternate interior angle property). We also know that $m\angle 1 + m\angle 3 + m\angle 2 = 180°$. Thus, by substitution, $m\angle A + m\angle 3 + m\angle B = 180°$ and the fact

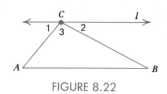

FIGURE 8.22

about the sum of the measures of the angles of any triangle has been deduced.

The fact that the sum of the measures of the angles of a triangle is 180° may be used to determine the sum of the measures of the angles of other convex polygons. For example, consider a quadrilateral $ABCD$, as illustrated in Figure 8.23. By drawing a diagonal (we used $\overline{DB}$, but $\overline{AC}$ could also have been used), we see that the sum of the measures of the angles of the quadrilateral is equal to the sum of the measures of the angles of two triangles. Thus, we conclude that $2(180°) = 360°$ is the sum of the measures of the angles of the quadrilateral. Perhaps you already see a general formula that may be used to find the sum of the measures of the angles of any convex polygon. If not, we have a problem in the next set of exercises that will allow you to pursue this idea.

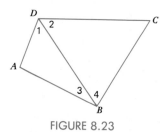

FIGURE 8.23

PROBLEM SET 8.3

1. Do the "lengths of the sides of an angle" affect its measure? Explain your answer.

2. For each of the following, decide which is the angle with the larger measure.

   a. $\angle ABD$ or $\angle DBC$?

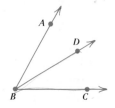

b. ∠ABC or ∠ABD?

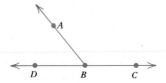

c. ∠ABC or ∠DEF?

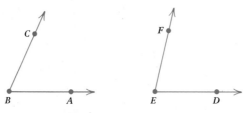

d. ∠ABC or ∠ADC?

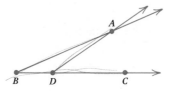

3. Draw a sketch of each of the following (some of these may not be possible):
   a. A triangle with three acute angles
   b. A triangle with one obtuse angle
   c. A convex quadrilateral with two right angles
   d. A convex quadrilateral with no acute angles
   e. A convex quadrilateral with four acute angles
   f. A convex pentagon with five obtuse angles
   g. A convex quadrilateral with three right angles and one acute angle
   h. A convex pentagon with three right angles

4. Classify each of the following true or false. If your answer is false, explain why.
   a. The complement of an acute angle is an obtuse angle.
   b. If two angles are adjacent, then they have the same measure.
   c. The supplement of an obtuse angle is an acute angle.
   d. If two angles are complementary, then they are adjacent angles.
   e. The supplement of a right angle is a right angle.
   f. If two angles are alternate interior angles, then they have the same measure.

g. A pair of alternate exterior angles formed by a transversal intersecting two parallel lines are equal in measure.

h. The supplement of an angle with a measure of 47° 16′ 17″ is an angle with a measure of 132° 43′ 43″.

5. Find the measure of each of the seven remaining angles in the accompanying figure if we know that $m\angle 2 = 65°$. ($l_1 \parallel l_2$ and l_3 is a transversal).

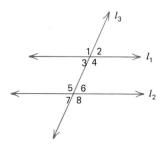

6. Find the measure of the supplementary angle for each of the following:
   a. 130° 15′   **b.** 67° 25′   **c.** 120° 45′ 15″
   d. 53° 13′ 17″   **e.** 57° 16″   **f.** 143° 42″

7. Suppose that two lines intersect so that the measure of one of the four angles formed is 74°. Find the measure of each of the other three angles.

8. Sketch each of the following:
   a. An obtuse isosceles triangle
   b. An isosceles right triangle
   c. An equilateral right triangle
   d. An equilateral acute triangle
   e. A scalene right triangle

9. **a.** Using a ruler and protractor draw a right triangle in which one acute angle has a measure of 40°. What is the measure of the other acute angle?

   b. One acute angle of a right triangle has a measure of 17°. Find the measure of the other acute angle.

10. **a.** Draw a triangle in which one angle measures 48° and a second angle measures 71°. What is the measure of the third angle?

    b. One of the angles of a triangle has a measure of 60°. Find the measure of the other two angles if the difference of their measure is 12°.

11. How many degrees are there in the sum of the measures of the interior angles of the following? (*Hint:* Draw the diagonals from *one* vertex in each polygon.)

a. Triangle   **b.** Quadrilateral   **c.** Pentagon
d. Hexagon   **e.** Heptagon   **f.** *n*-sided polygon
g. Fifteen-sided polygon

12. How many degrees are in each angle of the following regular polygon (all sides and angles equal)

   a. Triangle   **b.** Quadrilateral   **c.** Pentagon
   d. Hexagon   **e.** Heptagon   **f.** *n*-gon

13. a. Draw triangle *ABC* with the following angles: $m\angle A = 23°$, $m\angle B = 58°$, and $m\angle C = 99°$. Measure the lengths of the sides of the triangle. Which side is the longest? Which side is the shortest? Given the measures of the angles of a triangle, can you make any statements about the lengths of the sides of the triangle?

   b. If triangle *ABC* has $m\angle A = 76°$, $m\angle B = 45°$, and $m\angle C = 59°$, which side of the triangle is the longest? Which side is the shortest?

14. In the accompanying figure, $\angle 4$ is called an exterior angle of the triangle. (In general, an exterior angle of a triangle is formed by two rays, one containing a side and the other containing an extension of a second side.) Complete the following chart:

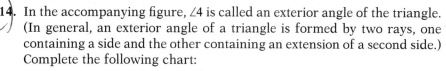

m∠	*m∠2*	*m∠3*	*m∠4*
62°	61°		
57°	48°		
72°	53°		
68°	71°		
64°	73°		

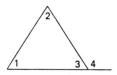

This type of activity may be used to help children realize that the measure of an exterior angle of a triangle equals the sum of the measures of the nonadjacent interior angles.

15. a. What is the sum of the three exterior angles of this equilateral triangle below? See Problem 14 for a definition of exterior angle.

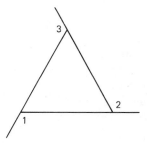

b. Make a scalene triangle and draw an exterior angle at each vertex. Is the sum of the three exterior angles of a scalene triangle the same as that for an equilateral triangle?

c. Consider the two types of quadrilaterals below. Draw an exterior angle at each vertex. What is the sum of the exterior angles for each?

Square   Parallelogram

d. If you had a pentagon and drew one exterior angle at each vertex, what do you think the sum of the measures would be?

e. What regular polygon has each of its exterior angles having a measure of 10°? What is the measure of each interior angle of this polygon?

Pedagogical Problems and Activities

16. One very familiar physical model that elementary school teachers use when discussing various angle relationships is the clock. What kind of angle (acute, obtuse, or right) is represented by the hands of a clock at the following?

a. Three o'clock

b. Fifteen minutes past one o'clock

c. Four o'clock

d. Five o'clock

e. Two o'clock

17. Estimation is involved with angular measure, just as it was with linear measure. Try sketching an angle with a measure of each of the following and then use a protractor to measure to see how well you did:

a. 60°   **b.** 120°   **c.** 150°   **d.** 45°   **e.** 30°

18. What kind of physical activities would you provide for children to help them realize that the "lengths of the sides of an angle" do not affect its measure?

19. Several activities are used in elementary school mathematics programs to help children see that the sum of the measures of the angles of a triangle is 180°. For example, draw a large scalene triangle on a sheet of paper and cut it out. Tear off each corner of the triangle. Draw a straight line on another sheet of paper and label some point P on the line. Place the vertices of the angles that you have torn from the triangle about point P on one side of the line.

20. Using a large scalene triangle cut from a sheet of paper, see if you can "fold" the triangle so as to demonstrate that the sum of the measures of the angles is 180°. Fold all corners to point *D*.

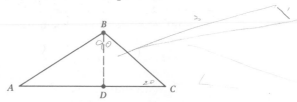

21. A child says, "I made a triangle and when I measured the angles my sum was 182°. Why didn't I get 180°?" What do you say?

22. **a.** A child says, "If you tell me the measures of any two angles of a triangle, I can tell you which side of the triangle is the longest and which side is the shortest." What do you say?

   b. Given the lengths of the two sides of triangle, can you predict which angle is the largest and which is the smallest?

8.4 CONSTRUCTIONS

The terms *sketch, draw,* and *construct* are used frequently to give directions for doing an activity involving certain geometric concepts. Many times sketch and draw are used interchangeably. The directions to "sketch or draw" would usually allow for either a freehand sketch or the use of a measuring instrument such as a meter stick or a protractor. However, in the field of geometry a unique meaning has been reserved for the concept of a *construction.* This meaning was given even before Euclid's time and has been passed along as a tradition. Constructions allow only the use of a compass for making circles or arcs of circles and an unmarked straightedge for making straight lines.

Probably the simplest of the constructions is that of copying a line segment (Construction 8.1). Suppose that we want to mark off on line *l* a segment of the same length as $\overline{AB}$. Choose some point *A'* on *l* to correspond with point *A*. Now place the point of the compass on *A* and open it so that the other

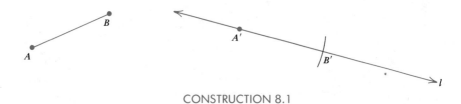

CONSTRUCTION 8.1

point is on B. Using this radius, one can mark off a segment $\overline{A'B'}$ on l so that $A'B' = AB$. Notice that the point B' could be on either side of A'.

Suppose you want to construct an angle of the same measure as $\angle ABC$ (Construction 8.2). First, make some line l that will contain one side of the angle. Choose point B' on line l to serve as a vertex of the angle. Place the point of the compass at B and strike an arc intersecting both sides of the angle. Using the same radius and B' as the center, construct a semicircle intersecting l in two points D' and E'. Now use the compass to "measure" $\overline{XY}$. With that radius, place the point of the compass at E' (D') and make an arc intersecting the semicircle at F' (G'). The points B' and F' (G') determine a ray that now gives us $\angle F'B'E'$ and $\angle G'B'D'$ so that $m\angle F'B'E' = m\angle ABC = m\angle G'B'D'$.

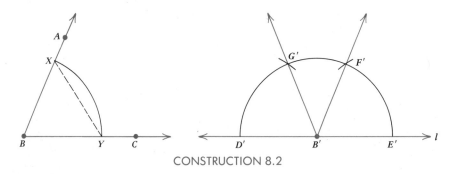

CONSTRUCTION 8.2

To construct a ray that bisects a given angle (Construction 8.3), begin by placing the point of the compass at B and striking an arc of some radius intersecting the two sides of the angle at E and D. Now using the same radius (or changing the radius if you like), place the compass point at D and make an arc in the interior of $\angle ABC$. Using this same radius and E as a center, strike an arc intersecting the other arc you made in the interior of $\angle ABC$. Point P is determined, and $\overrightarrow{BP}$ is the angle bisector.

What are the results of the angle bisector construction if the angle being bisected is a straight angle? In this case, each of the resulting angles is a right angle, and the line determined by the bisector ray is *perpendicular* to the line containing the straight angle (Construction 8.4). This construction is what we

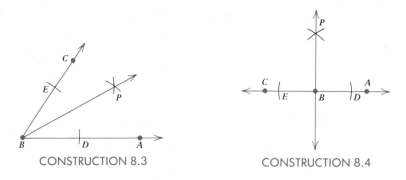

CONSTRUCTION 8.3   CONSTRUCTION 8.4

do if we are asked to construct a line perpendicular to a given line at some point on the line. Variations of this construction may be used to construct the perpendicular bisector of a line segment and to construct a line perpendicular to a given line through a point not on the given line.

Let us consider one final construction in this section. Suppose we want a line parallel to a given line and containing some point not on the given line. Property 8.7 gives several relationships that may be used for this construction (Construction 8.5). In Construction 8.5, line l is the given line and P is the point not on l. First, draw any line through P intersecting l at A. Now a line l_1 that is parallel to l may be determined by copying corresponding angles as indicated. We could use alternate interior or alternate exterior angles as well.

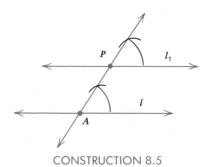

CONSTRUCTION 8.5

PROBLEM SET 8.4

1. **a.** On a line l construct line segments $\overline{A'B'}$ and $\overline{C'D'}$ that are equal in measure to $\overline{AB}$ and $\overline{CD}$, respectively, so that their intersection is empty.

   b. Do as in part a except the intersection is to be a point.

   c. Do as in part a except the intersection is to be a segment.

2. Draw an acute angle and then construct its angle bisector.

3. Draw an obtuse angle and then construct its angle bisector.

4. Construct a line perpendicular to a given line at a given point on the given line.

5. Construct a line perpendicular to a given line and containing a given point not on the given line.

6. Draw a line segment 10-cm long. Construct the perpendicular bisec-tor of the segment. Check the accuracy of your construction by mea-suring.

7. Draw an acute angle. Construct an angle with twice the measure of that angle.

8. Draw two acute angles. Construct an angle equal in measure to the sum of the measures of the two angles.

9. **a.** Review Construction 8.5.

   b. Use alternate interior angles to do Construction 8.5.

   c. Use alternate exterior angles to do Construction 8.5.

   d. Do you see any other way of constructing a line parallel to a given line and containing a given point not on the given line?

10. Construct an angle with the following measures:

    a. 90°   **b.** 45°   **c.** 135°

11. Draw an acute angle. Construct the complement of the angle.

12. **a.** Construct an equilateral triangle for which each side has the same measure as $\overline{AB}$.

   b. Construct a 30° angle.

13. Construct an isosceles right triangle for which the two sides of the same length have the measure of $\overline{AB}$.

Pedagogical Problems and Activities

14. Figure $ABCD$ is a quadrilateral with all four sides equal, that is, $AB = BC = CD = DA$. Such a quadrilateral is called a rhombus.

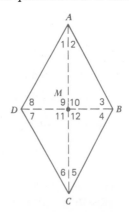

   a. Draw three different rhombi. (Label each *ABCD* is in the figure.)
   b. Draw the diagonals $\overline{AC}$ and $\overline{BD}$ in each rhombus.
   c. Measure all 12 angles, labeled as above. What do you notice?
   d. Measure $\overline{AM}$, $\overline{MC}$, $\overline{BM}$, and $\overline{MD}$. What do you notice?
   e. Refer to Construction 8.3. Can you "see" rhombus *BEPD* in this
       construction?

15. Figure *ABCD* is a special quadrilateral with *AB* = *BC* and *AD* = *DC*. Such
    a quadrilateral is called a *kite*.

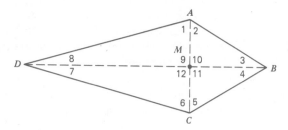

   a. Draw three different kites. (Label each *ABCD* as in the figure.)
   b. Draw the diagonals $\overline{AC}$ and $\overline{ED}$.
   c. Measure all 12 angles, labeled as above. State three relationships you
       notice.
   d. Measure $\overline{AM}$, $\overline{MC}$, $\overline{BM}$, and $\overline{MD}$. State two relationships you notice.

16. Children in the elementary school may use paper folding to simulate
    some of the basic constructions. For example, folding a sheet of paper
    in half both vertically and horizontally will produce a model that can be
    used to demonstrate perpendicularity as well as the idea of a perpendic-
    ular bisector of a line segment. Suggest how children could illustrate the
    following constructions by paper folding:
   a. A line perpendicular to a given line at a given point on the given line
   b. A line perpendicular to a given line and containing a given point not
       on the given line
   c. A line parallel to a given line and containing a given point not on the
       given line
   d. An angle bisector

8.5   CONGRUENCE AND SIMILARITY

The concept of congruence has always been a vital part of the study of
Euclidean geometry. However, many times we fail to realize that this same
notion of congruence also plays a very important role in everyday living. We

are able to replace worn-out spark plugs with new ones of "the same code number." A belt on the clothes dryer breaks, and in order to buy a new one we need to know "the brand name and model number" of the dryer. In both of these examples, the idea of "sameness of size and shape" is involved, and mathematically we call this notion *congruence*.

It should seem evident that two line segments of the same length do fit the notion of "sameness of size and shape." Thus, we say that if $AB = CD$, then the two segments are congruent, which is written as $\overline{AB} \cong \overline{CD}$. An analogous statement may be made pertaining to angles. If $m\angle ABC = m\angle DEF$, then the angles are congruent, and we write $\angle ABC \cong \angle DEF$.

The notion of congruence related to line segments and angles merely provides another way of stating that two line segments or two angles have the same measure. However, the simple tie-up between "having the same measure" and "congruence" does not extend to all geometric figures. For example, two triangles may have the same measure (area) but be of totally "different shapes," as illustrated in Figure 8.24. Thus, the relation of congruence becomes an important issue when studying geometric figures.

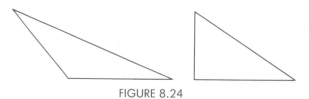

FIGURE 8.24

When we speak of two geometric figures as being congruent, we mean that they have exactly the same size and shape. For example, in Figure 8.25, the two triangles are congruent. You might establish this fact by cutting out one of the triangles and fitting it on the other one. This process of cutting out and superimposing may be described by using the concept of one-to-one corre-

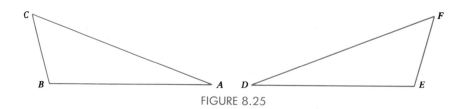

FIGURE 8.25

spondence. We could describe an attempt to place $\triangle ABC$ on $\triangle DEF$ by matching vertices A and D, B and E, and C and F. This matching may be indicated by the order in which the vertices are stated (Fig. 8.26).

In this matching, $\overline{AB}$ corresponds to $\overline{DE}$, $\overline{BC}$ matches with $\overline{EF}$, and $\overline{AC}$ is

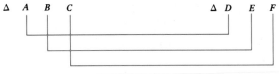

FIGURE 8.26

paired with $\overline{DF}$. Furthermore, it should be noted that by simply matching vertices, six different one-to-one correspondences between the two triangles may be described as follows:

$$\triangle ABC \leftrightarrow \triangle DEF \qquad \triangle ABC \leftrightarrow \triangle FDE$$
$$\triangle ABC \leftrightarrow \triangle DFE \qquad \triangle ABC \leftrightarrow \triangle EFD$$
$$\triangle ABC \leftrightarrow \triangle FED \qquad \triangle ABC \leftrightarrow \triangle EDF$$

If a matching can be found so that corresponding angles and corresponding line segments are congruent, then the correspondence is called a congruence between the two triangles. In Figure 8.25, the matching $\triangle ABC \leftrightarrow \triangle DEF$ is a congruence, and we write $\triangle ABC \cong \triangle DEF$.

In general, congruent polygons may be defined as follows.

Definition 8.2 Two polygons are congruent if and only if some one-to-one correspondence exists between the vertices of the polygons such that all pairs of corresponding angles and all pairs of corresponding sides are congruent.

Even though the definition for congruent triangles states that all six pairs of corresponding parts (three pairs of angles and three pairs of sides) must be congruent, fewer than six parts may be used to determine congruence. For example, suppose that we were to construct a number of different triangles, all having sides of the same length, as indicated in Figure 8.27. Two such triangles have been constructed with the indicated lengths of a, b, and c and appear to be congruent. In Figure 8.27, the congruence is indicated by $\triangle DEF \cong \triangle HGI$. Thus, we are saying that two triangles are congruent if the three sides of one are congruent, respectively, to the three sides of the other triangle. Let us state this as a property.

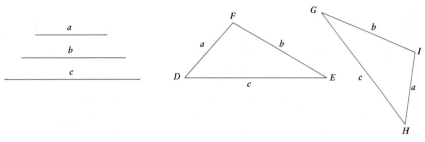

FIGURE 8.27

PROPERTY 8.8   In $\triangle ABC$ and $\triangle A'B'C'$, if $\overline{AB} \cong \overline{A'B'}$, $\overline{AC} \cong \overline{A'C'}$, and $\overline{BC} \cong \overline{B'C'}$, then $\triangle ABC \cong \triangle A'B'C'$ (this property is commonly referred to as the **SSS** property of congruent triangles).

Let us now investigate a situation that demonstrates the significance of Property 8.8. An isosceles triangle has been defined as a triangle having two sides of the same measure or, stated another way, a triangle with two congruent sides.

We might conjecture that the angles opposite the congruent sides of an isosceles triangle are also congruent. We will state this as a property and then exhibit a proof in which Property 8.8 plays a very important role.

PROPERTY 8.9   **In an isosceles triangle, the angles opposite the congruent sides are also congruent.**

Proof Consider $\triangle ABC$ for which $\overline{AC} \cong \overline{BC}$, as in Figure 8.28. Find the midpoint D of $\overline{AB}$. Draw line segment $\overline{CD}$. We know that $\overline{AC} \cong \overline{BC}$, $\overline{AD} \cong \overline{DB}$, and $\overline{CD}$ is a common side of $\triangle ADC$ and $\triangle BDC$. Thus, by Property 8.8, $\triangle ADC \cong \triangle BDC$. Now we know that the remaining corresponding parts of the two triangles are congruent. Thus, we have $\angle A \cong \angle B$, which is what we were attempting to establish.

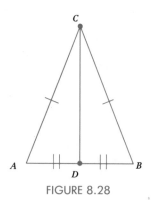

FIGURE 8.28

It should be noted that Property 8.9 also allows us to conclude that all three angles of an equilateral triangle are congruent. Thus, it is frequently stated that equilateral triangles are also equiangular. In addition to the *SSS* property, there are several other ways of determining congruent triangles by using fewer than all six parts of the triangles. We state two of these properties at this time and in the next problem set have you deduce some other properties.

PROPERTY 8.10   In $\triangle ABC$ and $\triangle A'B'C$, if $\overline{AC} \cong \overline{A'C'}$, $\overline{AB} \cong \overline{A'B'}$, and $\angle A \cong \angle A'$, then $\triangle ABC \cong \triangle A'B'C'$. (*SAS* property)

Property 8.10 is sometimes stated: If two sides and the included angle of one triangle are congruent, respectively, to two sides and the included angle of another triangle, then the triangles, are congruent.

PROPERTY 8.11   In $\triangle ABC$ and $\triangle A'B'C'$, if $\angle A \cong \angle A'$, $\angle B \cong \angle B'$, and $\overline{AB} \cong \overline{A'B'}$, then $\triangle ABC \cong \triangle A'B'C'$. (*ASA* property)

Property 8.11 is also stated: If two angles and the included side of one triangle are congruent, respectively, to two angles and the included side of another triangle, then the triangles are congruent.

> REMARK   For you who have previously had a "proof-oriented" geometry course, the *SSS*, *ASA*, and *SAS* properties should be familiar. They are used extensively in such a course to establish that certain triangles are congruent, and then the congruency of the triangles is used to deduce basic geometric relationships. The purpose of this book is to provide an intuitive look at the development of relationships involving congruence and not to dwell on proofs.

In Figure 8.29, the triangles in Parts (*a*) and (*b*) appear to be congruent, but neither of them seems to be congruent to the triangle in part (*c*). However, the triangles in parts (*a*) and (*b*) do have the same shape as the one in part (*c*). We refer to figures that have the same shape (but not necessarily the same size) as *similar* figures. No doubt many everyday situations come to mind when we think of the concept of similarity. For example, the figurine that is a model for a full-scale figure, a road map, and a toy train that is a scale model of a full-size train are all illustrations of the concept of similarity.

In general, we talk about three types of similarity. Given an object, there is an *enlargement* similarity, which is illustrated by the use of an overhead

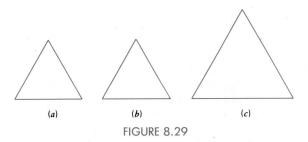

(a)   (b)   (c)

FIGURE 8.29

projector. We also have a *shrinking* similarity, which is illustrated by pictures taken by a camera. *Congruence*, which keeps objects the same size, is the third form of similarity.

Using the notion of the same shape to describe similar figures may provide a good intuitive background, but we need to be careful that it does not mislead students. For example, in Figure 8.30 are the two quadrilaterals similar? It is possible that some people would say yes because they both have four sides and are therefore of the same shape. However, this is not what we want to mean by the phrase "same shape." To avoid confusion, we offer the following definition for the concept of similarity.

FIGURE 8.30

Definition 8.3   Two polygons are said to be similar if and only if there is a one-to-one correspondence between their vertices such that corresponding angles are congruent and the measures of corresponding sides are proportional.

REMARK Recall that when some number a is divided by a nonzero number b, the quotient $\dfrac{a}{b}$ is called a ratio. The equality of two ratios is called a proportion. For example, $\frac{8}{10} = \frac{4}{5}$ is a proportion. Also recall that $\dfrac{a}{b} = \dfrac{c}{d}$ if and only if $ad = bc$.

EXAMPLE

When enlarged, 3-cm $\times$ 5-cm picture becomes 18 cm along the short side. What will be the length of the long side in the enlargement?

Solution Let s be the length of the large side. From similarity we know $\frac{3}{18} = \frac{5}{s}$. Solving, we find $s = 30$ cm. We could also have used the proportion $\frac{3}{5} = \frac{18}{s}$ to solve the problem.

Even though Definition 8.3 is in terms of polygons, we restrict our study of similarity to triangles. As one might suspect, certain conditions determine similarity of two triangles without using all six parts. It can be shown that two triangles are similar if two angles of one triangle are congruent respectively to two angles of the other triangle. Suppose that in Figure 8.31 we know that $\angle A \cong \angle D$ and $\angle B \cong \angle E$. This is enough information to guarantee that the two triangles are similar, and we will write this as $\triangle ABC \sim \triangle DEF$.

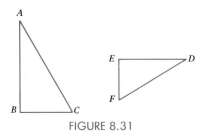

FIGURE 8.31

As with congruency, the order in which we indicated the vertices is significant; that is, A is matched with D, B with E, and C with F. Thus, we may also conclude that

$$\frac{AB}{DE} = \frac{AC}{DF} = \frac{BC}{EF}$$

Let us now examine two problems involving the concept of similarity.

EXAMPLE 1

Suppose that in Figure 8.32 we know that $\triangle ABC \sim \triangle DEF$. Furthermore, suppose that some of the lengths of the sides are known as indicated. Find the measures of $\overline{BC}$ and $\overline{DF}$.

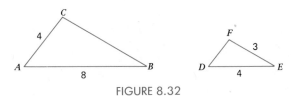

FIGURE 8.32

Solution First, let us use the proportion $\dfrac{AB}{DE} = \dfrac{AC}{DF}$. From this we have $\dfrac{8}{4}$

$= \dfrac{4}{DF}$ and therefore $8DF = 16$ or $DF = 2$. Then using the proportion

$\dfrac{BC}{EF} = \dfrac{AB}{DE}$ we have $\dfrac{BC}{3} = \dfrac{8}{4}$, therefore $BC = 6$.

EXAMPLE 2

In Figure 8.33 we are told that $\overline{BE}$ and $\overline{DC}$ are both perpendicular to $\overline{AC}$. It is also given that E is the midpoint of $\overline{AD}$ and $BE = 4$. Find CD.

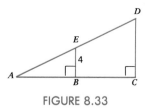

FIGURE 8.33

Solution We know that $\triangle ABE \sim \triangle ACD$ because $\angle A$ is common to both triangles and $\angle B$ and $\angle C$ are right angles. The fact that E is the midpoint of $\overline{AD}$ tells us that $\dfrac{AE}{AD} = \dfrac{1}{2}$. Thus, using the proportion $\dfrac{BE}{CD} = \dfrac{AE}{AD}$, we have $\dfrac{4}{CD} = \dfrac{1}{2}$ from which we conclude $CD = 8$.

One of the most frequently used relationships based on similarity of triangles is illustrated in Figure 8.34. Line l is parallel to $\overline{BC}$. It can be verified by using similar triangles ABC and ADE that $\dfrac{AD}{DE} = \dfrac{AE}{EC}$. This relationship is often stated as follows: If a line parallel to one side of a triangle intersects the other two sides, then it divides those sides proportionally.

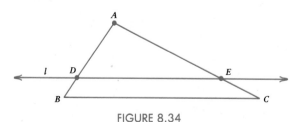

FIGURE 8.34

An extension of the previously stated relationship is illustrated in Figure 8.35. In this figure, l_1, l_2, and l_3 are parallel lines, and it can be shown that $\dfrac{a}{b} = \dfrac{c}{d}$. (Parallel lines intercept proportional line segments on two transversals.) For example, in Figure 8.35 suppose that $a = 3$, $b = 4$, and $c = 7$. The proportion $\dfrac{a}{b} = \dfrac{c}{d}$ becomes $\dfrac{3}{4} = \dfrac{7}{d}$, and d may be found to be $9\frac{1}{3}$.

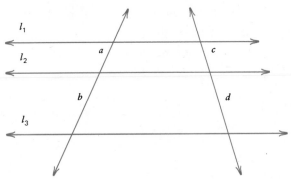

FIGURE 8.35

Let us conclude this section by looking at one application of this property. Suppose that we are given a line segment $\overline{AB}$ and we are asked to divide it into three congruent segments (Construction 8.6). We may begin by drawing a ray $\overrightarrow{AC}$ and on this ray marking off three congruent segments $\overline{AP_1}$, $\overline{P_1P_2}$, and $\overline{P_2P_3}$. Connect P_3 with B, and through P_2 and P_1 construct lines parallel to $\overline{P_3B}$. These lines intersect $\overline{AB}$ in points S and R, and it must be true that $\overline{AR} \cong \overline{RS} \cong \overline{SB}$.

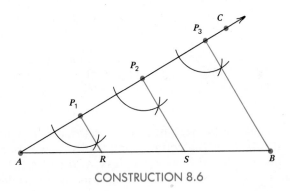

CONSTRUCTION 8.6

PROBLEM SET 8.5

1. Given that $\triangle DEF \cong \triangle HKP$, name the congruent angles and congruent sides.

2. **a.** What is the measure of each angle of an equilateral triangle?
   b. Are all equilateral triangles congruent? Explain your answer.

3. If $\triangle ABC$ is isosceles such that $\overline{AC} \cong \overline{BC}$ and $m\angle A = 70°$, find the measures of $\angle B$ and $\angle C$.

4. In △ABC, $\overline{AC} \cong \overline{BC}$ and the measure of ∠A is twice the measure of ∠C. Find the measures of ∠A, ∠B, and ∠C.

5. Construct an angle of measure
   a. 60°   b. 30°   c. 120°   d. 75°

6. In the accompanying figure, △ABC and △A'B'C' are right triangles with right angles at B and B', respectively. If ∠C ≅ ∠C' and $\overline{AC} \cong \overline{A'C'}$, why are the triangles congruent?

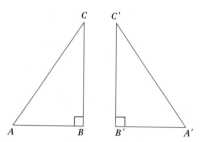

7. Property 8.10 states that if two angles and the included side of one triangle are congruent, respectively, to two angles and the included side of another triangle, then the triangles are congruent. Suppose that we have two angles and a side respectively congruent in two triangles, but it is not the "included" side. Will the triangles be congruent? Explain your answer.

8. Suppose that we have two right triangles with a hypotenuse and one acute angle of one triangle congruent to the hypotenuse and an acute angle of the other triangle. Are they congruent triangles? Explain your answer.

9. a. In the accompanying figure, $\overline{CB} \cong \overline{CD}$, $\overline{AC}$ is a common side of △ACB and △ACD. ∠A is a common angle of the two triangles, and as stated $\overline{CB} \cong \overline{CD}$. Are the two triangles △ACB and △ACD congruent? This is why Property 8.9 states that "it must be two sides and the *included* angle."

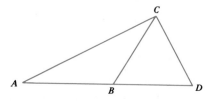

   b. Two noncongruent triangles can be made in which each satisfy the following three conditions. Draw both triangles.

   $$m\angle A = 45°, AB = 50 \text{ mm}, AC = 40 \text{ mm}$$

10. **a.** If two polygons are similar, does this assure us that they are congruent?

   b. If two polygons are congruent, does this assure us that they are similar?

11. **a.** Are any two equiangular triangles similar? Explain your answer.

   b. Are any two equilateral triangles similar? Explain your answer.

12. Suppose that a road map has a scale such that 1 centimeter represents 50 kilometers. Use proportions to find the following:

   a. 14 centimeters represent how many kilometers?

   b. 8.5 centimeters represent how many kilometers?

   c. 750 kilometers would be represented by how many centimeters?

13. The measures of the sides of a triangle are 3, 4, and 6 centimeters, respectively. If the longest side of a similar triangle is 18 centimeters, find the measures of the other two sides.

14. The sides of a pentagon are of length 4, 6, 7, 9, and 12 meters, respectively. If the longest side of a similar pentagon is of length 8 meters, find the length of the remaining sides.

15. The legs of a right triangle are of length 5 inches and 7 inches, respectively. If the shorter leg of a similar right triangle has a measure of 12 inches, find the measure of the other leg.

16. In the accompanying figure, $\overline{DE} \| \overline{AB}$.

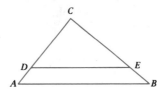

   a. Find BE if $CD = 6$, $DA = 2$, and $CE = 7$.

   b. Find CB if $AC = 14$, $DA = 5$, and $CE = 12$.

17. Using the procedure outlined in Construction 8.6, divide a line segment into five congruent parts.

18. Show two different constructions that might be used to divide a line segment into four congruent parts.

19. Consider the following pieces of information about triangle ABC. In each case, decide whether the information allows you to construct a triangle and, if it does, decide whether all triangles made under these conditions are congruent.

	$m\angle A$	$m\angle B$	$m\angle C$	AB	AC	BC
i.			40°	72 mm		83 mm

	$m\angle A$	$m\angle B$	$m\angle C$	AB	AC	BC
ii.	72°	83°				
iii.		98°	104°			88 mm
iv.	72°			72 mm		54 mm
v.	72°			72 mm		85 mm
vi.	35°	55°		65 mm		
vii.	35°	55°			65 mm	
viii.	35°	55°				65 mm

20. If $\overrightarrow{BD}$ is the bisector of $\angle ABC$, $\overline{PM} \perp \overrightarrow{BA}$ and $\overline{PN} \perp \overrightarrow{BC}$, how do we know that $\overline{PM} \cong \overline{PN}$.

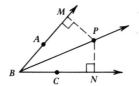

Pedagogical Problems and Activities

21. Very carefully construct different triangles that have two angles and the included side as indicated. Cut the triangles out and show that they are congruent by placing them so as to coincide. (This type of an activity may be used to help children understand the significance of Property 8.10.)

22. Very carefully construct different triangles that have two sides and the included angle as indicated. Cut the triangles out and show that they are congruent by placing them so as to coincide. (This should help children with Property 8.9.)

23. Give five examples from the physical world that suggest similarity but not congruence.

24. Grid paper or dotted paper simulating a geoboard may also be used to help children with the concept of similarity. Consider the two similar triangles on the grids shown. How do the lengths of their sides compare? How do their perimeters compare?

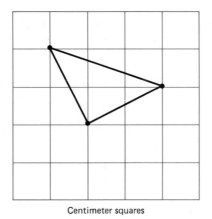

Centimeter squares   One-half centimeter squares

25. a. On the grid provided, make a figure similar to (but not congruent to) the one on the left so that the new figure touches 12 dots.

b. On the grid provided, make a figure similar to (but not congruent to) the one on the left so that the new figure touches 10 dots.

26. a. On the grid provided, "scale down" the pentagon by a factor of one-half.

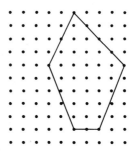

   b. On the "grid" provided, "scale up" the hexagon by a factor of 3.

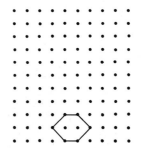

27. In the accompanying figure we indicate a way of constructing a triangle similar to a given triangle. The newly formed triangle ($\triangle A'B'C$) has sides of length twice those of the original triangle ($\triangle ABC$). Point O is chosen as some arbitrary point other than points A, B, or C. Then rays $\overrightarrow{OA}$, $\overrightarrow{OB}$, and $\overrightarrow{OC}$ are drawn. On these rays, lengths are marked off such that $OA' = 2(OA)$, $OB' = 2(OB)$, and $OC' = 2(OC)$. Use this technique to do each of the following:

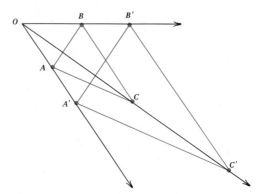

    a. "Scale up" a triangle by a factor of 3.

    b. "Scale down" a triangle by a factor of $\frac{1}{2}$.

    c. "Scale down" a triangle by a factor of $\frac{1}{3}$. (*Hint:* Make use of Construction 8.6.)

28. Pattern blocks consist of the following shapes:

    a. Using pattern block pieces, a child says that ⬭ and ⬭⬭ are similar. What do you say?

    b. Using only the ◊ pattern block pieces, make a figure similar, but not congruent, to this piece. How many pieces did you use?

    c. Using only one kind of pattern block piece, make a shape similar, but not congruent, to the following shape:

    d. Using only the ⬭ pattern block pieces, make a figure similar, but not congruent, to this piece.

8.6 CONGRUENCE VIA MOTION GEOMETRY

We now take a look at congruence from a different perspective, that of transformational, or motion, geometry. This approach more closely parallels the type of visual thinking and spatial ability that develops early in young children—that of movement of figures in space as well as mental transformations of figures. The purpose of this section is to introduce you to several of these concepts. The development of these ideas from an activity approach is suggested in the NCTM Standards.

    Suppose that we print the "letters" METRIC on a sheet of paper and then fold the paper before the ink dries completely, so that the folded-over part covers the printing. As the paper is unfolded, two printings appear, as illustrated in Figure 8.36. The two printings are called *line reflection* images of each other. If one were to hold the printing on the left side of Figure 8.36 up to a mirror, the right side would appear in the mirror. Thus, the terminology of "mirror image" is also being used to describe a line reflection. Some materials use the term "flip" instead of line reflection. Regardless of the terminology used, we want to develop the mental picture of flipping over.

FIGURE 8.36

Now let us look at the concept of a line reflection. In Figure 8.37, triangles *ABC* and *A'B'C'* are line reflection images of each other. The line *l* is the perpendicular bisector of $\overline{AA'}$, $\overline{BB'}$, and $\overline{CC'}$. The two triangles are congruent, and, in general, any two figures that are line reflection images of each other

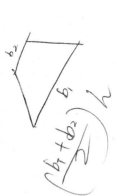

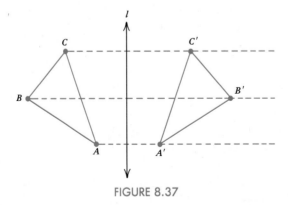

FIGURE 8.37

are congruent. Thus, in Figure 8.38 we might guess that the two quadrilaterals are congruent by mentally picturing them as line reflection images of each other.

Next, suppose that we have made a lettering stencil for the word METRIC. In Figure 8.39 we use the stencil on the left and then simply slide it across the paper and use it a second time. The two printings are called *slide* or *translational* images of each other. The slide could be made in any direction as long as there is no turning of the stencil (Fig. 8.40).

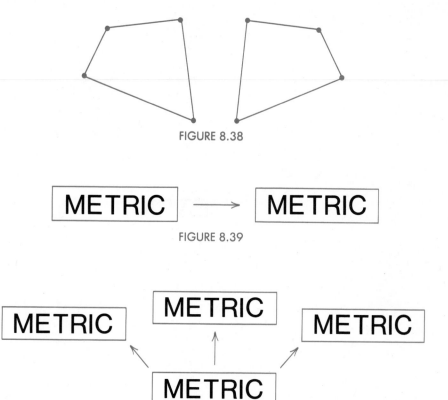

FIGURE 8.38

FIGURE 8.39

FIGURE 8.40

In Figure 8.41, we can view a translation from a construction viewpoint. The lines $\overleftrightarrow{AA'}$, $\overleftrightarrow{BB'}$, and $\overleftrightarrow{CC'}$ are parallel and $AA' = BB' = CC'$. We say that $\triangle ABC$ and $\triangle A'B'C'$ are translational images of each other and are congruent. Any two geometric figures that are translational images of each other are congruent.

Consider Figure 8.42. Note that the letter stencil positions are not translational images, nor are they line reflection images. Some sort of "turning" process has occurred. In fact, as illustrated in Figure 8.43, the stencil has been rotated 90° clockwise about a fixed point O. Thus, we say that the two positions of the stencil are 90° *rotational images* of each other. The direction of rotation is given in terms of being clockwise or counterclockwise.

Figure 8.44 shows a 60° clockwise *rotation* of a triangle. Point A has been

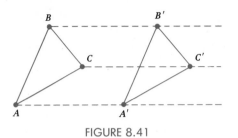

FIGURE 8.41

FIGURE 8.42

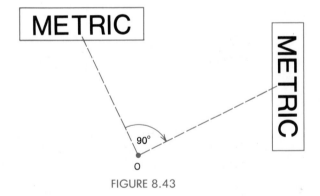

FIGURE 8.43

rotated to A', B to B', and C to C', thus making triangles ABC and $A'B'C'$ rotational images of each other. More specifically, $\triangle A'B'C'$ is a 60° clockwise rotational image of $\triangle ABC$, about point O, and $\triangle ABC$ can be considered as a 60° counterclockwise rotational image of $\triangle A'B'C'$. It should be noted that $m\angle AOA' = m\angle BOB' = m\angle COC' = 60°$. Furthermore, $OA = OA'$, $OB = OB'$, and $OC = OC'$. The triangles ($\triangle ABC$ and $\triangle A'B'C'$) in Figure 8.44 are congru-

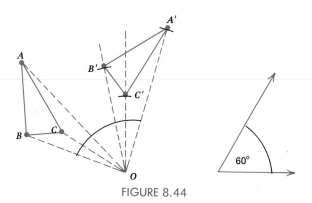

FIGURE 8.44

ent; in general, any two geometric figures that are rotational images of each other are congruent.

Consider Figure 8.45*a*. Note that the letter stencil positions are not line reflection images, nor translational images, nor rotational images of each other. However, consider sliding the stencil as indicated by the arrow and then reflecting it over line *l* (Figure 8.45*b*). This is called a *glide reflection*. A glide reflection is the successive application of a translation and a line reflec-

FIGURE 8.45*a*   FIGURE 8.45*b*

tion. In Figure 8.46 △*ABC* and △*A′B′C′* are glide-reflection images of each other and are congruent. In general, any two geometric figures that are glide-reflection images of each other are congruent.

It should be noted in Figure 8.46 that the translation is made parallel to the line of reflection. This allows us to make the translation and line reflection in either order. For example, in Figure 8.46 had we reflected △*ABC* over line *l* first and then translated it to the right, the final image would have been the same △*A′B′C′*.

For the purpose of summarizing this section, let us repeat four important statements:

1. If two geometric figures are *line reflection images* of each other, then they are congruent.

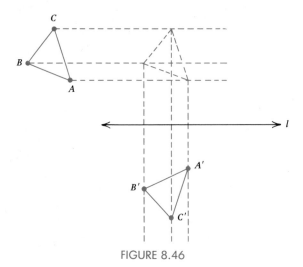

FIGURE 8.46

2. If two geometric figures are *translational images* of each other, then they are congruent.
3. If two geometric figures are *rotational images* of each other, then they are congruent.
4. If two geometric figures are *glide-reflection images* of each other, then they are congruent.

Finally, it can also be stated that if two geometric figures in the same plane are congruent, then they must be either line-reflection images, translational images, rotational images, or glide-reflection images of each other.

PROBLEM SET 8.6

1. Find the image for each of the following with respect to the given line of reflection:

a.
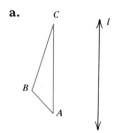

b.
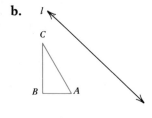

c.

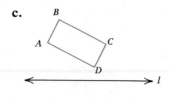

d.

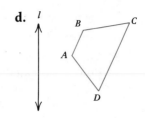

e.

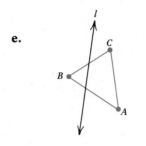

f.

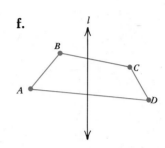

2. In each part of Problem 1 we labeled the original figure using a clock-wise orientation. For example, the quadrilateral in part **c** is labeled *ABCD* moving in a clockwise direction around the figure. Now look at your reflection images from Problem 1. Are they oriented in a clockwise or counterclockwise manner?

3. Find the translational image for each of the following (the arrow indicates the direction for the translation, and the length of the arrow indicates the distance to be translated):

a.

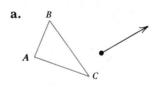

b.

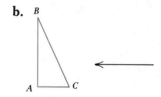

c.

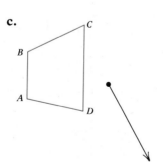

d.

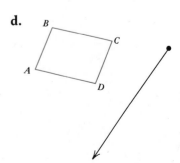

4. From your work in Problem 3, does orientation seem to be affected by translations?

5. Find the rotational image for each of the following. The amount of rotation is indicated by the accompanying angle, and the direction is indicated by the arrow in the angle. The point *O* is to be the center of rotation. You may want to copy the figure on another sheet of paper first.

a.

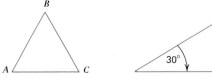

● *O*

b.

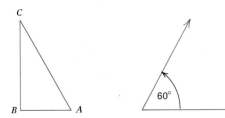

● *O*

c.

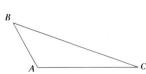

● *O*

d.

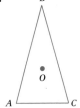

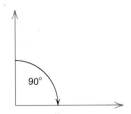

e.

• *O*

f.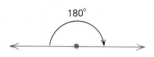

• *O*

6. From your work in Problem 5, does orientation seem to be affected by rotations?

7. Find the glide-reflection image for each of the following. The amount and direction of translation is indicated by the arrow, and *l* is the line of reflection. You may want to copy the figure on another sheet of paper first.

a.

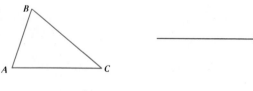

b.

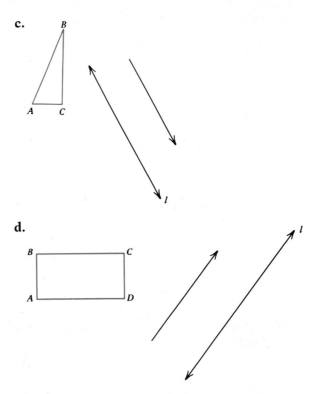

c.

d.

8. From your work in Problem 7, does orientation seem to be affected by glide reflections?

9. Which triangles seem to be congruent to △ABC? Indicate whether they appear to be line-reflection, translational, rotational, or glide-reflection images of △ABC.

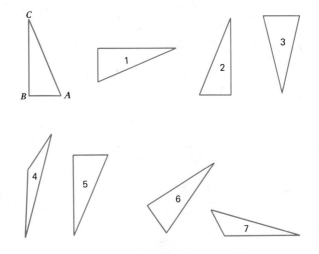

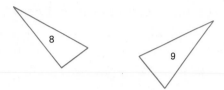

10. Find the glide-reflection image of the accompanying triangle by doing the following:

 a. First translating and then reflecting

 b. First reflecting and then translating

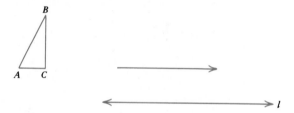

11. In the accompanying figure, $\triangle ABC$ and $\triangle A'B'C'$ are line-reflection images of each other. Construct the line of reflection.

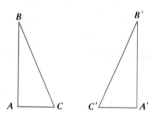

12. In the accompanying figure, $\triangle ABC$ and $\triangle A'B'C'$ are rotational images of each other. By a construction, find the center of rotation and then do the rotation.

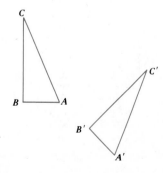

Pedagogical Problems and Activities

13. Children can be challenged to find physical examples of the motion-geometry concepts of this section. For example, the movement of an elevator is a model of a translation, and the turning of clock hands describes a rotation. Make a list of physical models for line reflections, translations, rotations, and glide reflections. For rotations, indicate whether the model normally allows for both clockwise and counterclockwise movement.

14. Sketch the line reflection image for each of the following:

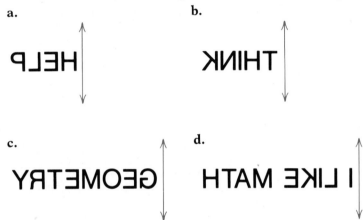

a.   **b.**

c.   **d.**

15. Using the following, find the images of the figures over the given line.

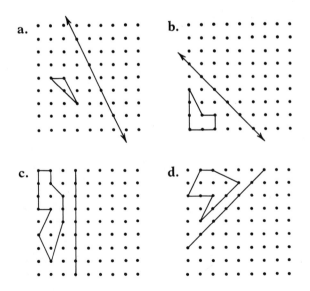

a.   **b.**

c.   **d.**

8.7   QUADRILATERALS

In Chapter 7, the concept of a polygon was introduced. Convex polygons were classified according to the number of sides (triangle, quadrilateral, pentagon, etc.). In this chapter we classified triangles according to length of sides and measure of angles, such as isosceles, acute, and equilateral. It is also possible and convenient to make some additional classifications for quadrilaterals.

Let us start with a definition for a *parallelogram;* it is a quadrilateral having both pairs of opposite sides parallel. A few parallelograms are illustrated in Figure 8.47. Looking at these figures, some ideas should be emphasized. First, we would probably agree at once that the figures in parts (*a*), (*b*), and (*c*) are parallelograms. However, we may look at part (*d*) and say that it is a rectangle. This is true, but we must realize that it does fit our definition of a parallelogram, and the fact that we call it a rectangle simply means that a further classification of parallelograms is being made. In other words, Figure 8.47*d* will possess all the properties of the figures in parts (*a*), (*b*), and (*c*), plus some additional ones. Likewise, the figure in part (*e*) is a rhombus and the one in (*f*) is a square, but they are also parallelograms. Also, figure (*f*), although a square, is also considered a rectangle.

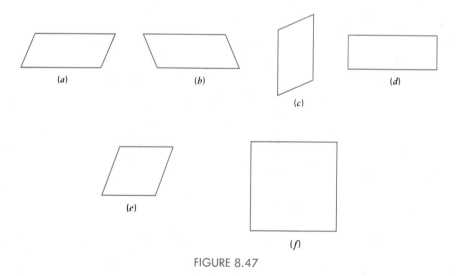

(*a*)   (*b*)   (*c*)   (*d*)   (*e*)   (*f*)

FIGURE 8.47

In Figure 8.47, it certainly appears that these figures possess properties other than the fact that both pairs of opposite sides are parallel. This is true, but rather than include a complete listing of properties in a definition, it is more reasonable to keep the definition as simple as possible and then deduce the additional properties by using previous information. For example, consider a parallelogram $ABCD$, as in Figure 8.48 with a diagonal $\overline{AC}$. Using $\overline{AC}$ as a transversal and the fact that $\overline{DC}\|\overline{AB}$, we know that $\angle 2 \cong \angle 1$. Again, using $\overline{AC}$ as a transversal and this time the fact that $\overline{AD}\|\overline{BC}$, it can be concluded that $\angle 3 \cong \angle 4$. Using $\overline{AC}$ as a common side, we conclude by the ASA congruence property that $\triangle ABC \cong \triangle CDA$. Thus, we know that $\overline{AB} \cong \overline{DC}$, $\overline{BC} \cong \overline{AD}$, and $\angle D \cong \angle B$.

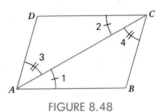

FIGURE 8.48

We now present a sequence of pictures and definitions indicating the usual classification scheme of quadrilaterals.

A *parallelogram* is a quadrilateral having both pairs of opposite sides parallel.

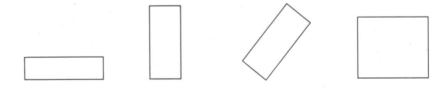

A *rectangle* is a parallelogram having one right angle.

A *square* is a rectangle having two adjacent sides congruent.

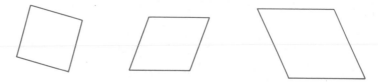

A *rhombus* is a parallelogram having two adjacent sides congruent.

REMARK In general usage with younger children a rectangle is considered a parallelogram with four right angles, a square is considered a rectangle with all sides equal, and a rhombus is considered a parallelogram with four sides equal. It should again be noted that in any case a square is also a rectangle.

A *trapezoid* is a quadrilateral having one and only one pair of parallel sides. If the nonparallel sides are congruent, then it is called an *isosceles trapezoid*. We will have you deduce some additional properties of some of these figures in the next problem set.

PROBLEM SET 8.7

1. Sketch each of the following:

   a. A rectangle that is not a square

   b. A parallelogram that is not a rectangle

   c. A rhombus that is not a square

   d. A trapezoid having three congruent sides

   e. An isosceles trapezoid

2. Answer each of the following true or false. If your answer is false, explain why.
   a. A square is a parallelogram.
   b. A trapezoid is a parallelogram.
   c. A square is a rhombus.
   d. A rhombus is a square.
   e. A parallelogram is a rhombus.
   f. A rhombus is a parallelogram.
   g. An isosceles trapezoid is a quadrilateral.

3. Are the opposite sides of a rectangle congruent? Explain your answer.

4. The definition for a rectangle stated that it was a parallelogram with one right angle. Argue that this implies that all four angles are right angles.

5. Provide an argument that the diagonals of a rectangle are congruent.

6. The definition for a square stated that it was a rectangle with two adjacent sides congruent. Argue that this implies that all four sides of a square are congruent.

7. Draw some different sizes of parallelograms and draw in both diagonals for each. Make a conjecture pertaining to some relationship that you observe about the two diagonals of a parallelogram. Attempt to justify your conjecture.

8. Make the following constructions:
   a. A square given the length of a diagonal
   b. A rectangle given the length of one side and one diagonal
   c. A parallelogram given the lengths of two adjacent sides and the measure of the included angle
   d. A rhombus given the lengths of the diagonals

   Recall that we had you do some "counting" type problems back in Chapter 7 involving line segments and triangles. Problems 9–11 pertain to "counting squres."

9. How many squares (all sizes) can you find in each of the following figures? (Do not forget to organize your counting process so that all squares are counted, but none is counted more than once!)

   a.   b.

c.   d.

10. Sometimes a complicated counting problem can be handled by first doing some *easier but analogous* problems and trying to find a pattern. For example, suppose that we want to know the total number of squares (all sizes) on the following checkerboard.

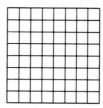

We could begin our analysis by considering some "smaller" situations first as follows:

1   square

4   1 by 1 squares
1   2 by 2 square
___
5

9   1 by 1 squares
4   2 by 2 squares
1   3 by 3 square
___
14

Complete each of the following:

_____1 by 1 squares
_____2 by 2 squares
_____3 by 3 squares
_____4 by 4 squares

_____1 by 1 squares
_____2 by 2 squares
_____3 by 3 squares
_____4 by 4 squares
_____5 by 5 squares

Now "count" the number of squares (all sizes) on the checkerboard shown at the beginning of this problem.

11. How many squares (all sizes) are there in the following figure?

Pedagogical Problems and Activities

12. Many squares of different sizes can be made on a geoboard. Often the square like that shown here is overlooked because it is not in "normal" position. Find as many different sized squares as you can in the dot paper on the right.

13. In the next chapter we work with the concept of area. An understanding of some of the area formulas relies on being able to see some relationships between geometric figures. A foundation for this work may be started with children as they are beginning to work with the various geometric shapes. Paper-folding and cutting is one vehicle that can be used to help develop some important concepts. For each of the following indicate how one cut can be made to accomplish the objective:

   a. Make one right triangle and one rectangle from the accompanying figure.

b. Make one parallelogram and one triangle from the accompanying figure.

c. Make two triangles from the accompanying figure.

d. Make one triangle and one trapezoid from the accompanying figure.

e. Make two trapezoids from the accompanying figure.

8.8   REGULAR POLYGONS AND SYMMETRY

The concepts of linear and angular measure have been the points of emphasis throughout this chapter. Various classifications of triangles and quadrilaterals have been based on either some kind of linear measure relationship or an angular measure concept. In fact, when working with triangles we concluded that an equilateral triangle (all sides of the same measure) was also equiangular (all angles of the same measure). This tie-up between equilateral and equiangular does not exist for all polygons. For example, a rhombus is equilateral but may not be equiangular. Furthermore a rectangle is an example of a polygon that is equiangular but not necessarily equilateral. Any polygon that is both equilateral and equiangular is called a *regular polygon*. This classification of polygons is our concern at this time.

Previously we deduced that the sum of the interior angles of any polygon is given by the expression $180(n - 2)$, where n represents the number of sides of the polygon.

Thus, if a polygon is regular, each angle should be of measure $\dfrac{180(n - 2)}{n}$. Using this formula, each angle of a regular pentagon is $\dfrac{180(5 - 2)}{5} = 108°$.

Let us use this information about regular polygons to investigate a problem. Suppose that we want to form a "tiling pattern" to cover a flat surface by repeatedly using a regular polygon of one kind. For example, in Figure 8.49 a pattern is illustrated using only squares. We have indicated with the dots that this pattern could go on infinitely in all directions. This is often called *tiling the plane.*

Can other regular polygons be used to tile a plane? Suppose that we try using equilateral triangles. As illustrated in Figure 8.49, they also work. Some points are darkened in both Figure 8.49 and Figure 8.50 in an attempt to help you focus on the key to the general problem of determining which regular polygons may be used for tiling the plane. We know that the sum of the measures of the angles about a point is 360°. In Figure 8.49 there are four 90° angles "surrounding" each point. In Figure 8.50 there are six 60° angles "surrounding" each point. What is the measure of each angle of a regular pentagon? Will we be able to use regular pentagons to cover the plane? What is the measure of each angle of a regular hexagon? Will we be able to use regular hexagons? Are there any other regular polygons that will work? From the investigation of angles about a point, we see that only equilateral triangles, squares, or regular hexagons will work.

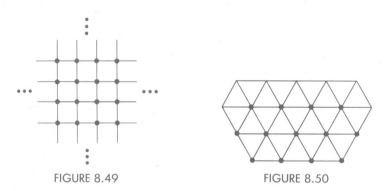

FIGURE 8.49　　　　　　　　　　　FIGURE 8.50

One other property of regular polygons plays a very important role. Every regular polygon has a point in its interior that is equidistant from all of its sides, and this point is also equidistant from all vertices. The point is called the *center* of the polygon. It is helpful to know that this point can always be found at the intersection of angle bisectors, as illustrated in Figure 8.51.

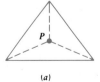

(a)　　　　　　　(b)　　　　　　(c)　　　　　　(d)

FIGURE 8.51

In Section 8.6, the notion of a line reflection was discussed. Suppose that in Figure 8.52 we consider the line reflection image of the rectangle with respect to the line l. The line l is the perpendicular bisector of $\overline{BC}$ and $\overline{AD}$. The image of the rectangle is the rectangle itself. We say that line l is a *line of symmetry* or that the rectangle is symmetrical with respect to the line l. In general, a plane geometric figure is said to be symmetric with respect to a line l if and only if the reflection of the figure with respect to l is the figure itself.

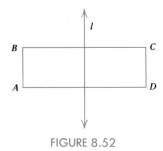

FIGURE 8.52

In Figure 8.53 parts (a), (b), (d), (e), and (g) illustrate lines of symmetry, but in parts (c) and (f) the indicated line of reflection is not a line of symmetry.

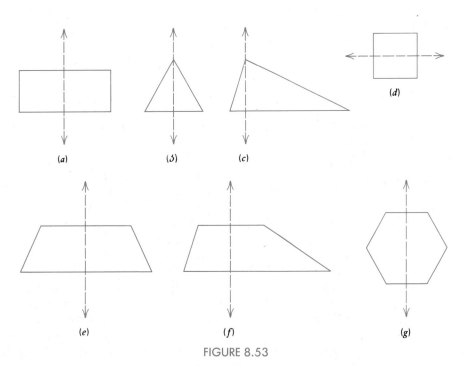

FIGURE 8.53

We could also check for symmetry in the polygons in Figure 8.53 by cutting out each and folding along the dashed lines and seeing whether the two parts fold together and coincide, or by placing a transparent mirror along the dashed lines to see if the reflection image coincides with the actual figure we see by looking through the mirror.

Consider the polygons and the indicated lines in Figure 8.54. Which of the figures appear to be symmetrical with respect to the indicated line? Certainly the use of a mirror or paper-folding would be helpful; however, perhaps you can simply form a mental picture of what would happen. Only in parts (a), (b), and (f) is the indicated line a line of symmetry. The concept of line sym-

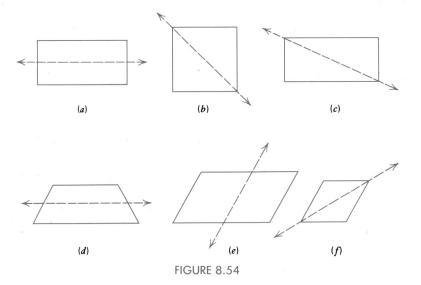

FIGURE 8.54

metry may be used as another setting for studying some characteristics of various geometric figures. For example, as illustrated in Figure 8.55, a square has four lines of symmetry, a rectangle has two lines of symmetry, and the isosceles triangle has one line of symmetry.

We have so far considered only lines of symmetry relative to polygons. From the general description of line symmetry we need not restrict our work to polygons. Consider the various plane curves in Figure 8.56. Do the curves in parts (a), (c), (d), (e), (f), and (g) have line symmetry? [Note that the curves in parts (d), (e) and (g) have two lines of symmetry.]

In Section 8.6 we also worked with the concept of a rotation. Consider a 90° clockwise rotation of a square using the point of intersection of the diagonals as the center of rotation. A physical model of this rotation is illustrated in Figure 8.57. In part (a) a square region has been cut from a sheet of cardboard and fastened to another piece of cardboard by placing a thumbtack at the point of intersection of the diagonals. The vertices of the square have been labeled on both pieces of cardboard as indicated in (a). Now suppose

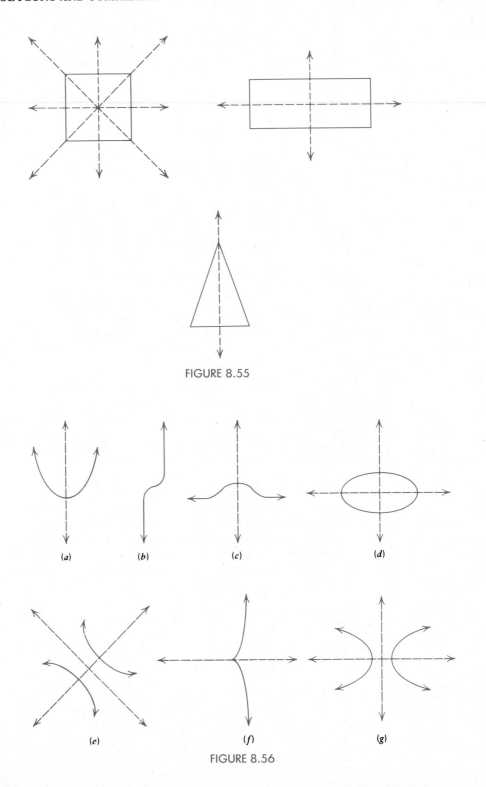

FIGURE 8.55

(a) (b) (c) (d)

(e) (f) (g)

FIGURE 8.56

(a)   (b)

FIGURE 8.57

that we trace (on the larger sheet) the square and then rotate it 90° clockwise and trace it again. [Part (b) illustrates the square after a clockwise rotation of 90°.] The two tracings should coincide, and thus we say that a square has 90° rotational symmetry. In other words, the result of a 90° clockwise rotation of a square, using the point of intersection of the diagonals as the center of rotation is the square itself.

Does a square have rotational symmetry other than 90°? A continuation of the experiment illustrated in Figure 8.57 should allow us to conclude that a square also has 180° and 270° rotation symmetry.

> REMARK Because the "direction" of rotation has no effect on the study of symmetry properties, we will continue in this section to consider only clockwise rotations. Furthermore, we will restrict the rotations to be between 0° and 360°. We state this restriction becasue it should be clear that a rotation of 360° will make any figure coincide with itself.

Now suppose we carry out the same experiment illustrated in Figure 8.57 except this time rotate a rectangular region 90°. The two tracings around the rectangular region would be as depicted in Figure 8.58. Thus, we would say that a rectangle (that is not a square) does not have 90° rotational symmetry. However, we should be able to conclude that a rectangle does have 180° rotational symmetry. Thus, we have another way of distinguishing between a

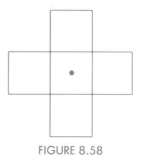

FIGURE 8.58

square and a rectangle that is not a square. A square has rotational symmetry of 90°, 180°, and 270°, whereas a rectangle that is not a square only has rotational symmetry of 180°.

One final idea needs to be mentioned in this section. The notion of 180° rotational symmetry is sometimes also called *point symmetry*. The reason for this is illustrated in Figure 8.59. Certainly points B and D are 180° rotational images of each other. However, because $OB = OD$, we could also think of them as *point reflection images* of each other with respect to the point O. Likewise, the points A and C can be considered point reflection images with respect to point O. In fact, for any point P of the rectangle, there is a point reflection image P' also on the rectangle. Consequently, we can mentally picture a 180° rotation in terms of "rotating" about a fixed point or also in terms of "reflecting" through the fixed point.

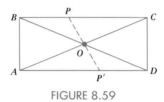

FIGURE 8.59

Having studied regular polygons in two-space, we now investigate analogous figures in three-space. Such figures are called *regular polyhedrons*. A regular polyhedron is composed of congruent regular polygonal regions put together to form a solid figure with identical corners. Probably the simplest regular polyhedron is the one made up of four equilateral triangles, as illustrated in Figure 8.60. (Keep in mind that we mean *regions* in the shape of equilateral triangles.) This figure is called a *regular tetrahedron*. Note that each corner is "surrounded" by three equilateral triangles.

Now suppose that we try to surround a point with four equilateral triangles. In so doing we can form a figure with eight faces, as illustrated in Figure 8.61. It is called a *regular octahedron*.

Using five equilateral triangles to surround a point produces the figure illustrated in Figure 8.62. Such a figure has 20 faces and is called a *regular icosahedron*. Visualizing all the faces of this figure from a two-dimensional

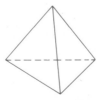

FIGURE 8.60   FIGURE 8.61   FIGURE 8.62

drawing is very difficult. A three-dimensional model constructed as suggested in Problem 24 of the next Problem Set would be very helpful.

It is impossible to form a polyhedron by surrounding a point with six equilateral triangles. This may not be at all obvious, but if you try to do it you will find that you must put all six equilateral triangles in the same plane. Thus, a three-dimensional figure is not formed. Therefore, we have exhausted the possibilities for forming regular polyhedrons from equilateral triangles.

Now suppose that we attempt to form a regular polyhedron made up of squares. By surrounding a point with three squares and then completing the figure, we form probably the most familiar of all regular polyhedrons, the *cube* (Fig. 8.63). Because it has six faces, it is also referred to as a *regular hexahedron*.

FIGURE 8.63

From your work with equilateral triangles, it should seem reasonable that any attempt to build a regular polyhedron by surrounding a point with four or more squares would be futile. Thus, the cube is the only regular polyhedron made up of squares.

Next let us see what happens when regular pentagons are used to build a regular polyhedron. Surrounding a point with three regular pentagons and then completing the figure produces a *regular dodecahedron* (Fig. 8.64). Again, a three-dimensional model would be very helpful to see all 12 faces of the figure. Because the measure of each angle of a regular pentagon is 108°, no more than three pentagons surrounding a point will work. Thus, the regular dodecahedron is the only regular polyhedron made up of regular pentagons.

At this time we reach an interesting conclusion: There are no other regular

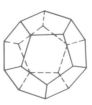

FIGURE 8.64

polyhedrons. Our reasoning for reaching this conclusion goes as follows. Suppose that we try to build a regular polyhedron by using regular hexagons. The measure of each angle of a regular hexagon is 120°. Thus, any attempt to surround a point with three hexagons would simply result in the three hexagons being placed in one plane, and no three-dimensional figure would be formed. This type of reasoning should also tell us that there is no need to try forming regular polyhedrons from regular heptagons, regular octagons, and so on. Therefore, there exist only five regular polyhedrons: tetrahedron, hexahedron (cube), octahedron, dodecahedron, and icosahedron.

It is interesting to note that the study of these regular polyhedron, as well as additional polyhedrons, has many applications. For example, the study of crystal structures makes extensive use of these shapes.

PROBLEM SET 8.8

1. Sketch each of the following:
   a. A quadrilateral that is equilateral but not equiangular
   b. A quadrilateral that is equiangular but not equilateral
   c. A regular quadrilateral
   d. A pentagon that is equilateral but not equiangular
   e. A pentagon that is equiangular but not equilateral

2. For each of the following find the measure of each interior angle and then sketch a figure:
   a. A regular pentagon
   b. A regular hexagon
   c. A regular heptagon
   d. A regular octagon
   e. A regular decagon
   f. A regular dodecagon

3. a. Use each of the following, to sketch a "tiling pattern" that covers a plane:
   (i) An isosceles triangle
   (ii) A right triangle that is not isosceles
   (iii) An isosceles right triangle
   b. Make a paper model of each of the following and trace around it to form a "tiling pattern" that covers a plane:
   (i) An acute scalene triangle
   (ii) An isosceles obtuse triangle
   (iii) A scalene obtuse triangle
   c. From your work in parts **a** and **b**, do you think that any triangle could be used to tile a plane? Explain your answer.

4. a. Use each of the following to sketch a "tiling pattern" that covers a plane:

  (i) A rectangle

 (ii) A parallelogram

(iii) A rhombus

 (iv) An isosceles trapezoid

b. Make a paper model and trace around it to form a "tiling pattern" that covers a plane:

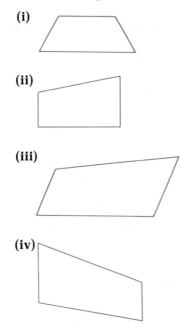

(i)

(ii)

(iii)

(iv)

c. From your work in parts **a** and **b,** do you think that any quadrilateral could be used to tile a plane? Explain your answer.

5. We have concluded that a regular pentagon cannot be used to tile a plane. Find a pentagon that is not regular that will work for tiling a plane.

6. We have also concluded that a regular hexagon can be used to tile a plane. See if you can find a hexagon that is not regular that will also work.

7. How many sides does a regular polygon have if each of its interior angles has a measure of 162°?

8. Do the following figures have any lines of symmetry? If so, about where are they? If you have a transparent mirror available, test your lines of symmetry with the mirror.

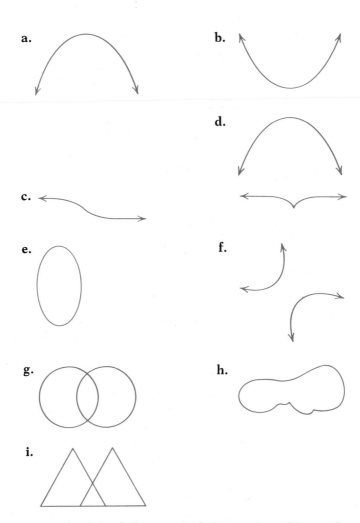

a.

b.

d.

c.

e.

f.

g.

h.

i.

9. For each of the following find the number of lines of symmetry. Draw figures to help you decide.

    a. Parallelogram   b. Rhombus

    c. Trapezoid   d. Isosceles trapezoid

    e. Scalene triangle   f. Isosceles triangle

    g. Equilateral triangle   h. Isosceles right triangle

10. Find the number of lines of symmetry for each of the following. Again, sketching figures may help you decide.

    a. Regular triangle   b. Regular quadrilateral

    c. Regular pentagon   d. Regular hexagon

    e. Regular heptagon   f. Regular n-sided polygon (n gon)

11. How many lines of symmetry does a circle possess? Defend your answer.

12. Describe the rotational symmetry of each of the following. For example, a square has rotational symmetry of 90°, 180°, and 270°.
    a. Equilateral triangle   b. Isosceles triangle   c. Scalene triangle
    d. Rectangle   e. Parallelogram   f. Rhombus
    g. Trapezoid   h. Regular pentagon   i. Regular hexagon
    j. Regular heptagon   k. Regular octagon

13. Which of the following figures has point symmetry? Remember that point symmetry is the same as 180° rotational symmetry.
    a. Rectangle   b. Parallelogram   c. Rhombus
    d. Isosceles trapezoid   e. Equilateral triangle f. Scalene triangle
    g. Isosceles triangle   h. Regular pentagon   i. Regular hexagon

14. Does a line segment have a point of symmetry? A line of symmetry?

15. Does an angle have a point of symmetry? A line of symmetry?

16. Sketch a concave quadrilateral that has a line of symmetry.

17. How many "small" cubes are indicated by each of the following figures?

a.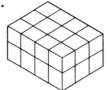

b.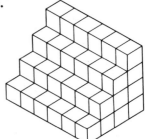

c.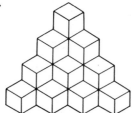

d.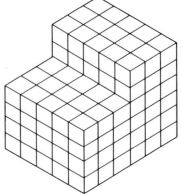

18. What is the total number of cubes (all sizes) indicated by each of the following figures?

a   b 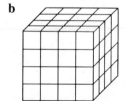   c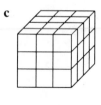

19. Suppose 27 small cubes are put together in a 3-by-3-by-3 cubical pile and the 6 outer surfaces are painted red. After the paint dries, the 17 cubes are "unpiled." Now answer the following questions:

  a. How many of the small cubes have 3 sides painted red?
  b. How many of the small cubes have 2 sides painted red?
  c. How many of the small cubes have 1 side painted red?
  d. How many of the small cubes do not have any sides painted red?

20. Using a calculator, find the measure of each interior angle of a regular polygon having the following number of sides. What is happening to the size of each interior angle as the number of sides of the regular polygon increases?
  a. 20 sides
  b. 50 sides
  c. 75 sides
  d. 150 sides
  3. 450 sides
  f. 1200 sides

Pedagogical Problems and Activities

21. Use paper-folding to establish the number of lines of symmetry for each of the following:
  a. Square   b. Rectangle
  c. Isosceles triangle   d. Equilateral triangle
  e. Regular pentagon   f. Regular hexagon

22. Use paper-folding to demonstrate each of the following:
    a. A diagonal of a rectangle is not a line of symmetry.
    b. A diagonal of a rhombus is a line of symmetry.
    c. An isosceles trapezoid has one line of symmetry.
    d. The angle bisectors of a scalene triangle are not lines of symmetry.

23. There is symmetry in many manmade objects of this world, but nature has also made great use of the concept of symmetry.
    a. Make a list of some manmade objects that possess symmetry. Indicate whether they have point symmetry or line symmetry or both.
    b. Make a list of some natural objects that possess symmetry. Indicate whether they have point symmetry or line symmetry or both.

24. The following are plane figures that may be folded as indicated to make models of the five regular polyhedrons. You may want to make your models on a larger scale than that illustrated.

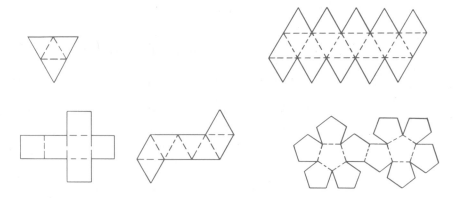

25. In Chapter 7 Euler's formula relative to polyhedrons (number of faces plus number of vertices minus number of edges equals two) was discussed. Use your models from Problem 24 and verify Euler's formula for each of them.

REVIEW PROBLEM SET

1. Convert as indicated within the metric system.
   a. 142 centimeters = _____ meters
   b. 31 meters = _____ centimeters
   c. 164 meters = _____ kilometers
   d. 0.34 decimeters = _____ meters
   e. 1.4 kilometers = _____ meters
   f. 163 hectometers = _____ dekameters

2. Why do we say that a measurement of 6 centimeters is more precise than a measurement of 8 meters?

3. Explain the meaning of the terms *accuracy* and *precision*.

4. Find the circumference of each of the following circles. Leave answers in terms of π.
   a. A circle with a radius of 17 centimeters
   b. A circle with a diameter of 13 meters

5. If $\angle A$ and $\angle B$ are supplementary angles and $m\angle A = 14° \ 17'$, find $m\angle B$.

6. If $\angle A$ and $\angle B$ are complementary angles and $m\angle B = 34° \ 16' \ 10''$, find $m\angle A$.

7. Construct an equilateral triangle and then construct the three angle bisectors.

8. Construct an angle whose measure is 150°.

9. How many degrees are there in the sum of the measures of the interior angles of a decagon?

10. Suppose you are told the $\triangle ABC \cong \triangle XYZ$. Complete the following:
    a. $\overline{AB} \cong$ _____
    b. $\angle C \cong$ _____
    c. $\overline{AC} \cong$ _____
    d. $\angle ABC \cong$ _____

11. The measures of the sides of a triangle are 5, 7, and 10 centimeters, respectively. If the shortest side of a similar triangle is 13 centimeters, find the measures of the other two sides.

12. Suppose you are told that $\triangle ABC \sim \triangle DEF$ and $AB = 14$ units, $DE = 8$ units, and $AC = 5$ units. Find DF.

13. How many lines of symmetry does each of the following possess?
    a. Square
    b. Rectangle
    c. Parallelogram
    d. Isosceles trapezoid
    e. Regular hexagon
    f. Isosceles triangle
    g. Equilateral triangle

14. Sketch each of the following:
    a. A right octagonal prism
    b. A regular pentagon

  c. A regular polyhedron having six faces
  d. An isosceles trapezoid
  e. A regular octahedron
  f. A hexagon that is equilateral but not equiangular

15. What is the measure of each interior angle of a regular hexagon?

16. From the diagram, construct a **90°** clockwise image of △*ABC* with respect to point *O*.

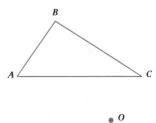

17. From the diagram, construct the line reflection image of △*ABC* with respect to the line *l*.

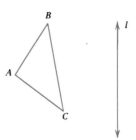

18. What does it mean to say that line reflections and glide reflections reverse orientation?

Solution to Sample Problem

How many dollar bills are there in a stack one kilometer tall?

1. *Understanding the Problem.* The question seems straightforward enough. It is asking how many dollar bills would it take to make a kilometer stack. Would it matter if the dollar bills were crumpled?

2. *Devising a Plan.* It does not seem reasonable to try and measure the thickness of a dollar bill. How many would I have to get in order to make a tall enough stack so that I would be comfortable with measuring it with any degree of confidence? The crumpled bills would soon flatten out if several hundred more of them were placed on top. I think I will model this with

paper seeing that I do not have enough dollar bills. I will measure the width of 500 sheets of paper and proceed from there.

3. *Solution.* I found a ream of 500 sheets of paper and measured its thickness. Interestingly enough, I found the 500 sheets to measure approximately 5 cm. Now, how many sheets would be needed for a kilometer thickness? First, we need to change 1 kilometer to centimeters, 1 km = 100 000 cm, and then set up a proportion to solve this: $\dfrac{500}{5} = \dfrac{n}{100\,000}$. Solving we find $n = 10\,000\,000$, and that there would be approximately 10 000 000 dollar bills in a stack one kilometer high.

4. *Looking Back.* If we measured a thick enough stack of paper, we are confident of this solution as being a reasonable approximation.

3. *Looking Ahead.* I wonder how much this stack of bills would weigh? I wonder what kind of polyhedron this stack is? I wonder how long a line this stack of bills would make if we laid them end to end? I wonder what the surface area and volume of this stack would be?

9 | AREA AND VOLUME

Sample Problem

A rectangular sheet of paper, 215 cm by 280 cm, can be rolled and taped along an edge in two different ways to make a cylinder. Which way, taped along the 215 cm or the 280 cm edge, should you roll it to give the larger volume?

9.1 INTRODUCTION AND AREA

The NCTM Standards again give us some insight into the types of experiences that should be provided for children to learn the measurement concepts of area and volume. Specifically, examples should be provided that include covering regions with squares and other units of area and filling of containers with cubes and other units of volume. Children should not be expected to learn these concepts from pictures in books. They should also develop procedures and formulas to determine area and volume by partitioning and rearranging figures. It is from this perspective that this chapter is organized.

Suppose we have five rectangular sheets of cardboard on the floor and that we try to cover each in a different manner, one with circular regions, one with square regions, one with rectangular regions, one with parallelograms, and one with equilateral triangles. A possible result of this activity is illustrated in Figure 9.1.

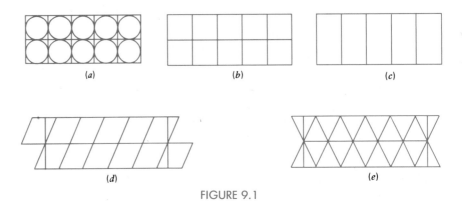

FIGURE 9.1

This type of activity could be used to lay the groundwork for a discussion of many different ideas pertaining to the concept of area. Some of the important notions that should be the result of such a discussion are as follows:

1. A basic unit plane region is needed to measure plane regions. Recall that a plane region is the union of a simple closed plane curve and its interior.
2. A number assigned to a plane region that describes how many unit regions are needed to cover it is called the *area* of the region. For example, in Figure 9.1*b*, the rectangular region has an area of approximately 10 unit squares, whereas in (*c*) it has an area of approximately 5 unit rectangles.
3. Many different shapes could be used for a basic unit of area. (Recall our work with tiling the plane in the previous chapter.)
4. Although many different shapes could be used, the square is the shape traditionally used for the basic unit of area.

Even after the square has been chosen as the basic shape of a unit of area, it is still necessary to adopt some standard-size squares. We normally choose as our standard squares those where the measure of a side is one of our standard linear units; for example, a square centimeter (a region bounded by a square, each side of which is one centimeter long), a square meter (a region bounded by a square, each side of which is one meter long), and a square inch (a region bounded by a square, each side of which is one inch long).

Suppose that we choose as our basic unit of area a square such as □ and form a grid (Fig. 9.2). The simple process of counting allows you to determine that the areas of the shaded regions in parts (*a*) through (*d*) are 6, 6, 7,

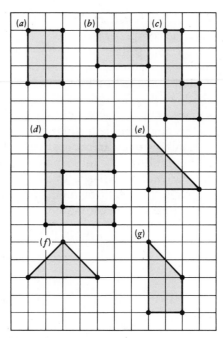

FIGURE 9.2

and 14 square units, respectively. Furthermore, the property that a diagonal of a square divides it into two congruent triangles allows one to determine the areas of the shaded regions in parts (e), (f), and (g) to be $4\frac{1}{2}$, 4, and 6 square units, respectively.

Now suppose that we have a triangular region BCD as indicated in Figure 9.3. Recall that a diagonal of a rectangle divides it into two congruent triangles. Thus, we know that the area of the triangular region BCD is one-half the area of the rectangular region ABCD.

Figure 9.4 illustrates a region having a boundary of a trapezoid. To "count" the square units in this region one could begin by forming rectangles as indicated by the dashed lines and determine that the shaded region contains eight square units. This process of sectioning regions into rectangular

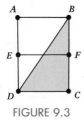

FIGURE 9.3

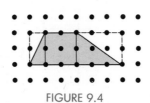

FIGURE 9.4

sections and then applying the diagonal property allows one to find the area of some complex figures.

Counting square units from a grid may also be used to approximate areas of regions enclosed by curves other than polygons. For example, consider the region indicated in Figure 9.5. There are nine complete square units (the shaded squares) in the region, in addition to a number of fractional parts of square units. When we consider the fractional parts, we see that in addition to the nine complete squares, fractional parts of 20 squares are inside the region. To make an accurate count of these fractional parts, we could subdivide each square into smaller squares or we could approximate the areas of the fractional parts. In any case, we would perhaps judge there is the equivalent of eight or nine squares units contained in the fractional parts. Therefore, a total estimate of 17 or 18 square units would seem reasonable.

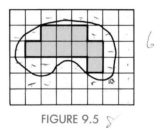

FIGURE 9.5

A second method for finding the area of the region in Figure 9.5 is called the *averaging method*. There are 9 squares totally inside the figure and parts of 29 squares inside the region. The average of these, $\dfrac{29 + 9}{2} = \dfrac{38}{2} = 19$, gives us a good estimate of the total area inside the curve and is close to the estimate made in the preceding paragraph.

PROBLEM SET 9.1

1. Find the number of square units in each shaded region.

(a)   (b)   (c)   (d)

2. Find the number of square units in each shaded region.

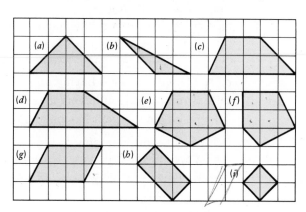

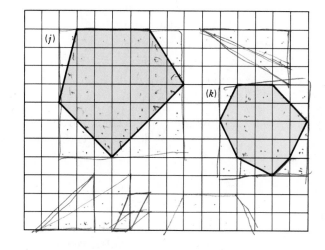

3. Estimate the area of each of the following enclosed regions.

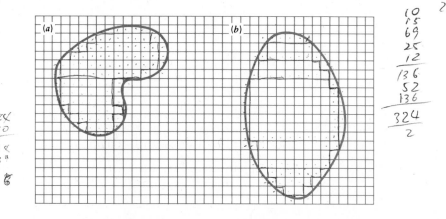

4. Using either paper with a grid or paper with dots simulating a geoboard, draw each of the following:

    a. A triangular region having an area of six square units

    b. A parallelogram region having an area of eight square units

    c. A parallelogram region having an area of one square unit

    d. A triangular region having an area of seven square units

    e. A trapezoid region having an area of eight square units

    f. A pentagonal region having an area of eleven square units

5. Using paper with dots simulating a geoboard, draw a square region having an area of the following. (*Hint:* These might not all be possible. Also, another look at Problem 2, parts **h** and **i**, might be helpful.)

    a. Four square units

    b. Nine square units

    c. Two square units

    d. Three square units

    e. Five square units

    f. Six square units

    g. Seven square units

    h. Eight square units

6. **a.** How many different square regions can be formed on the accompanying set of dots What is the area of each of these square regions?

                    .   .   .

                    .   .   .

                    .   .   .

    b. How many different square regions can be formed on the accompanying set of dots? What is the area of each of these square regions?

                    .   .   .   .

                    .   .   .   .

                    .   .   .   .

                    .   .   .   .

Pedagogical Problems and Activities

7. Complete the chart for each of the following regions, based on the accompanying diagram.

a.

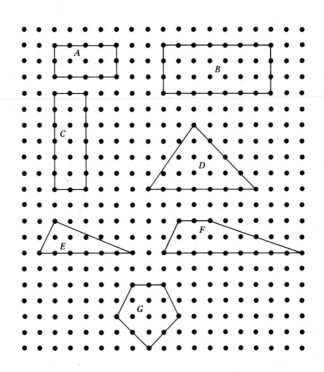

Region	Number of Dots on Boundary of Region (b)	Number of Dots in Interior of Region (i)	Area of Region (A)
A			
B			
C			
D			
E			
F			
G			

b. Pick's formula gives the area (A) of such figures in terms of interior (i) points and boundary (b) points. On dot paper, sketch figures that have the number of boundary points and interior points given below. Then choose which formula applies.

   (i) Which formula applies in this example?

b	i	A
4	0	1
5	0	
6	0	
7	0	

(a) $A = b - 2$

(b) $A = \frac{1}{2}b - 2$

(c) $A = b - 3$

(d) $A = \frac{1}{2}b - 1$

(ii) Which formula applies in this example?

b	i	A
4	1	2
5	1	
6	1	
7	1	
8	1	

(a) $A = b - 2$
(b) $A = \frac{1}{2}b - 1$
(c) $A = \frac{1}{2}b$
(d) $A = \frac{1}{2}b + 1$

(iii) What is a formula that applies here?

b	i	A
4	2	
5	2	
6	2	
7	2	
8	2	

(iv) What is a formula that applies here?

b	i	A
4	3	
5	3	
6	3	
7	3	
8	3	

c. If a polygon has 6 boundary points and 7 interior points, what is a formula that would yield the area?

d. Suppose a polygon has b boundary points, i interior point, and the area enclosed is represented by A. Write an equation relating A, b, and i. This is known as Pick's formula.

8. In the next section we develop some of the basic area formulas such as the one for rectangular regions—namely, $A = lw$. Without looking ahead to that material, describe some activities that could be used with elementary school children to allow them to "discover" the formula for themselves.

9. Describe activities that could be used with children to help them distinguish between a triangle and a triangular region, a rectangle and a rectangular region, and so on.

10. Using several triangles like the one below, other geometric shapes can be formed. If the length of the side of the triangle is 1, find:
   a. The perimeter of each shape.
   b. How many triangles are used to make the shape.

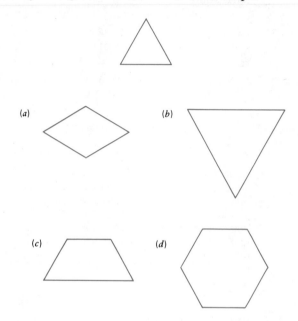

(a)   (b)

(c)   (d)

11. When given two triangles like the one here:

a child proceeded to make the following three shapes:

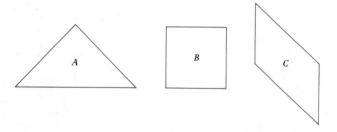

When asked which of the shapes had the largest area, the student picked piece C. What do you say?

9.2   DEVELOPING AREA FORMULAS

It was mentioned in the previous section that we normally choose as "standard squares" those for which the measure of a side is one of the standard linear units. In this country, although we are in the period of transition from the English system to the metric system, we should be familiar with both systems. Table 9.1 indicates some of the basic units and their relationships for the two systems. Table 9.1 need not be memorized because any of the relationships can be easily determined as illustrated in Figure 9.6.

TABLE 9.1

Metric Units	*English Units*
100 square millimeters = 1 square centimeter	144 square inches = 1 square foot
100 square centimeters = 1 square decimeter	9 square feet = 1 square yard
100 square decimeters = 1 square meter	$30\frac{1}{4}$ square yards = 1 square rod
100 square meters = 1 square dekameter	
100 square dekameters = 1 square hectometer	
100 square hectometers = 1 square kilometer	

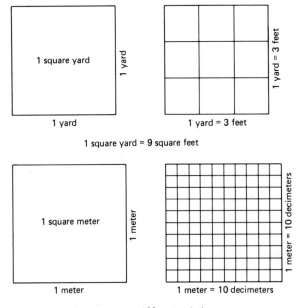

FIGURE 9.6

As with linear units, there are symbols for metric units of area. These are given in Table 9.2.

TABLE 9.2

Square millimeter	mm^2
Square centimeter	cm^2
Square decimeter	dm^2
Square meter	m^2
Square dekameter	dam^2
Square hectometer	hm^2
Square kilometer	km^2

Before discussing the development of area formulas, let us clarify a point regarding vocabulary. We do want children to realize that the concept of area refers to *regions*. Thus, a statement such as "find the area of the rectangle" is technically incorrect. Instead, it should read "find the area of the rectangular region." However, once we feel that the meaning is perfectly clear, we may, for the sake of convenience, use expressions such as "find the area of the triangle" knowing that you understand the intended meaning.

Inductively, an area formula for rectangular regions is fairly easy to develop. As a result of working with area problems using the counting approach described in the previous section, children naturally begin to relate the number of linear units in its length and the number of linear units in its width.

They may also relate the number of square units in a row to the length and the number of rows of square units to the width. Thus, finding the area of a rectangular region by multiplying the *number* of linear units in the length by the *number* of linear units in the width, provided length and width are expressed in the same linear unit, seems very reasonable. Let us state this as a property.

PROPERTY 9.1   **The area of a rectangular region having a length of *l* linear units and a width of *w* linear units is given by $A = lw$.**

It should be noted that the idea of designating a length and width of a rectangle is arbitrary. For example, in Figure 9.7a, most of us would probably designate length and width as indicated; however, in parts (*b*) and (*c*) we might not agree on which should be called the length and which the width.

Technically, the formula means "the product of the number of linear units of two adjacent sides." The terminology of *base* and *height* is also used when working with rectangular regions. The formula is then stated as $A = bh$. Even though the terminology of *length* and *width* may be used with rectangular regions, it becomes more convenient to switch to the *base* and *altitude*

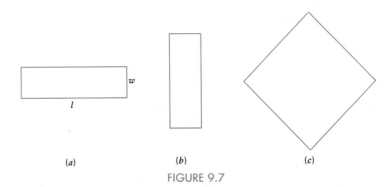

(a)   (b)   (c)

FIGURE 9.7

(height) terminology for some of the other regions. There is still a certain arbitrariness in the designations. For example, when working with a parallelogram, either pair of parallel sides may be designated as the bases. Then a corresponding altitude of the parallelogram is any perpendicular line segment joining the lines in which two parallel sides lie. Figure 9.8 illustrates these ideas.

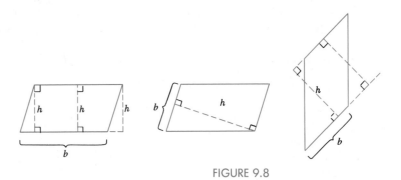

FIGURE 9.8

Many children will probably guess a formula for finding the area of a parallelogram region from their work with counting squares as described in the previous section. We can strengthen the validity of their guess by using some paper-folding and cutting activities. For example, consider the parallelogram region in Figure 9.9. Cutting off $\triangle BFC$ and placing it in the position AED "changes" a parallelogram into a rectangle. The area of the rectangle is given by $AB \cdot AE$ and this should also be the area of the original parallelogram.

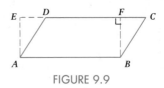

FIGURE 9.9

PROPERTY 9.2   The area of a parallelogram region is equal to the product of the measure of one side times the measure of an altitude to that side (we often state this as *A* = *bh*, where *b* = length of a base and *h* = length of corresponding altitude).

It should be noted that the area of a parallelogram will be the same for whichever pair of base and altitude is chosen. For example, to find the area of the parallelogram in Figure 9.10, either base *a* and altitude *b* or base *c* and altitude *d* could be used.

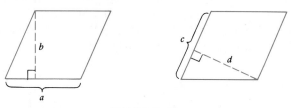

FIGURE 9.10

REMARK   We must realize that if the area formulas are being developed by using grids or dotted paper and the "counting-of-squares" process, then we are using only the whole numbers as dimensions of the figures. However, the formulas do apply for all real numbers, and children should be made aware of this fact. For example, the area formula will also be used to find the area of a parallelogram with base 3.2 cm and altitude of 1.7 cm.

Suppose that we have a triangular region with one side of length 4 centimeters and the altitude to that side having a length of 3 centimeters, as illustrated in Figure 9.11*a*. What is the area of the triangular region? As indicated in part (*b*), a parallelogram region can be formed having a base of 4 centimeters and a corresponding altitude of 3 centimeters. We know that the area of the parallelogram region is (4)(3) = 12 square centimeters, and therefore

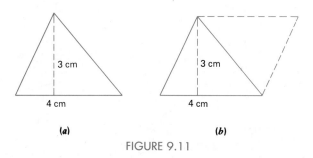

(*a*)   (*b*)

FIGURE 9.11

the area of the triangular region is one-half of this or 6 square centimeters. This relationship is expressed for all triangles in Property 9.3.

PROPERTY 9.3   **The area of a triangular region is given by the formula $A = \frac{1}{2}bh$, where b represents the measure of a side and h represents the measure of the corresponding altitude to that side.**

Each of the sides is a candidate to be called the base of a triangle. When this base is chosen, then the corresponding altitude can be identified. Thus, there are three pairs of bases and altitudes for each triangle. It is important to realize that whichever pair is chosen the area determined will be the same. In Figure 9.12*a*, *b*, and *c*, the three pairs of bases and altitudes are identified for the same triangle. In Figure 9.12*d*, *e*, *f*, each base and a corresponding altitude are shown for an obtuse triangle.

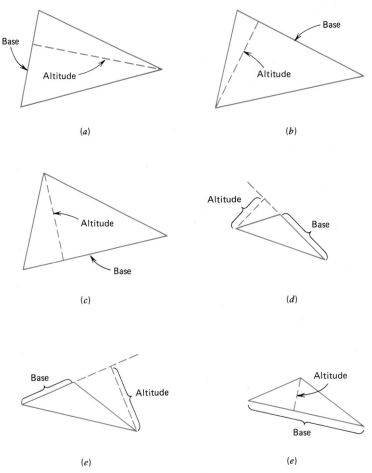

FIGURE 9.12

You will recall that a trapezoid is a quadrilateral with one and only one pair of parallel sides. These parallel sides are referred to as the *bases* of a trapezoid, and any perpendicular line segment joining the lines in which the bases lie is an *altitude*. An area formula for a trapezoid region can be determined by using the parallelogram formula. Consider the region in Figure 9.13. In this figure we have cut the trapezoid into two pieces by a line that is parallel to both bases and that cuts the height in two.

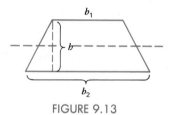

FIGURE 9.13

The two pieces in Figure 9.13 can be rearranged into a parallelogram as shown in Figure 9.14. Now we see that the base of the parallelogram has length $(b_1 + b_2)$ and has height $\frac{h}{2}$. Thus, the area of the parallelogram in Figure 9.14 is $(b_1 + b_2)(\frac{h}{2})$ which can also be written $(\frac{1}{2})h(b_1 + b_2)$. Indeed, this must also be the area for the trapezoid in Figure 9.13. We state this result as Property 9.4.

FIGURE 9.14

PROPERTY 9.4   **The area of a trapezoid region is given by $A = \frac{1}{2}h(b_1 + b_2)$ where b_1 and b_2 represent the measures of the bases and h the measure of an altitude.**

Throughout the remainder of this chapter our problem-solving efforts will be directed toward "area and volume" type problems. We offer the following suggestions as you tackle these problems.

Read the problem very carefully, making sure of the types of figures and units of measure being used.

Sketch the figure (or figures) and record the appropriate information on the figure.

Choose the appropriate area or volume formula to be used.

Analyze the problem, using the area or volume formula as a guideline. For example, if the problem involves finding the area of a triangle, then the formula $A = \frac{1}{2}bh$ serves as a guideline. Either the values of b and h are given in the problem or they can be found from the given informaton or by measuring.

Carry out the necessary computations.

Ask yourself one final question. Is my answer *reasonable?*

Keep these suggestions in mind as we consider a few problems.

EXAMPLE 1

A flower garden is in the shape of a trapezoid having bases of measure 6 meters and 10 meters. The distance between the bases is 4 meters. Find the area of the garden.

Solution Let us sketch a trapezoid and record the given information.

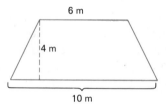

Notice that the phrase "distance between the bases" means the length of an altitude. The formula for finding the area of a trapezoid is $A = \frac{1}{2}h(b_1 + b_2)$ and the values of h, b_1, and b_2 are all given in the statement of the problem. Thus , we obtain

$$
\begin{aligned}
A &= \tfrac{1}{2}h(b_1 + b_2) \\
&= \tfrac{1}{2}(4)(6 + 10) \\
&= 2(16) \\
&= 32
\end{aligned}
$$

The area of the garden is 32 square meters.

EXAMPLE 2

Suppose that paint costs $2.00 per liter and that one liter will cover approximately 9 square meters of surface. We are going to paint (on one side only) 50 congruent pieces of wood that are rectangular in shape, having a length of 60 centimeters and a width of 30 centimeters. What will be the approximate cost of the paint?

Solution We can begin by sketching and labeling one of the 50 pieces of wood.

The area of one piece of wood is

$$A = lw$$
$$= 60(30)$$
$$= 1800 \text{ cm}^2$$

Therefore, the total area of all 50 pieces of wood is

$$50(1800) = 90,000 \text{ cm}^2$$

Because 1 square meter is equivalent to 10,000 square centimeters (1 m² = 10,000 cm²), we have

$$\frac{90,000}{10,000} = 9$$

Thus, we have **9** square meters of surface to paint and 1 liter of paint at a cost of $2 should do the job.

EXAMPLE 3

A lawn is in the shape of a triangle with one side 130 feet long and the altitude to that side 60 feet long. Will one sack of fertilizer, which covers 4000 square feet, be enough to fertilize the lawn?

Solution Let us sketch a triangle and record the information.

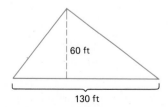

Using the formula $A = \frac{1}{2}bh$, we obtain

$$A = \frac{1}{2}bh$$
$$= \frac{1}{2}(130)(60)$$
$$= (65)(60)$$
$$= 3900 \text{ square feet}$$

Therefore, one sack of fertilizer should be enough.

PROBLEM SET 9.2

1. Find the area of each of the following rectangular regions:

a.

3 cm
5 cm

b.

$3\frac{1}{4}$ cm
$1\frac{1}{2}$ cm

c.
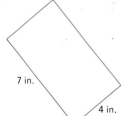
7 in.
4 in.

d.

3 cm
5 m

e.
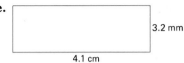
3.2 mm
4.1 cm

2. Find the area of each of the following regions (the figures are triangles, parallelograms, and trapezoids):

a.
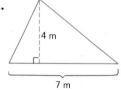
4 m
7 m

b.
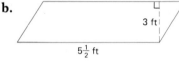
3 ft
$5\frac{1}{2}$ ft

c.

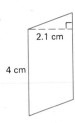

2.1 cm

4 cm

d.

4 mm

17 mm

e.

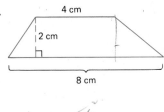

4 cm

2 cm

8 cm

f.

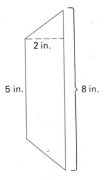

2 in.

5 in.   8 in.

3. If the measurements in the parallelogram are given, what is the length of the altitude to base $\overline{AB}$ in each figure below?

a.

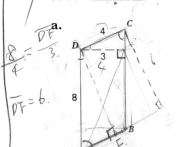

b.

$x + 3^2 = 4^2$

$\dfrac{16 - 9}{1}$ 7

$8^2 + 12^2 = x^2$

$9 \cdot 14$ 81

$\overline{DF} = \dfrac{27}{12} = \dfrac{9}{4}$

$\dfrac{3}{12} = \dfrac{\overline{DF}}{9}$

4. Convert each of the following as indicated:
   a. 4 square feet = _____ square inches
   b. 5 square yards = _____ square feet
   c. 6 square meters = _____ square decimeters
   d. 45 square decimeters = _____ square meter
   e. 32 square feet = _____ square yards
   f. 12 square inches = _____ square feet
   g. 1 square yard = _____ square inches
   h. 1 square kilometer = _____ square meters
   i. 1 square meter = _____ square kilometer

5. The area of a triangular region is 108 square dekameters. If the length of one side is 18 dekameters, find the length of the altitude to that side.

6. Find the length of a side of a square region that has the same area as a rectangular region that is 45 yards by 5 yards.

7. Find the length of an altitude of a trapezoid region having bases of 8 centimeters and 20 centimeters and an area of 96 square centimeters.

8. Use a ruler to measure, in mm, the necessary lengths so that you can determine the area of the following figures. With your measurements, find the approximate area of each figure.

a.   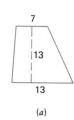   **b.**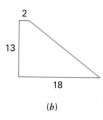

9. a. Which of the trapezoids below has the largest area?

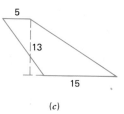

(a)   (b)   (c)

b. Find the area of a trapezoid region if the sum of its bases is 20 meters and an altitude is 13 meters long.

10. a. If you double the width of a rectangular region and leave the length the same, how is the area changed?

b. If you double both the width and the length of a rectangular region, how is the area changed?

11. How many square tiles, each 4 inches on a side, does it take to cover a floor that is 8 feet 4 inches long by 7 feet 8 inches wide?

12. Find the area of a cement walk 5 feet wide that surrounds a rectangular plot of ground 104 feet long and 73 feet wide.

13. One side of a parallelogram is 18 decimeters long and an altitude to that side is 7 decimeters long. Express the area of the region in square meters.

14. If you double the length of both bases of a trapezoid and keep the length of an altitude the same, how is the area affected?

15. In the accompanying figure, which of the two shaded triangular regions has the larger area?

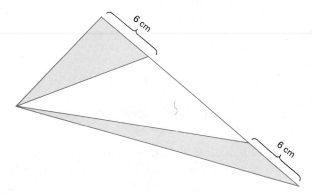

16. In triangle *ABC*, the median, $\overline{AD}$, from *A* to *D* the midpoint of $\overline{BC}$ has been drawn. How does the area of triangle *ABD* compare to the area of triangle *ADC*?

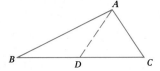

17. In the accompanying figure, *l* and *m* are parallel lines, and *AB* = *CD* = *EF*.

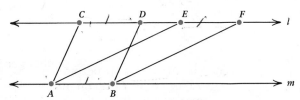

How does the area of parallelogram *ABDC* compare to the area parallelogram *ABFE*?

18. In the accompanying figure, *l* and *m* are parallel lines, and *AB* = *CD*. How does the area of triangle *ABP* compare to the area of parallelogram *ABDC*?

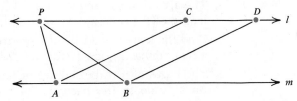

19. The accompanying diagram is found in some elementary texts when developing a formula for the area of a trapezoid region. Explain how the formula $A = \frac{1}{2}h(b_1 + b_2)$ can be found using the approach suggested by the figure.

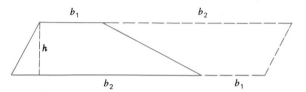

20. **a.** It is also possible to determine the area formula for a trapezoid region by using a diagonal of the trapezoid to section it into two triangles. Use this approach with a trapezoid having bases of b_1 and b_2 and an altitude of h to arrive at the same formula $A = \frac{1}{2}h(b_1 + b_2)$.

   b. The area of a trapezoid can also be determined by partitioning the trapezoid into a parallelogram and a triangle as shown below. Note that the height is the same for the trapezoid as well as the triangle and the parallelogram. From this information derive the formula for the area of the trapezoid.

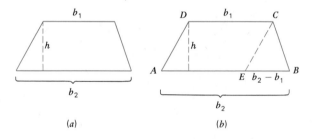

   c. The area of a trapezoid can also be determined by partitioning the trapezoid into a rectangle and two triangles as shown below. Use this approach to determine the formula for the area of the trapezoid.

21. **a.** The area of a rectangular region is 107.25 square centimeters. If the length of the rectangle is 14.3 centimeters, find the width.

   b. Find the length of a side of a square region that has the same area as a rectangular region 12 feet by 27 feet.

   c. The bases of a trapezoid are of length 14.6 meters and 22.9 meters. An altitude to the bases is 9.4 meters long. Find the area of the trapezoid.

Pedagogical Problems and Activities

22. Even after the area formulas have been presented, it is helpful to use the geoboard or dotted paper for reinforcement exercises. For example, using either paper with a grid or paper with dots simulating a geoboard, draw each of the following:

    a. Three triangular regions, each having an area of 8 square units

    b. Three parallelogram regions, each having an area of 12 square units

    c. One triangular region having an area of 7 square units

    d. Two trapezoid regions, each having an area of 12 square units

    e. A trapezoid region having an area of 15 square units

Find the area of each of the triangular regions *ABP, ABQ, ABR, ABS,* and *ABT* in the accompanying diagram. What do you think would be the reason for having children do such a problem?

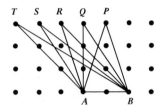

23. Children should be given the opportunity to estimate when working with areas. The following suggestions for making "area estimates" may be helpful:

    (1) Form a mental image of the desired unit (square centimeter, square inch, and so on) and "mentally picture" covering the region.

    (2) Use a convenient unit as a mental image and then make a conversion if necessary.

    (3) Use an appropriate area formula.

    (4) Use previous measurement experiences for comparison purposes.

Using the above suggestions, estimate the area of each of the following. Check by measuring.

    a. _____ cm²   Front cover of this book

    b. _____ cm²   A dollar bill

    c. _____ cm²   The "back side" of your calculator

    d. _____ m²   The floor of the room in which you are studying

    e. _____ dm²   One side of a door of the room in which you are studying

    f. _____ cm²   A "large" triangle that you have drawn on a sheet of paper

    g. _____ cm²   A "large" parallelogram that you have drawn on a sheet of paper

24. Some elementary texts include problems that have the children choose "the most reasonable answer." Such problems are designed to help children develop their estimation skills. Choose the most reasonable answer for each of the following:

  a. A garden plot has an area of (80 square meters, 80 square decimeters, 80 square centimeters).

  b. The area of a sheet of notebook paper is (500 square meters, 500 square decimeters, 500 square centimeters).

  c. The area of the state of Texas is (685,000 square kilometers, 685,000 square meters, 685,000 square centimeters.

  d. The area of one side of a stop sign is (47 square meters, 47 square decimeters, 47 square centimeters).

  e. The area of one side of a dollar bill is (102 square meters, 102 square decimeters, 102 square centimeters).

9.3   PYTHAGOREAN THEOREM

The triangle has long been known to be a very "practical" geometric figure. In building construction, for example, it is not uncommon to find the rafters of a house fastened together in the shape of triangles in order to help make the framework rigid. Perhaps you have noticed other examples of triangles being used in the construction of bridges, buildings, fence gates, and so forth.

The ancient Greeks also did a lot of work with triangles, particularly with right triangles. One very important relationship attributed to Pythagoras is illustrated in Figure 9.15. This relationship, known as the Pythagorean theorem, states that the number of unit squares found in the square built on the hypotenuse of a right triangle is the same as the sum of the number of unit squares found in the squares built on the legs. (The hypotenuse is the side opposite the right angle, and the other two sides are called legs.) This property is usually stated at the present time in a more algebraic form as follows.

PROPERTY 9.5   **Pythagorean Theorem**

If for a right triangle, a and b are the measures of the legs and c is the measure of the hypotenuse, then $a^2 + b^2 = c^2$.

An intuitive proof of Property 9.5 is offered by the following diagram. Consider a right triangle with legs of measure a and b and hypotenuse of measure c. In (i) and (ii) the same-size square has been partitioned in two ways. In (i) we find a square and four triangles all the same size. In (ii) we find two smaller squares and again four triangles all the same size. Therefore the square in (i) must have the same area as the sum of the squares in (ii). We

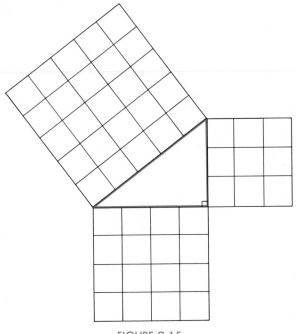

FIGURE 9.15

can write this relationship as c^2 [the area of the square in (i)] $= a^2 + b^2$ [the sum of the areas of the squares in (ii)], or $a^2 + b^2 = c^2$.

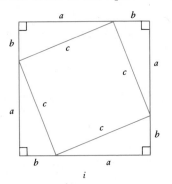

i

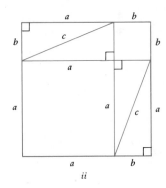

ii

The converse of the Pythagorean theorem is also true and is of great use. We state it as Property 9.6.

PROPERTY 9.6   Converse of Pythagorean Theorem

If the measures a, b, and c of the sides of a triangle are such that $a^2 + b^2 = c^2$, then the triangle is a right triangle with a and b the measures of the legs and c the measure of the hypotenuse.

Because $3^2 + 4^2 = 5^2$, a triangle having sides with measures of 3, 4, and 5 is a right triangle. This example motivates a natural question. Are there other triples of positive numbers that satisfy $a^2 + b^2 = c^2$? A logical guess might be to try some multiples of the 3-4-5 right triangle. For example, suppose that the measures of the sides of a triangle are 6, 8, and 10. Because $6^2 + 8^2 = 10^2$, we have found another triple of positive whole numbers that satisfies the Pythagorean relationship. This might lead us to suspect that *any* positive integral multiple of the 3-4-5 triangle will work. Are there still other triples of positive numbers that will work in $a^2 + b^2 = c^2$? It turns out that there are other possibilities, and we will have you find some of them in the next Problem Set.

The Pythagorean theorem also plays an important role in problem solving. In Chapter 1 we suggested some questions you might ask yourself when *devising a plan of attack* for solving some particular problem. Two of those questions are very appropriate at this time:

1. Is there a figure, diagram, chart, or some other visual aid that will help organize the data in the problem?
2. Is there a relationship suggested by the visual aid that can be used as a guideline for solving the problem?

Let us consider some problems for which these questions provide some helpful direction.

EXAMPLE 1

A 50-foot rope hangs from the top of a flagpole. When pulled out taut, the rope reaches a point on the ground 18 feet from the base of the pole. How high is the pole?

Solution Figure 9.16 pictures the situation described in the problem.

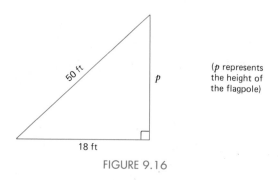

FIGURE 9.16

Using the Pythagorean theorem, we can solve for p as follows:

$$p^2 + 18^2 = 50^2$$
$$p^2 + 324 = 2500$$
$$p^2 = 2176$$
$$p = \pm\sqrt{2176}$$

The negative solution is disregarded, and we know that $p = \sqrt{2176}$. Using a calculator, we can find an approximation for $\sqrt{2176}$ to the nearest tenth. Thus,

$$p \doteq 46.6$$

EXAMPLE 2

Find the length of each leg of an isoscles right triangle having a hypotenuse with a measure of 6 centimeters.

Solution Because it is an *isosceles right* triangle, both legs are the same length. Thus, as indicated in Figure 9.17, we can let x represent the length of each of the legs and then apply the Pythagorean theorem.

$$x^2 + x^2 = 36$$
$$2x^2 = 36$$
$$x^2 = 18$$
$$x = \sqrt{18} \doteq 4.2 \text{ cm}$$

At this time we want to deduce one additional property pertaining to certain special right triangles. We will begin by constructing an angle bisector of an equilateral triangle $\triangle ABC$, as illustrated in Figure 9.18. Because $\overline{AC} \cong \overline{BC}$, $\angle 1 \cong \angle 2$, and $\overline{CD}$ is a common side, it can be concluded that $\triangle ADC \cong \triangle BDC$. From this we may conclude that $\overline{CD} \perp \overline{AB}$ and also $\overline{AD} \cong \overline{DB}$. Because $AD = \frac{1}{2}AB$, it is obvious that $AD = \frac{1}{2}AC$. This fact is summarized in the following property.

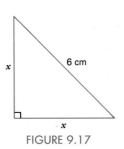

6 cm

x

x

FIGURE 9.17

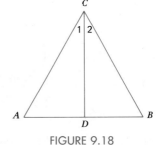

C

1 2

A D B

FIGURE 9.18

PROPERTY 9.7   **In a 30°-60° right triangle, the measure of the side opposite the 30° angle is equal to one-half the measure of the hypotenuse.**

Property 9.7, together with the Pythagorean theorem, provides the basis for solving a variety of problems pertaining to 30°–60° right triangles. Let us consider one such example.

EXAMPLE 3

Suppose that a 20-foot ladder is leaned against a building so as to make an angle of 60° with the ground. How far up on the building does the top of the ladder reach?

Solution Figure 9.19 depicts the situation: $m\angle B = 90° - 60° = 30°$, and we know that $AC = \frac{1}{2}(20) = 10$ feet. Therefore, using the Pythagorean theorem, we can find x as follows:

$$x^2 + 10^2 = 20^2$$
$$x^2 + 100 = 400$$
$$x^2 = 300$$
$$x = \sqrt{300}$$
$$x = 17.3 \text{ (nearest tenth)}$$

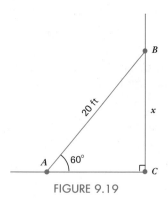

FIGURE 9.19

We now have the tools to solve problems involving relationships pertaining to the various kinds of quadrilaterals.

EXAMPLE 1

A rectangular lot is 130 feet long and 70 feet wide. Find, to the nearest foot, the distance from one corner of the lot to the diagonally opposite corner.

Solution The rectangular lot is illustrated in the following figure.

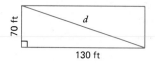

Using the Pythagorean theorem, we obtain

$$70^2 + 130^2 = d^2$$
$$4900 + 16900 = d^2$$
$$21800 = d^2$$
$$\sqrt{21800} = d$$
$$d = 148 \text{ (nearest foot)}$$

EXAMPLE 2

The bases of an isosceles trapezoid are 12 and 18 centimeters long. The non-parallel sides make angles of 60° with the longer base. Find the length of the nonparallel sides.

Solution The following figure depicts the situation described in the problem.

By drawing line segments from the upper vertices perpendicular to the lower base, we can form two congruent 30°–60° right triangles as indicated in the next figure. Because in each case the side opposite the 30° angle is 3 centimeters long, the hypotenuse must be 2(3)=6 centimeters long. Thus, the length of each of the nonparallel sides of the trapezoid is 6 centimeters.

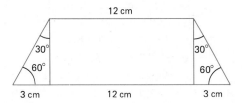

> REMARK Notice the importance of the figures in the analysis of example 2. The computational aspect of the problem is routine once the proper figures have been drawn.

EXAMPLE 3

Suppose that a room of a house is in the shape of a rectangular box with a length of 6 meters, a width of 5 meters, and a height of 3 meters (Fig. 9.20). Find the distance from a lower corner to the diagonally opposite upper corner.

Solution In Figure 9.20 we are looking for the length of $\overline{FC}$. By drawing $\overline{FB}$, a right triangle $\triangle FAB$ (right angle at A) is formed, having legs measuring 5 and 6 meters. Thus, by the Pythagorean theorem, the measure of $\overline{FB}$ is $\sqrt{5^2 + 6^2} = \sqrt{61}$ meters. Now using right triangle $\triangle FBC$ (right angle at B), we can find the measure of $\overline{FC}$ to be $(\sqrt{(\sqrt{61})^2 + 3^2} = \sqrt{70}$ meters. Therefore, the distance from F to C is approximately 8.4 meters.

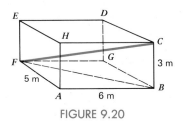

FIGURE 9.20

PROBLEM SET 9.3

Many of the following problems lend themselves to the use of a calculator.

1. Use the converse of the Pythagorean theorem to determine which of the triangles having sides with the following measures are right triangles:
   a. 4,5,6   b. 9,12,15
   c. 5,12,13   d. 10,24,26
   e. 6,8,17   f. 9,40,41

2. If △*ABC* has a right angle at *C* and sides *a*, *b*, *c*, find the missing side. Express all answers as rational approximations to the nearest tenth.

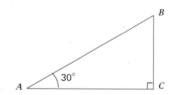

	a	*b*	*c*
a.	2	3	
b.	3		6
c.		4	6
d.	4	5	

3. Suppose △*ABC* has ∠*A* with a measure of 30° and ∠*C* is a right angle. Complete each of the following. Leave irrational numbers in radical form.

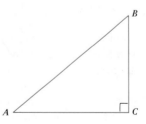

a. If *AB* = 4, find *AC* and *BC*.   **b.** If *BC* = 5, find *AC* and *AB*.
c. If *BC* = 6, find *AC* and *AB*.   **d.** If *AC* = 9, find *BC* and *AB*.

4. Suppose △*ABC* is an isosceles right triangle with the right angle at *C*. Complete each of the following. Express answers to the nearest tenth.

a. If *AC* = 5, find *AB*.   **b.** If *BC* = 4, find *AB*.
c. If *AB* = 6, find *AC* and *BC*.   **d.** If *AB* = 8, find *AC* and *BC*.

5. The length of the hypotenuse of an isosceles right triangle is 8 meters. Find, to the nearest tenth of a meter, the length of each leg.

6. The length of the hypotenuse of an isosceles right triangle is 11 centimeters. Find, to the nerest tenth of a centimeter, the length of each leg.

7. Find, to the nearest tenth of a centimeter, the length of an altitude of an equilateral triangle, each of whose sides has a measure of 8 centimeters.

8. Find, to the nearest tenth of a meter, the length of the sides of an equilateral triangle if an altitude has a measure of 6 meters.

9. An 18-foot ladder resting against a house just reaches a windowsill 16 feet above the ground. How far is the foot of the ladder from the foundation of the house? Express answer to the nearest foot.

10. A 42-foot guy wire makes an angle of 60° with the ground and is attached to a telephone pole. Find the distance from the base of the pole to the point on the pole where the wire is attached. Express the answer to the nearest tenth of a foot. (See accompanying figure.)

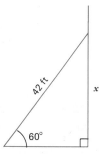

11. Is a triangle with sides measuring 12, 15, and 18 centimeters, respectively, a right triangle? Defend your answer.

12. A rectangular floor is 7 meters long and 5 meters wide. Find, to the nearest tenth of a meter, the distance from one corner to the diagonally opposite corner.

13. Given a square that is 4 cm by 4 cm, find the distance from the center of the square to a vertex.

14. One diagonal of a rectangle is 25 centimeters long and the width of the rectangle is 7 centimeters. Find the length of the rectangle.

a. A baseball diamond is a square and the distance from home plate to first base is **90** feet. How far is it from home plate to second base? Express answer to the nearest tenth of a foot.

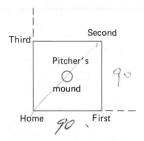

b. A second baseman catches a pop fly on the right field foul line 20 feet beyond first base. How far must he throw the ball to double a runner off of third base? (The ball must be thrown to third base to "double the runner off.") Express answer to the nearest foot.

16. The bases of an isosceles trapezoid are 10 meters and 18 meters long. The nonparallel sides are each 8 meters long. Find the length of a line segment that joins the two bases and is perpendicular to each of them. Express the answer to the nearest tenth of a meter.

17. Each side of a rhombus is 14 centimeters long, and one angle is 60°. Find the length of a line segment that joins the opposite sides and is perpendicular to each of them. Express the answer to the nearest tenth of a centimeter.

 18. Suppose that we are given a rectangular box with a length of 8 centimeters, a width of 6 centimeters, and a height of 4 centimeters. Find the length of a diagonal from a lower corner to the diagonally opposite upper corner. Express your answer as a rational approximation to the nearest tenth.

 19. Suppose that we are given a cube with edges of length 12 centimeters. Find the length of a diagonal from a lower corner to the diagonally opposite upper corner. Express your answer as a rational approximation to the nearest tenth.

 20. Find the length of each leg of an isosceles right triangle having a hypotenuse 16 centimeters long. Express answer to the nearest tenth of a centimeter.

 21. Find the length of a diagonal of a rectangle that is 9 meters long and 6 meters wide. Express the answer to the nearest tenth of a meter.

22. The length of the leg opposite the 30° angle in a 30°–60° right triangle is 4 centimeters. Find, to the nearest tenth of a centimeter, the length of the other leg.

23. Suppose that $\triangle ABC$ is a right triangle with the right angle at B If $AC = 12$ meters and $AB = 7$ meters, find BC. Express the answer to the nearest tenth.

Pedagogical Problems and Activities

24. Draw a right triangle with the legs having measures of 5 and 6 cm. Calculate the length of the hypotenuse by using the Pythagorean theorem and then measure it and compare answers.

25. Use paper-folding to demonstrate that the length of the side opposite the 30° angle in a 30°–60° right triangle is one-half the length of the hypotenuse.

26. Describe a physical model (or models) that children could easily make to help them understand the statement that "triangles are *rigid* figures."

27. Use a calculator to complete a table of squares for the counting numbers 1 through 50 ($1^2 = 1$, $2^2 = 4$, $3^2 = 9$, etc.). Now search the table to find all examples in it that will satisfy the Pythagorean relationship $a^2 + b^2 = c^2$.

28. Various patterns exist that can be used to generate Pythagorean triples. Look for patterns in the first three rows of the following table and then use these patterns to complete the table. (In each case, $a^2 + b^2 = c^2$.)

a	b	c
3	4	5
5	12	13
7	24	25
9	40	
11		
13		

29. Construct a 30°–60° right triangle where the length of the side opposite the 30° angle is as indicated.   _____

30. Construct a 30°–60° right triangle where the length of the side opposite the 60° angle is as indicated.   _____

31. President Garfield devised a proof of the Pythagorean theorem based on the concept of area. The accompanying figure indicates the basic approach he used in his argument. Note that $\angle ZPY$ is a right angle. Why is this true?

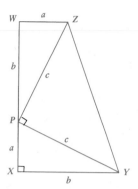

Using the measures a, b, and c do the following:

a. Express the area of right triangle PWZ.

b. Express the area of right triangle PXY.

c. Express the area of right triangle ZPY.

d. Indicate the sum of your results from parts **a**, **b**, and **c**.

e. Use the formula for a trapezoid and express the area of trapezoid $XYZW$.

f. Equate parts **d** and **e** and simplify.

9.4   AREA FORMULAS AND OTHER GEOMETRIC RELATIONSHIPS

Finding the area of a rectangle, parallelogram, triangle, or trapezoid by merely substituting the given values into the appropriate formula and then performing the necessary computations is usually an easy process. For example, finding the area of a rectangle ($A = lw$) that is 30 feet long and 20 feet wide simply requires finding the product of 30 and 20. Thus, the area is $30(20) = 600$ square feet. However, it is often necessary to first apply other geometric relationships before an area formula can be used. Consider the following problems.

EXAMPLE 1

Find the area of a rectangular region if the diagonals are 20 meters long and the width of the rectangle is 12 meters.

Solution The following figure depicts the situation described in the problem.

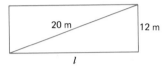

Applying the Pythagorean theorem, we obtain

$$l^2 + 12^2 = 20^2$$
$$l^2 + 144 = 400$$
$$l^2 = 256$$
$$l = \sqrt{256} = 16$$

(Remember that $l^2 = 256$ does have two solutions, 16 and ⁻16, but only the positive solution is meaningful for this type of problem.) Now we can apply the area formula.

$$A = lw$$
$$= 16(12)$$
$$= 192 \text{ m}^2$$

EXAMPLE 2

Find the area of a region in the shape of a rhombus, each side of which is 8 centimeters long: the measure of one angle is 30°.

Solution Let us sketch a rhombus and record the given information.

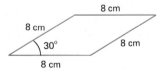

Because a rhombus is a special parallelogram, we can use the formula $A = bh$. The length of an altitude can be determined from the 30°–60° right triangle indicated in the following figure. Remember that in a 30°–60° right triangle the length of the side opposite the 30° angle is equal to one-half the length of the hypotenuse. Thus, $h = \frac{1}{2}(8) = 4$ centimeters. Now we can use the area formula and obtain

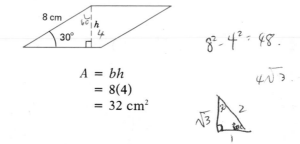

$$8^2 - 4^2 = 48.$$

$$4\sqrt{3}.$$

$$A = bh$$
$$= 8(4)$$
$$= 32 \text{ cm}^2$$

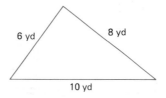

EXAMPLE 3

Find the area of a triangle region whose sides are of length 6 yards, 8 yards, and 10 yards.

Solution First, let us sketch a triangle and record the given information.

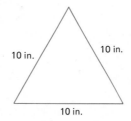

The "key" to this problem is recognizing that $6^2 + 8^2 = 10^2$: thus, it is a right triangle with legs of length 6 yards and 8 yards. The legs of a right triangle serve as the base and altitude in the formula $A = \frac{1}{2}bh$. Therefore, the area is

$$A = \frac{1}{2}bh$$
$$= \frac{1}{2}(6)(8)$$
$$= 24 \text{ yd}^2$$

EXAMPLE 4

Find the area of an equilateral triangle if each side is 10 inches long.

Solution The situation is as follows:

The length of an altitude can be found by applying the Pythagorean theorem to one of the right triangles indicated in the following figure.

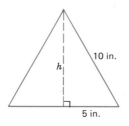

$$h^2 + 5^2 = 10^2$$
$$h^2 + 25 = 100$$
$$h^2 = 75$$
$$h = \sqrt{75}$$

Now the area formula can be used.

$$A = \tfrac{1}{2}bh$$
$$= \tfrac{1}{2}(10)\sqrt{75}$$
$$= 5\sqrt{75}$$

The area is $5\sqrt{75}$ square inches, which is 43.3 square inches to the nearest tenth of a square inch.

EXAMPLE 5

Find the area of an isosceles trapezoid having bases of 12 centimeters and 18 centimeters and the nonparallel sides of length 5 centimeters.

Solution We have the following situation.

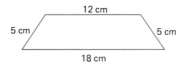

Let us label the vertices and also draw line segments from the upper vertices perpendicular to the lower base.

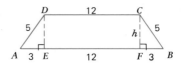

Because it is an isosceles trapezoid, we know that AE = FB = 3 cm. Thus,

$$h^2 + 3^2 = 5^2$$
$$h^2 + 9 = 25$$
$$h^2 = 16$$
$$h = 4 \text{ cm}$$

Therefore, the area is

$$A = \tfrac{1}{2}h(b_1 + b_2)$$
$$= \tfrac{1}{2}(4)(12 + 18)$$
$$= 2(30)$$
$$= 60 \text{ cm}^2$$

You will recall from an earlier section that an approximation for the area of regions bounded by curves other than polygons can be made by using grids, but this yields certainly no more than a rough estimate. For circular regions, it is desirable to have a formula that will give exact answers; however, the mathematical development of such a formula is beyond the scope of this book. Therefore, we will simply describe a procedure that helps to show the "reasonableness" of the formula.

In Figure 9.21a a circular region is cut into 4 "wedges" and then rearranged. In part (b) the number of wedges is 8, and in (c) 16 wedges are used. Notice that the figures resulting from the rearrangements of the wedges tend to look like parallelograms. In fact, as the number of wedges increases, the figure that results closely approximates a parallelogram. Then, as the number of wedges increases, the area of the figure, and therefore the area of the original circular region, must be closer and closer to the area of a parallelogram. However, notice that the altitude of the parallelogram is approaching r (the radius of the circle) and the length of the base is approaching one-half the circumference of the circle. (You will recall that $C = 2\pi r$.) Thus, the

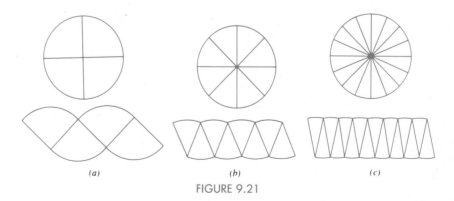

(a)   (b)   (c)

FIGURE 9.21

length of the base can be determined by $\frac{1}{2}(2\pi r) = \pi r$. Then the area of a par-allelogram formula yields $A = (\pi r) \cdot r = \pi r^2$. Let us state this result as a property.

PROPERTY 9.8   **The area of a circular region is equal to π times the square of the measure of a radius of the circle ($A = \pi r^2$).**

> **REMARK** It would probably be desirable to have elementary school children use paper-cutting activities to help with the above discussion. This would help them see the "approximating of a parallelogram" process as they divide circular regions into more and more wedges.

As we use the area formula for a circular region, we must keep in mind that π is an irrational number. Therefore, we may choose to leave an answer in terms of π or we may want to use a rational approximation for π. Consider the following examples.

EXAMPLE 6

Find the area of a circular region having a radius of 7 centimeters.

Solution By direct application of the area formula we obtain

$$A = \pi r^2$$
$$= \pi(7)^2$$
$$= 49\pi \text{ cm}^2$$

If we choose to use $3\frac{1}{7}$ as an approximation for π, then we obtain

$$A \doteq 49(\tfrac{22}{7})$$
$$\doteq 154 \text{ cm}^2$$

EXAMPLE 7

Find the area of the "shaded ring" in the following figure.

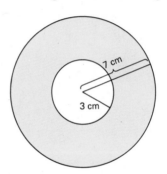

Solution The area of the "shaded ring" can be found by subtracting the area of the smaller circular region from the area of the larger circular region. Thus,

$$A = \pi(7)^2 - \pi(3)^2$$
$$= 49\pi - 9\pi$$
$$= 40\pi \text{ cm}^2$$

If we choose to use 3.14 as a rational approximation for π, then we obtain

$$A \doteq 40(3.14)$$
$$\doteq 125.6 \text{ cm}^2$$

REMARK Notice in Example 7 that although we are going to use a rational approximation for π, it is easier to first set up and simplify the problem in terms of π before making the substitution.

PROBLEM SET 9.4

1. Find the area of a rectangular region if the diagonals are 26 centimeters long and the length of the rectangle is 24 centimeters.

2. Find the area of a triangular region that has two sides of length 4 meters and 6 meters, and the angle included by those sides is of measure 30°.

3. Find the area of a region in the shape of a rhombus having sides 6 meters long and having a 30° angle.

4. Find the area, to the nearest tenth of a square foot, of a right triangular region having a 30° angle and a hypotenuse of length 8 feet.

5. Find the area of a region in the shape of an isosceles trapezoid having bases of 16 inches and 24 inches and two angles of 60°. Leave the answer in radical form.

6. Find the area of a triangular region whose sides are of length 9 yards, 12 yards and 15 yards.

7. The area of an isosceles right triangular region is 50 square meters. Find the length, to the nearest tenth of a meter, of the hypotenuse.

8. A circular pool is 25 feet in diameter and has a flagstone walk around it that is 3 feet wide. How many square feet of flagstone are in the walk? (Use $3\frac{1}{7}$ as an approximation of π.)

9. Find the area of each of the five regions of the following dartboard.

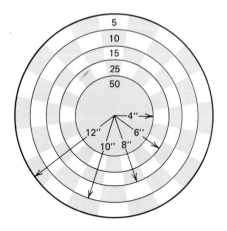

10. **a.** If the circumference of a circle is 12π units, find the measure of a radius.

b. Find the area of the circular region in part **a**.

c. If the area of a circle is 49π, what is the circumference of the circle?

d. If the area of a circle is 81π, what is the circumference of the circle?

e. What is the ratio of the area units in a circle to the circumference units for a circle of radius r

11. Find the area of each of the following regions (if the answer is irrational, leave it in radical form):

a.

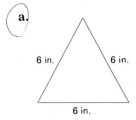

b.

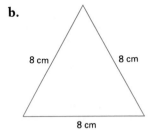

c.

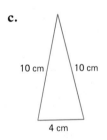

d.

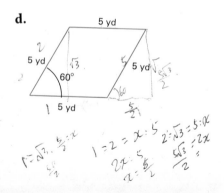

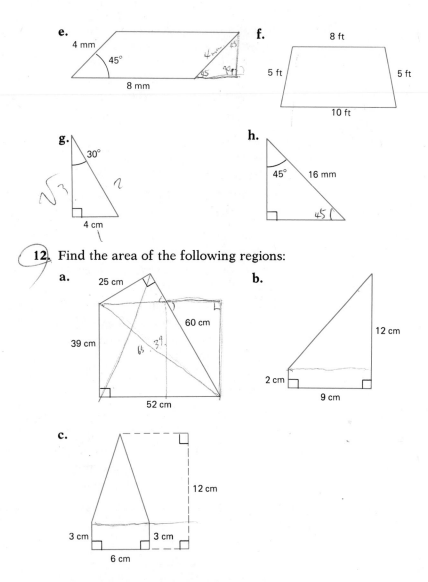

e.

4 mm
45°
8 mm

f.

8 ft
5 ft   5 ft
10 ft

g.

30°
4 cm

h.

45°   16 mm

12. Find the area of the following regions:

a.

25 cm
39 cm
60 cm
52 cm

b.

12 cm
2 cm
9 cm

c.

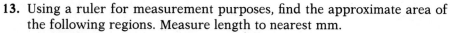

12 cm
3 cm   3 cm
6 cm

13. Using a ruler for measurement purposes, find the approximate area of the following regions. Measure length to nearest mm.

a.

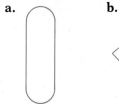

b.

c.

14. Find the area of a rectangular region if the diagonals are 18 centimeters long and the width of the rectangle is 7 centimeters. Express the answer to the nearest tenth of a square centimeter.

 15. A revolving lawn sprinkler sprays water for a distance of 8 meters from the sprinkler. Find the area, to the nearest square meter, of the lawn watered by the sprinkler. (Use 3.14 as an approximation for π.)

 16. Which of the following pizzas is the best buy. (Use 3.14 as an approximation for π).

    a. 10-inch diameter for $6.99

    b. 12-inch diameter for $9.99

    c. 14-inch diameter for $14.99

 17. Use a calculator to help with the following problems (express final answers to the nearest one-tenth of a unit):

    a. Find the area of a region in the shape of an equilateral triangle having sides of length 12.4 meters.

    b. Find the area of a region in the shape of a rhombus having sides of 21.4 centimeters and having a 30° angle.

    c. Find the area of a circular region having a radius of 14.3 meters (use 3.14 as an approximation for π).

    d. Find the area of a circular region having a circumference of 42.6π centimeters (use 3.14 as an approximation for π).

Pedagogical Problems and Activities

18. Draw a circle with a radius of 6 centimeters. Cut it up into 16 congruent wedges and reassemble them to approximate a parallelogram. What is an approximation of the area of the new figures?

19. From the following figure, show that the area of the circular region must be greater than $2r^2$ and less than $4r^2$.

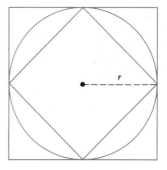

20. For each of the following, first estimate the area and then check your estimate by measuring.

  a. _____ mm²   A penny
  b. _____ mm²   A nickel
  c. _____ mm²   A quarter
  d. _____ cm²   A "large" circle that you have drawn on your paper
  e. _____ cm²   Any circular object in your room

9.5   SURFACE AREA OF PRISMS AND CYLINDERS

A prism was defined in Chapter 7, but we revisit it here from a little different viewpoint. Recall that a prism has its bases as congruent polygonal regions located in parallel planes. As indicated in Figure 9.22, the line segments connecting corresponding vertices are parallel.

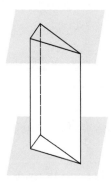 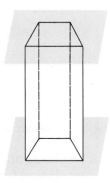 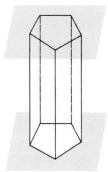

FIGURE 9.22

In Figure 9.22 the prisms are formed by starting with congruent triangles, quadrilaterals, and pentagons, but we could start with any two congruent polygons in parallel planes. In general, the line segments joining corresponding vertices of the bases of a prism need not be perpendicular to the bases. However, from a practical viewpoint, most of the real-world models of prisms to which elementary school children are exposed have these lines perpendicular to the bases and are called *right prisms*. Such physical models as rectangular boxes, children's building blocks, and file cabinets are examples of right prisms.

Consider the examples of right prisms in Figure 9.23. In each case the lateral faces are rectangular regions. Therefore, finding the *total surface area*

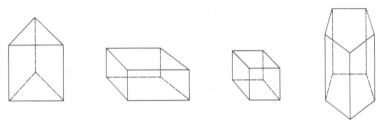

FIGURE 9.23

of a right prism involves finding the area of a number of rectangular regions (lateral faces of the prism) plus the area of two congruent polygonal regions (the bases of the prism).

EXAMPLE 1

Find the total surface area of the following right prism for which the bases and lateral faces are rectangles.

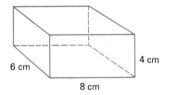

Solution The total surface area may be found as follows:

Area of two bases (top and bottom)	$2(6)(8) =$	96 cm^2
Area of two lateral faces (right side and left side)	$2(6)(4) =$	48 cm^2
Area of two lateral faces (front and back)	$2(8)(4) =$	$\underline{64}$ cm^2
Total surface area		208 cm^2

EXAMPLE 2

Find the total surface area of the following right prism for which the bases are equilateral triangles and the lateral faces are rectangles.

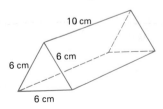

Solution First, let us find the area of one of the bases.

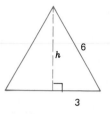

$$h^2 + 3^2 = 6^2$$
$$h^2 + 9 = 36$$
$$h^2 = 27$$
$$h = \sqrt{27}$$

Therefore, the area of a base is

$$A = \tfrac{1}{2}bh$$
$$= \tfrac{1}{2}(6)(\sqrt{27}) = 3\sqrt{27}$$

Now the total surface area of the prism can be found as follows:

Area of two bases	$2(3\sqrt{27}) = 6\sqrt{27}$ cm²
Area of three lateral faces	$3(6 \cdot 10) = 180$ cm²

The total surface area is $(180 + 6\sqrt{27})$ cm², or approximately 211.2 cm².

The concept of a cylinder may be described in much the same way as that of a prism. However, instead of starting with two congruent polygonal regions in parallel planes, let us start with two congruent regions bounded by simple closed plane curves other than polygons. Now, by connecting points on the two congruent curves in parallel planes with parallel line segments, we form three-space geometric figures called cylinders (Fig. 9.24). The two congruent regions are referred to as the *bases* of the cylinder and the parallel line segments joining points of the two congruent curves are called *elements*. If the bases are circles and the elements are perpendicular to the planes of the bases, then we have what is commonly called a *right circular cylinder.*

The right circular cylinder is the type of cylinder that frequently occurs in the environment. One very common model of a right circular cylinder is an unopened tin can. Also, such things as ordinary drinking straws, some glasses for drinking purposes, and beakers used in science laboratories have the basic shape of a right circular cylinder with one or both bases missing.

Analogous to a right prism, the total surface area of a right circular cylinder is equal to the sum of the areas of two congruent bases and the lateral

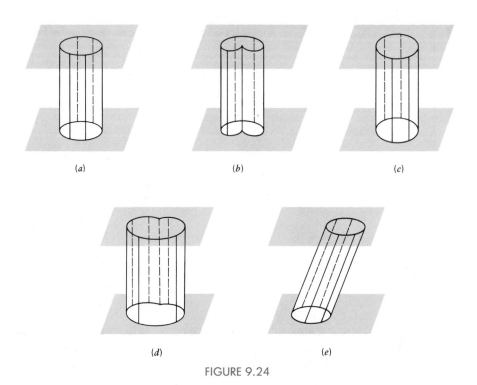

(a)   (b)   (c)

(d)   (e)

FIGURE 9.24

surface area. Because the bases of a right circular cylinder are congruent circular regions, their combined area is given by $2\pi r^2$. (Remember that the formula for the area of a circular region is $A = \pi r^2$.) Now what about the lateral surface? Consider the right circular cylinder illustrated in Figure 9.25. Suppose that a piece of paper covers the lateral surface (such as the label on a can of fruit). If one were to cut along some element such as $\overline{AB}$ and then lay the paper out flat, it would be a rectangular region. The width of the rectangle is h units (the height of the cylinder). Because the paper was

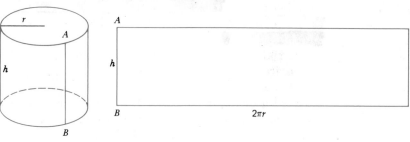

FIGURE 9.25

wrapped around the can, the length of the rectangle should be the same as the circumference of the cylinder, namely, $2\pi r$. Thus, the area of the rectangular region that is the lateral surface area of the cylinder is given by $2\pi rh$. Let us summarize this discussion with the following property.

PROPERTY 9.9 **The total surface area of a right circular cylinder is given by $T = 2\pi r^2 + 2\pi rh$, where r is the measure of a radius of a base and h is the height of the cylinder.**

EXAMPLE

Find the total surface area of a tin can if the radius of a base is 3 centimeters and the height of the can is 10 centimeters.

Solution Let us sketch the can and record the given information.

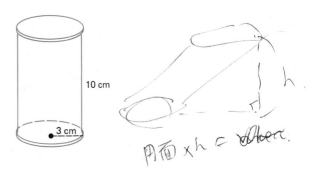

By a direct application of the total surface area formula given in Property 9.9 we obtain

$$T = 2\pi r^2 + 2\pi rh$$
$$= 2\pi(3)^2 + 2\pi(3)(10)$$
$$= 18\pi + 60\pi$$
$$= 78\pi \text{ cm}^2$$

Using 3.14 as a rational approximation for π, we can also say that the total surface area of the can, to the nearest tenth of a square centimeter, is 244.9 square centimeters.

PROBLEM SET 9.5

1. Sketch each of the following by starting with congruent bases in parallel planes:
   a. A right prism having bases that are isosceles triangles
   b. A right prism having bases that are isosceles right triangles
   c. A circular cylinder that is not a right cylinder

    d. A right cylinder that is not a circular cylinder

    e. A right prism having bases that are isosceles trapezoids

    f. A right prism having bases that are regular hexagons

2. Find the total surface area of each of the following right prisms:

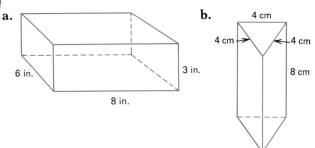

a.   **b.**   4 cm

6 in.   3 in.   4 cm ← →← 4 cm

8 in.   8 cm

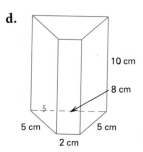

c.   **d.**   10 cm

6 cm   8 cm

4 cm   3 cm

5 cm   5 cm   5 cm

2 cm

3. Find the total surface area of a cube, each of whose edges is 6 inches.

4. Find the total surface area of a right prism whose bases are equilateral triangles 10 centimeters on a side and whose altitude is 12 centimeters.

5. Find the total surface area of each of the following right circular cylinders

    a. Radius of base is 4 meters and height of cylinder is 10 meters

    b. Radius of base is 6 feet and height of cylinder is 4 feet

    c. Diameter of base is 8 centimeters and height of cylinder is 20 centimeters

    d. Diameter of base is 7 inches and height of cylinder is 14 inches

6. Find the length of an edge of a cube whose total surface area is 294 square meters.

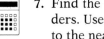

7. Find the total surface area of each of the following right circular cylinders. Use 3.14 as an approximation for π and express your final answers to the nearest tenth of a unit.

    a. Radius of base is 16.4 meters and the height of the cylinder is 24.7 meters.

b. Radius of base is 21.7 centimeters and the height of the cylinder is 37.8 centimeters.

c. Diameter of base is 28.6 meters and the height of the cylinder is 42.3 meters.

8. Find the total surface area of each of the following right prisms. Express answers to the nearest tenth of a unit. (Each prism makes use of properties of special triangles.)

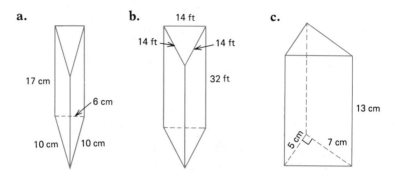

a.   17 cm   6 cm   10 cm   10 cm

b.   14 ft   14 ft   14 ft   32 ft

c.   13 cm   5 cm   7 cm

Pedagogical Problems and Activities

9. Using a piece of cardboard, follow the accompanying diagram and form a right rectangular prism. Cut along the solid line segments and fold along the dashed line segments.

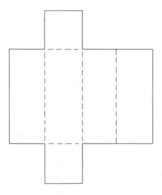

10. From your experience in Problem 9, make your own diagram and form a model of a cube each of whose edges is 10 centimeters.

11. Draw a diagram as in Problem 9 and form a model for a right prism whose bases are equilateral triangles 8 centimeters on a side and whose altitude is 12 centimeters.

12. Using a ruler for measuring length to nearest mm, find the surface area of the prism that can be made from the layout below. (Refer to problem 9.)

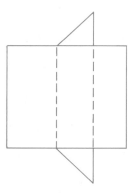

13. We know a rectangle "rolls" to make a cylinder. We might ask ourselves whether there are other shapes that also roll to make a cylinder.

    a. Does a general parallelogram roll to make a cylinder? Make a parallelogram, cut it out, and try to roll it to make a cylinder.

    b. Will a general trapezoid roll to make a cylinder?

    c. Will the following shape roll to make a cylinder?

    d. Will the following shape roll to make a cylinder?

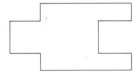

9.6 SURFACE AREA OF PYRAMIDS, CONES, AND SPHERES

Figure 9.26 is a reproduction of Figure 7.41 from Chapter 7. You will recall that there we defined a pyramid as a special kind of polyhedron. Now let us consider another way of forming a pyramid. In each part of Figure 9.27 we start with a polygonal region in a plane and a point not on the plane. Draw line segments connecting each point of the polygon to the point not on the plane. The resulting figures will be pyramids much like the ones in Figure

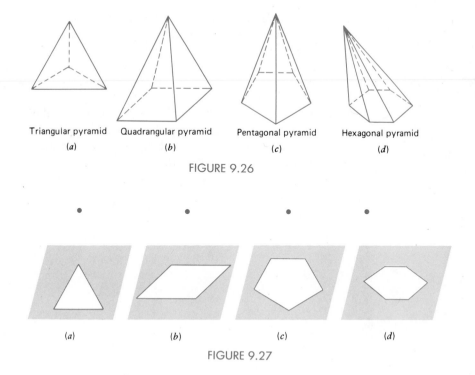

Triangular pyramid   Quadrangular pyramid   Pentagonal pyramid   Hexagonal pyramid
(a)   (b)   (c)   (d)

FIGURE 9.26

(a)   (b)   (c)   (d)

FIGURE 9.27

9.26. The original polygonal region is called the *base* of the pyramid and the point not on the plane of the base is called the *vertex*.

The altitude of a pyramid is a line segment drawn from the vertex perpendicular to the base. If the base of a pyramid is a regular polygon and the altitude intersects the base at its center, then the pyramid is referred to as a *regular pyramid*. Figure 9.28 illustrates some of the most frequently encountered regular pyramids.

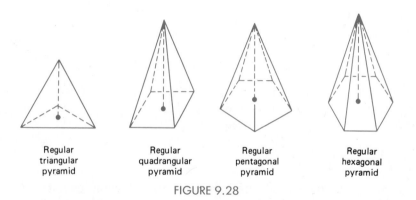

Regular   Regular   Regular   Regular
triangular   quadrangular   pentagonal   hexagonal
pyramid   pyramid   pyramid   pyramid

FIGURE 9.28

Because the lateral faces of a regular pyramid are congruent isosceles triangles and the base is a regular polygon, it is often a simple matter to find the total surface area. Let us consider an example.

EXAMPLE 1

Find the total surface area of the following regular pyramid that has a square base 4 centimeters on a side and a slant height that measures 8 centimeters. (An altitude of a lateral face drawn from the vertex of the pyramid is a *slant height* of the pyramid.)

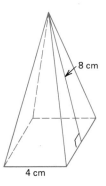

8 cm

4 cm

Solution First, find the area of one of the isosceles triangular faces.

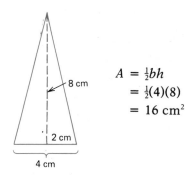

8 cm

2 cm

4 cm

$A = \frac{1}{2}bh$
$= \frac{1}{2}(4)(8)$
$= 16 \text{ cm}^2$

Thus, the total surface area can be found as follows:

Area of the square base $4(4) = 16 \text{ cm}^2$
Area of the four lateral faces $4(16) = 64 \text{ cm}^2$
Total surface area 80 cm^2

EXAMPLE 2

Find the total surface area of the following regular pyramid having a square base 6 meters on a side and an altitude of length 10 meters.

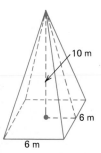

Solution   To find the area of the isosceles triangular faces, we need to find the slant height of the pyramid. (The slant height of the pyramid is the altitude of a face.) So, let us sketch the right triangle formed by the altitude and the slant height.

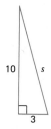

By applying the Pythagorean theorem we obtain

$$s^2 = 10^2 + 3^2$$
$$s^2 = 100 + 9$$
$$s^2 = 109$$
$$s = \sqrt{109} \doteq 10.4$$

Now we can find the area of an isosceles triangular face as follows:

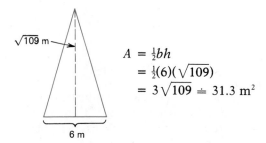

$$A = \tfrac{1}{2}bh$$
$$= \tfrac{1}{2}(6)(\sqrt{109})$$
$$= 3\sqrt{109} \doteq 31.3 \text{ m}^2$$

Thus, the total surface area can be found by adding the area of the base to the area of the four lateral faces. Recorded as follows we find the total surface area of this pyramid to be approximately 161.3 m²

Area of a square base   (6)(6)   = 36 m²   = 36 m²
Area of four lateral faces $4(3\sqrt{109}) = 12\sqrt{109}$ m² $\doteq$ 125.3 m²
Total surface area $(36 + 12\sqrt{109})$ m² $\doteq$ 161.3 m²

We found that a pyramid can be formed by starting with a polygonal region in a plane and a point not on the plane. Now let us start with a region bounded by a simple closed curve (other than a polygon) in a plane and a point not in the plane (Fig. 9.29). By drawing line segments connecting each

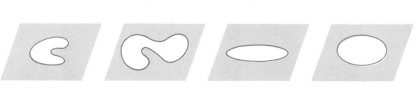

FIGURE 9.29

point of the curve to the point not on the plane, figures as indicated in Figure 9.30 are formed. Each of these figures is called a *cone*. The terminology used with a cone is analogous to that used with pyramids. The region bounded by the simple closed plane curve is called the *base*, and the line segments joining the points of the curve to the outside point *(vertex)* are referred to as *elements* of the cone.

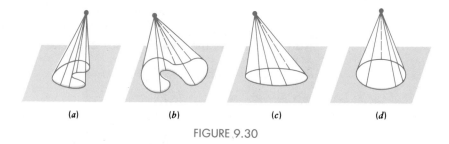

(a)   (b)   (c)   (d)

FIGURE 9.30

Even though all the illustrations in Figure 9.30 are cones, the one in part (d) is what most people think of when they use the term *cone*. It is a *right circular cone*. The base is a circular region, and the altitude (a line segment from the vertex perpendicular to the base) intersects the base at the center, as indicated in Figure 9.31.

The total surface area of a right circular cone is equal to the area of its

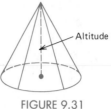

FIGURE 9.31

circular base plus its lateral surface area. To determine a general formula, let us "take a cone apart" as indicated in Figure 9.32. From part (*b*) to part (*c*) we have removed the circular base, cut the cone along a slant height, and flattened out the lateral surface. The lateral surface forms a *sector* of a cir-

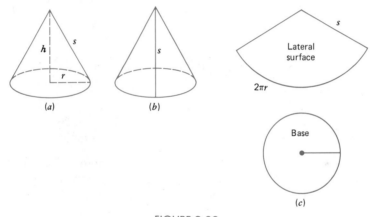

FIGURE 9.32

cular region—that is, a pie-shaped piece of a circular region. The area of the sector compares to the area of the entire circular region as the length of the arc of the sector compares to the circumference of the circular region. Thus, letting L represent the area of the sector, we have

$$\frac{L}{\pi s^2} = \frac{2\pi r}{2\pi s}$$

Solving this equation for L, we obtain

$$L = \frac{(2\pi r)(\pi s^2)}{2\pi s}$$
$$= \pi r s$$

Therefore, the following property can be stated.

PROPERTY 9.10   The lateral area of a right circular cone is given by $L = \pi rs$, where r is the measure of a radius of the base and s is the measure of the slant height of the cone. The total surface area is given by $T = \pi r^2 + \pi rs$.

EXAMPLE 3

Find the total surface area of the following right circular cone having a base with a radius of 4 centimeters and a slant height of 9 centimeters.

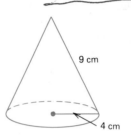

9 cm

4 cm

Solution Using the formula stated in Property 9.10 we obtain

$$T = \pi r^2 + \pi rs$$
$$= \pi(4)^2 + \pi(4)(9)$$
$$= 16\pi + 36\pi$$
$$= 52\pi \text{ cm}^2$$

Using 3.14 as a rational approximation for π, we obtain 163.3 square centimeters as an approximation, to the nearest tenth, for the total surface area of the cone.

EXAMPLE 4

Find the lateral surface area of the following right circular cone having a base with a radius of 3 meters and an altitude of 4 meters.

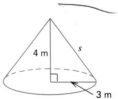

4 m s

3 m

Solution By applying the Pythagorean theorem we can find the length of the slant height as follows:

$$s^2 = 3^2 + 4^2$$
$$s^2 = 9 + 16$$
$$s^2 = 25$$
$$s = \sqrt{25} = 5$$

Therefore, the lateral area is

$$
\begin{aligned}
L &= \pi r s \\
&= \pi(3)(5) \\
&= 15\pi \ \mathrm{m}^2 \\
&\doteq 47.1 \ \mathrm{m}^2
\end{aligned}
$$

In Chapter 8 we defined a circle to be a set of points *in a plane* that are all at a given distance from some fixed point in the plane. The concept of a sphere may be defined simply by removing from the definition of cicle the condition that all points are in one plane. Thus, a sphere is a set of points in space such that all points are at some fixed distance from a given point. The terms *center, radius,* and *diameter* are used analogous to their usage with reference to a circle (Fig. 9.33).

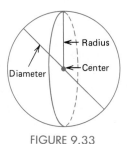

FIGURE 9.33

We have consistently attempted to provide some sort of "justification" for the development of various formulas. There does not seem to be a reasonably simple way of developing the formula for finding the surface area of a sphere, so we will simply state the formula and then put it to use.

PROPERTY 9.11 **The total surface area of a sphere having a radius of measure r is given by $T = 4\pi r^2$.**

EXAMPLE 5

Find the total surface area of a baseball having a radius of 4 centimeters.

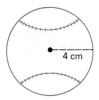

Solution Using the formula stated in Property 9.11 we obtain

$$T = 4\pi r^2$$
$$= 4\pi(4)^2$$
$$= 64\pi \text{ cm}^2$$
$$\doteq 201 \text{ cm}^2$$

> **REMARK** The relationship stated in Property 9.11 should not be viewed merely as a formula for finding the surface area of a sphere. In fact, if you had a circle of radius r and a sphere of radius r, the surface area of the sphere is exactly four times the area of the circle.

PROBLEM SET 9.6

For each of the following problems (1 through 7), first sketch a figure and insert the given information; then solve the problem.

1. Find the total surface area of a regular pyramid having a square base 7 centimeters on a side and a slant height of 12 centimeters.

2. Find the total surface area of a right circular cone having a base with a radius of 12 inches and a slant height of 18 inches.

3. Find the total surface area of a sphere having a radius of 9 meters.

4. Find the total surface area of a regular pyramid having a base that is an equilateral triangle 4 meters on a side and a slant height of 8 meters.

5. Find the total surface area of a regular pyramid having a square base 18 feet on a side and whose altitude is 40 feet.

6. Find the total surface area of a right circular cone having a base with a radius of 5 centimeters and whose altitude is 12 centimeters.

7. Find the total surface area of a regular pyramid having a hexagonal base 6 centimeters on a side and whose slant height is 13 centimeters. (*Hint:* A regular hexagonal region may be partitioned into six congruent equilateral triangular regions.)

8. How does doubling the radius of a sphere affect its surface area?

9. Sketch three pyramids that are not regular pyramids.

10. Sketch three cones that are not right circular cones.

 11. For each of the following problems, express answers to the nearest unit. Use 3.14 as an approximation for π when working with cones and spheres.

   a. Find the total surface area of a golf ball having a radius of 2 centimeters.

b. Find the total surface area of a regular pyramid having a base that is an equilateral triangle 14 inches on a side and a slant height of 17 inches.

    c. Find the total surface area of a right circular cone having a base with a radius of 10 meters and an altitude of 24 meters.

    d. Find the total surface area of a sphere having a diameter of 8000 miles. (The diameter of the earth is approximately 8000 miles.)

    e. Find the total surface area of a regular pyramid having a square base 14 feet on a side and an altitude of 14 feet.

 12. For each of the following, express answers to the nearest tenth of a unit. Use 3.14 as an approximation for π when working with cones and spheres.

    a. Find the total surface area of a softball having a circumference of 40 centimeters.

    b. Find the total surface area of a regular pyramid having a hexagonal base 22 inches on a side and a slant height of 17 inches.

    c. Find the lateral surface area of a right circular cone having a base with a radius of 7 centimeters and whose altitude is 19 centimeters long.

13. Consider the following figure that can be made into a pyramid.

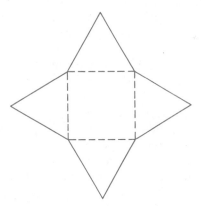

    a. Using a ruler to measure length to the nearest mm, determine the approximate surface area of this pyramid.

    b. Actually cut out and make the pyramid to determine the height of this pyramid.

Pedagogical Problems and Activities

14. a. Construct a circle having a radius of 10 centimeters. What is the area of the circular region?

b. Construct two radii perpendicular to each other. What is the area of the sector of the circle bounded by the two radii and the smallest arc of the circle?

c. Cut out that sector of the circle and fold it into a right circular cone. What is the lateral area of the cone?

d. What is the radius of the base of the cone? What is the slant height of the cone? Use these figures and the formula $L = \pi s r$ and find the lateral area of the cone.

This type of reasoning may also be used with children to "justify" the formula for finding the lateral area of a right circular cone.

15. Previously we investigated rolling shapes to make a cylinder. We might now ask what kind of shape will roll to make a cone. Does a triangle roll to make a cone? Make one, cut it out and try.

9.7   VOLUME

We have previously stated that a polyhedron separates three-space into sets of points commonly called the *interior* and the *exterior* of the polyhedron. The union of a polyhedron and its interior is called a *space region*. The notion of a space region may also be extended to the other three-dimensional concepts that we have studied—namely, the cylinder, cone, and sphere. Our problem now becomes one of attaching measurement concepts to space regions.

We used basic unit line segments to measure line segments, basic unit angles to measure angles, and basic unit plane regions to measure plane regions. In a similar fashion we must agree on some basic unit space regions to measure space regions. We could choose unit prisms, unit cylinders, unit pyramids, unit cones, unit spheres, or, in fact, unit polyhedrons of any shape. However, the one usually chosen is the "unit cube," such as a cubic centimeter (a cube all of whose edges are 1 centimeter long) and a cubic inch (a cube all of whose edges are 1 inch long) (Figure 9.34).

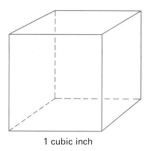

1 cubic centimeter   1 cubic inch

FIGURE 9.34

> REMARK Perhaps it would be advisable with elementary school children actually to do some "filling of space regions" using units such as spherical units (marbles). This might lead to a greater appreciation for the choice of unit cubes.

Figure 9.35 shows a rectangular box (right prism) 5 centimeters by 3 centimeters by 4 centimeters. Using a cubic centimeter as a basic unit we can place 15 such units in each layer. It would take 4 layers to "fill" the box, and thus the box has a volume of 60 cubic centimeters. For any right prism, knowing the number of cubes in one layer and knowing the number of layers allows us immediately to determine the volume. Thus, we state the following property.

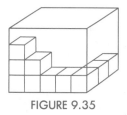

FIGURE 9.35

PROPERTY 9.12 The volume of any right prism is given by $V = Bh$, where B represents the area of a base and h is the measure of the altitude.

> REMARK 1 B in the formula tells us the volume of one layer as well as telling us the area of the base of a prism.
>
> REMARK 2 If the base of a right prism is a rectangle l units long and w units wide, then the area is given by lw. Thus, the formula in Property 9.12 becomes $V = lwh$, which may be one of the first volume formulas to which elementary school children are exposed.

EXAMPLE 1

Find the volume of a right prism whose bases are right triangles with legs of 4 centimeters and 7 centimeters and whose altitude is 12 centimeters long.

Solution First, let us sketch the prism and record the given information.

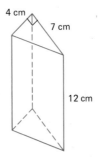

The area of a base is

$$A = \tfrac{1}{2}bh$$
$$= \tfrac{1}{2}(4)(7)$$
$$= 14 \text{ cm}^2$$

Thus, the volume is

$$V = Bh$$
$$= 14(12)$$
$$= 168 \text{ cm}^3 \text{ (cm}^3 \text{ is the symbol for cubic centimeters)}$$

Before we investigate other formulas for finding volume, let us insert a table that will be of use to us and briefly comment on it. In Table 9.3 we have indicated the basic units of volume used in both the English and metric systems. As with the table for area measurements, children need to realize that the numerical relationships in Table 9.3 need not be memorized, but can be easily figured out. For example, in Figure 9.36 we have shown that 1 cubic yard equals 27 cubic feet and 1 cubic decimeter equals 1000 cubic centimeters.

There are symbols for metric units of volume. These are given in Table 9.4. A liter, L, is typically used to measure volume or capacity (either liquid or

TABLE 9.3

Metric System	English System
1000 cubic millimeters = 1 cubic centimeter	1728 cubic inches = 1 cubic foot
1000 cubic centimeters = 1 cubic decimeter	27 cubic feet = 1 cubic yard
1000 cubic decimeters = 1 cubic meter	$166\tfrac{3}{8}$ cubic yards = 1 cubic rod
1000 cubic meters = 1 cubic dekameter	
1000 cubic dekameters = 1 cubic hectometer	
1000 cubic hectometers = 1 cubic kilometer	

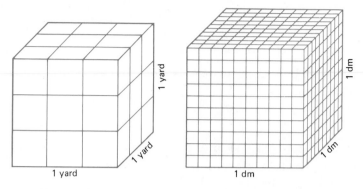

1 cubic yard = 27 cubic feet   1 cubic decimeter = 1000 cubic centimeters

FIGURE 9.36

TABLE 9.4

Volume unit	Symbol
Cubic millimeter	mm³
Cubic centimeter	cm³
Cubic decimeter	dm³
Cubic meter	m³
Cubic dekameter	dam³
Cubic hectometer	hm³
Cubic kilometer	km³

dry). For comparison purposes a liter can be thought of as approximately the same measure as the United States liquid quart. To help you have a visualization of a liter, consider a cubic decimeter, 1000 cm³, which is also called a liter. A decimeter cube, pictured in Figure 9.36, is also a block associated with base ten materials. A milliliter, mL, is 0.001 of a liter and the same volume as 1 cm³. Metric units of volume are given in Table 9.5.

TABLE 9.5

Unit	Symbol	Relation to Liter
kiloliter	kL	1000 liters
hectoliter	hL	100 liters
dekaliter	daL	10 liters
liter	L	1 liter
deciliter	dL	0.1 liter
centiliter	cL	0.01 liter
milliliter	mL	0.001 liter

EXAMPLE 1

Convert each of the following as indicated.

a. 43 L = _____ mL   **b.** 654 mL = _____ L
c. 9 mL = _____ cm^3 **d.** 5 m^3 = _____ L

Solutions

a. 43000; because 1 L = 1000 mL, then 43 L = 43000 mL.
b. 0.645; because 1 mL = 0.001 L, 654 mL = 654 $\times$ 0.001 L = 0.654 L.
c. 9; because 1 mL = 1 cm^3, 9 mL = 9 cm^3
d. 5000; because 1 m = 10 dm, 1 m^3 = 1000 dm^3 = 1000 L. Thus 5 m^3 = 5000 L.

The formula ($V = Bh$) for finding the volume of a right prism also holds true for right circular cylinders. Because the bases of right circular cylinders are circular regions, we have $B = \pi r^2$, and the formula is then usually stated as $V = \pi r^2 h$. Again, the interpretation of volume as number of units per layer times number of layers is useful here, even though it is more difficult to visualize the cubic units in the base of a cylinder than in the base of a prism. Let us state this as a property and then provide some justification for it.

PROPERTY 9.13   **The volume of any right circular cylinder is given by $V = \pi r^2 h$, where r is the measure of a radius of a base and h is the measure of the altitude of the cylinder.**

One way to realize the truth of Property 9.13 is illustrated in Figure 9.37. From the figure, as the number of sides of the prism increases, the volume becomes closer and closer to the volume of the cylinder. Because we know that the formula for volumes of prisms is $V = Bh$, this should also be the basic formula for right circular cylinders.

It may also be helpful to do some experimenting in order to know that our formula is working. For example, suppose that we have a right circular cyl-

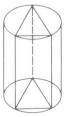 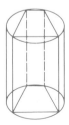  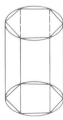

FIGURE 9.37

inder (without a top) having a base radius of 5 centimeters and a height of 10 centimeters (Fig. 9.38a). According to our formula, the volume should be $V = \pi(5)^2(10) = 250\pi$ cubic centimeters. Using 3.1 as an approximation for π, this would give us a volume of approximately 775 cubic centimeters. Thus, a right prism with a rectangular base 5 centimeters by 31 centimeters and a height of 5 centimeters should have the same volume (Fig. 9.38b). We could build models of these sizes and make a comparison of volumes by using sand, water, or some such substance.

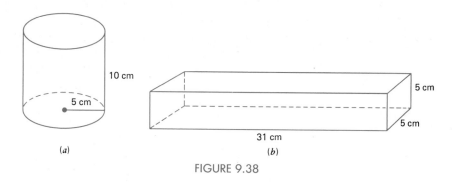

FIGURE 9.38

REMARK The formula $V = Bh$ holds for any prism and any cylinder, even though we have restricted our work to right prisms and right circular cylinders. Justification for the general cases is a little more difficult to establish.

EXAMPLE 2

Find the volume of a tin can having a base with a radius of 3 centimeters; the height of the can is 14 centimeters.

Solution First, let us sketch the can and record the given information.

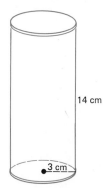

Using the formula stated in Property 9.13 we obtain

$$V = \pi r^2 h$$
$$= \pi(3)^2(14)$$
$$= 126\pi \ \text{cm}^3$$

If we use $3\frac{1}{7}$ as an approximation for π, then we obtain $V = 126(\frac{22}{7}) = 396$ cubic centimeters.

Determining the exact formula for finding the *volume of a sphere* is not an easy task. Suppose that we have a sphere of radius r as in Figure 9.39a. Let us put the sphere in a cubical box so that it touches all sides of the box as indicated in Figure 9.39b. The box would have dimensions of $2r$ by $2r$ by $2r$, and thus the volume of the box would be $8r^3$. This does not tell us the volume of the sphere, but it does indicate that the volume has to be less than $8r^3$.

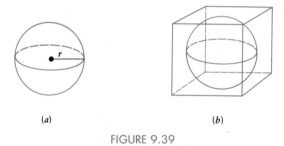

(a)   (b)

FIGURE 9.39

A second approximation may be made by relating a sphere to a cylinder. Suppose we have a sphere with a radius of length r and a right circular cylinder (no lid) having a base of radius r and a height of $2r$ (Fig. 9.40a). The volume of the cylinder is $V = \pi r^2(2r) = 2\pi r^3$. In 9.40b the sphere is shown placed inside the cylinder. Suppose the cylinder was filled with water. Then, as the sphere is lowered into the cylinder, water is displaced. The volume of displaced water is equal to the volume of the sphere. An attempt should now

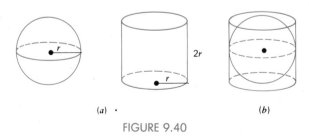

(a) ·   (b)

FIGURE 9.40

be made to relate the amount of water displaced with the amount of water the cylinder originally held. After several attempts we should begin to realize that the amount of water displaced is about two-thirds of the original amount. This is, in fact, the exact relationship. Therefore, the volume of the sphere is two-thirds of the volume of the cylinder and we have $V_{\text{sphere}} = \frac{2}{3}(2\pi r^3)$ $= \frac{4}{3}\pi r^3$. (An alternative justification of the volume formula is suggested in Question 20 of Problem Set 9.7.)

PROPERTY 9.14 **The volume of a sphere having a radius of measure r is given by $V = \frac{4}{3}\pi r^3$.**

EXAMPLE 3

Find the volume of a 5-inch softball.

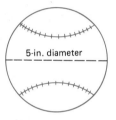

5-in. diameter

Solution A "5-inch softball" means a softball with a 5-inch diameter; thus, $r = 2.5$ inches and applying the formula in Property 9.14 we obtain

$$V = \frac{4}{3}\pi r^3$$
$$= \frac{4}{3}\pi(2.5)^3$$
$$= 20.8\pi \text{ cubic inches}$$
$$\doteq 65.3 \text{ cubic inches}$$

In each part of Figure 9.41 we indicate a pyramid that can be associated with a corresponding right prism having regular polygonal regions for bases. In Figure 9.41a, the shaded pyramid inscribed in the cube has a square base, *ABCD*, and a height *CG*. If you look carefully, you see that this pyramid, together with two other pyramids having bases *AEFB* and *AEHD* and vertex *C* fit together to make the cube. Therefore, the volume of one of these square pyramids is one-third of the volume of the cube. This relationship of one-third is true for pyramids and prisms in general, but you must keep in mind that we are comparing the volume of a pyramid to the volume of a prism where the prism has a base congruent to the base of the pyramid and the altitude of the prism is the same length as the altitude of the pyramid. We now state this as a property.

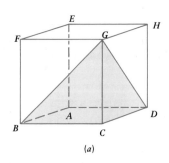

(a)

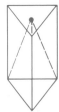 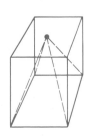 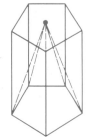

FIGURE 9.41

PROPERTY 9.15   **The volume of a regular pyramid is given by $V = \frac{1}{3}Bh$, where B is the area of the base and h is the measure of the altitude.**

EXAMPLE 4

Find the volume of the following regular pyramid having a square base 7 cm on a side and an altitude of 15 cm.

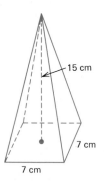

15 cm

7 cm

7 cm

Solution The base is a 7 cm by 7 cm square, so its area is $(7)(7) = 49$ cm². Then using the formula stated in Property 9.15, we obtain

$$V = \tfrac{1}{3}Bh$$
$$= \tfrac{1}{3}(49)(15)$$
$$= 245 \text{ cm}^3$$

In the previous section we derived the formula for finding the volume of a right circular cylinder directly from the formula for volume of a right prism. This same kind of approach may be used with right circular cones, as they are related to regular pyramids. From Figure 9.42 we see that as the number of sides of the pyramid increases, the volume of the pyramid approaches the volume of the cone. Indeed, the formula $V = \frac{1}{3}Bh$ will also work for a cone, and because the base of a right circular cone is a circle, we have $B = \pi r^2$. The volume formula for a right circular cone is then stated as $V = \frac{1}{3}\pi r^2 h$. This formula should be thought of as also expressing a relationship between a cone and a cylinder with the same radius and height of the cone. This relationship says that the volume of such a cone is $\frac{1}{3}$ of the volume of the related cylinder.

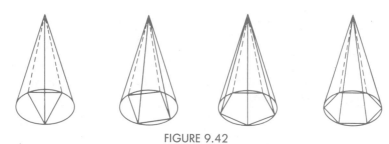

FIGURE 9.42

PROPERTY 9.16 **The volume of a right circular cone is given by $V = \frac{1}{3}\pi r^2 h$, where r is the measure of a radius of the base and h is the measure of the altitude of the cone.**

REMARK The general formula $V = \frac{1}{3}Bh$ holds true for any cone, even though it is the right circular cone that we work with most frequently in the elementary school program.

EXAMPLE 5

Find the volume of a right circular cone having a base with a radius of 5 meters and a slant height of 13 meters.

Solution Let us sketch the cone and record the given information.

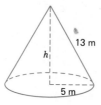

By applying the Pythagorean theorem we can find the value of h as follows:

$$h^2 + 5^2 = 13^2$$
$$h^2 + 25 = 169$$
$$h^2 = 144$$
$$h = 12$$

Then, using the formula stated in Property 9.16, we obtain

$$V = \tfrac{1}{3}\pi r^2 h$$
$$= \tfrac{1}{3}\pi(5)^2(12)$$
$$= 100\pi \text{ m}^3$$

PROBLEM SET 9.7

1. Find the volume of each of the following. Each figure represents a right prism, a right circular cylinder, a regular pyramid, a right circular cone, or a sphere

a.

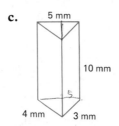

b.

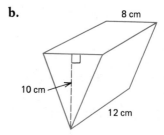

c.

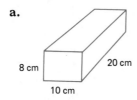

d.

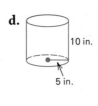

e.

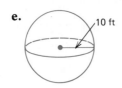

f.

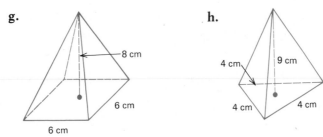

g.

8 cm

6 cm

6 cm

h.

4 cm

9 cm

4 cm

4 cm

2. A container in the shape of a right prism is 20 inches high and the volume is 3300 cubic inches.

    a. How many square inches are there in the base?

    b. If the base is a square, how long is each side?

3. **a.** How many cubic yards of sand are in a right circular conical pile that has a diameter of the base of 12 feet and a height of 5 feet?

    b. Could this sand all fit in a dump truck with a bed that is 6 feet by 10 feet by 3 feet?

4. An ice cream cone has the shape of a right circular cone with an altitude of 12 centimeters and a top diameter of 5 centimeters. A spherical scoop of ice cream having a radius of 2.5 centimeters is placed in the top of the cone.

    a. Draw a sketch of this cone and sphere

    b. Will the cone overflow if all the ice cream melts and runs into the cone?

5. Find the volume of a right circular cone having a base with a diameter of 12 centimeters and an altitude of 21 centimeters. Use $3\frac{1}{7}$ as an approximation for π.

6. Find the volume of a regular pyramid having a square base 7 meters on a side and an altitude of 27 meters.

7. Find the volume of a regular pyramid whose base is a square 6 centimeters on a side and whose slant height is 5 centimeters.

8. How many meters of wire that is 2 millimeters in diameter can be made from 10 cubic centimeters of copper?

9. A right circular cone and a right circular cylinder have altitudes of the same length. If the volumes are to be equal in measure, what relation must hold between the lengths of the radii of their bases?

10. How is the volume of a sphere affected by doubling the length of a radius?

11. Find the length of a side of a cube in which the volume equals the total surface area.

12. Find the volume of each of the following (when working with cylinders and cones, leave answers in terms of π):

a.

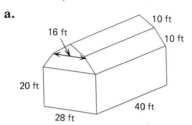

b.

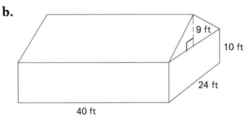

c.

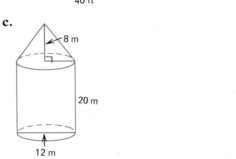

d.

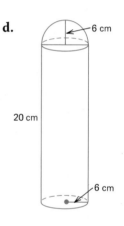

 13. A drain tile is made of clay. Each tile is a right cylindrical shell 36 centimeters long. The inside diameter is 12 centimeters and the outside diameter is 16 centimeters. How many cubic centimeters, to the nearest tenth of a cubic centimeter, of clay are used in each tile? (Use 3.14 as an approximation for π).

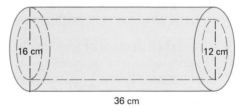

 14. Find the volume of a baseball, to the nearest cubic inch, having a diameter of 2.5 inches. (Use 3.14 as an approximation for π.)

15. Use a calculator to help with the following problems. Express final answers to the nearest one-tenth of a unit and use 3.14 as an approximation for π.

    a. Find the volume of a sphere having a radius of 14.3 centimeters.

    b. Find the volume of a right circular cylinder having a base with a radius of 23.7 meters and a height of 83.2 meters.

    c. Find the volume of a right circular cone having a base with a radius of 36.3 centimeters and a height of 57.3 centimeters.

16. Complete the following.

    a. $4 \, dm^3 =$ _____ L

    b. $52 \, mL =$ _____ cm^3

    c. $353 \, mL =$ _____ L

    d. $0.5 \, L =$ _____ mL

17. Place a decimal point so that the following is an accurate statement.

    a. A cup of coffee is about 25000 mL.

    b. A regular soft-drink can holds about 30000 L.

    c. A spoonful of medicine would hold about 1500 mL.

Pedagogical Problems and Activities

18. A child interprets $4 \, cm^3$ as a cube with 4 cm on an edge. What do you say?

19. A child says, "When we found the volume and surface area of a prism, the volume number was always smaller than the surface area number. Is this always the case?" What do you say?

20. Consider a sphere of radius r with a grid on it as indicated. Consider the figure formed by one section of the grid and the line segments joining its vertices to the center of the sphere. This figure approximates a pyramid with an altitude of r. Thus, the volume of any such pyramid is $\frac{1}{3}Br$. How can this information now be used to derive the volume formula for a sphere?

9.8 SUMMARY OF FORMULAS

The following list shows the formulas that have been presented in this chapter. We want to reemphasize that a knowledge of why the formulas work and how some of them are related to each other can greatly facilitate the memory process.

Area Formulas for Two-Dimensional Regions

$A = lw$ or $A = bh$	Rectangular region
$A = bh$	Parallelogram region
$A = \frac{1}{2}bh$	Triangular region
$A = \frac{1}{2}h(b_1 + b_2)$	Trapezoid region
$A = \pi r^2$	Circular region

Lateral Area (L) and Total Surface Area (T) Formulas for Three-Dimensional Figures

$$\left(\begin{array}{l} L = 2\pi rh \\ T = 2\pi rh + 2\pi r^2 \end{array} \right) \quad \text{Right circular cylinder}$$

$$\left(\begin{array}{l} L = \pi rs \\ T = \pi rs + \pi r^2 \end{array} \right) \quad \text{Right circular cone}$$

$$T = 4\pi r^2 \qquad \text{Sphere}$$

Volume Formulas for Three-Dimensional Figures

$V = Bh$	Right prism
$V = \pi r^2 h$	Right circular cylinder
$V = \frac{1}{3}Bh$	Right pyramid
$V = \frac{1}{3}\pi r^2 h$	Right circular cone
$V = \frac{4}{3}\pi r^3$	Sphere

REVIEW PROBLEM SET

1. Complete each of the following:
   a. 154 square centimeters = _____ square meters
   b. 14 square meters = _____ square decimeters
   c. 15 square kilometers = _____ square meters.
   d. 12 square inches = _____ square feet
   e. 14 square feet = _____ square yards

2. Find the area of a region in the shape of a rhombus having sides of length 8 centimeters and having a 30° angle.

3. Find the area of a circular region having a circumference of 10π units.

4. Find the area of a region in the shape of an isosceles trapezoid having bases of 14 inches and 22 inches and nonparallel sides of length 5 inches.

5. Find the area of a right triangular region having a hypotenuse of length 26 meters and one leg of length 10 meters.

6. Find the total surface area of a cube, each of whose edges is 8 inches.

7. Find the total surface area of a right circular cylinder having a base with a radius of 6 centimeters and a height of 14 centimeters.

8. Complete each of the following:
   a. 437 cubic centimeters = _____ cubic meters
   b. 38 cubic feet = _____ cubic yards
   c. 14 cubic meters = _____ cubic decimeters
   d. 4 cubic feet = _____ cubic inches
   e. 15.3 cubic dekameters = _____ cubic meters

9. Find the volume of a right prism whose bases are right triangles with legs of 5 meters and 9 meters and whose altitude is 14 meters.

10. Find the volume and total surface of a sphere having a radius of length 4 meters.

11. Find the volume of a regular pyramid having a square base 4 centimeters on a side and whose altitude is 14 centimeters.

12. Complete the following.
   a. 556 mL = _____ dm^3
   b. 556 mL = _____ L
   c. 0.345 L = _____ cm^3
   d. 0.345 L = _____ mL

Solution to Sample Problem.

A rectangular sheet of paper, 215 cm by 280 cm, can be rolled and taped along an edge in two different ways to make a cylinder. Which way, taped along the 215 cm or the 280 cm edge, should you roll it to give the larger volume?

1. *Understanding the Problem.* What is meant by rolling and taping along an edge? How would the cylinder hold anything without the ends? Are the ends needed to find the volume?

2. *Devising a plan.* Let me roll two identical pieces of paper up so that I can see what the cylinders will look like. The cylinders look quite different, but how can I determine the volume of either? Maybe I should make as good a cylinder as I can and then trace the circular ends so that I can use a ruler to measure.

   What do I need to know to find the volume of a cylinder. I need to know the area of the base and the height. I know the height of each cylinder, but I do not know the area of the base. However, I also know the perimeter of the base. Now, is there any other relationship between perimeter of the base and the area that I can use?

3. *Solution.* I recall that we were able to find the area of a circular region by knowing the perimeter of the circle. For the cylinder taped along the 280-cm edge, the other dimension, 215 cm, is actually the perimeter of the circular end. If 215 is the perimeter, then $2\pi r = 215$, and r is approximately 34.2 cm (using $\pi = 3.14$). Hence the area of the base is $\pi \times 34.2^2$ cm^2 = 3673 cm^2, and the volume is $3673 \times 280 = 1,028,440$ cm^3.

   Now for the rolling of the paper along the 215 cm edge, 280 cm is actually the perimeter of the circular end. In the same manner, we find $r = 44.6$ cm, the area of the base is approximately 6246 cm^2 and the volume is approximately 1,324,890 cm^3.

   Thus we see that the two rollings and taping provide cylinders that do generate different volumes, with the one taped along the shorter edge giving the larger volume.

4. *Looking Back.* We know the solution must be correct as we used the correct relationships to determine the actual values. Would we have been able to determine the same solution had we tried sketching the circular ends? We may not have found the same numerical values, but we would have still found the larger of the two.

5. *Looking Ahead.* I wonder what percent larger the volume of the shorter cylinder is than the larger cylinder?

   If we would have taken two identical sheets of paper and made creases in them so that one made a square prism and the other made a rectangular prism with bases like the ones shown here, I wonder which prism would have the larger volume or if the volumes would be the same?

10 | COORDINATE GEOMETRY

Sample Problem

A family with 100 meters of fencing decides to fence a rectangular area in which their dogs can run. As they begin to draw some plans, what size rectangle will give them the largest area for their dogs?

10.1   INTRODUCTION TO COORDINATE GEOMETRY

This chapter ties together several of the ideas from previous chapters. Similarly, the use of coordinate geometry should remind you of work you have completed in algebra. René Descartes is credited with being the first to relate geometric and algebraic ideas through the use of coordinate geometry. In this chapter we focus on several components mentioned in the NCTM Standards. Mathematics as communication is evident in our use of graphs to model situations and to represent ideas. Throughout the work with proportions in our investigation of slopes, mathematical reasoning is seen as a major emphasis. Patterns and functions are used in several ways within the chapter. In addition to these components, the Standards suggest informal investigation of linear equations and inequalities, beginning with the representation of concrete situations with number patterns and equations. All these are addressed in some way within this chapter.

We begin this development with a brief review. In Chapter 2 a correspondence was established between some points on a line (actually a ray) and the set of whole numbers (Fig. 10.1a). Then, when working with integers, the correspondence idea was extended as illustrated in part (b). The correspondence indicated by the number line in (c) was the result of our work with the set of rational numbers. Finally, as indicated in part (d), a one-to-one correspondence was established between the set of real numbers and all the points of a line. Each point on the line is associated with a distinct real number, and every real number is associated with a distinct point on the line.

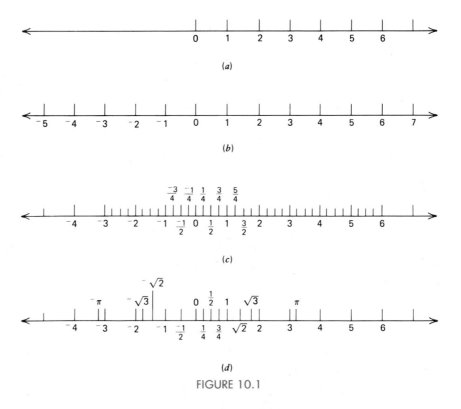

FIGURE 10.1

The distance between two points on a number line may be found by subtracting the numbers associated with the points. Consider the situations illustrated in Figure 10.2. We use the concept of *absolute value* to establish a positive number for this distance. The absolute value of a number is simply the distance that the point associated with the number is from zero without regard to direction. In other words, the absolute value of 5 is 5 (written $|5|$ = 5) and the absolute value of $^-5$ is also 5 (written $|^-5|$ = 5). Thus, $|9 - 4|$

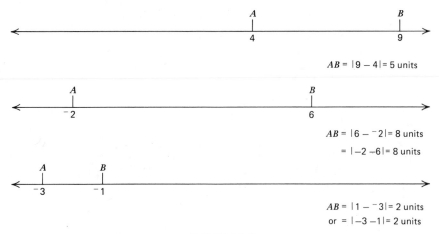

FIGURE 10.2

$= |4 - 9| = 5$ and the order in which the numbers associated with the points is taken is not important. In general, the distance between two points A and B on a number line associated with the numbers of x_1 and x_2, respectively, is given by either $|x_1 - x_2|$ or $|x_2 - x_1|$.

Let us review another notion. Suppose that we want to find a rational number between $\frac{1}{2}$ and $\frac{2}{3}$. One approach we used to handle this was to find the average of the two numbers.

It was shown that $\frac{1}{2}(\frac{1}{2} + \frac{2}{3}) = \frac{7}{12}$ is not only between $\frac{1}{2}$ and $\frac{2}{3}$, but is exactly midway between them. This idea may be generalized for any real numbers. Therefore, if A and B are any two points on a number line associated with the numbers x_1 and x_2, respectively, the number associated with the midpoint of $\overline{AB}$ is given by $\dfrac{x_1 + x_2}{2}$.

Suppose that we now consider two number lines perpendicular to each other at the point associated with zero on both lines (Fig. 10.3). These number lines are referred to as the *horizontal* and *vertical axes,* or together as the *coordinate axes.* The quadrants are numbered counterclockwise from I through IV, as indicated in Figure 10.3. The point of intersection of the two axes is called the *origin.*

It is now possible to set up a one-to-one correspondence between *ordered pairs* of real numbers and the points in a plane. To each ordered pair of real numbers there corresponds a unique point in a plane, and to each point in the plane there corresponds a unique ordered pair of real numbers. We have indicated part of this correspondence in Figure 10.4. The ordered pair $(3, 1)$ means that the point A is located *three units to the right* and *one unit up* from the origin, whereas the ordered pair $(1, 3)$ means that the point B is located *one unit to the right* and *three units up* from the origin. [The ordered pair $(0, 0)$ is associated with the origin.] The ordered pair $(^-5, ^-2)$ means that the

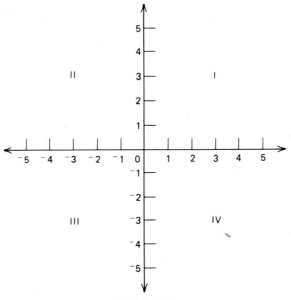

FIGURE 10.3

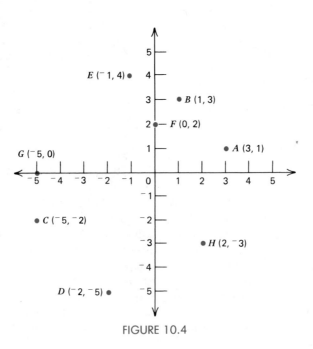

FIGURE 10.4

point C is located *five units to the left* and *two units down* from the origin, and the ordered pair $(^-2, \ ^-5)$ means that the point D is located *two units to the left* and *five units down* from the origin. Make sure that you agree with all the other locations labeled in Figure 10.4.

In general the real numbers a and b in an order pair (a, b) associated with a point are referred to as the *coordinates of the point*. The first number, a, called the abscissa, is the directed distance of the point from the vertical axis measured parallel to the horizontal axis. The second number, b, called the ordinate, is the directed distance of the point from the horizontal axis measured parallel to the vertical axis (Fig. 10.5a). Thus, in the first quadrant all points have a positive abscissa and a positive ordinate. In the second quandrant, all points have a negative abscissa and a positive ordinate. We have indicated the sign situations for all four quadrants in Figure 10.5b. This system of associating points in a plane with pairs of real numbers is called the *rectangular coordinate system* or the *Cartesian coordinate system*.

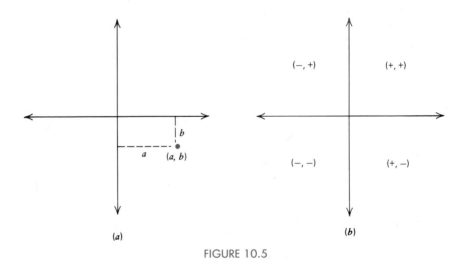

FIGURE 10.5

It is customary that the vertical number line be called the *y-axis* and the horizontal number line the *x-axis*. It is then convenient to be able to refer to some general points such as (x_1, y_1), (x_2, y_2), and (x_3, y_3) as in Figure 10.6.

We extend our work with finding the distance between points on a number line to finding the distance between two points in the coordinate plane. Suppose that the two points are located on a line parallel to one of the axes, as indicated in Figure 10.7. In such cases rectangles may be formed as indicated, and we can apply our knowledge of finding the distance between two points on a number line. That is, in Figure 10.7a, $AB = A'B'$ and $A'B' = |4 - \ ^-2| = |6| = 6$ units. Likewise, in 10.7b, $DC = D'C'$ and $D'C' = |4 - \ ^-3| = |7| = 7$ units.

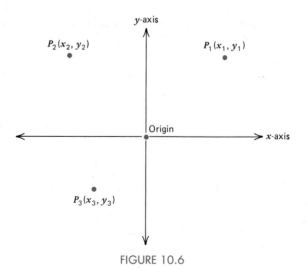

FIGURE 10.6

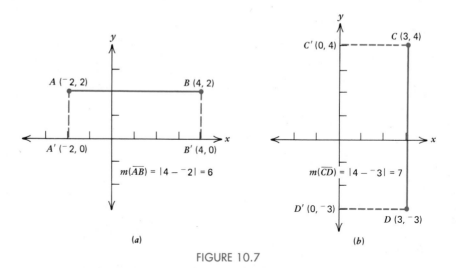

(a)   (b)

FIGURE 10.7

In Figure 10.8 the problem of finding the distance between two points is complicated somewhat by the fact that the points are not located on a line parallel to an axis. To solve this problem, first form a right triangle as indicated. Note that $\overline{AC}$ and $\overline{CB}$ are parallel to the x-axis and y-axis, respectively, and the coordinates of point C are $(6, 2)$. Thus, $AC = |6 - 2| = |4| = 4$ and $CB = |4 - 2| = |2| = 2$ units. By applying the Pythagorean theorem, $AB = \sqrt{4^2 + 2^2} = \sqrt{20}$ units.

The procedure used in the previous illustration may be generalized to

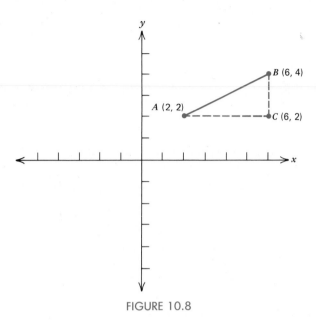

FIGURE 10.8

arrive at a distance formula. In Figure 10.9, we let $A(x_1, y_1)$ and $B(x_2, y_2)$ be any two points in a coordinate plane. Right triangle ACB is formed, and the coordinates of point C are (x_2, y_1). The length of $\overline{AC}$ is $|x_2 - x_1|$, and the length of $\overline{CB}$ is $|y_2 - y_1|$. Letting d represent the length of AB and applying

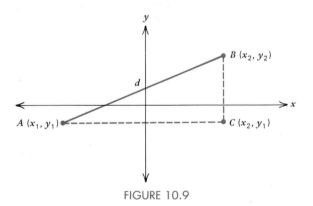

FIGURE 10.9

the Pythagorean theorem we obtain

$$d^2 = |x_2 - x_1|^2 + |y_2 - y_1|^2$$

Because $|a|^2 = a^2$, we can write

$$d^2 = (x_2 - x_1)^2 + (y_2 - y_1)^2$$

and then the *distance formula* can be stated as

$$d = \sqrt{(x_2 - x_1)^2 + (y_2 - y_1)^2}$$

The following two examples illustrate the use of the distance formula.

EXAMPLE 1

Find the distance between $A(^-2, \, ^-3)$ and $B(1, 7)$.

Solution　By applying the distance formula we obtain

$$
\begin{aligned}
AB &= \sqrt{(1 - {}^-2)^2 + (7 - {}^-3)^2} \\
&= \sqrt{3^2 + 10^2} \\
&= \sqrt{109} \text{ units}
\end{aligned}
$$

EXAMPLE 2

Verify that the points $A(^-3, 6)$, $B(3, 4)$, and $C(1, \, ^-2)$ are vertices of an isosceles triangle.

Solution　Let us plot the points and draw the triangle (Fig. 10.10). The distance formula can be used to find the lengths of the three sides.

$$
\begin{aligned}
AB &= \sqrt{(3 - {}^-3)^2 + (4 - 6)^2} &= \sqrt{36 + 4} &= \sqrt{40} \\
CA &= \sqrt{(^-3 - 1)^2 + (6 - {}^-2)^2} &= \sqrt{16 + 64} &= \sqrt{80} \\
CB &= \sqrt{(3 - 1)^2 + (4 - {}^-2)^2} &= \sqrt{4 + 36} &= \sqrt{40}
\end{aligned}
$$

Because $AB = CB$, the triangle is isosceles.

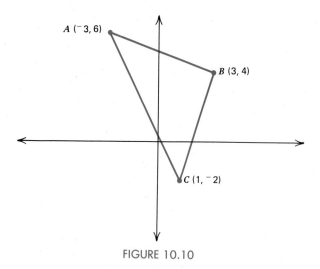

FIGURE 10.10

We can also use the distance formula to help us determine if a triangle is a right triangle. In Example 2 we have $AB = \sqrt{40}$, $CA = \sqrt{80}$, and $CB = \sqrt{40}$. Hence:

$$(AB)^2 + (CB)^2 = (\sqrt{40})^2 + (\sqrt{40})^2$$
$$= 40 + 40$$
$$= (\sqrt{80})^2$$
$$= (AC)^2$$

Therefore, triangle ABC is a right triangle.

Remember that if x_1 and x_2 are two points on a number line, then their average, $\dfrac{x_1 + x_2}{2}$, is the midpoint of the line segment determined by the two given points. The same "taking the average" procedure extends to a line segment on a coordinate plane, and the following statement can be made: If $A(x_1, y_1)$ and $B(x_2, y_2)$ are two points in a coordinate plane, then the coordinates of the midpoint of $\overline{AB}$ are

$$\left(\frac{x_1 + x_2}{2}, \frac{y_1 + y_2}{2} \right).$$

EXAMPLE 3

Find the coordinates of the midpoint of the line segment determined by the points $(^-2, 4)$ and $(6, ^-12)$.

Solution Finding the average of the x-coordinates and of the y-coordinates we obtain

$$\frac{^-2 + 6}{2} = \frac{4}{2} = 2$$

$$\frac{4 + ^-12}{2} = \frac{^-8}{2} = ^-4.$$

Thus, the coordinates of the midpoint are $(2, ^-4)$.

PROBLEM SET 10.1

1. If x_1 and x_2 are associated with points A and B, repectively, on a number line, find the number associated with the midpoint of AB.

   a. $x_1 = 4$, $x_2 = 16$ b. $x_1 = 7$, $x_2 = ^-6$

   c. $x_1 = ^-3$, $x_2 = ^-8$ d. $x_1 = \frac{5}{6}$, $x_2 = ^-\left(\frac{2}{3}\right)$

   e. $x_1 = 8.3$, $x_2 = 3.7$ f. $x_1 = 4.3$, $x_2 = ^-6.1$

2. On a coordinate plane, indicate the quadrant (I, II, III, or IV) containing each of the following ordered pairs:

   a. $(6, {}^-4)$ b. $(7, 2)$

   c. $({}^-7, 6)$ d. $({}^-4, {}^-3)$

   e. $(5, {}^-3)$ f. $({}^-3, 6)$

3. a. What is the first coordinate of any point on the vertical axis in a rectangular coordinate system?

   b. What is the second coordinate of any point on the horizontal axis?

4. a. In which quadrants do the coordinates of a point have the same sign?

   b. In which quadrants do the coordinates of a point have opposite signs?

   c. In which quadrants is the abscissa negative?

   d. In which quadrants is the ordinate negative?

5. Find the length of $\overline{AB}$ in a coordinate plane for each of the following. (Leave irrational numbers in radical form.)

   a. $A(3, 4)$, $B(0, 0)$ b. $A(4, 5)$, $B(7, 9)$

   c. $A({}^-2, 6)$, $B(8, {}^-4)$ d. $A(3, {}^-1)$, $B({}^-5, {}^-7)$

   e. $A(4, 5)$, $B(3, {}^-4)$ f. $A({}^-2, {}^-1)$, $B({}^-6, {}^-5)$

6. Find the coordinates of the midpoint of each line segment $\overline{AB}$ in Problem 5.

7. a. Verify that the points $({}^-1, 2)$, $(5, 4)$, and $(4, {}^-3)$ are vertices of an isosceles triangle.

   b. Is the triangle in (a) a right triangle?

8. Verify that the points $(2, 1)$, $(7, 1)$, $(8, 4)$ and $(3, 4)$ are vertices of a parallelogram.

9. Verify that the points $({}^-2, {}^-1)$, $(1, 0)$, $(2, 3)$, and $({}^-1, 2)$ are vertices of a rhombus.

10. Verify that the points $(7, 12)$ and $(11, 18)$ divide the line segment joining $(3, 6)$ and $(15, 24)$ into three segments of equal length.

11. Use the converse of the Pythagorean theorem to determine whether each of the following triangles is a right triangle.

    a. $A(3, 5)$, $B(6, 4)$, $C(0, {}^-4)$

    b. $A(4, 3)$, $B(5, 1)$, $C(3, 0)$

    c. $A(2, 2)$, $B(6, 4)$, $C(5, 6)$

    d. $A({}^-1, {}^-2)$, $B({}^-2, 4)$, $C(0, 6)$

12. Verify that $P({}^-4, {}^-3)$, $Q(0, 0)$, and $R(4, 3)$ lie in a straight line by showing that $PQ + QR = PR$.

13. Sketch the quadrilateral whose vertices are $A(1, 2)$, $B(5, 0)$, $C(7, 4)$, and $D(3, 8)$. Successively join the midpoints of the sides of this quadrilateral

to form another quadrilateral. Verify that the newly formed quadrilateral is a parallelogram.

14. Sketch the rectangle whose vertices are $A(0, 0)$, $B(6, 0)$, $C(6, 4)$ and $D(0, 4)$. Successively join the midpoints of the sides of this rectangle to form a quadrilateral. Verify that the newly formed quadrilateral is a rhombus.

15. The points $A(6, 6)$, $B(2, {}^-2)$, $C({}^-8, {}^-5)$, and $D({}^-4, 3)$ are vertices of a parallelogram. Verify that the diagonals of this parallelogram bisect each other.

16. **a.** Points $(2, 3)$, $(6, {}^-2)$, and $({}^-5, 1)$ and (a, b) are vertices of a parallelogram. One of the possible set of values for (a, b) is $({}^-1, {}^-4)$. What are the other two possible values for (a, b)?

    b. Show that the three points found in part **a** form a triangle and that the points given for the first three vertices are midpoints of the new triangle.

    c. Points $(1, 4)$, $(6, 3)$, $(10, 4)$ and (a, b) form the vertices of a kite. Find possible values for (a, b).

Pedagogical Problems and Activities

17. Some elementary texts begin their work with coordinate geometry in the early grades by using only counting numbers and the idea of locating points on a *grid*. The children are asked to "solve riddles" by using the letters located at different points on the grid. For example, consider the grid below that follows and solve the accompanying "riddles."

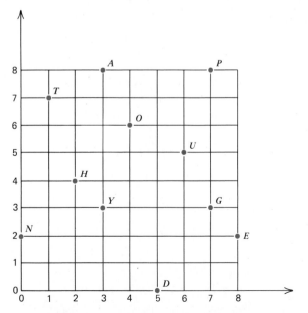

a. What kind of dog has no tail?: $(2, 4)$, $(4, 6)$, $(1, 7)$, $(5, 0)$, $(4, 6)$, $(7, 3)$

    b. What kind of fish can tune a piano?: (1, 7), (6, 5), (0, 2), (3, 8)

    c. What yesterday was, and what tomorrow will be: (1, 7), (4, 6), (5, 0), (3, 8), (3, 3)

    d. It has many eyes but never cries: (7, 8), (4, 6), (1, 7), (3, 8), (1, 7), (4, 6)

    e. How much dirt is there in a hole 4 feet deep and 3 feet across?: (0, 2), (4, 6), (0, 2), (8, 2)

18. Some ideas and approaches used to solve certain types of problems on a geoboard or dotted paper can also be used in coordinate geometry. Consider the following two problems:

    a. In the accompanying figure, find the area of the triangular region *ABC* by subtracting the areas of the right triangular regions from the area of the rectangular region.

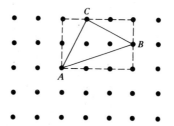

    b. On a coordinate plane, find the area of the triangular region determined by $A(^-3, 1)$, $B(^-1, 3)$, and $C(1, ^-1)$.

10.2 RELATIONS, FUNCTIONS, AND COORDINATE GRAPHING

We often must express relationships between objects or numbers. In earlier sections of this text we used such phrases as "is a subset of," "is less than," "is a factor of," "is a divisor of," "is the perimeter of," and "is the volume

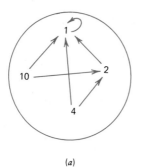

(a)

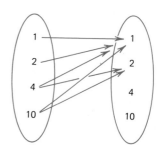

(b)

FIGURE 10.11

of." These phrases all expressed a relation between two sets of object. In Figure 10.11 two different arrow diagrams are used to express the relation "is a multiple of" on the set {1, 2, 4, 10}.

EXAMPLE 1

Complete an arrow diagram between the two sets below to express the relation "is president number."

Reagan   42
Ford   37
Johnson   35
Bush   39
Kennedy   40
Carter   38
Nixon   36
                  41
                  34

Solution Arrows should be drawn from Kennedy, Johnson, Nixon, Ford, Carter, Reagan, and Bush to 35, 36, 37, 38, 39, 40, and 41, respectively.

EXAMPLE 2

Draw an arrow diagram to express the relation "is a factor of" between the two sets below.

2   13
4   12
6   18
3   6
              9

Solution

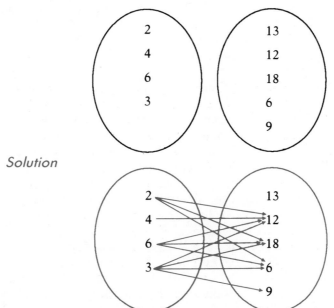

The concept of relation is used often in mathematics and society. For example, (1) each person is assigned a day of birth, (2) each book is assigned an ISBN number, (3) each student who completes the class you are in will be assigned a grade. The three examples given are special relations in that for each element in the first set there is a unique element in the second set. These special relations are called functions.

Definition 10.1   A function is a relation between two sets that assigns to each element in the first set a unique element in the second set.

The relation expressed in Example 1 is a function because each president is assigned a unique number. However, the relation expressed in Example 2 is not a function because the element 2 in the first set is assigned to 3 different numbers in the second set.

Functions can be expressed in ways different from an arrow diagram. For example, the following table expresses the "squared is " function from set A = $\{1, 3, 5, 6\}$ to B = $\{1, 9, 25, 36\}$

A	B
1	1
3	9
5	25
6	36

Functions are also expressed as pairs of numbers where the first number in the pair comes from the first set and the second number in the pair comes from the second set. The "squared is" function above expressed in ordered pair notation is written as $\{(1, 1), (3, 9), (5, 25), (6, 36)\}$, where the first element in each pair comes from set A and the second element in each pair comes from set B.

Functions are also expressed in formula form. In prior chapters we have seen formulas for finding area and volumes of various geometric figures. These formulas are always written in equation form. We now explore using graphing as another way to express functions.

Consider the solutions for the equation $y = x + 2$. A *solution* of an equation in two variables is an ordered pair of real numbers that satisfy the equation. When using the variables x and y, we agree that the first number of an ordered pair is a value for x and the second number is a value for y. Therefore, (1, 3) is a solution for $y = x + 2$ because if x is replaced by 1 and y by 3, the true numerical statement $3 = 1 + 2$ is obtained. Likewise, ($^-$1, 1) is a solution because $1 = {}^-1 + 2$ is a true statement.

However (3, 1) is not a solution because the numerical statement $1 = 3 + 2$ is false. Infinitely many pairs of real numbers that satisfy $y = x + 2$ can be found by arbitrarily choosing values for x, and for each value of x chosen, determining a corresponding value for y Let us use a table to record some of the solutions for $y = x + 2$. We can plot the ordered pairs on a coordinate

Choose x	Determine y from y = x + 2	Partial list of solutions for y = x + 2
0	2	(0, 2)
1	3	(1, 3)
3	5	(3, 5)
5	7	(5, 7)
⁻1	1	(⁻1, 1)
⁻2	0	(⁻2, 0)
⁻4	⁻2	(⁻4, ⁻2)

plane as indicated in Figure 10.12*a*. The straight line containing the points is called the *graph of the equation* $y = x + 2$ (Fig. 10.12*b*).

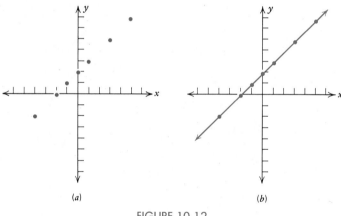

(a)   (b)

FIGURE 10.12

REMARK In Figure 10.12*b* we "connected" the points and drew a straight line. In some cases, this is inappropriate. For instance, if $y = x + 2$ would refer to the following relationship, "no matter how many ducks there are (x) there are 2 more geese (y)," it would be inappropriate to connect the points. It is inappropriate because although $(\frac{3}{2}, \frac{7}{2})$ would be a point on the line $y = x + 2$, we must keep in mind that $\frac{3}{2}$ refers to ducks. In this problem it is inferred that we would want whole numbers of ducks.

The remainder of this section consists of examples in which we suggest some different ideas for you as you develop some graphing techniques.

EXAMPLE 1

Graph $y = x^2$.

Solution First, let us set up a table indicating some of the solutions.

x	0	1	2	3	$^-1$	$^-2$	$^-3$
y	0	1	4	9	1	4	9

Second, we plot the points associated with the solutions (Fig. 10.13a). Again, because real numbers can be used for all values, we "connect" the points. However, in this case we cannot connect the points with straight lines. Instead, we connect the points with a smooth curve (Fig. 10.13b).

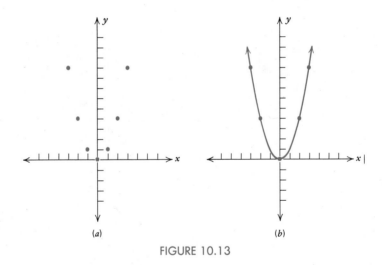

FIGURE 10.13

How many solutions do we need in a table of values? There is no definite answer to this question other than "a sufficient number so that the nature of the curve is determined."

EXAMPLE 2

Graph $2x + 3y = 6$.

Solution First, let us find the points of this graph that fall on the coordinate axes. Let $x = 0$; then

$$2(0) + 3y = 6$$
$$3y = 6$$
$$y = 2$$

Thus, (0, 2) is a solution and is a point on the y-axis. (In general, y-values obtained when 0 is substituted for x are called *y-intercepts*.)

Let $y = 0$; then

$$2x + 3(0) = 6$$
$$2x = 6$$
$$x = 3$$

Thus, (3, 0) is a solution and is a point on the x-axis. (In general, x-values obtained when 0 is substituted for y are called *x-intercepts*.)

Second, let us change the form of the equation to make it easier to find some additional solutions. We can either solve for x in terms of y or for y in terms of x. Solving for y we obtain

$$2x + 3y = 6$$
$$3y = 6 - 2x$$
$$y = \frac{6 - 2x}{3}$$

Third, a table of values can be formed including the intercepts found above.

	Intercepts		Other Solutions		
x	0	3	6	$^-3$	$^-6$
y	2	0	$^-2$	4	6

Finally, plotting the points associated with the ordered pairs from the table of values and joining the points with a "smooth curve" produces Figure 10.14.

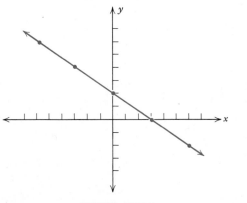

FIGURE 10.14

In the table for Example 2, notice that x-values were chosen so that integers were obtained for y. This is not necessary, but it does make things easier from a computational viewpoint.

EXAMPLE 3

Graph $y = \dfrac{1}{x}$

Solution First, let us find the intercepts. If we let $x = 0$, then $y = \dfrac{1}{x}$ becomes $y = \dfrac{1}{0}$ and $\dfrac{1}{0}$ is undefined. Thus, there is no y-intercept.

If we let $y = 0$, then $y = \dfrac{1}{x}$ becomes $0 = \dfrac{1}{x}$ and there are no values of x that will satisfy this equation. Therefore, there is no x-intercept. In other words, this graph has no points on either axis.

Second, we can set up a table of values keeping in mind that neither x nor y can equal 0.

x	$\frac{1}{2}$	1	2	3	$^-(\frac{1}{2})$	$^-1$	$^-2$	$^-3$
y	2	1	$\frac{1}{2}$	$\frac{1}{3}$	$^-2$	$^-1$	$^-(\frac{1}{2})$	$^-(\frac{1}{3})$

In Figure 10.15a we have plotted the points associated with the ordered pairs from the table. How do we decide what the graph will look like? Again, we should suspect that we cannot draw a "straight line." Furthermore, we have the condition that the graph does not intersect either axis. Hence, it must consist of two branches. Thus, connecting the points in the first quadrant with a smooth curve and then connecting the points in the third quadrant with a smooth curve, we obtain the graph in Figure 10.15b.

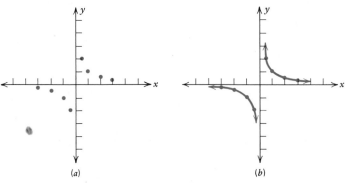

(a)   (b)

FIGURE 10.15

To summarize our work in the previous examples, we would suggest the following steps for graphing an equation in two variables.

1. Find the intercepts.
2. Solve the equation for y in terms of x or for x in terms of y if it is not already in such a form.
3. Set up a table of ordered pairs that satisfy the equation.
4. Plot the points associated with the ordered pairs.
5. Connect the points with a "smooth curve."

PROBLEM SET 10.2

1. Express the following relations in arrow form in their ordered-pair form.

   a.

   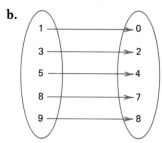

   b.

2. The following arrow form is to be completed using the following formula: For each number in the first set, square it and then subtract 4. Draw in the remaining arrows.

   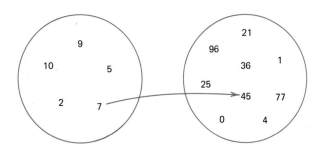

3. A 7% sales tax formula is often given as Tax = 7% of Cost. This is usually written as T = 0.07 × C. Complete the table based on a sales tax of 7%. Round up to the nearest cent.

C	T
$10	
24	
16	
9	

4. For any triangle, the area can be found. Complete the arrow diagram that assigns a triangle to its area.

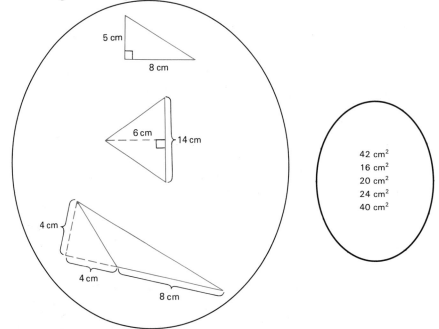

5. Graph each of the following on the same coordinate axis
   a. $y = 3x - 1$ **b.** $y = 3x + 5$ **c.** $y = 3x + 7$

6. Graph each of the following on the same coordinate axis
   a. $y = 3x + 2$ **b.** $y = 2x + 2$ **c.** $y = \frac{1}{3}x + 2$

7. Graph each of the following on the same coordinate axis.
   a. $y = x^2 + 4$ **b.** $y = x^2 - 1$ **c.** $y = {}^-x^2 + 4$

8. Graph each of the following on the same coordinate axis.
   a. $y = 2x + 5$ **b.** $y = {}^-2x + 5$

9. Graph each of the following on the same coordinate axis.
   a. $y = |x|$ **b.** $y = |x-1|$ **c.** $y = |x| - 1$
   d. $y = {}^-|x|$

10. Graph each of the following:
   a. $y = x$ **b.** $y = {}^-x$
   c. $3x - y = 6$ **d.** $y = |x - 1|^2$
   e. $2x - 5y = {}^-10$ **f.** $y = 2 - x^2$

Pedagogical Problems and Activities

11. Some elementary texts introduce "plotting points" using only the whole numbers as possible solutions. For example, suppose that we want to graph all ordered pairs of whole numbers that satisfy the equation $x + y = 4$. This solution set is $\{(1, 3), (3, 1), (2, 2), (0, 4), (4, 0)\}$, and its graph is as follows.

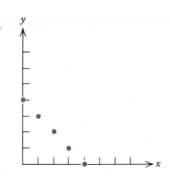

Graph the truth set for each of the following using only pairs of whole numbers.

a. $x + y = 6$ b. $x + y = 5$

c. $2x + 3y = 12$ d. $2x + y = 12$

e. $y = x$ f. $y = x^2$

12. Consider the following situation. Suppose that children from two classes, Ms. Trotter's class *(x)* and Ms. Standley's class *(y)* are to be selected to represent Logan School at a special ceremony. If a total of 9 children are to be selected, make a graph that expresses this relationship.

10.3 SLOPE

Many of the graphs in Problem Set 10.2 were lines. We are now going to begin the investigation of many relationships that exist between the equations of lines and the resulting graphs. Consider the lines illustrated in Figure 10.16. It is convenient to have some sort of coordinate geometry concept that will allow us to make the following kinds of statements: (1) lines l_1, l_2, and l_3 have a different "slant," (2) lines l_3 and l_4 are parallel, and (3) lines l_3 and l_4 are both perpendicular to l_1. The concept of *slope* will allow us to discuss these relationships in a meaningful way from the viewpoint of coordinate geometry.

The notion of slope may be introduced in a variety of ways using various terminology. For example, the ratio of "rise to run," the ratio of "vertical change to horizontal change," or the ratio of "a change in y to a change in x" are all common ways of describing the slope of a line. A precise definition for slope can be given by considering the coordinates of the points P_1, P_2, and

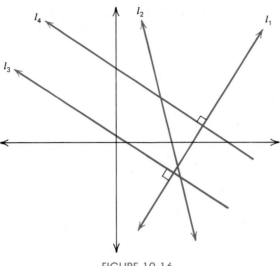

FIGURE 10.16

R as indicated in Figure 10.17. The horizontal change as we move from P_1 to P_2 is $x_2 - x_1$ and the vertical change is $y_2 - y_1$. Thus, the following definition for slope can be given.

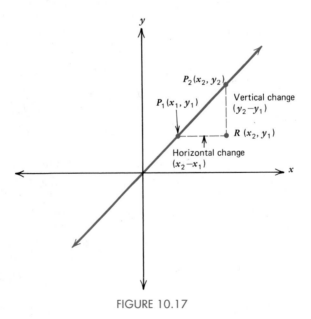

FIGURE 10.17

Definition 10.2 If points P_1 and P_2 with coordinates (x_1, y_1) and (x_2, y_2), respectively, are distinct points on a line, then the slope (denoted by m) of the line is the ratio

$$m = \frac{y_2 - y_1}{x_2 - x_1} \quad x_2 \neq x_1.$$

Because

$$\frac{y_2 - y_1}{x_2 - x_1} = \frac{y_1 - y_2}{x_1 - x_2}$$

how we designate P_1 and P_2 when using Definition 10.2 is not important. Furthermore, notice that a restriction, $x_2 \neq x_1$, is made. This restriction is necessary so that the denominator, $(x_2 - x_1)$, is not equal to zero. You should note that when $x_2 = x_1$ the two points would be on a vertical line. The significance of the restriction is that *slope is not defined* for vertical lines. Let us use Definition 10.2 to find the slopes of some lines.

EXAMPLE 1

Find the slope of the line determined by each of the following pairs of points and sketch the lines:

a. (1, 2) and (3, 5)   **b.** (⁻3, 1) and (2, ⁻2)   **c.** (4, 2) and (⁻1, 2)

Solutions **a.** Let P_1 be associated with (1, 2) and P_2 with (3, 5) (see Fig. 10.18).

$$m = \frac{y_2 - y_1}{x_2 - x_1} = \frac{5 - 2}{3 - 1} = \frac{3}{2}$$

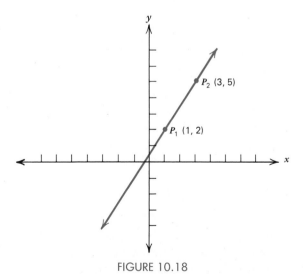

FIGURE 10.18

b. Let P_1 be associated with $(^-3, 1)$ and P_2 with $(2, ^-2)$ (see Fig. 10.19).

$$m = \frac{y_2 - y_1}{x_2 - x_1} = \frac{^-2 - 1}{2 - ^-3} = \frac{^-3}{5} = ^-\left(\frac{3}{5}\right)$$

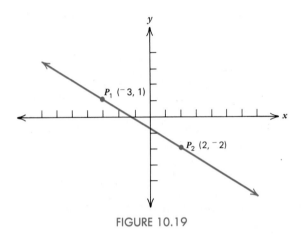

FIGURE 10.19

c. Let P_1 be associated with $(4, 2)$ and P_2 with $(^-1, 2)$ (see Fig. 10.20).

$$m = \frac{y_2 - y_1}{x_2 - x_1} = \frac{2 - 2}{^-1 - 4} = \frac{0}{^-5} = 0$$

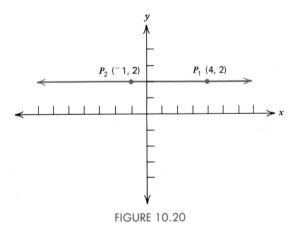

FIGURE 10.20

The various parts of Example 1 illustrate the three basic possibilities for slope; that is, the slope of a line can be positive, negative, or zero. A line having a *positive slope* rises as we move from left to right, as in Figure 10.18. A line having a *negative slope* falls as we move from left to right, as in Figure 10.19. A horizontal line, as in Figure 10.20 has a *slope of zero*.

It is important to remember that the slope of a line is a *ratio*, the ratio of vertical change compared to horizontal change. A slope of $\frac{3}{4}$ means that for every 3 units of vertical change there must be a corresponding 4 units of horizontal change. That is, starting at some point on a line having a slope of $\frac{3}{4}$ we can locate other points on the line as follows:

$\frac{3}{4} = \frac{6}{8}$: By moving 6 units *up* and 8 units to the *right*.

$\frac{3}{4} = \frac{15}{20}$: By moving 15 units *up* and 20 units to the *right*.

$\frac{3}{4} = \frac{^-3}{^-4}$: By moving 3 units *down* and 4 units to the *left*.

$\frac{3}{4} = \frac{1.5}{2}$: By moving 1.5 units *up* and 2 units to the *right*.

$\frac{3}{4} = \frac{\frac{3}{4}}{1}$: By moving $\frac{3}{4}$ units *up* and 1 unit to the *right*.

Likewise, if a line has a slope of $^-(\frac{2}{3})$, then by starting at some point on the line we can locate other points on the line as follows:

$^-\left(\frac{2}{3}\right) = \frac{^-2}{3}$: By moving 2 units *down* and 3 units to the *right*.

$^-\left(\frac{2}{3}\right) = \frac{2}{^-3}$: By moving 2 units *up* and 3 units to the *left*.

$^-\left(\frac{2}{3}\right) = \frac{^-4}{6}$: By moving 4 units *down* and 6 units to the *right*.

$^-\left(\frac{2}{3}\right) = \frac{8}{^-12}$: By moving 8 units *up* and 12 units to the *left*.

$^-\left(\frac{2}{3}\right) = \frac{(\frac{^-2}{3})}{1}$: By moving $\frac{2}{3}$ units *down* and 1 unit to the *right*.

From these two examples, we see that the slope of a line can be interpreted as the vertical change for a horizontal change of 1 to the right.

Two important relationships exist between lines and their slopes. We will state these two properties and then illustrate how they can be used to solve some problems.

If two lines have slopes m_1 and m_2, respectively, then:

1. The two lines are parallel if and only if $m_1 = m_2$.

2. The two lines are perpendicular if and only if $(m_1)(m_2) = {}^-1.$ $\left(\text{This is}\right.$

sometimes stated as "the slopes are negative reciprocals of each other and

written as $m_1 = \dfrac{{}^-1}{m_2}.$ $\left.\right)$

EXAMPLE 2

Verify that the points $A({}^-3, {}^-1)$, $B(4, 0)$, $C(5, 4)$, and $D({}^-2, 3)$ are the vertices of a parallelogram.

Solution Plotting the given points and joining them in succession produces Figure 10.21. The slopes of the four sides are as follows:

$$\text{slope of } \overline{AB}: \frac{0 - 1}{4 - {}^-3} \quad = \frac{1}{7}$$

$$\text{slope of } \overline{BC}: \frac{4 - 0}{5 - 4} \quad = \frac{4}{1} = 4$$

$$\text{slope of } \overline{DC}: \frac{4 - 3}{5 - {}^-2} \quad = \frac{1}{7}$$

$$\text{slope of } \overline{AD}: \frac{3 - {}^-1}{{}^-2 - {}^-3} \quad = \frac{4}{1} = 4$$

Sides $\overline{AB}$ and $\overline{DC}$ are parallel because their slopes are equal. Likewise, $\overline{BC}$ and $\overline{AD}$ are parallel because their slopes are equal. Therefore, the figure $ABCD$ is a parallelogram.

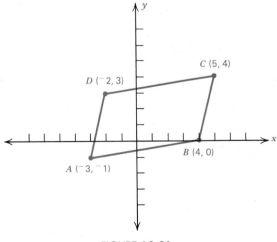

FIGURE 10.21

EXAMPLE 3

Verify that the triangle determined by the points $A(4, 3)$, $B(5, 1)$, and $C(3, 0)$ is a right triangle.

Solution The points are plotted and the triangle formed in Figure 10.22. The slope of $\overline{CB}$ is $\dfrac{1 - 0}{5 - 3} = \dfrac{1}{2}$ and the slope of $\overline{BA}$ is $\dfrac{3 - 1}{4 - 5} = {}^-2$. Because $(\frac{1}{2})({}^-2) = {}^-1$ (the product of the slopes is ${}^-1$), $\overline{CB} \perp \overline{BA}$ and $\triangle CBA$ is a right triangle with the right angle at B.

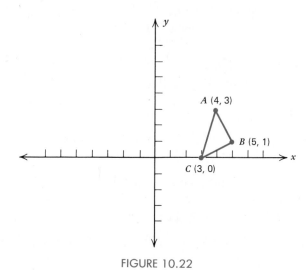

FIGURE 10.22

PROBLEM SET 10.3

1. Find the slope of the line determined by each pair of points:
   a. $(3, 1), (7, 4)$ **b.** $(1, 2), (6, 4)$
   c. $(2, 4), (6, 1)$ **d.** $({}^-2, 3), (1, {}^-1)$
   e. $({}^-1, 3), (4, 3)$ **f.** $({}^-2, {}^-4), (6, {}^-4)$
   g. $({}^-1, {}^-2), (6, 5)$ **h.** $({}^-7, 4), (3, {}^-2)$

2. For each of the following you are given one point on a line and the slope of the line. Find the coordinates of three other points on the line.

   a. $(1, 2), m = \dfrac{1}{2}$

   b. $(3, 4), m = \dfrac{3}{5}$

    c. $(^-4, 2)$, $m = 3$

    d. $(2, 4)$, $m = {}^-\left(\dfrac{1}{3}\right)$

    e. $(3, {}^-1)$, $m = {}^-\left(\dfrac{4}{5}\right)$

    f. $(^-2, {}^-4)$, $m = {}^-2$

3. Find x if the line through $(^-2, 4)$ and $(x, 6)$ has a slope of $\frac{2}{9}$.

4. Find y if the line through $(5, 2)$ and $(^-3, y)$ has a slope of ${}^-(\frac{7}{8})$.

5. For each of the following, decide whether $\overline{AB} \| \overline{CD}$, $\overline{AB} \perp \overline{CD}$, or whether they are neither parallel nor perpendicular:

    a. $A(2, 3)$, $B(5, 6)$, $C(^-1, 4)$, $D(5, 10)$

    b. $A(1, 2)$, $B(4, 5)$, $C(^-4, {}^-1)$, $D(^-10, 5)$

    c. $A(^-2, 3)$, $B(3, {}^-3)$, $C(4, 2)$, $D(^-2, {}^-3)$

    d. $A(2, {}^-3)$, $B(^-3, 3)$, $C(2, 3)$, $D(4, 2)$

    e. $A(3, 5)$, $B(4, {}^-2)$, $C(\frac{1}{2}, \frac{-3}{5})$, $D(\frac{2}{3}, \frac{-1}{3})$

6. Verify that the points $A(^-3, 8)$, $B(7, 4)$, and $C(5, {}^-1)$ are vertices of a right triangle. Find the area of the triangle.

7. a. Verify that the points $A(^-4, 6)$, $B(6, 10)$, $C(10, 0)$, and $D(0, {}^-4)$ are vertices of a square.

    b What is the area of the square?

8. Verify that the points $A(^-5, 1)$, $B(^-2, 7)$, $C(8, 3)$, and $D(5, {}^-3)$ are vertices of a parallelogram.

9. a. Verify that the quadrilateral determined by the points $A(0, 7)$, $B(^-2, {}^-1)$, $C(2, {}^-2)$, and $D(4, 6)$ is a rectangle.

    b. What is the area of the rectangle?

10. The points $A(4, 0)$, $B(4, 4)$, $C(0, 4)$, and $D(0, 0)$ are vertices of a square. Verify that the diagonals of this square are perpendicular.

11. Verify that the points $A(^-4, {}^-2)$, $B(0, 0)$, $C(2, 4)$, and $D(^-2, 2)$ are vertices of a rhombus.

Pedagogical Problems and Activities

12. Describe some activities that you might use with children to help them understand the significance of the fact that the slope of a line is a *ratio*.

13. Show how a geoboard or dotted paper could be used to demonstrate the following:

    a. Parallel lines have equal slopes.

    b. The product of the slopes of two perpendicular lines is ${}^-1$.

14. A child says "Because zero is nothing, a horizontal line has no slope." What do you say?

15. A sign on Interstate 70 near Denver, Colorado, says "7% downgrade next 6 miles." How is this to be interpreted? What drop in elevation in fact is likely to occur in that 6 miles of road?

10.4   STRAIGHT LINES

In the previous section and accompanying Problem Set we found that each of the equations $y = x + 2$, $2x + 3y = 6$, $y = 3x - 1$, $y = {}^-2x + 5$, $x - 2y = 4$, $3x - y = 6$, $3x + 4y = 12$, $2x - 5y = {}^-10$, $y = x$, and $y = {}^-x$ produced a straight-line graph. *In general, any equation of the form $Ax + By = C$, where A, B, and C are constants (A and B not both zero) and x and y are variables, is a linear equation and its graph is a straight line.* The choice of x and y for variables is arbitrary. Any two letters could be used to represent the variables. For example, an equation such as $3m + 2n = 7$ can be considered a linear equation in two variables. In fact, the equations $3m + 2n = 7$, $3a + 2b = 7$, $3x + 2y = 7$ are also representations of the same equation and will produce like graphs. The statement "any equation of the form $Ax + By = C$" technically means any equation of the form $Ax + By = C$ or *equivalent* to the form. For example, the equation $y = x + 2$ is equivalent to $x - y = {}^-2$ and thus is linear and its graph is a straight line.

The knowledge that any equation of the form $Ax + By = C$ produces a straight-line graph, along with the fact that two points determine a straight line, makes graphing linear equations a simple process. We simply find two solutions, such as the intercepts, plot the corresponding points, and connect the points with a straight line. It is usually wise to find a third point as a check point.

EXAMPLE 1

Graph $2x - y = 4$.

Solution Let $x = 0$; then

$$2(0) - y = 4$$
$${}^-y = 4$$
$$y = {}^-4$$

Thus, $(0, {}^-4)$ is a solution.
  Let $y = 0$; then

$$2x - 0 = 4$$
$$2x = 4$$
$$x = 2$$

Thus, (2, 0) is a solution.

Now let us find a third point to serve as a check point. Let $y = 2$; then

$$2x - 2 = 4$$
$$2x = 6$$
$$x = 3$$

Thus, (3, 2) is a solution.

Plotting the points associated with the three solutions and connecting them with a straight line produces the graph in Figure 10.23.

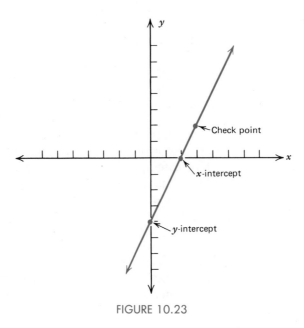

FIGURE 10.23

Notice that in our solution to Example 1 we did not solve the equation for y in terms of x or for x in terms of y. Because we know that the graph is a straight line, there is no need for an extensive table of values; thus, there is no need to change the form of the original equation. Furthermore, the solution (3, 2) serves as a check point. If it had not been on the line determined by the two intercepts, then we would have known that an error had been made.

EXAMPLE 2

Graph $x + 3y = {}^-3$.

Solution Without showing all the work, the following table indicates the intercepts and a check point.

	Intercepts		Check Point
x	0	⁻3	6
y	⁻1	0	1

The points from the table are plotted, and the graph is shown in Figure 10.24.

EXAMPLE 3

Graph $y = 2x$.

Solution The equation $y = 2x$ is equivalent to $2x - y = 0$ and therefore its graph is a straight line because it is of the form $Ax + By = C$. Obviously, $(0, 0)$ is a solution. Because both the x-intercept and y-intercept are determined by the point $(0, 0)$, another point must be found to determine the line. Then a third point should be found as a check point.

	Intercepts	Additional Point	Check Point
x	0	1	2
y	0	2	⁻4

The graph of $y = 2x$ is shown in Figure 10.25.

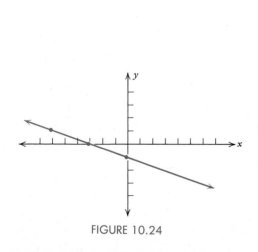

FIGURE 10.24

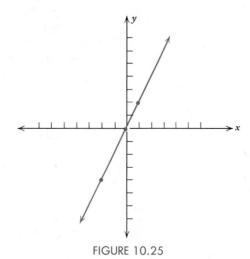

FIGURE 10.25

EXAMPLE 4

Graph $x = 3$.

Solution Because we are considering linear equations in *two variables*, the equation $x = 3$ is equivalent to $x + 0(y) = 3$. Now we can see that *any value of y* can be used, but the value of x must be 3. Thus, some of the solutions are $(3, 0)$, $(3, 1)$, $(3, 2)$, $(3, ^-1)$, and $(3, ^-2)$. The graph of all solutions of $x = 3$ is the vertical line in Figure 10.26.

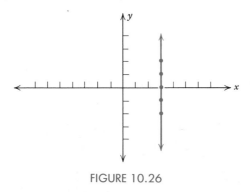

FIGURE 10.26

REMARK Just as $x = 3$ can be considered an equation in two variables, so can $y = 3$. Noting that the graph $x = 3$ is a vertical line should lead you to suspect that the graph of $y = 3$ will be a horizontal line. This is indeed the case.

In Section 10.3 we introduced the concept of slope and worked with two basic relationships involving the slopes of parallel and perpendicular lines. The following examples illustrate how those ideas are linked to the linear equations studied in this section.

EXAMPLE 5

Find the slope of the line determined by the equation $3x - 4y = 12$.

Solution The ordered pairs $(0, ^-3)$ and $(4, 0)$ are solutions for the equation. Thus, the slope of the line is

$$m = \frac{0 - ^-3}{4 - 0} = \frac{3}{4}.$$

EXAMPLE 6

Verify that $2x - 3y = 6$ and $4x - 6y = 24$ are equations of parallel lines.

Solution Using the same approach as in Example 5, the slopes of the two lines can be found as follows.

Equation	Two Points on the Line	Slope of the Line
$2x - 3y = 6$	$(0, {}^-2)$ and $(3, 0)$	$\dfrac{0 - {}^-2}{3 - 0} = \dfrac{2}{3}$
$4x - 6y = 24$	$(0, {}^-4)$ and $(6, 0)$	$\dfrac{0 - {}^-4}{6 - 0} = \dfrac{4}{6} = \dfrac{2}{3}$

Because the lines have equal slopes and are not the same line, they are parallel lines.

EXAMPLE 7

Verify that $4x - 5y = 20$ and $5x + 4y = 40$ are equations of perpendicular lines.

Solution

Equation	Two Points on the Line	Slope of the Line
$4x - 5y = 20$	$(0, {}^-4)$ and $(5, 0)$	$\dfrac{0 - {}^-4}{5 - 0} = \dfrac{4}{5}$
$5x + 4y = 40$	$(0, 10)$ and $(8, 0)$	$\dfrac{0 - 10}{8 - 0} = \dfrac{{}^-10}{8} = {}^-\left(\dfrac{5}{4}\right)$

Because $\left(\frac{4}{5}\right)\left(\frac{{}^-5}{4}\right) = {}^-1$ (the product of the slopes is negative one), the two lines are perpendicular.

PROBLEM SET 10.4

Graph each of the following linear equations (Problems 1–22).

1. $x - 3y = 6$ 2. $2x - y = 4$

3. $3x + 2y = 6$ 4. $2x - 3y = 12$

5. $4x - 5y = 20$ 6. $4x + 7y = 28$

7. $x + 2y = 5$ 8. $x - 3y = 4$

9. $2x - 3y = {}^-6$ 10. $5x - y = {}^-10$

11. $y = 3x - 4$ **12.** $y = 2x + 1$

13. $y = {}^-2x - 1$ **14.** $y = {}^-3x - 5$

15. $y = 3x$ **16.** $y = 4x$

17. $y = {}^-2x$ **18.** $y = {}^-3x$

19. $y = {}^-1$ **20.** $x = {}^-4$

21. $x = 0$ **22.** $y = 0$

23. Find the slope of each of the following lines and graph each line.

    a. $2x - y = 6$ **b.** $x + 3y = 9$

    c. $3x + 5y = 15$ **d.** $2x - 7y = 14$

    e. $y = 2x + 1$ **f.** $y = 3x + 5$

    g. $y = {}^-x - 4$ **h.** $y = {}^-2x - 3$

    i. $y = \frac{2}{3}x - \frac{3}{4}$ **j.** $y = {}^-\left(\frac{3}{4}\right)x + \frac{1}{3}$

    k. $y = 3$ **l.** $y = {}^-1$

24. For each pair of equations, determine whether they represent parallel lines, perpendicular lines, or intersecting lines that are not perpendicular.

    a. $3x + 5y = 15$ and $3x + 5y = 30$

    b. $2x - 3y = 6$ and $3x + 2y = 6$

    c. $x + 2y = 4$ and $2x - y = 2$

    d. $x - 3y = 6$ and $2x - 6y = 24$

    e. $5x - 2y = 10$ and $5x + 2y = 10$

    f. $4x + y = 8$ and $2x - y = 6$

25. Using the lines from Problem 23, we have listed the $Ax + By = C$ form of the line along with the slope, y-intercept, and x-intercept. From this information, state the relationship between the $Ax + By = C$ form and the slope, y-intercept, and x-intercept.

Equation in $Ax + By = C$ form	Slope	y-intercept	x-intercept
a. $2x - 1y = 6$	2	$^-6$	3
b. $x + 3y = 9$	$\frac{-1}{3}$	3	9
c. $3x + 5y = 15$	$\frac{-3}{5}$	3	5
d. $2x - 7y = 14$	$\frac{2}{7}$	$^-2$	7
e. $-2x + 1y = 1$	$\frac{2}{1}$	1	$\frac{-1}{2}$
f. $-3x + 1y = 5$	$\frac{3}{1}$	5	$\frac{-5}{3}$
g. $1x + 1y = -4$	$\frac{-1}{1}$	$^-4$	$^-4$
h. $2x + 1y = -3$	$\frac{-2}{1}$	$^-3$	$\frac{-3}{2}$
i. $Ax + By = C$	____	____	____

Pedagogical Activity

26. Several common situations are expressions of functions. A few of these are given here. These can be discussed with children so that a natural understanding of the uses of mathematics to model situations in life can be developed.

    a. A plumbing company sets its rates according to the following schedule. A fixed charge of $25 is made for any visit. In addition, a charge of $30 an hour is made for the services of one plumber. If a plumber came for 2 hours, what would her services cost? What would be the cost for 5 hours?, 7 hours?, n hours?

    b. A large entertainment facility charges an $8 cover charge to enter. Once inside the facility, it charges $0.50 per ride. What would be the cost for one person to enter and ride 3 rides?, 5 rides?, 9 rides?, n rides? How many rides would be taken to spend $20?

    c. A cab company charges a fixed fee of $0.75 plus $0.60 per mile. What is the cost of traveling 3 miles?, 5 miles?, 10 miles?, n miles?

    d. A power company has a basic charge of $4 per customer plus a rate of $0.40 per unit of energy used. What is the cost to a customer for 10 units of energy?, 50 units?, 125 units?, n units?

    e. For first-class postage less than 14 ounces, the postage is currently based on the following rate. The first ounce costs $0.25 and each additional ounce or fraction thereof costs $0.21. What is the cost of sending a first-class item that weighs 4 ounces?, 7 ounces?, n ounces?

10.5   DETERMINING EQUATIONS OF STRAIGHT LINES

There are two basic types of problems in coordinate geometry, namely:

1. Given an algebraic equation, find its geometric graph.
2. Given a set of conditions pertaining to a geometric figure, find its algebraic equation.

We have been working primarily with problems of type 1. In this section we want to concern ourselves with a few problems of type 2, specifically dealing with straight lines.

EXAMPLE 1

Find the equation of the line having a slope of $\frac{3}{4}$ and containing the point (2, 1).

Solution First, let us draw the line and record the given information (Fig. 10.27). Then choose a point (x, y) that represents any point on the line other than the given point $(2, 1)$. The slope determined by the two points $(2, 1)$ and (x, y) is $\frac{3}{4}$. Thus,

$$\frac{y - 1}{x - 2} = \frac{3}{4}$$
$$3x - 6 = 4y - 4$$
$$3x - 4y = 2$$

Therefore, the equation $3x - 4y = 2$ represents the line containing $(2, 1)$ and having a slope of $\frac{3}{4}$.

EXAMPLE 2

Find the equation of the line containing the points $(^-1, 3)$ and $(4, ^-2)$.

Solution The line is drawn in Figure 10.28. Because two points are given, the slope of the line can be found as follows:

$$m = \frac{y_2 - y_1}{x_2 - x_1} = \frac{3 - {^-2}}{{^-1} - 4} = \frac{5}{{^-5}} = {^-1}$$

Now we can use the same approach as in Example 1. Form an equation using a "variable" point (x, y), one of the two given points, and the slope of $^-1$.

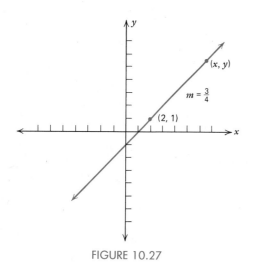

FIGURE 10.27

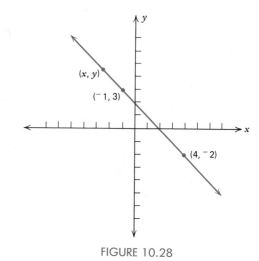

FIGURE 10.28

$$\frac{y-3}{x+1} = {}^-1$$
$$^-x - 1 = y - 3$$
$$x + y = 2$$

You may wonder if the same equation would result if we would use point (4, ⁻2) instead of point (⁻1, 3). The answer is yes and can be seen by the following:

$$\frac{y - ({}^-2)}{x - 4} = {}^-1$$
$$^-x + 4 = (y + 2)$$
$$x + y = 2$$

EXAMPLE 3

Find the equation of the line that has a slope of $\frac{2}{3}$ and a y-intercept of 1.

Solution A y-intercept of 1 means that the point (0, 1) is on the line (Fig. 10.29). Again, choosing a variable point (x, y), we can proceed as in the previous examples.

$$\frac{y-1}{x-0} = \frac{2}{3}$$
$$2x = 3y - 3$$
$$2x - 3y = {}^-3$$

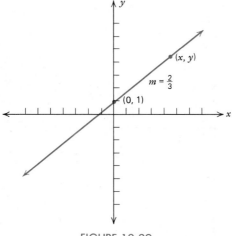

FIGURE 10.29

REMARK Perhaps it would be helpful for you to pause a moment and look back over Examples 1 through 3. Notice that the same basic approach is used in all three situations: that is, we choose a "variable" point (x, y) and use it to determine the equation that satisfies the conditions given in the problem.

EXAMPLE 4

Find the equation of the line having a slope of m and a y-intercept of b.

Solution A y-intercept of b means that the point $(0, b)$ is on the line (Fig. 10.30). We can proceed as in Example 3.

$$\frac{x - b}{x - 0} = m$$
$$y - b = mx$$
$$y = mx + b$$

The equation

$$y = mx + b$$

is referred to as the *slope-intercept* form of the equation of a straight line. It can be used for two primary purposes, as the next two examples illustrate.

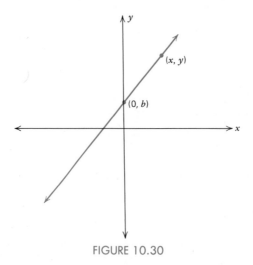

FIGURE 10.30

EXAMPLE 5

Find the equation of the line that has a slope of $\frac{2}{3}$ and a y-intercept of 1.

Solution This is a restatement of Example 3, but this time we will use the slope-intercept form ($y = mx + b$) of a line to write its equation. Because $m = \frac{2}{3}$ and $b = 1$, these values can be substituted into $y = mx + b$.

$$y = \tfrac{2}{3}x + 1$$
$$3y = 2x + 3 \qquad \text{Multiply both sides by 3}$$
$$^{-}3 = 2x - 3y \quad \text{Same result as in Example 3}$$

EXAMPLE 6

Find the slope and the y-intercept of the line whose equation is $3x - 7y = 10$.

Solution We can solve the given equation for y in terms of x and then compare it to the slope-intercept form.

$$3x - 7y = 10$$
$$^{-}7y = ^{-}3x + 10$$
$$y = \tfrac{3}{7}x - \tfrac{10}{7}$$

$$y = mx + b \qquad y = \frac{3}{7}x + \frac{^{-}10}{7}$$

The slope of the line is $\frac{3}{7}$ and the y-intercept is $^{-}(\frac{10}{7})$.

In general, if the equation of a nonvertical line is written in slope-intercept form ($y = mx + b$), the coefficient of x is the slope of the line and the constant term is the y-intercept. (Remember that the slope is not defined for a vertical line.)

In the final two examples, we again use the relationships involving slopes of parallel and perpendicular lines.

EXAMPLE 7

Find the equation of the line that contains the point (2, 5) and is parallel to the line determined by $2x + 3y = 6$.

Solution First let us draw a figure to help in our analysis of the problem (Fig. 10.31). Because the line through (2, 5) is to be parallel to the line

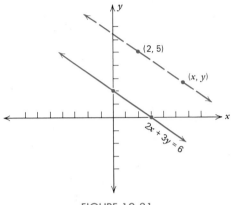

FIGURE 10.31

determined by $2x + 3y = 6$, it must have the same slope. We can find that slope by changing $2x + 3y = 6$ to slope-intercept form.

$$2x + 3y = 6$$
$$3y = {}^-2x + 6$$
$$y = {}^-\left(\frac{2}{3}\right)x + 2$$

The slope of both lines is ${}^-(\frac{2}{3})$. Now we can choose a variable point (x, y) on the line through $(2, 5)$ and proceed as we did in earlier examples.

$$\frac{y - 5}{x - 2} = \frac{2}{{}^-3} \text{ because } {}^-\left(\frac{2}{3}\right) = \frac{2}{{}^-3}$$
$$2x - 4 = {}^-3y + 15$$
$$2x + 3y = 19$$

EXAMPLE 8

Find the equation of the line that contains the point $({}^-1, {}^-2)$ and is perpendicular to the line determined by $2x - y = 4$.

Solution Figure 10.32 depicts the situation described in the problem. Since the line through $({}^-1, {}^-2)$ is to be perpendicular to the line determined by $2x - y = 4$, its slope must be the negative reciprocal of the slope of $2x - y = 4$. (The product of a number and its negative reciprocal is ${}^-1$.) The slope of $2x - y = 4$ can be found by changing it to the slope-intercept form.

$$2x - y = 4$$
$$^-y = {}^-2x + 4$$
$$y = 2x - 4 \qquad \text{(The slope is 2)}$$

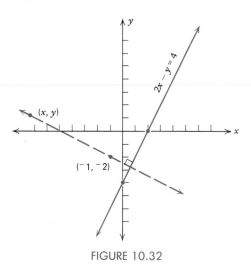

FIGURE 10.32

The slope of the desired line is $^-(\frac{1}{2})$ (the negative reciprocal of 2) and we can proceed as before by using a variable point (x, y).

$$\frac{y + 2}{x + 1} = \frac{1}{^-2} \text{ because } \; ^-\left(\frac{1}{2}\right) = \frac{1}{^-2}$$
$$x + 1 = {}^-2y - 4$$
$$x + 2y = {}^-5$$

Two forms of equations of straight lines are used extensively. They are referred to as the *standard form* and the *slope-intercept* form and can be described as follows.

Standard form: $Ax + By = C$, where B and C are integers and A is a nonnegative integer.

Slope-intercept form: $y = mx + b$, where m is a real number representing the slope and b is a real number representing the y-intercept.

There are also equations that resemble the standard form but when graphed do not produce a line. For example, consider the equation $|x + y| = 2$. Perhaps the easiest way to see what this will be when graphed is to consider a set of points that satisfy the equation like we did in Section 10.2.

x	0	2	$^-2$	0	1	1	$^-3$	$^-4$	2	$^-1$	$^-1$	3
y	2	0	0	$^-2$	1	$^-3$	1	2	$^-4$	$^-1$	3	$^-1$

The graph of these points is given in Figure 10.33, and they appear to fall on two distinct lines. This is indeed the case and reminds us that the equation

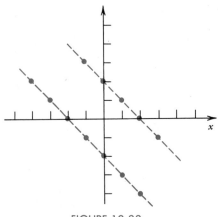

FIGURE 10.33

examined was not the standard form for a line. In these situations, the plotting of several points is the best practice to determine what the graph will
be. You will be provided with several examples to graph in the Problem Set
that follows.

PROBLEM SET 10.5

1. Write the equation of each of the following lines having the indicated
   slope and containing the indicated point. Express final equations in standard form.

   a. $m = \frac{2}{3}, (2, 6)$ **b.** $m = \frac{3}{5}, (2, {}^-1)$

   c. $m = 2, (1, 4)$ **d.** $m = {}^-3, ({}^-1, 4)$

   e. $m = {}^-(\frac{3}{5}), (2, {}^-4)$ **f.** $m = {}^-(\frac{1}{4}), ({}^-2, {}^-6)$

   g. $m = 0, (3, {}^-4)$ **h.** $m = \frac{5}{2}, ({}^-2, {}^-6)$

2. Write the equation of each line containing the indicated pair of points.
   Express final equations in standard form.

   a. $(2, 3), (4, 7)$ **b.** $(1, 2), (6, 7)$

   c. $(3,2), ({}^-2, 5)$ **d.** $(1, 1), ({}^-1, 7)$

   e. $({}^-2, {}^-3), (2, 6)$ **f.** $({}^-1, {}^-7), (1, 4)$

   g. $({}^-3, 4), (5, 4)$ **h.** $({}^-2, 5), (0, 0)$

3. Write the equation of each line having the indicated slope (*m*) and *y*-
   intercept (*b*). Express final equations in standard form.

   a. $m = \frac{1}{5}, b = 2$ **b.** $m = \frac{2}{7}, b = {}^-1$

   c. $m = {}^-(\frac{4}{5}), b = 1$ **d.** $m = {}^-(\frac{4}{3}), b = {}^-3$

   e. $m = 3, b = {}^-1$ **f.** $m = {}^-4, b = 5$

4. Write the equation of each line having the indicated slope (m) and y-intercept (b). Express final equations in slope-intercept form.

   a. $m = \frac{3}{7}, b = 5$ **b.** $m = \frac{3}{8}, b = {}^-4$

   c. $m = {}^-(\frac{3}{2}), b = {}^-1$ **d.** $m = {}^-(\frac{1}{2}), b = \frac{2}{5}$

   e. $m = 0, b = \frac{3}{4}$ **f.** $m = {}^-2, b = \frac{5}{9}$

5. Write the equation of each of the following lines satisfying the given conditions. Express final equations in standard form.

   a. x-intercept of 2 and y-intercept of 5

   b. y-intercept of 0 and slope of ${}^-(\frac{4}{7})$

   c. Contains the point $(2, {}^-3)$ and is parallel to the x-axis

   d. Contains the point $({}^-4, 1)$ and is parallel to the y-axis

   e. Contains the point $(4, 5)$ and is perpendicular to the y-axis

6. For each of the following pairs of lines, determine whether they are parallel, perpendicular, or intersecting lines that are not perpendicular.

   a. $y = \frac{3}{4}x - 2$ and $y = \frac{3}{4}x + 6$

   b. $y = 3x - 2$ and $y = {}^-(\frac{1}{3})x + 4$

   c. $2x - 3y = 9$ and $4x - 6y = 17$

   d. $3x + 5y = 4$ and $2x - y = 7$

   e. $4x + 3y = 1$ and $3x - 4y = 2$

   f. $y = 2x$ and $y = {}^-(\frac{1}{2})x$

   g. $y = \frac{2}{3}x$ and $y = \frac{3}{4}x$

   h. $y = \frac{5}{7}x - 2$ and $y = {}^-(\frac{5}{7})x + 3$

7. Write the equation of each of the following lines satisfying the given conditions. Express final answers in standard form.

   a. Containing $(1, 2)$ and parallel to $2x - y = 5$

   b. Containing $(3, 5)$ and parallel to $3x + y = 6$

   c. Containing $({}^-2, 4)$ and parallel to $4x + 5y = 20$

   d. Containing $({}^-4, {}^-5)$ and parallel to $2x - y = 8$

   e. Containing $(4, 3)$ and perpendicular to $x + y = 5$

   f. Containing $(2, 6)$ and perpendicular to $x - y = 3$

   g. Containing $(3, {}^-2)$ and perpendicular to $4x - 7y = 1$

   h. Containing $({}^-4, {}^-3)$ and perpendicular to $2x + 5y = 7$

8. A linear relationship exists between temperatures measured in °F and in °C. In fact letting (x, y) represent (°C, °F), we know two points $(0, 32)$ and $(100, 212)$ of the relationship. Using point-slope form, write the equation that represents this relationship.

9. Graph each of the following:

   a. $y = |x|$ **b.** $|x + y| = 1$ **c.** $|y| = x$ **d.** $|x| + |y| = 1$

10. **a.** On the same axes, graph the following pairs of equations:
     (i) $y = 2x - 5$ and $y = {}^-2x - 5$
     (ii) $y = 3x + 2$ and $y = {}^-3x + 2$
     (iii) $y = x + 3$ and $y = {}^-x + 3$
   b. How does it appear that the graphs of $y = mx + b$ and $y = {}^-mx + b$ are related?
   c. What is the point of intersection of the two lines $y = mx + b$ and $y = {}^-mx + b$?

11. **a.** On the same axes graph the following pairs of equations:
     (i) $y = 2x - 5$ and $y = {}^-2x + 5$
     (ii) $y = 3x + 2$ and $y = {}^-3x - 2$
     (iii) $y = x + 3$ and $y = {}^-x - 3$
   b. How does it appear that the graphs of $y = mx + b$ and $y = {}^-mx - b$ are related?
   c. What is the point of intersection of the two lines $y = mx + b$ and $y = {}^-mx - b$?

12. In Chapter 8 we dealt with reflections, translations and rotations. Answer each of the following questions concerning these ideas.
   a. Let line l be the x-axis. What is the image of each of the following points reflected over l?
     (i) $(3, 5)$ **(ii)** $({}^-2, 4)$ **(iii)** $(5, {}^-2)$
     (iv) $({}^-2, {}^-6)$ **(v)** $(4, 4)$ **(vi)** (x, y)
   b. Let line l be the y-axis. What is the image of each of the following points reflected over l?
     (i) $(3, 5)$ **(ii)** $({}^-2, 4)$ **(iii)** $(5, {}^-2)$
     (iv) $({}^-2, {}^-6)$ **(v)** $(4, 4)$ **(vi)** (x, y)
   c. Let l be the line $y = x$. What is the image of each of the following points reflected over l?
     (i) $(3, 5)$ **(ii)** $({}^-2, 4)$ **(iii)** $(5, {}^-2)$
     (iv) $({}^-2, {}^-6)$ **(v)** $(4, 4)$ **(vi)** (x, y)
   d. Let l be the line $y = {}^-x$. What is the image of each of the following points reflected over l?
     (i) $(3, 5)$ **(ii)** $({}^-2, 4)$ **(iii)** $(5, {}^-2)$
     (iv) $({}^-2, {}^-6)$ **(v)** $(4, 4)$ **(vi)** (x, y)
   e. Let R be a rotation about the origin of $180°$. What is the image of each of the following points in the rotation R?
     (i) $(3, 5)$ **(ii)** $({}^-2, 4)$ **(iii)** $(5, {}^-2)$
     (iv) $({}^-2, {}^-6)$ **(v)** $(4, 4)$ **(vi)** (x, y)
   f. Let R be a rotation about the origin of $90°$ counterclockwise. What is the image of each of the following points in the rotation R?

$$\textbf{(i) } (3, 5) \qquad \textbf{(ii) } (^-2, 4) \qquad \textbf{(iii) } (5, \, ^-2)$$
$$\textbf{(iv) } (^-2, \, ^-6) \qquad \textbf{(v) } (4, 4) \qquad \textbf{(vi) } (x, y)$$

13. a. Sketch the image of the line $y = 2x + 3$ reflected over the x-axis.
  b. What is the equation of the image drawn in part **a**?
  c. Sketch the image of the line $y = 2x + 3$ reflected over the y-axis.
  d. What is the equation of the image drawn in part **c**?

14. a. Consider the line $y = 2x + 3$. Translate each point of this line 4 units "up." Sketch the image of this translation.
  b. What is the equation of the image drawn in part **a**?

Pedagogical Problems and Activities

15. A rental company charges \$1 per hour for renting a movie projector. If you are a member of their club, there is no initial fee. However, non-members from out of the county must pay an initial fee of \$7 whereas nonmembers from the county must pay an initial fee of \$3. The graphs of these three rate structures is given in the accompany figure.
  a. Label the graphs correctly as to members, in-county nonmembers, and out-of-county nonmembers.
  b. Why is the slope of each of the lines of the same?
  c. How much more will it cost an out-of-county resident than a club member to rent the projector for 7 hours? Label the portion of the graph that shows this amount.
  d. Repeat part **c** for 10 hours, 3 hours.

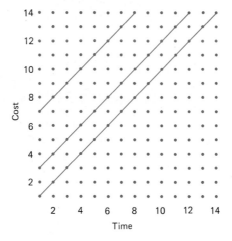

REVIEW PROBLEM SET

1. Verify that the points $A(3, 2)$, $B(6, 3)$, and $C(4, 9)$ are vertices of a right triangle.

2. One endpoint of a line segment is $(^-1, 4)$ and the midpoint of the segment is $(3, 2)$. Find the coordinates of the other endpoint.

3. Verify that the points $A(^-3, ^-2)$, $B(2, 0)$, $C(1, 4)$, and $C(^-4, 2)$ are vertices of a parallelogram.

4. Find the slope of the line determined by $(^-1, ^-4)$ and $(6, ^-3)$.

5. For each of the following, decide whether $\overleftrightarrow{AB} \| \overleftrightarrow{CD}$, $\overleftrightarrow{AB} \perp \overleftrightarrow{CD}$, or whether they are neither parallel nor perpendicular.

   a. $A(2, ^-1)$, $B(4, 2)$, $C(^-3, ^-2)$, $D(^-1, 1)$
   b. $A(^-1, 3)$, $B(1, 2)$, $C(^-4, ^-1)$, $D(7, 2)$
   c. $A(3, 2)$, $B(2, 4)$, $C(^-1, ^-3)$, $D(^-3, ^-4)$

6. Graph the solution set on a number line for each of the following open sentences involving one variable.

   a. $x > ^-4$ and $x \le 2$ b. $x < ^-1$ or $x > 4$

7. Graph the solution set on a coordinate plane for each of the following equations.

   a. $y = x^2 - 2$ b. $y = 3x - 4$ c. $x + 5y = ^-5$
   d. $y = ^-x^3 + 2$ e. $y = ^-2x$ f. $y = 2x^2$

8. Find the slope of the line that is the graph of the equation $2x - 3y = 30$.

9. Determine whether the graphs of the equations $5x - 2y = 7$ and $2x + 5y = 9$ are parallel lines, perpendicular lines, or intersecting lines that are not perpendicular.

10. Write the equation, in standard form, of the line that has a slope of $\frac{2}{5}$ and contains the point $(^-2, 6)$.

11. Write the equation, in standard form, of the line that contains the points $(2, 4)$ and $(^-6, 6)$.

12. Find the slope and y-intercept of the line $5x - 3y = 7$.

13. Write the equation, in standard form, of the line that is parallel to $3x - y = 6$ and contains the point $(2, 5)$.

14. Write the equation, in standard form, of the line that is perpendicular to $4x + 3y = 12$ and contains the point $(2, ^-7)$.

15. What is the image of $(4, ^-1)$ reflected over each of the following lines?

    a. x-axis   b. y-axis   c. line $y = x$ d. line $y = ^-x$

16. What is the image of the point $(^-3, 5)$ rotated $180°$ about the origin?

17. What is the image of the point $(^-3, 5)$ rotated $90°$ about the origin counterclockwise?

18. What is the equation of the line $y = 2x + 5$ reflected over the x-axis?

19. A car rental company charges a daily rate based on a fixed cost and miles driven. It charges \$20/day plus \$0.23/mile. What is the charge for 1 day of use and 50 miles driven?, 80 miles driven?, 200 miles driven? *n* miles driven?

Solution to Sample Problem

A family with 100 meters of fencing decides to fence a rectangular area in which their dogs can run. As they begin to draw some plans, what size rectangle will give them the largest area for their dogs?

1. *Understanding the Problem.* To what does the 100 meters of fencing refer? It must be talking about the perimeter of the rectangle. What types of rectangles could I make that would give me a perimeter of 100 meters?

2. *Devising a Plan.* We could make a list of several possible lengths and widths of rectangles or we could try to work with an algebraic equation that relates the length and width and perimeter of a rectangle.

3. *Solution.* A. A list of possible values relating length, width, and area is given here. Because the perimeter is 100 meters, the length plus the width must be 50.

Length	Width	Area
10	40	400
15	35	525
20	30	600
25	25	625
30	20	600

At this point, it appears that the largest area is when the length and width are both 25.

B. From the information gathered in Solution A, we could graph the relation length + width = 50, as shown here.

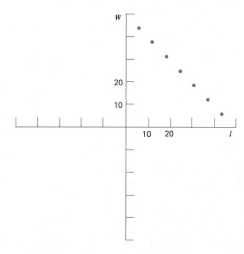

Now, because we know that a length × width = area, which we will abbreviate to $l \times w = A$, maybe we can work with this. We also know that $l + w = 50$, or $w = 50 - l$. Substituting this relation into $l \times w = A$, we have $l \times (50 - l) = A$. This equation is equivalent to $A = 50l - l^2$. The graph of this equation is presented below, using the l and A values from the table above.

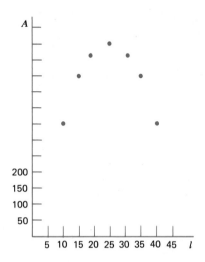

From this graph, it appears that the largest value for A is when $l = 25$.

4. *Looking Back.* In both cases, we may wish to know whether there may be some other value for the length that may make the area larger. In Solution B, because the graph is symmetric about the line $l = 25$, we may speculate that this indeed cannot happen and that the largest value does occur at $l = 25$ as suspected.

5. *Looking Ahead.* The dimensions we found for the largest rectangle actually turned out to be a square. I wonder what would have happened if one side of the rectangle was to be along the side of the house and we would only need to use the fencing to build three sides of the rectangle?

I wonder what would have happened if we would have been allowed to build a triangle, or hexagon, or some other closed-plane figure?

Is this problem related to the sample problem presented in the last chapter?

11 | PROBABILITY

Sample Problem

When rolling a standard pair of dice, there are 36 possible outcomes with sums from 2 to 12. The probability of rolling a 2 is $\frac{1}{36}$ and the probability of rolling a 3 is $\frac{2}{36}$ (a 1 and 2 or a 2 and 1). How could you mark a pair of dice differently so that the probability of throwing sums from 1 to 12 is the same?

11.1 INTRODUCTION

According to most historical accounts, the branch of mathematics known as probability had its origin in the middle of the seventeenth century when the gambler Chevalier de Mere sought the advice of the famous mathematician Blaise Pascal concerning some games of chance. One specific question was concerned with "how to divide the prize money between two equally skilled contestants if the game of chance is interrupted before completion." As the story goes, Pascal and another well-known mathematician, Pierre de Fermat, exchanged ideas in letters regarding the gambling questions. Supposedly, the beginnings of probability theory evolved from this correspondence. Regardless of the authenticity of the details of this story, the area of probability has become an important part of modern-day mathematics.

The National Council of Teachers of Mathematics Curriculum and Evaluation Standards outline the level of inclusion of probability concepts in the elementary school curriculum. The K–4 standards recommend that students be introduced to initial concepts of chance and use experiments and real-world examples to develop probability sense. In grades 5–8, the curriculum should include modeling situations and carrying out simulations to construct sample spaces and determine probabilities that lead to making predictions. In this chapter we introduce the basic concepts of probability that we feel should be a part of your mathematical background as an elementary school teacher.

We all use probability terms loosely in our everyday conversations when we estimate our chance for an outcome in our lives to occur. The terms chance and probability are often used to report the degree of "certainty" of a particular event occurring. There are events that we encounter that we may describe as certain, such as "on January 1st a New Year will begin." Other events are not certain, but are likely or even highly likely to occur. It is highly likely that you will teach in the elementary school upon certification, but unlikely that you will teach in a high school environment. To help us make decisions in life, we need to be able to understand the likelihood of events occurring. Although we may not know the outcome in advance, we may be able to investigate situations and list possible outcomes. From these listings, we can assign numbers to represent our chances or probabilities. You will be using your knowledge of fractions, decimals, and percents to make these numbers meaningful.

For some events we can actually perform an experiment to produce observable data. Using the simple experiment of tossing a die, we will introduce some terminology used in probability. There are six equally likely possible outcomes to this experiment: the 1 will come up, the 2 will come up, the 3 will come up, the 4 will come up, the 5 will come up, or the 6 will come up. We say these outcomes are equally likely because one outcome is just as likely to occur as the other. This set of possible outcomes is called a *sample space* and the individual elements of the sample space are called *sample points*. We will use S (sometimes with subscripts for identification purposes) to refer to a particular sample space of an experiment and then denote the number of sample points by $n(S)$. Thus, $S = \{1, 2, 3, 4, 5, 6\}$, where $n(S) = 6$, can be used as a sample space for the experiment of tossing a die.

Suppose that our experiment were one of tossing a coin. There are two possible outcomes (if the coin stands on its edge we will toss it again)—namely, heads or tails—and therefore a sample space of $S = \{H, T\}$, where $n(S) = 2$, is a natural one to use.

Consider the experiment of tossing two coins. (Tossing two coins once is to be considered the same as tossing one coin twice.) For clarification, let the coins be a penny and a nickel. The possible outcomes of this experiment are:

(1) a head on both coins, (2) a head on the penny and a tail on the nickel, (3) a tail on the penny and a head on the nickel, or (4) a tail on both coins. Using ordered pair symbolism, where the first entry of a pair records the result of the penny and the second entry records the result of the nickel, a sample space of $S = \{(H, H), (H, T), (T, H), (T, T)\}$, where $n(S) = 4$, can be used for this experiment.

Now suppose that in tossing two coins we are interested in some of the various possible outcomes (events) of this experiment. For example, suppose we are interested in the event "two heads occur." In this case, we are satisfied if (H, H) occurs and therefore the event "two heads occur" is the subset $E = \{(H, H)\}$, where $n(E) = 1$. Perhaps, instead, we are interested in the event "at least one head occurs." This would be the subset $F = \{(H, H), (H, T), (T, H)\}$, where $n(F) = 3$. In general, any subset of a sample space is called an *event*. If the event consists of exactly one element of the sample space, then it is called a *simple event*. Any nonempty event that is not simple is called a *compound event*. A compound event can always be represented as the union of simple events.

Now let us introduce the concept of probability via a few examples, and then present a more general definition.

EXAMPLE 1

A coin is tossed. What is the probability that a head turns up?

Solution Let the sample space $S = \{H, T\}$, where $n(S) = 2$. The event of "turning up a head" is the subset $E = \{H\}$, where $n(E) = 1$. Thus, we say that the probability of getting a head with a flip of one coin is given by

$$P(E) = \frac{n(E)}{n(S)} = \frac{1}{2}$$

EXAMPLE 2

Two coins are tossed. What is the probability that at least one head will turn up?

Solution Let $S = \{(H, H), (H, T), (T, H), (T, T)\}$, where $n(S) = 4$. Let E be the event of "at least one head." Thus, $E = \{(H, H), (H, T), (T, H)\}$ and $n(E) = 3$. Therefore, the probability of getting at least one head with the flip of two coins is given by

$$P(E) = \frac{n(E)}{n(S)} = \frac{3}{4}$$

EXAMPLE 3

What is the probability of obtaining an even number with one throw of a die?

Solution Let $S = \{1, 2, 3, 4, 5, 6\}$, where $n(S) = 6$ and let $E = \{2, 4, 6\}$, where $n(E) = 3$. Hence, $P(E) = \dfrac{3}{6}$.

REMARK Note that in Example 3 the fraction $\frac{3}{6}$ was not reduced to $\frac{1}{2}$. This is advantageous when working with probability because a reduction of the fraction will cause us to "lose" some information about the number of elements in the event space and sample space.

The events in rolling a die are said to be mutually exclusive. In other words, the occurrence of any one event precludes the occurrence of all the others. When a single die is rolled, there are six possible events, $\{1, 2, 3, 4, 5, 6\}$, of which one and only one can occur. Likewise, when a coin is tossed, one and only one of two possible events can occur (heads or tails). For this reason, we were able to define the probability of an event quite easily based on our sample space and the number of occurrences of a given event.

Definition 11.1 In a sample space of equally likely outcomes, the probability of an event can be expressed as

$$P(E) = \frac{\text{number of occurrences}}{\text{number of possible outcomes}} = \frac{n(E)}{n(S)}$$

The procedure for finding probabilities as shown in Examples 1–3 can only be used if we can define our sample space. We refer to this as *theoretical probability* because these probabilities determine what should theoretically happen in ideal situations with equally likely outcomes.

Sometimes we can only estimate the probability based on actual experiments or by examining data that has been collected from previous experiments. We will look at estimating probabilities later after further exploring theoretical probability.

No event has a probability greater than 1 because the number of ways the outcome of an event occurs cannot be greater than the total number of outcomes in the sample space. What is the probability that 1, 2, 3, 4, 5, or 6 will appear on a roll of a single die? An event such as this is called a certain event and has a probability of 1.

$$P(E) = \frac{n(E)}{n(S)} = \frac{6}{6} = 1$$

Likewise, no event has a probability less than 0. What is the probability that you will roll a 7 on a single die? This is an impossible event and its probability is 0.

$$P(E) = \frac{n(E)}{n(S)} = \frac{0}{6} = 0$$

PROPERTY 11.1   For all events E, $0 \le P(E) \le 1$.

Property 11.1 merely states that probabilities must fall in the range from 0 to 1, inclusive. This should seem reasonable as $P(E) = \dfrac{n(E)}{n(S)}$ and E is a subset of S.

It should be noted that Property 11.1 also serves as a check for "reasonableness" of answers. In other words, when computing probabilities we know that our answer must fall in the range from 0 to 1, inclusive. Any other probability answer is simply "not reasonable."

Having looked at a few examples, let us now formulate the concept of probability in a somewhat more general way. Consider a sample space $S = \{e_1, e_2, e_3, \dots, e_k\}$, where $n(S) = k$. Let us assume that each of the simple events in S is equally likely to occur. Thus, we associate with each simple event a real number $\dfrac{1}{k}$ called the probability of that event. We denote the probability of a simple event such as e_1 by $P(\{e_1\}) = \dfrac{1}{k}$. Furthermore, because a compound event is the union of simple events, the probability of a compound event is defined to be the sum of the probabilities of the simple events that comprise it. For example, if $E = \{e_1, e_2, e_3\}$ then

$$P(E) = P(\{e_1\}) + P(\{e_2\}) + P(\{e_3\})$$
$$= \frac{1}{k} + \frac{1}{k} + \frac{1}{k} = \frac{3}{k}$$

Let us look again at the probability of obtaining an even number on the roll of a die. We could get only one number on one roll of a die, but the event of rolling an even number occurs if we get either a 2 or 4 or 6. Therefore, the compound event of getting an even number is the union of the simple events and can be found by

$$P(2) + P(4) + P(6) \text{ or } \tfrac{1}{6} + \tfrac{1}{6} + \tfrac{1}{6} = \tfrac{3}{6}$$

If the probability of all simple events are added such as rolling a 1, 2, 3, 4, 5, or 6 on a die, the sum will equal 1.

$$P(1) + P(2) + P(3) + P(4) + P(5) + P(6) \text{ or } \tfrac{1}{6} + \tfrac{1}{6} + \tfrac{1}{6} + \tfrac{1}{6} + \tfrac{1}{6} + \tfrac{1}{6} = \tfrac{6}{6} = 1$$

Now let us consider a few more probability situations. In each of these we need to determine the number of elements in the sample space and in the event space. Sometimes this can be easily accomplished by actually listing all the elements and then counting them. At other times, we may see a pattern that will allow us to determine the number of elements without having to list all of them. Study these next examples very carefully.

EXAMPLE 1

Suppose that a committee of two is chosen at random from the four people Amy, Bob, Carol, and Dan. Find the probability that Amy is on the committee.

Solution The sample space for this problem consists of all 2-person committees that can be formed from a group of 4 people. Stated another way, the sample space consists of all 2-element subsets that can be formed from a set of 4 elements. This set of 2-element subsets can be listed as

$$S = \{\{A, B\}, \{A, C\}, \{A, D\}, \{B, C\}, \{B, D\}, \{C, D\}\}$$

where we have used the first letters of the names for the sake of simplicity. The event that "Amy is on the committee" is represented by

$$E = \{\{A, B\}, \{A, C\}, \{A, D\}\}$$

Because $n(S) = 6$ and $n(E) = 3$, the requested probability is given by

$$P(E) = \frac{n(E)}{n(S)} = \frac{3}{6}$$

EXAMPLE 2

Two dice are tossed. Find the probability of getting a sum of 7.

Solution For clarification purposes, let us use a red die and a white die. (It is not necessary to use different colored dice, but it does help when analyzing this type of problem.) Using ordered pairs, where the result on the red die is recorded as the first entry and the result on the white die as the second entry, we can represent the sample space as follows.

$$(1, 1), (1, 2), (1, 3), (1, 4), (1, 5), (1, 6)$$
$$(2, 1), (2, 2), (2, 3), (2, 4), (2, 5), (2, 6)$$
$$(3, 1), (3, 2), (3, 3), (3, 4), (3, 5), (3, 6)$$
$$(4, 1), (4, 2), (4, 3), (4, 4), (4, 5), (4, 6)$$
$$(5, 1), (5, 2), (5, 3), (5, 4), (5, 5), (5, 6)$$
$$(6, 1), (6, 2), (6, 3), (6, 4), (6, 5), (6, 6)$$

This 6 by 6 array indicates that there are 36 elements in the sample space. The event "sum of 7" is the set

$$E = \{(1, 6), (6, 1), (2, 5), (5, 2), (3, 4), (4, 3)\}.$$

Therefore, the probability of "getting a sum of 7" is

$$P(E) = \frac{n(E)}{n(S)} = \frac{6}{36}$$

EXAMPLE 3

A container contains 7 red marbles, 5 blue marbles, and 3 white marbles. If one marble is drawn at random from the container, find the probability that it is red.

Solution In this problem, $n(S)$ and $n(E)$ can be determined without any type of listing process. Because there is a total of 15 marbles, $n(S) = 15$. Seven of the marbles are red, so $n(E) = 7$. Thus, the probability of "drawing a red marble" is given by

$$P(E) = \frac{n(E)}{n(S)} = \frac{7}{15}$$

PROBLEM SET 11.1

For each of the following problems you should be able to determine a sample space and an event space so that the probability can be computed by using
$$P(E) = \frac{n(E)}{n(S)}$$

1. Two coins are tossed. Find the probability of each of the following events:
   a. One head and one tail
   b. Two tails
   c. At least one tail

2. Three coins are tossed. Find the probability of each of the following events:
   a. Three heads
   b. Two heads and a tail
   c. At least one head
   d. Exactly one tail

3. Four coins are tossed. Find the probability of each of the following events:
   a. Four heads
   b. Three heads and a tail
   c. Three tails and a head
   d. Two heads and two tails
   e. At least one head

4. If a coin is tossed twice, which of the following is most likely to occur?

   Tails on both tosses.

   Head on first toss, tail on second toss.

   Why?

5. Consider a true/false quiz on which you guessed at random.
   a. If there are two questions on the quiz, what are the possible ways you could have answered the quiz? What is the probability of getting 100% of the questions correct?
   b. If there are four questions on the quiz, would you have a higher or lower probability of getting all four questions correct by random guessing then if there were three questions on the test?

6. The probability of the birth of a child of a given sex is $\frac{1}{2}$. For a two-child family, what is the probability of
   a. Two girls?
   b. A boy and a girl?
   c. A girl then a boy?
   d. What is the probability that if a family consists of four children, that they will have all boys?

7. A die is tossed. Find the probability of each of the following events:
   a. A 4 showing (a 4 showing means a 4 on the up face)
   b. A multiple of 3 showing
   c. A prime number showing
   d. An even number showing
   e. A multiple of 7 showing

8. Two dice are tossed. Find the probability of each of the following events.
   a. A sum of 6
   b. A sum of 11
   c. A sum less than 5
   d. A 5 on exactly one die
   e. A 4 on at least one die
   f. A sum greater than 4

9. Suppose you have two spinners labeled A and B as shown.

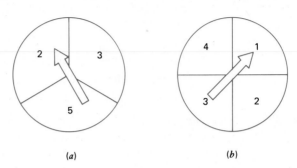

(a)   (b)

You spin A first and then B and record the numbers shown. If a spinner points to a line, you spin again. Record the resulting numbers as ordered pairs.

a. How many outcomes are possible?

b. List the possible outcomes.

c. What is the probability that the sum is prime?

d. What is the probability that the product is even?

10. a. Suppose you have a die labeled as pictured.

List the possible outcomes to determine:

  (i) $P(1)$

 (ii) $P(2)$

(iii) $P(3)$

b. If you have 2 dice, both labeled as pictured in **(a)**, find the probabilities of the following:

  (i) P(getting a sum of 4) _____

 (ii) P(getting an even sum) _____

(iii) P(sum that is a prime number) _____

11. One card is randomly drawn from a standard deck of 52 playing cards. Find the probability of each of the following events:

a. A heart is drawn.

b. A king is drawn.

c. A spade or a diamond is drawn.

d. A red jack is drawn.

12. Twenty-five slips of paper numbered 1 to 25, inclusive, are put in a hat and then one is drawn out at random. Find the probability of each of the following events:

   a. The slip with the 5 on it is drawn.

   b. A slip with an even number on it is drawn.

   c. A slip with a prime number on it is drawn.

   d. A slip with a multiple of 6 on it is drawn.

13. A bag contains 10 red marbles, 7 black marbles, and 6 green marbles. If one marble is drawn at random from the bag, find the probability of each of the following events:

   a. A red marble is drawn.

   b. A green marble is drawn.

   c. A green marble or a black marble is drawn.

   d. A yellow marble is drawn.

14. A poll was taken among students in mathematics courses. They were asked to choose the weekday at which they could perform the best academically. The results of the poll are recorded in the following table.

Day of the Week	Freshman	Sophomore	Junior	Senior
Monday	1	2	3	5
Tuesday	2	1	6	1
Wednesday	4	7	13	17
Thursday	2	1	1	4
Friday	1	2	1	1

If we choose a student at random from among all the students that were polled, what is a good estimate of the probability of the following?

   a. The student chooses Monday

   b. The student chooses Friday

   c. The student chooses Tuesday or Thursday

   d. The student is a sophomore

   e. The student is a sophomore who chooses Wednesday

15. A committee of two girls is to be chosen at random from the four girls Alice, Barb, Carol, and Denise. Find the probability that Barb but not Carol is on the committee.

16. Bill, Carol, and Alice are seated at random in a row of three seats. Find the probability that Bill and Carol are seated side by side.

17. A letter is chosen at random from the English alphabet. Find the probability of each of the following events:

   a. The letter is q.

   b. The letter is a vowel.

   c. The letter is a consonant.

18. Suppose that a committee of two boys is to be chosen at random from the five boys Al, Bill, Carl, Dan, and Elmer. Find the probability of each of the following events:

   a. 'Dan is on the committee.

   b. Dan and Elmer are on the committee.

   c. Bill and Carl are not both on the committee.

19. A committee of four boys is to be chosen at random from the five boys Al, Bill, Carl, Dan, and Elmer. Find the probability that Dan is not on the committee.

20. A subset of two letters is to be chosen at random from the set $\{a, b, c, d, e, f\}$. Find the probability that the letter a is in the subset.

21. A subset of two letters is to be chosen at random from the set $\{a, b, c, d, e, f, g\}$. Find the probability that the letter b is not in the subset.

Pedagogical Problems and Activities

22. Make a list of "probability situations" that might arise in everyday life.

23. Suppose that you proposed the following problem to a class of sixth-graders: "If one card is drawn at random from a deck of 52 playing cards, what is the probability that it is a heart?" Now suppose that two students reacted as follows:

Bill: There are 52 cards and 13 hearts; therefore, the answer is $\frac{13}{52}$.

Sue: There are 4 suits, one of which is hearts; therefore, the answer is $\frac{1}{4}$.

Who is correct, and what kind of discussion is needed at this time?

24. Following are some problems representative of the kinds found in elementary school mathematics texts for the purpose of introducing probability ideas. Solve each of the problems.

   a. A box contains 5 lemon, 4 orange, and 7 cherry popsicles. If you reach in and draw out one without looking, what is the probability that you will pick a lemon popsicle?

   b. A box contains cans of pop as illustrated.

| 7 lemon lime |
| 5 root beer |
| 11 creme soda |

   If you pick one can without looking, what is the probability that you will choose root beer?

   c. A box of candy contains "different kinds" as indicated on the cover.

   6 creams
   8 caramels
   6 nuts

   You choose one piece of candy without looking. What is the probability that you pick a caramel-filled piece of candy?

25. The dormitory rooms in Higgins Hall were all decorated for Christmas with red and green streamers. Some of the rooms had red streamers, some had green streamers, and some had both red and green streamers. The following situation existed: 72% of the rooms had red streamers, 58% of the rooms had green streamers, and 30% had both red and green streamers.

   a. Draw a Venn diagram to illustrate the situation.
   b. What percent of the rooms had red or green streamers?
   c. What percent of the rooms had only red streamers?
   d. If we walked into one of the rooms at random, what is the probability that a chosen room would have only green streamers?

26. Travis and Tanya play a game that involves tossing two coins. Tanya will get one point if there is a match. Because there are two ways to get a match, Travis will get two points if there is no match. Is this a fair game so that each player has an equal chance of winning? What would be the score based on theoretical probability after 100 tosses? Try it and see if your outcome is approximately the same.

27. Toss a fair coin 40 times recording a list of your results (e.g., *HHTH* . . .). From the information, complete the following table. Toss the coin 80 times and record again.

	For 40 Tosses		For 80 Tosses	
	Fraction	*Decimal*	*Fraction*	*Decimal*
Number of heads				
Number of tails				
Number of runs* of heads				
Number of runs of tails				
Total number of runs				
Average length of a run of heads				
Average length of a run of tails				
Average length of all runs				

*A run occurs when the same result happens two or more times.

   a. How many times do you think you need to toss the coin to approximate the probability of $\frac{1}{2}$ for obtaining a head?

b. Would the average length of run for 80 tosses tend to be twice that for 40?

c. Would the number of heads for 80 tosses tend to be twice that for 40?

28. In the case of rolling two dice, we can draw a grid with the top and left side indicating possible throws and each square inside showing the sum of the numbers on the two dice.

a. Complete the grid.

	1	2	3	4	5	6
1	2	3	4			
2	3	4				
3						
4						
5						
6						

b. From examining the grid, what sums are highly likely and what sums are unlikely?

c. Use the grid to determine which of the two events in each case is more likely.

   (i) sum > 8 or sum < 8

   (ii) sum = 3 or sum = 6

   (iii) sum = 7 or sum = 10

   (iv) sum < 7 or sum < 5

   (v) sum > 9 or sum < 7

   (vi) sum > 12 or sum < 12

   (vii) sum is 5, 6, or 7 or sum is 9, 10, or 11

29. Suppose you would play a game in which Player A gets a point if the sum on the dice is even and Player B gets a point if the sum on the dice is odd. Is it a fair game or would one of the players have an advantage?

30. A box contains several blocks. Some are purple, some are gold, and some are white. The probability of picking a purple block at random is $\frac{1}{4}$ and the probability of picking a gold block is $\frac{3}{8}$.

a. What is the probability of picking a white block at random?

b. What is the smallest number of blocks that could be in the box?

c. Could the box contain 32 blocks? If so, how many of each color would there be?

d. If the box contains 12 purple blocks and 18 gold blocks, how many white blocks does it contain?

11.2   COUNTING TECHNIQUES TO HELP WITH PROBABILITY

We have looked at some counting processes in Chapter 1 that involved the combination interpretation of multiplication. This process of counting the number of elements in a sample space is nicely illustrated through the use of a *tree diagram*. For example, suppose that Eric is shopping for a new bicycle and has two different models (5-speed, 10-speed) and four different colors (red, white, blue, silver) from which to make a choice. His different choices can be "counted" in terms of a tree diagram, as shown in Figure 11.1.

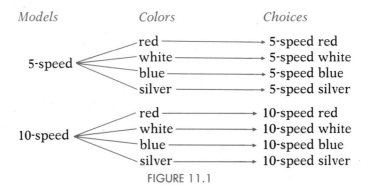

FIGURE 11.1

Thus, there are 2 · 4 or 8 combinations for Eric to choose.

EXAMPLE

There are two red marbles and one yellow marble in a box. You reach in and get a marble, record the color, replace it, and draw a second marble. What are the possible combinations for the first and second marbles you draw?

Solution

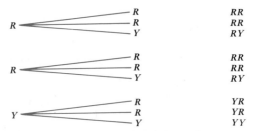

You can have 3 × 3 or 9 possible combinations for a first and second marble.

A tree diagram allows us to view the experiment of tossing three coins in the air as the tossing of one coin three times in succession.

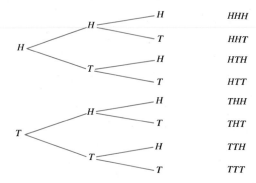

Because there are two things that can happen to each of the three coins, there are $2 \times 2 \times 2$ or 8 different results possible when tossing three coins.

This multiplication principle for counting will work any time one event can happen in m ways and then a successive event can happen in n ways. Specifically, in such cases, there will be $m \cdot n$ possible ways for the combined events to occur. This is commonly referred to as the Fundamental Principle of Counting.

FUNDAMENTAL PRINCIPLE OF COUNTING
If one task can be accomplished in m different ways, and, following this task, a second task can be accomplished in n different ways, then the first task followed by the second task can be accomplished in $m \cdot n$ different ways. (This counting principle extends to any finite number of tasks.)

Tree diagrams can become cumbersome for some problems for which the sample spaces and, perhaps also, the event spaces are large. Thus, the Fundamental Principle of Counting provides us with a systematic counting technique that will help us determine the number of elements without actually listing them.

The next three examples further illustrate the use of the Fundamental Principle of Counting.

EXAMPLE 1

Suppose that in a small town there are 9 "north-south" streets, each of which intersects 12 different "east-west" streets. How many intersections are there?

Solution Because each of the 9 "north-south" streets intersects each of the 12 "east-west" streets, there are $9(12) = 108$ intersections.

EXAMPLE 2

How many numbers of 3 different digits each can be formed by choosing from the digits 1, 2, 3, 4, 5, and 6?

Solution Let us analyze this problem in terms of three tasks as follows:

Task 1: Choose the hundred's digit, for which there are 6 choices.

Task 2: Choose the ten's digit, for which there are only 5 choices because one digit was used in the hundred's place.

Task 3: Choose the unit's digit, for which there are only 4 choices because two digits have been used for the other places.

Thus, there are (6)(5)(4) = 120 numbers of three different digits that can be formed.

Looking back over the solution for Example 2, it would be helpful for you to react to each of the following questions.

1. Could we have solved the problem by choosing the unit's digit first, then the ten's digit, and then the hundred's digit?

2. How many three digit numbers can be formed from 1, 2, 3, 4, 5, and 6 if we did not say that each one has to have three *different* digits?

3. Suppose that the digits from which to choose are 0, 1, 2, 3, 4, and 5. Now, how many numbers of three different digits each can be formed? (We do not want 0 in the hundred's place.)

EXAMPLE 3

In how many ways can Al, Bob, Carol, Dawn, and Ed be seated in a row of five chairs if Al is to be seated in the "middle" chair?

Solution Because Al must occupy the "middle" chair, we can do that task first and then proceed to fill the other chairs. Therefore, the problem can be analyzed in terms of five tasks as follows.

Task 1: Choose Al for the middle chair. This can be done in 1 way.

Task 2: Choose someone for the first chair on the left. There are 4 choices because Al has been seated.

Task 3: Choose someone for the second chair from the left. There are 3 choices because two people have already been seated.

Task 4: Choose someone for the second chair from the right. There are now only 2 choices left.

Task 5: Choose someone for the last chair on the right. There is only 1 choice left.

Therefore, by the Fundamental Principle of Counting, there are $(1)(4)(3)(2)(1) = 24$ ways of seating these five people so that Al is in the middle chair.

Up to this point, we have only used the Fundamental Principle of Counting to help us determine the number of ways certain events would happen. We will also consider some probability problems for which our newly acquired counting techniques will prove very helpful.

EXAMPLE 1

If 4 coins are tossed, what is the probability of getting 3 heads and 1 tail?

Solution The sample space consists of the possible outcomes for tossing 4 coins. By the Fundamental Principle, we know that tossing 4 coins can result in $2 \cdot 2 \cdot 2 \cdot 2 = 16$ different outcomes. The event of "getting 3 heads and 1 tail" is the subset $E = \{(H, H, H, T), (H, H, T, H), (H, T, H, H), (T, H, H, H)\}$, where $n(E) = 4$. Therefore.

$$P(E) = \frac{n(E)}{n(S)} = \frac{4}{16}$$

Notice that in this example we used the Fundamental Principle to determine the number of elements in the sample space without actually listing all the elements in it. For the event space, we then actually listed the elements and counted them in the usual way. There are no definite rules as to when to list the elements and when to apply some sort of counting technique. In general, we suggest that if you do not see a counting pattern for a particular problem, you begin the listing process. If a counting pattern then emerges as you are listing the elements, use the pattern at that time.

EXAMPLE 2

A pair of dice is tossed. Find the probability of getting a sum of 8.

Solution The sample space consists of all possible outcomes for rolling a pair of dice. In Section 11.1 we systematically enumerated these and concluded that there are 36 possible outcomes. The Fundamental Principle can also be used to arrive at this same conclusion. There are 6 things that can happen on the first die and 6 things on the second die; therefore, there are $6 \cdot 6 = 36$ possible outcomes. The event space can be listed as $E = \{(2, 6), (6, 2), (3, 5), (5, 3), (4, 4)\}$, where $n(E) = 5$. Thus, the probability of getting a sum of 8 is given by

$$P(E) = \frac{n(E)}{n(S)} = \frac{5}{36}$$

EXAMPLE 3

Suppose that we form all possible numbers of 3 different digits by choosing from the digits 1, 2, 3, 4, 5, and 6. If one of these three-digit numbers is chosen at random, what is the probability that it is greater than 400?

Solution The sample space consists of all possible numbers of three different digits that can be formed from 1, 2, 3, 4, 5, and 6. In an earlier example we found that there were (6)(5)(4) = 120 such numbers; thus, $n(S) = 120$. The event space consists of those three-digit numbers in the sample space that are greater than 400. Let us count these as follows:

Task 1: Choose the hundred's digit. It must be 4, 5, or 6; thus, there are 3 choices.

Task 2: Choose the ten's digit. After choosing a digit in Task 1, there are 5 choices for this digit.

Task 3: Choose the unit's digit. After choosing a digit in Task 1 and another digit in Task 2, there are 4 choices for this digit.

Therefore, there are (3)(5)(4) = 60 three-digit numbers greater than 400; so $n(E) = 60$. Thus, the required probability is

$$P(E) = \frac{n(E)}{n(S)} = \frac{60}{120}$$

PROBLEM SET 11.2

Problems 1–13 are counting problems. No probability questions are being asked.

1. Draw a tree diagram of the following: A student has a choice of three different mathematics classes at 9 A.M., two different humanities classes at 10 A.M., and four different science classes at 11 A.M. List the possible choices of class schedules that will include a mathematics class at 9 A.M., a humanities class at 10 A.M., and a science class at 11 A.M.

2. Draw a tree diagram and then see if the multiplication principle works on the following: A steak house has two kinds of salads, five kinds of steak, and four kinds of desserts. How many different dinners could you order, if a dinner includes a salad, a steak, and a dessert?

3. Use the multiplication principle to answer the following exercises. Check by using a tree diagram or listing.

   a. A basketball team of 10 players is warming up by making quick sharp passes. The three guards are lined up so they can pass to the other seven players. In how many ways could a pass be made from a guard to one of the other players?

    b. Suppose there are five roads from Los Angeles to San Francisco and six from San Francisco to Sacramento, how many routes are there from Los Angeles through San Francisco to Sacramento?

    c. A certain make of automobile has three body types, seven choices of upholstery, and five color schemes. In order to show all possible cars at an exhibit, how many cars are necessary?

4. If a man has 8 shirts, 5 pairs of slacks, and 3 pairs of shoes, how many different "shirt-slack-shoe" outfits does he have?

5. If 5 coins are tossed, in how many ways can they fall?

6. If 3 dice are tossed, in how many ways can they fall?

7. How many numbers of two different digits can be formed by choosing from the digits 1, 2, 3, 4, 5, 6, and 7?

8. How many even numbers of three different digits can be formed by choosing from the digits 2, 3, 4, 5, 6, 7, 8, and 9?

9. How many odd numbers of four different digits can be formed by choosing from the digits 1, 2, 3, 4, 5, 6, 7, and 8?

10. How many numbers of three different digits can be formed by choosing from the digits 0, 1, 2, 3, 4, and 5?

11. In how many ways can 4 people be seated in a row of 4 seats?

12. How many different batting orders can be formed from a team of 9 players?

13. How many different license plates are there with three places consisting of a letter followed by two digits? Do not allow zero as the first digit.

14. List all the outcomes possible when rolling a die and tossing a coin. (Use a tree diagram to help determine the outcomes.) Answer the following·

    a. What is the probability of a head on the coin and a three on the die?

    b. What is the probability that the number on the die is greater than 5 and the coin shows heads?

    c. What is the probability that the number on the die is prime and the coin shows tails?

    d. What is the probability that the number on the die is even and the coin is either heads or tails?

In Problems 15–24 use $P(E) = \dfrac{n(E)}{n(S)}$ to determine the requested probabilities.

15. Two dice are tossed. Find the probability of getting a sum of 10.

16. Two dice are tossed. Find the probability of getting a sum greater than 9.

17. Three dice are tossed. Find the probability of getting a sum of 4.

18. Three dice are tossed. Find the probability of getting a sum of 5.

19. A die and a coin are tossed. Find the probability of getting an even number on the die and a head on the coin.

20. A building has 5 doors. Find the probability that two people, entering the building at random, will choose the same door.

21. All possible numbers of three different digits are formed from the digits 1, 2, 3, 4, 5, 6, and 7. If one number is then chosen at random, what is the probability that it is an odd number?

22. All possible numbers of four different digits are formed from the digits 0, 1, 2, 3, 4, 5, and 6. If one number is then chosen at random, what is the probability that it is greater than 2000? (We do not want 0 in the thousand's place.)

23. Al, Barb, and Cindy are randomly seated in a row of three seats. Find the probability that Al is seated in the middle.

24. Al, Bob, Cindy, Dawn, and Eric are randomly seated in a row of five seats. Find the probability that Al and Bob occupy end seats.

25. As we have already determined, when a single coin is tossed, there are only two possible ways it can land—either heads up or tails up. With two coins, there are four different possibilities—*HH, HT, TH,* and *TT*. When three coins are tossed the possibilities are *HHH, HHT, HTH, THH, HTT, THT, TTH,* and *TTT*. The number of ways one, two and three coins can land can be shown in a triangular arrangement of numbers known as Pascal's Triangle.

Row 0				1			
Row 1			1		1		1 coin
Row 2		1		2		1	2 coins
Row 3	1		3		3		1 3 coins

Look at Row 1. With one coin there is 1 way to get a head and 1 way to get a tail. Row 2 shows 1 way to get two heads (*HH*), 2 ways to get a head and a tail (*HT* or *TH*), and 1 way to get two tails (*TT*).

a. What does Row 3 show about the possibilities for three coins?

b. How many possibilities are there from tossing four coins?

c. How many ways can you get four heads or four tails?

    d. How many ways can you get three heads and one tail?

    e. How many ways can you get two heads and two tails?

    f. How many ways can you get one head and three tails?

    g. Complete Row 4 in Pascal's Triangle.

26. a. Using the information generated in Problem 25, we can extend our use of Pascal's Triangle. The number of elements in the sample spaces can be related to the sum of the rows of Pascal's Triangle. Use Rows 4, 5, 6, and 7 to identify this relationship.

    b. Notice that if you draw a little triangle like the three shown, the sum of the top two numbers gives you the bottom number. Use this pattern to extend Pascal's Triangle through Row 7.

		Sum of #s in Row	*Exponential Form*
Row 0	1	1	2^0
Row 1	1 1	2	2^1
Row 2	1 2 1	4	2^2
Row 3	1 3 3 1	8	_____
Row 4	1 4 6 4 1	_____	_____
Row 5	1 5 10 10 5 1	_____	_____
Row 6		_____	_____
Row 7		_____	_____

27. Compare the sums found in rows 2, 3, and 4 and the tossing of coins. How does this relate to the Fundamental Counting Principle and the exponential form in Pascal's Triangle?

28. Because the sum of each row of Pascal's Triangle represents the number of possibilities of events for that number of coins, one can find probabilities very easily when there is a fixed number of trials, each trial results in a success or a failure ($P = \frac{1}{2}$), and the probability of success remains constant from one trial to the next. Using Row 6, we can find $P(6$ heads and 0 tails$) = \frac{1}{64}$ whereas the $P(4$ heads and 2 tails$) = \frac{15}{64}$.

    a. What is the $P(3$ heads and 3 tails$)$?

    b. What is the probability of one head and five tails?

    c. What is the probability of two heads and four tails?

29. a. Using the foregoing method, find the following probabilities for 5 coins.

    (i) What is the probability of five tails?

    (ii) What is the probability of two heads and three tails?

    (iii) What is the probability of four heads and one tail?

    (iv) What is the probability of five heads?

b. Find the following probabilities using 7 coins.
  (i) What is the probability of 7 tails?
  (ii) What is the probability of four heads and three tails?
  (iii) What is the probability of two heads and five tails?
  (iv) What is the probability of 6 heads and one tail?

Pedagogical Problems and Activities

30. In Chapter 8 we identified the five regular polyhedrons as follows:

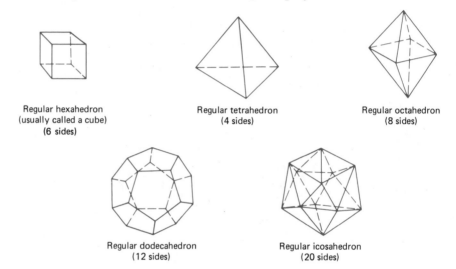

Regular hexahedron
(usually called a cube)
(6 sides)

Regular tetrahedron
(4 sides)

Regular octahedron
(8 sides)

Regular dodecahedron
(12 sides)

Regular icosahedron
(20 sides)

In addition to the standard cubical dice, you can also purchase dice in the shapes of the other regular polyhedrons. Such dice provide some variations to the typical "dice problems."

a. Consider a pair of dice each in the shape of a regular tetrahedron with sides numbered 1, 2, 3, and 4. If you toss such a pair of dice, what is the probability of getting a sum of 6 on the "down" faces?

b. Consider a pair of dice each in the shape of a regular octahedron with sides numbered 1, 2, 3, . . . , 8. If you toss such a pair of dice, what is the probability of getting a sum of 13 on the "up" faces?

c. Consider a pair of dice each in the shape of a regular dodecahedron with sides numbered 1, 2, 3, . . . , 12. If you toss such a pair of dice, what is the probability of getting a sum greater than 21?

d. Consider a pair of dice each in the shape of a regular icosahedron. On each die two sides are numbered 0, two sides are numbered 1, two sides are numbered 2, and so on, through 9. If you toss such a pair of dice, what is the probability of getting a sum of 17?

31. Through the use of 3 yellow cubes and 1 blue cube we can simulate successive spins on the spinner below. We can place the cubes in a bag and draw one cube at a time and record the results. Be sure to replace the cube after each trial.

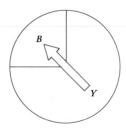

a. Use a tree diagram and list all the possible outcomes for two successive draws of the cubes.

b. Find the probabilities of the following.

(i) $P(BB)$_____	**(ii)** $P(YB)$_____
(iii) $P(BY)$_____	**(iv)** $P(YY)$_____
(v) P(blue on 1st)_____	**(vi)** P(yellow on 1st)_____

32. When asked, "What is the probability of rain?," a child says, "one-half! Either it happens or it doesn't." What do you say?

33. Is the statement P(one head and three tails) the same as $P(HTTT)$?

11.3 MORE ON THE FUNDAMENTAL PRINCIPLE OF COUNTING AND PROBABILITY

In this section we extend our use of the Fundamental Principle of Counting and offer some other suggestions for solving "counting" type problems.

EXAMPLE 1

In how many ways can Al, Barb, Carl, Don, and Edna be seated in a row of five seats if Al and Barb are to be side-by-side?

Solution This problem can be analyzed in terms of three tasks as follows:

Task 1: Choose the two adjacent seats to be occupied by Al and Barb. An illustration such as the one here helps us to see that there are **4** possible choices for the two adjacent seats.

Task 2: Determine the number of ways that Al and Barb can be seated in each of the "adjacent-seat" positions. Because Al can be seated on the left and Barb on the right, or vice versa, there are 2 ways to seat Al and Barb for each of the four choices of the two adjacent seats.

Task 3: The remaining three people must be seated in the remaining three seats. This can be done in $(3)(2)(1) = 6$ different ways.

We can use a diagram to show the choices at each stage.

STAGE	1st	2nd	3rd	TOTAL
Number of choices	4 $\cdot$	2 $\cdot$	6 =	48

Thus, by the Fundamental Principle, Task 1 followed by Task 2, followed by Task 3 can be done in $(4)(2)(6) = 48$ ways.

Sometimes a problem needs to be broken down into two or more smaller problems, as the next example illustrates.

EXAMPLE 2

How many numbers greater than 4000, for which no number contains repeated digits, can be formed by choosing from the digits 1, 2, 3, 4, and 5?

Solution The key for solving this problem is to recognize that *all* five-digit numbers formed will be greater than 4000, but only *some* of the four-digit numbers will be greater than 4000. Thus, we need to break the problem into two smaller problems as follows.

PROBLEM 1

Find the number of four-digit numbers, with different digits, greater than 4000 that can be formed from 1, 2, 3, 4, and 5.

Solution

Task 1: Choose the thousand's digit. There are 2 choices, the 4 or the 5.

Task 2: Choose the hundred's digit, for which there are 4 choices as one digit was used in the thousand's place.

Task 3: Choose the ten's digit, for which there are 3 choices as two digits have been used.

Task 4: Choose the unit's digit, for which there are 2 choices as three digits have been used.

The diagram below illustrates the choices at each stage.

STAGE	1st		2nd		3rd		4th	TOTAL
	Thousands		Hundreds		Tens		Units	
Number	digit		digit		digit		digit	
of choices	2	·	4	·	3	·	2	=	48

Thus, there are $(2)(4)(3)(2) = 48$ possible four-digit numbers.

PROBLEM 2

Find the number of five-digit numbers, with different digits, that can be formed from 1, 2, 3, 4, and 5.

> *Solution* Because these can be chosen in any order, there are $(5)(4)(3)(2)(1) = 120$ five-digit numbers. Altogether there are $48 + 120 = 168$ numbers, with different digits, greater than 4000 that can be formed by choosing from the digits 1, 2, 3, 4, and 5.

Recall that in Chapter 2, when working with sets, the concept of the complement of a set was discussed. This same idea of complement is used with reference to events and sample spaces where the sample space serves as the universal set. For example, if $S = \{1, 2, 3, 4, 5, 6\}$ and $E = \{1, 2\}$, then the *complement of E* (written E') is $E' = \{3, 4, 5, 6\}$. Likewise, if $S = \{1, 2, 3, 4\}$ and $E = \{1, 2, 3, 4\}$, then $E' = \emptyset$.

Complementary events are complementary sets for which S, the sample space, serves as the universal set. The following examples illustrate this idea.

Sample Space	Event Space	Complementary Event Space
$S = \{1, 2, 3, 4, 5, 6\}$	$E = \{1, 2\}$	$E' = \{3, 4, 5, 6\}$
$S = \{H, T\}$	$E = \{T\}$	$E' = \{H\}$
$S = \{2, 3, 4, \ldots, 12\}$	$E = \{2, 3, 4\}$	$E' = \{5, 6, 7, \ldots, 12\}$
$S = \{1, 2, 3, \ldots, 25\}$	$E = \{3, 4, 5, \ldots, 25\}$	$E' = \{1, 2\}$

In each row, note that E' (the complement of E) consists of all elements of S that *are not* in E. Thus, E and E' are called *complementary events*. Also note that for each row, the statement $P(E) + P(E') = 1$ can be made. For example, in the first row $P(E) = \frac{2}{6}$ and $P(E') = \frac{4}{6}$. Likewise, in the last row $P(E) = \frac{23}{25}$ and $P(E') = \frac{2}{25}$. The following general property can be stated.

PROPERTY 11.2 **If E is any event of a sample space S and E' is the complementary event, then**

$$P(E) + P(E') = 1$$

If we are able to compute either $P(E)$ or $P(E')$, then the other one is determined by subtracting from 1. For example, suppose that for a particular problem we can find that $P(E) = \frac{3}{13}$. Then we immediately know that $P(E') = 1 - P(E) = 1 - \frac{3}{13} = \frac{10}{13}$. The following examples further illustrate the use of Property 11.2.

EXAMPLE 1

Two dice are tossed. Find the probability of getting a sum greater than 3.

Solution Let S be the familiar sample space of ordered pairs for this problem, where $n(S) = 36$. Let E be the event of "obtaining a sum greater than 3." Then E' is the event of "obtaining a sum less than or equal to 3," which is $E' = \{(1, 1), (1, 2), (2, 1)\}$. Thus, $P(E') = \dfrac{n(E')}{n(S)} = \frac{3}{36}$ and this produces

$$P(E) = 1 - P(E') = 1 - \tfrac{3}{36} = \tfrac{33}{36}$$

EXAMPLE 2

Toss three coins. Find the probability of getting at least one head.

Solution The sample space S consists of all possible outcomes for tossing three coins. Using the Fundamental Principle of Counting we know that there are $(2)(2)(2) = 8$ outcomes, so $n(S) = 8$. Let E be the event of "getting at least one head"; then E' is the complementary event of "not getting at least one head." The set E' is easy to list—namely, $E' = \{(T, T, T)\}$. Thus, $n(E') = 1$ and $P(E') = \frac{1}{8}$. From this $P(E)$ can be determined to be

$$P(E) = 1 - P(E') = 1 - \tfrac{1}{8} = \tfrac{7}{8}$$

EXAMPLE 3

From a group of 5 women and 4 men a 2-person committee is chosen at random. Find the probability that the committee contains at least one woman.

Solution Let the sample space S be the set of all possible 2-person committees that can be chosen from 9 people. We know that there are $\dfrac{9 \cdot 8}{2} = 36$ such committees; thus, $n(S) = 36$. Let E be the event of "committee contains at least one woman"; then E' is the complementary event of "committee contains all men." Thus, E' consists of all 2-

man committees that can be chosen from 4 men. We know that there are $\dfrac{4 \cdot 3}{2} = 6$ such committees; thus, $n(E') = 6$. Therefore, $P(E') = \dfrac{n(E')}{n(S)} = \frac{6}{36}$, which determines $P(E)$ to be

$$P(E) = 1 - P(E') = \tfrac{36}{36} - \tfrac{6}{36} = \tfrac{30}{36}$$

REMARK We can use our knowledge of complements in problem solving by using this "backdoor" approach. For example, suppose we know that our classroom contains 50 seats. On a given day, it may be easier to count the number of empty seats and subtract from 50 to find the number of students in class rather than counting those present. In other words, you "count what you are not looking for" and subtract from a total to "find out what you are looking for."

When we are concerned with arranging a set of objects in a particular order, we are dealing with permutations. If we are using only two different objects, A and B, then there are two different arrangements or permutations: AB and BA. Taking three objects in a set and considering all possible arrangements gives us six permutations, ABC, ACB, BAC, BCA, CAB, CBA. We could also list all possible arrangements of four objects, finding that there are 24 permutations. Listing all the permutations becomes cumbersome when there are more than four things. The Fundamental Counting Principle is useful for calculating the number of permutations of five objects: $(5)(4)(3)(2)(1) = 120$ permutations. Recall from Chapter 4 that this product can be written another way, 5!, which is read "five factorial."

We can use a diagram to show the product of the different stages.

STAGE	1st		2nd		3rd		4th		5th		TOTAL
Number of choices	5	·	4	·	3	·	2	·	1	=	120

The number of permutations is the factorial of the number of objects in a set. Therefore, the number of permutations of n objects taken all together is $n!$. When the number of objects becomes quite large, a calculator will be very useful in finding permutations. The number of permutations of 9 is 9!: $(9)(8)(7)(6)(5)(4)(3)(2)(1) = 362{,}880$.

EXAMPLE

Using factorial notation, express the number of arrangements of the letters in the word MATH.

Solution Using a diagram we have the following.

STAGE	1st		2nd		3rd		4th		TOTAL
Number of choices	4	·	3	·	2	·	1	=	24

Because there are four letters that can be arranged in different order, we will use $4! = (4)(3)(2)(1) = 24$

We state our procedure for finding permutations as a property.

PROPERTY 11.3 **The number of permutations of n distinct objects, taken all together, is $n!$.**

EXAMPLE

How many different 6-digit license plates can be produced using the digits 3, 4, 5, 7, 8, 9 if no digits can be repeated? If a license plate is chosen at random, what is the probability it is the number 4 5 3 8 7 9?

Solution There are 6 digits that can be arranged in different order giving us $6!$ or 720 permutations. The probability that any one arrangement is chosen at random is $P(E) = \dfrac{n(E)}{n(S)} = \dfrac{1}{720}$.

We may have a situation where several of the objects being arranged are alike. If we made all the possible arrangements of the letters in the word TOP, we would have $3!$ or 6 (TOP, TPO, OTP, OPT, POT, PTO). However, if we used the word TOO, we would only have 3 possibilities, TOO, OOT, and OTO, because the two O's are the same.

Now consider the word TOOT to find all the different possible arrangements of letters. To help us keep track of the Os and Ts we will use subscripts (O_1, O_2 and T_1, T_2). The left-hand column that follows gives us six distinctly different arrangements of the letters of the word TOOT. When we use subscripts, there are 24 ways to arrange the letters (four for each of the six). Because there are four that are the same in each row, we can divide 24 by 4 to find our 6 distinctly different arrangements.

$T_1O_1O_2T_2$	$T_1O_2O_1T_2$	$T_2O_1O_2T_1$	$T_2O_2O_1T_1$
$T_1T_2O_1O_2$	$T_2T_1O_1O_2$	$T_1T_2O_2O_1$	$T_2T_1O_2O_1$
$T_1O_1T_2O_2$	$T_1O_2T_2O_1$	$T_2O_1T_1O_2$	$T_2O_2T_1O_1$
$O_1O_2T_1T_2$	$O_2O_1T_1T_2$	$O_1O_2T_2T_1$	$O_2O_1T_2T_1$
$O_1T_1O_2T_2$	$O_1T_2O_2T_1$	$O_2T_1O_1T_2$	$O_2T_2O_1T_1$
$O_1T_1T_2O_2$	$O_1T_2T_1O_2$	$O_2T_1T_2O_1$	$O_2T_2T_1O_1$

The 24 ways can be arrived at by finding the permutations of 4 objects (4!). However, because two Os and two Ts are the same, we need to divide the number of permutations (24) by the number of ways or permutations any letters are alike. For two Os we have 2! and for the two Ts we also have 2!. Therefore, to find all the distinctly different possible arrangement of letters in the word TOOT we have $\dfrac{4!}{2!\ 2!}$

EXAMPLE

Find the number of permutations of the letters in the word ILLINOIS.

Solution The word ILLINOIS has 8 letters with 3 Is and 2 Ls. The number of different permutations of ILLINOIS is $\dfrac{8!}{3!2!} = 3360.$

The preceding discussion and examples lead us to Property 11.4.

PROPERTY 11.4.   **The number of distinct permutations of n objects when p_1 are alike, p_2 are another kind that are alike, ... and p_k are yet another kind that are alike is**

$$\frac{n!}{p_1!p_2!\ldots p_k!}$$

Suppose we work with a set and we do not use all the elements. For example, use the digits 1, 2, 3, and 4 to form two-digit numbers. How many two-digit numbers having different digits could you form taking two of the digits at a time? A listing produces 12, 21, 13, 31, 14, 41, 23, 32, 24, 42, 34, 43. After choosing the first digit in four ways, there are three ways remaining to chose the second digit, $4 \cdot 3 = 12$. Therefore, we have 12 different two-digit numbers formed from the digits 1, 2, 3, and 4.

In a recent election there were four positions to be filled on a school board (president, vice president, secretary, and treasurer) from among six candidates. After one of the six people was elected for president, there were five people left for vice president, four for secretary, and three for treasurer. Using the Fundamental Counting Principle, we find that there were (6)(5)(4)(3) or 360 ways the four positions could be filled. The notation $_6P_4$ is used to denote the permutations of 6 objects taken 4 at a time. To evaluate $_6P_4$, we need to find 6! first and then divide that by the part of 6! that we are not counting, which is 2!. The computation for this is

$$_6P_4 = \frac{6!}{2!} = \frac{(6)(5)(4)(3)\cancel{(2)}\cancel{(1)}}{\cancel{(2)}\cancel{(1)}} = 360$$

EXAMPLE

Find the number of ways to seat 3 people in a row of 3 chairs selected from a group of 15 people.

Solution 1 A diagram illustrates use of the Fundamental Counting Principle.

STAGE	1st		2nd		3rd		TOTAL
Number of choices	15	·	14	·	13	=	2730

Solution 2 The solution requires using a permutation of 15 things taken 3 at a time. We need to find 15! first and then divide that by the part of 15! that we are not counting, which is 12!.

$$\frac{(15)(14)(13)(12)(11)(10)(9)(8)(7)(6)(5)(4)(3)(2)(1)}{(12)(11)(10)(9)(8)(7)(6)(5)(4)(3)(2)(1)}$$

Property 11.5 gives us the generalized procedure used to find the number of permutations of n different objects taken r at a time, denoted by $_nP_r$.

PROPERTY 11.5   **The number of permutations of r objects chosen from n objects where $0 \le r \le n$ is**

$$_nP_r = \frac{n!}{(n-r)!}$$

EXAMPLE

Consider 8 participants in a contest with four winning positions. In how many ways could there be four winning positions? (The positions are ordered from first to fourth).

Solution This situation requires a permutation, $_nP_r$, of 8 objects taken 4 at a time ($_8P_4$). Using Property 11.5 we have $\frac{8!}{(8-4)!} = \frac{8!}{4!} = 1680$.

Therefore, the four winners of the contest could be arranged in 1680 ways.

Let us examine Property 11.5 to see if it also works when $r = n$. For example, how many different ways may we arrange five elements of a set if we arrange them using all five at a time? We have already determined that the number of permutations of elements of a set is the factorial of the number of objects in the set. This means that $_nP_n = n!$. For five elements, using

$\dfrac{n!}{(n-r)!}$, we find $_5P_5 = \dfrac{5!}{(5-5)!} = \dfrac{5!}{0!}$. This leads us to define $0! = 1$ so that when $r = n$ occurs, we can still use $(n - r)!$

We have examined permutations, which are arrangements of objects where order is important. There are also times that we use arrangements when order is not important. These are called *selections* or *combinations*. Consider selecting two coins out of your coin purse that has a nickel, dime, and quarter. How many different sums are possible if we select two coins at a time? The selection of a quarter and a nickel would be the same as a nickel and a quarter because the sum in either case is 30 cents. The order of the coins is not important in this situation.

To examine arrangements where order may or may not be important, we will consider the permutations of 3 different coins, a penny (P), a nickel (N), and a dime (D), selected two at a time. We know the number of permutations is 3! or 6. These are PN (6 cents), PD (11 cents), NP (6 cents), ND (15 cents), DP (11 cents), and DN (15 cents). But as we can see, there are only 3 different sums or combinations. Therefore, there are three combinations of two coins chosen from three coins. This is written as $_3C_2 = 3$. The probability of picking 15 cents out of our coin purse is $\frac{1}{3}$ because one of our three selections, a nickel and a dime, will give us 15 cents.

Other situations in which selections or combinations are readily used involve choosing members of committees or participants in an event or project from a group of people. For instance, how many ways are there of selecting two people from a group of four? We will express this as $_4C_2$. Again, we could list them keeping in mind that selecting any two people in position 1 and 2 is the same as reversing their order of selection, as both situations produce a grouping with the same two people. Using A, B, C, D to represent the group of people from which we choose two, we have AB being the same as BA. The possible combinations are AB, AC, AD, BC, BD, CD.

Notice that if we selected all 4 people in the group as our participants, $_4C_4$, there would be only one combination of all four. The order of their selection is not important, only the fact that they were selected is important.

The difference between permutations and combinations can be illustrated by comparing permutations and combinations on a set of three elements. We will see that $_3P_3 = 3! = (3)(2)(1) = 6$ whereas $_3C_3 = 1$. Listing the permutations, we have $(1, 2, 3), (1, 3, 2), (2, 1, 3), (2, 3, 1), (3, 1, 2)$, and $(3, 2, 1)$. All six permutations, however, are associated with just one combination in which each one of the three elements is included in our set.

When the size of the group we are choosing is small, it will be relatively easy to determine the number of combinations. However, with larger numbers we need a method for calculating combinations. If we had a class of 20 and wanted to choose 3 participants at random to do a presentation, we are considering $_{20}C_3$. In developing a method for calculating, we can look at combinations as two stages. First we select our participants by using Property

11.5 to find the number of permutations $\dfrac{n!}{(n-r)!} = \dfrac{20!}{17!}$. We then divide by the number of ways in which each choice can be arranged (3!).

$$\frac{\dfrac{20!}{17!}}{3!} = \frac{(20)(19)(18)}{(3)(2)(1)} = 1140$$

EXAMPLE

Larry has 3 extra tickets to a concert. Six friends would like to go. How many ways could Larry pick 3 of his friends?

Solution First we find the permutations of the six friends taken three at a time $\dfrac{6!}{3!} = 120$. Then we divide by the number of ways each choice can be arranged $\dfrac{120}{3!} = 20$. Therefore, there are 20 ways Larry could pick 3 friends if order is not important.

The general form of combinations can be expressed as $_nC_r$, and the procedure we have used is generalized in Property 11.6.

PROPERTY 11.6   **The number of combinations of r objects chosen from n objects where $0 \leq r \leq n$ is**

$$_nC_r = \frac{_nP_r}{_rP_r} = \frac{\dfrac{n!}{(n-r)!}}{r!} = \frac{n!}{r!(n-r)!}$$

REMARK The notation $_nC_r$ is often written as $\dbinom{n}{r}$. Therefore, $\dbinom{5}{2}$ would mean the number of combinations of 2 objects chosen from a set of 5 or the combination of 5 objects taken 2 at a time.

EXAMPLE

Forming a committee of 7 from a faculty of 30 produces how many possible selections of committee members?

Solution We can apply Property 11.6 here because we have a combination problem $_nC_r = {_{30}}C_7 = \dfrac{30!}{7!23!} = \dfrac{(30)(29)(28)(27)(26)(25)(24)}{(7)(6)(5)(4)(3)(2)} = 2,035,800$. A calculator would be helpful to evaluate this number.

Mathematics consists of many patterns to enable us to organize our world. Let us look at Pascal's Triangle to explore the patterns and relate them to combinations. Earlier we worked with Pascal's Triangle in Problem 25 in Problem Set 11.2 when we looked at patterns as the results of tossing coins.

Observe Row 0 in the portion of Pascals Triangle shown in Figure 11.2. It gives combinations based on 0 objects. There is only one way to pick 0 objects—don't pick any. Row 1 looks at combinations of 1 object. The first 1 in Row 1 shows that there is only one way to pick 0 objects from 1 object—you don't pick any object or you have the empty set. The second 1 shows that there is only one way to pick 1 object from 1 object.

```
Row 0                        1
    1                     1   1
    2                   1   2   1
    3                 1   3   3   1
    4               1   4   6   4   1
    5             1   5  10  10   5   1
    6           1   6  15  20  15   6   1
    7         1   7  21  35  35  21   7   1
```
FIGURE 11.2

In Row 2 we see that there is 1 combination of 2 objects chosen 0 at a time $\{\ \}$, 2 combinations of 2 objects chosen 1 at a time $\{A\}$, $\{B\}$, and 1 combination of 2 objects chosen 2 at a time $\{A, B\}$.

In Figure 11.3, we see how Row 3 relates to combinations of three objects. Row 3 represents the combinations of 3 objects selected 0, 1, 2, and 3 at a time. If we have A, B, C as our objects, we see that taking them one at a time, (A, B, C), produces three combinations just as choosing them two at a time does (AB, AC, BC). Row 3 begins and ends with 1 (as do all the rows), illustrating that selecting 0 objects and all objects from a set result in 1 possible combination.

$$_3C_0 \quad {_3}C_1 \quad {_3}C_2 \quad {_3}C_3$$
$$1 \qquad 3 \qquad 3 \qquad 1$$

FIGURE 11.3

EXAMPLE

Use Pascal's Triangle to determine $_5C_3$ and $_5C_4$.

Solution Because $_5C_3$ and $_5C_4$ are combination situations that select from 5 objects, we can use Row 5 in Pascal's Triangle.

$$_5C_0 \quad _5C_1 \quad _5C_2 \quad _5C_3 \quad _5C_4 \quad _5C_5$$
$$1 \quad\quad 5 \quad\quad 10 \quad\quad 10 \quad\quad 5 \quad\quad 1$$

We see that the number of combinations of 5 objects 3 at a time is 10 and 5 objects 4 at a time is 5.

PROBLEM SET 11.3

For Problems 1–11, compute the probability by using $P(E) = \dfrac{n(E)}{n(S)}$. For some of these problems the property $P(E) + P(E') = 1$ will be helpful. Do not forget the Fundamental Principle of Counting.

1. Two dice are tossed. Find the probability of each of the following events:
   a. A sum of 6
   b. A sum greater than 2
   c. A sum less than 8
   d. A sum greater than 1

2. Three dice are tossed. Find the probability of each of the following events:
   a. A sum of 3
   b. A sum greater than 4
   c. A sum less than 17
   d. A sum greater than 18

3. Toss a pair of dice. What is the probability of not getting a double?

4. Four coins are tossed. Find the probability of each of the following events:
   a. Four heads
   b. Three heads and a tail
   c. At least one tail

5. Five coins are tossed. Find the probability of each of the following events:
   a. Five tails

    b. Four heads and a tail

    c. At least one tail

6. The probability that a certain horse will win the Kentucky Derby is $\frac{1}{20}$. What is the probability that it will not win the race?

7. One card is randomly drawn from a deck of 52 playing cards. What is the probability that it is not an ace?

8. Six coins are tossed. Find the probability of getting at least two heads.

9. A subset of two letters is chosen at random from the set $\{a, b, c, d, e, f, g, h, i\}$. Find the probability that the subset will contain at least one vowel.

10. From a group of 4 women and 3 men, a 2-person committee is chosen at random. Find the probability that the committee contains at least one woman.

11. From a group of 7 women and 5 men, a 2-person committee is chosen at random. Find the probability that the committee contains at least one man.

Problems 12–32 are counting problems. No probability questions are being asked.

12. In how many ways can 6 people be seated in a row of 6 seats?

13. In how many ways can Al, Bob, Carl, Don, Ed, and Fern be seated in a row of 6 seats if Al and Bob are to be seated side-by-side?

14. In how many ways can Amy, Bob, Cindy, Dan, and Elmer be seated in a row of five seats so that neither Amy nor Bob occupies an end seat?

15. Consider nine participants in a contest with three possible winning positions. In how many different ways could there be three winning positions?

16. In planning next semester's schedule, Jan needs to choose four courses, one each from 3 English courses, 2 math courses, 3 science courses, and 4 social science courses. How many different ways are possible for planning next semester's schedule?

17. How many numbers greater than 400, for which no number contains repeated digits, can be formed by choosing from the digits 2, 3, 4, and 5?

18. How many numbers greater than 5000, for which no number contains repeated digits, can be formed by choosing from the digits 1, 2, 3, 4, 5, and 6?

19. In how many ways can 12 people line up to pick up tickets for the Madrigal Dinner production?

20. At the Delta Deli you can order a sandwich with choices from nine different toppings—mustard, relish, cheese, sprouts, mushrooms, horseradish, pickle, lettuce, tomato. If a regular sandwich comes with four toppings, how many different combinations of four toppings are available as choices?

21. In how many ways can a sum less than 10 be obtained when tossing a pair of dice?

22. In how many ways can a sum greater than 5 be obtained when tossing a pair of dice?

23. In how many ways can a sum greater than 4 be obtained when tossing three dice?

24. Find the number of different arrangements of the letters in the following words:
   a. OHIO
   b. TENNESSEE
   c. ALABAMA
   d. STATISTICS

25. At commencement, seven students will be recognized as outstanding students. In the selection process, it was found that 52 students qualified for such awards. In how many different ways could the seven outstanding students be chosen?

26. Jay tends to be forgetful and cannot remember how to open his locker. Each of the three dials on his lock has the digits 0 through 9. How many different ways would Jay have to try to be assured that the three digits chosen will open the lock?

27. How many 2-person committees can be formed from a group of 10 people?

28. How many 2-element subsets can be formed from a set of 12 elements?

29. How many 2-person committees that do not include Al can be formed from the eight people Al, Bob, Carl, Dawn, Eve, Fern, George, and Hazel?

30. A baseball league consists of 6 teams. Each team is to play the other teams 9 games during the season. How many games will be necessary to complete the entire league schedule?

31. In how many ways can Al, Bob, Carl, Don, Ed, and Fern be seated in a row of six seats if Al and Bob are not to be seated side-by-side? (*Hint:* Al and Bob will either be seated side-by-side or not seated side-by-side).

32. The following people belong to a club and two bring refreshments each week: Bob, Ted, Carol, Alice, Ann.

      a. How many possible pairs of members are there for bringing refreshments?

      b. If Don decides to join the club, how many pairs can be made if 6 people are in the club?

33. On a commuter flight out of Bomcam, there are 5 seats left, but 7 people are scheduled for the flight.

      a. How many ways could the airline pick 5 people to seat?

      b. How many ways could the airline pick 2 people to leave off the flight?

      c. How does $_7C_5$ compare to $_7C_2$?

      d. Would the same thing be true if there are only four seats available?

34. a. Using a set of four objects, (A, B, C, D), list the possible combinations that correspond to the numbers in Pascal's Triangle.

      b. Look at Row 6: 1, 6, 15, 20, 15, 6, 1. Describe what each of the numbers represents regarding combinations.

      c. Continue Pascal's Triangle with Rows 8 and 9, indicating how the numbers relate to combinations of 8 and 9 objects.

      d. Why are some numbers the same in each row?

In Problems 35–44 use $P(E) = \dfrac{n(E)}{n(S)}$ to determine the requested probabilities. Assume that the outcomes are equally likely.

35. Amy, Bill, Cindy, and Don are randomly seated in a row of 4 seats. Find the probability that Amy and Bill will be seated side-by-side.

36. Two dice are tossed. Find the probability of getting a sum less than 9.

37. Two dice are tossed. Find the probability of getting a sum greater than 5.

38. Three dice are tossed. Find the probability of getting a sum greater than 5.

39. Three dice are tossed. Find the probability of getting a sum less than 17.

40. Amy, Bill, Chad, Dee, and Eric are randomly seated in a row of five seats. Find the probability that Amy and Bill will not be seated side-by-side.

41. A committee of 2 is to be chosen at random from the six people Amy, Beth, Chad, Dawn, Eric, and Francis. Find the probability that Beth is on the committee.

42. A committee of 2 is to be chosen at random from the eight people Ann, Bob, Cindy, Dee, Eleanor, Faye, Gladys, and Herschel. Find the probability that neither Ann nor Bob is on the committee.

43. A subset of 2 letters is chosen at random from the set {a, b, c, d, e, f, g, h, i, j, k}. Find the probability that the letter k is in the subset.

44. A subset of 2 letters is chosen at random from the set {a, b, c, d, e, f, g, h, i, j}. Find the probability that the subset contains two vowels.

Pedagogical Problems and Activities

45. Some probability results may seem not to agree with our intuition. For example, consider the following table.

Number of People	Probability That at Least Two of Them Have the Same Birthday
5	0.03
10	0.12
15	0.25
20	0.41
25	0.57
30	0.71
40	0.89
60	0.99

Note that for a group of 25 people, the probability is better than $\frac{1}{2}$ that at least two of them will have the same birthday. Having the same birthday means "same month and day of the month." Try this experiment with several groups of different sizes.

46. Simulate the following problem concretely. Using cards with letters R, O, O, T; list all possible arrangements of the letters in the word ROOT.

47. Put a blue, red, and yellow card behind a barrier on the table. Have a partner try to guess the order. Record the number of guesses needed. Do this several times.

    a. How many different orders are possible? List these with the help of the cards.

    b. How many wrong ways could you guess?

    c. How many right ways could you guess?

11.4 ADDITION AND MULTIPLICATION OF PROBABILITIES WITH INDEPENDENT AND DEPENDENT EVENTS

The successive events that we have considered thus far have had one common element. The outcome of one event did not affect the outcome of the successive event. When we tossed coins, the outcome for the first coin (H or T) was independent or not affected by the outcome of the toss of the second coin. The compound events to which we have applied the Fundamental Counting Principle all have been independent events.

Sometimes the outcome of one event affects successive events. We call situations like these *dependent events*. Suppose we have 5 notebooks on a shelf—4 red and 1 blue. The probability that we would randomly pick a red one is $\frac{4}{5}$. If we do not replace it, we now have 3 red and 1 blue notebooks and our probability for picking a red one becomes $\frac{3}{4}$ because our sample space has changed. The probability for the second event was dependent on the outcome of the first event.

Tree diagrams provide a convenient way of analyzing probability problems whether *drawing with replacement* (independent events) or *drawing without replacement* (dependent events). Consider the following experiment. Suppose that one marble is randomly drawn from a bag containing 2 red and 3 white marbles. Because there are 5 marbles of which 2 are red, the probability of drawing a red marble is $\frac{2}{5}$. Likewise, there are 3 white marbles; so the probability of drawing a white marble is $\frac{3}{5}$. These probabilities can be recorded on a tree diagram as in Figure 11.4.

FIGURE 11.4

Consider the following experiment. Suppose that we again have a bag containing 2 red and 3 white marbles. Furthermore, suppose that we draw one marble at random and record its color. The marble is then *replaced* in the bag (this is called "drawing *with* replacement") and a second marble is drawn and its color recorded. The tree diagram in Figure 11.5 shows this two-step experiment of independent events. Each path along the tree corresponds to a possible outcome of this experiment. For example, the *RW* path

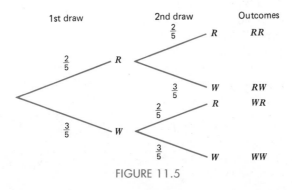

FIGURE 11.5

means that we obtain a red marble on the first draw and a white marble on the second draw.

Probabilities for each of the outcomes of the two-step experiment can be calculated from the tree diagram. Let us analyze the RW outcome. (We will use $P(RW)$ to symbolize the probability of the RW outcome.)

$P(RW)$: The probability of drawing a red marble on the first draw is $\frac{2}{5}$, and the probability of drawing a white marble on the second draw is $\frac{3}{5}$. This means that we expect to draw a red marble on the first draw $\frac{2}{5}$ of the time and then to draw a white marble on the second draw $\frac{3}{5}$ *of the times that we obtained a red marble on the first draw.* Thus, $P(RW) = \frac{2}{5}$ of $\frac{3}{5} = \frac{2}{5} \cdot \frac{3}{5} = \frac{6}{25}$.

In other words, the probability for each outcome of the two-step experiment can be found from the tree diagram by following the paths to each of the outcomes and by *multiplying the probabilities along the paths.* Thus, for the other three outcomes in Figure 11.5 we obtain

$$P(RR) = \frac{2}{5} \cdot \frac{2}{5} = \frac{4}{25}$$
$$P(WR) = \frac{3}{5} \cdot \frac{2}{5} = \frac{6}{25}$$
$$P(WW) = \frac{3}{5} \cdot \frac{3}{5} = \frac{9}{25}$$

Notice that

$$P(RR) + P(RW) + P(WR) + P(WW) = \frac{4}{25} + \frac{6}{25} + \frac{6}{25} + \frac{9}{25} = 1$$

which is as it should be.

From the tree diagram in Figure 11.5 we can also answer some other probability questions relative to this experiment. For example, suppose that we want to know the probability of drawing one red marble and one white marble. The two outcomes RW and WR both contain one red and one white marble. Because $P(RW) = \frac{6}{25}$ and $P(WR) = \frac{6}{25}$, then the probability of RW *or* WR occurring is the *sum* of the probabilities. Thus, $P(RW \text{ or } WR) = \frac{6}{25} + \frac{6}{25} = \frac{12}{25}$.

Tree diagrams also provide a convenient way of analyzing "drawing *without* replacement" situations. For example, suppose that we have a bag containing 5 red and 2 white marbles. Furthermore, suppose that we randomly draw one marble from the bag and record its color. Then, *without replacing* the marble, we draw another marble and record its color. The tree diagram in Figure 11.6 shows this two-step experiment of dependent events. Notice that the denominators of the probabilities on the second draw are all 6. Since after the first draw the marble is *not* replaced, there are only 6 marbles remaining for the second draw.

Again we can calculate probabilities for the various outcomes from the tree diagram as we did before.

$$P(RR) = \frac{5}{7} \cdot \frac{4}{6} = \frac{20}{42}$$
$$P(RW) = \frac{5}{7} \cdot \frac{2}{6} = \frac{10}{42}$$
$$P(WR) = \frac{2}{7} \cdot \frac{5}{6} = \frac{10}{42}$$
$$P(WW) = \frac{2}{7} \cdot \frac{1}{6} = \frac{2}{42}$$

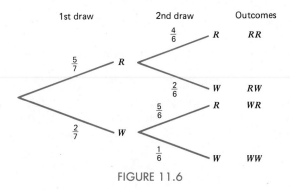

FIGURE 11.6

Notice again that

$$P(RR) + P(RW) + P(WR) + P(WW) = \tfrac{20}{42} + \tfrac{10}{42} + \tfrac{10}{42} + \tfrac{2}{42} = \tfrac{42}{42} = 1$$

As discussed earlier in this chapter, we can add the probabilities of events if outcomes are mutually exclusive. If we roll a die, what is the probability of a 3 or a 5 turning up? Because the two events are mutually exclusive (the intersection of the two sets is empty), we can add the two probabilities to find the combined probability. $P(3) = \tfrac{1}{6}$ and $P(5) = \tfrac{1}{6}$:

$$P(3 \text{ or } 5) = \tfrac{1}{6} + \tfrac{1}{6} = \tfrac{2}{6}$$

Using the spinner in Figure 11.7 in which R, B, and Y represent the colors red, blue, and yellow; we will consider some situations where we do not have mutually exclusive events. The possible numbers that will appear on the spinner are (1, 2, 3, 4, 5, 6). The possible colors are (R, R, B, B, Y, Y). The outcomes on the spinner can be listed as a set of ordered pairs (R, 4), (R, 1), (B, 2), (B, 3), (Y, 5), (Y, 6). We can see that there are 3 even possibilities and 2 red possibilities when we spin the spinner. The $P(\text{Even}) = \tfrac{3}{6}$ and the $P(\text{Red}) = \tfrac{2}{6}$ because we have a sample space of 6 outcomes.

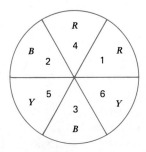

FIGURE 11.7

EXAMPLE 1

What is the probability of spinning both a red and an even outcome?

Solution The red outcomes give us a set of 2 ordered pairs $\{(R, 4), (R, 1)\}$ whereas the even outcomes give us $\{(R, 4), (B, 2), (Y, 6)\}$. To find the outcomes that are both red and even, we need the intersection of the two sets $R \cap E = (R, 4)$. Therefore, the $P(R \cap E) = \frac{1}{6}$.

We can use a Venn diagram to illustrate our outcomes and help us see the intersection of the two sets more easily.

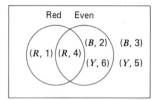

The previous example illustrates what we refer to as conditional probability. This means that a second event B occurs under the condition or after an event A has occurred. This is often written as $P(B$ given $A)$. In Example 1, event A was spinning a red and event B was an even outcome. Therefore, we wanted the probability that we could spin an even number under the condition that it was red.

Property 11.7 generalizes a procedure for determining conditional probability.

PROPERTY 11.7   For any two events A and B, $P(A \cap B) = P(A) \times P(B$ given $A)$.

Let us return to Example 1 and use Property 11.7. The $P(A)$, which is spinning a red, is $\frac{2}{6}$ whereas the probability of spinning an even number given a red has occurred is $\frac{1}{2}$ (there are two red outcomes and one of them is even). Therefore, Property 11.7 gives us $P(R \cap E) = P(R) \times P(E$ given $R) = \frac{2}{6} \times \frac{1}{2} = \frac{1}{6}$.

EXAMPLE 2

What is the probability of spinning a red or an even?

Solution

Looking back to the listing of outcomes for red and for even, we want all those that are red and all those that are even. $P(R) + P(E) = \frac{2}{6} + \frac{3}{6} = \frac{5}{6}$. However, looking at the spinner and the Venn diagram, we see that there are only 4 out of the 6 sections that have red or even possibilities. Care must be taken to count each outcome only once, so we must subtract any outcomes that belong in both sets. Red or even means the outcome is red or it is even, or it is both red and even, therefore

$$P(R) \text{ or } P(E) = P(R \cup E) = P(R) + P(E) - P(R \cap E)$$
$$= \tfrac{2}{6} + \tfrac{3}{6} - \tfrac{1}{6} = \tfrac{4}{6}$$

We can make a general statement about adding probabilities that holds true whether or not the events are mutually exclusive.

PROPERTY 11.8   **For any two events A and B, $P(A \cup B) = P(A) + P(B) - P(A \cap B)$.**

PROBLEM SET 11.4

For Problems 1–6 use tree diagrams to help analyze the probability situations.

1. A bag contains 3 red and 2 white marbles. One marble is drawn and its color recorded. The marble is then replaced in the bag and a second marble is drawn and its color recorded. Find the probability of each of the following:
   a. The first marble drawn is red, and the second marble drawn is white.
   b. The first marble drawn is white, and the second marble drawn is red.
   c. Both marbles drawn are white.
   d. At least one marble drawn is red.
   e. One red and one white marble are drawn.

2. A bag contains 5 blue and 6 gold marbles. Two marbles are drawn in succession, without replacement. Find the probability of each of the following:
   a. Both marbles drawn are blue.
   b. One marble drawn is blue, and the other is gold.
   c. At least one marble drawn is gold.
   d. Both marbles drawn are gold.

3. A bag contains 1 red and 2 white marbles. Two marbles are drawn in succession, without replacement. Find the probability of each of the following:
   a. One marble drawn is red, and one is white.
   b. Both marbles drawn are white.
   c. Both marbles drawn are red.

4. A bag contains 5 red and 12 white marbles. Two marbles are drawn in succession without replacement. Find the probability of each of the following:

a. Both marbles drawn are red.

b. Both marbles drawn are white.

c. One red and one white marble are drawn.

d. At least one marble drawn is red.

5. Two boxes with red and white marbles are shown here. A marble is drawn at random from Box 1, and then a marble is drawn from Box 2 and the colors recorded in order. Find the probability of each of the following.

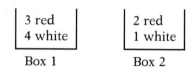

3 red	2 red
4 white	1 white
Box 1	Box 2

a. Both marbles drawn are white.

b. Both marbles drawn are red.

c. One red and one white marble are drawn.

6. Three boxes containing red and white marbles are shown here. Randomly draw a marble from Box 1 and put it in Box 2. Then draw a marble from Box 2 and put it in Box 3. Then draw a marble from Box 3. What is the probability that the last marble drawn, from Box 3, is red? What is the probability that it is white?

2 red	3 red	
2 white	1 white	3 white
Box 1	Box 2	Box 3

7. Answer the following questions assuming you had three dice in a container, one red, one white, and one green. Without looking, take one and roll it.

a. List the possible outcomes as ordered pairs using R for red, W for white, and G for green.

b. $P(R) =$

c. $P(W) =$

d. $P(G) =$

e. $P(\text{Even}) =$

f. $P(\text{Odd}) =$

g. $P(\text{White and Even}) =$

h. $P(\text{White or Even}) =$

8. Consider this spinner with 12 divisions:

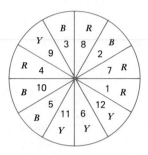

    a. List the possible numbers.
    b. List the possible colors.
    c. List the outcomes as a set of ordered pairs.

9. Find the following probabilities using the information in Problem 8.
    a. $P(Y$ or even$)$
    b. $P(B$ or prime$)$
    c. $P($red or factor of 12$)$
    d. $P(R)$
    e. $P($even$)$
    f. $P(R$ and even$)$
    g. $P(R$ or even$)$
    h. $P($red or prime$)$
    i. $P($multiple of 5 or blue$)$
    j. $P($multiple of 3 or even$)$
    k. $P($factor of 36 and prime$)$

Pedagogical Problems and Activities

10. Write the numbers given on slips of paper that are of the designated colors: 8 white slips of paper numbered 1–8, 7 yellow slips numbered 9–15, and 5 green slips numbered 16–20. Place these slips of paper in an envelope or paper bag. Answer the following questions about the probability of drawing slips of paper at random from the paper bag.
    a. What is the probability of drawing a yellow slip of paper?
    b. What is the probability of drawing an even-numbered slip of paper?
    c. $P($Yellow and Even$)$?
    d. $P($Green and numbered greater than 6$)$?
    e. $P($White and Odd$)$?
    f. $P($Green and Even$)$?

g. *P*(Green or Odd)?

h. *P*(Green or greater than 12)?

i. *P*(Even or White)?

j. *P*(Green or Even)?

11. Simulate the following classroom situation with the use of colored blocks or unifix cubes. Use red, green, and yellow blocks to represent the students in the classroom that are wearing clothing with those colors. In a given classroom, there are 17 students wearing red clothing, 12 students wearing green clothing, 15 students wearing yellow clothing, 8 students wearing both red and yellow, 4 students wearing green and yellow, 6 students wearing red and green, and 4 students that are wearing all three colors.

Use a large sheet of paper or loops of yarn to make a Venn diagram for placing the blocks into the three sets.

a. Determine the total number of students that will be in the sample space.

b. If a student walked out of the classroom, what would be the following probabilities?

(i) The student is wearing red

(ii) The student is wearing green

(iii) The student is wearing yellow

(iv) If the student is wearing red, then the student is wearing green

(v) If the student is wearing red, then the student is wearing yellow

(vi) If the student is wearing green, then the student is wearing yellow

(vii) If the student is wearing red, then the student is wearing yellow and green

11.5 ODDS AND MATHEMATICAL EXPECTATION

The term "odds" is frequently used in everyday conversation to express a probability statement. For example, we hear such statements as "The odds against the Cubs winning the pennant are 200 to 1," or "The odds in favor of Blue Streak winning the fifth race are 3 to 1." Such statements are often misinterpreted because of the term "odds." Thus, we need to be certain of the exact meaning of probability statements that use the "odds" vocabulary.

Let us consider the simple experiment of rolling a die. The following probability statements can be made.

1. The probability of getting a four is $\frac{1}{6}$.

2. The probability of not getting a four is $\frac{5}{6}$.

3. The *odds in favor* of getting a four are 1 to 5.

4. The *odds against* getting a four are 5 to 1.

Statement 1 indicates that there is one favorable outcome (getting a four) out of six possible outcomes when rolling a die. Statement 2 indicates that there are five unfavorable outcomes (ways of not getting a four) out of six possible outcomes. Statement 3 compares the number of favorable outcomes to the number of unfavorable outcomes. Statement 4 compares the number of unfavorable outcomes to the number of favorable outcomes.

"Odds in favor" and "odds against" for equally likely outcomes can be defined as follows:

Odds in favor = ratio of number of favorable outcomes to number of unfavorable outcomes

Odds against = ratio of number of unfavorable outcomes to number of favorable outcomes

Notice that when we compare the odds in favor of getting a four and the odds against getting a four, in each case, we compared the numerators of each probability by means of a ratio. The order in which the numerator occurs in each ratio is important in determining odds. The probability of getting a four is $\frac{1}{6}$, and the probability of not getting a four is $\frac{5}{6}$: therefore, odds in favor compares the numerator in $\frac{1}{6}$ with the numerator in $\frac{5}{6}$ and we have odds in favor to be 1 to 5.

> **REMARK** The odds in favor of rolling a four with one roll of a die are usually stated as 1 to 5 instead of $\frac{1}{5}$. The odds against rolling a four are stated as 5 to 1.

You may have noticed the use of complementary events in describing favorable and unfavorable events. Therefore, probabilities that are complementary, with a sum of one, form the basis of determining odds. If we know the probability in favor of getting a four, we can easily determine the probability of not getting a four by $1 - P(E)$.

The process of formulating odds for a particular problem simply involves determining the number of favorable and unfavorable outcomes. Consider the following examples.

EXAMPLE 1

What are the odds in favor of getting two heads with a toss of two coins?

Solution   There is 1 favorable outcome—namely, (H, H). The unfavorable outcomes can be listed and counted or, because there are 4 possible outcomes (both favorable and unfavorable), the number of unfavorable outcomes is $4 - 1 = 3$. Therefore, the *odds in favor* of getting two heads are 1 to 3.

EXAMPLE 2

What are the odds against getting 2 heads and 1 tail with a toss of three coins?

Solution There are 3 favorable outcomes—namely, (H, H, T), (H, T, H), and (T, H, H). Using the Fundamental Principle of Counting we can determine that there are $(2)(2)(2) = 8$ possible outcomes. This leaves $8 - 3 = 5$ unfavorable outcomes. Thus, the *odds against* getting 2 heads and 1 tail are 5 to 3.

EXAMPLE 3

What are the odds against rolling a double with a pair of dice?

Solution There are 6 favorable outcomes—namely, $(1, 1)$, $(2, 2)$, $(3, 3)$, $(4, 4)$, $(5, 5)$ and $(6, 6)$. Because there are $(6)(6) = 36$ possible outcomes, there are $36 - 6 = 30$ unfavorable outcomes. Therefore, the *odds against* rolling a double are 30 to 6, which can be expressed as 5 to 1.

Because probability statements can be made in terms of $\dfrac{n(E)}{n(S)}$ and in terms of "odds," we need to be able to change from one type of statement to the other. The following examples illustrate this process.

EXAMPLE 4

Suppose that $P(E) = \frac{4}{7}$ for some event E. What are the odds against E happening?

Solution The statement $P(E) = \frac{4}{7}$ indicates 4 favorable outcomes and a total of 7 possible outcomes. Therefore, there are $7 - 4 = 3$ unfavorable outcomes and the *odds against* E happening are 3 to 4.

EXAMPLE 5

Suppose that the odds against the Cubs winning the pennant are stated as 50 to 1. What is the probability of the Cubs winning the pennant?

Solution The "odds against" statement of 50 to 1 means that there are 50 unfavorable outcomes and 1 favorable; thus, there is a total of 51 outcomes. The probability of the Cubs winning can then be stated as $\frac{1}{51}$.

Another important concept related to probability is that of *mathematical expectation*, sometimes called *expected value*. Suppose that we toss a coin 500 times. Certainly we would expect to get approximately 250 heads. In other words, because the probability of getting a head with one toss of a coin is $\frac{1}{2}$, then in 500 tosses we should get approximately $500(\frac{1}{2}) = 250$ heads.

The word "approximately" when used with mathematical expectation conveys a key idea. As we all know, it is possible to toss a coin several times and get all tails. However, with a large number of tosses, things should "average out" so that we get about an equal number of heads and tails. In other words, mathematical expectation predicts an average result of an experiment when it is repeated many times, but expectation cannot be used to predict the outcome of a single experiment.

The next two examples further illustrate this idea of expected value.

EXAMPLE 1

If we toss a pair of dice 360 times, approximately how many times should we expect to get a sum of 6?

Solution The probability of getting a sum of 6 with one toss of a pair of dice is $\frac{5}{36}$. Therefore, if a pair of dice is tossed 360 times, we should expect to get a sum of 6 approximately $360(\frac{5}{36}) = 50$ times.

EXAMPLE 2

If 3 coins are tossed 800 times approximately how many times should we expect to get 2 heads and 1 tail?

Solution The probability of getting 2 heads and 1 tail with one toss of three coins is $\frac{3}{8}$. Therefore, if 3 coins are tossed 800 times, we should expect to get 2 heads and 1 tail approximately $800(\frac{3}{8}) = 300$ times.

Definition 11.2 For a single event, mathematical expectation is the product of the probability that an event will occur and the amount to be received on such occurrence.

Mathematical expectation is used with probability situations dealing with "fairness of games." Suppose you buy one ticket in a lottery for which 1000 tickets are sold. Three prizes are awarded, one of $500, one of $300, and one of $100. Because you bought 1 ticket, your probability of winning $500 is

$\frac{1}{1000}$, of winning \$300 is $\frac{1}{1000}$, and of winning \$100 is $\frac{1}{1000}$. Multiplying each of these probabilities times the corresponding prize money and adding the results yields your mathematical expectation—let us call it M.

$$M = \$500 \left(\frac{1}{1000} \right) + \$300 \left(\frac{1}{1000} \right) + \$100 \left(\frac{1}{1000} \right)$$
$$= \$0.50 \qquad\quad + \$0.30 \qquad\quad + \$0.10$$
$$= \$0.90$$

So, if you pay more than \$0.90 for a ticket it is not a *fair game* from your viewpoint.

Mathematically, a game is considered fair if the net winnings are \$0. In other words, if the expected value of the game equals the price of playing the game, then it is a *fair game*.

EXAMPLE

A "wheel of fortune" is divided into four colors, red, white, blue, and yellow. The probabilities of the spinner landing on each of the colors and the money you receive are given by the table. The price for spinning the wheel is \$1.50. Is it a fair game?

Color	Probability	Money You Receive
Red	$\frac{4}{10}$	\$0.50
White	$\frac{3}{10}$	\$1.00
Blue	$\frac{2}{10}$	\$2.00
Yellow	$\frac{1}{10}$	\$5.00

Solution Multiplying each probability by the corresponding "money you receive" and adding these results yields your mathematical expectation. Thus,

$$M = \frac{4}{10}(0.50) + \frac{3}{10}(1) + \frac{2}{10}(2) + \frac{1}{10}(5)$$
$$= 0.20 + 0.30 + 0.40 + 0.50$$
$$= \$1.40$$

Because your expected value is \$1.40, but you have to pay \$1.50 for a ticket, it is not a fair game. This does not mean the game is necessarily a crooked game. To be a fair game, the expected value minus the price of playing the game should equal zero.

PROPERTY 11.9 When an event has several possible outcomes with amounts of m_1, m_2, m_3 ... m_n that have probabilities of p_1, p_2, p_2, ... p_n, respectively, then the mathematical expectation, E, is given by

$$E = m_1 \cdot p_1 + m_2 \cdot p_2 + m_3 \cdot p_3 \ldots + m_n \cdot p_n$$

Probabilistic reasoning is used by business people, economists, and medical researchers to consider the relationship between a probability and the payoff or mathematical expectation of an experiment. They must be aware, however, of the possible deficiencies in the values caused by factors in the experiment such as lack of control over outside influences or lack of adequate information. These probabilities are not as accurate as those in situations where events are equally likely. However, decisions are made based on probabilities and whether the payoff will exceed the cost.

We conclude this chapter with a few general remarks about probability. Let us begin once again by considering a very simple "coin-tossing" experiment. Suppose that two coins are tossed and we want the probability of getting two heads. The sample space is $S = \{(H, H), (H, T), (T, H), (T, T)\}$, where $n(S) = 4$. The event space is $E = \{(H, H)\}$, where $n(E) = 1$. Thus, we say that the probability of the event "getting two heads" occurring is given by

$$P(E) = \frac{n(E)}{n(S)} = \frac{1}{4}$$

We are assuming that each of the possible outcomes for tossing two coins is *equally likely* to occur. All the problems of the previous sections dealing with coin tossing, rolling of dice, drawing of cards, and so on have been worked based on this "equally likely" condition. However, there are many probability situations, even some very simple ones, for which the "equally likely" condition does not apply.

Consider the spinner in Figure 11.8. Suppose we spin the hand and ask for the probability that it lands on white. The sample space for this experiment is $S = \{\text{white, red}\}$, where $n(S) = 2$. However, as can be seen from Figure 11.8, these two possible outcomes are not equally likely to occur. Therefore, it would not be reasonable to claim that the probability of "landing on white" is $\frac{1}{2}$.

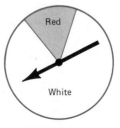

FIGURE 11.8

For such situations, something must be done to determine a reasonable probability assignment for each of the possible outcomes. In Figure 11.8, the red part of the circular region has been constructed to represent $\frac{1}{6}$ of the entire region. You could have determined this by measuring the central angle and finding it to be 60°. Thus, it would be reasonable to assign a probability of $\frac{1}{6}$ to the event of "landing on red" and $\frac{5}{6}$ to the event of "landing on white."

Now let us consider the experiment of "tossing a thumbtack" on a hard surface. Because it is a hard surface, so that the point of the tack cannot stick in the surface, there are only two possible outcomes. The thumbtack can land on its head ($\perp$) or on its side ($\diagdown$). Thus, the sample space is S = {head, side}, where $n(S)$ = 2; but again the equally likely condition may not apply. In other words, there is nothing about the physical makeup of a thumbtack to suggest how the tack will fall. We could make a guess; for example, we might guess that out of every 10 tosses it will land on its head 6 times. However, this is strictly a guess. What we need to do is gather some "empirical evidence." In other words, we need to toss the thumbtack a large number of times and record the results. Suppose that we toss it 5000 times and it lands on its head 3000 times and on its side 2000 times. Based on these results, it would be reasonable to assign a probability of $\frac{3}{5}$ to the event "land on head" and a probability of $\frac{2}{5}$ to the event "land on side." (The 3000 and 2000 figures are "made-up" and not the actual results of tossing a thumbtack.)

Probability is often classified as either (1) *empirical* or *experimental probability* or (2) *theoretical* or *a priori probability*. "A priori" refers to the idea of making probability assignments independent of any empirical evidence. For example, consider the experiment of rolling a die. We have used a sample space of S = {1, 2, 3, 4, 5, 6} with the assumption that each of the possible outcomes is *equally likely* to occur. This assumption is suggested by the physical makeup of a die without any support from empirical evidence.

Empirical or experimental probability refers to the idea of using empirical evidence to make the probability assignments. The "thumbtack problem" is a good example of empirical probability. The physical makeup of a thumbtack does not necessarily suggest an assumption of "equally likely" outcomes. Therefore as we suggested, one would need to gather empirical evidence (toss the tack a large number of times) first and then make the probability assignments.

We have concentrated more heavily on theoretical probability throughout this chapter, but in working with children, experiments should be performed to observe the outcomes. Children should realize that these observed probabilities may not exactly match with the theoretical probabilities. When we cannot determine theoretical probabilities, we can conduct experiments from which the frequency of the desired event can be determined. Empirical evidence should be gathered to establish probabilities for events about which we have little information. We can then make predictions based on probabilities that we formulate. Many such situations from which we can gather data exist in real life events. The next chapter on Statistics will look at statistical ideas to help us understand the meaning of data that have been gathered through experiments or that are presented to us through the media.

PROBLEM SET 11.5

1. Suppose the probability of an event occurring is $\frac{5}{9}$. What are the odds in favor of the event? What are the odds against the event?

2. The odds against Contrary Mary in the sixth race are 10 to 1. What is the probability of Contrary Mary winning the sixth race?

3. If the odds against an event occurring are 5 to 2, find the probability that the event will occur.

4. The weather bureau indicates that a certain area has a 20% probability for a tornado, which means that 80 times out of 100 a tornado would not happen. What are the odds in favor of a tornado happening?

5. Find the following probabilities.
   a. The odds in favor of winning a race are 7:4. What is the probability of winning?
   b. A candidate's chances of losing an election are 3 to 12. What is the probability that he will be defeated?
   c. If the chances for rain tomorrow are 1 to 4, what is the probability for rain tomorrow?

6. Suppose one card is drawn from a deck of 52 playing cards.
   a. Find the odds against drawing a heart.
   b. Find the odds against drawing a king.
   c. Find the odds in favor of drawing a red card.
   d. Find the odds in favor of drawing an ace.
   e. Find the odds against drawing an ace or a king.

7. Roll a pair of dice.
   a. Find the odds in favor of getting a sum of 12.
   b. Find the odds in favor of getting a sum less than 5.
   c. Find the odds against getting a sum of 8.
   d. Find the odds against getting a sum greater than 10.

8. For each of the following, find the odds against and the odds in favor of the event occurring:
   a. Drawing a queen with one draw from a deck of 52 playing cards
   b. Rolling a sum of 5 with a single roll of a pair of dice
   c. Getting 3 heads and 1 tail with one toss of four coins

    d. Rolling a pair of sixes with a single roll of a pair of dice

    e. Getting a head with one toss of a penny

9. a. Three coins are tossed. What are the odds against getting 3 heads?

    b. Four coins are tossed. What are the odds in favor of getting 4 tails?

10. A die is tossed 240 times. How many times would you expect to get a six?

11. Two dice are tossed 360 times. How many times would you expect to get a sum of 9?

12. Two dice are tossed 480 times. How many times would you expect to get a sum greater than 10?

13. Three dice are tossed 216 times. How many times would you expect to get a sum of 4?

14. Four coins are tossed 80 times. How many times would you expect to get 1 head and 3 tails?

15. Five coins are tossed 320 times. How many times would you expect to get 5 heads?

16. Suppose you buy one ticket in a lottery for which 5000 tickets are sold. Three prizes are awarded, one for $1000, one for $500, and one for $100. What is your mathematical expectation for winning?

17. Is $1 a fair price to pay for a ticket at a raffle for which 100 tickets are to be sold and one prize of $100 is offered?

18. Your friend challenges you with the following game. You are to roll a pair of dice and he will give you $5 if you roll a sum of 2 or 12, $2 if you roll a sum of 3 or 11, $1 if you roll a sum of 4 or 10; otherwise, you are to pay him $1. Should you play the game?

19. Suppose a player rolls one die and receives $1 for a one, $2 for a two, $3 for a three, and so on. What is the mathematical expectation?

20. Suppose a player rolls two dice and receives $2 for a sum of two, $3 for a sum of three, $4 for a sum of four, and so on up to $12 for a sum of 12. What is the mathematical expectation?

21. Suppose a person tosses two coins and wins $5 if either 2 heads or 2 tails come up, but pays $8 if 1 head and 1 tail come up. Is it a fair game?

Pedagogical Problems and Activities

22. Perhaps you and a friend (or friends) could do the following experiments:

    a. Toss a coin 500 times and record the number of heads you obtain. Does your result come close to the expected value for this experiment?

b. Toss two coins 200 times and record the number of times you get two heads. Does your result come close to the expected value?

c. Toss three coins 160 times and record the number of times you get 2 heads and 1 tail. Does your result come close to the expected value?

d. Toss a die 180 times and record the number of times a six appears on the up face. Does your result come close to the expected value?

e. Toss a pair of dice 360 times and record the number of times you get a sum of 7. Does your result come close to the expected value?

23. From our listing of possible outcomes when rolling two dice, we observe that the probability for throwing a double is $\frac{6}{36}$. Try rolling two dice to observe the greatest number of rolls possible without getting doubles.

a. Roll and write down the number of rolls you can make before getting doubles. Do this 25 times.

b. Does there seem to be a limit to the number of rolls you can make before getting a double?

c. Do you think it would be rare for the number of rolls to reach 40?

24. Take 10 thumbtacks and a paper cup. Shake the cup and turn it face down on the desk. Count the number of thumbtacks landing point up. Do this experiment 25 times. (This means you will have the results for 250 individual throws.) Record your results in the table.

Toss	*Number Pointing Up*			Toss	*Number Point Up*		
	Own	*Group*	*Class*		*Own*	*Group*	*Class*
1				14			
2				15			
3				16			
4				17			
5				18			
6				19			
7				20			
8				21			
9				22			
10				23			
11				24			
12				25			
13							

a. How many times did tacks land point up?

    b. Write this number over 250. This is the empirical or experimental probability of a tack landing point up.

    c. Write the probability as a decimal.

    d. Combine the results of those in your group and then the whole class and complete the table.

    e. Find the experimental probability for the class results.

    f. Write the probability as a decimal. How do they compare with individual results?

    g. How do you think your results would be affected if the point of the tacks were very long? Very short?

25. Place 25 chips in a container: 2 blue, 8 green, and 15 yellow (or some similar combination). Taking turns with a partner, each person reach into the cup 25 times and pick a chip. Record the color, place the chip back, and select again. Complete the following:

Color	Tallies Person 1	Tallies Person 2	Total Tallies	Prediction of No. in Cup	Actual No. in Cup
Blue					
Green					
Yellow					

26. In a paper bag, place 10 marbles (some red and some green). Draw five marbles from the bag, record the number of each color drawn, and replace the marbles in the bag. Do this 25 times, recording each result and returning the marbles to the bag after each drawing. Average the results of the trials and then make a statement of probability based on the experimental results.

    a. $P(\text{red}) = $ _____

    b. $P(\text{green}) = $ _____

    c. Now predict the actual number of red and green marbles in the bag. Check the bag to see how close you came.

    d. Should more marbles be drawn to predict the contents of the bag adequately?

    e. Could fewer marbles be drawn?

27. Place a penny on edge, spin and record your results. Which occurred more often (heads or tails)? How do you explain your results?

28. Perform an experiment where the outcomes are equally likely. Determine the experimental probabilities and compare them to the theoretical probabilities.

29. **a.** Describe a survey in which the theoretical probabilities of the outcomes are not known. Conduct the survey to determine the experimental probabilities.

   b. Describe your procedure, analyze your data, and make some predictions based on the probabilities you found.

   c. Repeat the experiment in a second situation to "verify" your empirical probabilities.

30. Make a list of experiments you could use with children in the middle grades to introduce the idea of empirical probability.

REVIEW PROBLEM SET

1. Three coins are tossed. Find the probability of getting 1 head and 2 tails.

2. Two dice are tossed. Find the probability of getting a sum of 8

3. A committee of two people is to be chosen at random from Alice, Barb, Chad, and Dennis. Find the probability that Alice is on the committee.

4. A die and a coin are tossed. Find the probability of getting a prime number on the die and a tail on the coin.

5. All possible numbers of three different digits are formed by choosing from the digits 1, 2, 3, 4, 5, and 6. If one number is chosen at random, what is the probability that it is greater than 500?

6. Agnes, Bertha, Carl, Dan, and Enos are randomly seated in a row of five seats. Find the probability that Agnes is seated next to Bertha on the left.

7. Two dice are tossed. Find the probability of getting a sum greater than 5.

8. A committee of two people is to be chosen at random from the seven people Al, Bob, Chad, Dan, Eric, Fern, and Gina. Find the probability that neither Al nor Bob is on the committee.

9. From a group of 5 women and 3 men, a 2-person committee is chosen at random. Find the probability that the committee contains at least one woman.

10. A bag contains 4 red and 3 white marbles. One marble is drawn, and its color recorded. The marble is then replaced in the bag and a second marble is drawn, and its color recorded. Find the probability that one marble drawn is red and the other is white. (Use a tree diagram.)

11. A bag contains 3 red and 6 white marbles. Two marbles are drawn in succession, without replacement. Find the probability that two white marbles are drawn. (Use a tree diagram.)

12. Three different shapes are chosen from a set of 7 shapes to use as a repeatable pattern. How many different ways can three shapes be used to form the pattern that will be used?

13. A club has a planning committee of 9 members. If three members of the committee are chosen to plan each of the three social events of the year, how many different ways can a group of 3 people be selected?

14. Suppose the probability of an event occurring is $\frac{5}{7}$. What are the odds in favor of the event? What are the odds against the event?

15. Find the odds in favor of getting a sum of five when rolling a pair of dice.

16. Two coins are tossed 500 times. How many times would you expect to get one head and one tail?

17. Suppose a player rolls a pair of dice and wins $5 for a "double" but loses $1 for anything else. What is the player's mathematical expectation?

One Solution to Sample Problem

When rolling a standard pair of dice, there are 36 possible outcomes with sums from 2 to 12. The probability of rolling a 2 is $\frac{1}{36}$ and the probability of rolling a 3 is $\frac{2}{36}$ (a 1 and 2 or a 2 and 1). How could you mark a pair of dice differently so that the probability of throwing sums from 1 to 12 is the same?

1. *Understanding the Problem.* We are to take a pair of unmarked dice and remark them with numbers so when they are rolled the sums from 1 through 12 will occur. Because there are 36 possible outcomes when rolling two dice, the probability of each sum from 1 through 12 being the same will be true if each sum occurs three times out of the 36 outcomes. This means that each sum from 1 through 12 has an equally likely chance of occurring.

2. *Devising a Plan.* We could look at a simpler problem by considering the sums 1 through 6. This will give us a more manageable number of sums with which we are working. We could also use a table to determine how the 36 possible outcomes can occur so that the sums from 1 through 12 are equally likely.

3. *Solution.* We can look at how to obtain sums from 1 to 6 when rolling a pair of dice. If we want these to be equally likely, each sum must occur 6

out of the 36 possible outcomes. To get 6 sums of 1 we will need a 0 on one die and 6 ones on the other die. Then to obtain 6 sums of 2 we need a 1 on the first die to match with the 6 ones on the second die. The table and listing below shows how we can obtain 6 of each of the sums from 1 through 6.

		Second die					
		1	1	1	1	1	1
First die	0	1	1	1	1	1	1
	1	2	2	2	2	2	2
	2	3	3	3	3	3	3
	3	4	4	4	4	4	4
	4	5	5	5	5	5	5
	5	6	6	6	6	6	6

First Die	Second Die
0	1
1	1
2	1
3	1
4	1
5	1

Now let us consider the sums from 1 through 12. Again, to obtain a 1 on a roll the pair of dice would have to be marked with a 0 on one of the die and a 1 on the other. Therefore to obtain the required three out of 36 sums, we must have three ones to match with the zero rather than the 6 ones we had for sums from 1 to 6. The three ones will match with 1 to produce three sums of 2, match with 2 to produce three sums of 3, match with 3 to produce three sums of 4, and so on for the sums to 6. After the sums from 1 to 6 have been obtained three times, we consider the three ways the sums from 7 to 12 can occur. This can be accomplished by matching three 7s with each of the numbers 0 to 5. The following table illustrates this.

	Second die					
	1	1	1	7	7	7
0	1	1	1	7	7	7
1	2	2	2	8	8	8
2	3	3	3	9	9	9
3	4	4	4	10	10	10
4	5	5	5	11	11	11
5	6	6	6	12	12	12

First die

Therefore, the pair of dice could be marked in the following way.

First Die	Second Die
0	1
1	1
2	1
3	7
4	7
5	7

```
      ┌───┐                    ┌───┐
      │ 0 │                    │ 1 │
  ┌───┼───┼───┐            ┌───┼───┼───┐
  │ 4 │ 1 │ 5 │            │ 7 │ 1 │ 7 │
  └───┼───┼───┘            └───┼───┼───┘
      │ 2 │                    │ 1 │
      ├───┤                    ├───┤
      │ 3 │                    │ 7 │
      └───┘                    └───┘
```

4. *Looking Back.* Because there are 36 possible outcomes for sums when rolling a pair of dice, the sample space $P(S)$ is 36. For each of 12 sums from 1 to 12 to be equally likely we need to have 3 of each occur. Therefore, the probability of each of the events occurring is $\frac{3}{36}$ and each sum from 1 to 12 has an equal probability.

5. *Looking Ahead.* If we tossed a pair of duodecagon (12-sided) dice, could we produce a similar situation. How many possible outcomes would there be? If we wanted equally likely sums beginning with 1 what would these sums be? How should the dice be marked?

12 | STATISTICS: USES AND MISUSES

Sample Problem

In a mathematics class of 35 students, the mean on the first exam of the semester was 67. Five of the students withdrew from the course because their scores of 43, 45, 32, 37, and 28 were so low. Two students enrolled late and took the makeup exam, scoring 69 and 71. What would the new mean for the class be?

12.1 INTRODUCTION AND ORGANIZING DATA

"Dave's *mean score* for his first five tests was 87."

"Monica ranked in the 94th *percentile* on the quantitative part of the SAT."

"Five thousand scores were *normally distributed* about a *mean* of 72 and the *standard deviation* of the scores was 6."

As teachers, we need to be able to interpret such statements involving *statistical concepts*.

"Buy Brand X soap and you will have a lovely complexion."

"Don't eat a certain kind of food because it raises your cholesterol level, which causes heart attacks."

As consumers, we are constantly bombarded with such statements, all of which are said to be backed by *statistical evidence*. It is apparent that we need to understand the concepts being used to interpret the statistical information that describes phenomena in our society.

As prospective classroom teachers, knowledge of statistics becomes more important in this age of information gathering. Statistics can become an integral part of the curriculum if we have a good working knowledge of the concepts involved. A major direction in the mathematics curriculum over the past years has been to include more statistics. In 1977, the National Council of Supervisors of Mathematics listed "reading, interpreting, and constructing tables, charts, and graphs" as one of its 10 basic mathematical skills. The National Council of Teachers of Mathematics (NCTM) indicated the need for data collection and interpretation in its 1980 Agenda for Action. The NCTM Curriculum Standards for School Mathematics place the collection, organization, and displaying of data along with applying statistics to solve problems within the K–4 curriculum. The Standards recommend that in grades 5–8, students need to extend the exploration of statistics in real-world situations by understanding how information is processed and translated into usable knowledge.

Through the knowledge of statistics gained by data analysis, students can become intelligent consumers who can make informed and critical decisions. Data analysis involves several steps: collecting and organizing the data, constructing and interpreting tables and graphs, drawing inferences to describe trends, developing convincing arguments, and evaluating the arguments of others.

In the elementary school, children need to acquire two basic types of graphing skills: (1) the ability to collect, organize, and display information, and (2) the ability to interpret information presented by a graph. Descriptive statistics refers to the techniques used to collect, organize, analyze, and present such data. The study of descriptive statistics should begin with the posing of questions that require the collection of data and then rely on efficient methods to organize and understand the information collected.

Suppose we are interested in the amount of sunshine in various parts of the United States. The data set in Table 12.1 provides raw data on the average percentage of possible sunshine in selected cities.

By using a line plot, we can have a better picture of the data, as well as summarize and communicate the numerical information. A line plot is a quick and simple way to organize data when there are 25 numbers or less. To make a line plot, first make a horizontal line and put a scale of numbers on this line that is appropriate for the data. In making a line plot, it is usual to number the scale in multiples of 5, 10, or 100. Because the smallest value in our data set is 30 and the largest is 85, we will run the scale from 30 to 90 in multiples of 10. By putting an X above the line at the appropriate numbers, we can plot the data as shown in Figure 12.1.

The line plot provides us with certain interpretations of data that cannot be obtained from the raw listing. From the line plot we can spot outliers that

TABLE 12.1 AVERAGE PERCENTAGE OF POSSIBLE SUNSHINE—SELECTED CITIES

Juneau, AK	30	Cleveland, OH	49
Phoenix, AZ	85	Oklahoma City, OK	67
Little Rock, AR	62	Portland, OR	47
Los Angeles, CA	73	Cheyenne, WY	65
Denver, CO	70	Portland, ME	57
Washington, DC	57	New York, NY	58
Miami, FL	72	El Paso, TX	83
Honolulu, HI	67	Wichita, KS	65
Chicago, IL	52	Great Falls, MT	65
Boston, MA	59	Detroit, MI	53
St. Louis, MO	57	New Orleans, LA	59
Reno, NV	79	Seattle, WA	46
Bismarck, ND	59		

Source: U.S. National Oceanic and Atmospheric Administration, Comparative Climatic Data Annual.

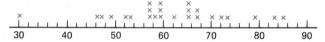

FIGURE 12.1 Line plot of average percentage of possible sunshine—selected cities

are substantially larger or smaller than the other values. Outliers such as Juneau, AK, are easy to spot. Along with outliers, we can observe where gaps or large spaces between points might exist.

Clusters or isolated groups of points can be examined for similar attributes from which the data were generated. As we examine the line plot, we can make observations and raise questions. If having a sunshiny day is important to us, we might be interested in parts of the country that have 70 to 80% possible sunshine and choose cities such as Phoenix, El Paso, or Reno. Because we have clusters in several places, it would be of interest to know if those cities are in the same part of the country. When we examine those cities with 59% sunshine, we find that they are in various locations across the United States—Boston, MA: Bismarck, ND: and New Orleans, LA. Often a line plot produces a graphic picture from which a narrative description could be written.

When the number of pieces of data exceeds 25, a line plot may not be the best method of organizing our data. The stem and leaf approach provides a way to organize and display data quickly that allows us to identify largest and smallest values, outliers, clusters, gaps, the relative position of important values, and also the shape of the distribution. Using Table 12.2, which lists the number of women in state legislatures in 1986 as our data set, we can organize the raw data for further interpretation with a stem and leaf plot.

To make a stem and leaf plot, we need to locate the smallest and largest values. The smallest value is 4 for Mississippi and the largest value is 140 for

TABLE 12.2 WOMEN HOLDING OFFICE IN STATE
LEGISLATURES

AL	9	IN	19	NE	8	RI	23
AK	11	IA	22	NV	10	SC	10
AZ	18	KS	30	NH	140	SD	15
AR	10	KY	9	NJ	12	TN	11
CA	15	LA	5	NM	13	TX	16
CO	24	ME	44	NY	23	UT	7
CT	41	MD	36	NC	20	VT	47
DE	10	MA	33	ND	18	VA	10
FL	31	MI	16	OH	12	WA	35
GA	23	MN	29	OK	13	WV	23
HI	14	MS	4	OR	18	WI	25
ID	24	MO	26	PA	13	WY	24
IL	30	MT	22				

Source: Center for the American Woman and Politics, Eagleton Institute of
Politics, Rutgers University, New Brunswick, NJ, information releases.

New Hampshire. Because 140 is such an extreme outlier, we will exclude it
for now and use the 47 for Vermont as our largest number on the stem and
leaf plot.

We can group the data by tens and use the tens digits as the stems written
vertically with a line to their right (see Fig. 12.2). With numbers less than 10
we use a 0 as our stem. For example the number of women state representatives for Alabama is 9, therefore the stem is 0 and the leaf is 9. From the
plot, we read 2|4 as 24 women. Note that each stem represents an interval.
For example, the stem "3" represents all the data for 30 through 39.

Stem	Leaf
0	9 9 5 4 8 7
1	1 8 0 5 0 4 9 6 0 2 3 8 2 3 8 3 0 5 1 6 0
2	4 3 4 2 9 6 2 3 0 3 3 5 4
3	1 0 0 6 3 5
4	1 4 7

FIGURE 12.2

To further interpret the data, it is convenient to arrange the leaves so they
are ordered from the smallest value to the largest value, as illustrated in Figure 12.3.

When there are too many leaves per stem, we can spread out the stem and
leaf plot by putting leaves 0, 1, 2, 3, and 4 on the first line for each stem and
the leaves 5, 6, 7, 8, and 9 on the second line. Figure 12.4 illustrates how this
technique works with our data in Figure 12.3. As you can see, no original
information is lost with a stem and leaf plot.

Stem and leaf plots are useful for displaying two sets of data for comparison. By constructing back-to-back stem and leaf plots with the stems in the
center of the plot we have a useful technique for organizing our data sets.

Stem	Leaf
0	4
.	5 7 8 9 9
1	0 0 0 0 0 1 1 2 2 3 3 3 4
.	5 5 6 6 8 8 8 9
2	0 2 2 3 3 3 3 4 4 4
.	5 6 9
3	0 0 1 3
.	5 6
4	1 4
.	7

Stem	Leaf
0	4 5 7 8 9 9
1	0 0 0 0 0 1 1 2 2 3 3 3 4 5 5 6 6 8 8 8 9
2	0 2 2 3 3 3 3 4 4 4 5 6 9
3	0 0 1 3 5 6
4	1 4 7

FIGURE 12.3   FIGURE 12.4

Using the information on wind speeds from Table 12.3, we can compare the average wind speeds in January with those in July for selected cities (Fig. 12.5).

TABLE 12.3   AVERAGE WIND SPEED—SELECTED CITIES

	Jan.	July	Annual		Jan.	July	Annual
Mobile, AL	10.5	7.0	9.1	Omaha, NE	10.9	8.9	10.6
Juneau, AL	8.3	7.5	8.4	Reno, NV	5.6	6.9	6.5
Phoenix, AZ	5.3	7.2	6.3	Concord, NH	7.3	5.7	6.7
Little Rock, AR	8.7	6.8	8.0	Atlantic City, NJ	11.3	8.6	10.2
Los Angeles, CA	6.7	7.7	7.5	Albuquerque, NM	8.1	9.1	9.0
San Francisco, CA	7.1	13.6	10.5	Buffalo, NY	14.3	10.4	12.1
Denver, CO	8.7	8.4	8.8	New York, NY	10.7	7.6	9.4
Hartford, CT	9.0	7.5	8.5	Charlotte, NC	7.9	6.6	7.5
Wilmington, DE	10.0	7.8	9.2	Raleigh, NC	8.6	6.6	7.7
Washington, DC	10.0	8.2	9.3	Bismarck, ND	10.0	9.2	10.3
Miami, FL	9.4	7.8	9.2	Cleveland, OH	12.4	8.7	10.7
Atlanta, GA	10.6	7.5	9.1	Columbus, OH	10.3	6.9	8.7
Honolulu, HI	9.7	13.5	11.6	Oklahoma City, OK	12.9	10.9	12.5
Boise, ID	8.1	8.4	8.9	Portland, OR	10.0	7.6	7.9
Chicago, IL	11.6	8.1	10.3	Philadelphia, PA	10.3	8.0	9.5
Peoria, IL	11.2	7.9	10.1	Providence, RI	11.3	9.5	10.6
Indianapolis, IN	11.0	7.4	9.6	Columbia, SC	7.2	6.3	6.9
Des Moines, IA	11.7	8.9	10.9	Sioux Falls, SD	11.0	9.7	11.1
Wichita, KS	12.2	11.1	12.3	Nashville, TN	9.2	6.4	8.0
Louisville, KY	9.6	6.7	8.4	Dallas, TX	11.1	9.5	10.8
New Orleans, LA	9.4	6.1	8.2	Houston, TX	8.2	6.8	7.9
Portland, ME	9.2	7.6	8.7	Salt Lake City, UT	7.6	9.5	8.8
Baltimore, MD	9.8	7.9	9.2	Burlington, VT	9.5	7.9	8.8
Boston, MA	13.9	10.9	12.4	Norfolk, VA	11.5	8.9	10.6
Detroit, MI	11.7	8.4	10.3	Richmond, VA	8.0	6.7	7.6
Minneapolis, MN	10.4	9.3	10.5	Seattle, WA	9.8	8.3	9.0
Jackson, MS	8.7	5.9	7.5	Charleston, WV	7.6	5.1	6.4
Kansas City, MO	11.1	8.9	10.7	Milwaukee, WI	12.8	9.6	11.6
St. Louis, MO	10.6	7.9	9.7	Cheyenne, WY	15.2	10.3	12.9
Great Falls, MT	15.2	10.2	12.8				

Source: U.S. National Oceanic and Atmospheric Administration, Comparative Climatic Data, annual.

January	Stem	July
6 3	5	1 7 9
7	6	1 3 4 5 6 6 7 7 8 8 9 9
9 6 6 3 2 1	7	0 2 4 5 5 6 6 6 7 8 8 9 9 9 9
7 7 7 6 3 2 1 1 0	8	0 1 2 3 4 4 4 6 7 9 9 9 9
8 8 7 6 5 4 4 2 2 0	9	1 2 3 5 5 5 6 7
9 7 6 6 5 4 3 3 0 0 0 0	10	2 3 4 9 9
7 7 6 5 3 3 2 1 1 0 0	11	1
9 8 4 2	12	
9	13	5 6
3	14	
2 2	15	

FIGURE 12.5

Numbers containing decimals often occur in data. Consider Table 12.4, which represents the average salary of teachers by states. The values range from 18.1 to 41.5, so we choose the stems to be 18, 19, 20 . . . 41. The data from Table 12.4 has been organized into a stem and leaf plot in Figure 12.6.

TABLE 12.4 AVERAGE SALARY OF CLASSROOM TEACHERS ($1000)

AL	22.9	IL	27.2	MT	22.5	RI	29.5
AK	41.5	IN	24.3	NE	20.9	SC	21.4
AZ	24.7	IA	21.7	NV	25.6	SD	18.1
AR	19.5	KS	22.8	NH	20.1	TN	21.8
CA	29.8	KY	20.9	NJ	28.2	TX	24.4
CO	25.9	LA	20.5	NM	22.5	UT	22.3
CT	26.6	ME	19.6	NY	30.2	VT	20.3
DE	24.6	MD	27.2	NC	22.5	VA	23.4
DC	34.0	MA	25.8	ND	20.8	WA	26.0
FL	22.3	MI	30.2	OH	24.5	WV	20.6
GA	22.1	MN	27.0	OK	21.4	WI	26.8
HI	25.8	MS	18.4	OR	25.8	WY	27.9
ID	21.0	MO	21.9	PA	26.0		

Source: National Education Association, Washington, DC, Estimates of School Statistics, 1985–86

Using Figure 12.6, we can easily locate the highest and lowest salaries. From Table 12.4, locate the average salary of teachers within the state in which you live. Now use Figure 12.6 to observe how your state compares to the rest of the United States with regard to average teachers' salaries. Notice that Alaska and Washington, DC, are both outliers and pay teachers considerably more than the rest of the states in the United States. As we interpret the data, we can try to explain reasons for outliers.

By adding frequency and cumulative frequency columns in Figure 12.6,

Stem	Leaf	Frequency	Cummulative Frequency
18	1 4	2	2
19	5 6	2	4
20	1 2 5 6 8 9 9	7	11
21	0 4 4 7 8 9	6	17
22	1 3 3 5 5 5 8 9	8	25
23	4	1	26
24	3 4 5 6 7	5	31
25	6 8 8 8 9	5	36
26	0 0 6 8	4	40
27	0 2 2 9	4	44
28	2	1	45
29	5 8	2	47
30	2 2	2	49
31			
32			
33			
34	0	1	50
35			
36			
37			
38			
39			
40			
41	5	1	51
	Total	51	

FIGURE 12.6

we have extended the information in our stem and leaf plot. Notice that following the 18-stem there are 2 leaves indicating salaries of 18.1 and 18.4 thousand dollars. The frequency of 2 accounts for these two entries in the 18.0–18.9 row, and the cumulative frequency column indicates there are two leaves up until the end of the interval 18.0–18.9. There are two more leaves on the 19-stem and 7 more on the 20-stem. The cummulative frequency of 11 tells us that up until the end of the interval 20.0–20.9 there is a total of 11 leaves (2 for the 18-stem, 2 for the 19-stem, and 7 for the 20 stem). This extension of the stem and leaf plot will be very useful as we construct various kinds of graphs.

Another way to display raw data is in a frequency table, as is shown in Table 12.5 where we have organized data collected from the heights of 20 children measured to the nearest centimeter. We could use data organized in a stem and leaf plot to construct a frequency table or it could be constructed without the use of a stem and leaf plot.

As long as the number of measurements is small, this is a useful way to handle data. However, the situation becomes somewhat more complicated as the amount of data increases. For example, suppose that instead of having

TABLE 12.5

Height	Frequency	Height	Frequency
100	1	116	0
101	0	117	2
102	2	118	1
103	0	119	0
104	1	120	0
105	1	121	1
106	1	122	0
107	0	123	0
108	0	124	2
109	0	125	0
110	0	126	0
111	1	127	1
112	1	128	1
113	0	129	0
114	0	130	1
115	3	Total	20

the heights of 20 people, we had the heights of 100 basketball players and, measured to the nearest centimeter, they ranged from 180 to 210 centimeters. A frequency table similar to Table 12.5 could be constructed but, because of the range and the number of measurements involved, it would become large and cumbersome. In such situations it is more convenient to group the data into several classes and then to construct a frequency table based on class frequencies. Table 12.6 illustrates such a grouped-data frequency table. The smallest and largest values for each class (interval) are

TABLE 12.6

Height (nearest centimeter)	Frequency
180–184	2
185–189	10
190–194	12
195–199	32
200–204	29
205–209	12
210–214	3
Total	100

called the *class limits;* more specifically, the smallest value is the lower-class limit and the largest value is the upper-class limit. In Table 12.6 the first class has a lower limit of 180 and an upper limit of 184.

The heights in Table 12.6 are rounded to the nearest centimeter. Thus, the interval 180–184 theoretically includes all measurements between 179.5 and 184.5. The numbers 179.5 and 184.5 are called the *lower-class boundary* and *upper-class boundary*, respectively.

Note that in Table 12.6 we use seven classes and that each class is of size 5. The choices for number of classes and size of classes to be used relative to a certain set of data are arbitrary. However, following are some "rules of thumb" that are frequently used:

1. We seldom use fewer than 6 or more than 20 classes.
2. We always choose classes so that each "score" is recorded in one and only one class.
3. We make the intervals of equal size.
4. Having intervals with a size that is an odd number facilitates some computations (this statement will become more meaningful shortly).

Now let us illustrate the process of constructing a grouped data frequency table from some raw data. Suppose that we have the following test scores from a group of sixty students: 81, 62, 44, 89, 73, 71, 72, 75, 44, 84, 82, 98, 45, 78, 68, 69, 75, 70, 46, 65, 64, 97, 79, 84, 77, 79, 58, 69, 75, 53, 90, 39, 78, 66, 69, 50, 67, 77, 49, 81, 54, 54, 94, 86, 67, 90, 79, 55, 38, 74, 78, 81, 62, 55, 56, 88, 86, 74, 91, and 58. We can "scan" the scores and find the largest and smallest scores to be 98 and 38, respectively. Thus, the range is 98 − 38 = 60. Choosing an interval of seven units allows us to group the data into nine classes and, because seven is an odd number, the *midpoint* of each interval falls at a whole number. (You will see a little later the convenience of having the midpoints associated with whole numbers.) Now let us construct a frequency table for these data (Table 12.7).

Frequency distribution tables exhibit organized data; however, from the human standpoint they may lack visual appeal. Consequently, *histograms*

TABLE 12.7

Test Scores	Tally Marks	Frequency
37–43	||	2
44–50	⧸⧸⧸⧸ |	6
51–57	⧸⧸⧸⧸ |	6
58–64	⧸⧸⧸⧸	5
65–71	⧸⧸⧸⧸ ⧸⧸⧸⧸	10
72–78	⧸⧸⧸⧸ ⧸⧸⧸⧸ ||	12
79–85	⧸⧸⧸⧸ ||||	9
86–92	⧸⧸⧸⧸ ||	7
93–99	|||	3
	Total	60

and *frequency polygons* are commonly used to represent frequency distributions graphically. Figure 12.7 is a histogram that "pictures" the data from Table 12.7. The rectangles used in the histogram are "centered" about the midpoints of the intervals on the horizontal scale.

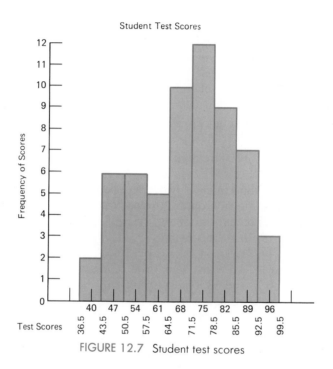

FIGURE 12.7   Student test scores

Another way of graphically representing a frequency distribution is by the use of a *frequency polygon* (Fig. 12.8). Here the class frequencies are plotted at the midpoints of the intervals and joined by line segments. An extra interval with a frequency of zero is added at each end of the distribution. This forms a polygon so that the area of the polygonal region is equal to the sum of the areas of the rectangular regions in the corresponding histogram.

Sometimes when working with frequency distributions we are interested in how many scores fall below (or above) a certain level. For example note that in Table 12.7, 14 scores fall below 57.5. How many scores are below 78.5? In general, the total frequency of scores less than the upper-class boundary of a given interval is called the *cumulative frequency* up to and including that interval. Table 12.8 summarizes the cumulative frequencies of Table 12.7.

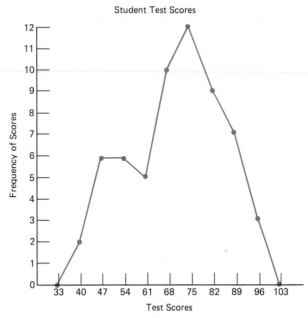

FIGURE 12.8 Student test scores

TABLE 12.8

Scores	Cumulative Frequencies
Less than 36.5	0
Less than 43.5	2
Less than 50.5	8
Less than 57.5	14
Less than 64.5	19
Less than 71.5	29
Less than 78.5	41
Less than 85.5	50
Less than 92.5	57
Less than 99.5	60

Now let us construct a graphic representation for the data in Table 12.7. This time we will plot the frequencies at the boundary points and not at the midpoints of the intervals as we did earlier with the regular frequency polygon. Thus, we get the line graph in Figure 12.9. Such a graph of a cumulative frequency distribution is called an *ogive*.

Often histograms can be quickly made from stem and leaf plots. Figure 12.10 listing the number of women state representatives is reproduced here with frequencies added.

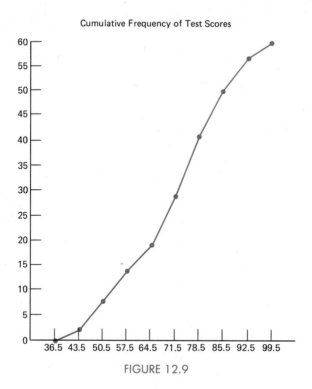

Cumulative Frequency of Test Scores

FIGURE 12.9

Stem	Leaf	Frequencies
0	4 5 7 8 9 9	6
1	0 0 0 0 1 1 2 2 3 3 3 4 5 5 6 6 8 8 8 9	21
2	0 2 2 3 3 3 3 4 4 4 5 6 9	13
3	0 0 1 3 5 6	6
4	1 4 7	3

FIGURE 12.10

By enclosing each row or set of leaves in a bar, we have a crude histogram (Fig. 12.11). The frequencies can then be shown along one axis of the graph (Fig. 12.12). Histograms are usually displayed with vertical bars rather than horizontal bars, so we will rotate our figure 90° and have a histogram with our intervals shown along the horizontal axis (Fig. 12.13).

Stem	Leaf
0	4 5 7 8 9 9
1	0 0 0 0 0 1 1 2 2 3 3 3 3 4 5 5 6 6 8 8 8 9
2	0 2 2 3 3 3 3 4 4 4 5 6 9
3	0 0 1 3 5 6
4	1 4 7

FIGURE 12.11

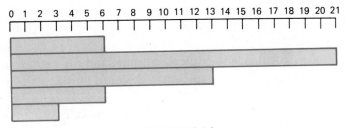

FIGURE 12.12

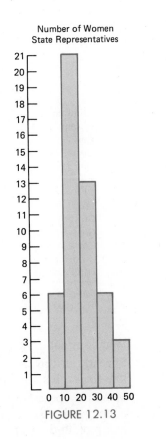

Number of Women
State Representatives

FIGURE 12.13

PROBLEM SET 12.1

1. Construct a line plot from the list of scores on a mathematics test.

78	99	85	89	95
67	95	89	91	81
62	84	82	61	84
77	76	85	92	95
95	93	80	78	76
42	79	87	91	83

   a. Identify any outliers, clusters, and the highest and lowest grades.

   b. Construct a stem and leaf plot to illustrate the data.

2. Using the data below on longevity of animals, construct a stem and leaf plot.

   ### AVERAGE LONGEVITY OF ANIMALS IN CAPTIVITY

Baboon	20	Horse	20
Black bear	18	Kangaroo	7
Grizzly bear	25	Leopard	12
Beaver	5	Lion	15
Camel	12	Monkey	15
Cat	12	Moose	12
Chimpanzee	20	Mouse	3
Chipmunk	6	Opossum	1
Cow	15	Pig	10
Deer	8	Rabbit	5
Dog	12	Rhonoceros	20
Elephant	35	Sea lion	12
Elk	15	Sheep	12
Fox	7	Squirrel	10
Giraffe	10	Tiger	16
Goat	8	Wolf	5
Gorilla	20	Zebra	15
Guinea pig	4		
Hippopotamus	25		

   Source: The World Almanac and Book of Facts 1986 (Figures supplied by Ronald T. Reuther).

   a. What animal may be considered an outlier?

   b. Spread out the stem and leaf plot by putting leaves 0–4 on the first line for each stem and the leaves 5–9 on the second line.

   c. Make the spread out stem and leaf plot into a histogram. Make a frequency column, determine the range and classes from the stem and leaf plot, and find the midpoint of each class.

3. Make back-to-back stem and leaf plots of the scores of Test I and Test II below.

Test I				Test II			
85	71	74	66	85	70	90	84
98	62	79	99	73	83	70	99
76	55	65	89	76	95	91	85
89	88	98	88	94	94	82	85
82	78	91	91	79	90	84	96
85	96	86	82	96	91	84	92

a. Did the students do better on Test I or Test II?

b. Find the high and low scores on each test, any clusters or outliers.

c. What observations can you make about the two exams from the stem and leaf plot? What are some possible explanations for the differences?

4. Using the test scores in Problem 3, construct back-to-back line plots.

5. Find the range of the following scores: 65, 48, 39, 38, 72, 45, 55, 56, 73, 74, 62, 33, 45, 44, 54, 73, and 65.

6. If the midpoints of the class intervals in a frequency distribution are 117, 124, 131, 138, 145, and 152, find:

a. Class size

b. Class limits

c. Class boundaries

7. Consider the following frequency distribution table:

Class Limits	Frequency
15–19	2
20–24	8
25–29	17
30–34	14
35–39	4
40–44	7
45–49	8

a. Construct a histogram.

b. Construct a frequency polygon.

c. Construct a cumulative frequency distribution table.

d. Construct an ogive for part **c.**

8. Suppose the daily temperature for the months of July and August in a given city is recorded (in Celsius) as in the following table:

```
38   19   38   26   27   33   42
19   21   29   27   29   21   38
24   22   28   24   31   19
36   21   26   41   30   26
40   27   25   32   32   28
18   28   32   32   34   29
34   31   31   34   28   27
36   19   19   31   29   34
36   24   24   22   35   38
33   38   26   24   34   38
```

   a. What is the range of temperatures?
   b. Group these temperatures into six classes using 17, 22, 27, 32, 37, and 42 as midpoints and form a frequency distribution table.
   c. Make a histogram for these data.
   d. Make a frequency polygon for these data.

9. The grades on a test taken by 100 students are as follows:

```
79   66   78   84   77   84   68   52   78   56
91   87   83   86   84   76   65   68   80   58
81   52   84   85   86   78   68   73   84   93
87   93   97   93   85   82   73   74   85   84
73   97   96   78   87   83   84   65   82   83
74   46   87   92   84   91   83   76   78   78
77   84   54   87   78   87   96   75   93   76
42   86   48   86   65   86   81   84   84   87
71   93   56   74   93   74   43   82   83   88
96   92   73   76   92   72   65   90   81   81
```

   a. Make a frequency distribution table starting the first class at 40 and using ten classes of size 6.
   b. Construct a histogram for the data.
   c. Construct a frequency polygon on the same axes as the histogram.
   d. Construct a cumulative frequency distribution table and its corresponding ogive.

10. The weights of 75 students are as follows to the nearest pound: 127, 134, 131, 176, 184, 129, 120, 194, 187, 176, 168, 210, 204, 163, 172, 181, 142, 125, 136, 145, 164, 200, 185, 175, 124, 136, 158, 155, 162, 188, 194, 150, 130, 173, 191, 202, 188, 167, 139, 145, 153, 158, 162, 168, 174, 181, 128, 137, 146, 149, 168, 188, 194, 143, 157, 184, 172, 164, 131, 132, 169, 208, 192, 148, 141, 161, 135, 154, 178, 192, 145, 201, 186, 168, 174.

a. Make a frequency distribution table using a "reasonable" number of intervals.

b. Construct a frequency polygon.

c. Construct a cumulative frequency distribution table and its corresponding ogive.

Scores	Cumulative Frequencies
More than 36.5	60
More than 43.3	58
.	.
.	.
.	.

11. The cumulative frequency distribution based on total scores less than the upper boundaries is sometimes called a "less-than" cumulative distribution. A "more-than" cumulative distribution could also be formed by considering scores more than the corresponding lower boundary. Refer to Table 12.8 in the text and complete the "more-than" cumulative frequency table started below. Also construct the corresponding ogive.

Pedagogical Problems and Activities

12. The following type of problem appears in some elementary textbooks: Make tally marks to record the scores 45, 82, 97, 56, 50, 62, 68, 49, 63, 74, 77, 80, 95, 99, 44, 48, 73, 75, 61, 63, 64, 92, 98, 95, 56, 63, 72, and 45 and then fill in the frequency column for the following table:

Scores	Tally Marks	Frequency
40–50		
50–60		
60–70		
70–80		
80–90		
90–100		

Do this problem and indicate the difficulty that arises. How can it be handled?

13. Collect data on the amount of change (coins) students in your class have with them. Make a line plot of the data and write a summary of the information displayed by the plot.

14. Measure the heights (in centimeters) of students in your class. Make a stem and leaf plot to display the data.

12.2   PRESENTING DATA

Statistical data can be presented in a variety of ways. For example, the frequency tables, histograms, and frequency polygons of the previous section could be used to present data as well as to organize it. However, to present data to the public in a way that "simplifies and dramatizes the facts," different kinds of *graphs* are frequently used. We will discuss four types of graphs in this section: circle graph, bar graph, line graph, and pictograph.

One of the simplest types of graphs is the *circle graph*, also referred to as a pie chart. It allows one to compare the component parts of some entity to the whole entity itself. For example, suppose that a family budget based on a monthly salary (take-home pay) is constructed as follows:

Food and housing: 40 percent

Clothing: 3 percent

Contributions and savings: 10 percent

Educational expenses: 15 percent

Automobile expenses: 7 percent

Insurance: 5 percent

Miscellaneous: 20 percent

In constructing a circle graph to portray this information, each part of the budget is represented by a sector of a circle. The measure of the central angle for each sector is the corresponding percent of 360 degrees. For example, because 40 percent of the budget is for food and housing, a central angle of 40 percent of 360°, which is 144°, is constructed for the sector that represents food and housing. It should be noted that in so doing we have constructed a sector having an area that is 40 percent of the area of the entire circular region. Likewise, the sector representing clothing would have a central angle of 3 percent of 360 degrees or $(\frac{3}{100})(360°) = 10.8°$. Figure 12.14 is a circle graph depicting the entire budget breakdown.

As mentioned before, the main thrust of a circle graph is to compare parts of something to the whole. The original information need not necessarily be given in percent form. For example, the information given in Table 12.9 lends itself to a circle graph presentation. A sector of a circle representing the A's given on the final exam would have a central angle of $\frac{8}{120}(360°) = 24°$. We will have you complete the circle graph for this table in the next set of exercises.

Another common way of presenting data is to use *bar graphs*. Basically, there are two types of bar graphs: the vertical bar graph (sometimes called a column chart) and the horizontal bar graph. Even though there are no definite rules that must be followed relative to the construction and use of bar

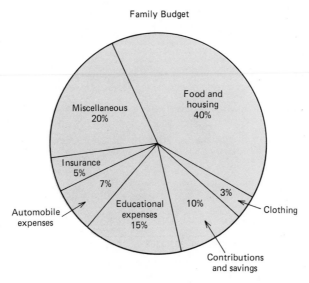

Family Budget

FIGURE 12.14

TABLE 12.9 GRADES ON A FINAL
EXAM

Grade	Number of People
A	8
B	20
C	72
D	15
F	5
	120

graphs, graphic analysts do have a few "rules of thumb" that they use as guidelines. Some of these are as follows:

1. Use a vertical bar graph if the data to be presented are to depict the fluctuation of the numerical value of some item over a sequence of time.
2. Use a horizontal bar graph if a number of different items are to be compared relative to a specified time.
3. When constructing bar graphs, make the spacing between bars approximately one-half of the width of a bar.
4. All bars in a particular graph should be of the same width.
5. All bars should begin at a zero line.

The vertical bar graph in Figure 12.15 and the horizontal bar graph in Figure 12.16 are constructed according to the foregoing guidelines.

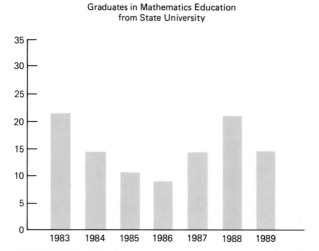

FIGURE 12.15 Graduates in mathematics education from State University

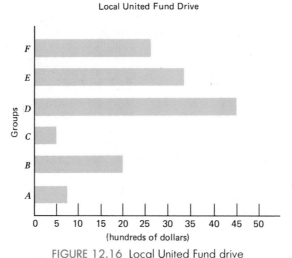

FIGURE 12.16 Local United Fund drive

In Figure 12.16 the vertical scale is called a *nominal scale*. This means that the data are not numerically ordered, but are simply categorized. The order in which the categories are distributed along the scale is immaterial. If a scale is numerically ordered but does not indicate "how much more or less" in the ordering, then it is called an *ordinal scale*. For example, suppose that we were to rank five people by their height from shortest to tallest. We could set up an ordinal scale that would rank the people but not give any information regarding "how much taller or shorter" between ranks. A scale that is numerically ordered and also possesses information regarding "how much more or less" is called an *interval scale*. Thus, on an interval scale there is significance attached, for example, to the fact that 7 is 2 greater than 5, and 6 is 3 less than 9. An interval scale that has an absolute zero is called a *ratio scale*. Having an absolute zero is another way of saying that the concept of ratio is meaningful; thus it is called a *ratio scale*. For example, on a ratio scale, 20 means twice as much as 10 and 60 means three times as much as 20. The vertical scale of Figure 12.15 and the horizontal scale of 12.16 are examples of ratio scales. It is correct to interpret from Figure 12.16 that group *B* collected four times as much as group *C*. A scale to record lengths (measured in some standard unit) is also an example of a ratio scale, as the origin of the scale is an absolute zero that corresponds to no length at all. It is correct to say that an object that is 6 meters long is twice as long as an object 3 meters long. An interval scale where ratio is not meaningful (no absolute zero) is usually used when recording something such as IQ scores. An IQ of 120 is not to be considered "twice as good" as an IQ of 60.

> REMARK This distinction between an interval scale and a ratio scale frequently causes misinterpretations of data. We need to be very sure that the ratio concept is meaningful before drawing implications based on the ratio idea.

Now let us refer back to Figure 12.15. Suppose that we wanted to show the number of graduates in mathematics education at State University over a much longer span of years, say, from 1974 through 1989. A bar graph presentation of that much information tends to become large and cumbersome; thus, we might use a *line graph*, as illustrated in Figure 12.17. Line graphs

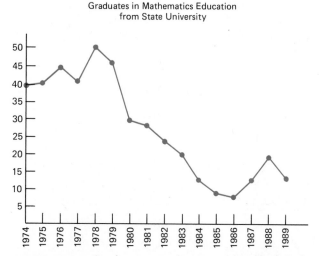

FIGURE 12.17 Graduates in mathematics education from State University

allow us to pick out specific information as well as to look for "trends." Furthermore, line graphs are very effective for depicting comparisons. For example, Figure 12.18 very clearly makes a comparison between the production of widgets and wadgets by the WW Company over a span of several years.

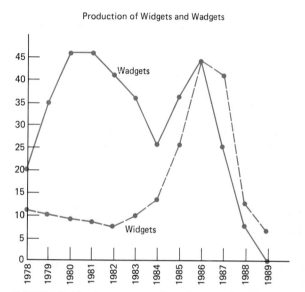

FIGURE 12.18   Comparison of production of widgets and wadgets by the WW Company

In addition to showing trends, line graphs are also appropriately used when we are dealing with continuous data. An example of continuous data would be recording the speed of a stationary bicycle as one begins to pedal towards full speed for maximum exercise (Fig. 12.19). The speedometer will pass through all possible speeds as we pedal faster and then again as we slow down.

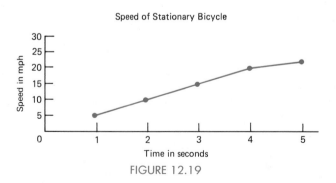

FIGURE 12.19

For discrete data such as number of students enrolled in selected classes, we should not use a line graph to display the data because only isolated values have meaning.

Pictographs (sometimes called picture graphs) are often used instead of bar graphs to "put a little more life" into an accumulation of cold facts. For example, suppose the owner of an ice cream shop wanted to illustrate that his sales had gone from 10 to 20 to 30 thousand dollars over a 3-year period. Certainly these facts could be represented by a bar graph, but perhaps a pictograph such as in Figure 12.20 would be a bit more "lifelike."

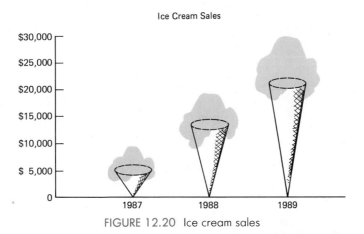

FIGURE 12.20 Ice cream sales

Care must be taken when interpreting pictographs. It is easy to "embellish" the facts by making a few slight changes. For example, Figure 12.21 shows another pictograph for the ice cream sales. In Figure 12.20 each cone

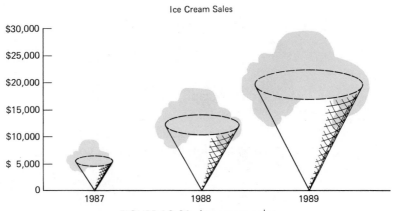

FIGURE 12.21 Ice cream sales

has the same radius: thus, the volume of the 1987 cone has been doubled in 1988 and tripled in 1989. However, in Figure 12.21 the radius of each cone has been increased proportionately. This means that the volume of the 1988 cone is 8 times the volume of the 1987 cone and the volume of the 1989 cone is 27 times the volume of the 1987 cone. The "facts" according to the vertical scales remain the same, but to the casual observer Figure 12.21 may be deceiving.

PROBLEM SET 12.2

1. Construct a circle graph to represent the grade distribution given in Table 12.9.

2. Geometric regions other than circular regions are sometimes used to present data such as in Table 12.9. Construct a rectangular region 10 centimeters long and 1 centimeter wide and divide it proportionally so as to represent the data in Table 12.9.

3. Construct a budget (using percentages) of your own and use a circle graph to present it.

4. The total land area of the earth is approximately divided according to the following table:

Land Mass	Area (%)
Africa	22
Asia (excluding USSR)	21
Europe	4
North America	18
Oceania	6
South America	13
USSR	16

Make a circle graph depicting this information.

5. Suppose that the following circle graphs are used to illustrate that the number of employees of a certain company has doubled from 1982 to 1989 and, furthermore, that the percent of female employees has risen from 20 to 40 percent. What is misleading about the way the graphs are constructed?

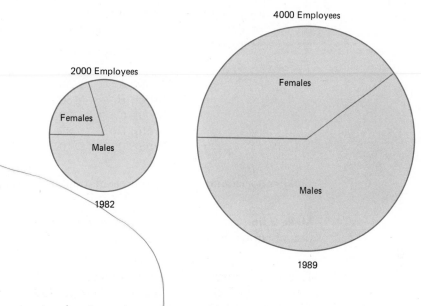

6. The number of snowmobiles produced by a particular firm over the
years 1983–1989, inclusive, is indicated in the following table:

1983	200
1984	200
1985	250
1986	300
1987	400
1988	600
1989	900

Make a vertical bar graph presentation of this data.

7. A community has collected the following amounts for the United Fund
during the years indicated:

1983	$10,000
1984	15,000
1985	15,000
1986	20,000
1987	25,000
1988	30,000
1989	35,000

Make a vertical bar graph presentation of this information.

8. A local Boy Scout troop divided into five groups and sold Christmas trees for one of their money-making projects. The money taken in by each group was as follows:

Group A	$ 50
Group B	150
Group C	30
Group D	85
Group E	110

Make a horizontal bar graph presentation of this data.

9. Make a line graph to represent the information given about the production of snowmobiles in Problem 6.

10. The WW Company referred to in Figure 12.8 also produces whistles and waggles. The following table gives their production figures for the years 1978 through 1989.

Year	Whistles (in millions)	Waggles (in millions)
1978	20	40
1979	35	45
1980	32	50
1981	35	50
1982	40	45
1983	37	40
1984	20	40
1985	10	20
1986	5	35
1987	5	45
1988	5	50
1989	5	50

Make a dashed line graph to show the production of whistles and, using the same axes, make a solid line graph to show the production of waggles.

11. We have stated that when constructing bar graphs involving arithmetic scales, it is essential that a zero baseline be used. Let us see why. Consider the following vertical bar graph:

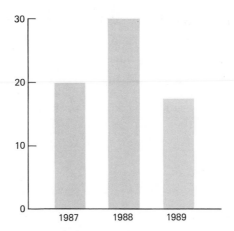

Now construct a vertical bar graph to depict the same information but omit the zero line, that is, start with the 10 line. How might such a graph be misleading to the casual observer?

12. One easy way of emphasizing or deemphasizing the trend depicted by a line graph is to expand or contract the vertical scale. Consider the following line graph.

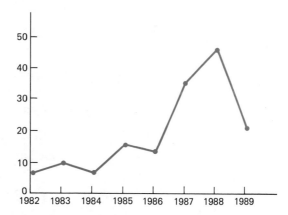

a. Construct a line graph to depict the same information as in the graph but expand the vertical scale by a factor of 2. How has the "trend" of the line been affected?

b. Construct another line graph to depict this information, but contract the vertical scale by a factor of $\frac{1}{2}$. How has the trend of the line been affected?

Pedagogical Problems and Activities

13. Solve the following problem, which illustrates the kind of problems found in elementary school textbooks combining work with circle graphs and a review of computational skills: The 500 students at Logan Elementary School chose their favorite sport to watch on TV. The results are shown on the circle graph. How many children chose baseball as their favorite sport? Basketball? Football? Golf? Tennis? Bowling? Soccer?

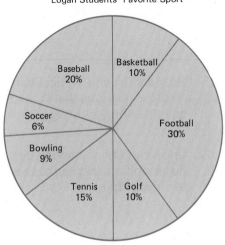

Logan Students' Favorite Sport

14. The following problem illustrates the type of problem found in some elementary texts when working with line graphs. It actually demonstrates the use of line graphs as a problem-solving technique.

Betty left home at 4:00 P.M., riding her moped at 30 kilometers per hour. Her sister, Dawn, left one hour later on her moped traveling at 50 kilometers per hour.

a. Make a table showing Betty's distance, hour by hour, from 4:00 P.M. to 7:00 P.M.

b. Make another table showing Dawn's distance, hour by hour, from 5:00 P.M. to 7:00 P.M.

c. Make a line graph for the data in Betty's table on a grid such as the one here.

d. On the same grid, make a line graph for Dawn's table.

e. From your graphs, tell about what time Dawn will overtake Betty.

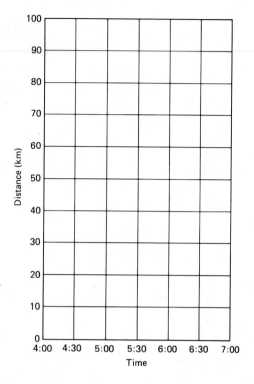

15. Collect examples of various graphs from newspapers or weekly news magazines to note the graphing techniques used.

12.3 ANALYZING DATA: MEASURES OF CENTRAL TENDENCY

In the previous sections we investigated various techniques that are used to organize and present accumulations of data. Our primary objective in the next three sections is to examine some statistical concepts that are useful for interpreting, analyzing, and describing sets of data. Basically, these concepts fall into two categories: measures of central tendency and measures of dispersion. In this section we will be concerned with three commonly used measures of central tendency—namely, mean, median, and mode.

Probably the most frequently used measure of central tendency is the *arithmetic mean*, sometimes simply called the mean. It is the arithmetical average of a set of scores. More precisely, if $x_1, x_2, x_3, \ldots, x_n$ represents n

scores, then the mean (designated by $\bar{x}$) is defined as

$$\bar{x} = \frac{x_1 + x_2 + x_3 + \cdots + x_n}{n}$$

In other words, to find the arithmetic mean of a group of scores, you add the scores and divide this sum by the number of scores.

EXAMPLE 1

If you have scores of 49, 52, 55, 58, and 61; what is the mean?

Solution $\bar{x} = \dfrac{49 + 52 + 55 + 58 + 61}{5} = \dfrac{275}{5} = 55$

EXAMPLE 2

If your scores are 32, 34, 37, 40, 44, and 48, what is the mean?

Solution $\bar{x} = \dfrac{32 + 34 + 37 + 40 + 44 + 48}{6} = \dfrac{235}{6} = 39\frac{1}{6}$

EXAMPLE 3

What is the mean of the scores 1, 2, 5, 6, 8, 13, and 91?

Solution $\bar{x} = \dfrac{1 + 2 + 5 + 6 + 8 + 13 + 91}{7} = \dfrac{126}{7} = 18$

By looking at Examples 1 and 2, we see that the mean may or may not be one of the original scores. Example 3 illustrates an important idea to remember about the mean: It can be greatly affected by extreme values. The one large score of 91 caused the mean to be larger than any of the other six scores. This characteristic of the mean will be discussed more later.

Now suppose that we want to calculate the mean of the scores given in Table 12.10. Because we have three scores of 23, five scores of 25, and so on, the mean is calculated as follows:

$$\bar{x} = \frac{3(23) + 5(25) + 2(28) + 4(31) + 2(34) + 4(35)}{20} = \frac{582}{20} = 29.1$$

TABLE 12.10

Scores	Frequency
23	3
25	5
28	2
31	4
34	2
35	4
	$n = 20$

In general, the formula for the mean of a set of scores organized in a frequency table is given by

$$\bar{x} = \frac{f_1 x_1 + f_2 x_2 + f_3 x_3 + \cdots + f_k x_k}{f_1 + f_2 + f_3 + \cdots + f_k}$$

where $x_1, x_2, x_3, \ldots, x_k$ are the scores and $f_1, f_2, f_3, \ldots, f_k$ are the corresponding frequencies.

Table 12.11 is a grouped frequency table. To calculate the mean of data organized in a grouped frequency table we simply assume that the scores of

TABLE 12.11

Interval	Midpoint	Frequency
40–44	42	3
45–49	47	6
50–54	52	7
55–59	57	4
60–64	62	2
		$n = 22$

each interval are "centered" around the midpoint of that interval. Thus, the mean of the scores in Table 12.11 is

$$\bar{x} = \frac{3(42) + 6(47) + 7(52) + 4(57) + 2(62)}{22} = \frac{1124}{22} = 51\frac{1}{11}$$

Obviously, this is an approximation, as we are assuming that the scores of each interval are centered about the midpoint of the interval. However, for many applications such an approximation is sufficiently accurate. Notice that the size of the intervals in Table 12.11 is an odd number (5). This makes the midpoints whole numbers, which helps the computational work a bit.

Measures of central tendency are used to indicate some sort of description about a set of data in terms of one specific value. For example, when we say that the mean of the five scores 40, 52, 54, 55, and 59 is 54, we are attempting to describe the entire set of scores by merely stating a "representative" score. In this particular example, the mean serves well as a "typical" score, but this is not always true. For example, suppose that on five tests a student had scores of 100, 99, 98, 97, and 15. The mean score is $81\frac{4}{5}$, which is not very "typical" of the five scores. In this case, the "middle score" of 98 would better represent the set of scores. The middle score is called the *median*. More specifically, if we arrange a group of numbers in either ascending or descending order of magnitude, *the median is the middle number if there is an odd number of scores or the mean of the two middle scores if the number of scores is even.*

EXAMPLE 1

What is the median of the scores 7, 9, 11, 13, and 15?

Solution The median is the middle score of 11.

EXAMPLE 2

Find the median of the scores 7, 9, 11, 13, 15, and 16.

Solution The median of the scores 7, 9, 11, 13, 15, and 16 is the mean of the two middle scores 11 and 13. Thus, the median is

$$\frac{11 + 13}{2} = 12$$

It should be evident that the median is *not affected by extreme values*, as is the mean. We could have infinitely many sets of five scores each having a median of 11 simply by making it the middle score. For example, the set of scores 1, 3, 11, 981, and 5217 has a median of 11 as does the set 5, 10, 11, 12, and 13.

REMARK There is a technique for calculating the median of a set of data organized in a frequency table; however, for our purposes in this text we will not need to discuss it.

Both the median and the mean summarize the data with a single number. It is helpful to consider both in the interpretation of the data. Whenever there are a few very large or very small values in the data, the median is probably more valuable than the mean.

A box and whiskers plot is an efficient graphing technique to describe information about the center and spread of a set of data. It relies on the use of the median along with four other summary numbers. Two of these numbers are the lower extreme and the upper extreme, which we have already used to find the range of the data. A stem and leaf plot can be constructed to order our data from the lower extreme to upper extreme. Then by counting we can easily locate the median and draw a vertical line through it. We then want to locate two other numbers that mark off the bottom quarter (first or lower quartile—Q_1) and the top quarter of the data (third or upper quartile—Q_3). This will divide the data into four groups of roughly the same size. The median represents Q_2 where 50% of the values are below the median. This is also referred to as the 50th percentile. Likewise, Q_1 is the 25 percentile (P_{25}) with 25% of the value below Q_1 and $Q_3 = P_{75}$ with 75% of the values below Q_3.

The vertical lines in the stem and leaf plot in Figure 12.22 show the data divided into four groups. The points of division for the quartiles are indicated below.

4	Lower extreme	
11	First or lower quartile	Q_1
18	Median	Q_2
24.5	Third or upper quartile	Q_3
47	Upper extreme	

Stem	Leaf
0	4 5 7 8 9 9
1	0 0 0 0 0 1|1 2 2 3 3 3 4 5 5 6 6 8 8 9
2	0 2 2 3 3 3 3 4 4 4|5 6 9
3	0 0 1 3 5 6
4	1 4 7

FIGURE 12.22

The box and whiskers plot in Figure 12.23 illustrates the summary numbers and "boxes in" the middle half of the data with whiskers showing the range of the data.

A box and whiskers plot does obscure some of the data, so clusters and gaps are no longer easily spotted. However, we can focus on relative positions of large sets of data and make comparisons on the variability. Even if

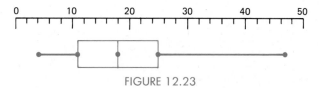

FIGURE 12.23

sets of data have unequal numbers of values, a box plot can still show comparisons. The stem and leaf plots in Figures 12.24*a* and *b*, illustrating the wind speeds from Table 12.3 in Section 12.1, can be used to construct box and whiskers plots that compare the three sets of numbers. Notice that the

January		July
6 3	5	1 7 9
7	6	1 3 4 5 6 6 7 7 8 8 9 9
9 6 6 3 2 1	7	0 2 4 5 5 6 6 6 7 8 8 9 9 9 9
7 7 7 6 3 2 1 1 0	8	0 1 2 3 4 4 4 6 7 9 9 9 9
8 8 7 6 5 4 4 2 2 0	9	1 2 3 5 5 5 6 7
9 7 6 6 5 4 3 3 0 0 0 0	10	2 3 4 9 9
7 7 6 5 3 3 2 1 1 0 0	11	1
9 8 4 2	12	
9	13	5 6
3	14	
2 2	15	

FIGURE 12.24 (*a*)

		Annual
	5	
	6	3 4 5 7 9
	7	5 5 5 6 7 9 9
	8	0 0 2 4 4 5 7 7 8 8 8 9
	9	0 0 1 1 2 2 2 3 4 5 6 7
	10	1 2 3 3 3 5 5 6 6 6 6 7 7 8 9
	11	1 6
	12	1 3 4 5 8 9

FIGURE 12.24 (*b*)

vertical lines in the stem and leaf plots that divide each set of numbers into four groups makes it easy to translate the data into a box and whiskers plot in Figure 12.25.

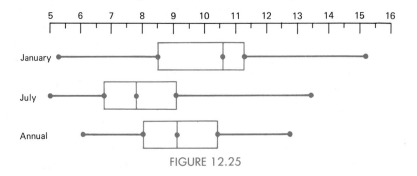

FIGURE 12.25

We can focus on the summary numbers as well as make some overall observations about the sets of data. In January the middle 50% of the data lies between 8.6 and 11.3, whereas in July the middle 50% of the data lies between 6.9 and 9.2. It is evident that, overall, the United States is windier in January than in July and there is less variability in wind speed in July, as shown by the width of the "box" in Figure 12.25. The box allows us to see where the middle half of each set of data is and the whiskers focus on the range of the numbers.

The final measure of central tendency to be considered in this section is the *mode. The mode of a set of numbers is that number that occurs most frequently.* We should immediately realize that the mode may not exist, or, if it does exist, it may not be unique. Consider the following examples.

EXAMPLE 1

What is the mode of the set of scores 3, 4, 5, 5, 5, 6, 10, and 14?

Solution   Because there are 3 scores of 5, the mode is 5.

EXAMPLE 2

Find the mode of the set of scores 63, 64, 68, 69, and 72.

Solution   The set of scores 63, 64, 68, 69, and 72 has no mode.

EXAMPLE 3

Indicate the mode of the set of scores 2, 3, 4, 5, 5, 8, 9, 10, 10, 11, 13 and 15.

Solution   The set of scores 2, 3, 4, 5, 5, 8, 9, 10, 10, 11, 13, and 15 has two modes, 5 and 10, and is called a *bimodal* distribution.

In the case of data tabulated in classes, we are frequently interested in the *modal class* or *modal interval*, that is, the interval with the greatest frequency. Again, grouped frequency distributions may have more than one modal class. The distribution in Table 12.11 has one modal class, 50–54, whereas the distribution in Table 12.12 has two modal classes, 10–14 and 20–24.

TABLE 12.12

Interval	Frequency
10–14	5
15–19	3
20–24	5
25–29	2
30–34	1

Now that we have introduced three measures of central tendency (mean, median, mode), a natural question arises: When do you use each measure and for what purpose? This is a difficult question and has no definite answer because it depends largely on the "purpose of the message" conveyed by the measure. However, we can make a few brief comments about each measure and illustrate some possible uses, as well as "abuses," made of them.

The mean is "central" to a set of scores in the sense that the algebraic sum of the deviations of the scores from their mean is zero. For example, consider the scores 3, 4, 6, 7, and 10, which have a mean of 6. The deviations of the scores from the mean are $10 - 6 = 4$, $7 - 6 = 1$, $6 - 6 = 0$, $4 - 6 = {}^-2$, and $3 - 6 = {}^-3$, and the sum of the deviations is $4 + 1 + 0 + {}^-2 + {}^-3 = 0$. Because of this property, a school board wanting to determine what a 7 percent cost-of-living raise for all teachers will cost the district could effectively use the mean salary as a representative salary for computational purposes. Likewise, the general manager of a baseball team may have a certain amount of money to be used for raises for the next season. If this amount is to be divided among 25 players, he can compute a "mean raise" and then begin working in terms of that figure. He knows that if one "star" gets a raise far above the mean, then some second-stringer is probably going to get a raise far below the mean to compensate for it.

We want to re-emphasize the point that the mean is affected by extreme values. Thus, a statement about the mean salary of a group of people may not tell much about the individual salaries of the people. For example, suppose you are told that the mean salary of five people is $50,000. The salaries may all be very similar, such as $48,000, $49,000, $50,000, $51,000, and $52,000; or they may be rather dissimilar, such as $10,000, $20,000, $40,000, $60,000, and $120,000; or one of them may be completely out of line with the rest, such as $5,000, $6,000, $9,000, $10,000, and $220,000. In other words, the mean by itself does not give much information about the individual numbers.

The median is the middle score; it is not an arithmetical average and is not affected by extreme values, but it, too, by itself, gives very little information about how the "scores" are scattered. For example, suppose that you are told that the median salary of five people is $30,000. This one salary gives no information about the other four salaries except that two of them are less than or equal to $30,000, and two of them are more than or equal to $30,000.

The median salary of all employees of some factory may be more useful as a typical figure than the mean salary because it is not affected by the high salaries of the executives, unless there are more executives than other workers. Likewise, the median salary of all major league baseball players might be considered more representative than the mean salary.

The mode is useful, as it is the most common value or values, if they exist; however, its usefulness is of a more general nature. For example, a dress-shop owner is probably going to stock more dresses in the popular sizes (modes) than in the extreme sizes. Likewise, it would be helpful for the owner of a men's shoe store to know that the previous year's shoe sales formed a bimodal distribution with peaks at sizes 9D and 10E.

The concepts of mean, median, and mode are really easy to understand. However, in everyday language the terms are often used incorrectly, especially mean and median. Then, to make matters worse, the term "average" is tossed around to refer to all three of the concepts. Consider the following situations.

1. The *average* rainfall for the month of June is 4.5 inches. (Here the word average is used instead of mean.)
2. Bill is an *average* student. (In this situation the word average probably refers to the idea of Bill's being in the middle of some sort of qualitative ranking.)
3. The *average* cap size for this year's graduation class was $7\frac{1}{8}$. (This is probably a statement about a mode, that is, the most common cap size is $7\frac{1}{8}$.)
4. The *average* salary for the faculty at a certain university is $35,000. (This type of statement really creates confusion. Unless more information is given, we simply do not know whether the "average" is a mean or a median. It may depend on who is making the statement and for what purpose. If a larger figure is advantageous, then probably the mean is being used, because the higher salaries of administrators would raise the average. However, if the statement is made by someone attempting to get faculty raises, then the "average" could be a median.)

PROBLEM SET 12.3

1. Find the mean, median, and mode for each of the following sets of scores:
   a. 1, 2, 2, 3, 4, 7, 11, 16, 19
   b. 4, 7, 10, 11, 12, 14, 15, 17, 19, 114, 114
   c. 2, 2, 2, 3, 4, 7, 10, 13, 14, 16
   d. 3, 4, 4, 4, 6, 9, 11, 13, 17, 18, 18, 20
   e. 5, 14, 3, 8, 26, 4, 17, 21, 8, 14, 17, 32, 14, 41, 9, 13, 32

2. Find the mean for the following distribution:

Scores	Frequency
70	2
75	3
80	7
85	5
90	4
95	2
100	2

3. Find the mean for each of the following grouped data distributions:

a.

Interval	Frequency
20–24	5
25–29	4
30–34	6
35–39	10
40–44	5
45–49	6
50–54	4

b.

Interval	Frequency
20–26	2
27–33	3
34–40	6
41–47	7
48–54	2

4. Find the mean and modal class for the following distribution:

Interval	Frequency
40–48	3
49–57	4
58–66	7
67–75	15
76–84	17
85–93	4

5. Give an example involving seven scores where the mean is greater than all but one of the scores.

6. The mean salary for 24 people is $8000. How much will one additional salary of $58,000 increase the mean salary for all 25 people?

7. Give an example of a set of 8 scores for which the mean is 30 and no two scores are the same.

8. The chamber of commerce advertises Ideal City as the "place to live" because it has a mean temperature of 60°F. How should you react to such a statement?

9. a. The mean score of a set of 30 tests is 82. Find the sum of the 30 test scores.

   b. Suppose that four students had scores of 60 and five students had scores of 100 on a test. Find the mean, median, and mode of the nine test scores.

   c. The total for the test scores of 30 students was 2610. What was the mean score?

10. The results of Sandy's fall semester grades are as follows:

Course	Credits	Grades
Math	5	B
History	3	C
English	3	A
Psychology	3	B
P.E.	1	A

Find her grade point average for the semester (A = 4, B = 3, C = 2, D = 1, F = 0).

11. How do you think the term "average" is being used in each of the following statements?

a. The *average* yearly snowfall is 40 inches.

b. Sue is an *average* basketball player.

c. Bill is of *average* height.

d. She is an *average* teacher.

e. Factory workers make an *average* of $7.50 per hour.

f. "Who Shot the Butler?" was an *average* movie.

g. On the *average*, children watch TV 3 hours a day.

12. Suppose three instructors, Mr. Ly, Ms. Demeanor, and Ms. Inturpret, gave the same test to five students in their classes. The results were as follows:

Mr. Ly's students: 90, 94, 95, 96, and 100

Ms. Demeanor's students: 52, 68, 85, 98, and 98

Ms. Inturpret's students: 74, 79, 96, 98, and 99

Each of the instructors claimed that "on the average" his or her class did the best job. What did each of them use as the "average?"

Use your calculator to help with Problems 13-16.

 13. Find the mean of the set of scores: 18, 20, 21, 26, 28, 32, 32, 34, 37, 42, 48, 51, 54, 57, 58, 62, 67, 69, 74, 82, 83, 86, 88, 89, and 94.

14. Find the mean for the following distributions:

a.

Scores	Frequency
42	31
47	47
52	69
57	85
62	62
67	51
72	37
77	19

b.

Intervals	Frequency
10–14	7
15–19	4
20–24	8
25–29	6
30–34	9
35–39	5
40–44	6
45–49	5

c.

Intervals	Frequency
95–100	3
89–94	8
83–88	5
77–82	6
71–76	2
65–70	1

15. **a.** Find the mean of the following set of scores: 75, 60, 67, 66, 78, 88, 97, 81, 88, 51, 74, 91, 81, 59, 72, 84, 80, 83, 76, 88, 91, 64, 73, 77, 94, 77, 56, 63, 96, 76, 68, 95, 75, 87, 71, 77, 81, 90, 76, and 78.

    b. Now construct a grouped frequency table using intervals of 10 units starting with a lower class of 50–59.

    c. Find the mean of the grouped frequency table in part **b.**

    d. Compare your results from parts **a** and **c**.

16. **a.** Find the mean of the following 50 scores: 67, 71, 78, 72, 88, 87, 68, 98, 94, 97, 84, 83, 74, 64, 69, 70, 85, 94, 98, 89, 87, 86, 78, 77, 84, 94, 98, 97, 96, 87, 82, 81, 72, 75, 78, 86, 91, 90, 99, 69, 79, 85, 87, 93, 98, 76, 78, 81, 89, and 87.

    b. Construct a grouped frequency table using intervals of size 7 starting with a lower class of 60–66.

    c. Find the mean of the grouped frequency table in part **b.**

    d. Compare your results from parts **a** and **c**.

17. **a.** Using the data set of heights (to the nearest cm) of 10 year olds, make a stem and leaf plot.

    b. Construct a box and whiskers plot.

    c. Indicate the lower and upper extremes, the median, and the first and third quartiles on both the stem and leaf plot and box and whiskers plot.

133	137	120	122	138	127
125	115	135	137	130	148
134	130	131	152	123	136
128	132	117	128	129	110

    d. What conclusions can be drawn from the two different plots? Discuss the strengths and weaknesses of each.

18. **a.** Using the test scores provided below, construct box and whiskers plots to compare the data. What are three observations you can make about the data from the box and whiskers plots?

    b. In what ways can the box and whiskers plots be used for interpreting and comparing the results on the tests?

Test A				Test B			
75	80	97	72	99	67	96	98
83	54	87	85	85	94	98	100
73	91	89	77	82	84	83	87
69	99	92	68	88	76	72	95
58	81	74	70	97	91	89	100

Pedagogical Problems and Activities

19. Find examples where measures of central tendency are used in the media. Discuss how they are used and the appropriateness of their use.

20. Gather prices from several brands of margarine of the same capacity (1 lb) at two different stores (wholesale versus retail supermarket). Find measures of central tendency (mean, median, and mode) of your two sets of data. Construct box and whiskers plots to observe the spread of data and make comparisons.

21. From the information that follows, a bar graph has been drawn showing the number of aluminum cans students have collected.

Andrea	24 cans
Brian	46 cans
Travis	60 cans
Tanya	42 cans
Jessica	30 cans
Erin	28 cans
Greg	50 cans
Jared	56 cans

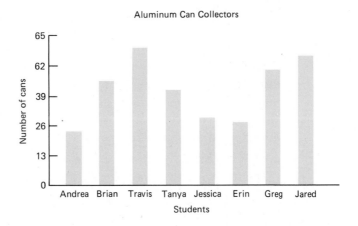

Aluminum Can Collectors

Illustrate or physically demonstrate by cutting and moving portions of the bars to explain why the mean number of cans collected is 42.

12.4 ANALYZING DATA: EXTENSIONS OF CENTRAL TENDENCY

Measures of central tendency tell us something about the "typical" score but do not give much information about how the scores are scattered around that measure. For example, both sets of scores {6, 12, 18, 24, 30} and {1, 2, 18, 34,

35} have a mean of 18, but are "scattered" differently. Even the knowledge of all three basic measures of central tendency (mean, median, mode) for a set of scores does not yield much information about the scattering of the scores. In this section, we investigate some measures of scatter, more commonly called *measures of dispersion*. Various measures of dispersion exist, but we will concentrate on two of them—namely, the *range* and *standard deviation*.

The *range* (defined in Section 12.1 as the difference between the smallest and largest score) is a measure of dispersion that is easy to calculate, but provides limited information regarding the scattering of the scores. For example, the sets of scores {0, 1, 2, 84, 100}, {25, 50, 75, 100, 125}, and {200, 218, 219, 280, 300} each have a range of 100. In other words, the range merely indicates the "distance" between the endpoints of a distribution, but yields no information about the distribution of scores between the endpoints.

Now let us concentrate on the *standard deviation*. In general terms, the standard deviation is a number that indicates how the scores are *scattered about the mean* of the distribution. It is hoped that this general statement will take on more meaning for you as we do problems involving the standard deviation.

Rather than starting our discussion by stating a definition, let us begin by indicating a step-by-step procedure that can be followed to compute the standard deviation for a set of scores.

Step 1 Find the mean of the set of scores.

Step 2 Find the deviation (difference) of each score from the mean.

Step 3 Square each deviation (difference).

Step 4 Find the mean of this set of squared deviations. This result is called the *variance*.

Step 5 Find the square root of the variance. This result is called the *standard deviation*.

The following two examples illustrate this procedure.

EXAMPLE 1

Find the standard deviation for the scores 3, 4, 7, 12, 13, and 15.

Solution First, let us calculate the mean.

$$\bar{x} = \frac{3 + 4 + 7 + 12 + 13 + 15}{6} = \frac{54}{6} = 9$$

Now we can arrange some of the work in a table (Table 12.13)

TABLE 12.13

Scores x	Deviations from the Mean $(x - \bar{x})$	Deviations Squared $(x - \bar{x})^2$
3	$^-6$	36
4	$^-5$	25
7	$^-2$	4
12	3	9
13	4	16
15	6	36
		126

$$V \text{ (variance)} = \frac{126}{6} = 21$$

Thus, to the nearest tenth, the standard deviation (s) is

$$s = \sqrt{21} = 4.6$$

EXAMPLE 2

Find the standard deviation for the scores 1, 5, 11, 30, 62, and 65.

Solution The mean of the scores is

$$\bar{x} = \frac{1 + 5 + 11 + 30 + 62 + 65}{6} = \frac{174}{6} = 29$$

The remainder of the computation is shown in Table 12.14

TABLE 12.14

x	$(x - \bar{x})$	$(x - \bar{x})^2$
1	$^-28$	784
5	$^-24$	576
11	$^-18$	324
30	1	1
62	33	1089
65	36	1296
		4070

$$V \text{ (variance)} = \frac{4070}{6} = 678.33 \text{ (nearest hundredth)}$$

$$s \text{ (standard deviation)} = \sqrt{678.33} = 16.0 \text{ (nearest tenth)}$$

Note the relative sizes of the standard deviations in Examples 1 and 2. The standard deviation will be affected by the "amount of scatter" of the scores. In other words, the more the scores deviate from the mean, the larger the standard deviation will be.

In general, if we are given n scores $x_1, x_2, x_3, \ldots, x_n$ having a mean of $\bar{x}$, then the standard deviation is

$$s = \sqrt{\frac{(x_1 - \bar{x})^2 + (x_2 - \bar{x})^2 + \cdots + (x_n - \bar{x})^2}{n}}$$

If a frequency table without intervals is used, the work for computing the standard deviation can be organized as in Table 12.15. The mean is

$$\bar{x} = \frac{3(5) + 5(7) + 7(10) + 4(12) + 1(32)}{20} = \frac{200}{20} = 10$$

TABLE 12.15

Scores x	Frequency f	$(x - \bar{x})$	$(x - \bar{x})^2$	$f \cdot (x - \bar{x})^2$
5	3	$^-5$	25	75
7	5	$^-3$	9	45
10	7	0	0	0
12	4	2	4	16
32	1	22	484	484
	20			620

$V \text{ (variance)} = \dfrac{620}{20} = 31$

$s \text{ (standard deviation)} = \sqrt{31} = 5.6 \text{ (nearest tenth)}$

Note that except for the one score of 32, the rest of the scores are closely grouped around the mean of 10. Consequently, a relatively small standard deviation was obtained.

If a frequency table with intervals is used, the deviations from the mean are computed by using the midpoints of the intervals. Table 12.16 illustrates this procedure.

Let us conclude this section with a few brief comments. Finding the standard deviation for a set of six scores (as we did in the first two examples of this section) is not a very realistic problem, but remember that in this section we are simply learning how to *compute* the standard deviation. More realistic sets of scores will be used in the next section for discussing some uses of the standard deviation.

Standard deviation is not a concept found in elementary school mathe-

TABLE 12.16

Intervals	Midpoints x_i	f	$f \cdot x_i$	$(x_i - \bar{x})$	$(x_i - \bar{x})^2$	$f \cdot (x_i - \bar{x})^2$
1–5	3	5	15	12.2	148.84	744.20
6–10	8	9	72	7.2	51.84	466.56
11–15	13	11	143	2.2	4.84	53.24
16–20	18	13	234	2.8	7.84	101.92
21–25	23	8	184	7.8	60.84	486.72
26–30	28	4	112	12.8	163.84	655.36
		50	760			2508.00

$$\bar{x} = \frac{760}{50} = 15.2 \quad \text{This is computed before the last three columns can be computed.}$$

$$V = \frac{2508}{50} = 50.16$$

$$s = \sqrt{50.16} = 7.1 \text{ (nearest tenth)}$$

matics textbooks. However, as a teacher, you will be reading and studying a variety of educational literature in which the concept of standard deviation will be used. Thus, we feel that the inclusion of the last two sections of this chapter is appropriate.

PROBLEM SET 12.4

1. Find the standard deviation, to the nearest tenth, for each of the following sets of scores:

   a. 2, 3, 8, 12, and 15
   b. 1, 2, 7, 11, and 14
   c. 1, 4, 6, 7, 8, 12, 13, 20, 22, and 27
   d. 2, 5, 8, 14, 24, 25, 40, and 42
   e. 1, 3, 5, 6, 8, 50, and 137
   f. 5, 10, 20, 35, 50, 55, 70, 90, and 115

2. Find the standard deviation, to the nearest tenth, for each of the following frequency distributions:

a.

Scores	Frequency
5	3
10	5
15	7
20	4
30	1

b.

Scores	Frequency
1	5
5	4
8	5
10	7
12	5
13	3
36	1

3. Find the standard deviation, to the nearest tenth, of the following grouped frequency distribution:

Intervals	Frequency
3–7	2
8–12	5
13–17	8
18–22	1
23–27	4

4. Consider the two sets of scores {1, 2, 3, 4, 5} and {1, 3, 5, 7, 9}.
   a. Predict which set of scores will have the greater standard deviation. Explain your choice.
   b. Compute the standard deviation for both sets of scores to check your prediction in part a.

5. Consider the two sets of scores {3, 4, 5, 6, 7} and {28, 29, 30, 31, 32}.
   a. Predict which set of scores will have the greater standard deviation. Why?
   b. Compute the standard deviation for both sets of scores to check your prediction in part a.

6. Consider the two sets of scores {1, 2, 3, 4, 5} and {10, 20, 30, 40, 50}.
   a. Predict which set of scores will have the greater standard deviation. Why?
   b. Compute the standard deviation for both sets of scores. Was your prediction correct in part a?

Use your calculator to help with problems 7-12.

7. For each of the following sets of scores, (1) find the mean to the nearest tenth, and (2) find the standard deviation to the nearest tenth:
   a. 78, 81, 63, 75, 76, 82, 67, 74, 78, 79, 82, 77, 78, 80, and 81
   b. 93, 94, 85, 87, 88, 82, 78, 76, 95, 99, 91, 97, 98, 84
   c. 24, 29, 35, 39, 43, 48, 55, 56, 71, 79, 85, 90
   d. 17, 25, 34, 36, 48, 57, 68, 71, 79, 86, 92, 99

8. For the following distribution, (a) find the mean to the nearest tenth, and (b) find the standard deviation to the nearest tenth:

Scores	Frequency
98	4
96	5
95	7
90	8
87	3

Scores	Frequency
85	6
83	2
80	8
77	5
76	2

9. The following table shows the results of a test given to 100 students:

Intervals	Frequency
40–49	3
50–59	2
60–69	15
70–79	30
80–89	35
90–99	15

   a. Compute the mean to the nearest tenth.
   b. Compute the standard deviation to the nearest tenth.

10. The following table shows the total points accumulated for a semester for a class of 50 students.

Intervals	Frequency
300–350	4
249–299	9
198–248	13
147–197	14
96–146	7
45–95	3

   a. Compute the mean to the nearest tenth.
   b. Compute the standard deviation to the nearest tenth.

11. Three classes of 20 students each took the same exam and the results were as follows:

   Class A: 70, 70, 71, 72, 74, 76, 76, 80, 81, 82, 83, 85, 86, 86, 90, 90, 90, 91, 92, 95

   Class B: 15, 23, 31, 45, 48, 56, 60, 62, 68, 70, 72, 75, 78, 80, 82, 83, 88, 88, 88, 88

   Class C: 30, 31, 31, 33, 34, 37, 37, 38, 39, 40, 42, 43, 43, 45, 47, 57, 48, 50, 52, 53

   a. Predict which class will have the greatest standard deviation.
   b. How do you think the standard deviations for Class A and Class C will compare? Why?
   c. Compute the standard deviation, to the nearest tenth, for each class.

12. The heights, measured to the nearest inch, of the traveling squads for two basketball teams are as follows:

Team A: 65, 66, 68, 70, 72, 76, 77, 78, 79, 80, 81, 82
Team B: 72, 73, 78, 79, 79, 80, 81, 81, 82, 82, 83

   a. Find the average (mean) height for each of the squads (nearest tenth).
   b. Find the standard deviation for each set of heights (nearest tenth).

Pedagogical Problems and Activities

13. a. What happens to the mean and standard deviation of a set of data when the same number is added to each value in the data?
   b. Verify your answer by finding the mean and standard deviation of a group of numbers. Now add a value to each number and find the mean and standard deviation of these numbers.

14. a. What happens to the mean and standard deviation of a set of data when a constant number is multiplied times each number in a set of data?
   b. Verify your answer by multiplying each number in the set of data in Problem 13b and finding the mean and standard deviation of these numbers.

12.5   USING THE STANDARD DEVIATION

It is not uncommon to hear a student say about a teacher that "he or she grades on a curve." This may be in reference to the *normal curve*. A certain distribution of scores, which is said to be a *normal distribution,* will produce a bell-shaped curve, commonly called the *normal curve,* as indicated in Figure 12.26. For such a distribution the mean, median, and mode all have the same value and the curve is symmetrical with respect to that value.

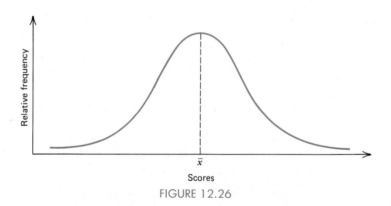

FIGURE 12.26

If a distribution is normal, or at least approximately normal, some statements about the spread of scores can be made, as indicated in Figure 12.27. Note the following statements:

1. Approximately 68.2 percent of the scores will fall in the interval between $\bar{x} - s$ and $\bar{x} + s$. (Remember that $\bar{x}$ represents the mean and s the standard deviation.)

2. Approximately 95.4 percent of the scores will fall in the interval between $\bar{x} - 2s$ and $\bar{x} + 2s$.

3. Approximately 99.8 percent of the scores will fall in the interval between $\bar{x} - 3s$ and $\bar{x} + 3s$.

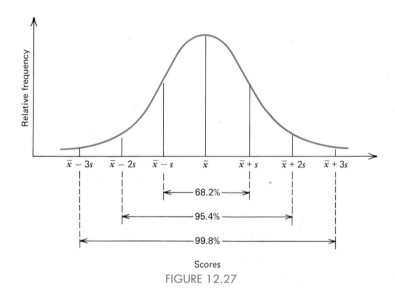

FIGURE 12.27

Now suppose that we have 100 scores having a mean of 65 and a standard deviation of 5. If we know that the distribution of the scores is approximately normal, then referring to Figure 12.27 we can draw the following conclusions:

1. Approximately 68 of the scores will fall in the interval between 60 and 70 ($\bar{x} - s = 65 - 5 = 60$ and $\bar{x} + s = 65 + 5 = 70$).

2. Approximately 95 scores will be in the interval between 55 and 75.

3. Approximately 99 scores will be in the interval between 50 and 80.

Figure 12.28 shows another way of looking at the facts about a normal distribution. Theoretically, the normal curve "tails off" in both directions beyond three standard deviations from the mean. However, for most practical purposes, a consideration of the scores between $\bar{x} - 3s$ and $\bar{x} + 3s$ is sufficient, because this includes more than 99 percent of the scores.

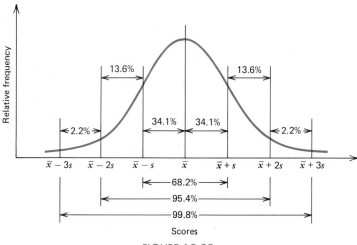

FIGURE 12.28

Using the distribution of scores indicated above the horizontal axis in Figure 12.28, the following statements about the previously mentioned set of 100 scores with a mean of 65 and a standard deviation of 5 can be made:

1. Approximately 2 scores fall in the interval between 75 and 80 ($\bar{x} + 2s = 65 + 10 = 75$ and $\bar{x} + 3s = 65 + 15 = 80$).
2. Approximately 14 scores fall in the interval between 70 and 75.
3. Approximately 34 scores fall in the interval between 65 and 70.
4. Approximately 34 scores fall in the interval between 60 and 65.
5. Approximately 14 scores fall in the interval between 55 and 60.
6. Approximately 2 scores fall in the interval between 50 and 55.

Referring back to Figure 12.28, let us pose another problem. Suppose we want to know the number of scores from a normal distribution that fall between the mean ($\bar{x}$) and one-half of the standard deviation above the mean—that is, between $\bar{x}$ and $\bar{x} + \frac{1}{2}s$. Thinking in terms of area under the curve, we should see that we cannot simply take one-half of 34.1 percent. However, there are tables available that can be used to handle such problems. Table 12.17 contains some values for this purpose. In this table, z represents the number of standard deviations away from the mean and P represents the percentage (to the nearest tenth of a percent) of the scores between the mean and z. For example, from the table we see that $P = 19.2$ when $z = 0.5$. This means that approximately 19.2 percent of the scores of a normal distribution will fall between the mean and 0.5 of a standard deviation *above* the mean. Because the normal curve is symmetrical about the mean, there are also approximately 19.2 percent of the scores between the mean and 0.5 of a standard deviation *below* the mean. Thus, we could say

TABLE 12.17 NORMAL CURVE PERCENTAGES

z	P	z	P	z	P
0.0	0.0	1.0	34.1	2.0	47.7
0.1	4.0	1.1	36.4	2.1	48.2
0.2	7.9	1.2	38.5	2.2	48.6
0.3	11.8	1.3	40.3	2.3	48.9
0.4	15.5	1.4	41.9	2.4	49.2
0.5	19.2	1.5	43.3	2.5	49.4
0.6	22.6	1.6	44.5	2.6	49.5
0.7	25.8	1.7	45.5	2.7	49.7
0.8	28.8	1.8	46.4	2.8	49.7
0.9	31.6	1.9	47.1	2.9	49.8
				3.0	49.9

that approximately 38.4 percent of the scores fall within one-half of a standard deviation of the mean. (Notice, for example, that $P = 34.1$ when $z = 1$.
This agrees with Fig. 12.28).

Let us conclude this section by illustrating how a table such as Table 12.17
can be used to calculate many different facts about a specific normal distribution. Suppose the weights, to the nearest pound, of 1000 male students
form a normal distribution having a mean of 160 and a standard deviation
of 10. This information can be recorded on the normal curve as indicated in
Figure 12.29.

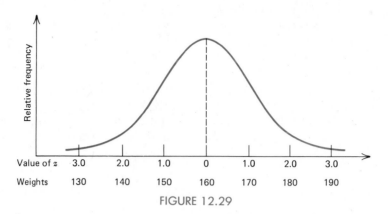

FIGURE 12.29

Now we can use Table 12.17 and establish the following (keep in mind that
these are "approximations"):

1. 341 male students weigh between 160 and 170. (This is found by letting z
   $= 1.0$ because 170 is one standard deviation above the mean of 160 and
   34.1 percent of 1000 is 341.)

2. 477 male students weigh between 160 and 180.

3. 136 male students weigh between 170 and 180. (This fact is found by subtracting the 341 in (1) from the 477 in (2).)

4. 682 male students weigh between 150 and 170. (This fact can be found by doubling the 341 in (1) because the curve is symmetrical about the mean.)

5. 192 male students weigh between 160 and 165. (Because 165 is one-half of a standard deviation above the mean, we let $z = 0.5$.)

6. 149 male students weigh between 165 and 170. (This can be found by subtracting the 192 in (5) from the 341 in (1).)

7. 258 male students weigh between 160 and 167. (Let $z = 0.7$, because 167 is 0.7 of a standard deviation above the mean.)

8. 385 male students weigh between 148 and 160. (Let $z = 1.2$, because 148 is 1.2 standard deviations below the mean.)

9. 643 male students weigh between 148 and 167. (Add the results of (7) and (8).)

A word of caution is in order here. The P values in Table 12.17 are percentages. We must be careful not to confuse percentages with *percentiles*. Percentages indicate what portion of a perfect score a person has achieved. For example, getting 30 items correct on a 50-item test produces a 60-percent score. Such a percentage score, by itself, gives no indication as to how this person did compared to others taking the same test. Suppose, for example, the 60-percent score ranked in the middle (at the median) of a distribution of the scores of all people taking the test. Then the 60-percent score would be said to rank this person in the *50th percentile*.

The concepts of *quartile, decile,* and *percentile* are used extensively in educational literature. Specifically, the *first quartile* of a distribution is a value such that one-fourth of the scores are less than it; the *first decile* is a value such that one-tenth of the scores are less than it; the *first percentile* is a value such that one one-hundredth of the scores are less than it. Obviously, these measures are interrelated. For example, the first decile is the same as the 10th percentile, and the first quartile is the same as the 25th percentile. The 5th decile, 2nd quartile, and the 50th percentile are all the same as the median.

PROBLEM SET 12.5

Use Figure 12.27 to help with Problems 1–4.

1. **a.** A set of scores is normally distributed about a mean of 85. The standard deviation of the distribution is 5. Find the intervals that contain approximately **(i)** 68.2 percent, **(ii)** 95.4 percent, **(iii)** 99.8 percent of the scores.

   b. How might this information be used?

2. **a.** A set of measurements is normally distributed about a mean of 1.7. The standard deviation is 0.3. Find the intervals that contain approximately **(i)** 68.2 percent, **(ii)** 95.4 percent, and **(iii)** 99.8 percent of the measurements.

   b. In what way is this information valuable?

3. A set of 1000 scores is normally distributed about a mean of 62 and has a standard deviation of 7. Find the number of scores in each of the following intervals.

   a. Between 63 and 77

   b. Between 56 and 84

   c. Between 49 and 91

4. A set of 2000 scores is normally distributed about a mean of 62 and has a standard deviation of 12. Find the number of scores in each of the following intervals:

   a. Between 50 and 74

   b. Between 38 and 86

   c. Between 26 and 98

Use Figure 12.28 to help with Problems 5–7.

5. A set of 1000 scores is normally distributed about a mean of 68. The standard deviation of the distribution is 7. Find the number of scores in each of the following intervals:

   a. Between 68 and 75

   b. Between 68 and 82

   c. Between 61 and 75

   d. Between 54 and 68

   e. Between 54 and 75

   f. Between 82 and 89

6. A set of 1000 measurements is normally distributed about a mean of 3.4. The standard deviation of the set is 0.6. Find the number of measurements in each of the following intervals:

   a. Between 3.4 and 4.0

   b. Between 2.8 and 4.6

   c. Between 2.2 and 3.4

   d. Between 1.6 and 2.2

   e. Between 2.2 and 5.2

   f. Between 4.0 and 5.2

7. A set of 2000 scores is normally distributed about a mean of 110. The standard deviation of the set is 8. Find the number of scores in each of the following intervals:

   a. Between 110 and 126
   b. Between 102 and 126
   c. Between 86 and 94
   d. Between 94 and 118
   e. Between 94 and 102
   f. Above 134

Use a figure such as Figure 12.29 and Table 12.17 to help with Problems 8–10.

8. A set of 1000 scores is normally distributed about a mean of 180. The standard deviation of the distribution is 10. Find the number of scores in each of the following intervals.
   a. Between 180 and 200
   b. Between 180 and 185
   c. Between 180 and 192
   d. Between 190 and 200
   e. Between 160 and 170
   f. Between 171 and 180
   g. Between 163 and 188
   h. Between 157 and 204

9. A set of 1000 scores is normally distributed about a mean of 120. The standard deviation of the distribution is 20. Find the number of scores in each of the following intervals:
   a. Between 120 and 130
   b. Between 120 and 150
   c. Between 130 and 150
   d. Between 108 and 120
   e. Between 88 and 110
   f. Between 64 and 120
   g. Between 112 and 134
   h. Between 122 and 176

10. A set of 3000 scores is normally distributed about a mean of 75, and the standard deviation of the distribution is 10. Find the number of scores in each of the following intervals:
   a. Between 70 and 75
   b. Between 60 and 75
   c. Between 60 and 70
   d. Between 46 and 75
   e. Between 58 and 67

  f. Between 87 and 101

  g. Between 59 and 94

  h. Between 47 and 103

11. Explain the difference between percentages and percentiles.

12. Sarah ranked in the 89th percentile of the quantitative part of the SAT exam. What does this tell you?

Pedagogical Problems and Activities

13. If possible, locate manuals for interpreting familiar standardized tests given in educational settings. Using what you have learned about statistics in this chapter, identify specific uses of measures of central tendency that are used in the normative data described in the manuals.

14. With your instructor's assistance, use the class test scores from your last test and determine if the distribution is approximately normal.

12.6   COLLECTING DATA: SAMPLING AND MISUSE OF STATISTICS

Suppose that we are interested in the political views of the youth of today. Obviously, the cost of interviewing *all* young people is prohibitive; thus, the usual procedure is to interview a sample of young people and from this sample draw some conclusions about the entire youth population. This process— drawing conclusions about an entire population based on a sample (or samples) of the population—involves some uncertainties, estimations, and predictions. *Inferential statistics* is the area of mathematics that deals with such problems. We might say that inferential statistics weave together many ideas from descriptive statistics and probability. For example, various concepts of descriptive statistics can be used to study a sample of a given population, and then conclusions (these conclusions are tentative and therefore involve uncertainties, estimations, and predictions) about the entire population are predicted according to probabilities.

A local industry manufactures ball bearings to be used in farm machinery. The ball bearings must meet certain specifications, but it is too expensive to check each one for these requirements. Therefore, the company has a *sampling technique* to assure their customers that the ball bearings are meeting the required specifications.

A TV station has introduced a new program entitled "What's Happening in our Community." The station is obviously interested in public reaction to the new program. Again, financially it is not reasonable to solicit the reactions of all viewers. So a *sample* of the TV audience is surveyed and the station draws some conclusions about public reaction to the new program from this sample.

In both these examples, two groups of people or objects are involved—namely, the entire set and a subset of the entire set. Statistically, the entire set of people or objects under consideration is called a *population* and a subset of the population is called a *sample*. A detailed study of sampling techniques is beyond the scope of this book, but we do want to make you aware of a general considerations relative to sampling procedures.

What is a correct *sample size*? If a sample is too small, it may not give a true picture of the entire population. On the other hand, very large samples are frequently expensive to acquire. So, a sample needs to be large enough to represent the population correctly and small enough to be affordable. There are statistical measures available to help assure correct sample size for particular situations.

Is it a *random* sample? Statistically, a sample is said to be a *random sample* if each member of the population has an equal chance of being drawn. Randomness may or may not be easy to achieve. For example, the industry manufacturing ball bearings should be able to acquire random samples without too much difficulty because of the availability of the population. On the other hand, the TV station wanting to sample its audience randomly faces some difficult problems. For one thing, determining the exact population may be hard to do. Also, deciding on a method of surveying a sample of the population produces some problems. Should they do the survey by mail, telephone, personal interviews, or in some other way? Each method has its strengths and weaknesses.

Should the sample be truly random or should it be a *stratified random* sample? A stratified sample represents the population in proportion to the way the population is stratified. For example, suppose the population consists of 7000 females and 3000 males. A stratified random sample of 1000 people would consist of 700 female and 300 males. The purpose for which the sample is to be used determines whether a stratified sample is desirable.

Is the sample *free of bias*? The concept of bias is an extremely important issue when it comes to sampling, and unfortunately it is very difficult to control. Suppose that we have determined a random sample of college professors and they are to be questioned about their TV viewing habits. Will a college professor admit watching night time "soap operas" as freely as he/she will admit to watching news commentaries on world affairs?

Now let us look at some hypothetical sampling situations and consider some pertinent questions and comments about each situation. A company producing Brand X facial soap makes the following claim: "From a sample of 1000 leading doctors, we found that 90 percent of them agreed that our Brand X facial soap is better for your complexion than any other soap on the market." How large was the sample? (Read the claim very carefully.) What is a doctor? Who are the "leading" doctors? How many other samples were taken that did not produce these results? What does "better for your complexion" mean? How was the information obtained from the sample of doctors? These and perhaps many other questions need to be answered before much credence can be given to such a claim.

Consider a newspaper article that states "a survey revealed that approximately 100 percent of the major league baseball players would vote to strike over the issue of compensation if necessary." Obviously, nothing in the claim indicates sample size or method of obtaining the information. There are other unanswered questions. What does "approximately" 100 percent mean? Was this a stratified random sample? Were as many "rookies" in the sample as "super stars"? Perhaps you can think of some additional questions about this claim that need to be answered.

Consider another hypothetical claim that "a survey of teenagers reveals that 75 percent of them smoke." Again the size of sample and method of gathering information need to be considered. What is the definition of a "teenager"? What does "smoke" mean? Was this a stratified sample according to age groups? Was this a stratified sample according to male versus female? Can you think of other "stratifications" that could be used for such a sampling situation?

We should make one final point regarding claims based on statistical evidence. A claim may be statistically valid, but "hidden factors" can exist that influence it. Suppose a placement bureau indicates that "they have 100 unemployed elementary school teachers in their files." On the surface, such facts seem to indicate a surplus of elementary school teachers; however, there may be a hidden factor. Suppose the placement bureau is located in a university town. There might be many spouses of university personnel who are looking for teaching positions, but who insist that these positions be within commuting distance of their homes. In other words, one area of the country may indeed have a surplus of teachers, but there may be other areas searching for teachers. Thus, a phrase such as "100 unemployed teachers" can be misleading.

We have already discussed the careless use of the word average and the unclear interpretations that accompany such a practice in statistics. The misuse of data for interpretation can also be misleading if all the facts are not present. An example of possible misinterpretation could occur from our data on women in state legislatures presented earlier in Table 12.2. New Hampshire, with 140 women in their state legislature, was excluded because it appeared to be such an outlier. However, it was not mentioned that the number of representatives vary from state to state, and how this might affect the number of women listed. New Hampshire has 400 state representatives; which is almost twice as many as any other state. Pennsylvania is the state with the next largest number of representatives, 203. Therefore, to give a fair picture of how women are represented in state legislatures, we should look at the percentage of women holding office. Some states with the smallest numbers of women in the state legislatures actually have a higher percentage of women representing their population because of their smaller total number of representatives. Table 12.18 lists the data with the additional information.

Using a stem and leaf plot of the percentages of women in state legislatures helps us interpret the information in Table 12.18. Figure 12.30 can be com-

TABLE 12.18 WOMEN HOLDING OFFICE IN STATE LEGISLATURES, 1986

	Number of Women	Total Rep.	% Women
AL	9	105	9
AK	11	40	28
AZ	18	60	30
AR	10	100	10
CA	15	80	19
CO	24	65	37
CT	41	151	27
DE	10	41	24
FL	31	120	26
GA	23	180	13
HI	14	51	27
ID	24	84	29
IL	30	118	25
IN	19	100	19
IA	22	100	22
KS	30	125	24
KY	9	100	9
LA	5	105	5
ME	44	151	29
MD	36	141	26
MA	33	160	21
MI	16	110	15
MN	29	134	22
MS	4	122	3
MO	26	163	16
MT	22	100	22
NE	8	49	16
NV	10	42	24
NH	140	400	35
NJ	12	80	15
NM	13	70	19
NY	23	150	15
NC	20	120	17
ND	18	106	17
OH	12	99	12
OK	13	101	13
OR	18	60	30
PA	13	203	6
RI	23	100	23
SC	10	124	8
SD	15	70	21
TN	11	99	11
TX	16	150	11
UT	7	75	9
VT	47	150	31
VA	10	100	10
WA	35	98	36
WV	23	100	23
WI	25	99	25
WY	24	64	38

Source: Center for the American Woman and Politics, Eagleton Institute of Politics, Rutgers University, New Brunswick, NJ, information release.

Stem	Leaf
0	3 5 6 8 9 9 9
1	0 0 1 1 2 3 3 5 5 5 6 6 7 7 9 9 9
2	1 1 2 2 2 3 3 4 4 4 5 5 6 6 7 7 8 9 9
3	0 0 1 5 6 7 8

FIGURE 12.30   Stem-and-leaf plot of percentages of women in state legislatures

pared to Figure 12.3 for similarities and differences in outliers, clusters, gaps, and largest and smallest value in each display of data. Depending on what our interest is in the subject of women legislators, we could choose either set of data and make our case based on statistics.

To add interest to the comparison of the actual number of women in state legislatures and the percentage of state representatives that are women, we can replace the leaves by symbols identifying the states as in Figures 12.31 and 12.32. Narrative descriptions could then be written from these stem and leaf plots. These narratives should include information on the total number of legislators in each state and how that may explain the differences in Figures 12.31 and 12.32. Possible explanations for various states' placement in the stem and leaf plots could be given.

STEM AND LEAF PLOT OF NUMBER OF WOMEN IN STATE LEGISLATURES

Stem	Leaf
0	MS LA UT NE AL KY
1	AR DE NV SC VA AK IN NJ OH NM OK PA HI CA SD MI TX AZ ND
2	NC IA MT GA NY RI WV CO ID WY WI MO MN
3	IL KS FL MA WA MD
4	CT ME VT
*	
*	
14	NH

FIGURE 12.31   Stem-and leaf plot of number of women in state legislatures

STEM AND LEAF PLOT OF PERCENTAGE OF WOMEN IN STATE LEGISLATURES

Stem	Leaf
0	MS LA PA SC AL KY UT
1	AR VA TN TX OH GA OK MI NJ NY MO NE NC ND CA IN NM
2	MA SD IA MN MT RI WV DE KS NV IL WI FL ND CT HI AK ID ME
3	AZ OR VT NH WA CO WY

FIGURE 12.32   Stem-and-leaf plot of percentage of women in state legislatures

TABLE 12.19 SCHOLASTIC APTITUDE TEST (SAT) SCORES
OF COLLEGE-BOUND SENIORS, 1970 TO 1985

Year	1970	1975	1980	1985
SAT scores in math	488	472	466	475

Source: College Entrance Examination Board, New York, NY, National
College-Bound Seniors, annual.

Using the information on SAT scores for 1970 to 1985 in Table 12.19, we
can demonstrate how the same data can be represented or misrepresented
using different vertical scales. From Figure 12.33, the change in SAT scores
can be interpreted as a concern. Whereas in Figure 12.34, we could feel comfortable with a little fluctuation in scores over time. Those who are know-
ledgeable in the use of statistics and have adequate information about the
source of the data would be able to make intelligent interpretations of the

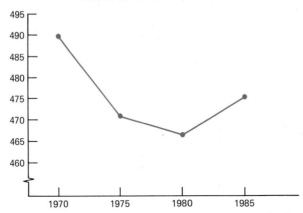

FIGURE 12.33 Scholastic aptitude test (SAT) scores of college-bound seniors, 1970 to 1985

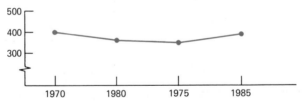

FIGURE 12.34 Scholastic aptitude test (SAT) scores of college-bound seniors, 1970 to 1985

two graphs. It is only the visual impact of the presentation that gives differing interpretations of the data.

The study of statistics is doubly important to those of us who will be responsible for the education of our young people. It is important to be able to make sense out of research and other reports of statistics that affect our lives, but even more important, we have a responsibility to our students to help them develop concepts and skills to organize and interpret the wealth of data and information that is a part of their world.

PROBLEM SET 12.6

1. Give the meaning of each of the following:
   a. Population   b. Sample
   c. *Random* sample   d. *Stratified random* sample
   e. A sample *free of bias*

2. Indicate some disadvantages for each of the following methods of taking a sample survey:
   a. Telephone calls
   b. Questionnaires though the mail
   c. House-to-house canvassing
   d. Street-corner interviewing

3. For each of the following fictitious claims, make a list of questions that could be asked about the claim to better establish its exact meaning.
   a. A survey of 1000 men between the ages of 35 and 50 revealed that 20 percent of them used a hair conditioner to cover up gray hair.
   b. A survey of farmers revealed that 10 percent of them play golf in their leisure time.
   c. A survey of college professors indicate that 75 percent of them are against using the strike as a negotiating weapon.
   d. A survey of college students indicates that 5 percent of them are involved in the local city politics.
   e. According to a recent poll, 40 percent of American housewives watch soap operas.
   f. A survey of high school students indicates that 60 percent of them plan to go on to college.
   g. A survey of elementary school teachers indicates that 35 percent of them believe that their salaries are adequate.
   h. A survey of college students majoring in elementary education reveals that 40 percent of them believe that a computer course should be a part of their requirements for graduation.
   i. According to a recent survey of placement bureaus, secondary school mathematics teachers are in great demand.

j. According to a recent poll, 60 percent of college students believe that college athletics are being overemphasized.

4. Suppose you have been put in charge of conducting a survey (by sampling) of the students at your university to determine what percentage of them favor a proposed change from the quarter to the semester system. Give your reaction to each of the following questions. Keep in mind that your objective is to get an accurate prediction based on your sample.

   a. Would you stratify the sample according to year in school? Give reasons for your answer.

   b. Would you stratify the sample according to female versus male? Give reasons for your answer.

   c. What other "stratifications" might you use?

   d. How would you conduct the survey?

5. Questionnaires were sent by mail to the 1989 graduates of a certain university. These people were asked to indicate their salary for the first year after graduation. Based on this information, reports were published to give the 1990 graduates some idea as to what beginning salary they might expect. What factors might contribute to misleading information in such a survey?

6. A city with a population of 20,000 reports that it has 100 unemployed people. What questions would you like to have answered to understand better the significance of the "100 unemployed" figure?

7. A company claims that "according to a recent survey, 95 percent of the people on their new Eat-All diet plan lost more than a pound per week." Indicate some questions that could be asked about this claim.

8. Suppose you were to conduct a random sampling of the full-time students at the university you attend. How would you ensure "randomness"?

9. To determine the need for in-service courses in mathematics for elementary school teachers, one state department of education sent out questionnaires to selected teachers. The teachers were selected at random from a list of all members of the state mathematics association. How might this survey be biased?

10. A claim has been made that 85 percent of the students at a certain university favor pro choice legislation. What facts about this survey would you like to know to better pinpoint the significance of the results?

11. Using the data that follows on school enrollment 1960–1985, construct two different graphs that present the data. Design your graphs in such a way that two different interpretations could be made.

SCHOOL ENROLLMENT—ALL
LEVELS PUBLIC AND PRIVATE (in
millions)

1960	46.3
1965	54.7
1970	60.4
1975	62.2
1980	58.6
1985	59.8

Source: U.S. Bureau of Census, Current
Population Reports

Pedagogical Problems and Activities

12. Locate a statistical report of a study in a newspaper or magazine in which you can identify the sampling technique used. Is the sample free of bias?

13. Examine the use of statistics in newspapers, magazines, or other media for presentations of statistics that are subject to misinterpretation.

14. In 1989, the National Education Association listed the average salaries of teachers in the states of Illinois and Wyoming to be $29,735 and $29,378, respectively. This could lead one to believe that most of the teachers in these two states have salaries that are approximately $29,000, and most teachers in these two states have the same standard of living. Do you think this an accurate interpretation of the statistics reported on teachers salaries in these two states? What information is not being reported that would give further interpretation to the issue of teacher salaries?

15. The Department of Education reports average Scholastic Achievement Test scores by states and then gives a state ranking. Do you think this information can be used to determine in which states overall student achievement is highest? What other information would be valuable to know for a more accurate interpretation of scholastic achievement?

REVIEW PROBLEM SET

1. Construct a circle graph to represent the following grade distribution on a test: 10 As, 18 Bs, 40 Cs, 15 Ds, and 17 Fs.

2. The following figures represent a university's budget over the past several years.

1984	$40,000,000		1987	$54,000,000
1985	$45,000,000		1988	$55,000,000
1986	$48,000,000		1989	$60,000,000

Make a vertical bar graph to represent these data.

3. Consider the following frequency distribution.

Intervals	Frequency
30–34	3
35–39	8
40–44	20
45–49	40
50–54	32
55–59	16
60–64	10
65–69	5

   a. Construct a histogram.
   b. Construct a frequency polygon.
   c. Construct a cumulative frequency table.
   d. Construct an ogive for part **c**.

4. Find the mean, median, and mode for each of the following:
   a. 1, 3, 4, 6, 8, 9, 13, 13, 13, 14, 16, 18, 18, 19, 20, and 21
   b. 3, 7, 11, 4, 8, 18, 41, 36, 21, 14, 2, 7, 16, 7, and 26

5. Construct a stem and leaf plot to organize the following values: 65, 30, 38, 53, 91, 31, 34, 40, 56, 69, 38, 39, 42, 46, 49, 54, 51, 72, 53, 58, 52, 49, 32.
   a. Identify the smallest and largest values, outliers, clusters, and any gaps.
   b. Using the stem and leaf plot, locate the upper and lower extremes, the median, and the lower and upper quartiles.

6. Find the mean of the following distribution.

Scores	Frequency
10–14	4
15–19	7
20–24	15
25–29	30
30–34	18
35–39	10
40–44	9
45–49	7

7. Find the standard deviation for the following set of scores: 3, 4, 6, 7, 10, 11, and 14.

8. A set of 1000 scores is normally distributed about a mean of 72 and the distribution has a standard deviation of 9. Use Figure 12.28 to help find the number of scores in each of the following intervals.
   a. Between 63 and 81
   b. Between 81 and 90
   c. Between 54 and 81
   d. Between 90 and 99
   e. Between 45 and 63

9. A set of 2000 scores is normally distributed about a mean of 130. The standard deviation of the distribution is 10. Use Table 12.28 to help find the number of scores in each of the following intervals.
   a. Between 130 and 137
   b. Between 130 and 152
   c. Between 137 and 152
   d. Between 112 and 130
   e. Between 118 and 141

Solution to the Sample Problem

In a mathematics class of 35 students, the mean on the first exam of the semester was 67. Five of the students withdrew from the course because their scores of 43, 45, 32, 37, and 28 were so low. Two students enrolled late and took the makeup exam, scoring 69 and 71. What is the new mean for the class?

1. *Understanding the Problem.* This problem involves the procedure for finding the arithmetic mean. The number of students in the class will change after the first exam. We need to understand how the number of students in the class and the mean are related.

2. *Devising a Plan.* Because we do not know the scores of all the students, we will need to devise a plan for working with the total number of students and the original mean. We then must consider how these numbers are affected when students withdraw from or add to the total number of students enrolled.

3. *Solution.* We can begin by making a partial list of the original class and the class after the first exam.

Results of Exam		*After Makeup Exam*	
Total # of students 35		Total # of students 32	
Mean 67		Mean ?	
Student	Score	Student	Score
1		1	
2		2	
3		3	
4		4	
5		5	
.		.	
.		.	
.		.	
31	43	31	69
32	45	32	71
33	32		
34	37		
35	28		

To find the mean, we add all the scores and divide the sum by the total number of entries. We can find the total sum of the scores on the first exam by multiplying the mean by the number of students ($35 \times 67 = 2345$). When 5 students withdrew, the total sum of the scores was reduced by the sum of the 5 scores or 185. This left the total sum to be 2160 for 30 students. The mean now is $2160 \div 30$ or 72.

Two students with scores of 69 and 71 took the makeup exam. Now we have 32 students, and the total sum of their scores is $2160 + 140$ or 2300. This gives us a mean for the class $2300 \div 32$ or 71.

4. *Looking Back.* Because the 5 students who withdrew all had scores below the mean and the two scores on the makeup exam were higher than the original mean, we would expect a higher class mean now. Our resulting mean of 71 is higher than the original mean of 67.

5. *Looking ahead.* Consider a class of 100 students. If we add 5 points to each score, how would the mean change? How would the standard deviation change? How would the mean change if we added 10% of a person's score to their original test score?

13

FURTHER MATHEMATICAL EXCURSIONS: EXTENDED PROBLEM SOLVING, NUMBER PATTERNS, AND MODULAR ARITHMETIC

13.1 INTRODUCTION

In this chapter we take a look at additional problem solving ideas that can be used in conjunction with previous chapters or be studied following the completion of other chapters. The material presented will be extensions of concepts previously covered as well as some new problems that can be solved by combining ideas in more than one chapter. Although all previous problem sets have had problem solving components, we believe that you will benefit from further examination of mathematical questions that are problem solving in nature. The problems presented here are intended to provide a broader perspective of mathematical problem solving. In this chapter you have the opportunity to examine problems from a variety of topics. At this time, you should feel more comfortable and confident when engaging in problem solving. As you work through the problems, we encourage you apply to Polya's four-step process for problem solving: (1) understanding the problem, (2) devising a plan, (3) carrying out the plan, and (4) looking back, which is described in Chapter 1. Also, do not forget the various strategies, such as acting it out, using a formula, solving a simpler problem, using trial and error, or working backward, mentioned in the devising-a-plan phase.

737

The problems and questions that arise in mathematics provide a fertile ground for developing the curiosity with which we are born. In addition, problem solving activities can encourage creativity as well as help structure thought processes. We provide these activities so that you personally have a chance to interact with this view of problem solving and can later provide similar experiences for the students you will teach.

We wish to remind you that the answer to a problem solving question need not be the end of the discussion. Indeed, many people believe that the answer is only the beginning for the next question to explore. Such persons often seek to find a different approach to solving the same problem. Therefore, after you have determined a solution, be prepared for extensions to the problem. We call this the iceberg analogy. As you may be aware, only about 10 percent of an iceberg is above the waterline. The rest is hidden below the water. You will find many interesting discoveries when you are curious enough to extend the problem in which you are engaged. This is often how many of the discoveries in mathematics have occurred.

EXAMPLE 1

Each year Euclid Elementary school has a spelling bee for its third-grade students. Students are paired off against one another until a champion speller emerges. In each pairing the loser is eliminated. This year there are 64 students in the third grade. How many pairings will be necessary to complete the spelling bee?

We use the four-step problem solving process as we try to solve the problem. Is the question clearly stated, and do we understand how to proceed? Well, someone may think that if you had 64 people only 32 pairings are possible. This person will need to be reminded that as no champion would emerge at this point, another round of pairings would be needed. Thus we know we must keep the pairing process going, and no student has a "second chance." Now that the problem is understood, let us look at two different strategies for solution.

Solution 1 If you pair the 64 students up, 32 pairings will be needed initially—call this the first round. At the end of the first round there will be 32 students left to pair in the second round. This will necessitate 16 pairs in the second round. Continuing this pattern, there will be 8 pairs needed in the third round, 4 pairs in the fourth round, 2 pairs needed in the fifth round, and 1 pair needed in the sixth round, which will be the championship round. We can find the total of pairings needed by adding up the number of pairings in each round, 32 + 16 + 8 + 4 + 2 + 1, which equals 63.

Notice that Solution 1 depended on a model that correctly portrayed the setting of the contest. The model in this case was extremely helpful, but other attempts at a solution are also possible, as can be seen by examining Solution 2.

Solution 2 Notice that of the 64 students who started the spelling bee, only one will be the champion speller. Thus all the remaining 63 students must each lose one time. But in each pairing there can be only one loser. Hence, there must be 63 pairings used to produce 63 losses.

At this point, we have solved the problem and looking back we know the solution is correct. These steps in the problem-solving process should not be forgotten. However, we also look forward and use this solution to generate our next problem.

What observations and comments can we make about this problem? First, note that one solution to this problem was found in adding terms of the sequence, (1, 2, 4, 8, 16, 32, . . .). It is interesting that the sum, $1 + 2 + 4 + 8 + 16 + 32 = 63$, is equal to one less than the next term of the sequence, namely 64. In the spirit of inquiry one might think to ask "Does this result hold for other sums found this way from this sequence?" Also, we should ask ourselves, "What would happen if we did not have 64 students at the beginning, but instead had 35, or 29, or 7, or . . . ?," or "What would happen if we had a double-elimination spelling contest (one in which a person is not eliminated until he/she has accumulated two losses)?" You should not be limited by the questions we have asked and should try hard to answer the following question, "Can you think of other questions to ask?"

EXAMPLE 2

If you were offered the following two choices of payment for your first teaching job, which would you choose?

Option 1 $24,000 per year with a $400 raise/year after each year of successful service.

Option 2 $24,000 per year with a $100 raise/6 months after each 6 months of successful service.

The question does not even seem like a problem because the solution seems obvious. However, you have probably learned to be a bit skeptical about problem solving situations and may be wondering where the catch is in this problem. Well, think through the two options and convince yourself of the best choice, if there is one, before proceeding to the solution.

Solution Remember that the first step in the problem-solving process is to understand the problem. Are you clear on the difference between a raise/year and a raise per 6 months? Did you remember to think that the $400 raise would not all be received until the end of the second year? What kind of plan should we use? We will begin the solution plan by breaking down the time periods into 6-month intervals of time and record the amount of money each person will receive during a specific 6-month interval. Because of the way raises are paid, if you chose Option 1 none of the raise will be paid during the first year. If you chose Option 2, a raise of $100 will be paid during the second 6-month period. This information is recorded here.

MONEY PAID DURING THIS PERIOD OF TIME

	0–6 Months	6–12 Months
Option 1	$12,000	$12,000
Option 2	$12,000	$12,100

Hence, for the first year, Option 2 looks like the best deal. Does this agree with your conjecture? Do you think Option 2 will also be the better deal by the end of year 2? Let us investigate. At the end of year 1, the $400 raise will go into effect, and $200 of it will be paid during the first 6-month period and the remaining $200 paid during the next 6-month period. In Option 2, an additional $100 will be paid during each 6-month period of time. Hence during the next two 6-month periods of time, the options will accumulate the following amounts of money.

MONEY PAID DURING THIS PERIOD OF TIME

	12–18 Months	18–24 Months
Option 1	$12,200	$12,200
Option 2	$12,200	$12,300

Again, Option 2 pays more money during the second year, in fact, $100 more just as it did in year one. Are you willing to believe that Option 2 will always be the best choice? Investigate the third year and see what happens.

EXAMPLE 3

In Figure 13.1 a survey related to traffic patterns shows that for every 14 cars that arrive at point E, 9 turn toward point D and 5 turn toward point C. Of every 9 that arrive at point D, 6 turn toward point B and 3 turn toward point A. Of 98 cars arriving at point E, how many are eventually expected to turn toward point B?

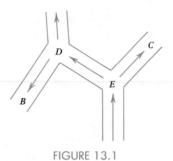

FIGURE 13.1

Solution To solve this problem we must look at two components. Of the 98 that arrive at point E, 63 would be expected to turn toward point D. Why? Of the 63 arriving at point D, 42 would be expected to turn toward point B.

PROBLEM SET 13.1

1. Each of the arcs pictures here is a semicircle with radius 4, and point P is the midpoint of each of the two arcs on which it lies. What is the area of the shaded region?

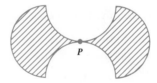

2. A farmer is planning to build a 350-meter-long fence, and plans to put the posts 5-meters apart. How many posts will be needed?

3. A bacteria was placed in a jar at 10:00 A.M. The bacteria had the property that it doubled in size every minute. At 11:00 A.M. on the same day it was observed that the bacteria now filled the jar completely.

   a. At what time of the morning was the jar half full of bacteria?

   b. At 10:55 what fractional part of the jar was filled?

4. In the figure, quadrilateral $ABCD$ is a square and P is the midpoint of side BC. What is the ratio of the areas of the following regions?

   a. Region I:Region II
   b. Region I:Region III
   c. Region I:Region IV

5. A chemist is working with a 2-percent saline solution that consists of 2 milliliters of salt and 98 milliliters of water. The chemist decides that what is really needed is a 1-percent solution, so she decides to make it by adding water to the current solution. How much water must be added so that a 1-percent solution is reached?

6. Going into the final part of the softball season at State University, Loretta is batting approximately 0.342 based on 161 at bats—that is, her number of hits divided by 161 is 0.342. If Loretta has 50 official at bats during the rest of the season, how many hits must she get to end the season with a batting average of 0.350 or better?

7. In a class of 400 students, 5 were running for the position of president. Every student in class voted for exactly one candidate, and the distribution of votes is given in the table. What is the maximum possible value for *m*?

Candidate	Number of Votes Received
1	50
2	75
3	142
4	*m*
5	*n*

8. To the nearest thousand, what is the number of seconds in a week?

9. The figure here is a square divided into 9 congruent smaller squares. If the perimeter of the large square is 1, what is the perimeter of a small square?

10. On her desk, Judy has a container of pencils. There are 10 pencils in the container, some of which are sharpened and some of which are not. Which of the following could represent the ratio of sharpened to unsharpened pencils in her container?

    a. 9:1

    b. 3:2

    c. 7:7

    d. 5:1

    e. 1:4

    f. 2:1

11. A cube has the volume of 64 cubic units. If point A is the center of one face of the cube and point B is the center of the opposite parallel face, what is the length of line segment $\overline{AB}$.

12. A zoologist was observing monkeys in a tree eating bananas. One monkey started the eating and ate $\frac{1}{4}$ of the 32 bananas. A second monkey ate $\frac{1}{4}$ of the bananas that were left. How many bananas are still on the tree?

13. Diane was to calculate $\frac{a}{b} + \frac{c}{d}$, but instead calculated $\frac{b}{a} + \frac{d}{c}$. She calculated the value of $\frac{b}{a} + \frac{d}{c}$ to be 4 before she realized her mistake. On seeing the mistake, she quickly wrote down $\frac{1}{4}$ as the answer to the problem. Was this correct reasoning? Justify your answer.

14. If points B and C are placed to the right of A on the line that follows so that $2\,AB = 3\,AC$,

a. Which of the points B or C is closest to point A?

b. What is the ratio of $CB{:}AC$?

15. The area of the square shown here is 144 square units; X is the center of the square; $\angle ZXY$ is a right angle; and $YC = 3$. What is the area of quadrilateral $ZXYC$?

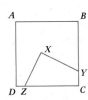

16. Travis found that his calculator could not handle the following computation, $2^{20} \times 5^{17}$. However, with a quick mind, Travis quickly determined the correct solution. What was the solution?

17. Suppose p is a number from column A and q is a number from column B in the table.

a. How many values are possible for the value of $p + q$?

b. What are these values?

A	B
2	3
3	5
4	7
5	11

18. Four lines are intersecting, as demonstrated in the figure. What is the sum of the degree measures of the marked angles?

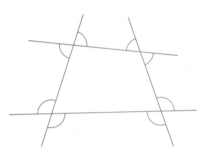

19. A cable of uniform diameter and composition that weighes 48 kilograms is cut into two pieces. One piece is 90 meters long and weighs 36 kilograms. What is the length of the other piece?

20. Glenn and Bill were about to roll a fair six-sided die with faces numbered 1 through 6. They were going to roll it twice, and Glenn thought that the probability of obtaining a 5 on the top face on the first roll and a 4 on the top face on the second roll was larger than the probability of obtaining a 4 on the top face on both the first and second rolls. Bill, of course, thought the opposite was true. Who, if either, was correct?

21. Mary was looking at the mean average that would be obtained from the positive numbers a, b, and c, as well as the mean average of the three numbers a^2, b^2, and c^2. She was wondering if the mean average of a, b, and c would ever be larger than the mean average of a^2, b^2, and c^2. What is your response?

22. If in the figure the radius of the smaller circle is $\frac{2}{3}$ the radius of the larger circle, what is the ratio of the area of the shaded region to the area of the larger circle?

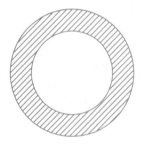

23. If you have a 9 L bucket and a 4 L bucket which of the following amounts can you take exactly from a pond of water?

    a. 1 L   **b.** 2 L   **c.** 3 L   **d.** 5 L

    e. 6 L   **f.** 7 L   **g.** 8 L

24. A line contains (0, 0) and (12, 8). What other points, (x, y), with whole number values for x and y, with $y < 28$, does it contain?

25. In the multiplication problem that follows, if $\bigcirc$, $\triangle$, and $\square$ represent digits, what digit does $\square$ represent?

$$
\begin{array}{r}
235 \\
4\bigcirc7 \\
\hline
1645 \\
1\triangle10 \\
940 \\
\hline
10\square745
\end{array}
$$

26. Ima Hungry ate $\frac{1}{4}$ of a sandwich at noon and then ate $\frac{1}{3}$ of the *remainder* at night. What part of the sandwich remained uneaten?

27. If the diameter of a wheel is 0.5 meters, how many meters has the center of the wheel traveled when the wheel has made 4 complete revolutions along a straight road?

28. In the figure Kerry traveled from point A to point B along the large semicircle, whereas Adam traveled along the several small semicircles. If the diameter of the large semicircle is 14, and the diameter of the small semicircles are 3, 4, 5, and 2 from left to right, who traveled the longer distance in getting from point A to point B?

29. Farmer Dondee wants to put in an irrigation system on a square piece of land. He wants to put in a circular system like the one shown in figure **a**. His children with whom he farms disagree with him and want to put in a system like in figure **b**. Which system will allow for the largest total amount of land to be irrigated?

(a)　　　　　(b)

30. Two students were discussing which of the following would be the larger answer.

    i. The average speed, in kilometers per hour, required to travel a distance of 200 kilometers in 3 hours, or

    ii. The average speed, in kilometers per hour, required to travel a distance of 200 kilometers in $\frac{1}{3}$ hour.

Which option produces the larger answer?

31. Two students were discussing which of the following options would produce the larger answer?

    i. 15% of 2000

    ii. 2000% of 15

Which option produces the larger answer?

32. If n is an integer greater than 2, decide whether the following integers are always even, always odd, or could be either even or odd.

    a. n^3

    b. $n(n - 1)$

    c. $6n + 3$

    d. $n^2 + n$

    e. $5n + 3$

33. In the rectangle illustrated, $\overline{EF}$ and $\overline{GH}$ are parallel to $\overline{AD}$. If the lengths of $\overline{AE}$, $\overline{EG}$, $\overline{GB}$, and $\overline{BD}$ are 2, 1, 3, and 10, respectively, what is the area of rectangle $EGHF$?

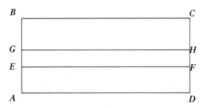

34. Sam was going to run a sale on some merchandise in his clothing store. Sam added 30 percent to the cost of the merchandise he received, then discounted that price 20 percent. What would be the cost to a customer of a piece of clothing that cost Sam $30?

35. At State University the math club has 22 members and the chess club has 15 members. If a total of 13 members belong to only one of the two clubs, how many students belong to both clubs?

36. The population of Itsy, the largest city in Bitsy, is 50% of the rest of the population of Bitsy. The population of Itsy is what percent of the entire population of Bitsy?

37. A machine can insert letters in envelopes at the rate of 240 per minute whereas another machine can stamp the envelopes at a rate of 3 per second. How many stamping machines are needed to keep up with 36 inserting machines of this kind?

38. The United States Department of Defense building, commonly called the Pentagon, has a shape of a pentagon with sides of 200 meters. The maintenance people at the Pentagon decide to build a fence around its pentagon, always keeping the fence 3 meters from the building. Draw the shape that the fence will take, and find the perimeter of the fence.

39. **a.** A circular track for two runners has a 50-meter radius to the center of the inside running lane and a 51-meter radius to the center of the second running lane. If two runners each run in the center of their respective lanes, how much of a "head start" should the runner in the outside lane be given?

   b. Would the "head start" change if the radius were 99 and 100 meters, respectively, for the inside and outside lanes?

40. What would be the fewest number of games necessary for a double-elimination tournament with:

   a. 3 teams?

   b. 10 teams?

   c. n teams?

41. What would be the largest number of games necessary for a double-elimination tournament with:

   a. 3 teams?

   b. 10 teams?

   c. n teams?

42. There are three spinners with numbers equally spaced. Spinner A has the numbers 9, 7, and 2. Spinner B has the numbers 8, 6, and 4. Spinner C has the numbers 10, 5, and 3.

   a. If only spinners A and B were used in a contest to see which spinner would have the larger number shown, what is the probability of spinner A winning?

   b. If only spinners A and C were used, what is the probability of spinner A winning?

   c. If only spinners B and C were used, what is the probability of spinner C winning?

   d. If all three spinners were used, what is the probability of winning for each of them?

43. From a string that is 18-units long the following four shapes were made at different times with all the string used each time:

   a. A square

   b. An equilateral triangle

   c. A rectangle with one side 7

   d. A circle

What would be the area of each of the shapes? Which shape, if any, had the largest area?

44. Kevin and Wayne ran a 100-meter race in which Kevin won by crossing the finish line at the same time that Wayne was at the 97-meter mark. In their next race, in order to be fair, Kevin decides to give Wayne a 3-meter handicap by starting his race 3-meters behind the starting line. In the second race both Kevin and Wayne ran at the same constant speed as they did in the first race. Who won the second race?

45. Every student at State University who studies mathematics receives exactly one of the grades A, B, C, or D. If $\frac{1}{5}$ of the students receive As, $\frac{1}{4}$ receive Bs, $\frac{1}{2}$ receive Cs, and 10 students receive Ds, how many students in the school study mathematics?

46. From the columns that follow, if a, b, and c are numbers chosen from columns A, B, and C, respectively, what is the greatest possible value of $\dfrac{(a + c)}{b}$?

A	B	C
1	3	4
5	4	6
11	5	9
15	6	13

47. If the length and width of rectangle X are 10-percent less and 30-percent less, respectively, than the length and width of rectangle Y, what is the ratio of the area of rectangle X to the area of rectangle Y?

48. To make an orange dye, 5 parts of red dye are mixed with 3 parts of yellow dye. To make green dye, 2 parts of yellow dye are mixed with 4 parts of blue dye. If equal amounts of orange and green are mixed,
   a. What is the ratio of yellow dye in the mixture?
   b. What is the ratio of blue dye in the mixture?
   c. What is the ratio of red dye in the mixture?

49. In a sorority of 80 students, there are 3 mathematics majors for every 5 nonmathematics majors. In a fraternity, there are 3 mathematics majors for every 2 nonmathematics majors. If the two groups are combined, it is found that there are an equal number of mathematics majors and nonmathematics majors. How many students are there in the fraternity?

50. One mathematics class of 20 students had a mean average of 60 whereas a second class of 35 students had a mean average of 80. What would be the mean average if the two groups would be combined?

51. When they run, Frick runs 80 meters during the time that Frack runs 60 meters. In a 100-meter race, how much of the race will Frack have left when Frick crosses the finish line?

52. Mary, Bill, Glenn, and Judy each have some pencils. Mary has 6 more pencils than Bill, Bill has 3 more pencils than Glenn, and Glenn has 4 more pencils than Judy. What is the least number of pencils that must change hands if each person is to have an equal number of pencils?

53. A, B, and C indicate points accurately placed on a number line as shown in the figure. On which of the line segments $\overline{AB}$ or $\overline{BC}$ will the point D, with the coordinate of the average (mean) of the coordinates of A, B, and C, fall?

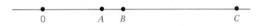

54. Twenty-one children start to count off "one, two, three, four, five" in a game. Each child who calls five "drops out" and the next child starts over at "one." Yvette starts the counting.
   a. At which of her calls will Yvette drop out?
   b. At which of her calls will the first person who counted "three" drop out?

55. In the figure, point E is on segment $\overline{AD}$. Which of the following distances will be the longest?

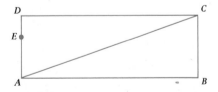

   a. Length of diagonal $\overline{AC}$, or
   b. Length of a line segment from E to a point on $\overline{BC}$.

56. The longest of 4 rods of unequal integer lengths is 80 centimeters and the shortest is 60 centimeters.
   a. What is the smallest value possible for the mean average of the 4 rods?
   b. What is the largest value possible for the mean average of the 4 rods?

57. In the figure, which is formed by connecting perpendicular line segments that have the lengths as shown, what is the length of the dotted line segment?

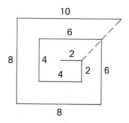

58. If the ratio of Pete's income to Vince's income is 2 to 5, and the ratio of Vince's income to Duane's income is 3 to 7, what is the ratio of Pete's income to Duane's income?

59. In a certain mathematics class for two testing periods, 15 students received no As and Bs, 22 students received at least one A, and 18 received at least one B. If 10 students received both As and Bs, how many students are there in the class?

60. In chess, the knight piece is allowed to move as shown by the arrows. The game board consists of 64 squares on an 8-by-8 board. On an empty board, what is the number of spaces from which all 8 such moves are *not* possible?

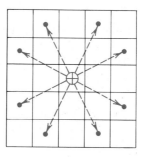

61. a. What is the largest finite number of points in which two triangles can intersect?

b. What is the largest finite number of points in which two quadrilaterals can intersect?

13.2   NUMBER PATTERNS

The study of number patterns has interested mathematicians as well as non-mathematicians for centuries. Very early in the study of mathematics children become familiar with number patterns. Consider the child who counts by 10. The child verbally says, "Ten, twenty, thirty, forty, fifty, ..." and knows quite well that this pattern is similar to the "One, two, three, four, five, ..." pattern with which he or she is already familiar. Similarly, consider the pattern of counting by fives, "Five, ten, fifteen, twenty, twenty-five, thirty, ..." which also has a pattern to it, as does the counting by five pattern that goes like "Twenty-six, thirty-one, thirty-six, forty-one, forty-six, ..." Often in a problem-solving situation it is advantageous to set up a number pattern to investigate possible solutions. This section will provide you with such an opportunity.

EXAMPLE 1

Suppose someone asked you to find the following sum

$$1 + 2 + 4 + 8 + 16 + 32 + 64 + \cdots + 32{,}768$$

Solution If you had the patience, you could try to write all the elements in the sequence and add them. Another strategy is to consider the following pattern.

$$
\begin{aligned}
1 &= 1 \\
1 + 2 &= 3 \\
1 + 2 + 4 &= 7 \\
1 + 2 + 4 + 8 &= 15 \\
1 + 2 + 4 + 8 + 16 &= 31 \\
1 + 2 + 4 + 8 + 16 + 32 &= 63
\end{aligned}
$$

At this point, it appears that a pattern emerges. There can be several ways to specify the pattern. If we do not give your method, that does not mean you are wrong. The pattern we mention is "The total sum written on the right side appears to be one less than the largest addend in the sum that follows." Based on this observation, we may be willing to "guess" that the answer to the original question is $(2 \times 32\,768) - 1 = 65\,535$. Indeed this is correct. From this exploration, we may be brave enough to ask ourselves the following question.

What would be the formula for the following sum?

$$1 + 2 + 4 + 8 + 16 + \cdots : 2^n$$

From the pattern, we would formulate the response $2^{(n+1)} - 1$. We have been able to use a number pattern to discover a very nice numerical relationship that can be written in the form of a formula.

EXAMPLE 2

The use of number patterns come at unsuspecting times. Consider the following question. What is the following product?

$$111111 \times 111111$$

Solution At first this does not seem like a very hard question, but a calculator with an eight-digit display cannot produce the answer. What are we to do? Let us try a pattern; but what pattern is there to try? This is where experience helps. Consider the following:

$$1 \times 1 = 1$$
$$11 \times 11 = 121$$
$$111 \times 111 = 12321$$
$$1111 \times 1111 = 1234321$$

Can you predict what 111111×111111 will produce? Can you also see a limitation of this pattern? If not, predict what will happen to $111111111 \times 11111111$. This is an important lesson to remember. When we try a pattern, we should be sure that the generalization will be correct. Obviously, in this case, seeing that we only have 10 digits, we will encounter a problem when we go beyond the answer 12345678987654321. This limitation should not deter us from looking for patterns to use, but to remind us to use patterns with care.

The strategy used in the foregoing examples can be thought of as looking for a simpler case. Here simpler may only refer to using fewer numbers in the hopes of generating a pattern while at the same time reducing the numbers to ones with which you can more readily manipulate.

EXAMPLE 3

How could we use a pattern to determine the following number:

$$4334314^2 - 4334313^2$$

Solution What relationships do we see that are worth exploring. Looking carefully, we see that the two numbers involved differ by 1. Let us explore this relationship with some patterns—but how? What would be the simplest case to explore? Next simpler? Let us try the following:

$$1^2 - 0^2 = 1$$
$$2^2 - 1^2 = 3$$
$$3^2 - 2^2 = 5$$
$$4^2 - 3^2 = 7$$

Have you seen enough for a pattern to emerge? Also, can you see a relationship between the numbers on the left side and the odd numbers that are emerging on the right side? It appears in all cases that the sum of the numbers to be squared is the answer to the question. Hence, it would seem that the solution to our original problem would be $4334314 + 4334313 = 8668627$.

PROBLEM SET 13.2

1. a. What would be the following sum?

$$\tfrac{1}{2} + \tfrac{1}{4} + \tfrac{1}{8} + \tfrac{1}{16} + \cdots + \tfrac{1}{1024}$$

b. What would be the formula for the following sum?

$$\tfrac{1}{2} + \tfrac{1}{4} + \tfrac{1}{8} + \tfrac{1}{16} + \cdots + \tfrac{1}{2^n}$$

c. What would be the following sum?

$$1 + 3 + 9 + 27 + 81 + \cdots + 2187?$$

d. What would be the formula for the following sum?

$$1 + 3 + 9 + 27 + 81 + \cdots + 3^n$$

e. What would be the following sum?

$$\tfrac{1}{3} + \tfrac{1}{9} + \tfrac{1}{27} + \cdots + \tfrac{1}{2187}?$$

f. What would be the formula for the following sum?

$$\tfrac{1}{3} + \tfrac{1}{9} + \tfrac{1}{27} + \cdots + \tfrac{1}{3^n}$$

g. Can you determine similar patterns in the sums using 4 and 5 instead of 2 and 3 as were done in 1a–f?

2. Gerald sets out to write all the numbers 1 to 1 000 000. However, he tires of the task and quits after writing a total of one-million digits. In what number and at the end of which digit did he quit? (In writing the numbers 1, 2, 3, 4, 5, 6, 7, 8, 9, 10, 11, 12, 13, 14, 15, Gerald would have written a total of 21 digits.)

3. a. What is the remainder when 7^{99} is divided by 4?
   b. What is the remainder when 7^{99} divided by 3?
   c. What is the remainder when 7^{99} divided by 5?
   d. What is the remainder when 7^{99} divided by 7?

4. Travis was hoping to use a calculator to calculate 42! but the number was too large for the display. Seeing that he could not get the exact number, he began to wonder how many zeros there were "at the end" of the 42!. How many are there? (For example, 32 000 has 3 zeros "at the end.")

5. Melissa wrote a computer program to examine the numbers 1 through 540. She sorted this set of numbers into three categories. Category A contained the numbers whose remainder when divided by 6 were larger than the remainder when divided by 9. Category B contained the numbers whose remainder when divided by 6 were less than the remainder when divided by 9. Category C contained those numbers whose remainder when divided by 6 was equal to the remainder when divided by 9. Which of the categories A, B, or C contained the most numbers?

6. What would be the thousandth term in the sequence (1, 2, 2, 3, 3, 3, 4, 4, 4, 4, 5, 5, 5, 5, 5, . . .)?

7. When two single-digit numbers are multiplied, the largest possible number of digits in the product is 2. When two two-digit numbers are multiplied, the largest possible number of digits in the product is 4. What is the largest number of digits possible from a product of two 15-digit numbers?

8. What would be the sum of the following sequence of numbers that is made up of all the positive proper fractions with denominators less than or equal to 100?

$$\left(\tfrac{1}{2} + \tfrac{1}{3} + \tfrac{2}{3} + \tfrac{1}{4} + \tfrac{2}{4} + \tfrac{3}{4} + \cdots + \tfrac{1}{100} + \tfrac{2}{100} + \tfrac{3}{100} + \cdots + \tfrac{99}{100}\right)$$

9. What is the sum of the digits in the integers 1 through 1000. (For example, the sum of the digits in the integers 12, 13, 14, and 15 is $1 + 2 + 1 + 3 + 1 + 4 + 1 + 5 = 18$.)

10. How many six-digit numbers are there in which the sum of the digits is greater than 50?

11. **a.** After the first bounce, a ball always bounces $\tfrac{2}{3}$ of the height of its previous bounce. If the height on its fifth bounce is 2 meters, what was the height of its second bounce?

    b. Suppose the rebound is $\tfrac{1}{2}$ of the height of the bounce. If the height is 1 meter, how far will the ball have traveled after it rebounds the eighth time?

12. A cartoon artist worked on a production that consisted of 4500 drawings. The artist did the first drawing, the sixth drawing, and every fifth drawing thereafter.

    a. How many of the 4500 drawings did the artist complete?

    b. What is the sum of the numbers of the drawings that the artist completed?

13. How many "different" arrangements of counting numbers are there whose sum is 15? In this case, $7 + 8$ and $8 + 7$ are considered different arrangements, and arrangements like $2 + 2 + 3 + 3 + 2 + 2 + 1$ are also possible.

14. Compute the following:
  a. $222222245^2 - 222222243^2$
  b. $222222245^2 - 222222242^2$
  c. $222222245^2 - 222222241^2$
  d. $222222245^2 - 222222240^2$

13.3   PROBLEM SOLVING IN A FINITE SYSTEM

We now investigate a finite mathematical system. A finite mathematical system consists of a finite set of elements together with an operation, some relations (such as equality), and some rules under which the system operates. Of course, the study of arithmetic is based on a mathematical system, so you already have some experience with systems. We begin by examining a system based on ideas with which you are somewhat familiar.

For example, consider the following statement, which is true in the system we will investigate: $8 + 6 = 2$. Perhaps this does not sound correct to you. However, consider the following scenario. If school starts at 8 A.M. and lasts 6 hours, at what time will school end? It appears that $8 + 6 = 2$ models this statement. In fact, the statement is true and represents a basic addition fact if we are talking about time related to a 12-hour clock.

Thus we begin our investigation of finite systems by considering the numerals 1 through 12 as the elements of the set under consideration. Specifically, we let set $C = \{1, 2, 3, 4, 5, 6, 7, 8, 9, 10, 11, 12\}$ and consider our operation as addition, denoted $\oplus$, where the addition is based on counting in a clockwise direction.

Figure 13.2a shows a clock and how we may think of the addition of $8 \oplus 6 = 2$. If we start at 8 and add 6 to it, we end up at 2. Similarly, $9 \oplus 9 = 6$ is shown in Figure 13.2b and $8 \oplus 11 = 7$ is shown in Figure 13.2c.

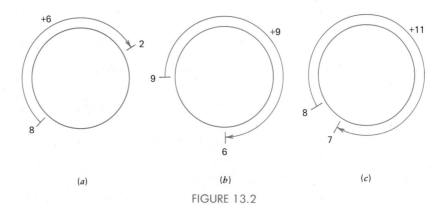

(a)   (b)   (c)

FIGURE 13.2

EXAMPLE 1

What are the following sums according to a 12-hour clock?

a. 4 ⊕ 9
b. 7 ⊕ 12
c. 8 ⊕ 8
d. 11 ⊕ 10

Solution (a) 1 (b) 7 (c) 4 (d) 9

We could calculate several "number facts" from the arithmetic on the clock. Table 13.1 represents the addition facts based on a 12-hour clock.

TABLE 13.1

⊕	1	2	3	4	5	6	7	8	9	10	11	12
1	2	3	4	5	6	7	8	9	10	11	12	1
2	3	4	5	6	7	8	9	10	11	12	1	2
3	4	5	6	7	8	9	10	11	12	1	2	3
4	5	6	7	8	9	10	11	12	1	2	3	4
5	6	7	8	9	10	11	12	1	2	3	4	5
6	7	8	9	10	11	12	1	2	3	4	5	6
7	8	9	10	11	12	1	2	3	4	5	6	7
8	9	10	11	12	1	2	3	4	5	6	7	8
9	10	11	12	1	2	3	4	5	6	7	8	9
10	11	12	1	2	3	4	5	6	7	8	9	10
11	12	1	2	3	4	5	6	7	8	9	10	11
12	1	2	3	4	5	6	7	8	9	10	11	12

You should examine this table to see how many patterns you can find. Specifically, can you see:

1. That regardless of what number you add to 12 you get that number back as an answer?
2. The number 1 occurs only in a diagonal row in the table?
3. A diagonal sequence that goes 2, 4, 6, 8, 10, 12, 2, 4, 6, 8, 10, 12?
4. A diagonal sequence that begins as 3, 5, 7, . . . ?
5. Adding 11 to a number is just like "subtracting" 1 from the number?

After having defined addition, you should not be surprised that we would also be thinking about multiplication or subtraction. In fact, what meaning could you give to $4 \otimes 3$ in this system? One meaning that can be attached is $4 \otimes 3 = 3 \oplus 3 \oplus 3 \oplus 3$, which indeed turns out to be 12.

EXAMPLE 2

"Compute" the following multiplications.

a. $3 \otimes 6$
b. $2 \otimes 7$
c. $5 \otimes 4$
d. $8 \otimes 8$
e. $7 \otimes 7$

Solutions (a) 6 (b) 2 (c) 8 (d) 4 (e) 1

You should know that it would be possible to complete a table of basic multiplication facts for this system just as we completed a set of basic addition facts. Table 13.2 has been started for you. You may wish to complete the table for future reference. A completed table will be helpful for later work in multiplication.

You may have noticed that finding a $5 \otimes 10$ on a 12-hour clock can be thought of as the arithmetic of remainders. For example, $5 \times 10 = 50$, and

TABLE 13.2

⊗	1	2	3	4	5	6	7	8	9	10	11	12
1		2										
2	2	4	6	8	10	12	2	4	6	8	10	12
3		6				6			6			
4		8	0						12			
5		10		8	1			4				
6		12				12	6					
7		2				6	1					
8		4			4			4				
9		6							9			
10		8	6									
11		10										
12		12										

$50 = (4 \times 12) + 2$. This is the same as saying 50 divided by 12 leaves a remainder of two. This is pictured as moving 4 times around the clock, which brings us back to the start, but there is a remainder of 2 left to consider. Hence $5 \otimes 10 = 2$.

Subtraction can be introduced into this system just as it is introduced in the arithmetic system of the elementary school. We give three possible ways here:

1. The *missing addend approach* asks you to solve the following sentence, $6 \oplus x = 3$. Just using counting properties, or by looking it up in the table, we see that $x = 9$ is the solution. We can get this by starting at 6 and keeping track of how many hours we count until we get to 3. Thus, $6 \oplus 9 = 3$, $3 \ominus 9 = 6$, and $3 \ominus 6 = 9$.

2. The *take-away or counting backward* approach asks us to think about the subtraction $3 \ominus 6$ as "three take-away 6." That may seem hard to do, but if we begin at 3 and "count backward" 6 hours we end up at 9, which we call our solution.

3. Of course, you can use the addition table to find the answer to any subtraction problem, too. To find x where $6 \oplus x = 3$, we can look across the 6 row until you find an answer of 3 recorded. That answer is recorded in the row under 9, so $x = 9$.

EXAMPLE 3

Solve the following subtraction problems using the 12-hour clock.

a. $7 \ominus 9$
b. $2 \ominus 11$
c. $5 \ominus 10$
d. $4 \ominus 12$
e. $9 \ominus 9$

Solutions (a) 10 (b) 3 (c) 7 (d) 4 (e) 0

After looking at subtraction and multiplication, there is only one of the usual operations left to consider. Although it makes sense to write $6 \ominus 2 = 3$ in the 12-hour clock, how do you think we could calculate $4 \oplus 5$ in the 12-hour clock? We do so by restating the division problem $4 \oplus 5 = n$ as the multiplication $n \otimes 5 = 4$. This can be interpreted as how many groups of 5 are needed to obtain a 4 on the 12-hour clock? The answer to this is 8. Now as $8 \otimes 5 = 4$, we also know that $4 \oplus 5 = 8$.

Interestingly, although all addition, subtraction, and multiplication problems had solutions, in division we may not always have a solution, just as happened in the set of integers. For example, there is not a solution to the problem $5 \oplus 4 = n$. To see why, consider the equivalent multiplication prob-lem, $n \otimes 4 = 5$. If you start looking at groups of 4 on a 12-hour clock, you will obtain, 4, 8, 12, 4, 8, 12, 4, 8, 12, . . . , which demonstrates that no multiple of 4 will ever end up at five.

EXAMPLE 4

If possible, solve the following division problems using the 12-hour clock. If no solution is possible, state that.

a. $3 \oplus 5$

b. $6 \oplus 3$

c. $11 \oplus 4$

d. $8 \oplus 7$

e. $3 \oplus 8$

Solutions (a) 3 (b) 2 (c) not possible (d) 8 (e) not possible

You can make use of the multiplication tables to tell whether a division problem can be solved, and also to find the solution when an answer is pos-sible. For example, if we want to find the solution x where $3 \oplus 8 = x$, we look across the 8 row in search of a 3. Because there is not one in that row, we conclude that $3 \oplus 8$ is not possible.

PROBLEM SET 13.3

1. Complete a table of multiplication facts for the 12-hour clock.

2. Compute the following on a 12-hour clock.

    a. $5 \oplus 9$

    b. $9 \oplus 9$

    c. $12 \oplus 12 \oplus 3 \oplus 4 \oplus 12 \oplus 5 \oplus 8$

    d. $7 \oplus 9 \oplus 3 \oplus 9$

    e. $5 \oplus 4 \oplus 6 \oplus 7$

    f. $2 \ominus 5$

    g. $5 \ominus 2$

    h. $7 \ominus 11$

    i. $8 \ominus 12 \ominus 5 \ominus 7$

    j. $4 \ominus 10 \ominus 5 \ominus 6$

    k. $4 \otimes 9$

    l. $5 \otimes 6$

    m. $4 \otimes 4 \otimes 6 \otimes 2 \otimes 5$

    n. $2 \otimes 2 \otimes 2 \otimes 2 \otimes 2 \otimes 2$

 o. $9 \otimes 6 \otimes 2 \otimes 9$
 p. $3 \oplus 5$
 q. $9 \oplus 7$
 r. $6 \oplus 5$
 s. $(5 \oplus 7) \oplus (3 \oplus 5)$
 t. $[(9 \oplus 6) \oplus 2] \oplus 3$
 u. $9 \oplus [6 \oplus (2 \oplus 3)]$

3. Find all the values from 1 through 12 that make each number sentence true.

 a. $n \oplus 9 = 5$
 b. $3 \oplus n = 7$
 c. $3 \ominus n = 3 \oplus n$
 d. $n \otimes 7 = 11$
 e. $5 \ominus n = 3 \oplus n$
 f. $n \ominus 6 = 11$
 g. $n \otimes 5 = 11$
 h. $n \oplus 8 = 7$
 i. $n \otimes 3 = 3$
 j. $n \otimes 5 = 5$

13.4 MODULAR ARITHMETIC

Often, in the 12-hour clock, it is convenient to use the numerals 0 through 11 instead of 1 through 12. You probably saw why in the exercises. For example, although $2 + 0 = 2$ is true, on a 12-hour clock a similar statement is $2 \oplus 12 = 2$. We are now going to consider a clock with fewer numbers. In Figure 13.3, a clock with 5 numerals, 0, 1, 2, 3, and 4, is shown. We can now consider addition, subtraction, multiplication, and division on this system in the same way as we did on the 12-hour system. For example, $3 \oplus 2 = 0$, $3 \ominus 2 = 1$, $3 \otimes 2 = 1$, and $3 \oplus 2 = 4$ on a 5-clock.

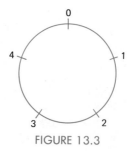

FIGURE 13.3

Part of the addition and multiplication tables, for a 5-clock are given in Tables 13.3a and 13.3b. Complete the missing entries.

The arithmetic of the 5-clock is called arithmetic modulo 5 and operates on the same principle as 12-hour clock arithmetic. For example, we know that any whole number divided by 5 will have a remainder of 0, 1, 2, 3, or 4.

TABLE 13.3a

$\oplus$	0	1	2	3	4
0					
1			3		
2					
3			0	1	
4		0			3

TABLE 13.3b

$\otimes$	0	1	2	3	4
0			0		
1		1			
2			4		3
3			1		
4					1

In general, two numbers are called congruent modulo 5 if and only if they have the same remainder when divided by 5. This is equivalent to saying that two numbers are congruent modulo 5 if the two numbers differ by a multiple of 5. We write this symbolically as follows:

$$12 \equiv 17 \text{ (mod 5) [Read this as 12 is congruent to 17 modulo 5.]}$$

EXAMPLE 1

Solve the following in modulo 5 arithmetic.

a. $1 \ominus 3$
b. $2 \ominus 3$
c. $1 \ominus 4$

Solutions (a) 3 (b) 4 (c) 2

EXAMPLE 2

Solve the following in modulo 5 arithmetic.

a. $n \oplus 1 = 0$
b. $n \oplus 3 = 2$
c. $n \otimes 3 = 2$
d. $3 \oplus n = 2$

Solutions (a) 4 (b) 4 (c) 4 (d) 4

You should be aware that we often make use of modular systems in our daily lives. For example, if today is a Friday, what day of the week will it be in 33 days? Here we are clearly considering the days of the week as modeling a modulo seven system. In fact, as $33 \div 7$ gives a remainder of 5, we know that 33 days from Friday will be a Wednesday. We can determine that by considering that in 28 days the day of the week will still be Friday, and 5 days after a Friday is a Wednesday.

Similarly, traffic signal lights usually operate on some modular system. A common modular system in a noncongested area is modulo 3—red, green, and yellow. Hence, if a light is green, in 17 changes the light will be red.

PROBLEM SET 13.4

1. Solve the following in arithmetic modulo 5
   a. $3 \oplus 3$
   b. $2 \oplus 4$
   c. $4 \otimes 2$
   d. $2 \ominus 4$
   e. $3 \ominus 4$
   f. $1 \ominus 3$
   g. $2 \ominus 3$
   h. $3 \oplus 2$

2. Solve the following, if possible, in the modular system indicated.
   a. $4 \oplus n \equiv 1 \pmod 5$
   b. $4 \oplus n \equiv 1 \pmod 6$
   c. $4 \oplus n \equiv 1 \pmod 7$
   d. $n \oplus n \equiv 3 \pmod 8$
   e. $n \ominus 4 \equiv 1 \pmod 9$
   f. $2 \ominus n \equiv 3 \pmod 7$
   g. $n \oplus 3 \equiv 1 \pmod 8$
   h. $2 \otimes n \equiv 3 \pmod 7$
   i. $3 \ominus n \equiv 2 \pmod 7$
   j. $2 \otimes n \equiv 3 \pmod 9$
   k. $(n \otimes 2) \oplus 3 \equiv 5 \pmod 7$
   l. $3 \ominus (5 \otimes n) \equiv 7 \pmod 9$
   m. $6 \oplus (2 \otimes n) \equiv 2 \pmod 7$
   n. $2 \oplus (3 \otimes n) \equiv 5 \oplus (2 \otimes n) \pmod 7$

14

14.1   ENTERING THE TURTLE GRAPHICS ENVIRONMENT

Although microcomputers are well established in schools and society, instructional uses of computers in education are still being defined and redefined. The National Council of Teachers of Mathematics (NCTM) Curriculum and Evaluation Standards for school mathematics provide clear directions for the use of technology in the teaching of mathematics. According to NCTM, students are to use the computer as a tool for processing information and performing calculations in order to investigate and solve problems. One of the assumptions of the NCTM standards is that computers are used throughout the school mathematics curriculum.

Increasing amounts and higher quality of software are becoming available for the classroom that use the capabilities of the computer for teaching mathematics. We encourage the use of software that allows the computer to be used as a tool to teach mathematical concepts while the students are active participants in the learning process. In our opinion, it would not be useful to provide a list of such software or use specific examples within this text because there is so much variability of hardware and software available.

However, there are some uses of the computer for teaching mathematics that are available in most elementary school classrooms. Programming languages, such as Logo, are being viewed in light of their capabilities as tools for teaching mathematics through a problem-solving approach.

Logo has been available on microcomputers since the early 1980s and has found its place within the elementary and junior high mathematics curriculum. Logo was designed in 1968 for use on large computer systems and has been continually refined since 1979 when it first became available on microcomputers. Students using Logo are not required to have a great store of mathematical or computer knowledge to enter the "Turtle Graphics" world of Logo. Because many different versions of Logo exist for use on microcomputers, it is accessible in most elementary schools. In order to make full use of Logo for instructional purposes, it will be necessary to be familiar with the structure of the language so that you can communicate with the computer. Because Logo is a software package and its use in schools is not universal, we devote some time to the language and its use in mathematics. Although learning to program is not the major emphasis here, a review for some and an introduction for others is presented to provide for explorations and extensions of mathematical topics.

Logo's Turtle Graphics allows students to write mathematical statements that produce interesting visual effects. An environment can be simulated that allows the study of geometry to take place in a natural way. The Logo turtle draws shapes on the screen by leaving a trail of its movements. This allows you to examine and reflect on the visualization of shapes, use attributes to describe the shapes, see the relationships among classes of figures, and experiment with geometric concepts.

Logo is characterized as "easy to get into," and students can use Logo without a complicated set of language elements. A few simple commands, called *primitives*, are used as building blocks for defined lists of commands written as procedures.

Although various versions of Logo are available, two major versions designed for microcomputers are used in most elementary school classrooms. The two most common are Terrapin Logo or Logo Plus (developed at the Massachusetts Institute of Technology and essentially the same as MIT Logo) and the LCSI (Logo Computer Systems Inc.) version of Logowriter. We have chosen to use a Terrapin version or MIT Logo for development here, although the examples and exercises can be used in any Turtle Graphics environment.

Most versions of Logo are quite similar and only slight modifications in instructions need to be made when using versions other than Terrapin or MIT Logo. However, if you are using LogoWriter, you will need to consult your manual for instructions on clearing the screen, using the "flip side" of the page for writing procedures, differences in stopping procedures, and specifics for naming pages to be saved on your LogoWriter Scrapbook (files) disk. Other minor differences also exist, but you can become familiar enough with your version of Logo after a short introduction, so that you should be able to work through the examples and exercises without much difficulty.

To start Logo, insert a Logo language disk into the disk drive and turn on the computer. When you see a question mark and a flashing cursor appear, the computer is waiting for instructions. We call this the *no-draw mode;* you must type DRAW to have the turtle appear in the center of the screen. The question mark is now at the bottom of the screen with room for four lines of text. This indicates that you are in SPLIT-SCREEN mode. The top part of the screen is for graphics whereas the bottom four lines will display the commands you type and the computer's responses. To view all the text, hold the CONTROL key down and press the T key (we abbreviate this as CTRL-T). Using CTRL-F will allow you to see the graphics screen only, whereas CTRL-S will return you to the SPLITSCREEN mode.

You are now in the *immediate mode* and can begin moving the turtle around to draw using a series of primitive commands such as FORWARD (FD), BACKWARD (BK), RIGHT (RT), or LEFT (LT). The number following FD and BK indicates how far the turtle will move in turtle steps whereas the number following RT and LT indicates the amount of turn in degrees made by the turtle. An angle measurement must follow RT and LT; a length measure must follow FD and BK. Figure 14.1 illustrates the use of these commands.

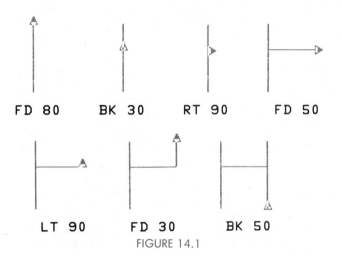

FIGURE 14.1

Therefore, to draw a square, we could use the following commands FD 40 RT 90 FD 40 RT 90 FD 40 RT 90 FD 40 RT 90 typed all on one line as in Figure 14.2*a* or typed on separate lines as in Figure 14.2*b*. In either case, we get the same result as shown in Figure 14.2*c*. However, if we use separate lines, we can observe the turtle's movement after pressing return at the end of each line, whereas commands all on one line are executed only after we press return following the list of commands.

The last two commands, FD 40 RT 90, return the turtle to its initial or "home" position in this case because we began our commands from the tur-

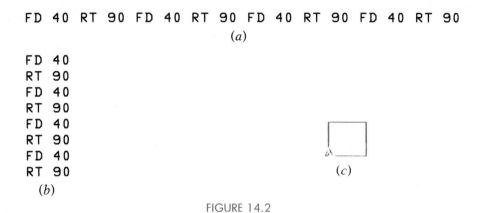

```
FD 40 RT 90 FD 40 RT 90 FD 40 RT 90 FD 40 RT 90
```
                              (a)

```
FD 40
RT 90
FD 40
RT 90
FD 40
RT 90
FD 40
RT 90
```
    (b)
                                                              (c)

FIGURE 14.2

tle's "home" position on the screen. The command HOME is another way to ensure that the turtle is in its original position in the center of the screen. However, by typing HOME, the turtle will leave a "trail" to the center of the screen from its current position. This trail can be eliminated by using the command PENUP (PU). Using PU before typing HOME will prevent the turtle from drawing while it moves home. The command PENDOWN (PD) can then be used when you wish to have the turtle draw with its next moves. As we can see in Figure 14.3, there are situations when it is useful for the turtle to leave a trail as it returns home whereas other times the PU command is used to prevent the turtle from drawing as it returns to home position. Remember by typing DRAW, the turtle will return home and the screen will be cleared. Also, we can hide the turtle with the HIDETURTLE (HT) command and make it reappear with SHOWTURTLE (ST).

Whenever the turtle points straight up or north, it has a heading of 0 (as it does in the "home" position). We can learn the turtle's heading by typing the primitive HEADING or PRINT HEADING. When the turtle turns RT 90 from the 0 heading, we say the turtle has a heading of 90 and it is facing directly east. A heading of 180 has the turtle facing down or south while a heading of 270 faces west. The command SETHEADING (SETH) can be used

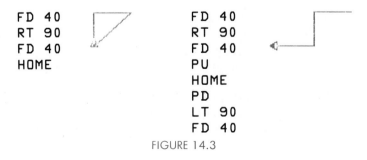

```
FD 40
RT 90
FD 40
HOME
```

```
FD 40
RT 90
FD 40
PU
HOME
PD
LT 90
FD 40
```

FIGURE 14.3

to turn the turtle in a direction from the 0 heading. Therefore, SETH 120 turns the turtle so it has a heading of 120. Figure 14.4 illustrates the use of HEADING and SETHEADING.

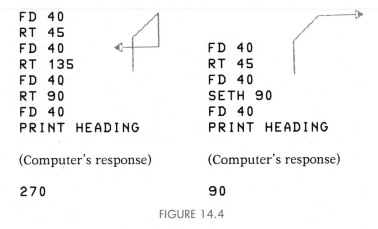

```
FD 40                        FD 40
RT 45                        RT 45
FD 40                        FD 40
RT 135                       SETH 90
FD 40                        FD 40
RT 90                        PRINT HEADING
FD 40
PRINT HEADING
```

(Computer's response)   (Computer's response)

270   90

FIGURE 14.4

Notice that when using the RT command the turtle is turned a given number of degrees to the right of its current heading and not the number of degrees from 0 or necessarily to your right as you face the screen. In Figure 14.5*a* the heading is 180°, whereas in 14.5*b*, the heading is 135°.

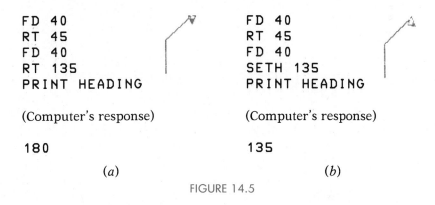

```
FD 40                        FD 40
RT 45                        RT 45
FD 40                        FD 40
RT 135                       SETH 135
PRINT HEADING                PRINT HEADING
```

(Computer's response)   (Computer's response)

180   135

(*a*)   (*b*)

FIGURE 14.5

REMARK The PRINT (PR) command may be used to print words or numbers. When this is desired, quotation marks are used preceding what you want to print, for example PRINT "HELLO produces the word HELLO. For a list of words, you must use brackets as PRINT [HELLO AND GOODBYE].

The sequence of commands for the square we drew earlier can be shortened by using the REPEAT command. We can command the turtle to repeat 4 times the drawing of the sides of the square. By typing REPEAT 4 [FD 40 RT 90] the commands within the brackets are executed 4 times. As before in Figure 14.2, the turtle's final position and heading is the same as its initial position and heading. To help us keep track of the turtle's position and heading after drawing a figure, it is convenient to have the turtle's final state to be the same as its initial state. We define a set of commands that accomplishes this to be *state transparent*.

The REPEAT command can be useful in drawing regular polygons. Before drawing polygons, we need to note that the number of degrees in a complete turn of the turtle, which is essentially going around in a circle, is 360. Therefore, it takes 360 degrees to complete the turns necessary to make a closed shape.

In Figure 14.6 an equilateral triangle is used to illustrate the degrees the turtle turns as it draws the sides of the triangle. We know that each of the angles of an equilateral triangle has a measure of 60 degrees. However, the degrees of turn would be equal to the exterior angle of the polygon rather than the interior angle.

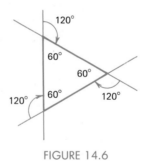

FIGURE 14.6

When we draw an equilateral triangle, the turtle must make three turns of 120 degrees to complete the 360 degrees. Using the REPEAT command, we can use the following to draw an equilateral triangle.

REPEAT 3 [FD 30 RT 120]

What would be the result if we typed REPEAT 3 [RT 120 FD 30]? Type in the commands to check your answer.

In Figure 14.7 we can observe the two triangles and see that only the posi-

FIGURE 14.7

tion with respect to the turtle changed. The first listing of commands resulted in the top triangle, whereas the second set of commands resulted in the bottom triangle. If it is important for the turtle to return to the initial position or the home position (if that is where the turtle started); you will want to use a set of commands that are state transparent.

Remember to clear the screen when you need a clean slate on which to draw.

EXAMPLE 1

Use the REPEAT command to draw a regular hexagon and a regular octagon.

Solution

REPEAT 6 [FD 30 RT 60]

REPEAT 8 [FD 30 RT 45]

Notice that the number following REPEAT multiplied by the degree turned gave us the necessary 360 degrees. This is called the *Total Turtle Trip Theorem* (TTTT) because each time the turtle makes a polygon and returns to its original position it will have turned a total of 360 degrees. This theorem is a restatement of the property that the sum of the exterior angles, one at each vertex of our polygon, is 360 degrees.

EXAMPLE 2

Write commands to draw the following rhombus, which consists of two congruent equilateral triangles. Use REPEAT where possible.

One Solution

REPEAT 2 [FD 30 RT 60 FD 30 RT 120]

Can you use another series of turtle moves to draw the rhombus?

PROBLEM SET 14.1

1. Type in the following commands and describe the results.
   a. FD30
   b. FD 60
   c. SETH 360
   d. SETH (20)
   e. HEADING 120
   f. PD 20
   g. RT 60
   h. LT 300

2. When we choose numbers to follow the FORWARD or PRINT and other commands accepting a numerical input, we can assign other real number quantities besides whole numbers. We could use decimals or values obtained as a result of an arithmetic operation. For example we could use FD 35.5 or FD 300/60. Other commands such as SQRT 100, which produces 10, can be used for generating numerical values. Other commands are listed here.

SQRT	Computes the square root of a nonnegative quantity
INTEGER	Computes the integer part of a quantity
QUOTIENT	Computes the integer quotient of two inputs
REMAINDER	Computes the integer remainder

   a. Type in the following commands using real-number inputs along with operations. Record the results given or the movement of the turtle.
      i. FD -25
      ii. BK -25
      iii. FD SQRT 100
      iv. PR 5 - 6 * 3
      v. PR 5 - 6 * (3 + 2)
      vi. PR QUOTIENT 47 6
      vii. PR REMAINDER 47 6
      viii. PR INTEGER 35.5
      ix. RT 9*40
      x. BK 3*20

   b. Try other inputs and operations for further exploration of the use of real numbers.

3. Study the following commands and sketch what the turtle will draw. Verify your prediction by typing in commands.

a. FD 40
   RT 120
   FD 40
   HOME

b. FD 40
   LT 145
   FD 50
   LT 145
   HOME

c. REPEAT 5 [FD 30 RT 360/5]

d. REPEAT 18 [FD 10 RT 10]

e. RT 60
   FD 30
   LT 90
   FD 30
   RT 90
   FD 30

f. REPEAT 4 [FD 20 RT 90]
   REPEAT 4 [FD 20*2 RT 90]

g. REPEAT 3 [FD 15 LT 90 FD 45 RT 90]

h. REPEAT 4 [FD 60 PU FD 10 PD]

i. REPEAT 10 [FD 40 RT 36]

4. Write commands to draw the following. Then continue the commands until the turtle goes off the screen.

a. 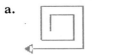   b.

5. It is helpful to know what direction the turtle is facing after a series of commands are given. Determine the heading of the turtle after each set of commands. Use the command PRINT HEADING to check your answer. Type DRAW before each set of commands to return the heading of the turtle to home position.

a. RT 50 LT -50

b. RT 120 LT 30

c. REPEAT 3 [RT 50]

d. REPEAT 3 [RT 50 LT 80 RT 30]

e. FD 30 RT 60 FD 40 RT 40 FD 20 LT 20

f. FD 50 RT -20 FD 20 LT -40 BK 60

g. LT 270 RT 30

h. RT 360

i. LT 720

j. RT 360/60 FD 60

6. Predict the final turtle state after each set of commands is executed. Before typing in the commands, clear the screen and return the turtle to the home position. Check your answers by typing in the commands.

a. REPEAT 2 [FD 20 RT 90 FD 40 RT 90]

b. REPEAT 5 [RT 360/5 FD 40]

c. SETH 120 REPEAT 3 [FD 20 RT 120]

d. RT 60 REPEAT 2 [FD 30 RT 60 FD 30 RT 120]

e. RT 60 REPEAT 3 [FD 30 RT 120] SETH 0

7. Explore with the turtle to determine the dimensions of the screen in turtlesteps.

8. Use the REPEAT command to draw the following polygons: hexagon, octagon, rhombus, and trapezoid.

9. Use the REPEAT command to draw a five-sided star.

10. Draw a set of perpendicular lines.

11. Use the REPEAT command to draw polygons that approximate a circle.

12. On the line provided, fill in the missing commands in each example so that your drawing will approximate the one shown. The screen should be cleared and the turtle in the home position before each set of commands is typed.

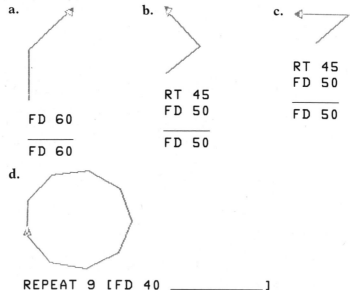

a.

FD 60

‾‾‾‾‾‾

FD 60

b.

RT 45
FD 50

‾‾‾‾‾‾

FD 50

c.

RT 45
FD 50

‾‾‾‾‾‾

FD 50

d.

REPEAT 9 [FD 40 _____]

13. Write commands that will draw an acute angle, a right angle, and an obtuse angle.

14. Write commands to draw a set of parallel lines.

15. Write commands to draw each of the sets of parallel lines that are cut by a transversal.

a.

b.

c. What did you notice about the turns the turtle made in drawing the parallel lines in (a)?

d. What did you notice about the turns the turtle made in drawing the parallel lines in (b)?

e. How were the turns similar or different in (a) and in (b)?

f. How do the commands for the drawings in (a) and (b) relate to angles formed by parallel lines cut by a transversal?

16. Use turtle commands to draw two line segments that are parallel and a third line segment that is a transversal and perpendicular to the set of parallel lines.

Pedagogical Activities

17. The Turtle Graphics of Logo can be made more meaningful for elementary school students by having them participate in activities in which their body movements relate to the Logo commands. On a flat surface or the floor, place marks to be used as corners of a square. Walk around these corners or connect them with lines as you issue commands that could be used in Logo to draw such a shape. Use other shapes in the same way.

18. Various activities can be helpful to better estimate angles and lengths used with the primitive commands for changing position and direction. Draw a maze on transparent plastic and attach it to the computer screen so that you can move the turtle through the path. Find the path through the maze with the shortest possible moves.

19. Place a piece of clay or other object on the screen and move the turtle to it in the fewest moves.

20. Explore various polygons to discover how they fit on a circle or if they will cover 360°. This will help you determine the interior angle measurement at each of the vertices. Using commercially designed pattern blocks or the following shapes, place the polygons on top of a circle.

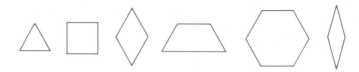

Notice that it takes four squares to cover the circle. Because there are 360 degrees in a circle, there are $\frac{1}{4}$ of 360° in one angle or corner of one square. How many triangles cover the circle? Each angle measures $\frac{1}{6}$ of 360° or 60°.

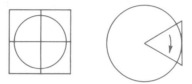

Try this procedure with the hexagon, both angles of the trapezoid, the rhombus, and the kite to find the number of degrees in the angles of each of the pattern block pieces.

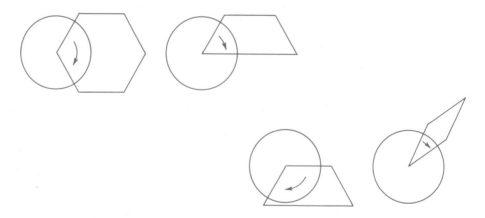

21. In a Logo environment, the turtle must turn the exterior angle to draw the next side of a polygon. The interior angle and exterior angle can be easily seen using pattern blocks or cut-out shapes and straight lines. The hexagon and the small angle of the rhombus together form a straight line or 180°. The interior (inside) angle (turn) of the rhombus is equal to the exterior (outside) angle (turn) of the hexagon.

   a. What is the measure of the interior angle of the hexagon?

   b. What is the measure of the exterior angle?

   c. What about the measures of the interior and exterior angles of the rhombus?

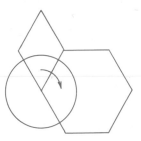

Try the same procedure with the two different angles of a trapezoid to determine the turn of the turtle necessary to go around the outside of the trapezoid.

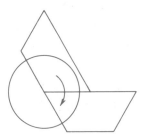

14.2   DEFINING PROCEDURES AND USING VARIABLE INPUTS

As you now know, when the screen is cleared the figure you had drawn is lost. To redraw the picture or shape, the entire sequence of commands must be typed. However, we can create procedures consisting of a group of one or more instructions (using primitives) that can be stored in the computer's memory to be used at a later time. The following instructions for creating and saving procedures are specifically for Terrapin Logo. In most versions, the instructions will be similar, however LogoWriter is considerably different so you will need to consult your manual.

To create a procedure, type TO followed by any name you wish to call the procedure. The name must contain no spaces, so if you wish to use two words, place a period between them. For example, you may use TO TRI, TO EQUITRI, or TO EQUI.TRI; but not TO EQUI TRI.

After you have typed TO and a name, press RETURN and you will be in edit mode or the "teaching mode." You may now enter the set of commands that are needed to produce the desired picture. The commands that you type will not be executed immediately, as they were in the immediate interactive mode we previously used. The last line of the procedure should be END to signify that you have completed the procedure. For an equilateral triangle, you could have the following procedure:

```
TO TRI
  REPEAT 3 [FD 30 RT 120]
END
```

To define and store a procedure and exit the edit mode, press the CONTROL key and the C key (this is called CTRL-C). At this point, you will return to the DRAW mode and the words TRI DEFINED will appear. When you see the ? and the blinking cursor, you can type the word TRI and the turtle will draw a triangle from the definition you used in the procedure.

To change or edit any part of the procedure, type EDIT TRI and you will be back in the edit mode. At this point, you may make changes to the procedure, if you choose. The following list of editing commands will help you edit more easily. These can only be used while in the edit mode.

CTRL-A	Moves cursor to start of current line
CTRL-E	Moves cursor to end of current line
CTRL-N	Moves cursor to next line
CTRL-P	Moves cursor to previous line
CTRL-X	Erases to end of current line
ESC or	
Delete	Erases preceding character.
→	Moves cursor to right
←	Moves cursor to left

EXAMPLE 1

Write a procedure to draw a 10-sided regular polygon (decagon).

One Solution

```
TO DECAGON
  REPEAT 10 [FD 30 RT 36]
END
```

Use CTRL-C and the computer will respond DECAGON DEFINED. When a ? appears, type in DECAGON and you will observe the turtle drawing the following figure.

EXAMPLE 2

Write a procedure to draw a rhombus.

One Solution

```
TO RHOMBUS
  REPEAT 2 [FD 30 RT 120 FD 30 RT 60]
END
```

After a procedure has been defined, it can be used in a manner similar to the way primitives are used. In other words, it can become a Logo command. For example, TRI can be used with the REPEAT command REPEAT 6 [TRI RT 60]. Procedures can then be written that use previously defined procedures. SPIN.TRI in Figure 14.8 is an example of such a procedure.

A procedure may be erased from memory, by typing ERASE followed by the name of the procedure. ERASE ALL will erase all the procedures presently in the computer's memory.

```
TO SPIN.TRI
  REPEAT 6 [TRI RT 60]
END
```

FIGURE 14.8

The procedures you have defined are saved in the computer's work space, but when you turn off the computer they will be lost. Logo procedures can be saved on an initialized disk to be read into the computer's memory at a later time. The SAVE command is used to save files that contain all the procedures currently in the computer's work space. Therefore, if you have several procedures, for example, TRI, SQUARE, HEXAGON, OCTAGON in memory, you could type SAVE "POLYGONS. The file POLYGONS will be created on your disk and contain each individual procedure (as well as any others in the computer's memory at this time). Therefore, if there are any procedures that you do not wish to save under POLYGON, be sure to erase them before using the SAVE command.

After the file has been saved on your disk, you can read it back into the work space of the computer by typing READ "POLYGONS. Typing CATALOG gives you a list of files on your disk. Remember that under each file name may be several different procedures, so you must read the file to get the procedures into the computer's memory before you can type the procedure name.

Following is a summary of work-space and file management commands.

CATALOG	Prints the names of the files on the currently mounted disk.
EDIT (ED)	Enters edit mode. If a procedure name is included as an input, that procedure will be in the editor.
ERASE (ER)	Erases designated procedure from workspace. May use ERASE ALL to erase all procedures from the workspace.
ERASEFILE	Removes from the disk a file saved with SAVE. Takes the file name as input, which must begin with a quotation mark.
PRINTOUT TITLES (POTS)	Lists all procedures currently in the work space.
READ	Reads a file from disk into the work space. Also takes the file name as an input, which must begin with a quotation mark.
SAVE	Saves all current procedures in the work space as a file under the given name. File name must begin with a quotation mark.

We can write a single procedure that allows us to input the number of sides we want our polygon to have. The computer can also compute the angle that needs to be turned to draw a regular polygon by dividing 360 by the varying number of sides in the polygon. Such a procedure alerts the computer that a variable input will be used. The computer understands that when a colon is used, a variable will follow. We will call this procedure POLY :SIDES indicating that the number of sides will vary as we choose. For example, we can define POLY :SIDES and use it to draw the polygons in Figure 14.9.

```
TO POLY :SIDES
  REPEAT :SIDES [FD 30 RT 360/ :SIDES]
END
```

Typing POLY 4 will produce a square whereas POLY 8 will draw an octagon.

The variable input SIDES could have been any word or letter. The proce-

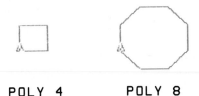

POLY 4   POLY 8

FIGURE 14.9

dure that follows produces the same figures as the one preceding. Here we have used N instead of SIDES.

```
TO POLY :N
  REPEAT :N [ FD 30 RT 360/ :N]
END
```

We can also use a variable for the length of the sides of the polygon because Logo procedures may contain variables to input several numbers. For instance, in the POLY procedure, we may also want to vary the length of the sides of a given polygon. To do this, we use a variable for the distance the turtle moves forward. It will be helpful to use POLY1 in this procedure to set it apart from our first polygon procedure.

```
TO POLY1 :N :DISTANCE
  REPEAT :N [FD :DISTANCE RT 360/ :N]
END
```

If two variables are used, two inputs are required. Now typing POLY1 3 30 will produce a three-sided regular polygon with a side of 30 (Fig. 14.10). Try this.

We can experiment by leaving the triangle on the screen and drawing a triangle that is similar (same shape, but a different size). For example, Figure 14.11 illustrates the results of POLY1 3 30 and POLY1 3 60 typed without using DRAW between them. As you can see, similar triangles with one having sides twice the length of the sides of the other were produced.

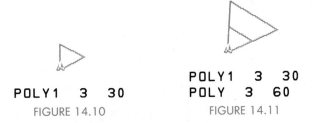

POLY1   3   30
POLY 1   3   30   POLY   3   60
FIGURE 14.10   FIGURE 14.11

Investigate other similar figures using the POLY1 procedure. Use the POLY1 procedure to draw a circle.

As we did earlier, we can define a procedure to call on another procedure that has already been defined. We can edit POLY1 :N :DISTANCE to include the command TRI before the END line. At this point, we may want to have all the variables as single letters so we will change the word DISTANCE to the letter S. Our procedure now is the following:

```
TO POLY1 :N :S
  REPEAT :N [FD :S RT 360/ :N]
  TRI
END
```

When you type POLY1 4 30, the turtle will draw a square with a triangle inside it, as seen in Figure 14.12.

POLY1   4   30

FIGURE 14.12

Use this procedure varying the inputs and then editing it to call on other procedures. It may be necessary to change the turtle's direction and position before calling another procedure. This allows us to build onto polygons. The procedures COMBINE and COMBINE1 in Figure 14.13 provide examples of building onto polygons.

```
TO COMBINE
  SQUARE
  FD 30 RT 90
  FD 30 LT 30
  RHOMBUS
END
```

```
TO COMBINE1
  SQUARE
  FD 30 LT 30
  RHOMBUS
  LT 150
  RHOMBUS
END
```

FIGURE 14.13

It may be helpful to use cutouts of shapes or actual polygon blocks to build the designs on a flat surface before typing them into the computer. This will allow you to reflect on the position and turn of the turtle that will be necessary before you draw the next shape.

EXAMPLE 1

Write a procedure to draw the sequence of squares with triangles inside.

One solution

```
TO SEQUENCE
 REPEAT 2 [SQUARE TRI RT 90
 FD 30 LT 90 SQUARE RT 30 TRI RT 60
 FD 30 LT 90]
END
```

EXAMPLE 2

Write a procedure to draw the following combined shapes using the POLY procedure.

One solution

```
TO HEXS
 POLY 6
 LT 90
 POLY 4
 FD 30
 LT 30
 POLY 6
 RT 120
END
```

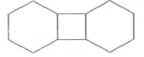

Most of the procedures we have defined thus far used only RT. If we define a POLY procedure that turns the turtle to the left, we can write a procedure that makes use of the POLY procedures turning the turtle both RT and LT.

```
TO POLYL :SIDES
 REPEAT :SIDES [FD 30 LT 360/ :SIDES]
END
```

```
TO HEXS1
  POLY 6
  POLYL 4
  LT 90
  FD 30
  RT 90
  POLYL 6
END
```

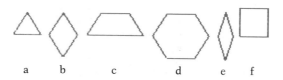

PROBLEM SET 14.2

1. Write procedures for a set of pattern blocks as shown here. Save these as the file Pattern.Blocks on your disk. You will be using these in other exercises.

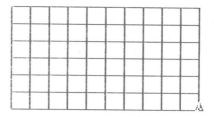

    a   b   c   d   e f

2. Write Logo procedures to tessellate (fill the screen with no holes and no overlapping) the screen with squares. Triangles and hexagons can also be tessellated. Write procedures for each of these and also try some tessellations using more than one shape.

3. Write a procedure to draw a rectangle with sides of length 30 and 50. Use variables so you may draw rectangles with varying lengths for the sides.

4. The following procedure can be used to create any parallelogram:

```
TO PARALLELOGRAM :LENGTH :WIDTH :ANGLE
  REPEAT 2 [FD :LENGTH RT :ANGLE FD :WIDTH
  RT 180 - :ANGLE]
END
```

Use this procedure to answer the following questions.

    a. What command will draw a square with side length of 20 turtle steps?

    b. Using the parallelogram procedure, draw a rhombus with side length of 60 and an angle of 45 degrees.

    c. Draw a rectangle with sides of 30 and 60.

    d. Draw a parallelogram with sides of 40 and 70 and one angle of 55 degrees.

    e. Draw a square similar to the square in (**a**), but three times the perimeter. How much larger in area will the square be?

    f. Draw a rhombus similar to the rhombus in (**b**), but half the perimeter. What will the relationship in area be?

    g. Draw a rectangle similar to the rectangle in (**c**), but 1.5 times the perimeter. What will the relationship in area be in this case?

5. Use the POLY1 procedure to draw five polygons with various number of sides. Enter the commands you used in the chart and compute the perimeter of each.

```
    COMMAND              PERIMETER
EX. POLY1 5 20             100
1.
2.
3.
4.
5.
```

6. Using your defined procedure that draws an equilateral triangle, write procedures for the following designs.

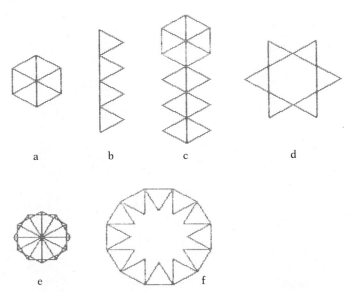

a   b   c   d

e   f

7. Use the parallelogram procedure to draw the following.

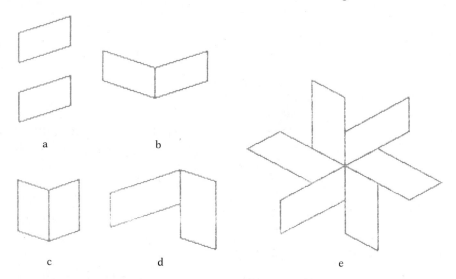

8. **a.** Write a procedure to draw a parallelogram using your equilateral triangle procedures.

   b. Write a procedure to draw a hexagon using a parallelogram procedure.

   c. Write a procedure to draw a trapezoid using the parallelogram and equilateral triangle procedures.

9. Write procedures to draw the following designs.

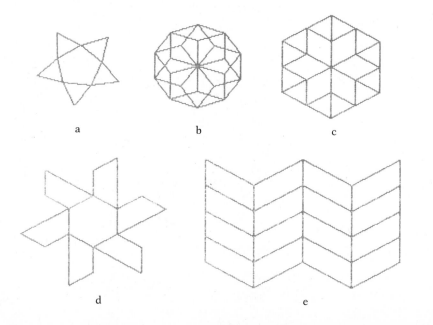

10. **a.** Write a procedure with variables that will draw a set of parallel lines in a Z shape cut by a transversal.

   b. Write a procedure with variables that will draw a set of parallel lines in a C shape cut by a transversal.

11. Draw several rectangles with the following perimeters:
   a. 180 turtle steps
   b. 250 turtle steps
   c. 199 turtle steps
   d. 129 turtle steps

   Write a procedure using variables to help you generate many rectangles with each given perimeter.

12. Although several versions of Logo have a FILL command, we can fill shapes by repeatedly drawing lines back and forth. For example, using a rectangle of length 50 and width 30 we have the following procedure:

```
TO FILL.REC
  REPEAT 30 [FD 50 BK 50 RT 90 FD 1 LT 90]
END
```

   a. Why did we REPEAT 30?
   b. How are the length and the width used in the filling process, and what is their relationship to the area of the rectangle?

13. Using the concepts involved in the area of rectangles that were explored in problem 12, write procedures for the rectangles described here.
   a. Write procedures to draw several rectangles with an area of 1800. Using variables will allow you to draw many different rectangles. Find the perimeter of each rectangle you drew.
   b. Write a procedure to fill one of the rectangles you drew in (*a*).
   c. Write procedures to draw several rectangles with areas of 960, 983, and 225.
   d. Write a procedure using variables that will fill any rectangle with a given area.

14. Write procedures using pattern blocks to draw the following designs. Edit your PATTERN.BLOCK file to vary the size of the sides of each polygon. Use those procedures to make the following designs bigger and smaller by various scale factors.

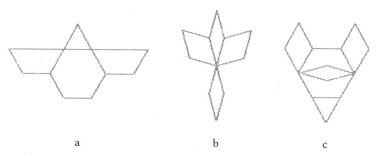

a   b   c

15. Write a circle procedure using variables that can be used in drawing the following designs.

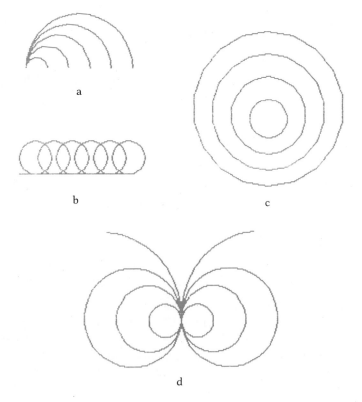

a

b   c

d

16. We can move objects around on the screen by sliding them a given direction and distance. Using a procedure such as SLIDE will move a shape when that procedure name is inserted within the SLIDE procedure.

```
TO SLIDE :DIRECTION :DISTANCE
  RT :DIRECTION
  FD :DISTANCE
  LT :DIRECTION
END
```

For example, to slide a trapezoid we could use the following procedure.

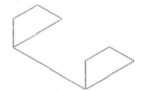

```
TO SLIDEON :DIRECTION :DISTANCE
TRAPEZOID
SLIDE :DIRECTION :DISTANCE
TRAPEZOID
END

?SLIDEON 120 60
```

a. Use the SLIDEON procedure to perform a slide that translates the image in a direction heading 60 degrees with a distance of 90 turtle steps.

Using the TRAPEZOID procedure, perform the following slides and record the results:

	DIRECTION	DISTANCE
b.	90	60
c.	180	60
d.	60	60
e.	270	90

f. What would SLIDE 60 90 followed by SLIDE 180 90 produce?

17. a. Write a procedure that will draw the following shape.

b. Write a procedure that will draw the shape and then turn or rotate it a varying degrees as shown below.

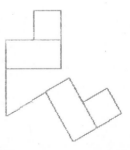

    c. Rotate the shape you have drawn 45 degrees.

    d. Rotate the shape 90 degrees.

    e. Rotate the shape 270 degrees.

18. Draw a vertical line up and down the screen through HOME. Use this line as the line of reflection.

    a. Write a procedure to flip the shape you drew in Problem 17 to the left across the line of reflection.

    b. Experiment with rotating the shape after flipping it across the line of reflection.

19. Write procedures for each individual shape that has been used to assemble the triangle. Use 30 turtle steps for the smaller length of side. Write a procedure using all the shapes to assemble the triangle on the screen.

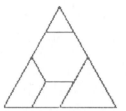

Pedagogical Activities

20. Build the following designs with pattern blocks on one side of the line of symmetry and then create a symmetrical pattern on the other side of the line. Create your own symmetrical designs with pattern blocks that can then be created on the screen using Logo and the pattern-block procedures.

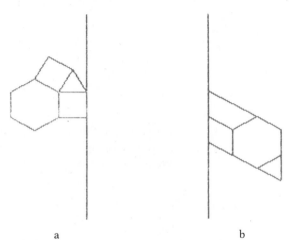

a   b

21. Cut out several rhombuses from three different colors of construction paper and use them to create the cube designs shown here. Use the rhombus procedure from the pattern-block file to draw the cube designs in Logo.

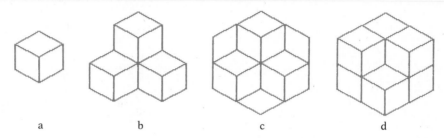

a   b   c   d

22. a. This triangle △ from a set of pattern blocks is one unit on each side. Make a similar triangle that is two units on each side. Make a similar triangle that is three units on each side.

   b. Using this rhombus ◇ with one unit on each side, make a similar rhombus with two units and then one with three units on each side.

   c. With this trapezoid, which is 1 unit on the top and sides and 2 units on the bottom, make a similar trapezoid that is 2 units on the top and sides and 4 units on the bottom.

   d. Note what measurement the angles of the similar figures have when compared to the original shape.

23. We can use the Logo procedures written with a variable side input for a square, an equilateral triangle, and a rhombus to explore the area and perimeter of similar figures.

   a. Have the turtle draw SQUARE 20 and then draw SQUARE 40. How many of the smaller squares will fit in the larger square? How is the perimeter of the large square related to the perimeter of the small square?

b. Now using the triangle, rhombus, and square procedures, draw figures like those below to explore the effect on the area when the perimeter of the figure is doubled or tripled. Explain what you observed in each of the five figures.

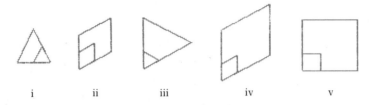

i   ii   iii   iv   v

14.3   MULTIPLE VARIABLES, TAIL-END RECURSION, AND CONDITION STATEMENTS

In this section, we further explore the process of calling procedures and subprocedures to investigate more mathematical concepts. It is also possible for a procedure to call on a copy of itself. In the TRI2 procedure, we can call the procedure TRI2 as a subprocedure before the END statement. This will start the TRI2 procedure anew each time the turtle encounters the word TRI2.

The process of a procedure calling on a copy of itself is called *recursion*. The example that follows is called *tail-end recursion* because only one recursive call is made within the body of the procedure, and it is the final step before the END statement. This procedure will continue indefinitely unless we do something to stop the turtle. Using CTRL-G will stop the procedure at any point.

```
TO TRI2
  REPEAT 3 [FD 30 RT 120]
  TRI2
END
```

Any procedure can be edited to call on a copy of itself. We can use any of the pattern block procedures we have defined and add a line to turn the turtle right a fixed number of degrees followed by a line to call a copy of itself. Figure 14.14 shows the procedure E.TRI spinning an equilateral triangle. You may want to enter this procedure and examine what transpires.

The POLY procedure we used earlier could have several subprocedures of which one is a copy of itself. Figure 14.15 shows the POLY1 procedure calling a copy of itself. Enter this procedure to observe the turtle as it draws the design.

As you can see, recursion can be useful if we do not know how many times

```
TO E.TRI :S
  REPEAT 3 [FD :S RT 120]
  RT 20
  E.TRI :S
END
```

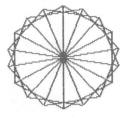

```
?E.TRI 60
```

FIGURE 14.14

```
TO POLY1 :N :S
  REPEAT :N [FD :S RT 360/ :N]
  TRI :S
  RT 90
  POLY1 :N :S
END
```

```
?POLY1 4 40
```

FIGURE 14.15

to repeat a sequence of instructions to accomplish some goal. The procedure will continue until you use CTRL-G, so you will obtain a completed design and can observe the number of repeats necessary to accomplish this.

We can add a third variable to the POLY1 procedure to increase the size of the side while the angle and number of sides remains constant. To do this we add a variable called INCREMENT that will be added to the size of the side whenever the POLY procedure calls itself. We now call this procedure POLY2, as defined in Figure 14.16 and use it to draw nested similar triangles. After you begin the procedure, you will want to use CTRL-G to stop the turtle when the drawing reaches the top of the screen.

```
TO POLY2 :N :S :INCREMENT
 REPEAT :N [FD :S RT 360/ :N]
 POLY2 :N :S + :INCREMENT :INCREMENT
END
```

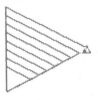

?POLY2 3 30 10

FIGURE 14.16

It is possible to include a "stop" command, rather than using CTRL-G. This can be done with the IF and STOP primitives. IF :S > 100 STOP will check to see how large the side is getting and stop the procedure when it becomes > 100. Therefore, we can write a POLY3 procedure as in Figure 14.17 to include the IF STOP statement as the second line. You should enter the procedure and try several different inputs.

```
TO POLY3 :N :S :INCREMENT
 IF :S > 100 STOP
 REPEAT :N [FD :S RT 360/ :N]
 POLY3 :N :S + :INCREMENT :INCREMENT
END
```

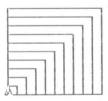

?POLY3 4 10 10

FIGURE 14.17

In the POLY3 procedure, the side of the polygon was increased after each smaller polygon was drawn. Suppose we increment the sides after each turn the turtle makes. This will produce "polygons" that change in size as they spiral outward, which we will call a *polyspiral*. Because we are not repeating a complete polygon, the REPEAT command would not be used. We will use an ANGLE input rather than an input for number of sides to make our investigations more interesting. In the POLYSPI procedure in Figure 14.18, SIZE is the input for the initial forward movement the turtle makes, ANGLE indicates the degrees the turtle will make each time it turns, and the INCREMENT increases the forward movement after each turn. The IF STOP statement on the second line will check for size of the side and stop the procedure when the side is greater than 100.

```
TO POLYSPI : SIZE :ANGLE :INCREMENT
 IF :SIZE >100 STOP
 FD :SIZE
 RT :ANGLE
 POLYSPI :SIZE + :INCREMENT :ANGLE :INCREMENT
END
```

```
?POLYSPI 5 120 6
```

FIGURE 14.18

The POLY procedures with variables provide opportunities for investigations of angles and sides when various inputs are used. Changes in the amount incremented or incrementing the :ANGLE rather than :SIDE may be an interesting investigation.

PROBLEM SET 14.3

1. Below is a POLY procedure that does not use a REPEAT statement but rather incorporates the use of recursion. This procedure can be used to draw a polygon when we do not know how many times to repeat a set of instructions because we are just asking the turtle to go forward some fixed distance and then turn right some fixed angle.

```
TO POLY4 :SIDE :ANGLE
 FD :SIDE RT :ANGLE
 POLY4 :SIDE :ANGLE
END
```

Predict which of the following inputs produced the figures **a-h.**

```
A.  POLY4  40  72
B.  POLY4  60  144
C.  POLY4  60  135
D.  POLY4  40  60
E.  POLY4  60  120
F.  POLY4  2  2
G.  POLY4  60  108
H.  POLY4  60  160
```

a.   **b.**

c.

e.

d.

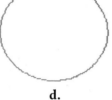

f.

h.

g.

2. a. Edit the pattern block procedures with variable inputs for the size of the side to include a line to increment the size. Write a procedure using recursion to draw the following nested polygons that includes a STOP command.

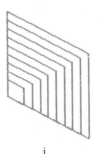

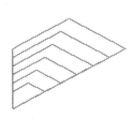

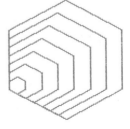

i   ii   iii

b. Are these nested polygons similar? Why?

3. Write procedures using recursion to draw the following polygons that spiral outward.

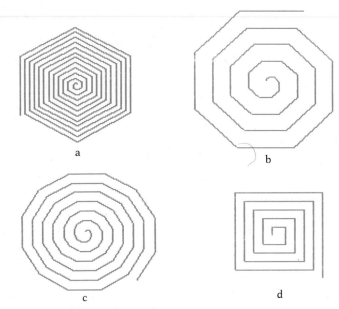

a

b

c

d

4. Write a recursive procedure to draw the staircase.

5. Write recursive procedures that draw the following polygons and then spin the polygons while they grow in size.

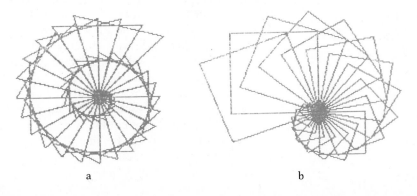

a

b

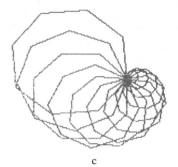

c

6. Using the POLY3 procedure in Figure 14.17, begin with a large number for the size of the side, subtract an increment and use < in your IF STOP statement. Describe what happens when you run the procedure.

7. Use several different inputs for the POLYSPI procedure in Figure 14.18.
   a. What type of spiral will an angle of 120 produce?
   b. What type of spiral will angles of 60, 40, 90, and 36 produce?

8. Vary the inputs for SIZE and INCREMENT in the POLYSPI procedure. Try large and small numbers as well as negative inputs. In what ways did the changes affect your spirals?

9. Which of the three inputs in the POLYSPI procedure seems to have the most potential for affecting changes?

10. Try POLYSPI 10 90 3. This is what we can call a perfect spiral or nested spiral. Find other perfect spirals.

11. Some spirals generated will not be perfect spirals. These will be of two types: (1) nonnested, such as 5 75 1, and (2) stars, such as 3 108 2. Draw approximately 20 spirals and make a record of your finding as you keep track of the length of side with which you began, the angle used, and the increment input. Use a table similar to the one following to keep your records. The first three entries will be your inputs whereas the last two you will gather from the figure produced on the screen. You will be able to categorize your spirals into nested, nonnested, or stars. Make sure you have some of each in your table. For each count either the sides, the branches, or the points of the star. Be sure to try inputs that are both whole numbers and decimals.

INPUTS			FINDINGS	
SIZE	ANGLE	INCREMENT	# OF SIDES, BRANCHES OR POINTS	TYPE OF SPIRAL
10	90	3	4	Perfect

12. In problem 11, what changes in your inputs produced the different types of spirals?

13. Rewrite the POLYSPI procedure to increment the angle rather than the side. Call this procedure INSPI. Vary the angle and the amount that the angle increases. Use some large numbers, small numbers, and negative numbers. Find inputs that will produce the following designs.

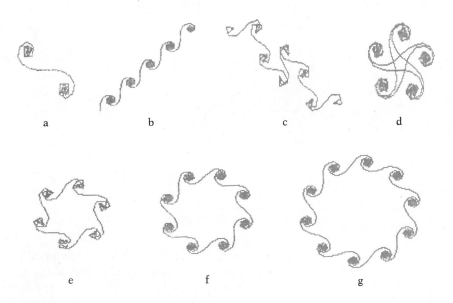

a   b   c   d

e   f   g

Pedagogical Activities

14. Use graph paper to draw a spiral with 90° angles. By using graph paper, it will be easy to see that each side gets just a little longer than the one preceding it.

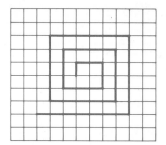

15. The following activity can help you see a relationship between straight lines and curves. Using drawings of a square, regular hexagon, and regular octagon; connect the midpoints on the sides. Continue this process, marking the new midpoints and connecting them until the figures get too small to work with. Shade in the triangles as they spiral inward as shown in the square. Notice in what ways the figures are the same and in what ways they differ. Compare the triangles formed in each figure as they become smaller.

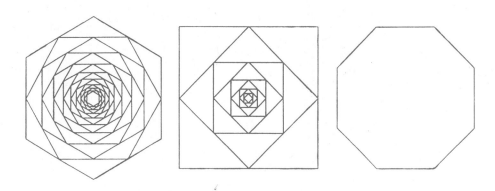

14.4   THE COORDINATED WORLD OF LOGO

The home position of the turtle on the computer screen is located at (0,0) on a rectangular coordinate plane. Each point of the screen is associated with an ordered pair of numbers *(x,y)* in relation to the turtle's home at (0,0). The turtle can be moved to any point on the coordinate system using the commands SETX, SETY, and SETXY.

SETX is used to move the turtle in a horizontal direction to the position of the given input for the x-coordinate. SETY moves the turtle vertically to the point of the given *y*-coordinate. These commands do not change the turtle's heading. Therefore, by typing SETX 40 and SETY 60, we can move the turtle to the position (40, 60) on the coordinate system. This could have been accomplished by typing SETXY 40 60. The final position will be the same;

however, if the pen is down when the commands are given, the turtle leaves a different trail. Figure 14.19 shows the difference when each command is given to move the turtle from the home position.

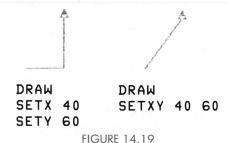

```
DRAW          DRAW
SETX 40       SETXY 40 60
SETY 60
```

FIGURE 14.19

We can draw shapes by moving the turtle around on the screen using SETX and SETY commands. If we start with the turtle at home and type SETX 40 SETY 60 SETX (-40) SETY (-70), we will have the drawing as shown in Figure 14.20.

FIGURE 14.20

By typing PRINT XCOR and PRINT YCOR, you will be able to determine the *x*-coordinate and *y*-coordinate of the turtle in the final position. The turtle could also have been moved to this position by using SETXY (-40) -70.

By using the SETXY command, we now have another way to construct an equilateral triangle, as shown in Figure 14.21.

```
TO TRIANGLE
  SETXY 0 0
  SETXY 0 (-40)
  SETXY (-30) (-20)
  SETXY 0 0
END
```

FIGURE 14.21

TRIANGLE will always be drawn in the same position and in the same orientation. In previously defined triangle procedures we could construct a triangle in any position or any orientation relative to the turtle's position when the procedure was executed. Using the coordinate points of the vertices of shapes, we now have another means for constructing polygons and moving them around on the turtle screen.

We can construct triangles at any point on the coordinate system when certain conditions are known. For instance, if we are given the three sides of the triangle, the triangle can be constructed side-side-side. When two sides and the angle included between those two sides (side-angle-side) or two angles and the included side (angle-side-angle) are given, the triangle can also be constructed.

The MAKE command will be needed to assign the coordinates of the turtle's initial position to variables. For example, MAKE "X 30 assigns the variable X the value of 30. The MAKE command is used with XCOR and YCOR so the turtle will remember the position and can return to it later. Figure 14.22 demonstrates the use of MAKE to draw a triangle knowing two sides and the included angle (side-angle-side).

```
TO TRI.SAS :SIDE1 :ANGLE :SIDE2
  MAKE "X XCOR
  MAKE "Y YCOR
  FD :SIDE1
  RT 180 - :ANGLE
  FD :SIDE2
  SETXY :X :Y
END
```

```
?TRI.SAS 70 40 40
```
FIGURE 14.22

In the foregoing procedure, the two MAKE commands assign the coordinates of the turtle's initial position to variables X and Y. The turtle then proceeds to draw the given side, angle, and side. Using the SETXY command with X and Y, the turtle is returned to its initial position.

PROBLEM SET 14.4

1. Write a procedure using the MAKE command to draw a right triangle in which the lengths of its legs are used as variable inputs.

2. Write a procedure using SETXY to draw a square and its diagonals.

3. Write a procedure to draw the coordinate axes with the origin at home.

4. Use variables to write a procedure to draw a quadrilateral in which the vertices are inputs.

5. Use coordinates to draw intersecting perpendicular lines.

6. Use coordinates to draw a pair of parallel lines.

7. Sketch what you think the turtle will construct. Type in the procedure to check your prediction.

   a. ```
TO CHECK
   SETXY 40 0
   SETY 40
   SETX (-40)
   SETY 0
   SETX 40
END
```

   b. ```
TO CHECK2
   SETXY 0 0
   SETXY 30 60
   SETXY (-30) 120
   SETXY 0 0
END
```

   c. ```
TO CHECK3
   SETXY 30 10
   SETXY 30 (-10)
   SETXY (-30) (-10)
   SETXY 30 10
END
```

   d. ```
TO CHECK4
   PU SETXY (-40) (-40) PD
   SETXY 0 40
   SETXY 40 40
   SETXY (-20) 0
   SETX 40
   SETXY (-40) (-40)
END
```

8. Run the axes procedure from Problem 3.

   a. Write a procedure to draw a triangle whose vertices have coordinates (10,5), (40,4), and (40,60).

   b. Write a procedure to flip the triangle over the y-axes.

   c. Write a procedure to flip the triangle over the x-axes.

9. Write a procedure to draw a square that has a side of 50 turtle steps with one of its vertices at (10,15). Now write a procedure that moves the square 20 turtle steps down and 10 turtle steps to the right.

Pedagogical Activities

10. Use graph paper with the coordinate system marked and draw the shapes at each of the given points on the graph.

   a. Go to X = 10 and Y = 10

   ```
   REPEAT 4 [FD 10 RT 90]
   ```

   c. Go to X = −5 and Y = 0

   ```
   REPEAT 4 [FD 10 RT 90]
   ```

   b. Go to X = −10 and Y = 10

   ```
   REPEAT 4 [ FD 10 LT 90]
   ```

   d. Go to X = −7 and Y = −20

   ```
   REPEAT 2 [FD 7 RT 90 FD 14 RT 90]
   ```

Turtle Commands	Action of the Turtle
FORWARD (FD)	Sends turtle forward
BACK (BK)	Sends turtle back
RIGHT (RT)	Turns turtle to the right
LEFT (LT)	Turns turtle to the left
PENUP (PU)	Puts the turtle's pen up
PENDOWN (PD)	Puts the turtle's pen down
HIDETURTLE (HT)	Hides the turtle
SHOWTURTLE (ST)	Shows the turtle
DRAW	Clears screen with turtle home
SETX	Moves turtle to indicated x-coordinate
SETY	Moves turtle to indicated y-coordinate
SETXY	Moves turtle to indicated coordinates
SETH	Sets turtle's heading
XCOR	Gives turtle's x-coordinate
YCOR	Gives turtle's y-coordinate
REPEAT	Repeats what is in brackets
PRINT	Prints what is inside brackets
SCREEN DISPLAY	Top of screen for turtle drawings

Turtle Commands	Action of the Turtle
SPLITSCREEN <CTRL>S	Bottom of screen for text
FULLSCREEN <CTRL>F	Entire screen for turtle drawings
TEXTSCREEN <CTRL>T	Entire screen for text
<CTRL> G	Stops program execution
DEFINING PROCEDURES	
TO (procedure name)	Enters edit mode to define procedure
EDIT (procedure name)	Enters edit mode to edit procedure
<CTRL> C	Defines a procedure
<CTRL> G	Returns to direct mode; no changes made
END	Ends definition of procedure
EDITING COMMANDS	
ESC or DELETE	Delete character to left of cursor
← or →	Moves cursor left or right
<CTRL> A	Moves cursor to start of line
<CTRL> E	Moves cursor to end of line
<CTRL> N	Moves cursor to next line
<CTRL> P	Moves cursor to previous line
<CTRL> X	Erases to end of current line
<CTRL> O	Opens a line
FILING/MANAGING	
POTS	Prints out titles of procedures
PO (procedure)	Prints out the procedure
PO ALL	Prints out all procedures
ERASE (procedure)	Erases procedure named
ERASE ALL	Erases all procedures
SAVE "(filename)	Saves all procedures as a file
READ "(filename)	Reads file from disk
ERASEFILE "(filename)	Erases file from disk
CATALOG	Prints names of files on disk

ANSWERS FOR
SELECTED PROBLEMS

CHAPTER 1

Problem Set

1. a. 4   b. 11   c. 1
3. 50
5. a. 9:59   b. There are many solutions to this one. (In fact, 67 of them.) For example, 00:19, 00:28, 3:07.
7. 36 angles having measures greater than 0° and less than 180°.
9. a. 8   b. 96 ways
11. a. 6 miles   b. $1\frac{1}{4}$ hours
13. 56
15. 202, 222, 242, 262, and 282 are solutions.
17. 93
19. 16 posts
21. 20

CHAPTER 2

Problem Set 2.1

1. a. T   c. T   e. F

2. a. $\{m, a, t, h, e, i, c, s\}$ **c.** $\{\triangle, \square, \bigcirc, 2, 6\}$ **e.** $\{\,\}$

3. c, d

4. a. $D = \{a, b, c, d\}$ **c.** $b \in D$

5. a. $\{6, 7, 8, 9, 10, 11, 12, 13, 14\}$ **c.** $\{501, 502, 503, 504, \ldots\}$
   e. $\{1, 3, 5, 7, 9, 11, \ldots\}$

6. a. F   **c.** T   **e.** F   **g.** T   **i.** T

7. Answers will vary. The following is only one of many correct
   responses.
   a. All students   **c.** All sweaters

8. c. $5 + 4 + 3 + 2 + 1 = 15$

9. a. $\dfrac{15 \times 16}{2} = 120$ **c.** 720,600

11. a. {small blue circle, large blue circle, small blue diamond, large blue
   diamond, small blue square, large blue square, small blue triangle,
   large blue triangle}
   c. all large pieces, small pieces, etc.

13. a. Could list a variety of musical instruments, bird calls, animal noises,
   etc.
   c. Answers will vary.

15. {pencil}   {pencil, eraser}   {pencil, eraser, crayons}
   {eraser}   {pencil, crayons}
   {crayons}   {eraser, crayons}

17. Answers will vary. Among the acceptable answers would be:
   a. Farm animals   **c.** Fruit

Problem Set 2.2

1. a. T   **c.** T   **e.** T   **g.** T   **i.** T

2. a.

   $B \subset A$ $A \cap B \neq \phi$
                          $A \not\subset B$
                          $B \not\subset A$

3. a. $\in$ **c.** $=$ (or $\subseteq$)   **e.** $=$ (or $\subseteq$ or $\supseteq$)   **g.** $\subset$ (or $\subseteq$)
   i. $\subset$ (or $\subseteq$)

4. a. T   **c.** F   **e.** T   **g.** T   **i.** F

5. a. $A = \{2, 4, 6, 8, 10, 12, 14, 16, 18, 20\}$ **c.** $B \subset A$

6. a. T   **c.** T   **e.** F   **g.** T   **i.** T

7. a. Yes, Yes   **c.** $E = \emptyset$ **e.** Yes

8. a. $B = \{a, b, \{a, b\}\}$ (many other answers possible)

9. a.

Set	Tabulation of Two-Element Subsets	Number of Two-Element Subsets
$\{a, b, c, d, e\}$	$\{a, b\}\,\{b, c\}\,\{c, d\}\,\{d, e\}$ $\{a, c\}\,\{b, d\}\,\{c, e\}$ $\{a, d\}\,\{b, e\}$ $\{a, e\}$	$4 + 3 + 2 + 1 = 10$
$\{a, b, c, d, e, f\}$	$\{a, b\}\,\{b, c\}\,\{c, d\}\,\{d, e\}\,\{e, f\}$ $\{a, c\}\,\{b, d\}\,\{c, e\}\,\{d, f\}$ $\{a, d\}\,\{b, e\}\,\{c, f\}$ $\{a, e\}\,\{b, f\}$ $\{a, f\}$	$5 + 4 + 3 + 2 + 1 = 15$

    c. $19 + 18 + 17 + 16 + \cdots + 3 + 2 + 1 = 190$

10. a.

Set	Three-Element Subset	Number of Three-Element Subsets
$\{a, b, c, d, e, f\}$	$\{a, b, c\}\,\{a, c, d\}\,\{a, d, e\}\,\{a, e, f\}$ $\{a, b, d\}\,\{a, c, e\}\,\{a, d, f\}$ $\{a, b, e\}\,\{a, c, f\}$ $\{a, b, f\}$ $\{b, c, d\}\,\{b, d, e\}\,\{b, e, f\}$ $\{b, c, e\}\,\{b, d, f\}$ $\{b, c, f\}$ $\{c, d, e\}\,\{c, e, f\}$ $\{c, d, f\}$ $\{d, e, f\}$	$(4 + 3 + 2 + 1) + (3 + 2 + 1)$ $+ (2 + 1) + 1 = 20$

    c. 120

11. a. C, G

    c. Yes. An easy matching is simply to match an element to itself.

12. a. $B = \{1, 2\}$ (many other answers possible)

    c. $D = \{1, 2\}$ and $E = \{1, 2\}$ (many other sets possible) $D = E$

13. a. No. If $A = \{1, 2, 3, 4\}$ and $B = \{1, 2, 3\}$, then $A \not\subseteq B$ but $B \subseteq A$.

15. a. 11   **c.** 9   **e.** 126

16. a. (i) a **(ii)** $a\ b$ $a\ b$ **(iii)** $a\ b\ c$ $a\ b\ c$ $a\ b\ c$

(iv)

a b c d   a b c d   a b c d   a b c d

1 2 3 4   1 2 3 4   1 2 3 4   1 2 3 4

a b c d   a b c d   a b c d   a b c d

1 2 3 4   1 2 3 4   1 2 3 4   1 2 3 4

a b c d   a b c d   a b c d   a b c d

1 2 3 4   1 2 3 4   1 2 3 4   1 2 3 4

a b c d   a b c d   a b c d   a b c d

1 2 3 4   1 2 3 4   1 2 3 4   1 2 3 4

a b c d   a b c d   a b c d   a b c d

1 2 3 4   1 2 3 4   1 2 3 4   1 2 3 4

a b c d   a b c d   a b c d   a b c d

1 2 3 4   1 2 3 4   1 2 3 4   1 2 3 4

  c. 40,320

17. a. (i) 1   **(ii)** $3 \cdot 2 \cdot 1 = 6$ **(iii)** $4 \cdot 3 \cdot 2 \cdot 1 = 24$

  c. $17 \cdot 16 \cdot 15 \ldots 3 \cdot 2 \cdot 1$

19. a. No, neither the reflexive nor the symmetric properties hold.

20. a. Transitive. Yes, it is correct.

  c. Reflexive property. No, it is not correct.

21. a. There is not a one-to-one correspondence between children and chairs. One child will be left without a chair to sit in.

23. Perhaps he could place a stone in a pile for each sheep that leaves the corral in the morning, then take one out for each sheep returning.

Problem Set 2.3

1. a. 3   **c.** 6   **e.** 52   **g.** 6   **i.** 50

3. a. Yes. If two sets are equal, they have exactly the same elements and therefore the same cardinal number.

5. No. If $A = \{1, 2, 3\}$ and $B = \{a, b, c, d, e\}$, $n(A) = 3$ and $n(B) = 5$ but $A \not\subset B$.

6. a. Cardinal   **c.** Cardinal   **e.** Ordinal   **g.** Ordinal

7. a. The empty set is a set; the number zero is a whole number.

  c. Yes   **e.** No

8. a. It is not a one-to-one correspondence; therefore, untrue.

9. a.

Set	Number of subsets having 0 el.	1 el.	2 el.	3 el.	Total number of subsets
$\{a, b, c\}$	1	3	3	1	8

c.

Set	Number of subsets having 0 el.	1 el.	2 el.	3 el.	4 el.	5 el.	Total number of subsets
$\{a, b, c, d, e\}$	1	5	10	10	5	1	32

10. a.

No. of Elements in Original Set	Number of Subsets
0	1
1	2
2	4
3	8
4	16
5	32
6	64
7	128

c. 256   **e.** 2^n

11-13. Answers will vary.

14. a. 7   **c.** No

Problem Set 2.4

1. a. $\{1, 2, 3, 4, 6, 7\}$

c. $\{$Alice, Todd, Beth, Joe, Jane, Jennifer$\}$

2. a. $\{2, 4\}$ **c.** $\emptyset$

3. a. $\{1, 3\}$ **c.** $\emptyset$ **e.** $\{0, 5, 6, 7, 8, \ldots, 12\}$ **g.** $\{0, 2, 4, 5, 6, \ldots, 12\}$
i. $\emptyset$

4. a. $\{d, e, f\}$ **c.** $\{g, h, i, j\}$ **e.** $\{a, o, p\}$

5.

a.
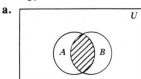
$A \cap B$

c.
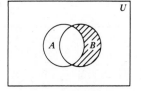
$A' \cap B$

e.
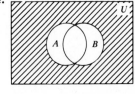
$A' \cap B'$

6. a.

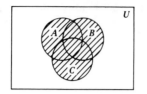

c.

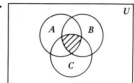

$(A \cup B) \cup C$

e.

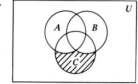

$(A \cup B)' \cap C$

7. a. $A \cup B$ **c.** $A \cap B'$ **e.** $(A \cup B)'$
  g. B' **i.** $(A \cap B') \cup (B \cap A')$

8. a. A **c.** $A \cap B$ **e.** $A \cup C$
  g. $A \cap B' \cap C'$

9. a. Boys with curly hair   **c.** Girls   **e.** The empty set

10. a.

$n(A)$	$n(B)$	$n(A \cap B)$	$n(A \cup B)$
4	3	2	5
2	4	2	4
1	5	0	6
4	0	0	4

  c. $n(A) + n(B) = n(A \cup B) - n(A \cap B)$

11. a.

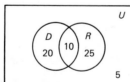

12. a.

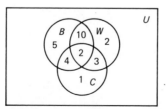

13. 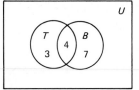 11 trips to Boston

15.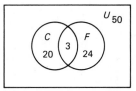

a. 3   c. 47

16.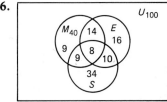

a. 48   c. 34

17. 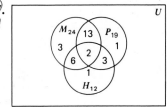 29 students

19.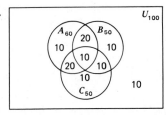

a. 20   c. 10

20. a. (i) 4   **(ii)** 1   **(iii)** 6   **(iv)** 5   **(v)** 2   **(vi)** 7   **(vii)** 8
    c. 45

21. a.   10

22. a.

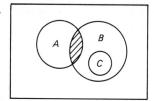

c.

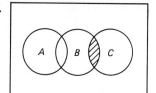

e.

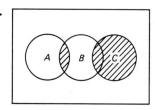

23. a. $(A \cap B) \cup (B \cap C)$

26. a.

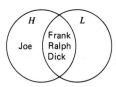

27. a.

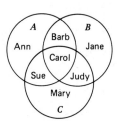

c. 3

Problem Set 2.5

1. a. $A \cap B = \{a, c\}, B \cap A = \{a, c\}$

   c. $A \cup (B \cap C) = \{a, b, c\} \cup \{c, e\} = \{a, b, c, e\}$

       $(A \cup B) \cap (A \cup C) = \{a, b, c, e\} \cap \{a, b, c, d, e, f\} = \{a, b, c, e\}$

2. a.

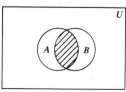

$A \cap B$

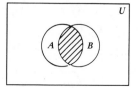

$B \cap A$

3. a. A and A' are disjoint, so $A \cap A' = \emptyset$. Because A' contains all the elements of the universe not in A, then $A \cup A' = U$.

4. a. T by Property 2.4 (1)

c. F

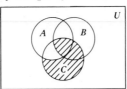 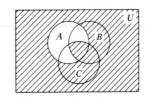

$$(A' \cup B) \cap C \neq A' \cup (B \cap C)$$

e. F

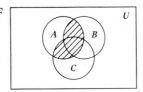 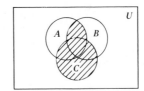

$$A \cap (B \cup C) \neq (A \cap B) \cup C$$

5. a. U **c.** U **e.** $A \cap B'$ **g.** $\emptyset$ **i.** A

7. a. $\{1, 2, 3, 4\}$ **c.** $\{2, 4, 5\}$ **e.** $\{1, 2, 4, 5\}$ **g.** No

8. a. No. For example, if $A = \{1, 2, 3\}$ and $B = \{3, 4\}$, then $A \cup B = \{1, 2, 3, 4\}$ and $A \cap B = \{3\}$.

9. a.

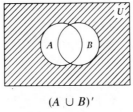 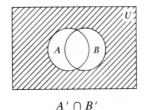

$(A \cup B)'$ $A' \cap B'$

10. a. Red ten-speed bikes. No

c. Bikes that are not red

e. Bicycles that are not red or are not ten-speed.

Problem Set 2.6

1. a. Let $A = \{1, 2, 3\}$ and $B = \{4\}$
$A \cup B = \{1, 2, 3, 4\}$
$n(A \cup B) = 4$
Thus $3 + 1 = 4$

c. Let $A = \{1, 2, 3, 4\}$ and $B = \{5, 6, 7\}$
$A \cup B = \{1, 2, 3, 4, 5, 6, 7\}$
$n(A \cup B) = 7$
Thus $4 + 3 = 7$

Note: Any sets A and B equivalent to those chosen will be acceptable.

2. a. No   c. Yes   e. No   g. Yes

3. a. Commutative   c. Commutative   e. Commutativeg.   **Associative**
   g. Associative

4. a. Let $A = \{1, 2, 3\}$ and $B = \{2, 3, 4, 5\}$. Then $n(A) + n(B) = 3 + 4 = 7$ and $n(A \cup B) = 5$.

   c. No

5. a. No   c. Yes

6. a. $\{4\}$ c. $\{10\}$ e. $\emptyset$ g. $\emptyset$ i. $\emptyset$

8. a.

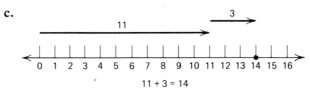

$3 + 2 = 5$

c.

$11 + 3 = 14$

9. a. (i) $\{4\}$ (ii) $\{0\}$ (iii) U

Problem Set 2.7

1. a. $5 + 5 + 5 = 15$ c. $8 + 8 + 8 = 24$ c. $0 + 0 + 0 + 0 + 0 = 0$

2. a. XXX   c. XX   e. XXX
      XXX   XX
      XXX   XX
      XXX   XX
      XXX

3. a. XXX   XXXX   c. X   XXXX
      XXX   XXXX   X $1 \cdot 4$
      XXX   XXXX   X
      XXX $3 \cdot 4$ X
      $4 \cdot 3$ $4 \cdot 1$

4. a. $4 \times 2 = 2 + 2 + 2 + 2 = 8$
      $2 \times 4 = 4 + 4 = 8$

   c. $7 \times 2 = 2 + 2 + 2 + 2 + 2 + 2 + 2 = 14$
      $2 \times 7 = 7 + 7 = 14$

5. a. No   **c.** Yes   **e.** Yes   **g.** Yes

6. a. xx 00000   xx   00000
        xx 00000   xx   00000
        xx 00000   xx   00000
        xx 00000   xx   00000
        4(2 + 5)   4 · 2   4 · 5

    c. xxxxx 00   xxxxx   00
        xxxxx 00   xxxxx   00
        xxxxx 00   xxxxx   00
        xxxxx 00   xxxxx   00
        xxxxx 00   xxxxx   00
        xxxxx 00   xxxxx   00
        6(5 + 2)   6 · 5   6 · 2

7. a. Commutative for multiplication   **c.** Distributive
   e. Commutative for addition   **g.** Distributive
   i. Distributive

8. a. **(i)** Associative property for multiplication
     (ii) Commutative property for multiplication
     (iii) Associative property for multiplication

9. a. 5 · (3 + 4) = (5 · 3) + (5 · 4)   **c.** 8 · (3 + 6) = (8 · 3) + (8 · 6)

10. a. xxxx   **c.** xxx
      xxxx   xxx
      xxxx

                   xxx
                   xxx

                   xxx
                   xxx

                   xxx
                   xxx

11. a. No. Because 2 + (3 · 5) = 17 and (2 + 3) · (2 + 5) = 35, 2 + (3 · 5)
   ≠ (2 + 3) · (2 + 5).

12. a. 4 · (3 + 5)   **c.** (8 + 3) · 5   **e.** 9 · (8 + 2)   **g.** 8 · (6 + 4)

13. a. 270,216   **c.** a is easier.

15. a. {5}   **c.** {7}   **e.** {7}   **g.** {2}   **i.** Ø

17. $11

18. a. 12

19. 510

21. a.

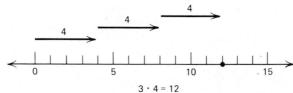

$3 \cdot 4 = 12$

c.

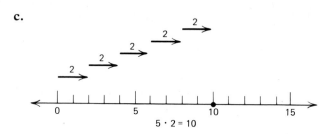

$$5 \cdot 2 = 10$$

e.

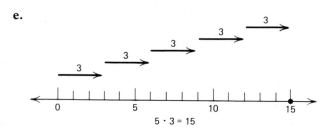

$$5 \cdot 3 = 15$$

Problem Set 2.8

1. $1 + \square = 4$ **c.** $5 + \square = 18$ **e.** $6 + \square = 17$
    $\square = 3$ $\square = 13$ $\square = 11$

2. a. $3 + 7 = x$ **c.** $x + 1 = 4$ **e.** $x + 9 = 6$ (No whole num-
    $\{10\}$ $\{3\}$ $\varnothing$ ber makes it true.)
  g. $47 + 63 = x$
    $\{110\}$

3. a. Let $a = b$

4. a. $f = 0$ and d and e are whole numbers for which $d - e$ is defined. For example, if $d = 12$, $e = 7$, and $f = 0$, $(d - e) - f = (12 - 7) - 0 = 5$ and $d - (e - f) = 12 - (7 - 0) = 12 - 7 = 5$.

5. Yes, because $a + 0 = a$, Definition 2.11 assures us that the difference is 0.

6. a. 75   **c.** 1403

7. a. $3 \cdot \square = 12$ **c.** $6 \cdot \square = 24$ **e.** $4 \cdot \square = 56$
    $\square = 4$ $\square = 4$ $\square = 14$

8. a. $x \cdot 4 = 24$ **c.** $4 \cdot 11 = x$ **e.** $3 \cdot x = 21$ **g.** $3 \cdot 7 = x + 1$
    $\{6\}$ $\{44\}$ $\{7\}$ $\{20\}$

9. a. For all whole numbers different from 0. That is, $a \cdot 1 = a$ for any whole number $a \neq 0$.

  c. $a = b$ or $a = {}^{-}b$

  e. $a = 0$ or $c = 1$

10. a. 9 letters and 6 postcards

11. a. $\{3\}$ **c.** $\{3\}$ **e.** $\{2\}$

12. a. 173,664   **c.** Yes

13. a. Answers will vary.

15. a.

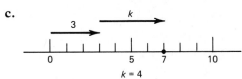

$k = 5$

c.

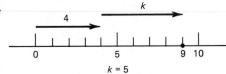

$k = 4$

e.

$k = 8$

Problem Set 2.9

1. a. XXX
   | |
   OO $2 < 3$

c.
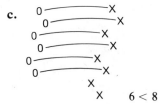

$6 < 8$

e. XXXXX
   XXXX
   | |
   OO $2 < 9$

2. a. $2 + 4 = 6$ **c.** $7 + 5 = 12$ **e.** $84 + 12 = 96$
   $2 < 6$ $7 < 12$ $84 < 94$

3. There exists some whole number k greater than zero such that $a = b + k$.

4. a. $(7 + 3)a = 10a$ **c.** $(3 + 2 + 5)\square = 10\square$
   e. $(5 + 2)a + (3 + 7)b = 7a + 10b$

5. a. $4x + 4$ **c.** $2x^2 + 6xy$ **e.** $2a^3 + 8a^2 + 10a$
   g. $10x^2 + 19x + 6$ **i.** $x^2 + 8x + 16$

6. a. $7(x + 2)$ **c.** $a(2b + 3)$ **e.** $x(x + 3 + y)$
   g. $(2 + 5)(x + 3) = 7(x + 3)$ **i.** $x(x + 2) + a(x + 2) = (x + a)(x + 2)$

7.

$0 < 1$

9. **a.** $\{0, 1, 2, 3, \ldots, 9\}$ **c.** $\{15, 16, 17, \ldots\}$ **e.** $\{5, 6, 7, 8, \ldots\}$
   g. $\{8, 9, 10, \ldots\}$ **i.** $\{4, 5, 6, 7, \ldots\}$ **k.** $\{6, 7, 8, 9, \ldots\}$
   m. $\{0, 1, 2, 3, 4, 5, 6, 7, 8, 9\}$ **o.** $\{0, 1, 2, \ldots, 19\}$ **q.** $\{0, 1, 2, 3, 4\}$

10. **a.** $\{4, 5, 6, 7, \ldots\}$ **c.** $\{0, 1, 2, 3, 4\}$ **e.** $\{3, 4, 5, 6, \ldots\}$
    g. $\emptyset$

11. **a.** $\{2, 4\}$ **c.** $\emptyset$ **e.** $\{3\}$ **g.** $\emptyset$ **i.** U

12. **a.** Cannot tell.   **c.** T   **e.** T

13. **a.** $(3 + 2) \times 5 + 4 = 29$ **c.** $3 + (2 \times 5) + 4 = 17$

14. **a.** 34   **c.** 42   **e.** 28

15. Each whole number associates with a point. Two points are the same or one is further to the right than the other. Thus, the numbers are the same or one is bigger than the other.

17. Choices of sets will vary.

19. $2(x + 2) = (x + 2) + (x + 2)$
    $$= x + x + 2 + 2$$
    $$= 2x + 4$$

Problem Set 2.10

1. **a.** T   **c.** F   **e.** Not a statement
   g. Not a statement

2. **a.** $q \wedge r$ F
   c. $r \vee p$ T
   e. $\sim p \wedge q$ F

3. **a.** T   **c.** T   **e.** T   **g.** F

4. **a.**

p	$\sim p$	$\sim(\sim p)$
T	F	T
F	T	F

5.

p	q	$p \vee q$	$\sim(p \vee q)$	$\sim p$	$\sim q$	$\sim p \wedge \sim q$
T	T	T	F	F	F	F
T	F	T	F	F	T	F
F	T	T	F	T	F	F
F	F	F	T	T	T	T

$$\sim(p \vee q) \equiv \sim p \wedge \sim q$$

6. Let p: John is happy and q: Alice is happy
   a. $p \wedge q$ **c.** $\sim(\sim p \wedge \sim q)$

Problem Set 2.11

1. **a.** If it rains, then I wear my raincoat.

   c. If I do not study, then I will fail this course.

   e. If a figure is a square, then it is a rectangle.

4. a. F   **c.** F   **e.** T
5. No
7. Yes
8. a. Valid   **c.** Not valid   **e.** Valid
9. a. Yes

Review Problem Set 2.12

1. a. $\{x \mid x$ is a third-grade teacher in District 163$\}$
  b. $\{x \mid x$ is an even whole number less than 9$\}$
  c. Depends on each person's family.
2. a. {lion, bear, monkey, elephant} (many other possible answers)
  b. $\{b, c, d, f\}$ (many other choices of answers)
  c. {Huron, Erie, Michigan, Superior, Ontario}
3. a. T   **b.** T   **c.** F   **d.** T   **e.** T   **f.** F   **g.** T
  h. T   **i.** T   **j.** F
4. a. 4   **b.** 7   **c.** 9   **d.** 4
5. a. {1, 2, 3, 4, 5}   **b.** {1, 3}   **c.** Ø   **d.** {2, 4, 6, 8, 10}
  e. U **f.** Ø   **g.** E **h.** Ø   **i.** {2, 4, 5, 6, 7, 8, 9, 10, 11}
  j. E
6. a.

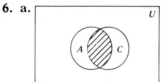

b.

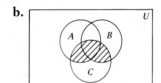

c.

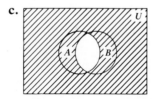

d.

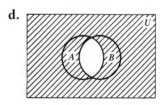

7. a.

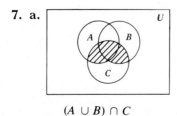

$(A \cup B) \cap C$

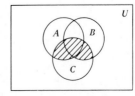

$(A \cap C) \cup (B \cap C)$

b.

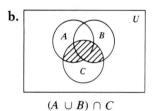

$(A \cup B) \cap C$

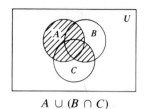

$A \cup (B \cap C)$

c.

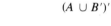

$(A \cup B')'$

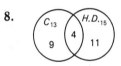

$A' \cap B$

8.

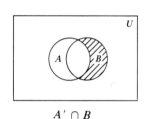

24

9. a. Let $A = \{1, 2, 3, 4, 5, 6, 7, 8\}$ and $B = \{9, 10, 11, 12, 13, 14\}$.
Then $A \cup B = \{1, 2, 3, 4, \ldots, 14\}$ and $n\{A \cup B) = 14$.
Therefore, $8 + 6 = 14$.

b. $4 \cdot 6 = 6 + 6 + 6 + 6 = 24$

10. a. Commutative for addition

b. Commutative for addition

c. Distributive

d. Associative for addition

e. Additive identity

f. Commutative for addition

g. Commutative for addition

11. a. $\{4\}$ **b.** $\{0\}$ **c.** U **d.** $\{7\}$ **e.** $\{3\}$ **f.** $\{1, 2\}$
g. $\emptyset$ **h.** $\{10\}$ **i.** $\{48\}$ **j.** $\{0, 1, 2\}$

12. a. $2a + 6$ **b.** $2x^2 + 4x$ **c.** $6x^3 + 9x^2$ **d.** $x^2 + 5x + 6$
e. $x^2 + 4x + 4$

13. a. $5(x + 3)$ **b.** $a(2 + 3b)$ **c.** $x(x + 4)$ **d.** $(x + 3)(x + 2)$
e. $x(x + 4) + a(x + 4) = (x + a)(x + 4)$

14. a. $17 - 9 = k$ **b.** $21 \div 7 = x$
$\qquad 9 + k = 17 \qquad\qquad 7 \cdot x = 21$
$\qquad\quad k = 8 \qquad\qquad\qquad x = 3$

15. a. 6 **b.** $D = \{1, 3, 5, 7, 9, \ldots, a, \ldots, 19\}$ and $E = \{4, 10, 16, \ldots, 3a + 1, \ldots, 58\}$

16. **a.** Let $A = \{a, b, c, d, e\}$
and $B = \{1, 2, 3, 4, 5, 6, 7, 8$
Therefore $5 < 8$

b. If $k = 155$, then $265 + 155 = 420$

17. 12

CHAPTER 3

Problem Set 3.1

1. **a.** $2 \cdot 10 + 8$ **c.** $8 \cdot 100 + 4 \cdot 10 + 5$ **e.** $4 \cdot 10{,}000 + 1 \cdot 1000 + 8 \cdot 100 + 5 \cdot 10 + 2$ **g.** $4 \cdot 100{,}000 + 5 \cdot 10{,}000 + 2 \cdot 1000 + 1 \cdot 100 + 5 \cdot 10 + 3$

2. **a.** 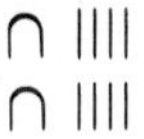 **c.**  **e.** 

g. 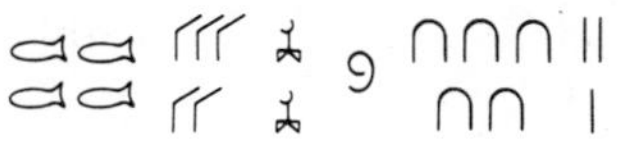

3. **a.** XXVIII **c.** DCCCXLV **e.** $\overline{\text{XLI}}$DCCCLII
g. $\overline{\text{CDLII}}$CLIII

4. **a.** 41,867 **c.** 234 **e.** 1,610,216

5. **a.** 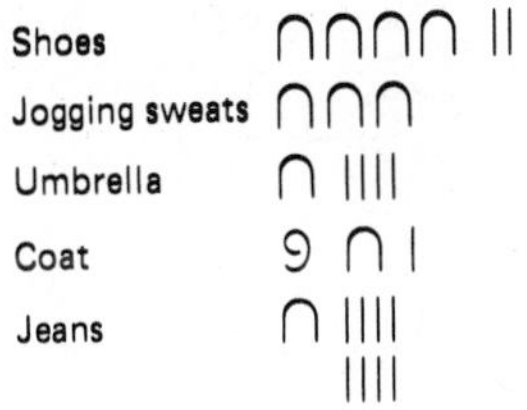
Shoes
Jogging sweats
Umbrella
Coat
Jeans

c. 

6. **a.**

car	$\overline{\text{V}}$ID
auto transmission	CCC
deluxe interior	CL
power steering	CC
power brakes	CLXXV
air condition	CCCLV

c. $\overline{\text{VII}}$DCLXXX

7. **a.**  **c.** LXXIII **e.** MMCCLIX

8. **a.**  **c.** 1 **e.** 691

9. **a.** $4632 > 4589$ **c.** $463{,}214 > 463{,}198$

Problem Set 3.2

1. a. 2^4 **c.** 2^5 **e.** $(2a)^4$

2. a. 2^4 **c.** $2^0 = 3^0$, etc. **e.** 5^3 **g.** 3^4

3. a. 7 **c.** 4 **e.** 13 **g.** 0 **i.** 6 **k.** 2

4. a. 81 **c.** 9 **e.** 850 **g.** 5184

5. a. No $2^3 = 8$, but $3^2 = 9$

6. a. $8 \cdot 10^3$ **c.** $6 \cdot 10^2 + 8 \cdot 10$
  e. $12a^3$ **g.** $4 \cdot 10^4$ **i.** $5a^2$
  k. $4 \cdot 10^4 + 9 \cdot 10^3 + 4 \cdot 10^2 + 7 \cdot 10$

7. a. $4^3 \cdot 4^5 = 64 \cdot 1024 = 65{,}536 = 4^8$
  c. $(3^2)^5 = 9^5 = 59{,}049 = 3^{10}$

9. a. Hundreds **c.** Tens **e.** Ten thousands

10. a. 430,851 **c.** 470,642

11. a. 63,089 63,809 63,890 63,980
  c. 3,005,000 3,050,000 3,050,100 3,500,900

Problem Set 3.3

1. a.
24_{five}
c.
32_{four}

e.
16_{eight}

2. a. $(1, 2, 3, 4, 10, 11, 12, 13, 14, 20, 21, 22, 23, 24, 30, 31)_{\text{five}}$
  c. $(1, 10, 11, 100, 101, 110, 111, 1000, 1001, 1010, 1011, 1100, 1101, 1110,$
  $1111)_{\text{two}}$

3. a.
c.
e.
g.

4. a.
41_{five}
c.
35_{six}

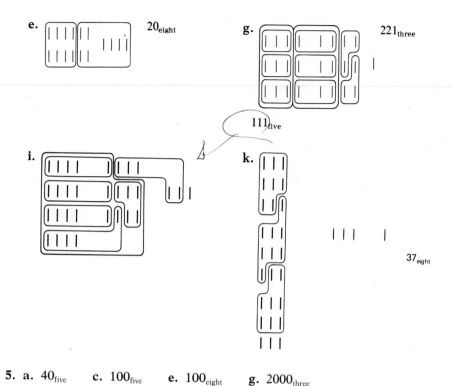

5. a. 40_{five} **c.** 100_{five} **e.** 100_{eight} **g.** 2000_{three}

6. a. (i) 31_{eight} **(ii)** 100_{five} **(iii)** 132_{five} **(iv)** 14_{five}

7. a. 320_{five} **c.** 2200_{four} **e.** 108 **g.** 52 **i.** 221_{eight}

8. a. 5 **c.** 3

9. a. (i) △   **(ii)** /⊥   **(iii)** △□   **(iv)** ⊥○
   c. (i) 11 **(ii)** 103 **(iii)** 283

10. a. 5)325 $325_{\text{ten}} = 2300_{\text{five}}$ **c.** 8)450 $450_{\text{ten}} = 702_{\text{eight}}$
   5)65 0   8)56 2
   5)13 0   7 0
    2 3

e. 2)200 $200_{\text{ten}} = 11001000_{\text{two}}$
   2)100 0
   2)50 0
   2)25 0
   2)12 1
    2)6 0
    2)3 0
     1 1

11. a. (i) 30_{twelve} **(ii)** 100_{twelve} **(iii)** $3\#4_{\text{twelve}}$ **(iv)** $10\#*_{\text{twelve}}$

12. a. $12\overline{)350}$ $350_{ten} = 252_{twelve}$

   $12\overline{)29}$ 2

        2 5

   c. $12\overline{)54852}$ $54{,}852_{ten} = 278{*}0_{twelve}$

   $12\overline{)4571}$ 0

   $12\overline{)380}$ $\,$ 11

   $12\overline{)31}$ 8

        2 7

13. a. (i) **(ii)** **(iii)** **(iv)**

14. a.(i) two longs and four unit cubes   **(ii)** one flat, four longs, and two unit cubes   **(iii)** four flats, three longs, and one unit cube **(iv)** two blocks, one flat, two longs, and three units cubes
   c. A block similar to that used for 1000, but ten times as long. Long block.

15. a. Four bundles and three single sticks

16. a. One dollar bill, 6 dimes, and 4 pennies

17. a. 16   8   4   2   1

18. a. *B* and *D*   **e.** 63

19. a. (i) 5   **(ii)** 7   **(iii)** 12   **(iv)** 5   **(v)** 12   **(vi)** 24   **(vii)** 3 **(viii)** 12

Problem Set 3.4

1. a.   2 tens and 3 ones   **c.**   1 hundred and 2 tens and 3 ones
   $+$6 tens and 5 ones $+$1 hundred and 4 tens and 5 ones

      8 tens and 8 ones   2 hundreds and 6 tens and 8 ones
           88   268

   e.   2 hundreds and   3 tens and 4 ones
      $+$ 5 tens and 6 ones
      1 hundred and   4 tens and 3 ones

      3 hundreds and 12 tens and 13 ones
      4 hundreds and   3 tens and   3 ones
                433

2. a.

$$\begin{array}{r} 47 \\ +26 \\ \hline 13 = 7 + 6 \\ 60 = 40 + 20 \\ \hline 73 \end{array}$$

c.

$$\begin{array}{r} 143 \\ 178 \\ \hline 11 = 3 + 8 \\ 110 = 40 + 70 \\ 200 = 100 + 100 \\ \hline 321 \end{array}$$

e.

$$\begin{array}{r} 456 \\ + 35 \\ 157 \\ \hline 18 = 6 + 5 + 7 \\ 130 = 50 + 30 + 50 \\ 500 = 400 + 100 \\ \hline 648 \end{array}$$

3. a.

$$\begin{array}{l} (2 \text{ base and } 3 \text{ units})_{\text{five}} \\ + (1 \text{ base and } 4 \text{ units})_{\text{five}} \\ \hline (3 \text{ base and } 12 \text{ units})_{\text{five}} \\ (4 \text{ base and } 2 \text{ units})_{\text{five}} \\ \quad 42_{\text{five}} \end{array}$$

c.

$$\begin{array}{l} (3 \text{ base and } 2 \text{ units})_{\text{five}} \\ + (4 \text{ base and } 3 \text{ units})_{\text{five}} \\ \hline (12 \text{ base and } 10 \text{ units})_{\text{five}} \\ (1 \text{ base}^2 \text{ and } 3 \text{ base and } 0 \text{ units})_{\text{five}} \\ \quad\quad 130_{\text{five}} \end{array}$$

e.

$$\begin{array}{l} (1 \text{ base}^2 \text{ and } 2 \text{ base and } 4 \text{ units})_{\text{five}} \\ + (2 \text{ base}^2 \text{ and } 3 \text{ base and } 3 \text{ units})_{\text{five}} \\ \hline (3 \text{ base}^2 \text{ and } 10 \text{ base and } 12 \text{ units})_{\text{five}} \\ (4 \text{ base}^2 \text{ and } 1 \text{ base and } 2 \text{ units})_{\text{five}} \\ \quad\quad\quad 412_{\text{five}} \end{array}$$

4. a.

$$\begin{array}{r} 13_{\text{five}} \\ +24_{\text{five}} \\ \hline 12 = (3 + 4)_{\text{five}} \\ 30 = (10 + 20)_{\text{five}} \\ \hline 42_{\text{five}} \end{array}$$

c.

$$\begin{array}{r} 32_{\text{five}} \\ + 24_{\text{five}} \\ \hline 11 = (2 + 4)_{\text{five}} \\ 100 = (30 + 20)_{\text{five}} \\ \hline 111_{\text{five}} \end{array}$$

e.

$$\begin{array}{r} 134_{\text{five}} \\ +142_{\text{five}} \\ \hline 11 = (4 + 2)_{\text{five}} \\ 120 = (30 + 40)_{\text{five}} \\ 200 = (100 + 100)_{\text{five}} \\ \hline 331_{\text{five}} \end{array}$$

5. a.

$$\begin{array}{r} 12_{\text{five}} \\ +22_{\text{five}} \\ \hline 34_{\text{five}} \end{array}$$

c.

$$\begin{array}{r} {}^143_{\text{five}} \\ 33_{\text{five}} \\ \hline 131_{\text{five}} \end{array}$$

e.

$$\begin{array}{r} {}^14{}^132_{\text{five}} \\ + 1\,44_{\text{five}} \\ \hline 11\,31_{\text{five}} \end{array}$$

6. a. XXX 00000   **c.** XXXX 00000 $4_{\text{six}} + 5_{\text{six}} = 13_{\text{six}}$

7. a. 55_{six} **c.** 123_{six} **e.** 514_{six} **g.** 4403_{six}

8. a. 1000_{two} **c.** $11{,}011_{\text{two}}$ **e.** $1{,}011{,}010_{\text{two}}$

9. a. XXXXXXX 00000000   **c.** XXXXXX 00000

e. (XXXXXXXXXX 0) 000000000* $_{\text{twelve}} + \#_{\text{twelve}} = 19_{\text{twelve}}$

10. a. 99_{twelve} **c.** 121_{twelve} **e.** 839_{twelve} **g.** 7997_{twelve}

11. a. Lay out 4 longs and 6 cubes, then 3 longs and 9 cubes. Now regroup the cubes, making 1 long and 5 cubes. Thus we have 8 longs and 5 cubes or 85.

   c. One flat, 4 longs, and 8 cubes are used along with 3 flats, 9 longs, and 6 cubes. Regroup the 14 cubes to make 1 long and 4 cubes, then the 14 longs to make 1 flat and 4 longs. We now have 5 flats, 4 longs, and 4 cubes, or 544.

12. a.   **c.**

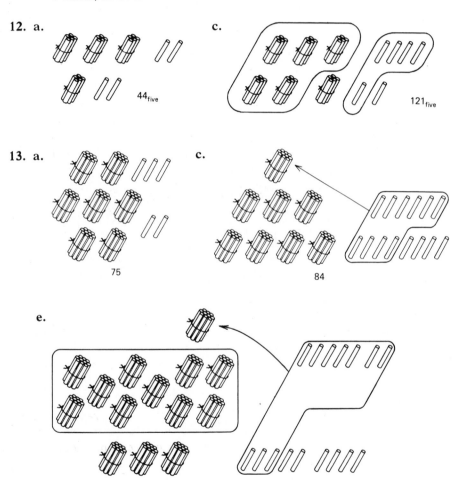

13. a.   **c.**

e.

14. a.   463   **c.**   467
           +532   +548
           ─────   ─────
            995   9̸0̸5
                           101

15. Answers will vary.

Problem Set 3.5

1. a.

Tens	Ones
$^3\cancel{4}$	^{13}
-1	6
2	7

c.

Tens	Ones
$^7\cancel{8}$	^{13}
-3	8
4	5

e.

Hundreds	Tens	Ones
$^2\cancel{3}$	$^{\cancel{10}9}$	^{12}
-1	2	7
1	7	5

2. a.

Base	Units
4	4
-1	2
3	2_{five}

d.

Base	Units
$^3\cancel{4}$	^{12}
-2	4
1	3_{five}

e.

Base^2	Base	Units
$^2\cancel{3}$	$^{\cancel{10}4}$	^{12}
$-$	2	3
2	2	4_{five}

3. a. $^2\cancel{3}^13_{\text{five}}$ **c.** $^1\cancel{2}^13_{\text{five}}$ **e.** $1^2\cancel{3}^11_{\text{five}}$

     $-\ 1\ 4_{\text{five}}$ $-\ \ \ 31_{\text{five}}$ $-\ \ 4\ 2_{\text{five}}$

     $1\ 4_{\text{five}}$ $1\ 32_{\text{five}}$ $3\ 4_{\text{five}}$

4. a. 35_{six} **c.** 35_{six} **e.** 233_{six}

5. a. 10_{two} **c.** 1100_{two}

6. a. 55_{twelve} **c.** 77_{twelve}

7. a. We would like to have 14 units rather than 4 in order to be able to subtract 8. We add 10 units and then subtract one extra 10. Thus, what we add we immediately subtract out.

  c. 41^13_{five}

     $-1^1\cancel{0}4_{\text{five}}$ Check 1^104_{five}

        304_{five} $+3\ 04_{\text{five}}$

                            $4\ 13_{\text{five}}$

8. a. (i) 46 **(ii)** 5^14 **(iii)** 8^15 **(iv)** 1^16^13 **(v)** 4^16^12

         -34 $-1\ 8$ $-2\ 7$ $-\ \ 8\ 8$ $-1\ 8\ 5$

         12 $\cancel{4}\ 6$ $\cancel{6}\ 8$ $\cancel{1}\ \cancel{8}\ 5$ $\cancel{3}\ \cancel{8}\ 7$

                      3 5 $0\ 7$ $2\ 7$

10. a.   342   **c.**   8000
     -255 -2345

        7 (262)   5 (2350)
      80 (342)   50 (2400)
         87   600 (3000)
                      5000 (8000)
                      5655

11. a. **(i)** 15   **(ii)** 37   **(iii)** 49   **(iv)** 168   **(v)** 396

    c. No subtraction facts greater than 10-k are needed.

12. a. $\cancel{X}$ $\cancel{A}$ $\cancel{3}$ **c.** $\cancel{2}$ $\cancel{A}$ $\cancel{3}$
     0 13 13   1 13 13
    $-$ 9   7 $-$ 8   5
        4   6   1   5   8

13. b. **(i)**   43 $=$ 46   **(iii)**   76 $=$ 78
       -17 -20 -18 -20
             26   58

    c. Yes 32_{five} $=$ 33_{five}
              -14_{five} -20_{five}
                       13_{five}

14. a. From 4 longs and 6 cubes we remove 2 longs and 5 cubes, leaving 2 longs and 1 cube, or 21.

    c. We have 5 longs and 4 cubes but wish to remove 8 cubes. Exchange 1 long for 10 cubes, making 14 cubes. Taking 8 away leaves 6 cubes. Then 4 longs $-$ 3 longs $=$ 1 long. Our answer is 16.

    e. Regroup one of the 3 flats, making 10 longs. Then trade 1 long for 10 cubes making 15 cubes. $15 - 8 = 7$ cubes. Then 7 longs from 9 longs $=$ 2 longs and 1 flat from 2 flats $=$ 1 flat. Thus, 127 is the answer.

15. a.

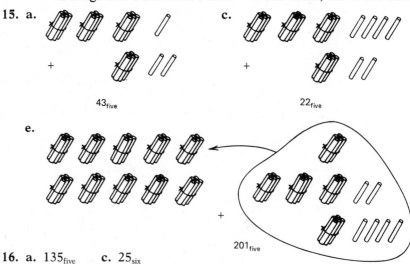

43_{five} 22_{five}

e.

201_{five}

16. a. 135_{five} **c.** 25_{six}

Problem Set 3.6

1. a.   23
        $\times\ 3$
      ─────
        69

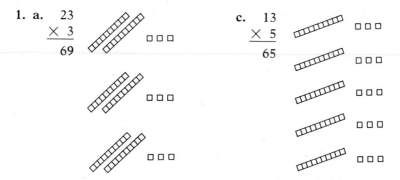

c.   13
        $\times\ 5$
      ─────
        65

2. a. $4 \cdot 19 = 4(10 + 9)$
         $= 4 \cdot 10 + 4 \cdot 9$
         $= 40 + 36$
         $= 76$

c. $9 \cdot 16 = 9(10 + 6)$
       $= 9 \cdot 10 + 9 \cdot 6$
       $= 90 + 54$
       $= 144$

3. a.   27
        $\times\ 3$
      ─────
        21 $= 3 \cdot 7$
        60 $= 3 \cdot 20$
      ─────
        81

c.   28
        $\times\ 9$
      ─────
        72 $= 9 \cdot 8$
       180 $= 9 \cdot 20$
      ─────
       252

4. a.

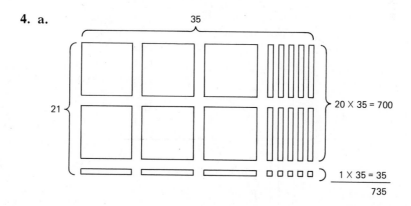

$20 \times 35 = 700$

$1 \times 35 = 35$

735

5. a. ^{1}42
        $\times\ 5$
      ─────
        210

c. $_2$^{1}1$_1$^{1}76
         32
      ─────
        352
        528
      ─────
       5632

6. a.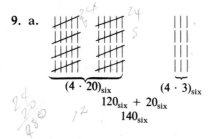

$$(3 \cdot 20)_{\text{five}} \quad (3 \cdot 4)_{\text{five}}$$
$$110_{\text{five}} + 22_{\text{five}}$$
$$132_{\text{five}}$$

c.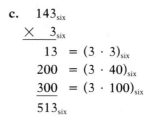

$$(10 \cdot 14)_{\text{five}} = 140_{\text{five}}$$

$$(2 \cdot 14)_{\text{five}} = 33_{\text{five}}$$
$$223_{\text{five}}$$

8. a. $(4 \cdot 3)_{\text{six}} = (3 + 3 + 3 + 3)_{\text{six}} = 20_{\text{six}}$

c.

·	0	1	2	3	4	5
0	0	0	0	0	0	0
1	0	1	2	3	4	5
2	0	2	4	10	12	14
3	0	3	10	13	20	23
4	0	4	12	20	24	32
5	0	5	14	23	32	41

9. a.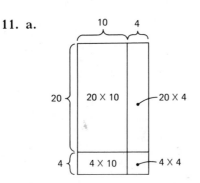

$$(4 \cdot 20)_{\text{six}} \qquad (4 \cdot 3)_{\text{six}}$$
$$120_{\text{six}} + 20_{\text{six}}$$
$$140_{\text{six}}$$

c.
$$143_{\text{six}}$$
$$\times \quad 3_{\text{six}}$$
$$13 \;=\; (3 \cdot 3)_{\text{six}}$$
$$200 \;=\; (3 \cdot 40)_{\text{six}}$$
$$\underline{300} \;=\; (3 \cdot 100)_{\text{six}}$$
$$513_{\text{six}}$$

10. a.

·	0	1
0	0	0
1	0	1

11. a.

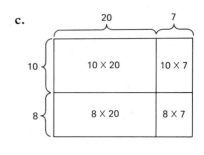

$$24 \times 14 = 200 + 80 + 40 + 16 = 336$$

c.

$$18 \times 27 = 200 + 70 + 160 + 56 = 486$$

12. a.
$$\begin{array}{r} 32 \\ \times\ 17 \\ \hline 14 = 7 \times 2 \\ 210 = 7 \times 30 \\ 20 = 10 \times 2 \\ 300 = 10 \times 30 \\ \hline 544 \end{array}$$

c.
$$\begin{array}{r} 145 \\ \times\ 23 \\ \hline 15 = 3 \times 5 \\ 120 = 3 \times 40 \\ 300 = 3 \times 100 \\ 100 = 20 \times 5 \\ 800 = 20 \times 40 \\ 2000 = 20 \times 100 \\ \hline 3335 \end{array}$$

13. a. (i)

14. a. (i)

1	25
2	50
4	100
8	200
16	400
→32	800←
	800

(ii)

1	12
2	24
4	48
→ 8	96←
→16	192←
→32	384←
	672

(iii)

1	50
2	100
4	200
8	400
→16	800←
→32	1600←
	2400

15.

	0	1	2	3	4	5	6	7	8	9	#	*
0	0	0	0	0	0	0	0	0	0	0	0	0
1	0	1	2	3	4	5	6	7	8	9	#	*
2	0	2	4	6	8	#	10	12	14	16	18	1#
3	0	3	6	9	10	13	16	19	20	23	26	29
4	0	4	8	10	14	18	20	24	28	30	34	38
5	0	5	#	13	18	21	26	2*	34	39	42	47
6	0	6	10	16	20	26	30	36	40	46	50	56
7	0	7	12	19	24	2*	36	41	48	53	5#	65
8	0	8	14	20	28	34	40	48	54	60	68	74
9	0	9	16	23	30	39	46	53	60	69	76	83
#	0	#	18	26	34	42	50	5#	68	76	84	92
*	0	*	1#	29	38	47	56	65	74	83	92	#1

a. 672_{twelve} **c.** $15*3_{\text{twelve}}$ **e.** $304\#2_{\text{twelve}}$

18. a. 2   **c.** 5

19. a. The child is not realizing that the second partial product is $20 \cdot 34$, but is using $2 \cdot 34$ instead.

c.   34
    × 21
    ───────
        34 = 1 · 34
       680 = 20 · 34
    ───────
       714

20. a. The product 320 · 15 has been found by finding 5 · 0 = 0, then 1 · 32. In 517 · 34, 4 · 7 = 28, so write 8 and carry 2. Then 3 · 1 = 3 plus the 2 carried gives 5. Then 3 · 5 = 15.

21. a.

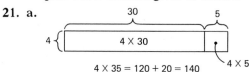

c.

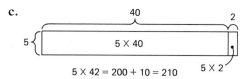

22. a.

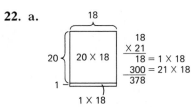

c.

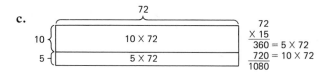

Problem Set 3.7

1. a. Place one long in each of four piles. Replace the remaining long with ten unit cubes, making 13 unit cubes in all. Give three of these cubes to each of four piles leaving one remaining.
   Thus, 53 ÷ 4 = 13 r1.

   c. Place one long in each of three piles. Convert the remaining long to unit cubes making 13. Place four in each of three piles leaving one undistributed.
   Thus, 43 ÷ 3 = 14 r1.

e. Place one flat in each of four piles, then replace the remaining flat by ten longs. Give three longs to each of the four piles, then convert the 2 that remain to unit cubes making 23 of them. Give 5 to each of the four piles leaving 3 undistributed.

Thus, $543 \div 4 = 135$ r3.

2. a. No, there are only four thousands. Yes. There are 46 hundreds, so distribute one to each of the 30.

3. a. 13 r38   **c.** 176 r4   **e.** 184 r326

4. a.

$$2_{\text{five}} \overline{)23} \quad \begin{array}{r} 11 \\ \hline 2 \\ \hline 3 \\ \hline 2 \\ \hline 1 \end{array}$$

One set of base to each of two piles leaves ||| units. Place one in each pile with one unit remaining. $23_{\text{five}} \div 2_{\text{five}} = 11_{\text{five}}$ r1_{five}.

c.

$$4_{\text{five}} \overline{)43_{\text{five}}} \quad \begin{array}{r} 10 \\ \hline 4 \\ \hline 3 \end{array}$$

$43_{\text{five}} \div 4_{\text{five}} = 10_{\text{five}}$ r3_{five}

e.

$$3_{\text{five}} \overline{)102_{\text{five}}} \quad \begin{array}{r} 14 \\ \hline 3 \\ \hline 22 \\ \hline 22 \end{array}$$

We have so cannot distribute any of the base X base groups. However, we have 10 groups of base so can give one group of base to each of three of three piles.

We now have 22 units. Give four to each pile.

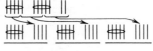

Thus $102_{\text{five}} \div 3_{\text{five}} = 14_{\text{five}}$

5. a. $(11 \text{ r}1)_{\text{six}}$ **c.** $(50 \text{ r}45)_{\text{six}}$ **e.** $(140 \text{ r}4)_{\text{six}}$

6. a. $(1 \text{ r}10)_{\text{two}}$ **c.** $(11 \text{ r}100)_{\text{two}}$ **e.** 100_{two}

7. a. 22_{twelve} **c.** $(81 \text{ r}49)_{\text{twelve}}$ **e.** $(763 \text{ r}138)_{\text{twelve}}$

8. a. $q = 54$ and $r = 1$

9. a. 2   **c.** 1

10. a.

	Quotient	Remainder
$(14 \div 2)_{five}$	4_{five}	1_{five}
$(13 \div 2)_{five}$	4_{five}	
$(12 \div 2)_{five}$	3_{five}	1_{five}
$(11 \div 2)_{five}$	3_{five}	
$(24 \div 2)_{five}$	12_{five}	
$(23 \div 2)_{five}$	11_{five}	1_{five}
$(22 \div 2)_{five}$	11_{five}	
$(21 \div 2)_{five}$	10_{five}	1_{five}

11. a. Yes

    c. If the units digit is even, the two-digit number is even; if it is odd, then the two-digit number is odd.

12. a. The same rule holds as for base five numbers.

13. a. It is not correct.   **c.** Yes. 1362   **e.** 138

15. a. $3\lfloor 140_{five}$ (Use base five tables.)   **c.** $4\lfloor 47$ (Use base eight table.)

        $3\lfloor 30$ 0 $4\lfloor 11$ 3

          $3\lfloor 10$ 0   2 1 $47_{eight} = 213_{four}$

              1   2 $140_{five} \div 1200_{three}$

    e. $12\lfloor 45$ (Use base six table.)

             3 5 $45_{six} = 35_{eight}$

16. a.

$26 \div 4 = 6 \ r2$

17. a.
```
  7) 36
     35 5
      1
     5r1
```
c.
```
  22) 254
      220  10
       34
       22   1
       12  11
      11r  12
```

19. a.
```
  6) 146
  -  96  16
      50
      48   8
       2  24
```
                            $1 \times 6 = 6$

                            $2 \times 6 = 12$

                            $4 \times 6 = 24$

                            $8 \times 6 = 48$

                          $16 \times 6 = 96$

                          $32 \times 6 = 192$

So $146 \div 6 = 24 \ r2$

c. $7\overline{)596}$

448	64	
148		
112	16	
36		
28	4	
8		
7	1	
1	85	

$1 \times 7 = 7$
$2 \times 7 = 14$
$4 \times 7 = 28$
$8 \times 7 = 56$
$16 \times 7 = 112$
$32 \times 7 = 224$
$64 \times 7 = 448$
$128 \times 7 = 896$

$596 \div 7 = 85 \text{ r}1$

20. a. (i) Q10R3   **(ii)** Q4R13   **(iii)** Q20R22   **(iv)** Q44R5

Review Problem Set 3.8

1. a. $3 \cdot 1000 + 1 \cdot 100 + 6 \cdot 10 + 2$
   c. MMMCLXII

2. a. 14,267   **b.** 230,676

3. a. $2^3 \cdot 3^2$ **b.** $3^1 \cdot 7^2$ **c.** $5^2 \cdot 11^1$ **d.** $2^2 \cdot 3^1 \cdot 5^2$

4. a. 4   **b.** 9   **c.** 3   **d.** 3   **e.** 8

5. a. 30_{five} **b.** 120_{three} **c.** 21_{seven}

6. a.   **b.** ...   **c.** ...

d. ...

7. a. 56_{eight} **b.** 1100_{five} **c.** 117   **d.** 21   **e.** 451_{six}

8. a.

463	
284	
+798	
15	
230	
1300	
1545	

b. $63 \cdot 26 = (60 + 3)26$
$= 60 \cdot 26 + 3 \cdot 26$
$= 60(20 + 6) + 3(20 + 6)$
$= 60 \cdot 20 + 60 \cdot 6 + 3 \cdot 20 + 3 \cdot 6$
$= 1200 + 360 + 60 + 18$
$= 1638$

c.

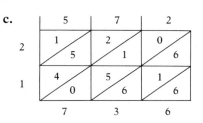

d.
$$\begin{array}{r} 25\ r9 \\ 23\overline{)584} \\ 46 \\ \hline 124 \\ 115 \\ \hline 9 \end{array}$$

9. a.

+	0	1	2	3
0	0	1	2	3
1	1	2	3	10
2	2	3	10	11
3	3	10	11	12

b. 3112_{four} **c.** 111_{four} **d.** 203_{four}

10. a.

·	0	1	2	3
0	0	0	0	0
1	0	1	2	3
2	0	2	10	12
3	0	3	12	21

b. $32 \cdot 3 = (30 + 2)3_{\text{four}}$
$$= 30 \cdot 3 + 2 \cdot 3_{\text{four}}$$
$$= 210 + 12_{\text{four}}$$
$$= 222_{\text{four}}$$

c. 20202_{four} **d.** 102 r11

11. a. odd   **b.** even   **c.** odd

CHAPTER 4

Problem Set 4.1

1. a. T   **c.** F   **e.** F

2. a. T   **c.** T   **e.** T   **g.** T

3. Property 4.1. Two examples are: If 2 | 4 and 4 | 8, then 2 | 8, and if 2 | 6 and 6 | 24, then 2 | 24.
Property 4.2. If 2 | 6 and 2 | 16, then 2 | (6 + 16).
Property 4.3. An example: If 3 | 6 and 3 | (6 + 3) then 3 | 3.
Property 4.4. An example: If 5 | 15 and 5 ∤ 6, then 5 ∤ (15 + 6).
Property 4.5. An example: If 2 | 6 then 2 | 6.5.

5. a. F   2 | 6 and 3 | 6 but (2 + 3) ∤ 6   **c.** T   **e.** T

6. a. T   **c.** T   **e.** T

8. a. Yes   **c.** No [6 ∤ 2 and 6 ∤ 3 but 6 | (2 · 3)]
    e. No [6 ∤ 3 and 6 | 3 · 2) but 6 ∤ 2]

Problem Set 4.2

1. a. Yes **c.** No **e.** Yes **g.** Yes **i.** No

2. a. Yes **c.** No **e.** No **g.** No **i.** Yes

3. a. No **c.** No **e.** Yes **g.** Yes **i.** No

4. a. No **c.** No **e.** Yes **g.** Yes **i.** No

5. a. No

6. a. Because $9 \mid 99$ and $9 \mid 9$, then $9 \mid 99c$ and $9 \mid 9b$. Therefore, $9 \mid (99c + 9b)$.

   c. A number is divisible by 9 if and only if the sum of the digits of its base-ten numeral is divisible by 9.

7. a. Yes **c.** No **e.** Yes

8. a. Yes **c.** No **e.** No

9. a. Yes **c.** No **e.** Yes

10. a. 8 **c.** 7 **e.** 6

11. a. T If $(a \cdot b) \mid c$, then $a \mid c$ and $b \mid c$.

   c. T If $a \mid c$ and $b \mid c$ and a and b are relatively prime, then $ab \mid c$.

   e. T This is really the same as part **a.**

12. a. $1000 = 994 + 4$ **c.** $6 \mid (6b + 96c + 996d + 9996e)$. If $a \mid b$ and
   $10,000 = 9996 + 4$ $a \mid c$ and $a \mid d$ and $a \mid e$, then $a \mid (b + c + d + e)$.

13. a. Yes **c.** Yes (Property 4.2)

   e. It is the three-digit number obtained by using the three digits on the right of our original number.

14. a. Yes, yes, yes

15. a. Yes. If $a \mid b$ and $a \mid c$, then $a \mid (b + c)$.

   c. If $a \mid b$ and $a \nmid c$, then $a \nmid (b + c)$.

   e. (i) $6 + 3 \cdot 9 + 2 \cdot 8 = 49$. Because $7 \mid 49$, then $7 \mid 896$.
   (ii) $4 + 3 \cdot 7 + 2 \cdot 5 = 35$. Because $7 \mid 35$, then $7 \mid 574$.
   (iii) $6 + 3 \cdot 9 + 2 \cdot 4 = 41$. Because $7 \nmid 41$, then $7 \nmid 496$.

16. a. $100,000 = 99,995 + 5$
   $1,000,000 = 999,999 + 1$
   $10,000,000 = 9,999,997 + 3$

   c. (i) $3 + 3 \cdot 2 + 2 \cdot 4 + 6 \cdot 7 = 59$; $7 \nmid 59$ so $7 \nmid 7423$.
   (ii) $5 + 3 \cdot 1 + 2 \cdot 0 + 6 \cdot 1 = 14$. Because $7 \mid 14$, then $7 \mid 1015$.
   (iii) $3 + 3 \cdot 5 + 2 \cdot 9 + 6 \cdot 1 = 42$. Because $7 \mid 42$, then $7 \mid 1953$.
   (iv) $0 + 3 \cdot 4 + 2 \cdot 5 + 6 \cdot 2 + 4 \cdot 1 = 38$. Because $7 \nmid 38$, then $7 \nmid 12540$.
   (v) $2 + 3 \cdot 3 + 2 \cdot 6 + 6 \cdot 4 + 4 \cdot 8 = 79$. Because $7 \nmid 79$, then $7 \nmid 84,632$.
   (vi) $5 + 3 \cdot 4 + 2 \cdot 8 + 6 \cdot 3 + 4 \cdot 6 + 5 \cdot 4 = 95$. Because $7 \nmid 95$, then $7 \nmid 463,845$.

17. 27,720

19. a. Yes. 2 | 2142 and 3 | 2142 so 6 | 2142.

　　c. Use the rule for 7 developed in Problem 16. Because $2 + 3 \cdot 4 + 2 \cdot 1 + 6 \cdot 2 = 28$ and 7 | 28, then 7 | 2142.
　　　Now 2 | 2142 and 7 | 2142, so 14 | 2142.

21. 480

23. a. Two darts in each region would produce $2 \cdot 9 + 2 \cdot 6 + 2 \cdot 2 = 34$.

Problem Set 4.3

1. 101, 103, 107, 109, 113, 127, 131, 137, 139, 149

2. a.　　　　　　　　　**c.**

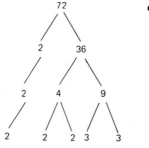 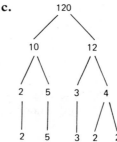

e.

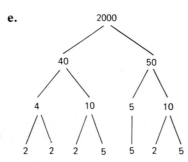

3. a. $3 \cdot 5 \cdot 5$　　**c.** $2 \cdot 2 \cdot 2 \cdot 2 \cdot 2 \cdot 3$　　**e.** $7 \cdot 17$　　**g.** $3 \cdot 3 \cdot 3 \cdot 19$
　i. $2 \cdot 2 \cdot 2 \cdot 2 \cdot 2 \cdot 2 \cdot 2 \cdot 2 \cdot 2$　　**k.** $3 \cdot 3 \cdot 3 \cdot 3 \cdot 3 \cdot 3 \cdot 3 \cdot 3$

4. a. Not prime　　**c.** Not prime　　**e.** Not prime

5. a. 24, 25, 26, 27　　**c.** 90, 91, 92, 93, 94, 95, 96

7. a. Composite: $1517 = 37 \cdot 41$

9. No. Every number has a unique prime factorization.

11. a. Yes, 2 and 3.

13. a. 1, 2, 4, 8, 16, 32, and 64

　　c. 1, 2, 3, 4, 6, 8, 9, 12, 18, 24, 36, 72

　　e. 72

14. a. (3, 5), (5, 7), (11, 13), (17, 19), (29, 31), (41, 43), (59, 61), (71, 73)

    c. Yes. Every other number is a multiple of 2. Thus, consider the three consecutive whole numbers p, $p + 1$, and $p + 2$. Because p is prime, it is not a multiple of 2. Therefore, $p + 1$ is a multiple of 2. Similarly, every third number is divisible by 3. Thus, exactly one of the numbers p, $p + 1$, and $p + 2$ is divisible by 3. Because p and $p + 2$ are prime, $p + 1$ must be divisible by 3.

15. a. Each prime factor appears an even number of times.

17. Note that 8 | 24 and 6 | 24, but 48 ∤ 24.

Problem Set 4.4

1. a. $7! + 2 = 5042$
    $7! + 3 = 5043$
    $7! + 4 = 5044$
    $7! + 5 = 5045$
    $7! + 6 = 5046$
    $7! + 7 = 5047$

2. a.

n	4
$2^n - 1$	15

    $= 3 \cdot 5$

3. a. $3 + 11$ **c.** $13 + 5$ **e.** $19 + 3$ **g.** $19 + 7$

4. a. $3 + 3 + 11$ **c.** $3 + 5 + 13$ **e.** $3 + 5 + 47$ **g.** $3 + 3 + 71$

5. a. 1, 2, 5   **c.** 1, 2, 3, 6, 9   **e.** 1, 2, 4, 7, 8, 14, 28

6. a. Perfect   **c.** Abundant   **e.** Perfect   **g.** Abundant

7. a. $(11! + 2)$, $(11! + 3)$, $(11! + 4)$, . . . , $(11! + 11)$

    c. $39{,}916{,}803 \div 3 = 13{,}305{,}601$

8. a. $(21)^2 = (20 + 1)^2 = 20^2 + 2(20)(1) + 1^2 = 400 + 40 + 1 = 441$

    c. $(24)^2 = (20 + 4)^2 = 20^2 + 2(20)(4) + (4)^2 = 400 + 160 + 16 = 576$

    e. $(92)^2 = (90 + 2)^2 = 90^2 + 2(90)(2) + (2)^2 = 8100 + 360 + 4 = 8464$

9. a. $15^2 = 100 \cdot 1 \cdot 2 + 25 = 225$ **c.** $35^2 = 100 \cdot 3 \cdot 4 + 25 = 1225$

    e. $95^2 = 100 \cdot 9 \cdot 10 + 25 = 9025$

10. a. 1, 121, 12321, 1,234,321   **c.** Yes

11. a. 15, 21, 28   **c.** 1, 5, 12, 22, 35, 51

13. a. $1 + 3 = 4$ The sum of the first two numbers in the sequence produce the second square number, the sum of the first three produce the third square number, etc.
    $(1 + 3) + 5 = 9$
    $(1 + 3 + 5) + 7 = 16$

    c. 36, 625, n^2

15. a. 12   **c.** 48

16. a. 20   **c.** 225

Problem Set 4.5

1. a. {1, 2, 3, 4, 6, 8, 9, 12, 18, 24, 36, 72}   **c.** {1, 2, 4, 23, 46, 92}
   e. {1, 2, 3, 4, 6, 8, 12, 16, 24, 48}

2. a. 24   **c.** 4   **e.** 2

3. a. 12   **c.** 2   **e.** 9

4. a.   **c.**

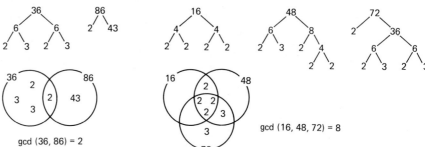

5. $3 \cdot 7^2 \cdot 31$

6. a. 6   **c.** 6

7. a. $7 \cdot (2^3 \cdot 3^{17} \cdot 5^{93})$, etc.   **c.** No

8. a. 2^3 or $2^3 \cdot 3$ or $2^3 \cdot 3^2$

9. a. 16   **c.** 36   **e.** 24

10. a. 168   **c.** 336   **e.** 468

11. a.   **c.**

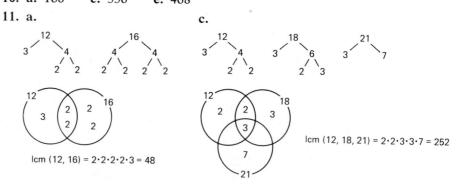

12. a. $\gcd(a, b) = 1$

13. 2520

14. a. $a \cdot b$ **c.** $a \cdot b$

15. a. 1, 2, 3, 4, 5, 6, 7, 8, 9, and 10
    c. 1, 5, 7, 11, 13, 17, 19, and 23

16. a. 9 | 18 and 6 | 18, but (9 · 6) ∤ 18   **c.** (i), (iii), (v)

17. a.

a	b	gcd(a, b)	lcm(a, b)	a · b
2	3	1	6	6
3	6	3	6	18
6	12	6	12	72
6	15	3	30	90
12	18	6	36	216

18. a.

n	Prime Factorization	Divisors of n	Number of Divisors of n
80	$2 \cdot 2 \cdot 2 \cdot 2 \cdot 5 = 2^4 \cdot 5$	1, 2, 4, 5, 8, 10, 16, 20, 40, 80	10
84	$2 \cdot 2 \cdot 3 \cdot 7 = 2^2 \cdot 3 \cdot 7$	1, 2, 3, 4, 6, 7, 12, 14, 21, 28, 42, 84	12
100	$2 \cdot 2 \cdot 5 \cdot 5 = 2^2 \cdot 5^2$	1, 2, 4, 5, 10, 20, 25, 50, 100	9
210	$2 \cdot 3 \cdot 5 \cdot 7$	1, 2, 3, 5, 6, 7, 10, 14, 15, 21, 30, 35, 42, 70, 105, 210	16

19. a. Yes   **c.** No   **e.** 1_{six} and 215_{six}

21. 10, yes

22. a. 42

23. a. 3 or 15, etc.

24. a. In 12 minutes   **c.** lcm(m, n) minutes

Problem Set 4.6

1. a. ⁻1   **c.** 6   **e.** ⁻7
    g. ⁻10   **i.** ⁻4   **k.** ⁻9
    m. ⁻5

2. a. >   **c.** <   **e.** <

3. a.   **c.**

    e.

4. a. 5   **c.** 9   **e.** 8   **g.** 7

5. a. 2   **c.** ⁻8   **e.** 4

7. a. 15   **c.** ⁻28   **e.** 2
    g. ⁻43   **i.** 2

8. a. A negative integer

9. a. ⁻5   **c.** 7   **e.** ⁻7
    g. ⁻2   **i.** 0   **k.** ⁻7

10. a. A negative integer if $r > 0$, zero if $r = 0$.

11. a. {2}   **c.** {$^-1$}   **e.** {10}
   g. {$^-4$}   **i.** {17}   **k.** {$^-5, ^-4, ^-3, ^-2, ^-1, 0, \ldots$}

12. a.

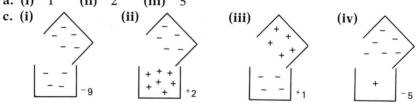

       −1   0   1   2   **c.**   5   6   7   8

e.   3

13. a. 3   **c.** $^-9$

14. a. Deviations from 80 would be 4, $^-2$, 2, and $^-5$. The sum would be (4.80) $+ (4 + ^-2 + 2 + ^-5) = 320 + ^-1 = 319$.

   c. Deviations from 60 would be $^-4$, 3, 1, $^-2$, $^-8$, and 7. The sum would be $(6 \cdot 60) + (^-4 + 3 + 1 + ^-2 + ^-8 + 7) = 360 + ^-3 = 357$.

15. a. 1   **c.** $^-7$

16. a. $^-7$ **c.** $^-5$

17. a. $3 + ^-8 = ^-5$ **c.** $125 + ^-30 + 45 = 140$
   e. $12 + ^-20 + 8 = 0$

18. a.

       2   3   4 $\cdots$ **c.** $^-2$ $^-1$ 0   1   2   3   4

       { 2, 3, 4, $\cdots$ }   { $^-2, ^-1, 0, 1, 2,$ }

e. $\cdots$ $^-2$ $^-1$ 0   1   2 $\cdots$

       { $\cdots, ^-2, ^-1, 0, 1, 2, 3, 4, \cdots$ } = U

19. a. (i) $^-120$ (ii) $^-5457$ (iii) $^-636$ (iv) $^-16$

20. a. Winning 10 points then losing four $(10 + ^-4)$ gives the same result as first losing four, then gaining 10 $(^-4 + 10)$.

21. a. Gain 16   **c.** Gain of 4   **e.** Gain 5

22. a. (i) $^-1$ (ii) $^+2$ (iii) $^-5$
   c. (i)   (ii)   (iii)   (iv)

Problem Set 4.7

1. a. 20   **c.** $^-18$ **e.** $^-30$ **g.** $^-15$

2. a. No   **c.** {$^-1, 0, 1$}

3. a. 37   **c.** 58   **e.** $^-1700$ **g.** 170   **i.** 42

4. a. $2 \cdot 2 = 4$

$2 \cdot 1 = 2$

$2 \cdot 0 = 0$

$2 \cdot {}^-1 = {}^-2$

$2 \cdot {}^-2 = {}^-4$

$2 \cdot {}^-3 = {}^-6$

5. a. Yes. ${}^-(4 + 3) = {}^-7 = {}^-4 + {}^-3$

6. a. Commutative property for multiplication

c. Multiplicative identity

e. Distributive property

g. Commutative property for addition

i. Distributive property

7. a. $\{5\}$ **c.** $\{{}^-6\}$ **e.** $\{{}^-4\}$ **g.** $\emptyset$ **i.** $\{\ldots, {}^-7, {}^-6, {}^-5\}$

8. a. ${}^-10 \cdot {}^-3 = 30$. Ten days ago it was $30°$ warmer than it is now. The temperature was $12°$ below zero (i.e., ${}^-42 + ({}^-3)({}^-10) = x$).

c. ${}^-42 + {}^-3\,\square$

9. a. ${}^-105 < 7r < {}^-35$

10. a. $5 + {}^-5 = 0$

$2(5 + {}^-5) = 2 \cdot 0 = 0$

$2 \cdot 5 + 2 \cdot {}^-5 = 0$

$10 + 2 \cdot {}^-5 = 0$

$2 \cdot {}^-5$ is the additive inverse of 10.

but ${}^-10$ is the additive inverse of 10.

Therefore,

$2 \cdot {}^-5 = {}^-10$

11. $1 + {}^-1 = 0$

$(1 + {}^-1) \cdot r = 0 \cdot r = 0$

$1 \cdot r + {}^-1 \cdot r = 0$

Because $1 \cdot r = r$, we may write $r + {}^-1 \cdot r = 0$. Therefore, ${}^-1 \cdot r$ is the additive inverse of r. But ${}^-r$ is the additive inverse of r.

$${}^-1 \cdot r = {}^-r.$$

12. a. ${}^-113,072$

13. a. $2 \cdot ({}^-3 + {}^-2) \overset{?}{=} (2 \cdot {}^-3) + (2 \cdot {}^-2)$

$2 \cdot {}^-5 \overset{?}{=} {}^-6 + {}^-4$

${}^-10 = {}^-10$

c. ${}^-5({}^-2 + {}^-6) \overset{?}{=} ({}^-5 \cdot {}^-2) + ({}^-5 \cdot {}^-6)$

${}^-5 \cdot {}^-8 \overset{?}{=} 10 + 30$

$40 = 40$

15. $(^-a \cdot b) + (a \cdot b) = 0$ Distributive property
   Therefore, (^-ab) is the additive inverse of (ab). Additive inverse property

   But $^-(ab) + (ab) = 0.$ Property 4.8
   Therefore, $^-(ab)$ is the additive inverse of (ab). Additive inverse property

17. a. Four plays with a gain of 3 on each results in a gain of 12 points.
   c. Four plays with a loss of 2 on each results in a loss of 8 points.
   e. Five plays with a loss of 3 on each results in a loss of 15 points.

19. $2 \cdot {}^-1 = {}^-2$
       $1 \cdot {}^-1 = {}^-1$
       $0 \cdot {}^-1 = 0$
       $^-1 \cdot {}^-1 = 1$

20. a. $^-10$ **c.** 180

21. a. No

Problem Set 4.8

1. a.

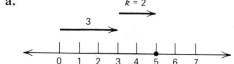

c.

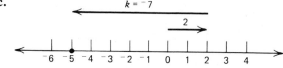

e.

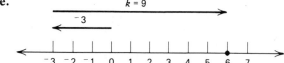

g.

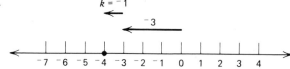

i.

2. a. $^-1$ **c.** 1   **e.** $^-24$ **g.** $^-2$
   i. 7   **k.** 13

3. a. Any example like $^-15 - (7 - 9)$ and $(^-15 - 7) - 9$ would suffice.
   Note that $^-15 - (7 - 9) = ^-13$ and $(^-15 - 7) - 9 = ^-31$.

4. a. 7   **c.** $^-3$ **e.** 5   **g.** $^-7$ **i.** $^-1$ **k.** $^-1$

5. a. No. $4 \div 2 = 2$, but $2 \div 4$ is not an integer.

7. 2609 B.C. (based on copyright date 1991)

8. a. 0   **c.** 58,200   **e.** 2,700

9. a. $\{11\}$ **c.** $\{18\}$ **e.** $\{8\}$ **g.** $\{^-70\}$ **i.** $\{89\}$

11. If $a = b$ or $a = ^-b$ and $a \neq 0$ and $b \neq 0$.

12. a. $(^-8 - 12) \cdot 2 \overset{?}{=} (^-8 \cdot 2) - (12 \cdot 2)$
   $$^-20 \cdot 2 \overset{?}{=} ^-16 - 24$$
   $$^-40 = ^-40$$

   c. $(8 - ^-12) \cdot ^-2 \overset{?}{=} (8 \cdot ^-2) - (^-12 \cdot ^-2)$
   $$(8 + 12) \cdot ^-2 \overset{?}{=} ^-16 - 24$$
   $$20 \cdot ^-2 \overset{?}{=} ^-16 + ^-24$$
   $$^-40 = ^-40$$

13. a. $^-8(12 - 2) \overset{?}{=} (^-8 \cdot 12) - (^-8 \cdot 2)$
   $$^-8 \cdot 10 \overset{?}{=} ^-96 - ^-16$$
   $$^-80 \overset{?}{=} ^-96 + 16$$
   $$^-80 = ^-80$$

   c. $8(^-12 - ^-2) \overset{?}{=} (8 \cdot ^-12) - (8 \cdot ^-2)$
   $$8(^-12 + 2) \overset{?}{=} ^-96 - ^-16$$
   $$8 \cdot ^-10 \overset{?}{=} ^-96 + 16$$
   $$^-80 = ^-80$$

14. a. Yes   **c.** Yes

15. a. $x^2 - 3x - 40$ **c.** $x^2 - 5x + 6$

17. You might be advised to use the number line approach. That is, $6 - ^-4$
   means "what must I add to $^-4$ to obtain 6?"

19. a. 6   **c.** $^-4$ **e.** $^-7$

20. a. $^-1$ **c.** 2   **e.** $^-105$

21. a.

c.

Problem Set 4.9

1. a. $9 > 7$ **c.** $^-12 > ^-14$ **e.** $^-2 > ^-4$

2. a. If $a = b$, then $a + c = b + c$.
   c. If $a > b$ and $c > 0$, then $ac > bc$.
   e. If $a > b$ and $c < 0$, then $ac < bc$.

3. a. {8}   **c.** {3}   **e.** {2}   **g.** {5}   **i.** {⁻3}   **k.** {4}
4. a. Sally
5. a. {7, 8, 9, 10, . . .}   **c.** {. . . , ⁻13, ⁻12, ⁻11}
   e. {. . . , ⁻7, ⁻6, ⁻5}   **g.** {. . . , ⁻7, ⁻6, ⁻5}
   i. {. . . , ⁻10, ⁻9, ⁻8}   **k.** {⁻3, ⁻2, ⁻1, 0, 1, . . . ,}
6. a. {3, 4, 5, 6, . . .}   **c.** {2, 3, 4, 5, . . .}
   e. {0, 1, 2, 3, 4, . . .}
7. a. $r > t$ **c.** $rt > st$
9.

r is to the right of s. If we add the same integer to each, they will both be shifted to the right, or to the left, by the same amount, so they will have the same relative position.

Review Problem Set

1. a. True   **b.** True   **c.** True   **d.** False   **e.** True   **f.** True
2. a. Yes   **b.** Yes   **c.** Yes   **d.** No   **e.** Yes   **f.** Yes
3. a. $2 \cdot 2 \cdot 13$ **b.** $3 \cdot 3 \cdot 7$ **c.** $2 \cdot 3 \cdot 3 \cdot 3 \cdot 3 \cdot 3$ **d.** $3 \cdot 37$
   e. $3 \cdot 97$ **f.** $2 \cdot 11 \cdot 2161$
4. It is prime. The last prime that we need to test is 19.
5. $(9! + 2), (9! + 3), . . . , (9! + 9)$.
6. a. 28   **b.** 168   **c.** gcd (21, 110) = 1
                              lcm (21, 110) = 21 · 110 = 2310
7. a. ⁻10   **b.** 9   **c.** 48   **d.** ⁻4   **e.** ⁻4
8. a. {2}   **b.** {2}   **c.** {8}   **d.** {⁻2}   **e.** {2}
   f. {3}   **g.** {⁻5}   **h.** {⁻3}
9. a. Yes   **b.** Yes   **c.** No
   d. 5 ÷ 2 is not an integer
10. a. True   **b.** False   **c.** True   **d.** True
11. a. D_{28} = {1, 2, 4, 7, 14, 28}, D_{35} = {1, 5, 7, 35}
   b. {1, 7}, gcd (28, 35) = 7   **c.** M_{28} = {0, 28, 56, . . .},
   M_{35} = {0, 35, 70, 105, . . .}
   d. $M_{28} \cap M_{35}$ = {0, 140, 280, . . .}
   e. lcm (28, 35) = 140
12. a. ⁻6   **b.** 3   **c.** 0   **d.** ⁻3   **e.** ⁻k **f.** m **g.** 2   **h.** 12
13. a. {. . . , ⁻1, 0, 1, 2}   **b.** {. . . , ⁻2, ⁻1, 0, 1}   **c.** {. . . , ⁻2, ⁻1, 0, 1}
   d. {. . . , ⁻1, 0, 1, 2, 3}   **e.** {⁻1, 0, 1, 2, . . .}   **f.** {. . . , ⁻3, ⁻2, ⁻1, 0}
   g. {9, 10, 11, 12, . . .}   **h.** {. . . , ⁻3, ⁻2, ⁻1, 0}
14. a. No   **b.** We just produced a counterexample.
15. a. Yes   **b.** Yes   **c.** Equal

CHAPTER 5

Problem Set 5.1

1. a. $\frac{2}{4}$ c. $\frac{5}{8}$ e. $\frac{3}{9}$ g. $\frac{4}{8}$

2. a.   c.

   e.    g.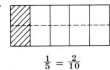

3. a. $\frac{1}{4} = \frac{2}{8}$ c. $\frac{2}{6} = \frac{6}{18}$ e. $\frac{1}{4} = \frac{2}{8}$

4. a.   c.

   $\frac{1}{2} = \frac{2}{4}$ $\frac{1}{5} = \frac{2}{10}$

5. a.   c.

   $\frac{1}{4} = \frac{2}{8}$

   $\frac{2}{3} = \frac{8}{12}$

6. a.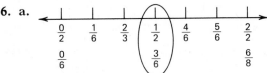

   c.

7. a. Yes   c. No
   e. Yes   g. No

8. a. $\frac{6}{10}, \frac{9}{15}, \frac{12}{20}$ c. $\frac{1}{1}, \frac{2}{2}, \frac{3}{3}$
   e. $\frac{8}{6}, \frac{12}{9}, \frac{16}{12}$ g. $\frac{6}{4}, \frac{9}{6}, \frac{12}{8}$ i. $\frac{6}{8}, \frac{9}{12}, \frac{12}{16}$

9. a. $\frac{1}{4}$ c. $\frac{2}{3}$ e. $\frac{3}{7}$
   g. $\frac{3}{5}$ i. $\frac{1}{3}$

10. a. 4   c. 1   e. 42
    g. 3 or $^{-}3$ i. 0

11. a. No   **c.** Yes   **c.** No
    g. Yes   **i.** Yes

12. a. 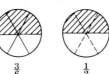   **c.** Not possible because we do not have three equal regions.

13. a. $\frac{15}{35}$ **c.** $\frac{10}{35}$ **e.** $\frac{5}{15}$

14. a. $\dfrac{1}{c}$ **c.** $\dfrac{b}{ac}$ **e.** $\dfrac{a}{b}$

15. a. Yes

c.
$$\frac{a}{b} = \frac{c}{d} \qquad\qquad \frac{c}{d} = \frac{e}{f}$$
$$ad = bc \qquad\qquad cf = de$$
$$f(ad) = f(bc) \qquad\qquad b(cf) = b(de)$$

$$f(ad) = b(de)$$
$$fad = bde$$
$$fa = be$$
$$\frac{a}{b} = \frac{e}{f}$$

17. In the case of a region or a number line, the whole that is being partitioned is together—a unit. In the case of a set, the elements are not attached in any way.

19. a. Use one orange and three purple.

    c. Use three green and nine white.

20. a.   **c.**

21. a.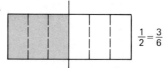

    c.

22. a. Use a physical model.

23. a. $\frac{4}{8}$ **c.** $\frac{2}{6}$

Problem Set 5.2

1. a.

c.

e.

$\frac{1}{3} + \frac{1}{3} = \frac{2}{3}$ $\frac{1}{6} + \frac{4}{6} = \frac{5}{6}$ $\frac{1}{8} + \frac{4}{8} = \frac{5}{8}$

2. a. 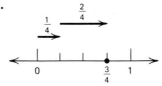   **c.**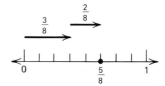

e.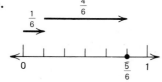

3. a. $\frac{7}{12}$ **c.** $\frac{3}{4}$ **e.** $\frac{3}{6} = \frac{1}{2}$

4. a.

$$\frac{1}{3} + \frac{1}{4} = \frac{7}{12}$$

c.

$$\frac{1}{3} + \frac{1}{5} = \frac{8}{15}$$

5. a. $\frac{3}{5}$ **c.** $\frac{7}{10}$ **e.** 1

6. a. $\frac{1}{6} + \frac{1}{4} = \frac{2}{12} + \frac{3}{12} = \frac{5}{12}$ **c.** $\frac{2}{3} + \frac{7}{8} = \frac{16}{24} + \frac{21}{24} = \frac{37}{24}$ **e.** $\frac{2}{5} + \frac{3}{4} = \frac{8}{20} + \frac{15}{20}$
$= \frac{23}{20}$ **g.** $\frac{2}{3} + \frac{1}{4} + \frac{5}{6} = \frac{8}{12} + \frac{3}{12} + \frac{10}{12} = \frac{21}{12} = \frac{7}{4}$

7. a. $6\frac{1}{2}$ **c.** $6\frac{1}{2}$ **e.** $23\frac{1}{3}$

8. a. $\frac{11}{5}$ **c.** $\frac{41}{5}$ **e.** $\frac{95}{4}$

9. a. $7\frac{1}{2}$ **c.** $5\frac{7}{12}$ **e.** $11\frac{3}{10}$ **g.** $10\frac{7}{30}$

10. a. $\dfrac{a + bc}{b}$ **c.** $\dfrac{a^2d + bc^2}{bd}$ **e.** $\dfrac{4 + 5a + 6b}{ab}$

11. c. $\dfrac{3}{4} + \dfrac{1}{6} = \dfrac{3 \cdot 6 + 4 \cdot 1}{4 \cdot 6} = \dfrac{22}{24} = \dfrac{11}{12}$. Yes   **e.** $\dfrac{8167}{6675}$

12. a. To add two fraction of the form $\dfrac{1}{a} + \dfrac{1}{a + 1}$, we write $a + (a + 1)$ as
the numerator and $a \cdot (a + 1)$ as the denominator. $\dfrac{1}{17} + \dfrac{1}{18} =$
$\dfrac{17 + 18}{17 \cdot 18} = \dfrac{35}{306}$

13. a. No

14. a. $\frac{1}{8} + (\frac{3}{8} + \frac{5}{8}) = \frac{1}{8} + \frac{8}{8} = \frac{9}{8}$ and $(\frac{1}{8} + \frac{3}{8}) + \frac{5}{8} = \frac{4}{8} + \frac{5}{8} = \frac{9}{8}$

15. No. $\frac{1}{7} + \frac{1}{8} = \frac{15}{16}$

16. a.

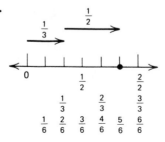

17. a. 1 green and 2 yellow = 11 white

$$\frac{1}{4} + \frac{2}{3} = \frac{11}{12}$$

c. 1 purple and 2 yellow = 5 purple

$$\frac{1}{6} + \frac{2}{3} = \frac{5}{6}$$

18. a. The sets representing $\frac{1}{2}$ and $\frac{1}{3}$ must be disjoint.

19. a.

$$2\frac{1}{3} = \frac{7}{3}$$

c.

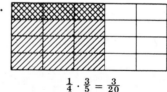

$$3\frac{1}{4} = \frac{13}{4}$$

e. To change from a mixed number to an equivalent improper fraction, take the product of the whole number and the denominator of the fraction, then add the numerator of the fraction and use the resulting number as the numerator of the improper fraction. The denominator of the improper fraction is the same as in the original fraction.

20. a. $\frac{2}{3}$ **c.** $\frac{3}{3}$

21. a. (i) $\frac{7}{12}$ **(ii)** $\frac{8}{15}$ **(iii)** $\frac{5}{12}$ **(iv)** $\frac{5}{18}$

22. a. (i) $\frac{2}{15}$ **(ii)** $\frac{1}{8}$ **(iii)** $\frac{3}{10}$ **(iv)** $\frac{5}{8}$

Problem Set 5.3

1. a.

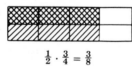

$$\frac{1}{2} \cdot \frac{3}{4} = \frac{3}{8}$$

c.

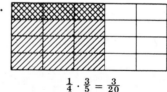

$$\frac{1}{4} \cdot \frac{3}{5} = \frac{3}{20}$$

e.

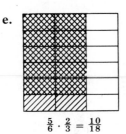

$$\frac{5}{6} \cdot \frac{2}{3} = \frac{10}{18}$$

2. a. $\frac{2}{3} \cdot \frac{1}{4} = \frac{2}{12}$ **c.** $\frac{2}{3} \cdot \frac{5}{6} = \frac{10}{18}$ **e.** $\frac{1}{3} \cdot \frac{2}{8} = \frac{2}{24}$

3. a. $\frac{3}{8}$ **c.** $\frac{2}{3}$ **e.** $\frac{3}{2}$ **g.** $\frac{5}{4}$ **i.** 1

4. a. $6\frac{2}{3}$ **c.** 3   **e.** $23\frac{5}{8}$ **g.** $14\frac{15}{28}$

5. a. $\dfrac{{}^{1}\cancel{3}}{5} \cdot \dfrac{1}{\cancel{3}_{1}} = \dfrac{1}{5}$ **c.** $\dfrac{{}^{1}\cancel{4}}{\cancel{9}_{3}} \cdot \dfrac{{}^{1}\cancel{3}}{\cancel{8}_{2}} = \dfrac{1}{6}$ **e.** $\dfrac{9}{\cancel{2}_{1}} \cdot \dfrac{\cancel{6}^{3}}{5} = \dfrac{27}{5}$

    g. $\dfrac{{}^{1}\cancel{3}}{1} \cdot \dfrac{5}{\cancel{3}_{1}} = \dfrac{5}{1}$

7. a. $1\frac{1}{4}$ cups of flour and $\frac{3}{8}$ cup of sugar

8. a. Commutative property of multiplication

    c. Distributive property

    e. Commutative property of multiplication

9. a. $12(\frac{1}{2} + \frac{1}{3}) = (12 \cdot \frac{1}{2}) + (12 \cdot \frac{1}{3})$

    c. $\frac{5}{3} \cdot (\frac{1}{4} + \frac{1}{2}) = (\frac{5}{3} \cdot \frac{1}{4}) + (\frac{5}{3} \cdot \frac{1}{2})$

    e. $\frac{1}{4} \cdot \frac{2}{3} + \frac{1}{4} \cdot \frac{1}{3} = \frac{1}{4}(\frac{2}{3} + \frac{1}{3})$

10. a. 10   **c.** $\frac{5}{4} = 1\frac{1}{4}$ **e.** $\frac{1}{4}$

11. a. $2 \cdot 3\frac{1}{3} = 2 \cdot (3 + \frac{1}{3})$ **c.** $3\frac{1}{2} \cdot 4\frac{3}{5} = (3 + \frac{1}{2}) \cdot (4 + \frac{3}{5})$

           $= 2 \cdot 3 + 2 \cdot \frac{1}{3}$ $= 3 \cdot 4 + 3 \cdot \frac{3}{5} + \frac{1}{2} \cdot 4 + \frac{1}{2} \cdot \frac{3}{5}$

           $= 6 + \frac{2}{3}$ $= 12 + \frac{9}{5} + 2 + \frac{3}{10}$

           $= 6\frac{2}{3}$ $= 16\frac{1}{10}$

12. a. (i)

$$\frac{1}{3} \cdot \frac{3}{4} = \frac{1}{4}$$

(ii)

$$\frac{1}{4} \cdot \frac{4}{5} = \frac{1}{5}$$

(iii)

$$\frac{2}{3} \cdot \frac{3}{5} = \frac{2}{5}$$

(iv)

$$\frac{3}{4} \cdot \frac{4}{7} = \frac{3}{7}$$

13. a. $\dfrac{a^2}{bd}$ **c.** $\dfrac{a}{b}$

15. a.

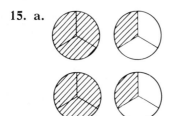

$$2 \cdot 1\tfrac{1}{3} = 2\tfrac{2}{3}$$

16. a. Suggest that he try $\frac{40}{1} \cdot \frac{3}{4} = 30$.

17. a. $\frac{1}{2}(1 - \frac{1}{4}) = n; \; n = \frac{3}{8}$

18. a. Cancellation applied incorrectly to addition of fractions

   c. This is an addition problem, so cancellation does not apply.

19. So we received three pieces, but how much is each worth, $\frac{1}{4}$ or $\frac{1}{12}$?

21. a. 500

22. a. $\frac{1}{6}$

23. a. Less   **c.** $\frac{11}{12}$

Problem Set 5.4

1. a. 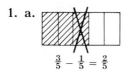   **c.** 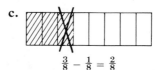   **e.**

$\frac{3}{5} - \frac{1}{5} = \frac{2}{5}$ $\frac{3}{8} - \frac{1}{8} = \frac{2}{8}$ $\frac{3}{4} - \frac{1}{4} = \frac{2}{4}$

2. a. $\frac{3}{7}$ **c.** $\frac{11}{6}$ **e.** $\frac{24}{35}$ **g.** $\frac{17}{24}$

3. a. $\frac{7}{4} \div \frac{1}{4} = 7$ **c.** $\frac{2}{8} \div \frac{1}{8} = 2$ **e.** $\frac{16}{6} \div \frac{4}{6} = 4$

4. a. $\frac{8}{9}$ **c.** $\frac{24}{5}$ **e.** $\frac{5}{24}$ **g.** 6

5. a. $\frac{1}{9}$ **c.** $\frac{5}{6}$ **e.** $2\frac{1}{4}$ **g.** $2\frac{1}{2}$ **i.** $\frac{55}{54}$ **k.** 1

6. a. $\frac{11}{8}$ **c.** $\frac{3}{16}$

7. a. $\dfrac{a - d}{bc}$ **c.** $\dfrac{a}{b^2}$ **e.** $\dfrac{5}{2b}$

8. a. Yes. $\dfrac{3}{8} \div \dfrac{3}{4} = \dfrac{3}{8} \cdot \dfrac{4}{3} = \dfrac{1}{2}$ and $\dfrac{3 \div 3}{8 \div 4} = \dfrac{1}{2}$ also. Therefore, $\dfrac{3}{8} \div \dfrac{3}{4} = \dfrac{3 \div 3}{8 \div 4}$.

   c. Yes. $\dfrac{5}{11} \div \dfrac{3}{11} = \dfrac{5}{11} \cdot \dfrac{11}{3} = \dfrac{5}{3}$ and $\dfrac{5 \div 3}{11 \div 11} = \dfrac{\frac{5}{3}}{1} = \dfrac{5}{3}$

   e. (i) $\dfrac{12}{7} \div \dfrac{3}{7} = \dfrac{12 \div 3}{7 \div 7} = 4$ (ii) $\dfrac{15}{17} \div \dfrac{5}{17} = \dfrac{15 \div 5}{17 \div 17} = 3$

(iii) $\dfrac{13}{17} \div \dfrac{19}{17} = \dfrac{13 \div 19}{17 \div 17} = \dfrac{13}{19}$ **(iv)** $\dfrac{5}{8} \div \dfrac{3}{4} = \dfrac{5}{8} \div \dfrac{6}{8} = \dfrac{5 \div 6}{8 \div 8} = \dfrac{5}{6}$

9. a. No   **c.** No

10. a. No. $\frac{3}{8} - \frac{1}{8} \neq \frac{1}{8} - \frac{3}{8}$

11. a. $\{\frac{1}{2}\}$ **c.** $\{\frac{1}{3}\}$ **e.** $\{\frac{2}{15}\}$

12. a. If $\dfrac{a}{b}$ and $\dfrac{c}{d}$ are rational numbers, then a, b, c, and d are integers. Therefore, ad, bc, and bd are integers. (The set of integers is closed under multiplication.) Then $(ad + bc)$ is an integer. (The set of integers is closed under addition.) Because $b \neq 0$ and $d \neq 0$, $b \cdot d \neq 0$. Therefore, $\dfrac{ad + bc}{bd}$ is a rational number and we may conclude that the set of rational numbers is closed under addition.

c. Yes. $\left(\dfrac{a}{b} \cdot \dfrac{c}{d} = \dfrac{a \cdot c}{b \cdot d} \text{, and } a \cdot c \text{ and } b \cdot d \text{ are integers.} \right)$

13. a. $\frac{7}{40}$

15. a. (i) $3 - \frac{1}{2} = 2\frac{1}{2}$
$2\frac{1}{2} - \frac{1}{2} = 2$
$2 - \frac{1}{2} = 1\frac{1}{2}$
$1\frac{1}{2} - \frac{1}{2} = 1$
$1 - \frac{1}{2} = \frac{1}{2}$
$\frac{1}{2} - \frac{1}{2} = 0$
Thus, there are six $\frac{1}{2}$'s in 3.

(ii) $2 - \frac{2}{3} = 1\frac{1}{3}$
$1\frac{1}{3} - \frac{2}{3} = \frac{2}{3}$
$\frac{2}{3} - \frac{2}{3} = 0$
Thus, there are three $\frac{2}{3}$'s in 2.

(iii) $\frac{3}{4} - \frac{1}{4} = \frac{2}{4}$
$\frac{2}{4} - \frac{1}{4} = \frac{1}{4}$
$\frac{1}{4} - \frac{1}{4} = 0$
There are three $\frac{1}{4}$'s in $\frac{3}{4}$.

(iv) $\frac{9}{2} - \frac{3}{4} = \frac{18}{4} - \frac{3}{4} = \frac{15}{4}$
$\frac{15}{4} - \frac{3}{4} = \frac{12}{4}$
$\frac{12}{4} - \frac{3}{4} = \frac{9}{4}$
$\frac{9}{4} - \frac{3}{4} = \frac{6}{4}$
$\frac{6}{4} - \frac{3}{4} = \frac{3}{4}$
$\frac{3}{4} - \frac{3}{4} = 0$
There are six $\frac{3}{4}$'s in $\frac{9}{2}$.

(v) $2 - \frac{2}{5} = \frac{10}{5} - \frac{2}{5} = \frac{8}{5}$
$\frac{8}{5} - \frac{2}{5} = \frac{6}{5}$
$\frac{6}{5} - \frac{2}{5} = \frac{4}{5}$
$\frac{4}{5} - \frac{2}{5} = \frac{2}{5}$
$\frac{2}{5} - \frac{2}{5} = 0$
There are five $\frac{2}{5}$'s in 2.

16. a. Yes   **c.** Yes. $\dfrac{1}{a} - \dfrac{1}{a + 1} = \dfrac{1(a + 1)}{a(a + 1)} - \dfrac{a \cdot 1}{a(a + 1)}$
$$= \dfrac{a + 1 - a}{a(a + 1)} = \dfrac{1}{a(a + 1)}$$

17. a. (X X X X X) X X

c.

$$\tfrac{3}{4} - \tfrac{1}{6} = \tfrac{7}{12}$$

19. a. Three $\tfrac{1}{3}$'s in 1   **c.** Three $\tfrac{1}{3}$'s in 1 $\therefore$ six $\tfrac{1}{3}$'s in 2.
   e. Eight $\tfrac{1}{8}$'s in 1 $\therefore$ 40 $\tfrac{1}{8}$'s in 5

20. a. More than 1   **c.** Less than 1   **e.** More than 1

21. a. No

Problem Set 5.5

1. a. $<$ **c.** $>$ **e.** $<$ **g.** $<$ **i.** $<$

2. a. $\tfrac{7}{8}, \tfrac{9}{10}, \tfrac{17}{18}$ **c.** $\tfrac{17}{24}, \tfrac{21}{26}, \tfrac{35}{40}$

3. a.

$$\tfrac{36}{48}, \tfrac{37}{48}, \tfrac{38}{48}, \tfrac{39}{48}, \tfrac{40}{48}$$

c.

$$\tfrac{15}{30}, \tfrac{16}{30}, \tfrac{17}{30}, \tfrac{18}{30}, \tfrac{19}{30}, \tfrac{20}{30}$$

4. a. $\tfrac{5}{9} - \tfrac{7}{11} = \tfrac{55}{99} - \tfrac{63}{99} \not> 0$,
   but $\tfrac{7}{11} - \tfrac{5}{9} = \tfrac{63}{99} - \tfrac{55}{99} = \tfrac{8}{99} > 0$.
   So $\tfrac{7}{11} > \tfrac{5}{9}$.

c. $\tfrac{7}{9} - \tfrac{5}{7} = \tfrac{49}{63} - \tfrac{45}{63} = \tfrac{4}{63} > 0$
   Therefore, $\tfrac{7}{9} > \tfrac{5}{7}$

5. a. $\dfrac{m}{n} = \dfrac{2+3}{3+4} = \dfrac{5}{7}$

c. $\dfrac{m}{n} = \dfrac{38}{45}$

6. a. $<$ **c.** $=$ **e.** $<$

7. a. $\dfrac{r}{s} = \tfrac{1}{2}(\tfrac{2}{3} + \tfrac{5}{6}) = \tfrac{3}{4}$. Yes   **c.** $\dfrac{r}{s} = \tfrac{1}{2}(\tfrac{17}{20} + \tfrac{21}{25}) = \tfrac{169}{200}$. Yes

8. a. As $\tfrac{3}{4} = \tfrac{9}{12}$ and $\tfrac{9}{12} > \tfrac{8}{12}$, then $\tfrac{3}{4} > \tfrac{8}{12}$.
   c. $\tfrac{5}{9} < \tfrac{25}{44}$ and $5 \cdot 44 < 9 \cdot 25$
   e. $\tfrac{488}{5423} > \tfrac{323}{3782}$ because $488 \cdot 3782 = 1{,}845{,}616$ and $5423 \cdot 323 = 1{,}751{,}629$.

9.

A ————————— B
   M_2 M_3 M_1

We can continue selecting midpoints of the segments formed.

11. a.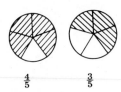

$\frac{4}{5}$ $\qquad$ $\frac{3}{5}$

c. Suppose you cut one pizza into 15 pieces and another into 17 pieces. Each piece of the first one (15ths) is larger than the pieces of the second (17ths). Therefore, $\frac{13}{15} > \frac{13}{17}$.

12. a. $\frac{1}{2}(\frac{1}{4} + \frac{5}{6}) = \frac{13}{24}$. Because $\frac{13}{24} - \frac{1}{4} = \frac{7}{24}$ and $\frac{5}{6} - \frac{13}{24} = \frac{7}{24}$, then $\frac{13}{24}$ is midway between $\frac{1}{4}$ and $\frac{5}{6}$.

$$\xleftarrow{\hspace{1cm}} \overset{|}{\underset{\frac{1}{4}}{}} \quad \overset{|}{\underset{\frac{13}{24}}{}} \quad \overset{|}{\underset{\frac{5}{6}}{}} \xrightarrow{\hspace{1cm}}$$

13. a. Answers will vary.

Problem Set 5.6

1. a. 15   c. 60   e. 5   g. 14   i. 40   k. 8
2. a. 500   c. $4.50
3. a. 140
4. a. 175
5. a. 8 lb
6. a. 330   c. 15
7. a. $\frac{2}{3}$ c. $\frac{f}{f + m} \cdot n$
8. a. 18
9. a. 12 grams of yellow and 4 grams of red   c. 4 grams
10. a. 104   c. 476.2 revolutions   e. 3.96 hours
11. a. $14.70   c. $4\frac{1}{2}$ hours
13. a. 2250 men   c. 750   e. 1800
14. a. 40 mph   c. 20 hr
15. a. 12 cm   c. 6 cm
16. a. What is the meaning of $\frac{2}{7}$? Does the + symbol mean addition in this situation?   c. 16 hits in 29 at bats.
17. 0.96 m
19. Wingspan: 0.28 m; length: 0.20 m

Review Problem Set

1. a.    b.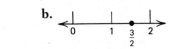

c.

d.

e.

2. a.

b. $3 \cdot 4 = 2 \cdot 6$ assures us that $\frac{3}{2} = \frac{6}{4}$

3. a. $\frac{10}{16}, \frac{15}{24}, \frac{20}{32}$ **b.** $\frac{3}{7}$

4. a.

b.

c.

d. (x x x x x)x x x

5. a. $\frac{7}{5}$ **b.** $\frac{39}{40}$ **c.** $4\frac{1}{12}$ **d.** $\frac{7}{20}$
   e. $1\frac{19}{24}$ **f.** $\frac{6}{35}$ **g.** 1   **h.** $3\frac{3}{5}$ **i.** $\frac{10}{9}$ **j.** $\frac{1}{8}$ **k.** $1\frac{7}{8}$
6. a. Yes   **b.** Yes. (Division by zero is excluded.)   **c.** No
7. Change to a common denominator and compare numerators
   $\frac{5}{6} = \frac{10}{12}$ and $\frac{3}{4} = \frac{9}{12}$. Thus $\frac{5}{6} > \frac{3}{4}$.
8. Many possible answers.
9. a. $\frac{5}{8}, \frac{7}{10}, \frac{8}{11}$ **b.** $\frac{3}{5}, \frac{5}{7}, \frac{9}{11}$
10. a. 3   **b.** 8   **c.** 9   **d.** 24   **e.** 16   **f.** 3   **g.** 12
   h. $\frac{15}{2} = 7\frac{1}{2}$
11. a. 8   **b.** 2   **c.** 16

CHAPTER 6

Problem Set 6.1

1. a. 0.2   **c.** 2.42

2. a.   **c.** 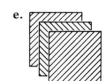   **e.**

3. a. $\frac{1}{10} + \frac{8}{100} + \frac{3}{1000}$　　**c.** $\frac{2}{10} + \frac{8}{100} + \frac{3}{1000}$　　**e.** $2 + \frac{1}{10} + \frac{3}{100}$

4. a. $>$　　**c.** $>$　　**e.** $<$　　**g.** $>$　　**i.** $<$　　**k.** $>$

5. a. 0.23　　**c.** 0.5　　**e.** 5.6　　**g.** 5.62　　**i.** 0.076　　**k.** 35.42

6. a. $\frac{7}{10}$　　**c.** $\frac{463}{1000}$　　**e.** $\frac{62}{100}$

　　g. $\frac{34}{1000}$　　**i.** $\frac{163}{100}$　　**k.** $\frac{1431}{100}$

7. a. 0.3　　**c.** 1.4　　**e.** Not possible　　**g.** Not possible　　**i.** 0.3

　　k. Not possible

8. a. 29.5　　**c.** 66.9　　**e.** 56.257　　**g.** 2.684　　**i.** 5.3988

9. a. 51.84　　**c.** 0.0126　　**e.** 0.03624　　**g.** 0.6414　　**i.** 30.3875

　　approximately

10. a. 12.3, 12.3498, 12.35, 12.3567, 12.4

　　c. 0.4036, 0.4063, 0.4306, 0.4360, 0.4603

11. a. $6^2 = 36$　　　　　　　　**c.** $10^2 = 100$

　　　　$6^1 = 6$　　　　　　　　　　　$10^1 = 10$

　　　　$6^0 = 1$　　　　　　　　　　　$10^0 = 1$

　　　　$6^{-1} = \dfrac{1}{6}$　　　　　　　　　$10^{-1} = \dfrac{1}{10}$

　　　　$6^{-2} = \dfrac{1}{36} = \dfrac{1}{6^2}$　　　　$10^{-2} = \dfrac{1}{100} = \dfrac{1}{10^2}$

　　　　$6^{-3} = \dfrac{1}{216} = \dfrac{1}{6^3}$　　　$10^{-3} = \dfrac{1}{1000} = \dfrac{1}{10^3}$

　　　　　　　　　　　　　　　　　　$10^{-4} = \dfrac{1}{10,000} = \dfrac{1}{10^4}$

12. a. $1.05 \cdot 10^2$　　**c.** $5.86 \cdot 10^8$　　**e.** $1.05 \cdot 10^{-4}$

13. a. $4.0 \cdot 10^2$　　**c.** $1.9 \cdot 10^5$　　**e.** $4.37 \cdot 10^5$

14. a. $1.403 \cdot 10^{10}$　　**c.** $2.542 \cdot 10^9$　　**e.** $2.73 \cdot 10^{13}$

15. a. Yes. (Unless both happen to be zero!)

17. a. The power to which 10 is being raised in scientific notation

　　c. $1.4637 \times 10^{-3} = 0.0014637$　　It is not an approximation.

18. a. 0.463　　**c.** 0.2134

21. a. Note that $76 \times 32 = 2432$, so the remainder was 21.

　　b. (i) 22　　**(iii)** 2

22. a. 0.46　　**c.** 6.43　　**e.** 0.34　　**g.** 0.06

23. a. 0.4　　**c.** 3.2　　**e.** 0.3　　**g.** 32.1

25. a.

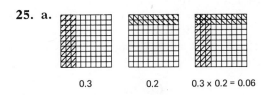

　　　　0.3　　　　　　0.2　　　0.3 x 0.2 = 0.06

c.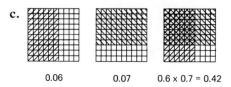

0.06   0.07   0.6 x 0.7 = 0.42

Problem Set 6.2

1. a. $0.\overline{285714}$
    c. $4.\overline{857142}$
    e. $4.\overline{0}$
    g. $.2\overline{142857}$
    i. $0.\overline{2}$

2. a. $\frac{5}{9}$ **c.** $\frac{7}{9}$ **e.** $\frac{2}{1}$ **g.** $\frac{2}{11}$ **i.** $\frac{2522}{999}$

3. a. $\frac{16}{45}$ **c.** $\frac{6}{55}$
    e. $\frac{1}{225}$

4. a. $3.45\overline{0},\ 3.\overline{453},\ 3.\overline{45},\ 3.4\overline{5}$ **c.** $1.451\overline{0},\ 1.45\overline{1},\ 1.\overline{451},\ 1.45\overline{1}$

5. Many possible answers

6. a. Many choices possible   **c.** Density

7. a. $0.\overline{49}$ Yes, 2 digits long or less.
    c. $0.\overline{373545462654}$ Yes.
    e. Yes. An infinite cycling decimal is a representation for a rational number and the rational numbers are closed under addition. Thus, the answer must be a cycling decimal.
    g. $0.\overline{6}$ Note that $0.\overline{6} = 0.\overline{666}$.

8. a. $\frac{2}{7} = 0.\overline{285714}$ and $\frac{5}{7} = 0.\overline{714285}$ **c.** $0.\overline{285714} + 0.\overline{714285} = 0.\overline{9}$

9. a. $0.\overline{1}$ **c.** $0.\overline{001}$

10. a. $\frac{5}{26}$

11. 27-digit repetition

12. a. $\frac{4}{9}$ **c.** $\frac{230}{999}$ **e.** $\frac{122}{99}$

13. a. $\frac{2}{11} < \frac{3}{13}$ **c.** $\frac{19}{42} > \frac{23}{51}$

15. a. Yes, yes, yes

17. a. $\frac{2}{3} \times 3 = 1.99999998$ because $\frac{2}{3}$ is computed by the calculator as 0.66666666 and the remaining digits are discarded. When 0.66666666 is multiplied by 3 the result is 1.99999998.
    c. $\frac{2}{3} \times 3 = 2$ because $\frac{2}{3}$ is computed as 0.6666666667 as the calculator rounds up, but it does not display the last two digits. Then 0.6666666667 × 3 yields 2.0000000001, which shows as 2 on the calculator since the last two digits are not displayed.

18. a. Answers will vary.

b. (i) $\dfrac{a}{b} = 0.341\overline{3}$

$10\,\dfrac{a}{b} = 3.41\overline{3} = 3.41\overline{33}$

$-\quad \dfrac{a}{b} = 0.341\overline{3} = 0.341\overline{3}$

$9\,\dfrac{a}{b} = \qquad\quad = 3.072$

$\dfrac{a}{b} = \dfrac{3.072}{9} = \dfrac{3072}{9000}$

(iii) $\dfrac{a}{b} = 0.5\overline{67}$

$100\,\dfrac{a}{b} = 56\overline{67} = 56.6\overline{767}$

$-\quad \dfrac{a}{b} = 0.5\overline{67} = 0.5\overline{67}$

$99\,\dfrac{a}{b} = \qquad\qquad 56.11$

$\dfrac{a}{b} = \dfrac{56.11}{99} = \dfrac{5611}{9900}$

Problem Set 6.3

1. **a.** Rational **c.** Irrational **e.** Rational
   g. Rational **i.** Rational **k.** Irrational
   m. Irrational

2. **a.** $2.44 < \sqrt{6} < 2.45$ because $2.44^2 = 5.9536$ and $2.45^2 = 6.0025$.
   $2.449 < \sqrt{6} < 2.450$ because $2.449^2 = 5.997601$ and $2.450^2 = 6.0025$.

   c. $4.24 < \sqrt{18} < 4.25$ because $4.24^2 = 17.9776$ and $4.25^2 = 18.0625$.
   $4.242 < \sqrt{18} < 4.243$ because $4.242^2 = 17.9946$ and $4.243^2 = 18.003$.

   e. $2.080 < \sqrt[3]{9} < 2.081$ because $2.080^3 = 8.9989$ and $2.081^3 = 9.0119$.

3. **a.** 2.2   **c.** 9.2   **e.** 27.4

4. **a.** 68.41 and 68.42   **c.** 7.66 and 7.67   **e.** 4.61 and 4.62

5. **a.** 4.123

6. **a.** $\frac{60}{25}$, $2\frac{1}{3}$, 2.3333, 2.33   **c.** 3.4623233, $3.46\overline{23}$, $\frac{68}{20}$, $\frac{2}{3}\sqrt{15}$

7. Many possible answers

9. **c.** $^-0.434\overline{2}$

10. **a.** Assume $2\sqrt{2}$ is rational. Then

    $$2\sqrt{2} = \frac{a}{b}$$

    $$\sqrt{2} = \frac{a}{2b}$$

    which contradicts the fact that $\sqrt{2}$ is irrational.

c. Assume $2 + \sqrt{2}$ is rational. Then

$$2 + \sqrt{2} = \frac{a}{b}$$

$$\sqrt{2} = \frac{a}{b} - 2 = \frac{a - 2b}{b}$$

which is a contradiction. Each of the others follow a similar pattern.

11. a. Assume $\sqrt{3}$ is rational. Then write $\sqrt{3} = \frac{a}{b}$, where a and b are relatively prime. Then

$$3 = \frac{a^2}{b^2}$$

$$3b^2 = a^2$$

Thus, a^2 is a multiple of 3 and it follows that a is a multiple of 3. Let

$$a = 3k$$
$$a^2 = 9k^2$$
$$3b^2 = 9k^2$$
$$b^2 = 3k^2$$

Thus, b^2 is a multiple of 3, and therefore b must also be a multiple of 3. But if both a and b are multiples of 3, they are not relatively prime. Therefore, our original assumption must be false. Therefore, $\sqrt{3}$ is irrational.

12. a. $g_1 = 9$, $q_1 = \dfrac{86}{9} = 9.555$, $g_2 = \dfrac{9 + 9 \cdot 555}{2} = 9.278$, $q_2 = \dfrac{86}{9.278} = 9.269$. Therefore, $\sqrt{86} \doteq 9.3$.

    c.   **(i)** 3.16   **(ii)** 5.92   **(iii)** 8.83

          (iv) 28.81   **(v)** 70.57   **(vi)** 89.44

13. $g_1 = 2$ $q_1 = \dfrac{80}{2} = 40$

$g_2 = \dfrac{2 + 40}{2} = 21$ $q_2 = \dfrac{80}{21} \doteq 3.8$

$g_3 = \dfrac{21 + 3.8}{2} = 12.4$ $q_3 = \dfrac{80}{12.4} \doteq 6.45$

$g_4 = \dfrac{12.4 + 6.45}{2} = 9.425$ $q_4 = \dfrac{80}{9.425} \doteq 8.488$

$g_5 = \dfrac{9.425 + 8.488}{2} \doteq 8.957$ $q_5 = \dfrac{80}{8.957} \doteq 8.932$

Problem Set 6.4

1. a. Yes   **c.** No   **e.** Density

2. a. $\{1.1\overline{3}\}$ **c.** $\{^-1.625\}$ **e.** $\{\frac{13}{4}\}$

3. a. $x > {}^-1.1\overline{3}$ **c.** $x < 3$ **e.** $x < \frac{20}{3}$

4. a. $x = \frac{1}{4}$ **c.** $x = \frac{11}{12}$ **e.** $x = \frac{33}{20}$
5. a. $x = 0.13$ **c.** $x = 4.38$ **e.** $x = 3.46$
6. a. F **c.** F **e.** T **g.** F
7. a. Four   **c.** An infinite number
9. a. False.   0.333333... This sum is irrational.
                    $+0.101001000...$
                    $\overline{0.434334333...}$
    c. False.   0.14144144414444... This sum is rational.
                    $+0.52522522252222...$
                    $\overline{0.6666...}$
    e. True

Problem Set 6.5

1. a. 0.46   **c.** 0.18   **e.** 0.03   **g.** 1.43   **i.** 0.142   **k.** 0.002
2. a. $\frac{3}{5}$ **c.** $\frac{12}{25}$ **e.** $\frac{11}{20}$ **g.** $1\frac{1}{4}$ **i.** $\frac{3}{50}$ **k.** $\frac{1}{200}$
3. a. 25%   **c.** 80%   **e.** 5%   **g.** 70%   **i.** 2.1%   **k.** $83\frac{1}{3}$%
5. a. 15   **c.** 102   **e.** $33\frac{1}{3}$%   **g.** 120%   **i.** 48   **k.** $113\frac{7}{11}$
6. a. 40%   **c.** \$7.54   **e.** 72%   **g.** 36
7. a. 40
9. a. \$38.25
10. a. 150   **c.** 15   **e.** 2.4
11. 32.5%
13. a. $<$ **c.** $>$ **e.** $<$ **g.** $<$
14. a. $13\% = \frac{13}{100} = 0.13$ **c.** $60\% = \frac{60}{100} = 0.6$
15. Answers will vary.
17. Answers will vary.
18. a. 15%   **c.** 64%

Review Problem Set

1. a. 1.25   **b.** 0.56   **c.** 0.375   **d.** 175   **e.** $0.\overline{63}$ **f.** $2.\overline{142857}$
2. a. $\frac{1}{5}$ **b.** $\frac{17}{50}$ **c.** $\frac{3}{2000}$ **d.** $\frac{5}{33}$ **e.** $\frac{937}{300}$ **f.** $\frac{43}{990}$
3. a. 64.13   **b.** 33.06   **c.** 0.05538   **d.** $3508.\overline{6}$
4. a. $\left\{\frac{5}{3}\right\}$ **b.** $\{5\}$ **c.** $\left\{\frac{-5}{12}\right\}$ **d.** $\{5\}$ **e.** $\left\{\frac{-1}{12}\right\}$
5. a. 0.582929..., 0.58229994, 0.583   **b.** $0.6\overline{2}$, 0.623, $0.6\overline{231}$
6. a. $5.\overline{393120}$ **b.** $0.\overline{342}$ **c.** $1.\overline{57}$ **d.** $2.\overline{03}$ **e.** $0.\overline{148}$
7. Many possible answers
8. $0.\overline{8}$ Rational

9. **a.** 3.9

10. **a.** $19,080   **b.** 20 percent

11. **a.** 11%   **b.** 6%   **c.** 67%   **d.** 44%   **e.** 52%   **f.** 89%

12. **a.** $\frac{23}{100}$ **b.** $\frac{1}{4}$ **c.** $\frac{7}{10}$ **d.** $\frac{4}{5}$ **e.** $\frac{23}{25}$ **f.** $\frac{7}{20}$

13. **a.** 0.13   **b.** 0.37   **c.** 0.41   **d.** 0.58   **e.** 0.79   **f.** 0.85

14. **a.** 2.12   **b.** 5.112   **c.** 0.364   **d.** 0.03362

15. $\frac{1}{2}$

16. 20%

17. Not true because 3:24 does not represent a decimal.

18. **a.** The quotient is 20 and the remainder is 2.
    b. The quotient is 17 and the remainder is 9.

19. **a.** $\frac{4}{100} = 0.04 = 4\%$ **b.** $\frac{32}{100} = 0.32 = 32\%$ **c.** $\frac{73}{100} = 0.73 = 73\%$

CHAPTER 7

Problem Set 7.1

2. **a.** $\overline{AC}$ **c.** $\{C\}$ **e.** $\overline{BC}$ **g.** $\overline{AB}$ **i.** ∅

5. **a.** $\overline{AD}, \overline{AB}, \overline{AC}, \overline{AE}, \overline{DC}, \overline{DB}, \overline{DE}, \overline{CE}, \overline{CB},$ and $\overline{EB}$
   b. $\overline{AB}, \overline{AD}, \overline{AE}, \overline{AF}, \overline{AG}, \overline{BD}, \overline{BG}, \overline{BC}, \overline{CE}, \overline{CG}, \overline{CF}, \overline{DE}, \overline{DF}, \overline{DG}, \overline{EF}, \overline{EG},$ and $\overline{FG}$
   c. $\overline{AB}, \overline{AC}, \overline{AG}, \overline{AD}, \overline{AF}, \overline{AE}, \overline{BG}, \overline{BE}, \overline{BC}, \overline{CG}, \overline{CF}, \overline{CD}, \overline{CE}, \overline{DG}, \overline{DE}, \overline{EG},$ $\overline{EF},$ and $\overline{FG}$.

7. **a.** 1, 4, 6   **c.** No

11.

Problem Set 7.2

2. Answers will vary

5. **a.** Yes   **c.** No

7. Yes

9. No

Problem Set 7.3

1. **a.** $\overleftrightarrow{AB}$ (the line could be named other ways)
   c. $\overleftrightarrow{AB}$ **e.** $\overleftrightarrow{BC}$ **g.** ∅   **i.** $\overleftrightarrow{BC}$ **k.** $\overleftrightarrow{BC}$

3. **a.** $\angle GOH$ and $\angle COB$ or $\angle GOC$ and $\angle HOB$ or $\angle FCE$ and $\angle OCB$ or $\angle FCO$ and $\angle ECB$
   c. They do not have a common vertex.

5. ∠*AOB* and ∠*BOC*, ∠*BOC* and ∠*COD*, ∠*AOB* and ∠*BOD*, ∠*AOC* and ∠*COD*

9. No

11. a. 3, 6, 10, 15

Problem Set 7.4

3. a. All except **(ii)** and **(iv)**.

    c. **(i,)**, **(v)**, **(vii)**, **(x)**, and **(xii)**

    e. **(v)**, **(vii)**, and **(x)**

    g. **(vii)** and **(x)**

10. a. 0   **c.** 5   **e.** 14   **g.** 54

11. a. $\overline{CE}$

13. a. Interior   **c.** Exterior

15. a. Yes

16. a. *A*, *G*, and *H*   **c.** *C*, *I*, and *B*   **e.** *D*, *E*, *F*, *J*, *K*, and *L*   **g.** *B* and *C*   **i.** *A*, *E*, *F*, *G*, and *H*   **k.** *E* and *F*   **m.** *J* and *K*

19. a.   **c.** 16

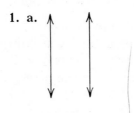

Problem Set 7.5

1. a. 4   **c.** 4

5. Triangular 6, 5, 9
    Pentagonal 10, 7, 15
    Heptagonal 14, 9, 21
    Nineteen-gonal 38, 21, 57

7. a. 129   **c.** 360

15 ↔ : □

Review Problem Set

1. a.   **b.**

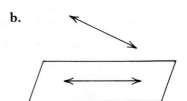

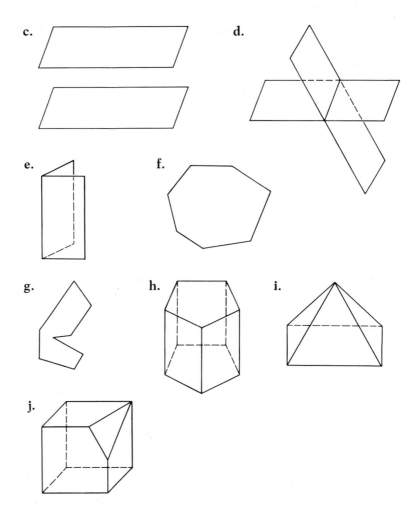

2. **a.** A line segment is the set of all points on a line between two given points, including the two points.

b. A ray is the union of a half-line and the point of separation.

c. A plane angle is the union of two rays with a common endpoint.

d. A simple closed plane curve is a curve in a plane that does not intersect itself and the starting point and the endpoint of the curve is the same point.

e. A polygon is a simple closed polygonal curve.

f. A convex polygon is a polygon, all of whose diagonals, except for their endpoints, are in the interior of the polygon.

g. Vertical plane angles are two plane angles whose sides form two pairs of opposite rays.

h. An octagon is an eight-sided polygon.

     i. An octagonal prism is a prism having octagons for bases.

     j. An octagonal pyramid is a pyramid having an octagon for a base.

3. a. 6   **b.** 8   **c.** 21   **d.** 56   **e.** 442, 444, 446, 448

4. Four points will determine 1, 4, or 6 *lines* depending on the location of the points. Four points will always determine 6 *line segments*.

5. 10

6.
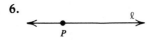
Point *P* is said to separate line *l* because any line segment joining a point on one half-line to a point on the other half-line must intersect *P*.

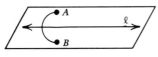
Line *l* is said to separate the plane because any curve joining a point in one half-plane to a point in the other half-plane must intersect *l*.

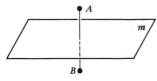
Plane *m* is said to separate space because any curve joining a point in one half-space to a point in the other half-space must intersect the plane *m*.

7. 0; 2; 1

8. a. Yes   **b.** Yes   **c.** No   **d.** No, not if the points are collinear.

CHAPTER 8

Problem Set 8.1

1. a. 100   **c.** 100   **e.** 0.01

2. a. 1700   **c.** 140   **e.** 5000

3. a. 36   **c.** 1760   **e.** $\frac{2}{11}$

4. a. $6\frac{1}{2}$ or 6.5   **c.** $49\frac{1}{2}$ or 49.5   **e.** $1\frac{1}{2}$ or 1.5

5. a. 1.9   **c.** 1.47   **e.** 0.2   **g.** 0.71   **i.** 11.3

6. a. 52   **c.** 640, 64000   **e.** 45.6, 4.56   **g.** 0.03, 0.0003

7. a. Donna

8. a. (ii)   **c.** (i)   **e.** (iii)

9-11. Answers and work will vary

12. a. millimeter   **c.** kilometer   **e.** millimeter   **g.** centimeter

13. 559 millimeters, 88 centimeters, 9.5 decimeters, 4.5 meters, 0.34 kilometers

Problem Set 8.2

1. a. 0.1 m   **c.** 0.001 km   **e.** 0.1 in.

2. a. 5 cm   **c.** 14 ft   **e.** 7.23 cm

3. a. An error of $\frac{1}{2}$ cm in a measurement of 8 cm   c. Same accuracy

4. a. 14π cm   c. 12π dm

5. a. 22 cm; 24.1 cm; 24.24 cm   c. 0.22 m; 0.241 m; 0.2424 m

7. 2π meters (about 6.3 meters)

11. a. 4   c. 3   e. 2

12. a. 51.5 cm   c. 39.6 cm

13. a. $2\pi, 4\pi, 6\pi$ c. 2 × (your height) × π

17. a. 30.4 cm   c. 0.8 m   e. 13.5 cm

19. Height of can and circumference of the ball should be about the same.

20. a. 4π c. 12k-12 = 12(k-1)

Problem Set 8.3

1. No

2. a. $\angle DBC$ c. $\angle DEF$

4. a. False   c. True   e. True   g. True

5. $m\angle 1 = m\angle 4 = m\angle 5 = m\angle 8 = 115°$ and $m\angle 2 = m\angle 3 = m\angle 6 = m\angle 7 = 65°$

6. a. $49°45'$ c. $59°14'45''$ e. $122°59'44''$

7. $74°, 106°, 106°$

9. a. $50°$

10. a. $61°$

11. a. $180°$ c. $540°$ e. $900°$ g. $2340°$

12. a. $60°$ c. $108°$ e. $128\frac{4}{7}°$

13. a. $\overline{AB}$ is shortest, $\overline{BC}$ is longest

15. a. $360°$ c. $360°$ e. 36-gon, $170°$

Problem Set 8.4

Almost all the problems in this set are constructions or measurements oriented that require class discussion.

Problem Set 8.5

1. $\angle D \cong \angle H, \angle E \cong \angle K, \angle F \cong \angle P, \overline{DE} \cong \overline{HK}, \overline{EF} \cong \overline{KP}, \overline{DF} \cong \overline{HP}$

3. $m\angle B = 70°$ and $m\angle C = 40°$

7. Yes

9. a. No

10. a. No

11. a. Yes   b. Yes

12. a. 700 km   c. 15 cm

13. 9 and 12

15. $16\frac{4}{5}$ in.

16. a. $2\frac{1}{3}$

19. **(i)** 2 noncongruent triangles can be formed

   (iii) 1 triangle

   (v) 1 triangle

   (vii) 1 triangle

25. a.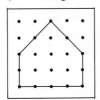

26. a.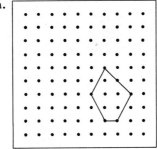

Problem Set 8.6

These problems are of the type that require class discussions.

Problem Set 8.7

2. a. True   **c.** True   **e.** False   **g.** True

3. Yes

9. a. 5   **c.** 10

11. 112

Problem Set 8.8

2. a. 108°   **c.** $128\frac{4}{7}°$ **e.** 144°

7. 20 sides

8. a. Yes   **c.** No   **e.** Yes   **g.** Yes   **i.** Yes

9. a. 0   **c.** 0   **e.** 0   **g.** 3

10. a. 3   **c.** 5   **e.** 7

11. Infinitely many

12. **a.** 120° and 240°   **c.** None   **e.** 180°   **g.** None   **i.** 60°, 120°, 180°, 240°, and 300°   **k.** 45°, 90°, 135°, 180°, 225°, 270°, and 315°

13. **a.** Yes   **c.** Yes   **e.** No   **g.** No   **i.** Yes

15. Only a straight angle has a point of symmetry, but any angle has a line of symmetry—namely, the angle bisector.

17. **a.** 24   **c.** 20

18. **a.** 36   **c.** 50

19. **a.** 8   **c.** 6

20. **a.** 162°   **c.** 175.2°   **e.** 179.2°

Review Problem Set

1. **a.** 1.42   **b.** 3100   **c.** 0.164   **d.** 0.034   **e.** 1400   **f.** 1630

2. A unit of measure of 1 cm is smaller than a unit of measure of 1 m.

3. Accuracy refers to relative error, a comparison of an error to the measurement involved. Precision refers to the unit of measure being used. The smaller the unit of measure the more precision is involved.

4. **a.** 34π cm   **b.** 13π m

5. 165°43′

6. 55°43′50″

9. 1440°

10. **a.** $\overline{XY}$ **b.** $\angle Z$ **c.** $\overline{XZ}$ **d.** $\angle XYZ$

11. 18.2 cm and 26 cm

12. $2\frac{6}{7}$ units

13. **a.** 4   **b.** 2   **c.** 0   **d.** 1   **e.** 6   **f.** 1   **g.** 3

15. 120°

CHAPTER 9

Problem Set 9.1

1. **a.** 4   **c.** 12

2. **a.** 4   **c.** 7   **e.** 8   **g.** 6   **i.** 2   **k.** $16\frac{1}{2}$

6. **a.** Four having an area of 1 square unit, one having an area of 2 square units, and one having an area of 4 square units

7. **a.**

A	3	12	8
B	12	20	21
C	5	16	12
D	9	12	14
E	3	8	6
F	5	14	11
G	7	8	10

c. $A = \frac{1}{2}b + 6$

10. a. 4, 2 triangles **c.** 5, 3 triangles

Problem Set 9.2

1. a. 15 cm^2 **c.** 28 in.^{2} **e.** 131.2 mm^2 or 1.312 cm^2

2. a. 14 m^2 **c.** 8.4 cm^2 **e.** 12 cm^2

3. a. 6

4. a. 576 **c.** 600 **e.** $3\frac{5}{9}$ **g.** 1296 **i.** 0.000001

5. 12 dam

7. $6\frac{6}{7}$ cm

9. a. All the same

10. a. Doubled

11. 575 tiles

13. 1.26 m^2

15. Same area

17. Same area

19. The area of the parallelogram is $h(b_1 + b_2)$. Thus, the area of the one trapezoid is $\frac{1}{2}h(b_1 + b_2)$.

21. a. 7.5 cm **c.** 176.25 m^2

24. a. 80 m^2 **c.** 685,000 km^2 **e.** 102 cm^2

Problem Set 9.3

1. a. No **c.** Yes **e.** No

2. a. 3.6 **c.** 4.5

3. a. $BC = 2$ and $AC = \sqrt{12}$ (3.46) **c.** $AB = 12$ and $AC = \sqrt{108}$ (10.39)

4. a. 7.1 **c.** 4.2

5. 5.7 m

7. 6.9 cm

9. 8 ft

11. No

13. 2.8 cm

15. a. 127.3 ft

17. 12.1 m

19. 20.8 cm

21. 10.8 m

23. 9.8 m

31. a. $\frac{1}{2}ab$ **b.** $\frac{1}{2}ab$ **c.** $\frac{1}{2}c^2$ **d.** $\frac{1}{2}ab + \frac{1}{2}ab + \frac{1}{2}c^2 = ab + \frac{1}{2}c^2$ **e.** $\frac{1}{2}(a + b)(a + b)$

f. $\frac{1}{2}ab + \frac{1}{2}c^2 = \frac{1}{2}a^2 + ab + \frac{1}{2}b^2$
$\frac{1}{2}c^2 = \frac{1}{2}a^2 + \frac{1}{2}b^2$
$c^2 = a^2 + b^2$

Problem Set 9.4

1. 240 cm² **3.** 18 m²

5. $20\sqrt{48}$ in.² (138.6 in²)

7. 14.1 m

9. 44π in.², 36π in.², 28π in.², 20π in.², 16π in.²

10. a. 6 units **c.** 7 units **e.** $\dfrac{r}{2}$

11. a. $3\sqrt{27}$ in.² $(3\sqrt{27} = 9\sqrt{3})$

    c. $2\sqrt{96}$ cm² $(2\sqrt{96} = 8\sqrt{6})$

    e. $8\sqrt{8}$ mm² $(8\sqrt{8} = 16\sqrt{2})$

    g. $2\sqrt{48}$ cm² $(2\sqrt{48} = 8\sqrt{3})$

12. a. 1764 cm² **c.** 45 cm²

15. 201 m²

17. a. 66.6 m² **c.** 642.1 m²

Problem Set 9.5

2. a. 180 in.² **c.** 84 cm²

3. 216 in.²

5. a. 112π m² **c.** 192π cm²

7. a. 4233.0 m² **c.** 5082.9 m²

8. a. 499.2 cm² **c.** 302.8 cm²

13. a. Yes **c.** No

Problem Set 9.6

1. 217 cm²

3. 324π m²

5. 1800 ft²

7. $(234 + 18\sqrt{27})$ cm² (327.5cm²)

11. a. 50 cm² **c.** 1116 m² **e.** 634 ft²

12. a. 509.6 cm² **c.** 445.1 cm²

Problem Set 9.7

1. a. 1600 cm³ **c.** 60 mm³ **e.** $\frac{4000}{3}\pi$ ft³ **g.** 96 cm³

2. a. 165 in.₂

3. a. $\dfrac{20\pi}{9}$ yd^3

5. 792 cm^3

7. 48 cm^3

9. The radius of the cone must be $\sqrt{3}$ times the radius of the cylinder.

11. 6 units

12. a. 31,360 ft^3 **c.** 816π m^3

13. 3165.1 cm^3

15. a. 12242.7 cm^3 **c.** 79027.1 cm^3

16. a. 4   **c.** 0.353

17. a. 250   **c.** 15

Review Problem Set

1. a. 0.0154   **b.** 1400   **c.** 15,000,000   **d.** $\frac{1}{12}$ **e.** $1\frac{5}{9}$

2. 32 cm^2

3. 25π

4. 54 in.^{2}

5. 120 m^2

6. 384 in.^{2}

7. 240π cm^2

8. a. 0.000437   **b.** $1\frac{11}{27}$ **c.** 14,000   **d.** 6912   **e.** 15,300

9. 325 m^3

10. $V = \frac{256}{3}\pi$ m^3, $A = 64\pi$ m^2

11. $\frac{224}{3}$ cm^3

12. a. 0.556   **b.** 0.556   **c.** 345   **d.** 345

CHAPTER 10

Problem Set 10.1

1. a. 10   **c.** $-\left(\frac{11}{2}\right)$ **e.** 6

2. a. IV   **c.** II   **e.** IV

3. a. 0

4. a. I and III   **c.** II and III

5. a. 5   **c.** $\sqrt{200}$ **e.** $\sqrt{82}$

6. a. $\left(\frac{3}{2}, 2\right)$ **c.** (3, 1)   **e.** $\left(\frac{7}{2}, \frac{1}{2}\right)$

7. Lengths are $\sqrt{40}$, $\sqrt{50}$, $\sqrt{50}$. Therefore it is isosceles.

9. All sides are of length $\sqrt{10}$, hence a rhombus.

11. a. Yes   **c.** Yes

13. Two sides are of length $\sqrt{17}$ and the other two are of length $\sqrt{10}$. Thus, it is a parallelogram.

15. Midpoint of each diagonal is $(^-1, \frac{1}{2})$

16. a. $(1, ^-4), (13, 0), (^-9, 6)$ **c.** $(6, 5)$

17. a. Hotdog   **c.** Today   **e.** None

18. a. $2\frac{1}{2}$ square units

Problem Set 10.2

1. a. $\{(2, 6), (2, 2), (2, 4), (4, 4), (4, 6), (6, 6)\}$

3.

C	T
\$10	\$0.70
\$24	\$1.68
\$16	\$1.12
\$ 9	\$0.63

5. a.

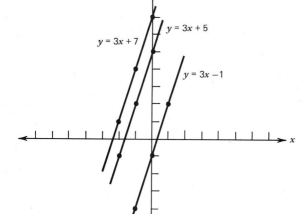

7. a.

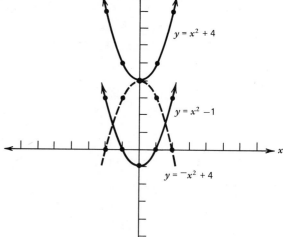

9. a.
b.

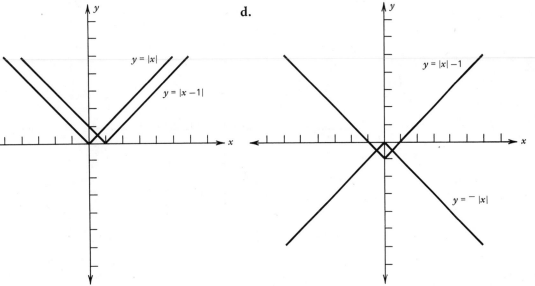

c.
d.

10. a.

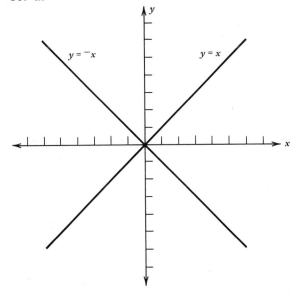

c.

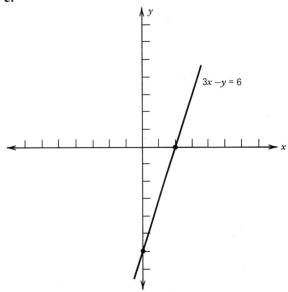

e.

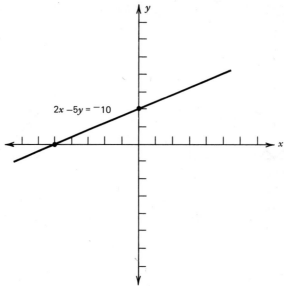

$2x - 5y = {}^-10$

11. a.

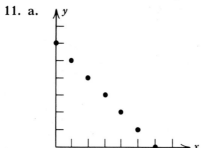

c.

e.

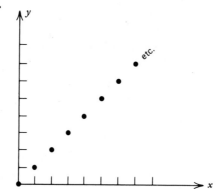

etc.

Problem Set 10.3

1. a. $\frac{3}{4}$ c. $^-(\frac{3}{4})$ e. 0   g. 1

3. 7

5. a. Parallel   c. Perpendicular   e. Intersecting lines that are not perpendicular.

7. All four sides are of length $\sqrt{116}$ units. The slope of $\overline{DA}$ is $^-(\frac{5}{2})$ and the slope of $\overline{DC}$ is $\frac{2}{5}$. Therefore, it is a rhombus with a right angle, which means that it is a square.

9. a. The slope of $\overline{BA}$ is 4 and the slope of $\overline{CD}$ is 4. The slope of $\overline{BC}$ is $^-(\frac{1}{4})$ and the slope of $\overline{AD}$ is $^-(\frac{1}{4})$. Therefore it is a parallelogram. Furthermore, because the slope of $\overline{BA}$ is a negative reciprocal of the slope of $\overline{BC}$, there is a right angle at B. Thus, it is a rectangle because it is a parallelogram with a right angle.
   b. area is 34 square units

11. All four sides are of length $\sqrt{20}$ units. Therefore, it is a rhombus.

Problem Set 10.4

1.   3.

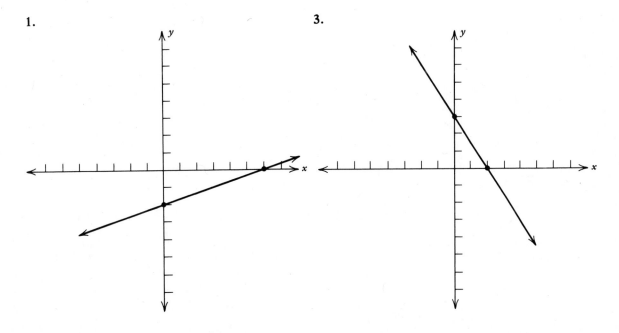

5.

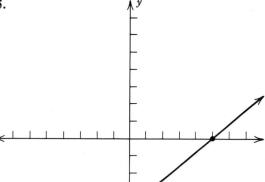

7.

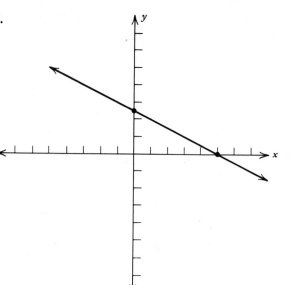

9.

11.

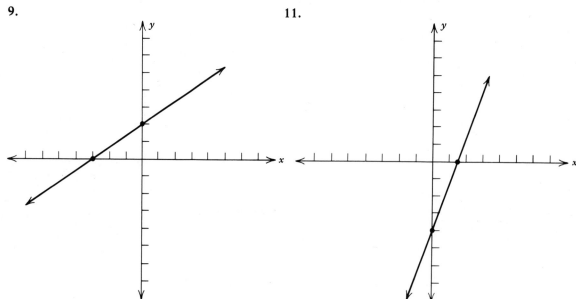

13.

15.

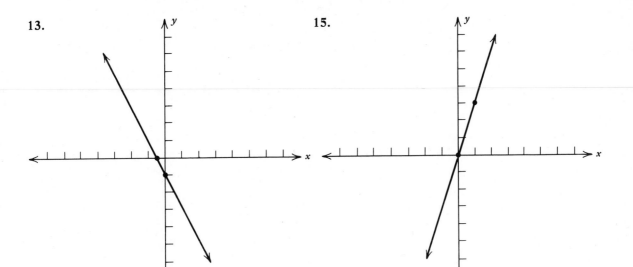

17.

19.

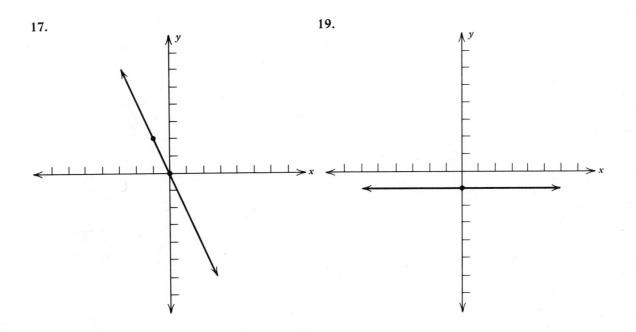

21.

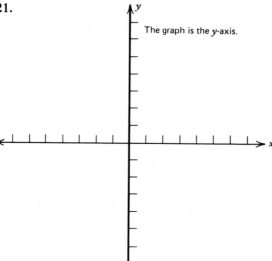

The graph is the *y*-axis.

23.

a. 2

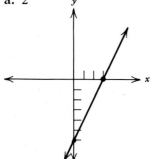

c. $^{-}\left(\frac{3}{5}\right)$

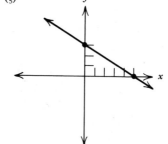

e. 2

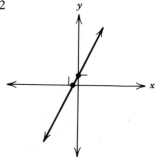

g. $^{-}1$

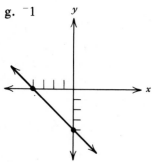

i. $\frac{2}{3}$

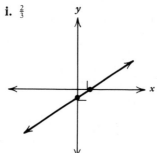

k. 0

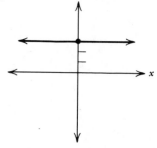

24. **a.** Parallel   **c.** Perpendicular   **e.** Intersecting lines that are not perpendicular

25. Slope is $-\dfrac{A}{B}$, y-intercept is $\dfrac{C}{B}$, x-intercept is $\dfrac{C}{A}$

26. **a.** \$85, \$75, \$235, $25 + 30n$ **c.** \$2.55, \$3.75, \$6.75, $0.75 + 0.60n$
    e. \$0.88, \$1.51, $0.25 + (n - 1)(0.21)$

Problem Set 10.5

1. **a.** $2x - 3y = {}^-14$ **c.** $2x - y = {}^-2$ **e.** $3x + 5y = {}^-14$
   g. $y = {}^-4$

2. **a.** $2x - y = 1$ **c.** $3x + 5y = 19$ **e.** $9x - 4y = {}^-6$ **g.** $y = 4$

3. **a.** $x - 5y = {}^-10$ **c.** $4x + 5y = 5$ **e.** $3x - y = 1$

4. **a.** $y = \frac{3}{7}x + 5$ **c.** $y = {}^-(\frac{3}{2}x) - 1$ **e.** $y = \frac{3}{4}$

5. **a.** $5x + 2y = 10$ **c.** $y = {}^-3$ **e.** $y = 5$

6. **a.** Parallel   **c.** Parallel   **e.** Perpendicular   **g.** Intersecting lines that are not perpendicular

7. **a.** $2x - y = 0$ **c.** $4x + 5y = 12$ **e.** $x - y = 1$ **g.** $7x + 4y = 13$

9.

a.

c.

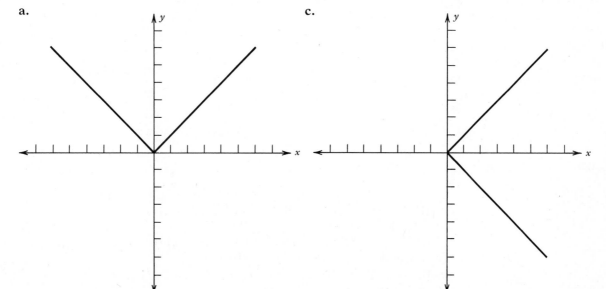

11.

a. (i)

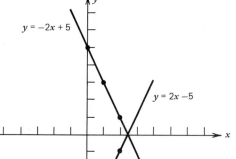

(ii)

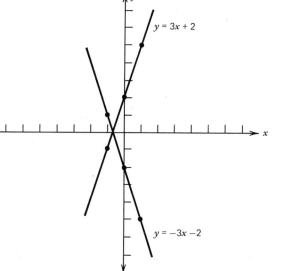

(iii)

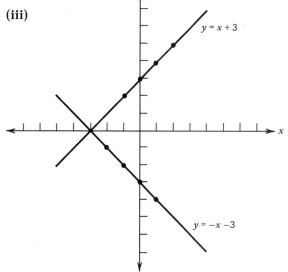

c. always intersect at $y = 0$

12. a. (i) $(3, {}^-5)$ **(ii)** $({}^-2, {}^-4)$ **(iii)** $(5, 2)$ **(iv)** $({}^-2, 6)$
      (v) $(4 \; {}^-4)$ **(vi)** $(x, {}^-y)$
      c. (i) $(5, 3)$ **(ii)** $(4, {}^-2)$ **(iii)** $({}^-2, 5)$ **(iv)** $({}^-6, {}^-2)$ **(v)** $(4, 4)$
      (vi) (y, x)
      e. (i) $({}^-3, {}^-5)$ **(ii)** $(2, {}^-4)$ **(iii)** $({}^-5, 2)$ **(iv)** $(2, 6)$
      (v) $({}^-4, {}^-4)$ **(vi)** $({}^-x, {}^-y)$

13.

a.

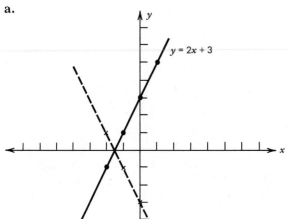

c.

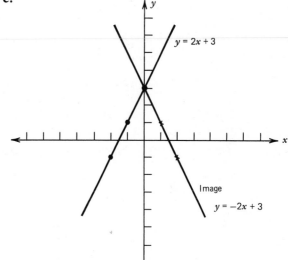

14.

a.

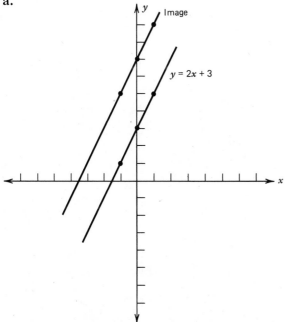

15. a. "Top" line—out of county nonmember

"Middle" line—in county nonmember

c. $7

Review Problem Set

1. The slope of $\overline{AB}$ is $\frac{1}{3}$ and the slope of $\overline{BC}$ is $^-3$. Because these two slopes are negative reciprocals of each other, there is a right angle at B and it is a right triangle.

2. (7,0)

3. The slope of $\overline{AD}$ is $^-4$ and the slope of $\overline{BC}$ is $^-4$. The slope of $\overline{AB}$ is $\frac{2}{5}$ and the slope of $\overline{DC}$ is $\frac{2}{5}$. Thus, both pairs of opposite sides are parallel and it is a parallelogram.

4. $\frac{1}{7}$

5. a. Parallel   **b.** Intersecting lines that are not perpendicular

c. Perpendicular

6. a.

b.

7.

a.   **b.**

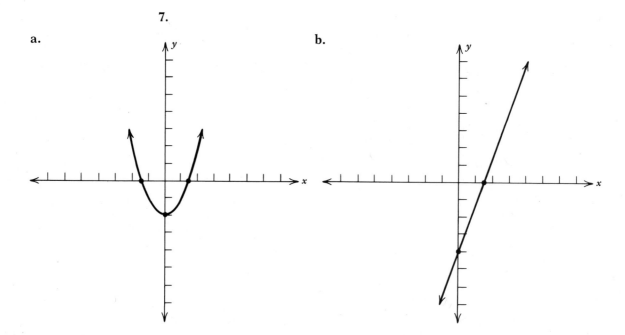

c.

d.

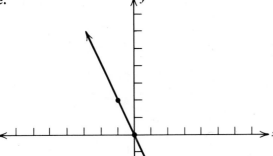
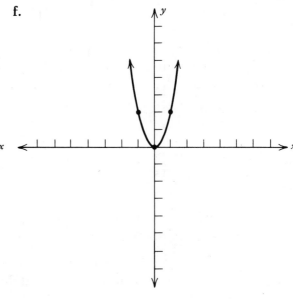

e.

f.

8. $\frac{2}{3}$

9. Perpendicular

10. $2x - 5y = {}^-34$

11. $x + 4y = 18$

12. $m = \frac{5}{3}$ and $b = {}^-\left(\frac{7}{3}\right)$

13. $3x - y = 1$

14. $3x - 4y = 34$

15. a. $(4, 1)$ **b.** $(^-4, ^-1)$ **c.** $(^-1, 4)$ **d.** $(1, ^-4)$

16. $(3, ^-5)$

17. $(^-5, ^-3)$

18. $y = ^-2x - 5$

19. $31.50, \$38.40, \$66, 20 + 0.23n$

CHAPTER 11

Problem Set 11.1

1. a. $\frac{2}{4}$ **c.** $\frac{3}{4}$

2. a. $\frac{1}{8}$ **c.** $\frac{7}{8}$

3. a. $\frac{1}{16}$ **c.** $\frac{4}{16}$ **e.** $\frac{15}{16}$

5. a. TT, FF, TF, FT—4 ways; $\frac{1}{4}$ probability of getting 100%

6. a. $\frac{1}{4}$ **c.** $\frac{1}{4}$

7. a. $\frac{1}{6}$ **c.** $\frac{3}{6}$ **e.** 0

8. a. $\frac{5}{36}$ **c.** $\frac{6}{36}$ **e.** $\frac{11}{36}$

9. a. 12   **c.** $\frac{5}{12}$

10. a. (i) $\frac{3}{6} = \frac{1}{2}$ **(ii)** $\frac{2}{6} = \frac{1}{3}$ **(iii)** $\frac{1}{6}$

11. a. $\frac{13}{52}$ **c.** $\frac{26}{52}$

12. a. $\frac{1}{25}$ **c.** $\frac{9}{25}$

13. a. $\frac{10}{23}$ **c.** $\frac{13}{23}$

14. a. $\frac{11}{75}$ **c.** $\frac{18}{75}$ **e.** $\frac{7}{75}$

15. $\frac{2}{6}$

17. a. $\frac{1}{26}$ **c.** $\frac{21}{26}$

18. a. $\frac{4}{10}$ **c.** $\frac{9}{10}$

19. $\frac{1}{5}$

21. $\frac{15}{21}$

23. Both are correct and this type of problem leads into a discussion of different sample spaces for the same problem.

24. a. $\frac{5}{16}$ **c.** $\frac{8}{20}$

25. a.   **c.** 42%

28. c. (i) sum < 8 **(ii)** sum $= 6$ **(iii)** sum $= 7$ **(iv)** sum < 7
    (v) sum < 12 **(vi)** sum is 5, 6, or 7

29. Fair game

30. a. $\frac{3}{8}$ **c.** yes; 8 purple, 12 gold, 12 white

Problem Set 11.2

1.

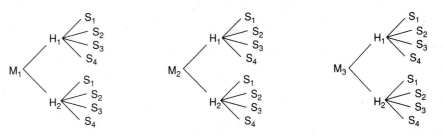

$3 \times 2 \times 4 = 24$ choices

3. a. 21   **c.** 105

5. 32

7. 42

9. 840

11. 24

13. $26 \times 9 \times 10 = 2340$

14. a. $\frac{1}{12}$ **c.** $\frac{3}{12}$

15. $\frac{3}{8}$

16. $\frac{3}{36}$

17. $\frac{3}{216}$

19. $\frac{3}{12}$

21. $\frac{120}{210}$

23. $\frac{2}{6}$

25. a. 1 way for 3 heads, 3 ways for 2 heads and 1 tail, 3 ways for 1 head
    and 2 tails, and 1 way for 3 tails

    c. 1 way each

    e. 6

    g. 1 4 6 4 1

27. Good discussion question

29. a. (i) $\frac{1}{32}$ **(ii)** $\frac{10}{32}$ **(iii)** $\frac{5}{32}$ **(iv)** $\frac{1}{32}$

30. a. $\frac{3}{16}$ **c.** $\frac{6}{144}$

31. a.

$\{YY,YY,YY,YB,YY,YY,YY,YB,YY,YY,YY,YB,BY,BY,BY,BB\}$

b. (i) $\frac{1}{16}$ **(ii)** $\frac{3}{16}$ **(iii)** $\frac{3}{16}$ **(iv)** $\frac{9}{16}$ **(v)** $\frac{1}{4}$ **(vi)** $\frac{3}{4}$

33. No

Problem Set 11.3

1. a. $\frac{5}{36}$ **c.** $\frac{21}{36}$

2. a. $\frac{1}{216}$ **c.** $\frac{212}{216}$

3. $\frac{30}{36}$

4. a. $\frac{1}{16}$ **c.** $\frac{15}{16}$

5. a. $\frac{1}{32}$ **c.** $\frac{31}{32}$

7. $\frac{48}{52}$

9. $\frac{21}{36}$

11. $\frac{45}{66}$

13. 240

15. 504

17. 36

19. 12!

21. 30

23. 212

24. a. 6   **c.** 210

25. $_{52}C_7$

27. 45

29. 21

31. 480

32. a. 10

33. a. 21   **c.** equal

34. a. 1—$\emptyset$

       4—$\{A\}, \{B\}, \{C\}, \{D\}$

       6—$\{AB\}, \{AC\}, \{AD\}, \{BC\}, \{BD\}, \{CD\}$

       4—$\{BCD\}, \{ACD\{, \{ABD\}, \{ABC\}$

       1—$\{ABCD\}$

c.   1   8   28   56   70   56   28   8   1

      1   9   36   84   126   126   84   36   9   1

35. $\frac{12}{24}$

37. $\frac{26}{36}$

39. $\frac{212}{216}$

41. $\frac{5}{15}$

43. $\frac{10}{55}$

47. a. 6   **c.** 1

Problem Set 11.4

1. a. $\frac{6}{25}$ **c.** $\frac{4}{5}$ **e.** $\frac{12}{25}$

2. a. $\frac{20}{110}$ **c.** $\frac{90}{110}$

3. a. $\frac{4}{6}$ **c.** 0

4. a. $\frac{20}{272}$ **c.** $\frac{120}{272}$

5. a. $\frac{4}{21}$ **c.** $\frac{11}{21}$

7. a. $\{(R, 1), (R, 2), (R, 3), (R, 4), (R, 5), (R, 6), (W, 1), (W, 2), (W, 3), (W, 4),$
$(W, 5), (W, 6), (G, 1), (G, 2), (G, 3), (G, 4), (G, 5), (G, 6)\}$

    c. $\frac{1}{3}$

    e. $\frac{1}{2}$

    g. $\frac{1}{6}$

8. a. $\{1, 2, 3, 4, 5, 6, 7, 8, 9, 10, 11, 12\}$

    c. $\{(R, 3), (R, 8), (B, 2), (R, 7), (R, 1), (Y, 12), (Y, 6), (Y, 11), (B, 5),$
$(B, 10), (R, 4), (Y, 9)\}$

9. a. $\frac{8}{12}$ **c.** $\frac{7}{12}$ **e.** $\frac{6}{12}$ **g.** $\frac{8}{12}$ **i.** $\frac{4}{12}$ **k.** $\frac{2}{12}$

10. a. $\frac{7}{20}$ **c.** $\frac{3}{20}$ **e.** $\frac{4}{20}$ **g.** $\frac{13}{20}$ **i.** $\frac{14}{20}$

11. a. 30

    b. (i) $\frac{17}{30}$ **(iii)** $\frac{15}{30}$ **(v)** $\frac{8}{17}$ **(vii)** $\frac{4}{17}$

Problem Set 11.5

1. 5 to 4; 4 to 5

3. $\frac{2}{7}$

5. a. $\frac{7}{11}$ **c.** $\frac{1}{5}$

6. a. 3 to 1   **c.** 1 to 1   **e.** 11 to 2

7. a. 1 to 11   **c.** 31 to 5

8. a. 12 to 1 against and 1 to 12 in favor

    c. 3 to 1 against and 1 to 3 in favor

    e. 1 to 1 against and 1 to 1 in favor

9. a. 7 to 1

11. 40

13. 3

15. 10

17. Yes

19. $3.50

21. No

Review Problem Set

1. $\frac{3}{8}$

2. $\frac{5}{36}$

3. $\frac{3}{6}$ **4.** $\frac{3}{12}$ **5.** $\frac{40}{120}$

6. $\frac{24}{120}$ **7.** $\frac{26}{36}$ **8.** $\frac{10}{21}$

9. $\frac{25}{28}$ **10.** $\frac{24}{49}$ **11.** $\frac{30}{72}$

12. 210   **13.** 84   **14.** 5 to 2; 2 to 5

15. 1 to 8   **16.** 250   **17.** 0

CHAPTER 12

Problem Set 12.1

1. a.

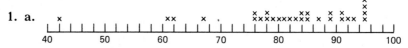

Highest 99; lowest 42; clusters between 76 and 95, inclusive

2. a. elephant

c.

Longevity	Frequency
0–4	3
5–9	8
10–14	10
15–19	7
20–24	5
25–29	2
30–34	0
35–39	1

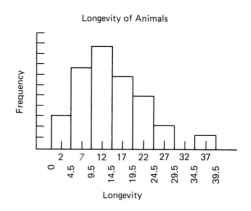

3.

Test I	Stem	Test II
5	5	
5 2 6	6	
8 6 9 4 1	7	0 3 0 6 9
2 6 5 2 8 8 9 9 5	8	5 4 3 5 2 5 4 4
6 1 1 8 9 8	9	0 9 5 1 4 4 0 6 6 1 2

a. Test II

5. 41

7.

a.

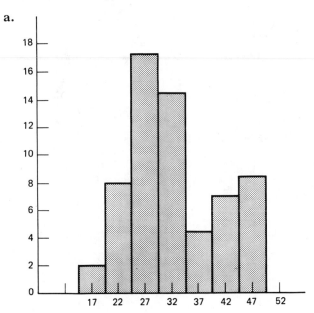

c.

Scores	Cumulative Frequency
Less than 14.5	0
Less than 19.5	2
Less than 24.5	10
Less than 29.5	27
Less than 34.5	41
Less than 39.5	45
Less than 44.5	52
Less than 49.5	60

8. a. 24

c.

Daily Temperatures

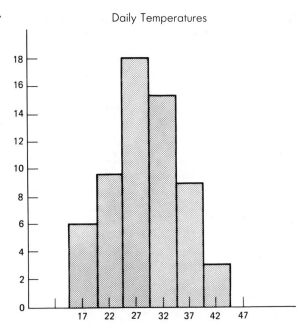

9.

a.

Intervals	Tallies	Frequency
40 to 45	//	2
46 to 51	//	2
52 to 57	TH	5
58 to 63	/	1
64 to 69	TH ///	8
70 to 75	TH TH /	11
76 to 81	TH TH TH ////	19
82 to 87	TH TH TH TH TH TH ////	34
88 to 93	TH TH ///	13
94 to 99	TH	5
		Total 100

b. and c.

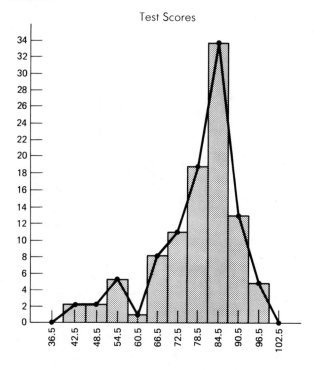

Test Scores

10. Answers will vary for this problem depending on the size of interval used. Ten intervals of size 9 would be "reasonable," but certainly there are other possibilities.

11.

Scores	Cumulative Frequency
More than 36.5	60
More than 43.5	58
More than 50.5	52
More than 57.5	46
More than 64.5	41
More than 71.5	31
More than 78.5	19
More than 85.5	10
More than 92.5	3
More than 99.5	0

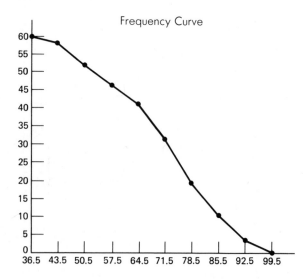

Frequency Curve

Problem Set 12.2

1. Final Grades

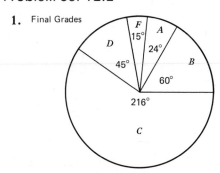

5. The length of the radius of the large circle is twice the length of the radius of the small circle. This makes the area of the large circle *four* times the area of the small circle and misrepresents the doubling of the number of employees.

7.

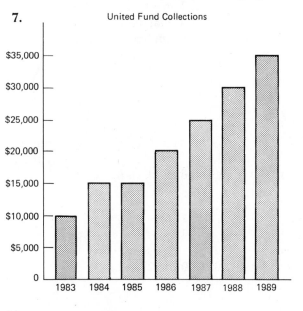

United Fund Collections

9.

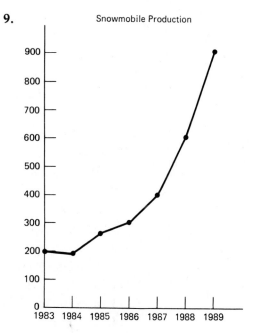

Snowmobile Production

11.

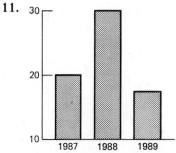

11. The 1988 bar is now twice as long as the 1987 bar and a little more than twice as long as the 1989 bar. This misrepresents the figures.

13. 100; 50; 150; 50; 75; 45; 30

Problem Set 12.3

1. a. Mean $\doteq$ 7.2, median is 4, mode is 2.
   c. Mean $\doteq$ 7.3, median is 5.5, mode is 2.
   e. Mean $\doteq$ 16.4, median is 14, mode is 14.

3. a. 37

9. a. 2460   **c.** 87

13. Approximately 54.1

14. a. Approximately 58.2   **c.** Approximately 85.7

15. a. 77.6   **c.** 77.5

16. a. 83.7   **c.** 83.4

17. a.

Stem	Leaf
11	0 57
12	0 23:57889
13	0:012345:6778
14	8
15	2

c. Lower extreme 110
Upper extreme 152
Median 130
First quartile 124
Third quartile 135.5

Problem Set 12.4

1. a. 5.0   **c.** 8.1   **e.** 46.5

2. a. 6.0

3. 6.1

5. b. Both sets of scores have the same standard deviation of $\sqrt{2}$.

7. a. 76.7 and 5.2   **c.** 54.5 and 21.3

8. a. 87.4

9. a. 78.2

10. a. 202.6

11. c. 6.8 for Class A, 21.8 for Class B, and 7.0 for Class C

12. a. 74.5 for Team A and 79.0 for Team B

13. a. Remains the same

14. a. The mean and standard deviation are also multiplied by the same constant.

Problem Set 12.5

1. a. (i) 80 to 90   **b. (ii)** 75 to 95   **c. (iii)** 70 to 100

3. a. 682   **c.** 998

4. a. 1364   **c.** 1996

5. a. 341   **c.** 682   **e.** 818

6. a. 341   **c.** 477   **e.** 976
7. a. 954   **c.** 44   **e.** 272
8. a. 477   **c.** 385   **e.** 136   **g.** 743
9. a. 192   **c.** 241   **e.** 253   **g.** 546
10. a. 576   **c.** 723   **e.** 501   **g.** 2748

Problem Set 12.6

These questions require class discussion.

Review Problem Set

1.   Test Grades

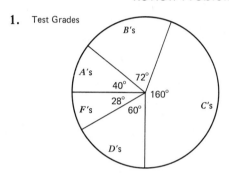

2.   University Budget

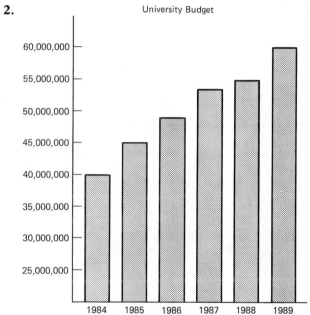

3. a.

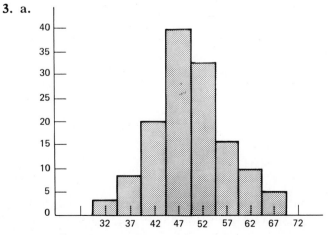

b.

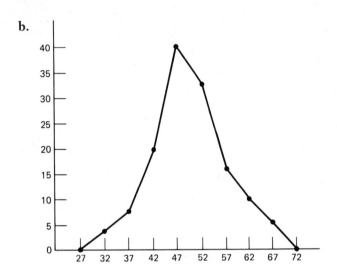

c.

Scores	Cumulative Frequency
Less than 29.5	0
Less than 34.5	3
Less than 39.5	11
Less than 44.5	31
Less than 49.5	71
Less than 54.5	103
Less than 59.5	119
Less than 64.5	129
Less than 69.5	134

d.

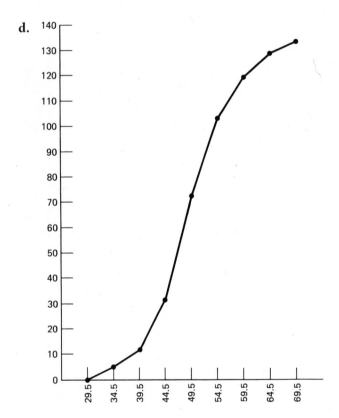

4. a. Mean is approximately 12.2, the median is 13, and the mode is 13.
   b. Mean is approximately 14.7, the median is 11, and the mode is 7.

5.

Stem	Leaf
3	0 8 1 4 8 9 2
4	0 2 6 9 9
5	3 6 4 1 3 8 2
6	5 9
7	2
8	
9	1

a.	Largest value	91	**b.**	Median	49
	Smallest value	30		Upper extreme	91
	Outlier	91		Lower extreme	30
	Cluster	30–60		Lower quartile	39
	Gap	73–90		Upper quartile	58

6. 29.6

7. 3.7

8. a. 682   **b.** 136   **c.** 818   **d.** 22   **e.** 158

9. a. 516   **b.** 972   **c.** 456   **d.** 928   **e.** 1498

CHAPTER 13

Problem Set 13.1

1. 64

3. a. 10:59

5. 100 mL

7. 133

9. $\frac{1}{3}$

10. a. Yes   **c.** Yes   **e.** Yes

11. 4

13. No

15. 36

17. a. 12 values

19. 30 meters

21. Yes

23. All are possible.

25. Value of   is 6,   is 4, and   is 9.

27. 2π meters

29. Same

31. Same

32. a. Either   **c.** Always odd   **e.** Either

33. 8 square units

35. Three belong to only chess, 10 to only math, and 12 to both.

37. 48

39. a. π meters

40. a. 4   **c.** $2(n - 1)$

41. a. 5   **c.** $2(n - 1) + 1$

42. a. $\frac{5}{9}$ **c.** $\frac{4}{9}$

43. a. 20.25 square units   **c.** 14 square units

45. $\frac{1}{20}$ receive Ds; therefore, 200 study mathematics.

47. 63:100

48. a. 5:14   **c.** 5:14

49. 100 students; 60 mathematics majors

51. 25 meters

53. $\overline{BC}$

55. AC

56. a. 65.75 cm

57. $4\sqrt{2}$

59. 45

61. a. 6

Problem Set 13.2

1. a. $\frac{1023}{1024}$ **c.** 3280   **e.** $\frac{1093}{2187}$

3. a. 3   **c.** 3

5. B

7. 30 digits

9. 18001

11. a. $\frac{250}{27}$ meters

12. a. 900 paintings

13. $2^{14} - 1$

14. a. $2 \times (22222225 + 22222223)$

    c. $4 \times (22222225 + 22222221)$

Problem Set 13.3

2. a. 2   **c.** 8   **e.** 10   **g.** 3   **i.** 8   **k.** 12   **m.** 12   **o.** 12
    q. 3   **s.** No solution   **u.** No solution

3. a. 8   **c.** 6, 12   **e.** 1   **g.** 7   **j.** 1

Problem Set 13.4

1. a. 1   **c.** 3   **e.** 4   **g.** 4

2. a. 2   **c.** 4   **e.** 4   **g.** 6   **i.** 5   **k.** 1   **m.** 5

Problem Set 14.1

1. **a.** Computer response:
   THERE IS NO PROCEDURE NAMED FD30

   b. Turtle moves forward
      60 turtle steps.

   c. Turtle makes complete turn while remaining in the same location on
      the screen. SETH 360 and SETH 0 result in the same Heading.

   d. Turtle turns 20 degrees from HOME or 0 position.

   e. Computer response:
      YOU DON'T SAY WHAT TO DO WITH 0
      (or the number that represents the current heading)
   f. Computer response:
      RESULT: 20
      PD does not require a number to follow it.
   g. This is the Turtle's position provided it was located at HOME initially.

   h. This is the Turtle's position, provided the Turtle's initial position was
      HOME.

2. **a.** (i)   (ii)   (iii)   (iv) −13   (v) −25

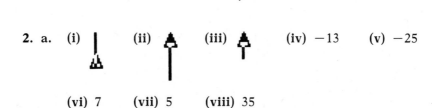

   (vi) 7   (vii) 5   (viii) 35

(ix) The Turtle makes one complete turn and remains in the same place.

(x)

3. a.

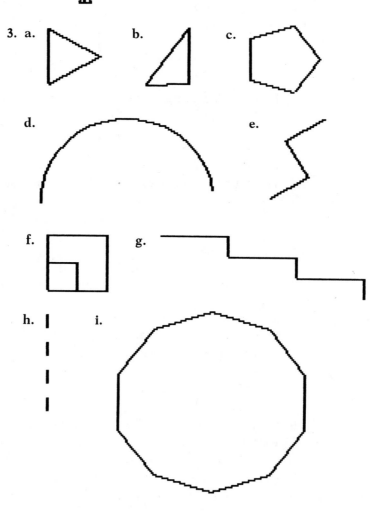

b.

c.

d.

e.

f.

g.

h.

i.

4. a. FD 20   RT 90   FD 25   RT 90   FD 30
      RT 90   FD 35   RT 90   FD 40   RT 90
      FD 45   RT 90   FD 50   RT 90   FD 55

5. a. 100   b. 90   c. 150   d. 360   e. 80
   f. 20   g. 120   h. 0   i. 0   j. 6

6. a. 0   **c.** 120   **e.** 0

7. 240 × 280

9. REPEAT 5 [FD 30 RT 144]

11. REPEAT 36 [FD 10 RT 10] or
REPEAT 360 [FD 1 RT 1]
Answers may vary as long as the number following REPEAT × the number following RT equals 360.

12. a. RT 45   **c.** LT 135

13. Answers will vary. Some possible answers follow.
Acute angle: FD 40 RT 120 FD 40
(RT or LT must be > 90.)
Right angle: FD 40 RT 90 FD 40
Obtuse angle: FD 40 RT 60 FD 40
(RT or LT must be < 90.)

15. a. Answers may vary. One possible set of commands follows
RT 90
FD 50
RT 60
FD 50
RT 120
FD 50

b. Answers may vary
RT 90
FD 50
RT 120
FD 50
LT 120
FD 50

c. The sum of the two right turns equals 180.

d. The right and left turns require the same number of degrees.

e. In (a) the turns were made so the Turtle was facing in the opposite direction. The sum of the two turns was 180. In (b) the right and left turns were the same, so the Turtle faced the same direction in which it began.

f. In (a) we see that interior angles on the same side of the transversal are supplementary. In (b) we can see that alternate interior angles are equal.

20. 6
Hexagon angles are 120°:
Trapezoid angles are 60° and 120°.
Rhombus angles are 60° and 120°.
Kite angles are 30° and 150°.

21. a. Interior angle of the hexagon is 120°.

   c. Interior angles of the rhombus are 60° and 120° and corresponding exterior angles are 120° and 60°.

Problem Set 14.2

1. a. Answers may vary.

```
TO TRI
  RT 30
  REPEAT 3 [FD 30 RT 120]
END
```

  b.
```
TO RHOM
  RT 30
  REPEAT 2 [FD 30 RT 120 FD 30 RT 60]
END
```

  c.
```
TO TRAP
  RT 30
  REPEAT 2 [FD 30 RT 60]
  FD 30 RT 120 FD 60 RT 120
END
```

  d.
```
TO HEX
  RT 30
  REPEAT 6 [FD 30 RT 60]
END
```

  e.
```
TO KITE
  RT 15
  REPEAT 2 [FD 30 RT 150 FD 30 RT 30]
END
```

  f.
```
TO SQ
  REPEAT 4 [FD 30 RT 90]
END
```

3.
```
TO REC
  REPEAT 2 [FD 30 RT 90 FD 50 RT 90]
END

TO REC !S1 !S2
  REPEAT 2 [FD !S1 RT 90 FD !S2 RT 90]
END
```

4. a. PARALLELOGRAM 20 20 90

  c. PARALLELOGRAM 30 60 90

  e. PARALLELOGRAM 60 60 90

     The area will be 9 times larger

  g. PARALLELOGRAM 45 90 90

     The area is 2.25 times as large.

5. Answers will vary. The product of the two inputs will be equal to the perimeter.

6. Possible answers:

a.
```
TO SPIN.TRI
   REPEAT 6 [TRI RT 60]
END
```

c.
```
TO TRI.PLUS
   TRI
   SPIN.TRI
   RT 180
   TRI
END
```

e.
```
TO DESIGN1
   REPEAT 12 [TRI RT 360/12]
END
```

7. The answers to a–e use the PARAR and PARAL procedures listed below. Possible answers:

```
TO PARAR !L !W !A
  REPEAT 2 [FD !L RT !A FD !W RT 180 − !A]
END

TO PARAL !L !W !A
  REPEAT 2 [FD !L LT !A FD !W LT 180 − !A]
END
```

a.
```
TO PARA1
   PARAR 35 60 70
   PU BK 70 PD
   PARAR 35 60 70
END
```

b.
```
TO PARA2
   PARAR 35 60 70
   PARAL 35 60 70
END
```

c.
```
TO PARA3
   PARAR 60 35 70
   PARAL 60 35 70
END
```

d.
```
TO PARA4
   PARAR 80 40 110
   FD 40
   PARAL 40 80 110
END
```

e.
```
TO PARA5
   REPEAT 6 [PARA 40 80 60 RT 60]
END
```

8. Possible answers:

a.
```
TO TRI
   REPEAT 3 [FD 30 RT 120]
END

TO TRI.L
   REPEAT 3 [FD 30 LT 120]
END
```

```
TO TRI.PARA
  TRI
  TRI.L
END
```

c. ```
   TO TRAP.PARA
     TRI.PARA
     RT 60
     TRI
   END
   ```

9. Possible procedures are listed.

   a. ```
      TO STAR
        REPEAT 6 [TRI RT 60 FD 30]
      END
      ```

   b. ```
      TO PENT
        REPEAT 5 [FD 30 RT 360/5]
      END
      ```

      ```
      TO SPIN.PENT
        REPEAT 10 [POLY 5 RT 36]
      END
      ```

   c. ```
      TO SPIN.TRI.RHOM
        REPEAT 6 [RHOM RT 60]
        REPEAT 6 [TRI RT 60]
      END
      ```

   d. ```
      TO SPIN.TRAP
        REPEAT 6 [TRAP RT 120 FD 30 LT 60]
      END
      ```

   e. ```
      TO PARA :L :W :A
        REPEAT 2 [FD :L RT :A FD :W RT 180 — :A]
      END
      ```

      ```
      TO PARAL :L :W :A
        REPEAT 2 [FD :L LT :A FD :W LT 180 — :A]
      END
      ```

      ```
      TO PAR.FENCE :X :L :W :A
        REPEAT :X [PARAL :L :W :A FD :L]
        BK :X * :L
        REPEAT :X [PARA :L :W :A FD :L]
      END
      ```

      ```
      TO PAR.FENCES :X :L :W :A
        PAR.FENCE :X :L :W :A
      ```

```
            BK 80 RT 60 FD 35 RT 60 FD 35 LT 120
            PAR.FENCE :X :L :W :A
            END
```

10. Possible solutions:

    a.
```
      TO PAR.Z.LINE :S :A
        RT 90
        FD :S RT :A FD :S LT :A FD :S
      END
          i. PARA.Z.LINE 50 60
        (ii) PARA.Z.LINE 50 90
       (iii) PARA.Z.LINE 50 150
```

11. Although answers will vary, some possible answers are given. The sum of numbers following FD should equal one half of the perimeter.

    a.
```
      TO REC
        REPEAT 2 [FD 60 RT 90 FD 30 RT 90]
      END

      TO REC
        REPEAT 2 [FD 45 RT 90 FD 45 RT 90]
      END

      TO REC
        REPEAT 2 [FD 10 RT 90 FD 80 RT 90]
      END

      TO REC
        REPEAT 2 [FD 30.5 RT 90 FD 59.5 RT 90]
      END
```

    b.
```
      TO REC
        REPEAT 2 [FD 100 RT 90 FD 25 RT 90]
      END

      TO REC
        REPEAT 2 [FD 33 RT 90 FD 92 RT 90]
      END
```

    c.
```
      TO REC
        REPEAT 2 [FD 20 RT 90 FD 79.5 RT 90]
      END

      TO REC
        REPEAT 2 [FD 65.25 RT 90 FD 34.25 RT 90]
      END
```

    d.
```
      TO REC
        REPEAT 2 [FD 60 RT 90 FD 4.5 RT 90]
      END
```

```
TO REC
  REPEAT 2 [FD 34.5 RT 90 FD 30 RT 90]
END


TO REC :P :L
  REPEAT 2 [FD :L RT 90 FD ( :P/2 - :L)
RT 90]
END
```

12. a. REPEAT 30 determines the width of the filled rectangle

13. Possible answers are listed:
    a.
    ```
    TO REC2 :A :L
      REPEAT 2 [FD :L RT 90 FD :A/ :L RT 90]
    END


    REC2 1800 90 perimeter is 220
    REC2 1800 24 perimeter is 198
    REC2 1800 18.75 perimeter is 229.5
    REC2 1800 40 perimeter is 180
    ```
    b.
    ```
    TO FILL.REC
      REPEAT 18.75 [FD 96 BK 96 RT 90 FD 1
    LT 90]
    END
    ```
    c. Use REC2 procedure from (a). Try inputs such as the following:
    ```
    REC2 960 34.122
    REC2 983 7.5
    REC2 225 (-60)
    ```
    d.
    ```
    TO FILL.REC :A :L
      REPEAT :L [FD :A/ :L BK :A/ :L RT 90
            FD 1 LT 90]
    END
    ```

14. Possible solutions:
    ```
    TO HEXAGON
      REPEAT 6 [FD 30 RT 60]
    END


    TO TRI
      REPEAT 3 [FD 30 RT 120]
    END


    TO TRAPEZOID
      REPEAT 2 [FD 30 RT 60]
      FD 30 RT 120 FD 60 RT 120
    END
    ```

```
TO TRAPEZOID.LEFT
 REPEAT 2 [FD 30 LT 60]
 FD 30 LT 120 FD 60 LT 120
END
```

a.
```
TO SHAPE1
   RT 30
   HEXAGON
   FD 30
   TRI
   RT 180
   TRAPEZOID
   LT 120
   FD 30
   RT 60
   TRAPEZOID.LEFT
  END
```

```
  TO RHOMBUS.LEFT
   REPEAT 2  [FD 30 LT 60  FD 30 LT 120]
  END
```

```
  TO KITE
   REPEAT 2 [FD 30 RT 30 FD 30 RT 150]
  END
```

```
  TO TRI.LEFT
   REPEAT 3 [FD 30 RT 120]
  END
```

```
  TO RHOMBUS
   REPEAT 2 [FD 30 RT 60 FD 30 RT 120]
  END
```

c.
```
TO SHAPE3
   RT 30
   HEXAGON
   RHOMBUS.LEFT
   RT 45
   KITE
   RT 75
   FD 30
   TRI.LEFT
   FD 30 LT 120 FD 60 LT 60
   RHOMBUS
  END
```

15. Possible solutions:
```
TO CIRC IN IS IA
  REPEAT IN [FD IS RT IA]
END
```

   a.
```
TO ARC
   CIRC 36 1 5
   PU HOME PD
   CIRC 36 2 5
   PU HOME PD
   CIRC 36 3 5
   PU HOME PD
   CIRC 36 4 5
   PU HOME PD
   CIRC 36 5 5
END
```

   b.
```
TO SLINKY
   REPEAT 5 [CIRC 30 3 12 RT 90 PU FD 18 LT
   90 PD]
END
```

   c.
```
TO CONCEN
   PU LT 90 FD 10 RT 90 PD
   CIRC 30 2 12
   PU HOME LT 90 FD 20 RT 90 PD
   CIRC 30 4 12
   PU HOME LT 90 FD 30 RT 90 PD
   CIRC 30 6 12
   PU HOME LT 90 FD 40 RT 90 PD
   CIRC 30 8 12
END
```

   d.
```
TO EYES
   CIRC 36 2 10
   CIRC 36 4 10
   CIRC 36 6 10
   CIRC 10 10 9
   PU HOME PD
   CIRCL 36 2 10
   CIRCL 36 4 10
   CIRCL 36 6 10
   CIRCL 10 10 9
END
```

16. a. 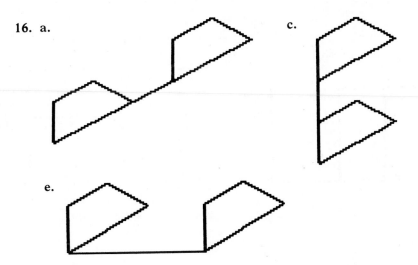 c.

e.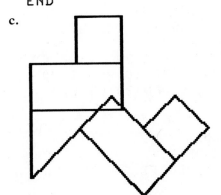

17. Possible answers:

a.
```
TO FLAG
   FD 40
   REPEAT 2 [FD 30 RT 90 FD 60 RT 90]
   FD 30 RT 90 FD 30 LT 90
   REPEAT 4 [FD 30 RT 90]
END
```

b.
```
TO ROTATE.FLAG
   FLAG
   PU HOME PD
   RT 60
   FLAG
END
```

c. d.

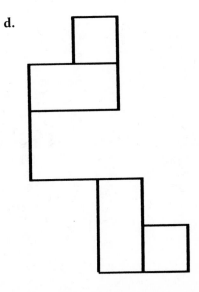

e.   **18.**

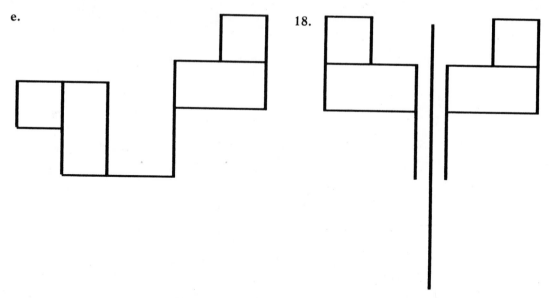

     a. Possible answers:

```
TO FLIP.FLAG
  PD BK 70 FD 170
  HOME
  RT 90 PU FD 10 LT 90 PD
  FLAG
  PU HOME
  LT 90 FD 10 RT 90
  PD
  FLAG.LEFT
END

TO FLAG.LEFT
  FD 45
  REPEAT 2 [FD 30 LT 90 FD 60 LT 90]
  FD 30 LT 90 FD 30 RT 90
  REPEAT 4 [FD 30 LT 90]
END
```

19. Possible solution:

```
TO TRAPEZOID
  FD 30 RT 60 FD 30 RT 120 FD 60 RT 120 FD 30
  RT 60
END

TO HEXAGON
  REPEAT 6 [FD 30 RT 60]
END
```

```
TO RHOMBUS
  REPEAT 2 [FD 30 RT 60 FD 30 RT 120]
END

TO TANGRAM.COUSIN
  RT 30
  HEXAGON
  FD 30
  LITTLE.TRI
  REPEAT 2 [RT 60 FD 30]
  BIG.TRI
  RT 60 FD 30
  RHOMBUS
  RT 60 FD 30 LT 60
  TRAPEZOID
END

TO LITTLE.TRI
  REPEAT 3 [FD 30 RT 120]
END

TO BIG.TRI
  REPEAT 3 [FD 60 RT 120]
END
```

20. Possible procedures to use.

a.
```
TO DESIGN.SYM1
  BK 70 FD 170 HOME
  SQUARE.LEFT
  FD 30 RT 30 LT 60
  TRI.LEFT
  FD 30 LT 30
  SQUARE.LEFT
  LT 90 FD 30 RT 90
  HEXAGON.LEFT
END

TO TRI.LEFT
  REPEAT 3 [FD 30 LT 120]
END

TO SQUARE.LEFT
  REPEAT 4 [FD 30 LT 90]
END

TO HEXAGON.LEFT
  REPEAT 6 [FD 30 LT 60]
END
```

21. Possible solution:
```
TO RHOMBUS
  REPEAT 2 [FD 30 RT 60 FD 30 RT 120]
END
```

    a.
```
TO CUBE
  RHOMBUS
  REPEAT 2 [FD 30 RT 60 FD 30 RT 60 RHOMBUS]
END
```

    b.
```
TO CUBES
  CUBE RT 120 CUBE
  FD 30 RT 60 FD 30 RT 60
  FD 30 LT 60 FD 30 RT 60
  CUBE
END
```

    c.
```
TO CUBE.STAR
  CUBES
  RT 120 RHOMBUS
  REPEAT 2 [LT 120 FD 30 RT 60 FD 30 LT 60
  RHOMBUS]
END
```

    d.
```
TO CUBE.RING
  CUBE FD 30 RT 60 FD 60 RT 60 RHOMBUS
  FD 30 CUBE RT 120 CUBE
  LT 60 FD 30 RT 60 RHOMBUS
  FD 30 RT 120 FD 60 LT 60
  FD 30 RHOMBUS
END
```

22. a. 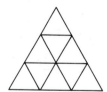   **c.**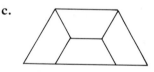

23. a.   **(i)** Four smaller squares fit in the larger square
      (ii) The perimeter of the large square is twice as large as the perimeter of the small square.

    b.   **(i)** TRI 20   **(ii)** RHOMBUS 20   **(iii)** TRI 20
             TRI 40   RHOMBUS 40   TRI 60
      (iv) RHOMBUS 20   **(v)** SQUARE 20
           RHOMBUS 60   SQUARE 60

      As the perimeter is doubled, the area is squared. If the perimeter is increased three times, the area is cubed.

Problem Set 14.3

1. a. h   b. c   c. f   d. b
   e. g   f. d   g. e   h. a

2. Possible procedures:
   a.   (i) TO RHOMBUS :S
             IF :S > 100 STOP
             REPEAT 2 [FD :S RT 120 FD :S RT 60]
             RHOMBUS :S + 10
          END
       (ii) TO TRAPEZOID :S
             IF :S > 70 STOP
             REPEAT 2 [FD :S RT 60]
             FD :S
             RT 120
             FD :S * 2
             RT 120
             TRAPEZOID :S + 10
          END
      (iii) TO HEXAGON :S
             IF :S > 80 STOP
             REPEAT 6 [FD :S RT 60]
             HEXAGON :S + 10
          END

3. Possible solutions:
   a. TO POLYSPI.L :SIZE :ANGLE :INCREMENT
         IF :SIZE > 55 STOP
         FD :SIZE
         LT :ANGLE
         POLYSPI.L :SIZE + :INCREMENT :ANGLE
         :INCREMENT
      END

      POLYSPI.L 1 60 1
   b-d. TO POLYSPI :SIZE :ANGLE :INCREMENT
         IF :SIZE > 55 STOP
         FD :SIZE
         RT :ANGLE
         POLYSPI :SIZE + :INCREMENT :ANGLE
         :INCREMENT
      END

   b. POLYSPI 2 45 2   c. POLYSPI 1 30 1
   d. POLYSPI 10 90 3

5. Use a procedure such as the following:
```
TO SPIRAL :N :S
  IF :S > 80 STOP
  REPEAT :N [FD :S RT 360/ :N] RT 20
  SPIRAL :N :S + 2
END
```
  a. SPIRAL 3 10

  b. Change RT to LT in SPIRAL and IF :S > 60. Use SPIRAL 4 20.

  c. Change IF :S > 35 in SPIRAL. Use SPIRAL 8 10.

7. a. Triangular   **b.** 60: Hexagonal

                                   40: 9-sided spiral

                                   90: Squiral

                                   36: 12-sided spiral

9. The angle input changes the shape of the spiral.

11. Answers will vary.

13.
```
TO POLY.INSPI :SIZE :ANGLE :INCREMENT
  FD :SIZE
  RT :ANGLE
  POLY.INSPI :SIZE :ANGLE + :INCREMENT
  :INCREMENT
END
```

Some possible inputs are the following:

  a. POLY.INSPI 10 40 10   **b.** POLY.INSPI 5 6 12

  c. POLY.INSPI 10 120 35   **d.** POLY.INSPI 10 9 10

  e. POLY.INSPI 10 110 30   **f.** POLY.INSPI 5 1 8

  g. POLY.INSPI 5 6 10

Problem Set 14.4

1. Possible procedure:
```
TO RT.TRI :SIDE1 :SIDE2
  MAKE "X XCOR
  MAKE "Y YCOR
  FD :SIDE1
  RT 90
  FD :SIDE2
  SETXY :X :Y
END
```

3. Possible procedure:
```
TO AXES
  PU SETXY -140 (-70)
  REPEAT 14 [PD FD 180 RT 90 PU FD 10 RT 90 PD
```

```
FD 180 LT 90 PU FD 10 PD LT 90]
 PU SETXY -140 (-70)
 PU RT 90 REPEAT 10 [PD FD 270 LT 90 PU FD 10
LT 90 PD FD 270 RT 90 PU FD 10 RT 90]
 PU HOME
END
```

5. Possible procedure:
```
TO INTER.PERPEND
 PU SETXY 30 50
 PD SETXY 30 (-50)
 SETXY 30 0
 SETXY (-50) 0
 SETXY 50 0
END
```

7. a.   b.

  c.   d.

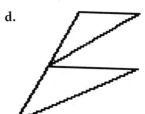

9. Possible solutions:
```
TO CORD.SQ
 PU SETXY 10 15
 PD REPEAT 4 [FD 50 RT 90]
END

TO MOVE.CORD.SQ
 CORD.SQ
 PU SETXY 20 (-5) PD
 REPEAT 4 [FD 50 RT 90]
END
```

INDEX

METRIC MEASUREMENT

Basic Prefixes

kilo-	$10^3 = 1000$	*kilo* means 1000 times basic unit
hecto-	$10^2 = 100$	*hecto* means 100 times basic unit
deka-	$10^1 = 10$	*deka* means 10 times basic unit
deci-	$10^{-1} = \frac{1}{10} = 0.1$	*deci* means 0.1 times basic unit
centi-	$10^{-2} = \frac{1}{100} = 0.01$	*centi* means 0.01 times basic unit
milli-	$10^{-3} = \frac{1}{1000} = 0.001$	*milli* means 0.001 times basic unit

Length

The *meter* is the basic unit

1 *kilo*meter = 1000 meters	1 km	= 1000 m
1 *hecto*meter = 100 meters	1 hm	= 100 m
1 *deka*meter = 10 meters	1 dam	= 10 m
1 *deci*meter = $\frac{1}{10}$ of a meter	1 dm	= 0.1 m
1 *centi*meter = $\frac{1}{100}$ of a meter	1 cm	= 0.01 m
1 *milli*meter = $\frac{1}{1000}$ of a meter	1 mm	= 0.001 m

Area

1 square *kilo*meter = 1,000,000 square meters	1 km^2	$= 1,000,000 \text{ m}^2$
1 square *hecto*meter = 10,000 square meters	1 hm^2	$= 10,000 \text{ m}^2$
1 square *deka*meter = 100 square meters	1 dam^2	$= 100 \text{ m}^2$
1 square *deci*meter = $\frac{1}{100}$ of a square meter	1 dm^2	$= 0.01 \text{ m}^2$
1 square *centi*meter = $\frac{1}{10,000}$ of a square meter	1 cm^2	$= 0.0001 \text{ m}^2$
1 square *milli*meter = $\frac{1}{1,000,000}$ of a square meter	1 mm^2	$= 0.000001 \text{ m}^2$